D1084225

3 SAINT☆YOUNG MEN

C O N T E N T S

FOREWORD

By Sam Humphries

This is a story about the human condition. Yes, I am fully aware that the book in your hands is about Jesus and Buddha. But listen—

Saint Young Men is my first exposure to Hikaru Nakamura's work, and it is brilliant. Buddha and Jesus are two young men, roommates and pals, living and exploring modern-day Japan. As far as high concepts go, this one reaches up to the highest heaven.

Yes, she's packed this book with religious references and Easter eggs, and to me the most sacred type of humor: puns. The physical comedy and facial expressions will make you literally LOL. She knows when to hit you with laughs, and when to dazzle you with a beautiful image, which more often than not, delivers an emotional punch.

But to me, her most stunning talent is characterization. When your characters are Jesus and Buddha, that's a tightrope walk in any century!

There's plenty of jokes, sure. But the lion's share of humor is character-based. In my opinion that's the best kind of humor. A punchline is one thing. But when a character says something that's only funny when it comes out of their mouth? That's the good stuff. You laugh, and you find yourself connected to the characters. The jokes illuminate who they are. You relate to them on a human level.

And yes, Nakamura-sensei does this with Jesus and Buddha. These are titanic religious figures whose shadows stretch across human civilization, but in the end, you think of them...well, as pals.

In this sense, Nakamura-sensei is in the tradition of Monty Python and Phoebe Waller-Bridge. Over in Canada, she is in harmony with Denys Arcand's film, *Jesus of Montreal*. Here in America, I think of the comic *Binky Brown Meets the Holy Virgin Mary* by Justin Green, or the musical *Godspell*.

To relate to Buddha and Jesus as humans is to enrich their holy power. Were they not, according to their own tradition, once regular dudes among their people? Despite their celestial provenance, did they not face hard choices that strike to the heart of what it is to be human? In a parable, psalm, or comic book, to walk by their side is to exalt them.

In that sense, Nakamura-sensei might have found allies in spiritual figures like Martin Luther King, Jr., or Mister Rogers. When we can comprehend the divine as more human, we get closer to discovering the divine in ourselves.

Watching Buddha and Jesus struggle as roommates, we embrace the struggles in our own lives. Seeing them wonder at modern-day Japan, we may be stupefied by astonishment at our own world. And laughing at them, we can laugh at ourselves.

That, my friends, is how *Saint Young Men* is a story about the human condition. But don't let all my lofty blathering fool you: it's also funny as hell. Enjoy.

Los Angeles, California
April 2020

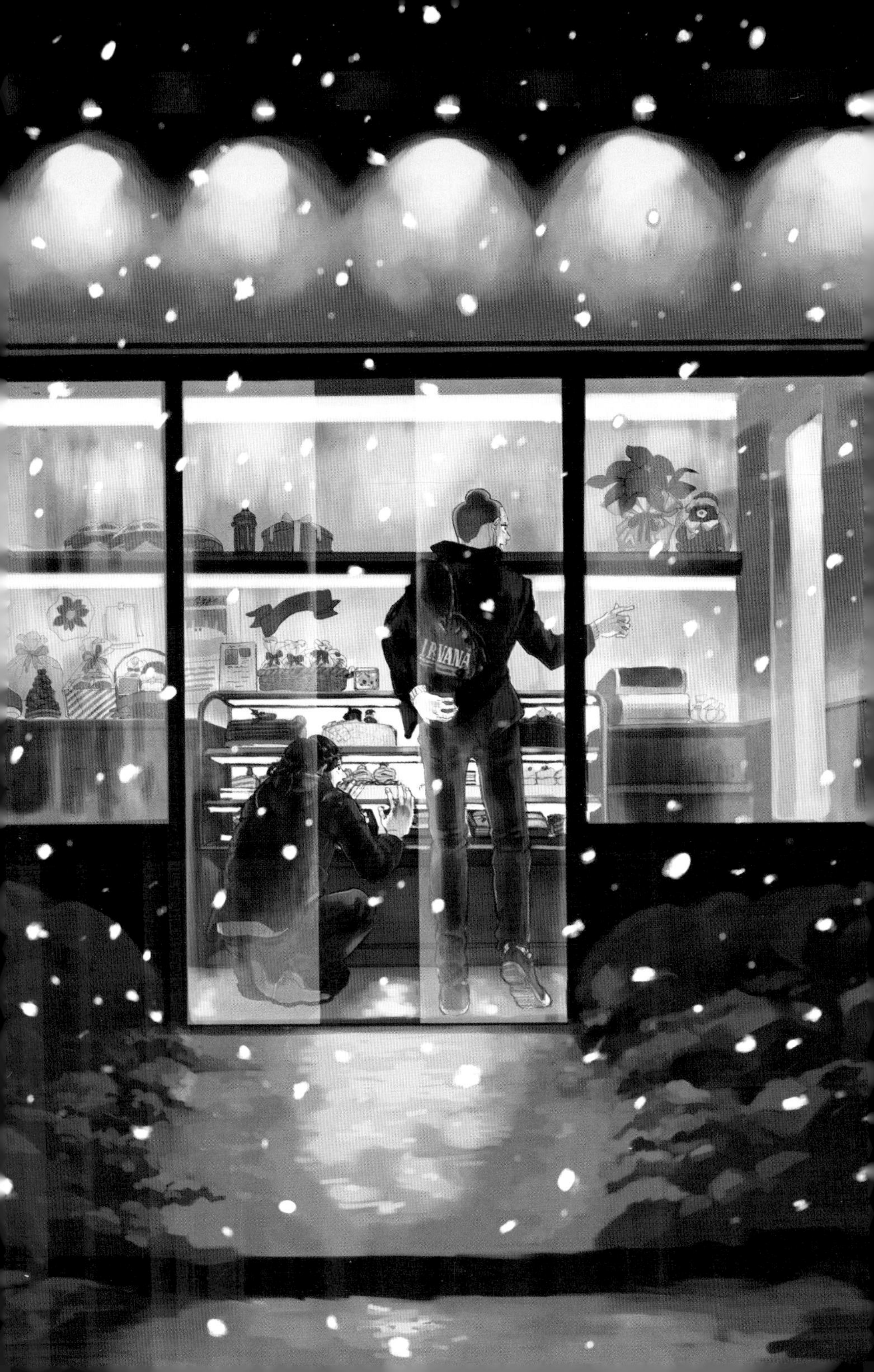
IRVANA

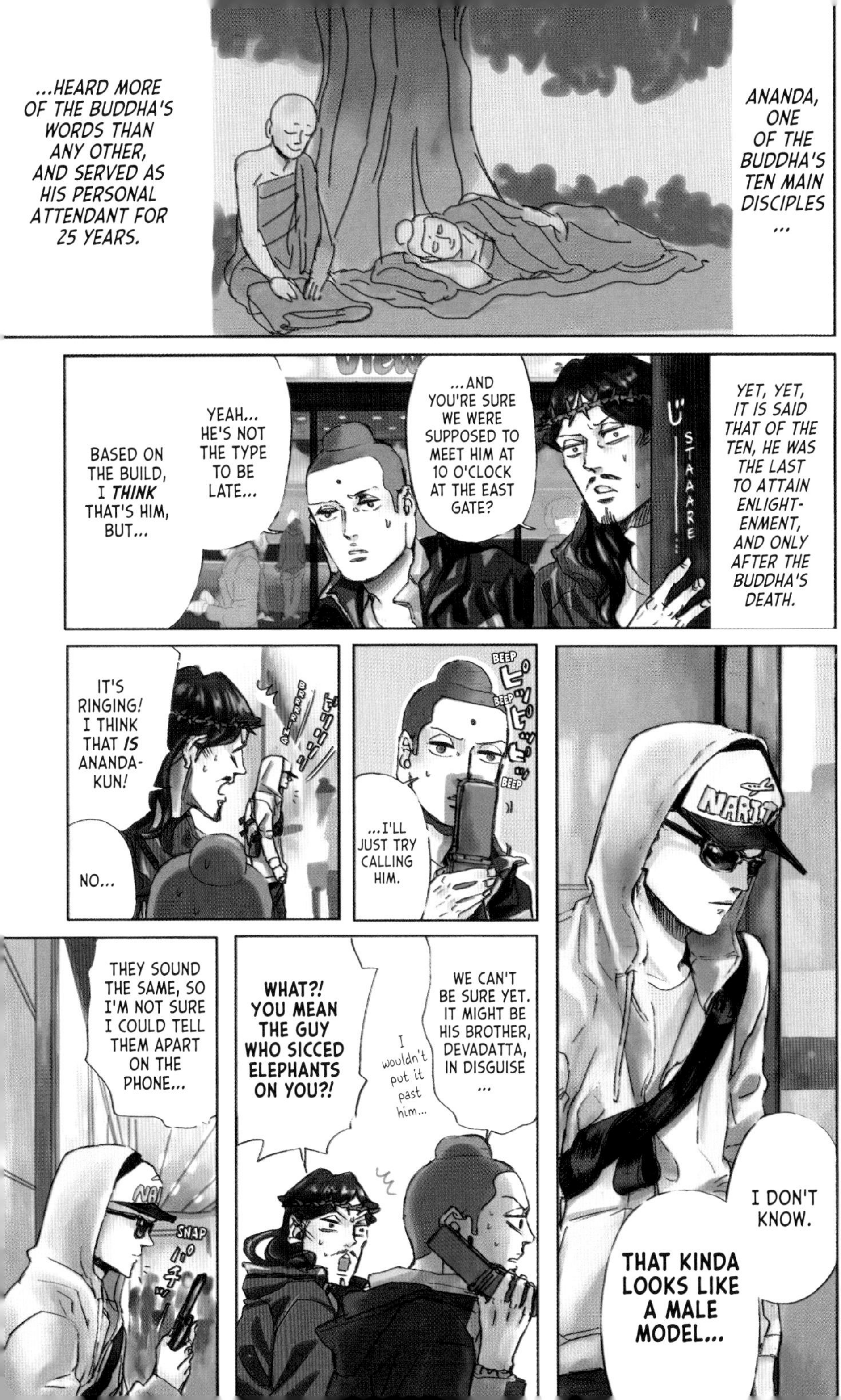
ANANDA, ONE OF THE BUDDHA'S TEN MAIN DISCIPLES...
...HEARD MORE OF THE BUDDHA'S WORDS THAN ANY OTHER, AND SERVED AS HIS PERSONAL ATTENDANT FOR 25 YEARS.
YET, YET, IT IS SAID THAT OF THE TEN, HE WAS THE LAST TO ATTAIN ENLIGHT-ENMENT, AND ONLY AFTER THE BUDDHA'S DEATH.
STAAARE
...AND YOU'RE SURE WE WERE SUPPOSED TO MEET HIM AT 10 O'CLOCK AT THE EAST GATE?
YEAH... HE'S NOT THE TYPE TO BE LATE...
BASED ON THE BUILD, I *THINK* THAT'S HIM, BUT...
I DON'T KNOW.
THAT KINDA LOOKS LIKE A MALE MODEL...
BEEP
BEEP
BEEP
...I'LL JUST TRY CALLING HIM.
BRRRING
IT'S RINGING! I THINK THAT *IS* ANANDA-KUN!
NO...
WE CAN'T BE SURE YET. IT MIGHT BE HIS BROTHER, DEVADATTA, IN DISGUISE...
I wouldn't put it past him...
WHAT?! YOU MEAN THE GUY WHO SICCED ELEPHANTS ON YOU?!
THEY SOUND THE SAME, SO I'M NOT SURE I COULD TELL THEM APART ON THE PHONE...
SNAP

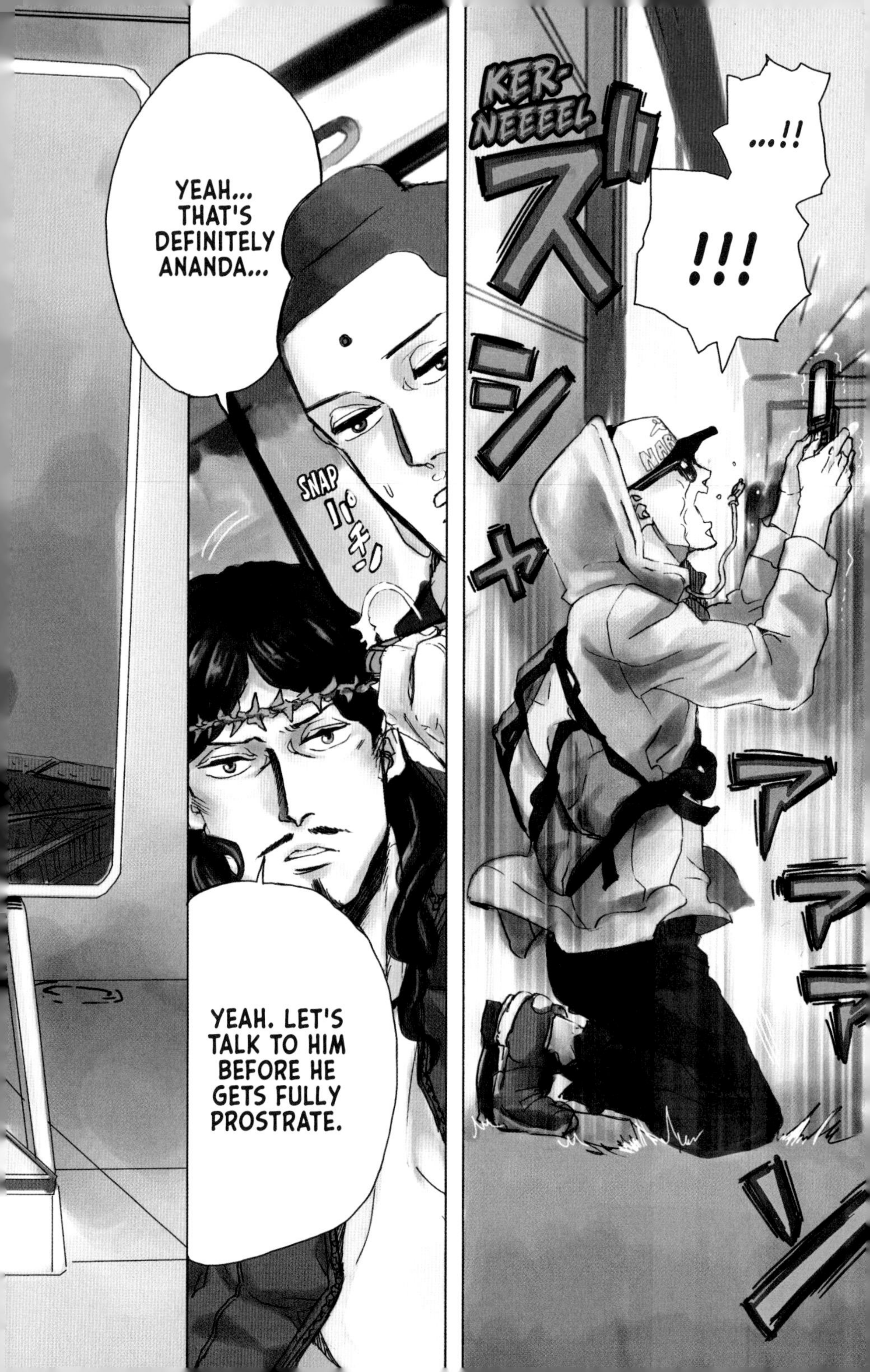
KER-NEEEEL
...!!
!!!
YEAH... THAT'S DEFINITELY ANANDA...
SNAP
YEAH. LET'S TALK TO HIM BEFORE HE GETS FULLY PROSTRATE.

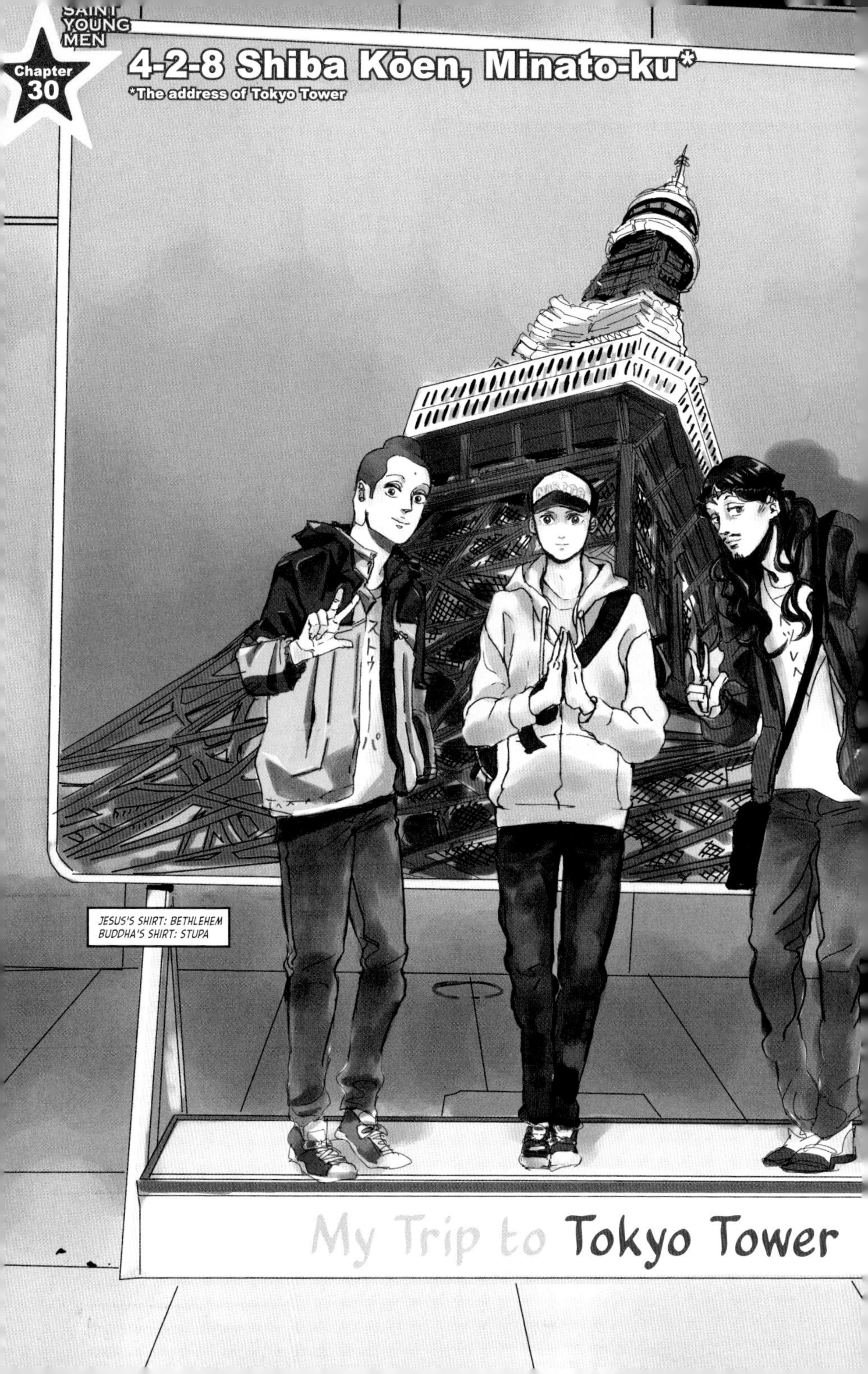
SAINT YOUNG MEN
Chapter 30
4-2-8 Shiba Kōen, Minato-ku*
*The address of Tokyo Tower
JESUS'S SHIRT: BETHLEHEM
BUDDHA'S SHIRT: STUPA
My Trip to Tokyo Tower

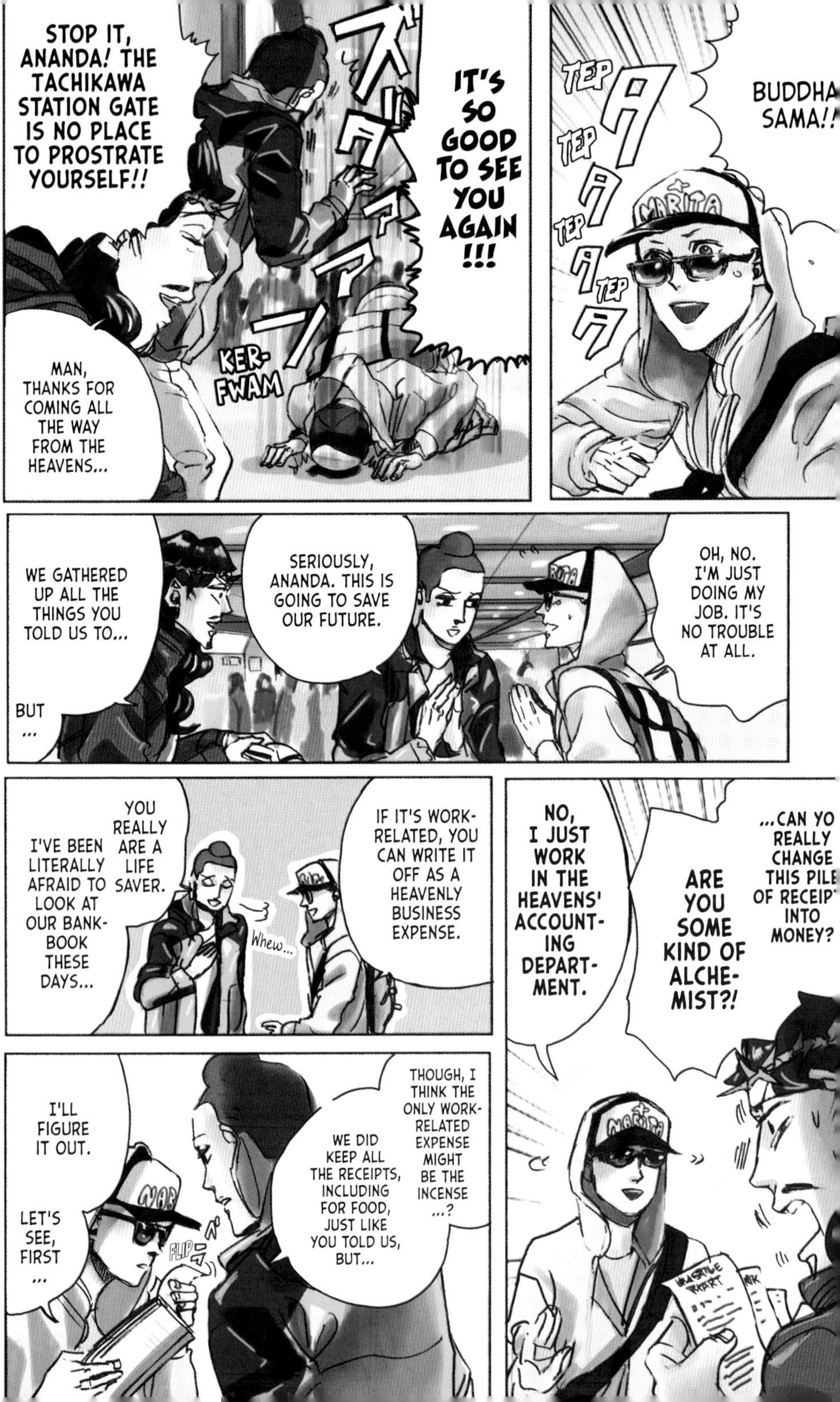

TEP TEP TEP TEP
BUDDHA SAMA!!
IT'S SO GOOD TO SEE YOU AGAIN!!!
STOP IT, ANANDA! THE TACHIKAWA STATION GATE IS NO PLACE TO PROSTRATE YOURSELF!!
KER-FWAM
MAN, THANKS FOR COMING ALL THE WAY FROM THE HEAVENS...
OH, NO. I'M JUST DOING MY JOB. IT'S NO TROUBLE AT ALL.
SERIOUSLY, ANANDA. THIS IS GOING TO SAVE OUR FUTURE.
WE GATHERED UP ALL THE THINGS YOU TOLD US TO...
BUT ...
...CAN YO REALLY CHANGE THIS PILE OF RECEIP INTO MONEY?
ARE YOU SOME KIND OF ALCHE-MIST?!
NO, I JUST WORK IN THE HEAVENS' ACCOUNT-ING DEPART-MENT.
IF IT'S WORK-RELATED, YOU CAN WRITE IT OFF AS A HEAVENLY BUSINESS EXPENSE.
YOU REALLY ARE A LIFE SAVER.
I'VE BEEN LITERALLY AFRAID TO LOOK AT OUR BANK-BOOK THESE DAYS...
Whew...
THOUGH, I THINK THE ONLY WORK-RELATED EXPENSE MIGHT BE THE INCENSE ...?
WE DID KEEP ALL THE RECEIPTS, INCLUDING FOR FOOD, JUST LIKE YOU TOLD US, BUT...
I'LL FIGURE IT OUT.
FLIP
LET'S SEE, FIRST ...

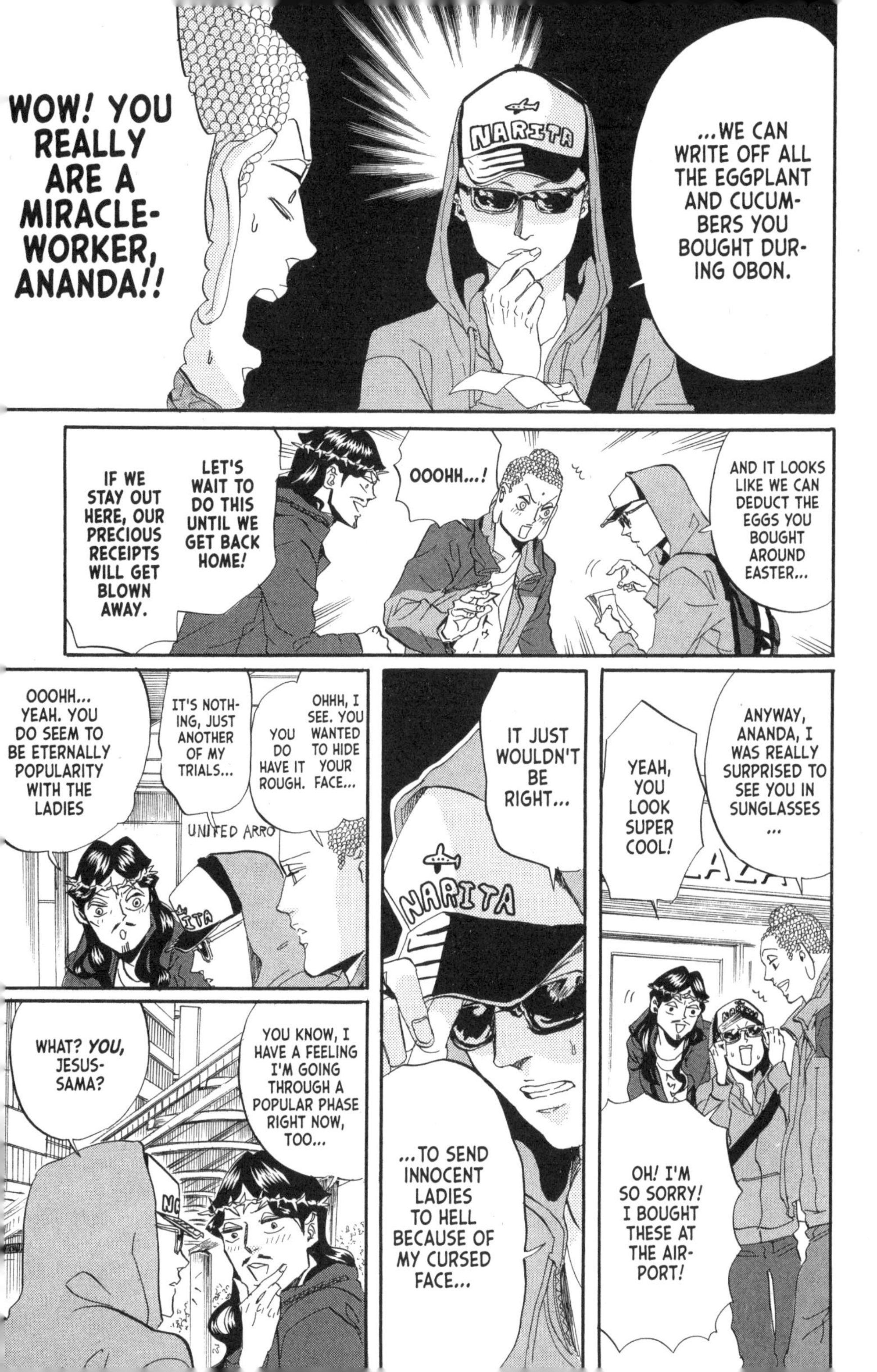
NARITA
...WE CAN WRITE OFF ALL THE EGGPLANT AND CUCUMBERS YOU BOUGHT DURING OBON.
WOW! YOU REALLY ARE A MIRACLE-WORKER, ANANDA!!
AND IT LOOKS LIKE WE CAN DEDUCT THE EGGS YOU BOUGHT AROUND EASTER...
OOOHH...!
LET'S WAIT TO DO THIS UNTIL WE GET BACK HOME!
IF WE STAY OUT HERE, OUR PRECIOUS RECEIPTS WILL GET BLOWN AWAY.
ANYWAY, ANANDA, I WAS REALLY SURPRISED TO SEE YOU IN SUNGLASSES...
YEAH, YOU LOOK SUPER COOL!
OH! I'M SO SORRY! I BOUGHT THESE AT THE AIRPORT!
NARITA
IT JUST WOULDN'T BE RIGHT...
...TO SEND INNOCENT LADIES TO HELL BECAUSE OF MY CURSED FACE...
OHHH, I SEE. YOU WANTED TO HIDE YOUR FACE...
YOU DO HAVE IT ROUGH.
IT'S NOTHING, JUST ANOTHER OF MY TRIALS...
OOOHH... YEAH. YOU DO SEEM TO BE ETERNALLY POPULARITY WITH THE LADIES
UNITED ARRO
YOU KNOW, I HAVE A FEELING I'M GOING THROUGH A POPULAR PHASE RIGHT NOW, TOO...
WHAT? YOU, JESUS-SAMA?

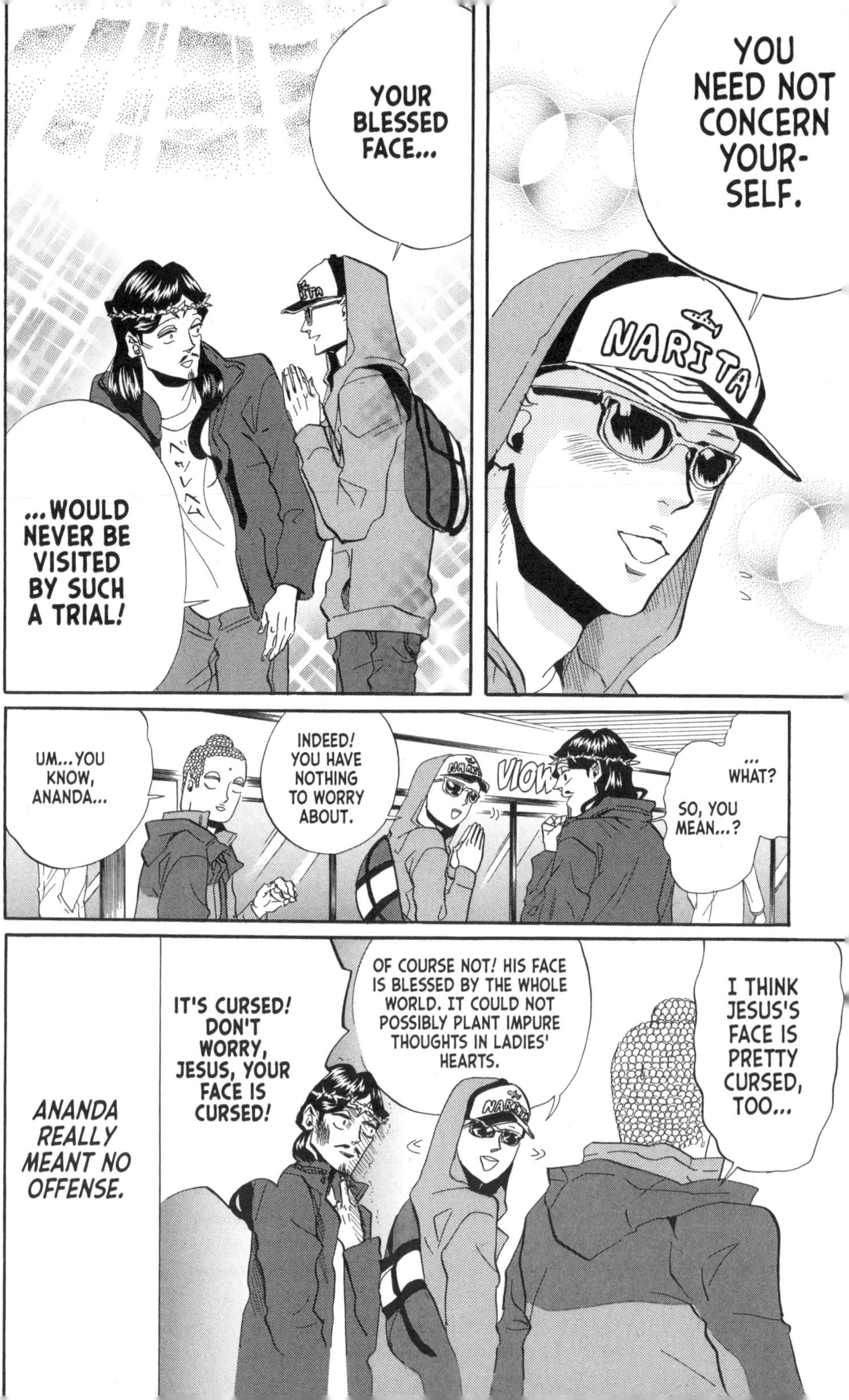
YOU NEED NOT CONCERN YOUR-SELF.
YOUR BLESSED FACE...
...WOULD NEVER BE VISITED BY SUCH A TRIAL!
... WHAT?
SO, YOU MEAN...?
INDEED! YOU HAVE NOTHING TO WORRY ABOUT.
UM...YOU KNOW, ANANDA...
I THINK JESUS'S FACE IS PRETTY CURSED, TOO...
OF COURSE NOT! HIS FACE IS BLESSED BY THE WHOLE WORLD. IT COULD NOT POSSIBLY PLANT IMPURE THOUGHTS IN LADIES' HEARTS.
IT'S CURSED! DON'T WORRY, JESUS, YOUR FACE IS CURSED!
ANANDA REALLY MEANT NO OFFENSE.

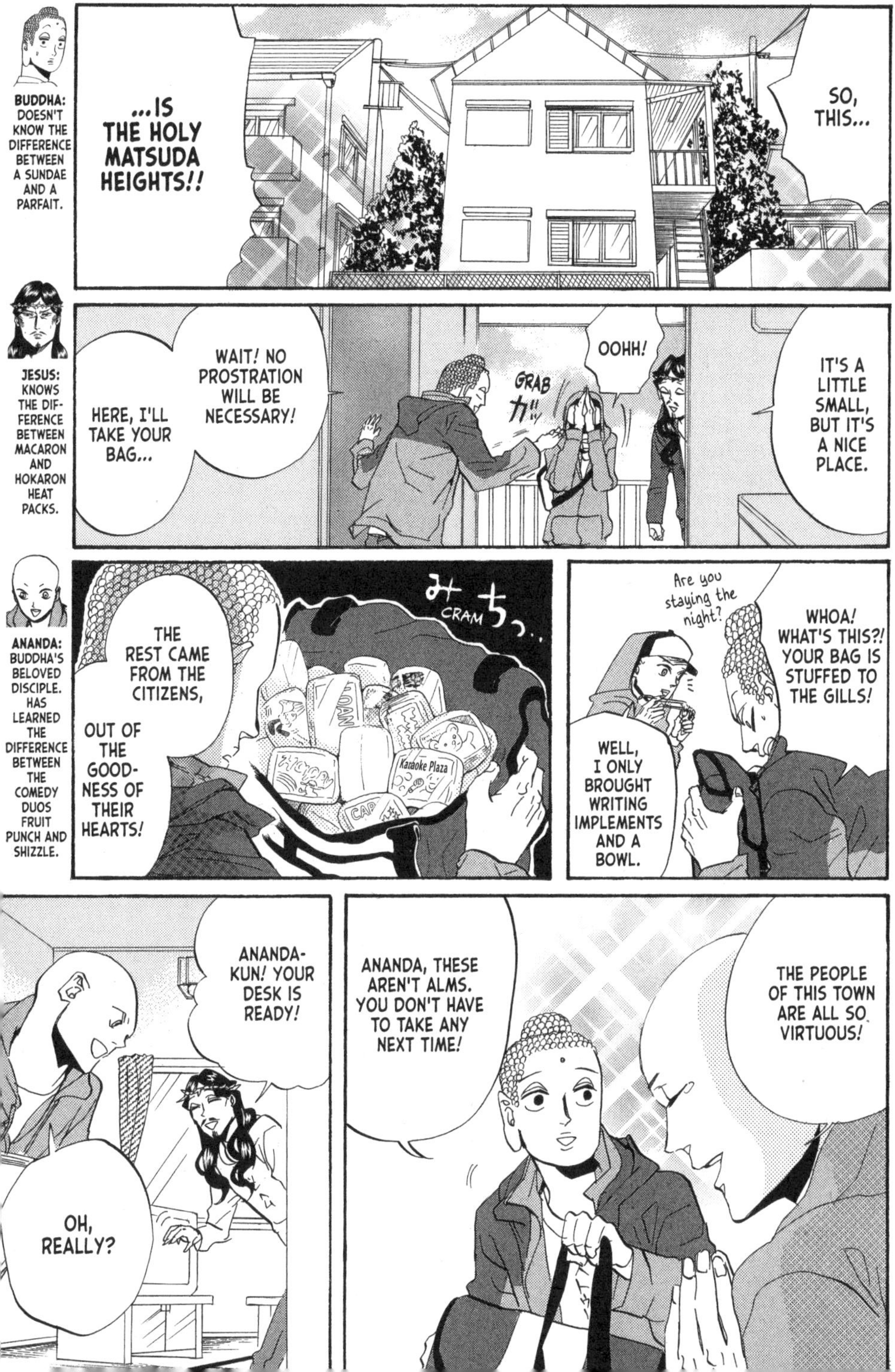

SO, THIS...
...IS THE HOLY MATSUDA HEIGHTS!!
BUDDHA: DOESN'T KNOW THE DIFFERENCE BETWEEN A SUNDAE AND A PARFAIT.
IT'S A LITTLE SMALL, BUT IT'S A NICE PLACE.
OOHH!
GRAB
WAIT! NO PROSTRATION WILL BE NECESSARY!
HERE, I'LL TAKE YOUR BAG...
JESUS: KNOWS THE DIFFERENCE BETWEEN MACARON AND HOKARON HEAT PACKS.
WHOA! WHAT'S THIS?! YOUR BAG IS STUFFED TO THE GILLS!
Are you staying the night?
WELL, I ONLY BROUGHT WRITING IMPLEMENTS AND A BOWL.
CRAM
THE REST CAME FROM THE CITIZENS,
OUT OF THE GOODNESS OF THEIR HEARTS!
ANANDA: BUDDHA'S BELOVED DISCIPLE. HAS LEARNED THE DIFFERENCE BETWEEN THE COMEDY DUOS FRUIT PUNCH AND SHIZZLE.
THE PEOPLE OF THIS TOWN ARE ALL SO VIRTUOUS!
ANANDA, THESE AREN'T ALMS. YOU DON'T HAVE TO TAKE ANY NEXT TIME!
ANANDA-KUN! YOUR DESK IS READY!
OH, REALLY?

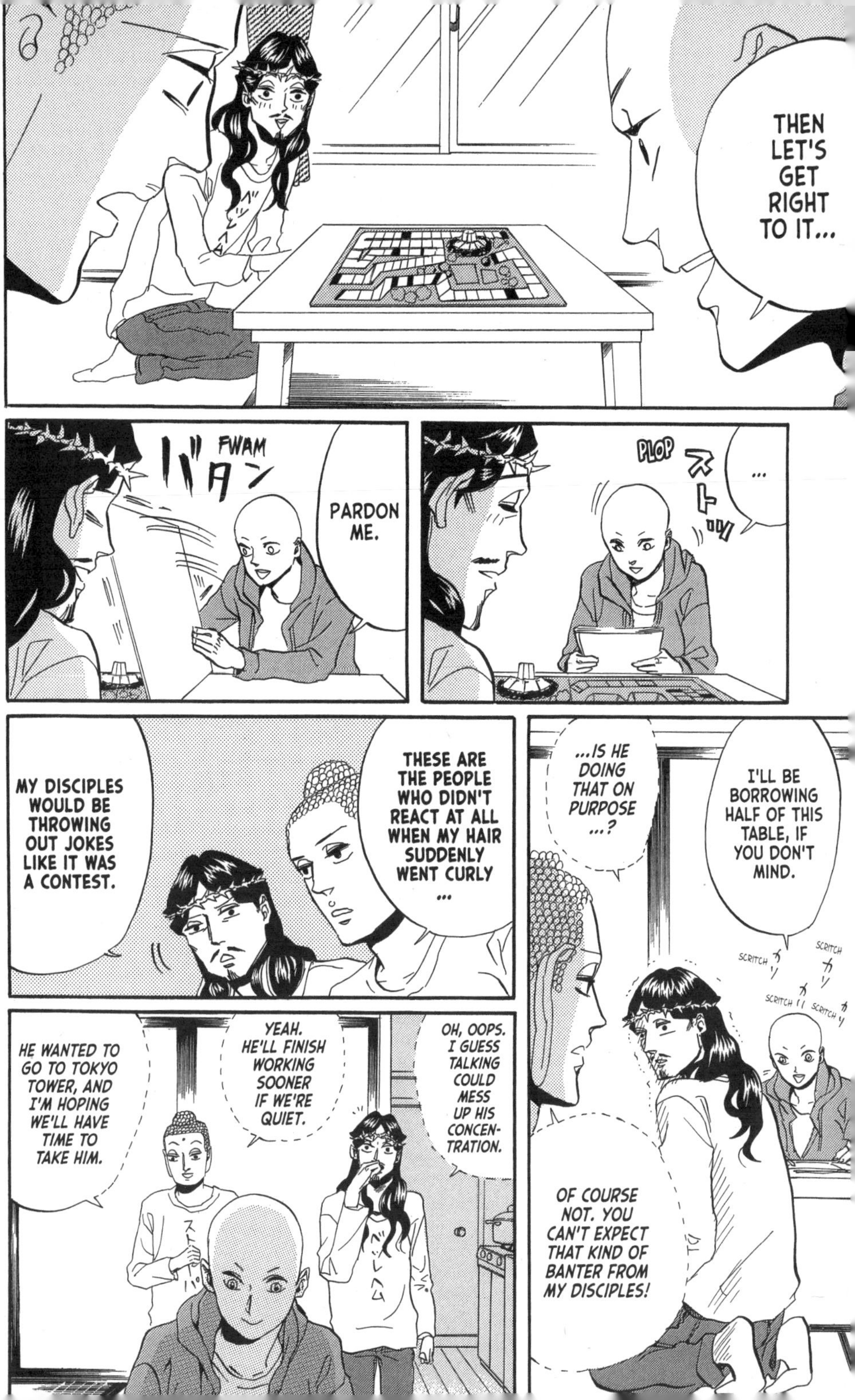
THEN LET'S GET RIGHT TO IT...
...
ストッ
PLOP
バタン
FWAM
PARDON ME.
I'LL BE BORROWING HALF OF THIS TABLE, IF YOU DON'T MIND.
...IS HE DOING THAT ON PURPOSE ...?
SCRITCH
SCRITCH
SCRITCH
SCRITCH
OF COURSE NOT. YOU CAN'T EXPECT THAT KIND OF BANTER FROM MY DISCIPLES!
THESE ARE THE PEOPLE WHO DIDN'T REACT AT ALL WHEN MY HAIR SUDDENLY WENT CURLY ...
MY DISCIPLES WOULD BE THROWING OUT JOKES LIKE IT WAS A CONTEST.
OH, OOPS. I GUESS TALKING COULD MESS UP HIS CONCEN-TRATION.
YEAH. HE'LL FINISH WORKING SOONER IF WE'RE QUIET.
HE WANTED TO GO TO TOKYO TOWER, AND I'M HOPING WE'LL HAVE TIME TO TAKE HIM.

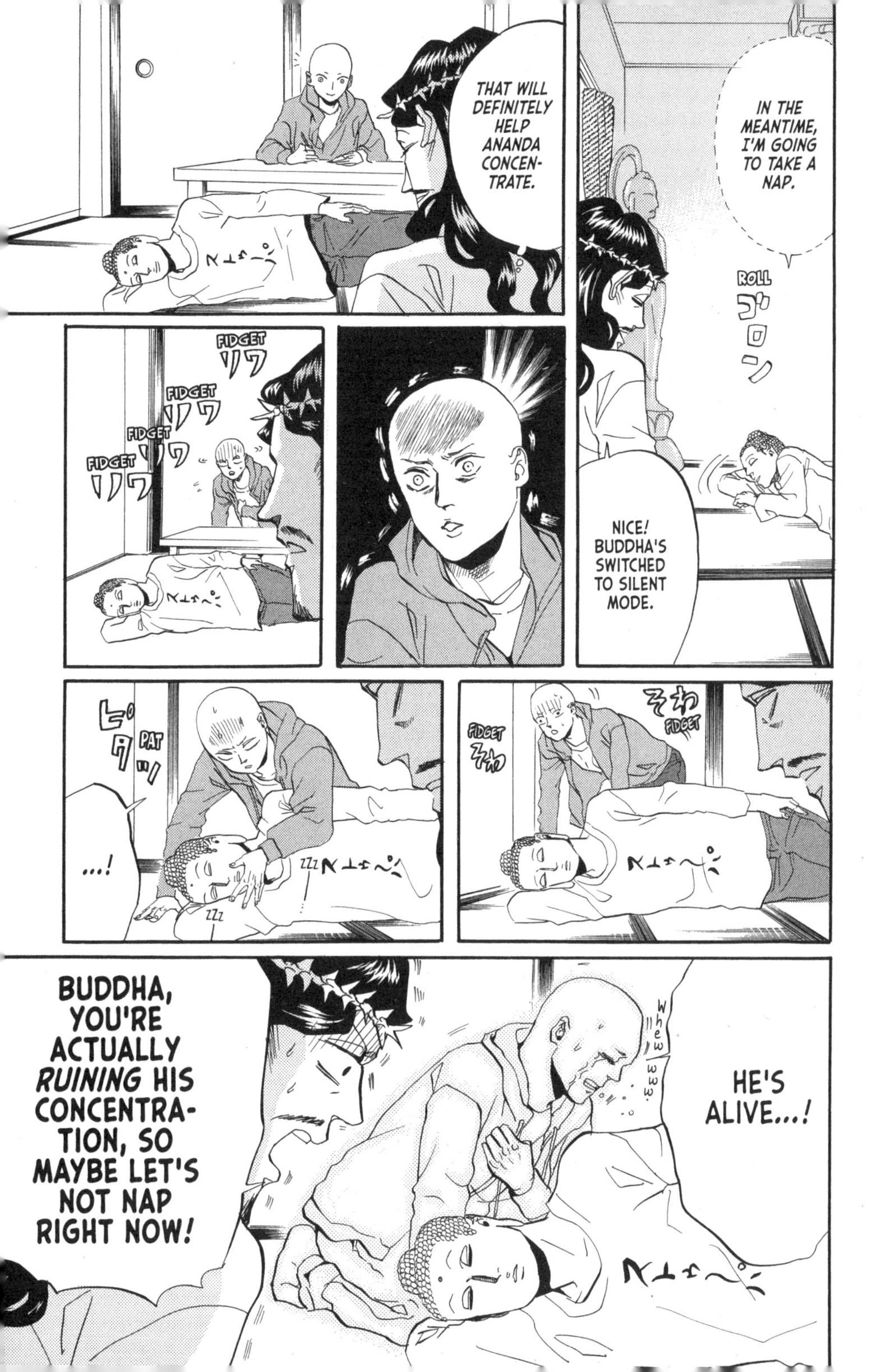

IN THE MEANTIME, I'M GOING TO TAKE A NAP.
ROLL
ゴロン
NICE! BUDDHA'S SWITCHED TO SILENT MODE.
THAT WILL DEFINITELY HELP ANANDA CONCENTRATE.
FIDGET
ソワ
FIDGET
ソワ
FIDGET
ソワ
FIDGET
ソワ
そわ
FIDGET
FIDGET
そわ
ピタッ
PAT
...!
ZZZ
ZZZ
HE'S ALIVE...!
Whew
BUDDHA, YOU'RE ACTUALLY *RUINING* HIS CONCENTRATION, SO MAYBE LET'S NOT NAP RIGHT NOW!

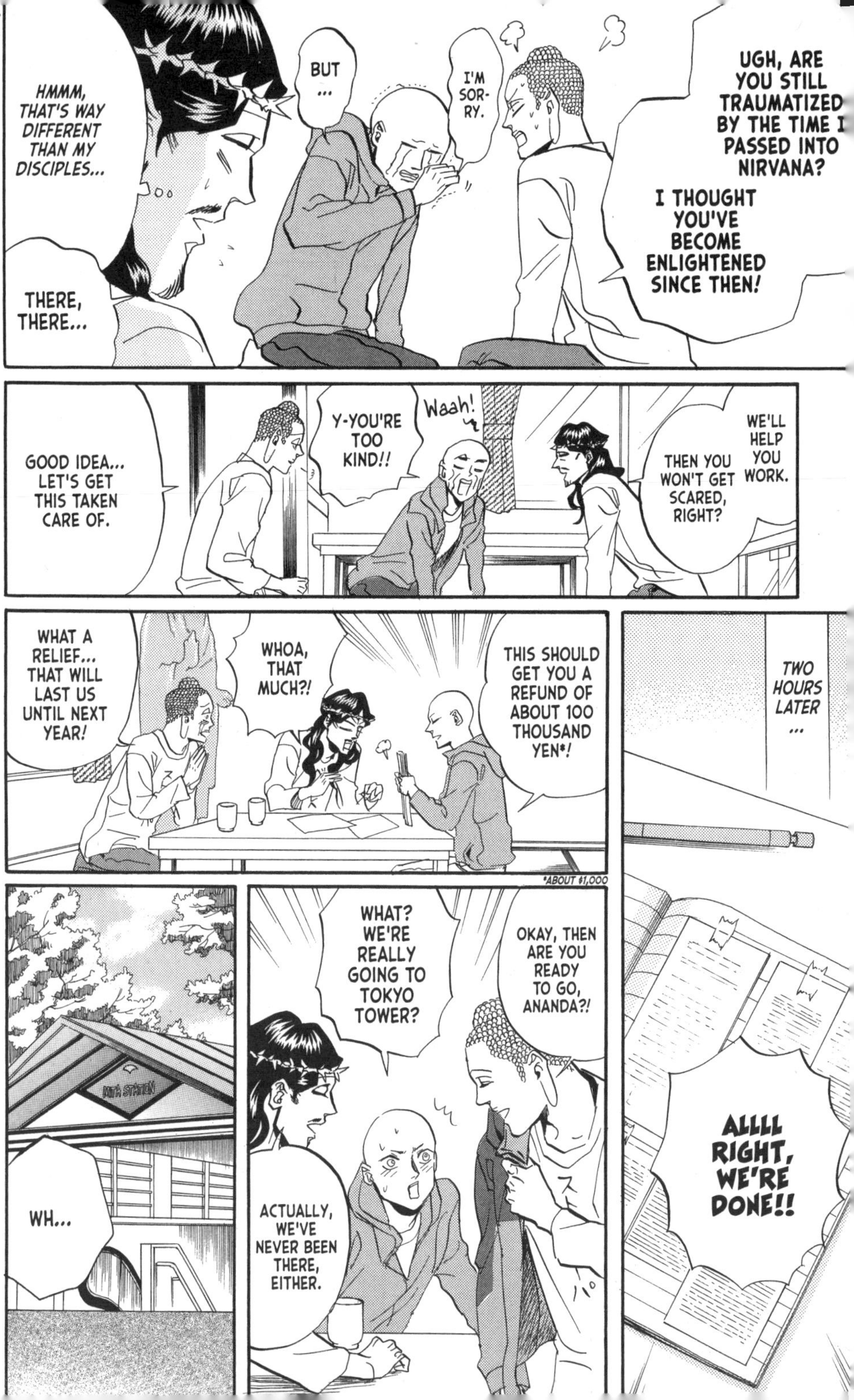
UGH, ARE YOU STILL TRAUMATIZED BY THE TIME I PASSED INTO NIRVANA?
I THOUGHT YOU'VE BECOME ENLIGHTENED SINCE THEN!
I'M SOR-RY.
BUT ...
HMMM, THAT'S WAY DIFFERENT THAN MY DISCIPLES...
THERE, THERE...
WE'LL HELP YOU WORK.
THEN YOU WON'T GET SCARED, RIGHT?
Waah!
Y-YOU'RE TOO KIND!!
GOOD IDEA... LET'S GET THIS TAKEN CARE OF.
TWO HOURS LATER ...
ALLLL RIGHT, WE'RE DONE!!
THIS SHOULD GET YOU A REFUND OF ABOUT 100 THOUSAND YEN*!
WHOA, THAT MUCH?!
WHAT A RELIEF... THAT WILL LAST US UNTIL NEXT YEAR!
*ABOUT $1,000
OKAY, THEN ARE YOU READY TO GO, ANANDA?!
WHAT? WE'RE REALLY GOING TO TOKYO TOWER?
ACTUALLY, WE'VE NEVER BEEN THERE, EITHER.
WH...

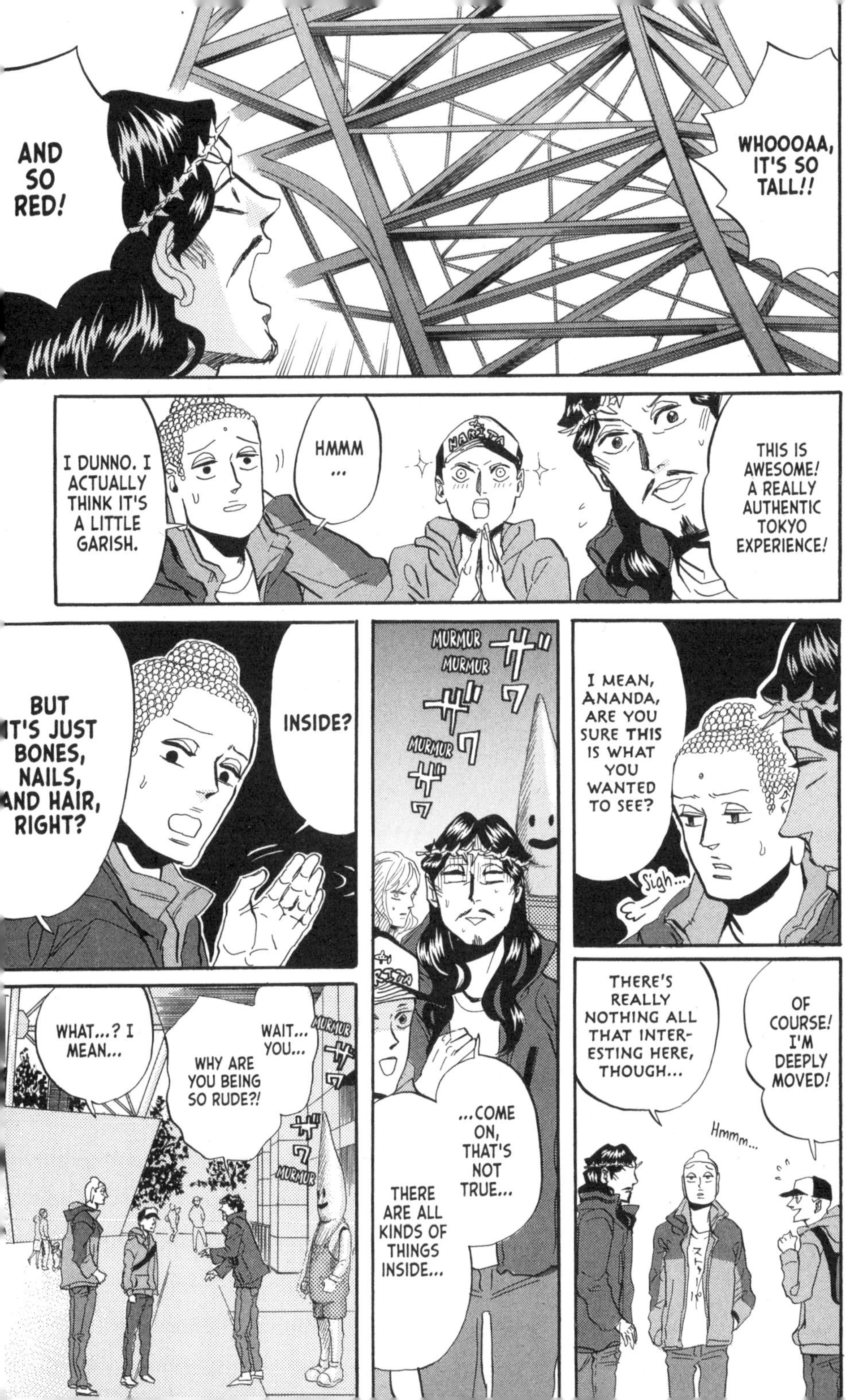
WHOOOAA, IT'S SO TALL!!
AND SO RED!
THIS IS AWESOME! A REALLY AUTHENTIC TOKYO EXPERIENCE!
HMMM ...
I DUNNO. I ACTUALLY THINK IT'S A LITTLE GARISH.
I MEAN, ANANDA, ARE YOU SURE THIS IS WHAT YOU WANTED TO SEE?
Sigh...
OF COURSE! I'M DEEPLY MOVED!
THERE'S REALLY NOTHING ALL THAT INTERESTING HERE, THOUGH...
Hmmm...
MURMUR MURMUR
MURMUR
...COME ON, THAT'S NOT TRUE...
THERE ARE ALL KINDS OF THINGS INSIDE...
INSIDE?
BUT IT'S JUST BONES, NAILS, AND HAIR, RIGHT?
WAIT... YOU...
WHY ARE YOU BEING SO RUDE?!
WHAT...? I MEAN...
MURMUR
MURMUR

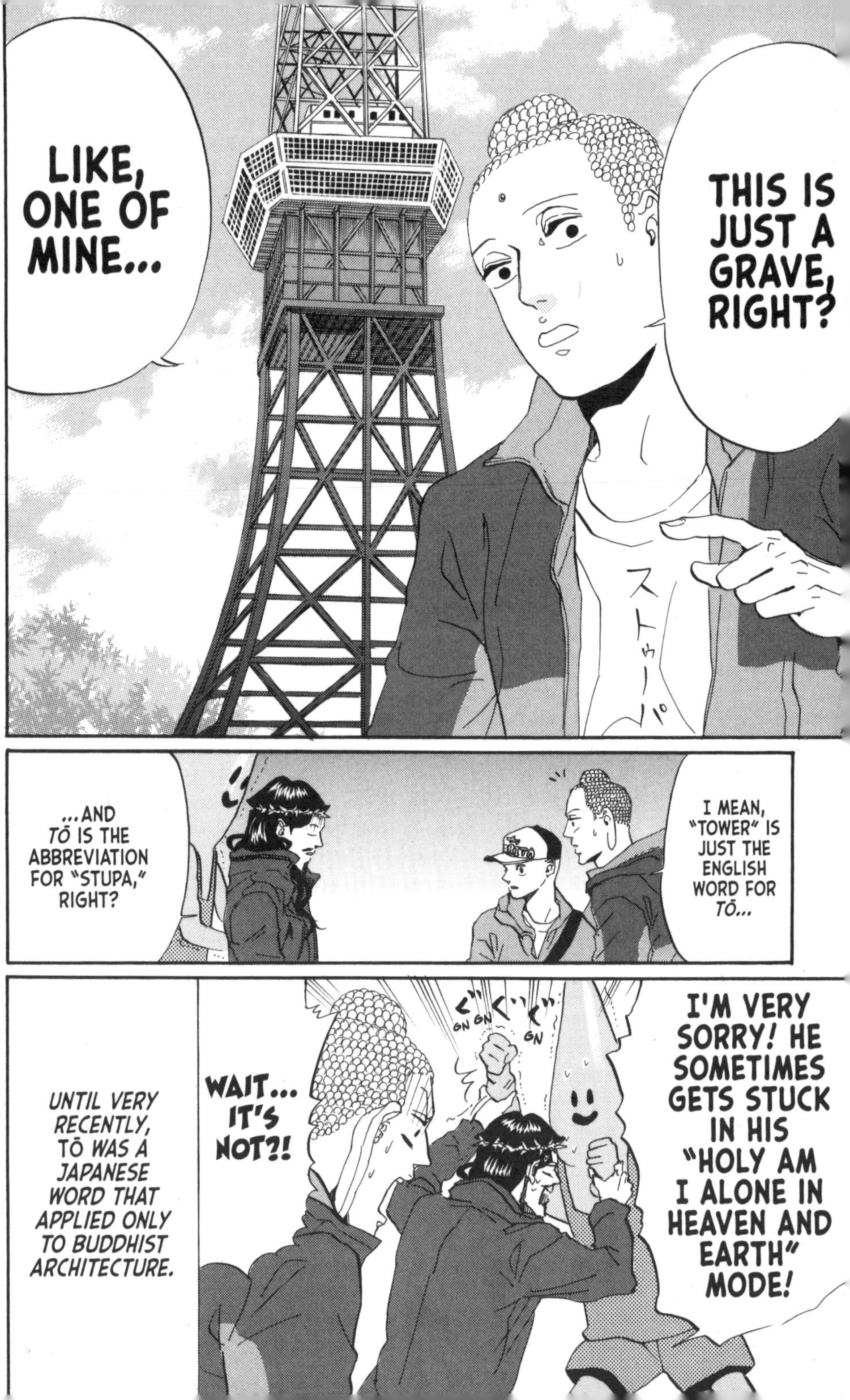
THIS IS JUST A GRAVE, RIGHT?
ストゥーパ
LIKE, ONE OF MINE...
I MEAN, "TOWER" IS JUST THE ENGLISH WORD FOR *TŌ*...
...AND *TŌ* IS THE ABBREVIATION FOR "STUPA," RIGHT?
I'M VERY SORRY! HE SOMETIMES GETS STUCK IN HIS "HOLY AM I ALONE IN HEAVEN AND EARTH" MODE!
GN GN GN
WAIT... IT'S NOT?!
UNTIL VERY RECENTLY, *TŌ* WAS A JAPANESE WORD THAT APPLIED ONLY TO BUDDHIST ARCHITECTURE.

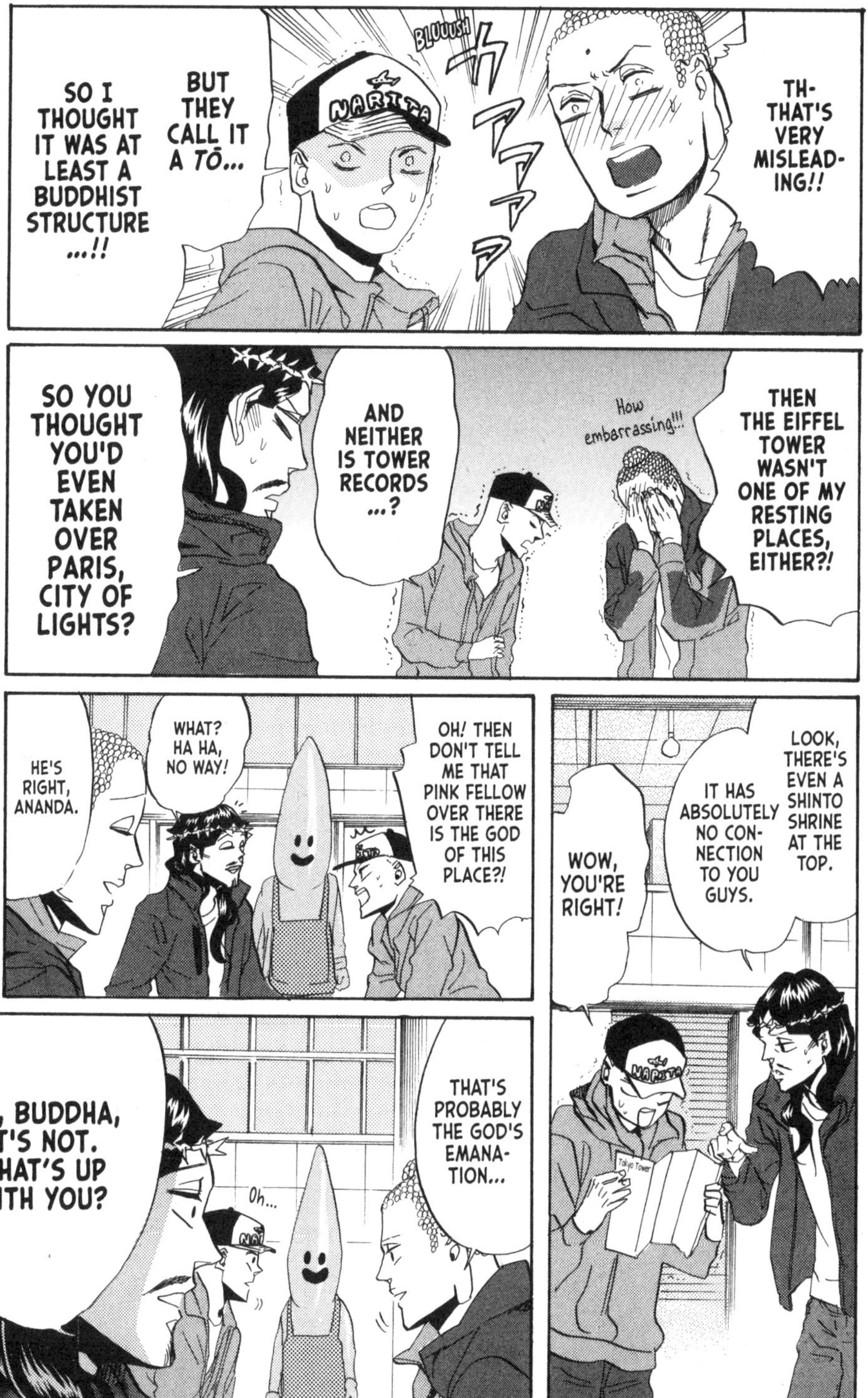
TH-THAT'S VERY MISLEAD-ING!!
BLUUUSH
BUT THEY CALL IT A *TŌ*...
SO I THOUGHT IT WAS AT LEAST A BUDDHIST STRUCTURE ...!!
THEN THE EIFFEL TOWER WASN'T ONE OF MY RESTING PLACES, EITHER?!
How embarrassing!!!
AND NEITHER IS TOWER RECORDS ...?
SO YOU THOUGHT YOU'D EVEN TAKEN OVER PARIS, CITY OF LIGHTS?
LOOK, THERE'S EVEN A SHINTO SHRINE AT THE TOP.
IT HAS ABSOLUTELY NO CON-NECTION TO YOU GUYS.
WOW, YOU'RE RIGHT!
Tokyo Tower
OH! THEN DON'T TELL ME THAT PINK FELLOW OVER THERE IS THE GOD OF THIS PLACE?!
WHAT? HA HA, NO WAY!
HE'S RIGHT, ANANDA.
THAT'S PROBABLY THE GOD'S EMANA-TION...
Oh...
NO, BUDDHA, IT'S NOT. WHAT'S UP WITH YOU?

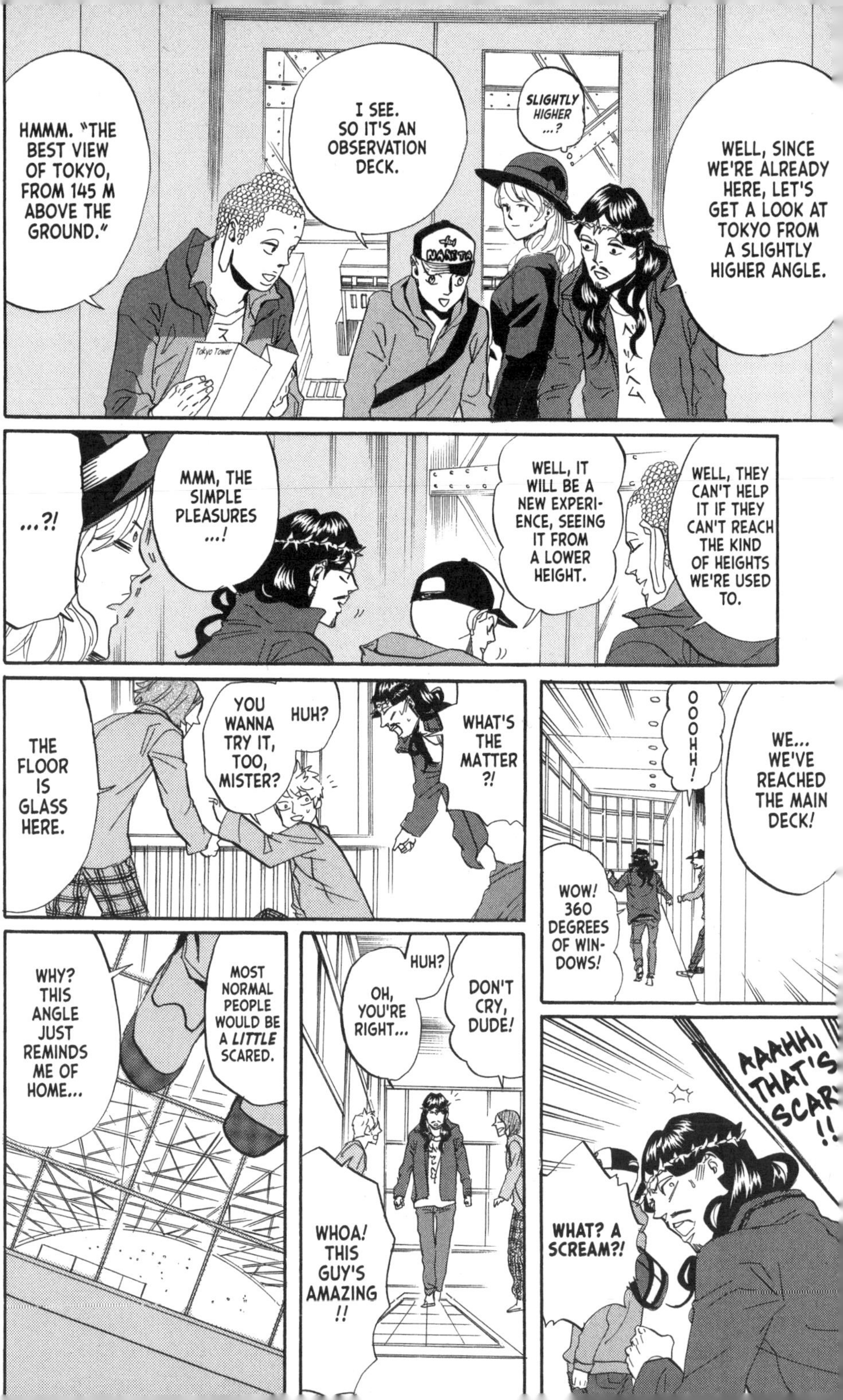
WELL, SINCE WE'RE ALREADY HERE, LET'S GET A LOOK AT TOKYO FROM A SLIGHTLY HIGHER ANGLE.
SLIGHTLY HIGHER ...?
I SEE. SO IT'S AN OBSERVATION DECK.
HMMM. "THE BEST VIEW OF TOKYO, FROM 145 M ABOVE THE GROUND."
Tokyo Tower
WELL, THEY CAN'T HELP IT IF THEY CAN'T REACH THE KIND OF HEIGHTS WE'RE USED TO.
WELL, IT WILL BE A NEW EXPERIENCE, SEEING IT FROM A LOWER HEIGHT.
MMM, THE SIMPLE PLEASURES ...!
...?!
WE... WE'VE REACHED THE MAIN DECK!
OOOOHH!
WOW! 360 DEGREES OF WINDOWS!
WHAT'S THE MATTER ?!
HUH?
YOU WANNA TRY IT, TOO, MISTER?
THE FLOOR IS GLASS HERE.
AAAHH, THAT'S SCAR !!
WHAT? A SCREAM?!
DON'T CRY, DUDE!
HUH?
OH, YOU'RE RIGHT...
WHOA! THIS GUY'S AMAZING !!
MOST NORMAL PEOPLE WOULD BE A *LITTLE* SCARED.
WHY? THIS ANGLE JUST REMINDS ME OF HOME...

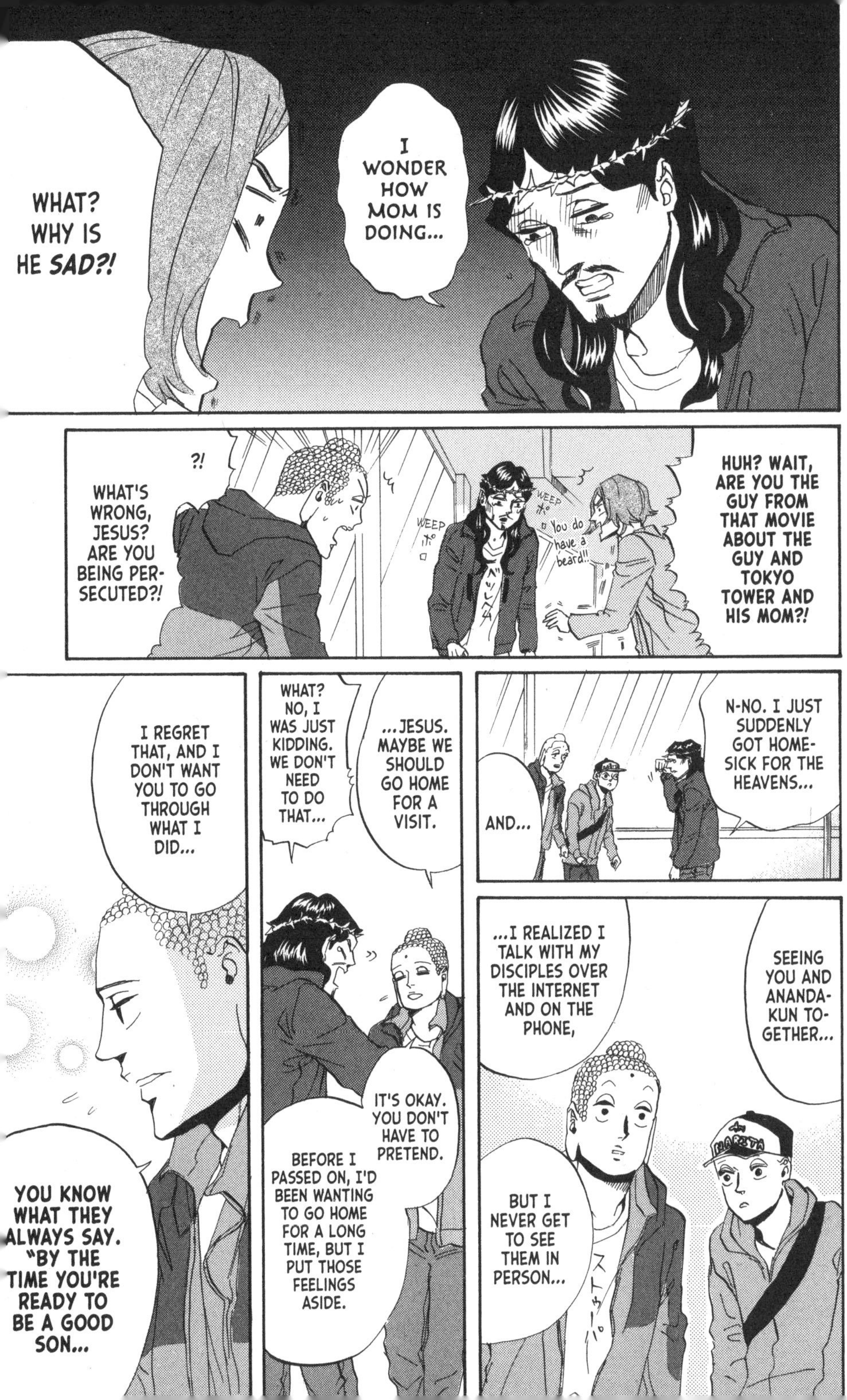
I WONDER HOW MOM IS DOING...
WHAT? WHY IS HE *SAD?!*
HUH? WAIT, ARE YOU THE GUY FROM THAT MOVIE ABOUT THE GUY AND TOKYO TOWER AND HIS MOM?!
WEEP
You do have a beard!!
WEEP
?!
WHAT'S WRONG, JESUS? ARE YOU BEING PER-SECUTED?!
N-NO. I JUST SUDDENLY GOT HOME-SICK FOR THE HEAVENS...
AND...
SEEING YOU AND ANANDA-KUN TO-GETHER...
...I REALIZED I TALK WITH MY DISCIPLES OVER THE INTERNET AND ON THE PHONE,
BUT I NEVER GET TO SEE THEM IN PERSON...
...JESUS. MAYBE WE SHOULD GO HOME FOR A VISIT.
WHAT? NO, I WAS JUST KIDDING. WE DON'T NEED TO DO THAT...
IT'S OKAY. YOU DON'T HAVE TO PRETEND.
BEFORE I PASSED ON, I'D BEEN WANTING TO GO HOME FOR A LONG TIME, BUT I PUT THOSE FEELINGS ASIDE.
I REGRET THAT, AND I DON'T WANT YOU TO GO THROUGH WHAT I DID...
YOU KNOW WHAT THEY ALWAYS SAY. "BY THE TIME YOU'RE READY TO BE A GOOD SON...

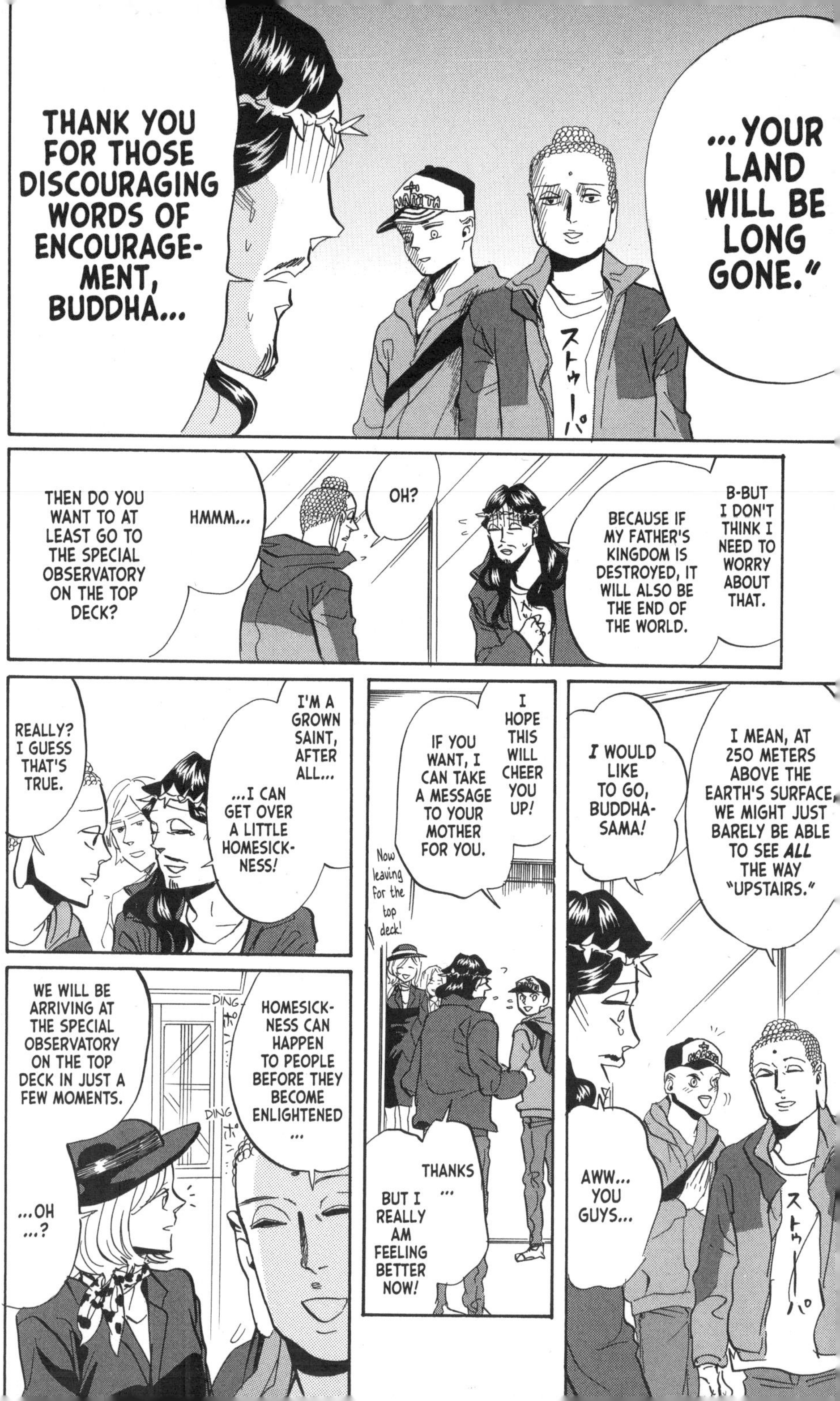
...YOUR LAND WILL BE LONG GONE."
ストゥーパ
THANK YOU FOR THOSE DISCOURAGING WORDS OF ENCOURAGE-MENT, BUDDHA...
B-BUT I DON'T THINK I NEED TO WORRY ABOUT THAT.
BECAUSE IF MY FATHER'S KINGDOM IS DESTROYED, IT WILL ALSO BE THE END OF THE WORLD.
OH?
HMMM...
THEN DO YOU WANT TO AT LEAST GO TO THE SPECIAL OBSERVATORY ON THE TOP DECK?
I MEAN, AT 250 METERS ABOVE THE EARTH'S SURFACE, WE MIGHT JUST BARELY BE ABLE TO SEE *ALL* THE WAY "UPSTAIRS."
I WOULD LIKE TO GO, BUDDHA-SAMA!
AWW... YOU GUYS...
I HOPE THIS WILL CHEER YOU UP!
IF YOU WANT, I CAN TAKE A MESSAGE TO YOUR MOTHER FOR YOU.
Now leaving for the top deck!
THANKS...
BUT I REALLY AM FEELING BETTER NOW!
I'M A GROWN SAINT, AFTER ALL...
...I CAN GET OVER A LITTLE HOMESICK-NESS!
REALLY? I GUESS THAT'S TRUE.
HOMESICK-NESS CAN HAPPEN TO PEOPLE BEFORE THEY BECOME ENLIGHTENED...
DING
DING
WE WILL BE ARRIVING AT THE SPECIAL OBSERVATORY ON THE TOP DECK IN JUST A FEW MOMENTS.
...OH ...?

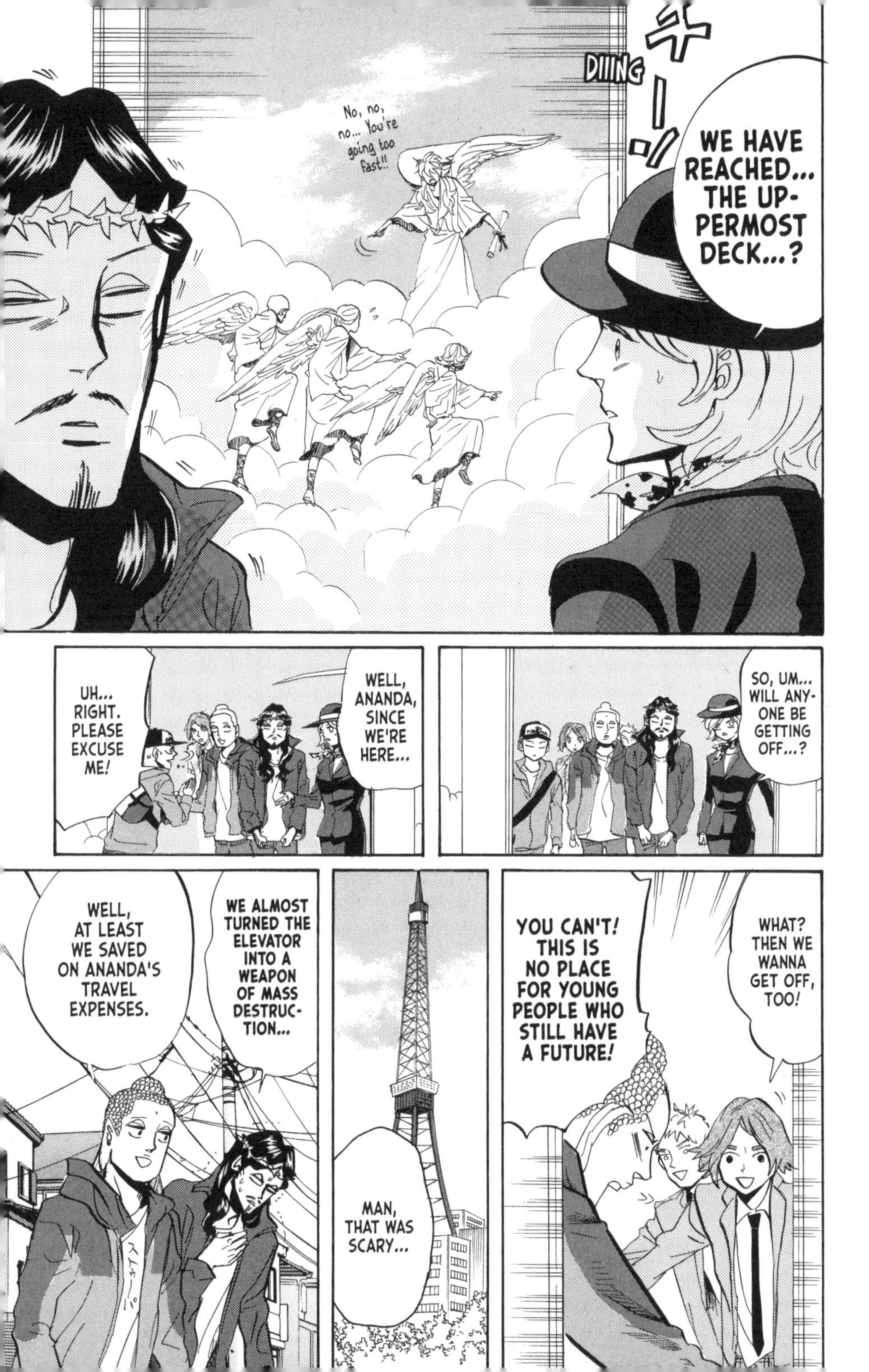
DIIING
WE HAVE REACHED... THE UPPERMOST DECK...?
No, no, no... You're going too fast!!
SO, UM... WILL ANYONE BE GETTING OFF...?
WELL, ANANDA, SINCE WE'RE HERE...
UH... RIGHT. PLEASE EXCUSE ME!
WHAT? THEN WE WANNA GET OFF, TOO!
YOU CAN'T! THIS IS NO PLACE FOR YOUNG PEOPLE WHO STILL HAVE A FUTURE!
MAN, THAT WAS SCARY...
WE ALMOST TURNED THE ELEVATOR INTO A WEAPON OF MASS DESTRUCTION...
WELL, AT LEAST WE SAVED ON ANANDA'S TRAVEL EXPENSES.

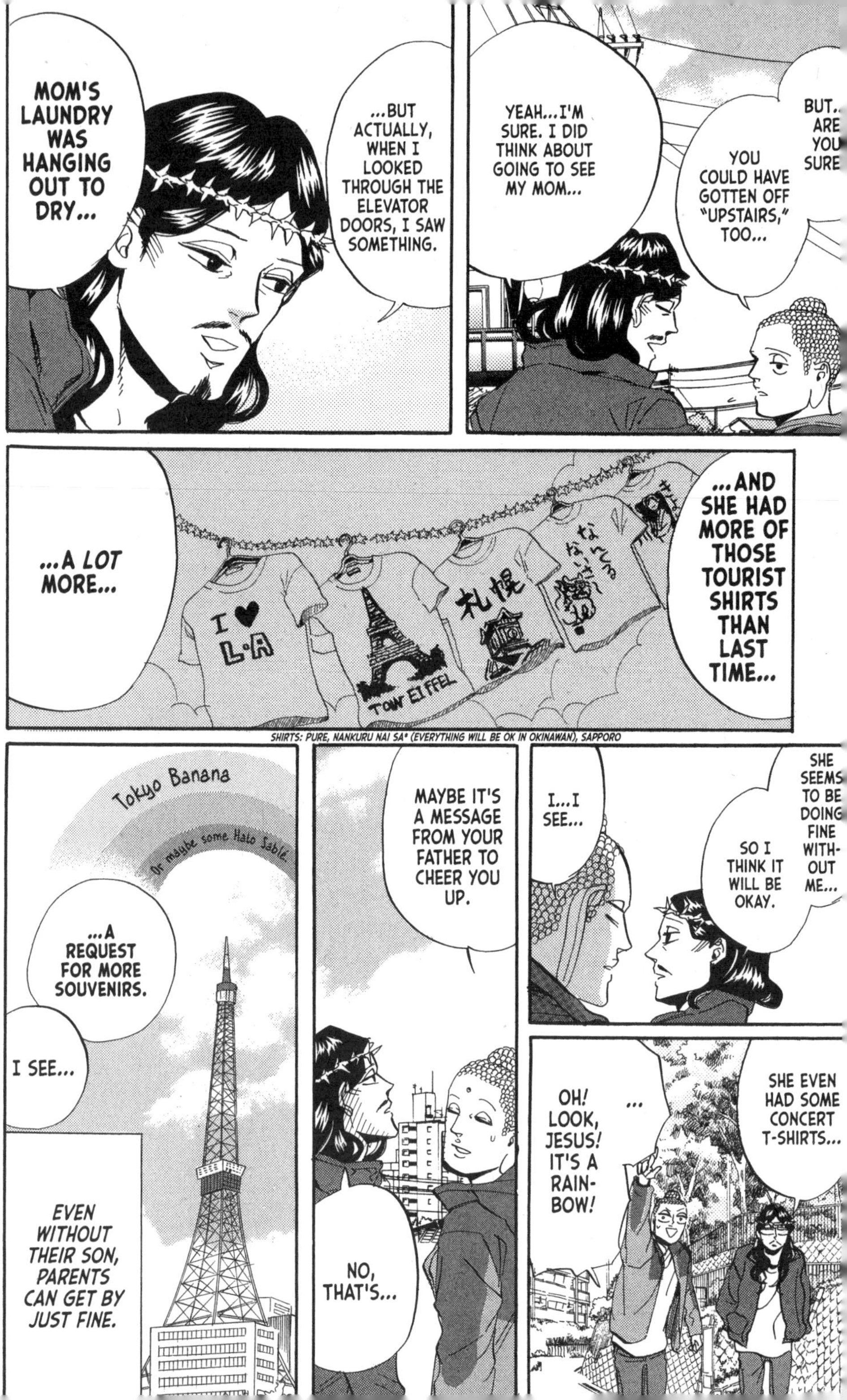
BUT.. ARE YOU SURE
YOU COULD HAVE GOTTEN OFF "UPSTAIRS," TOO...
YEAH...I'M SURE. I DID THINK ABOUT GOING TO SEE MY MOM...
...BUT ACTUALLY, WHEN I LOOKED THROUGH THE ELEVATOR DOORS, I SAW SOMETHING.
MOM'S LAUNDRY WAS HANGING OUT TO DRY...
...AND SHE HAD MORE OF THOSE TOURIST SHIRTS THAN LAST TIME...
...A *LOT* MORE...
I ♥ LA
札幌
SHE SEEMS TO BE DOING FINE WITHOUT ME...
SO I THINK IT WILL BE OKAY.
I...I SEE...
SHE EVEN HAD SOME CONCERT T-SHIRTS...
...
OH! LOOK, JESUS! IT'S A RAINBOW!
MAYBE IT'S A MESSAGE FROM YOUR FATHER TO CHEER YOU UP.
NO, THAT'S...
Tokyo Banana
Or maybe some Hato Sablé.
...A REQUEST FOR MORE SOUVENIRS.
I SEE...
EVEN WITHOUT THEIR SON, PARENTS CAN GET BY JUST FINE.

SHIRTS: PURE, NANKURU NAI SA (EVERYTHING WILL BE OK IN OKINAWAN), SAPPORO*

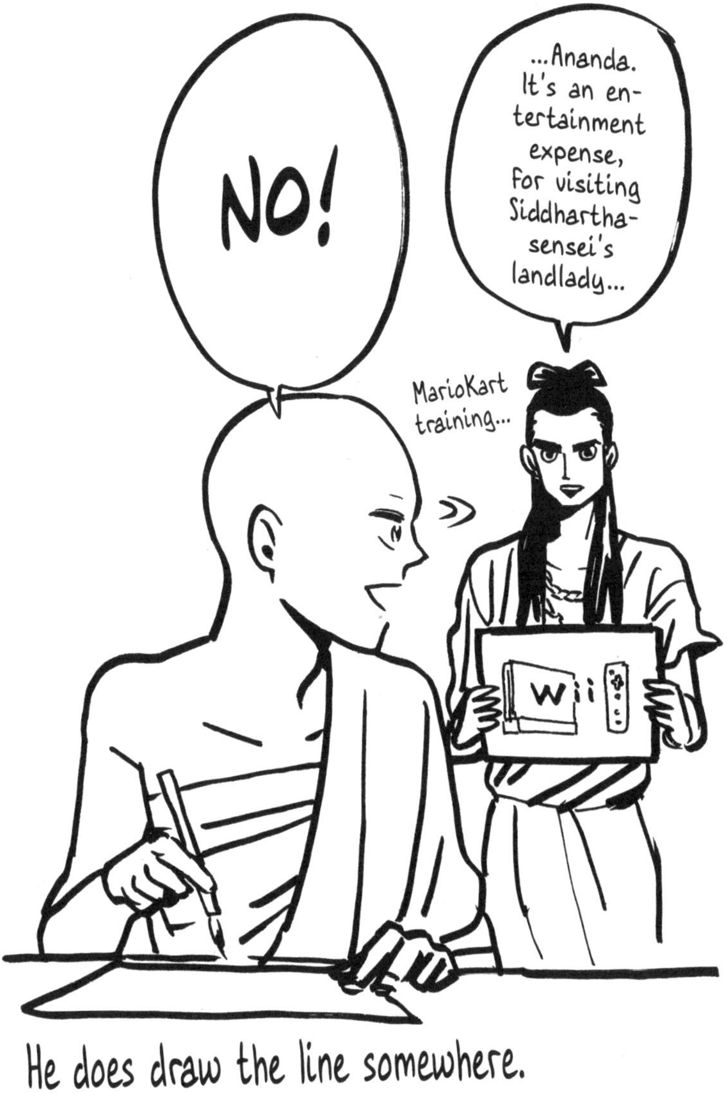
...Ananda. It's an entertainment expense, for visiting Siddhartha-sensei's landlady...
MarioKart training...
NO!
Wii
He does draw the line somewhere.

CHAPTER 30 TRANSLATION NOTES

Stupa, page 7
A stupa is a mound-like structure created as a memorial to the Buddha or other important figures in Asian religious tradition, which often contain their relics or remains. After his death, Gautama Buddha was cremated and his remains were buried in eight different stupas. These remains were recovered by Emperor Ashoka and redistributed into thousands of stupas all over the world.

Jesus's face, page 10
When prophesying about the coming Messiah's earthly ministry, the Old Testament prophet Isaiah states, "he hath no form nor comeliness [attractiveness]; and when we shall see him, there is no beauty that we should desire him." (Isaiah 53:2)

The townspeople's show of affection, page 11
Busier neighborhoods in Tokyo will often have salespeople handing out packets of tissues with advertisements on them to promote local businesses.

Tower, tō, and stupa, page 16
In Japanese, the word used for "tower" in Tokyo Tower is a phoetically rendered English term native to Japanese (*wasei-eigo*). The English word then shares a common pronounciation with the Japanese word for stupa, *sotoba*, which have over the course of their history come to resemble towers. The character of "to" as well is present in other words referring to buildings not associated with Buddhism.

Paris, City of Lights, page 17
One of the nicknames for Paris is "City of Lights," because it was one of the first cities to have electricity. However, that is not the nickname Jesus actually used in the original text. In Japan, Paris is often referred to as the "city of flowers," because it is so *hanayaka*. *Hana* means "flower," and the word *hanayaka* (flower-like) is used to describe things that are brilliantly beautiful.

The god of this place, page 17
The "pink personage" in question is actually one of the Noppon Brothers, the twin mascots of Tokyo Tower. The Shinto shrine in Tokyo Tower, Tower Daijingu, is dedicated to the sun goddess in Japanese mythology, Amaterasu. Shinto shrines and Buddhist sacred spaces have a long shared history in Japan, but were separated by government edict during the reforms of the late 19th century.

The guy from the movie, page 19
In the original Japanese, this young man asks, "Are you Lily Franky?!" Lily Franky is the author of an autobiographical novel called *Tokyo Tower: Mom and Me, and Sometimes Dad*, about an irresponsible man who reorganizes his life when he must take care of his cancer-stricken mother. The book was made into a movie in 2007.

Your nation is long gone, page 20
The more commonly known version of this expression in Japanese translates to, "By the time you're ready to be a good son, your parents are long gone."

Discouraging words of encouragement, page 20
A more literal translation of this line is, "Thank you for those lead-like words of gold, Buddha." "Words of gold" is a Japanese metaphor referring to a maxim, proverb, aphorism, or other such pieces of good advice. More specifically, "words of gold" also refers to the valuable teachings spoken by Buddha.

Tokyo Banana and Hato Sablé, page 22

These are popular souvenirs from Japan, where many culinary souvenirs are specific to a place. Tokyo Bananas are miniature sponge cakes filled with banana custard cream and shaped like bananas. Hato Sablé are shortbread cookies (or *sablé* in French) shaped like doves (*hato* in Japanese) that can be found in the city of Kamakura.

SAINT☆YOUNG MEN

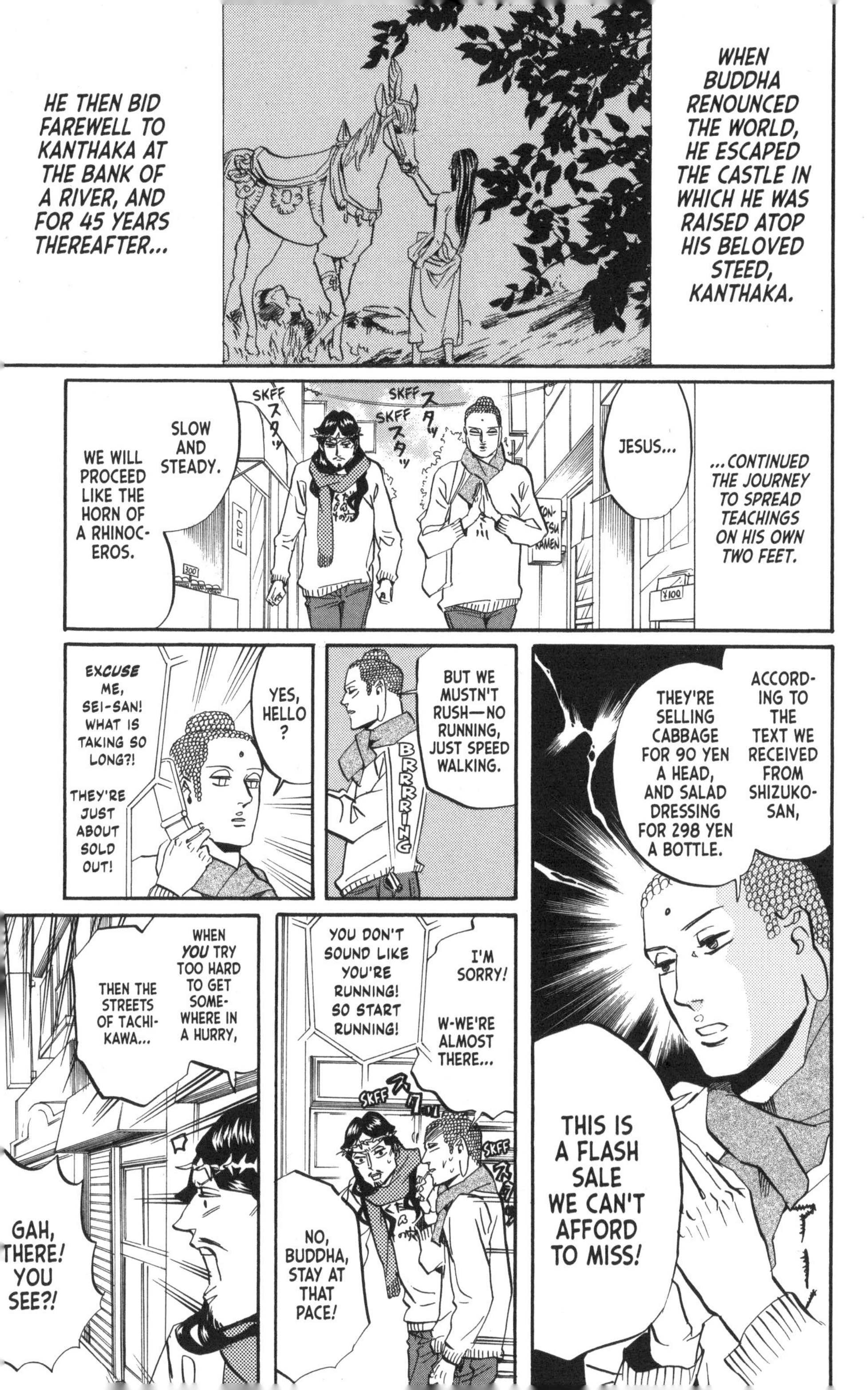

WHEN BUDDHA RENOUNCED THE WORLD, HE ESCAPED THE CASTLE IN WHICH HE WAS RAISED ATOP HIS BELOVED STEED, KANTHAKA.
HE THEN BID FAREWELL TO KANTHAKA AT THE BANK OF A RIVER, AND FOR 45 YEARS THEREAFTER...
...CONTINUED THE JOURNEY TO SPREAD TEACHINGS ON HIS OWN TWO FEET.
¥100
JESUS...
SKFF
SKFF
SKFF
SLOW AND STEADY.
WE WILL PROCEED LIKE THE HORN OF A RHINOCEROS.
TOFU
300
ACCORDING TO THE TEXT WE RECEIVED FROM SHIZUKO-SAN,
THEY'RE SELLING CABBAGE FOR 90 YEN A HEAD, AND SALAD DRESSING FOR 298 YEN A BOTTLE.
THIS IS A FLASH SALE WE CAN'T AFFORD TO MISS!
BUT WE MUSTN'T RUSH—NO RUNNING, JUST SPEED WALKING.
BRRRRING
YES, HELLO?
EXCUSE ME, SEI-SAN! WHAT IS TAKING SO LONG?!
THEY'RE JUST ABOUT SOLD OUT!
I'M SORRY!
YOU DON'T SOUND LIKE YOU'RE RUNNING! SO START RUNNING!
W-WE'RE ALMOST THERE...
SKFF
SKFF
NO, BUDDHA, STAY AT THAT PACE!
WHEN *YOU* TRY TOO HARD TO GET SOMEWHERE IN A HURRY,
THEN THE STREETS OF TACHIKAWA...
GAH, THERE! YOU SEE?!

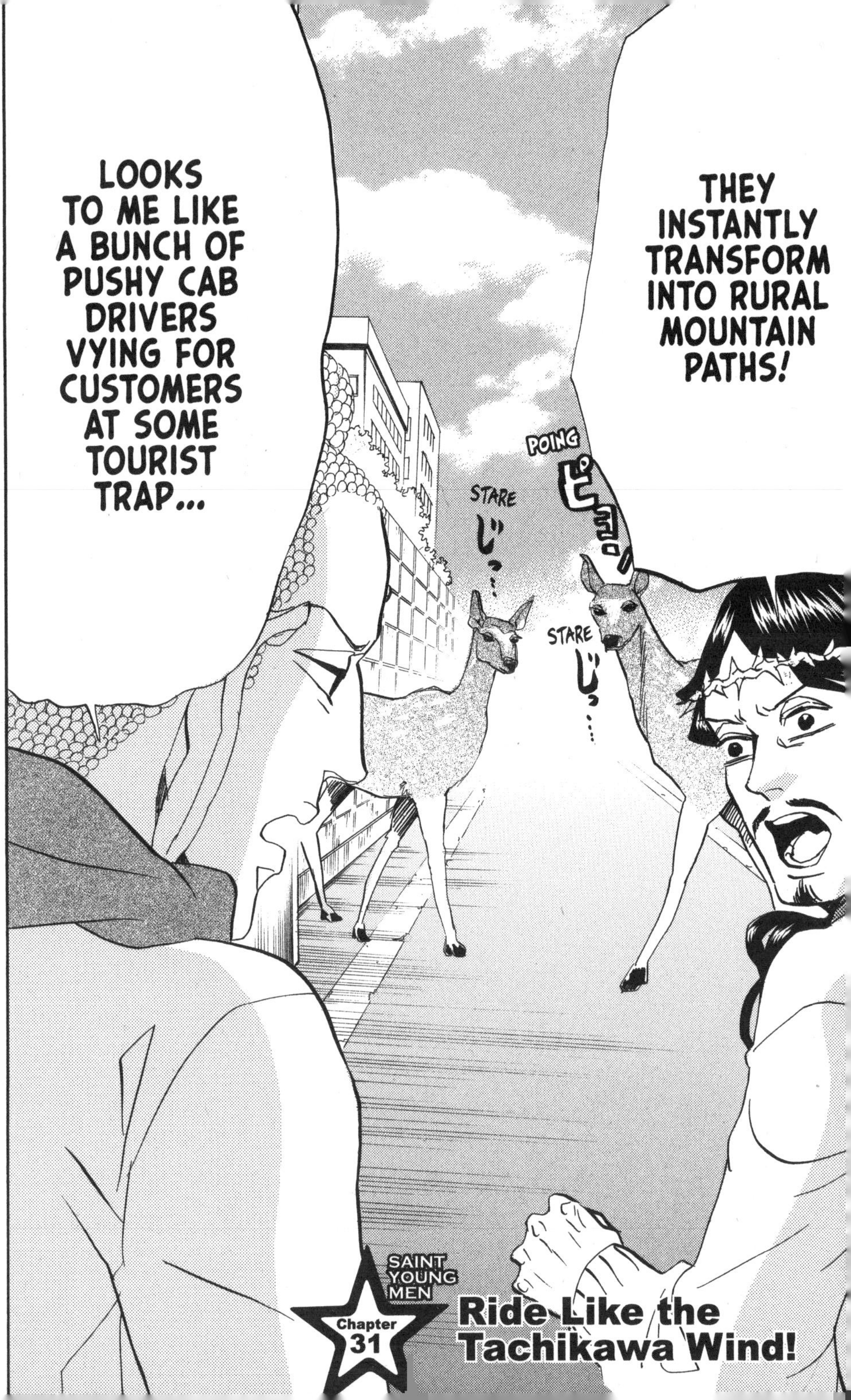
THEY INSTANTLY TRANSFORM INTO RURAL MOUNTAIN PATHS!
LOOKS TO ME LIKE A BUNCH OF PUSHY CAB DRIVERS VYING FOR CUSTOMERS AT SOME TOURIST TRAP...
POING
STARE
STARE
SAINT YOUNG MEN
Chapter 31
Ride Like the Tachikawa Wind!

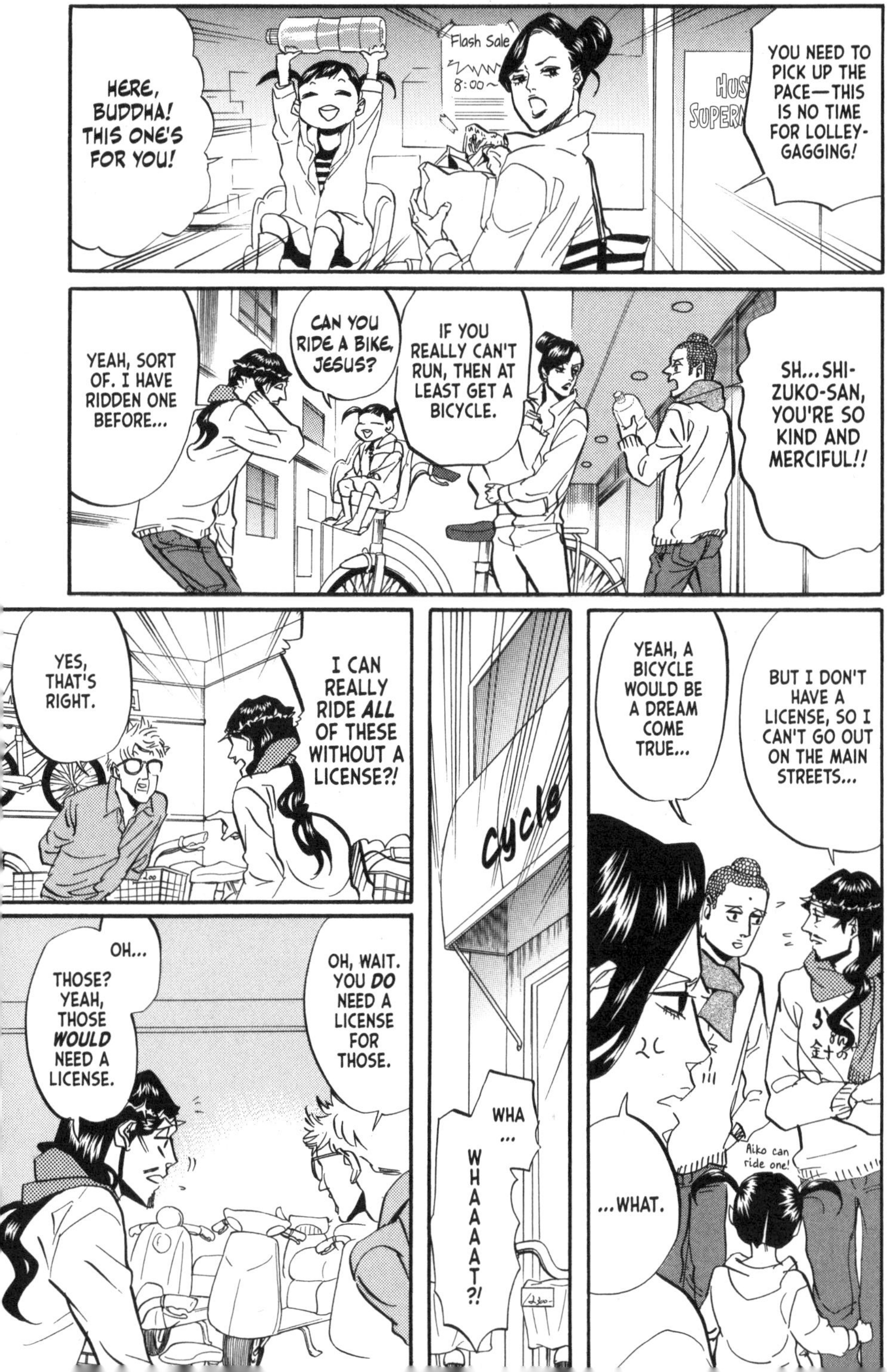
YOU NEED TO PICK UP THE PACE—THIS IS NO TIME FOR LOLLEY-GAGGING!
Flash Sale
8:00~
HERE, BUDDHA! THIS ONE'S FOR YOU!
SH... SHI-ZUKO-SAN, YOU'RE SO KIND AND MERCIFUL!!
IF YOU REALLY CAN'T RUN, THEN AT LEAST GET A BICYCLE.
CAN YOU RIDE A BIKE, JESUS?
YEAH, SORT OF. I HAVE RIDDEN ONE BEFORE...
BUT I DON'T HAVE A LICENSE, SO I CAN'T GO OUT ON THE MAIN STREETS...
YEAH, A BICYCLE WOULD BE A DREAM COME TRUE...
Aiko can ride one!
...WHAT.
Cycle
WHA...
WHAAAAAT?!
I CAN REALLY RIDE *ALL* OF THESE WITHOUT A LICENSE?!
YES, THAT'S RIGHT.
OH, WAIT. YOU *DO* NEED A LICENSE FOR THOSE.
OH... THOSE? YEAH, THOSE *WOULD* NEED A LICENSE.

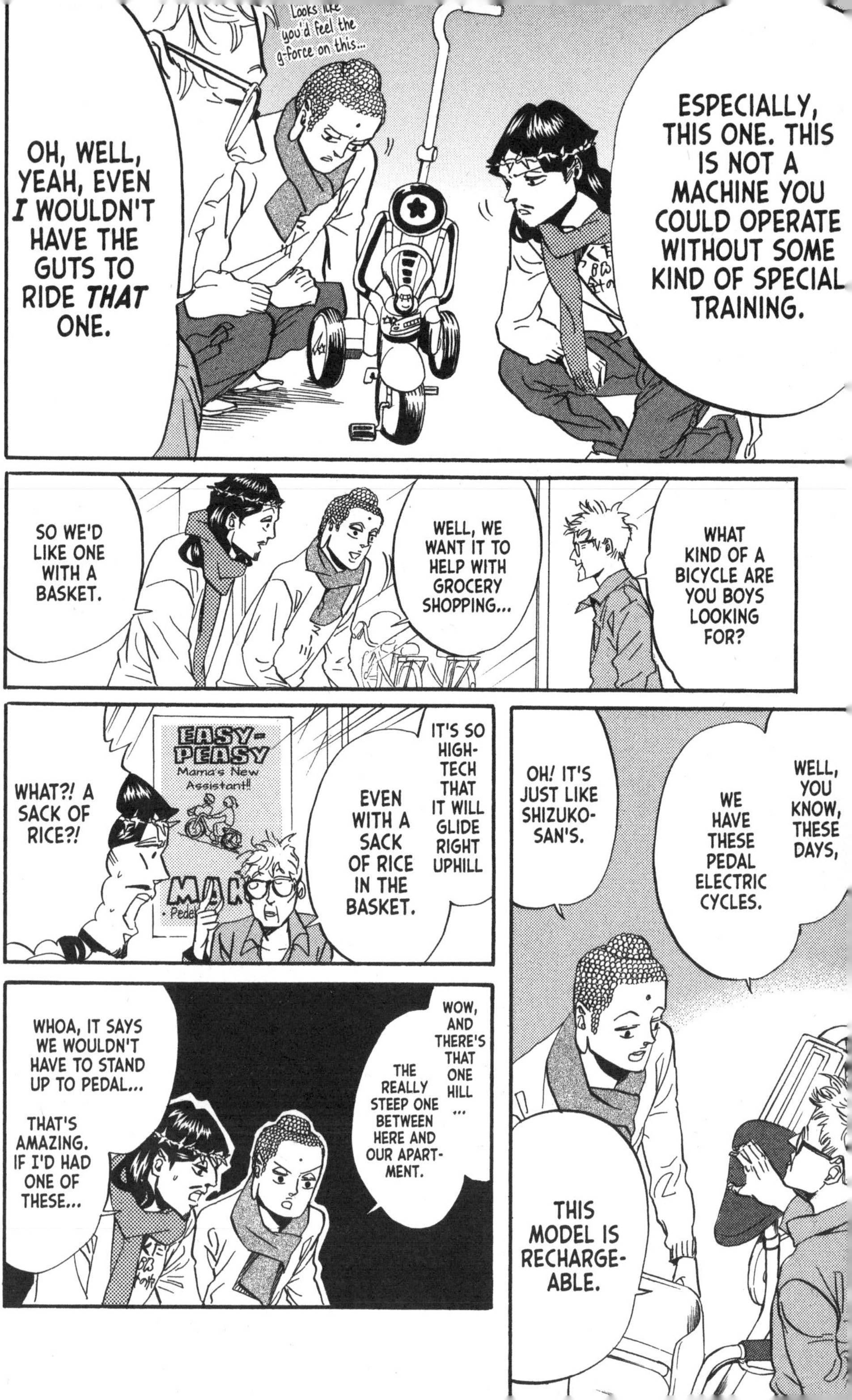
ESPECIALLY, THIS ONE. THIS IS NOT A MACHINE YOU COULD OPERATE WITHOUT SOME KIND OF SPECIAL TRAINING.
Looks like you'd feel the g-force on this...
OH, WELL, YEAH, EVEN *I* WOULDN'T HAVE THE GUTS TO RIDE *THAT* ONE.
WHAT KIND OF A BICYCLE ARE YOU BOYS LOOKING FOR?
WELL, WE WANT IT TO HELP WITH GROCERY SHOPPING...
SO WE'D LIKE ONE WITH A BASKET.
WELL, YOU KNOW, THESE DAYS,
WE HAVE THESE PEDAL ELECTRIC CYCLES.
OH! IT'S JUST LIKE SHIZUKO-SAN'S.
THIS MODEL IS RECHARGE-ABLE.
IT'S SO HIGH-TECH THAT IT WILL GLIDE RIGHT UPHILL
EVEN WITH A SACK OF RICE IN THE BASKET.
WHAT?! A SACK OF RICE?!
EASY-PEASY
Mama's New Assistant!!
WOW, AND THERE'S THAT ONE HILL...
THE REALLY STEEP ONE BETWEEN HERE AND OUR APART-MENT.
WHOA, IT SAYS WE WOULDN'T HAVE TO STAND UP TO PEDAL...
THAT'S AMAZING. IF I'D HAD ONE OF THESE...

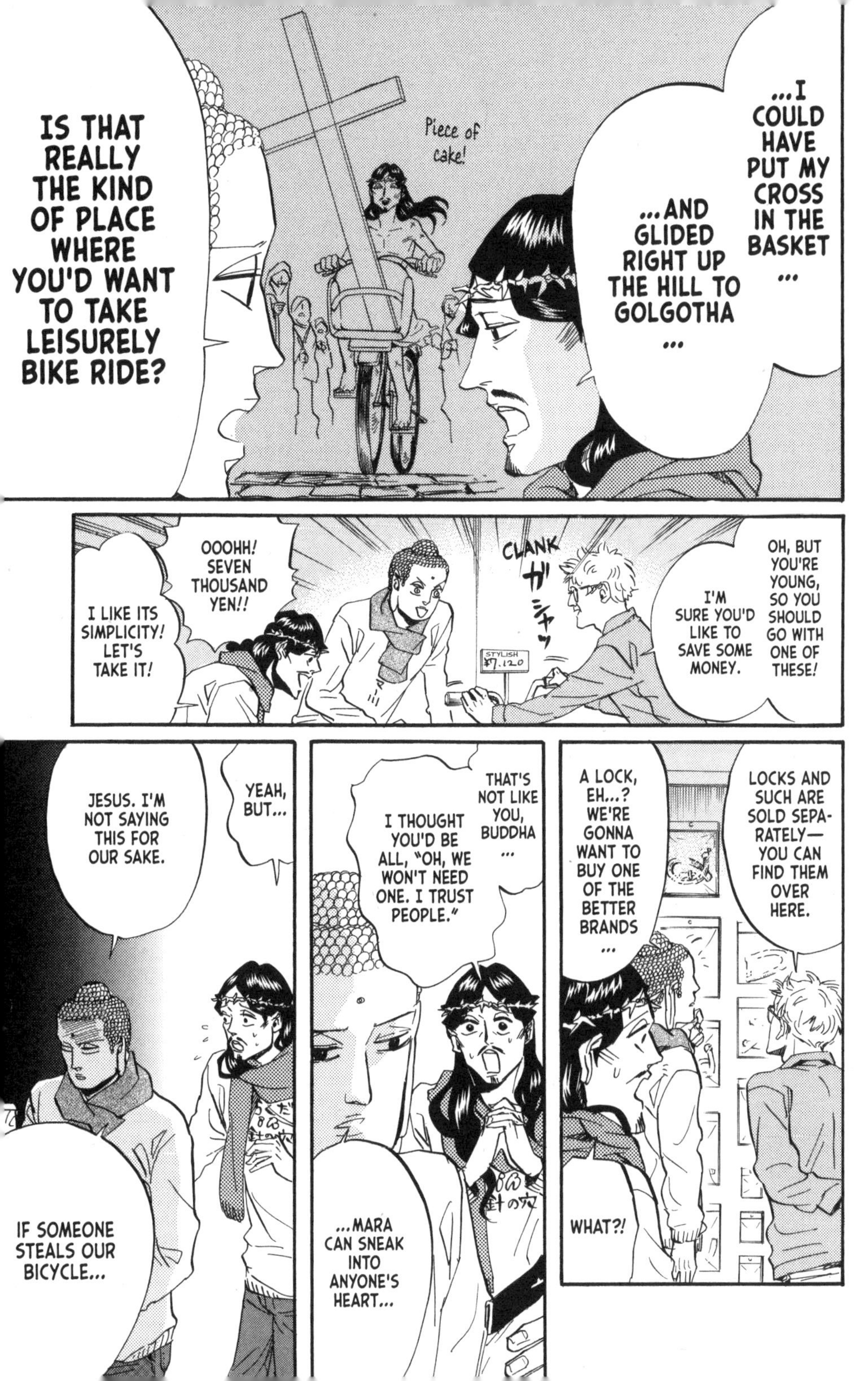
...I COULD HAVE PUT MY CROSS IN THE BASKET...
...AND GLIDED RIGHT UP THE HILL TO GOLGOTHA...
Piece of cake!
IS THAT REALLY THE KIND OF PLACE WHERE YOU'D WANT TO TAKE LEISURELY BIKE RIDE?
OH, BUT YOU'RE YOUNG, SO YOU SHOULD GO WITH ONE OF THESE!
I'M SURE YOU'D LIKE TO SAVE SOME MONEY.
CLANK
ガシャッ
STYLISH ¥7,120
OOOHH! SEVEN THOUSAND YEN!!
I LIKE ITS SIMPLICITY! LET'S TAKE IT!
LOCKS AND SUCH ARE SOLD SEPA-RATELY—YOU CAN FIND THEM OVER HERE.
A LOCK, EH...? WE'RE GONNA WANT TO BUY ONE OF THE BETTER BRANDS...
WHAT?!
THAT'S NOT LIKE YOU, BUDDHA...
I THOUGHT YOU'D BE ALL, "OH, WE WON'T NEED ONE. I TRUST PEOPLE."
...MARA CAN SNEAK INTO ANYONE'S HEART...
YEAH, BUT...
JESUS. I'M NOT SAYING THIS FOR OUR SAKE.
IF SOMEONE STEALS OUR BICYCLE...

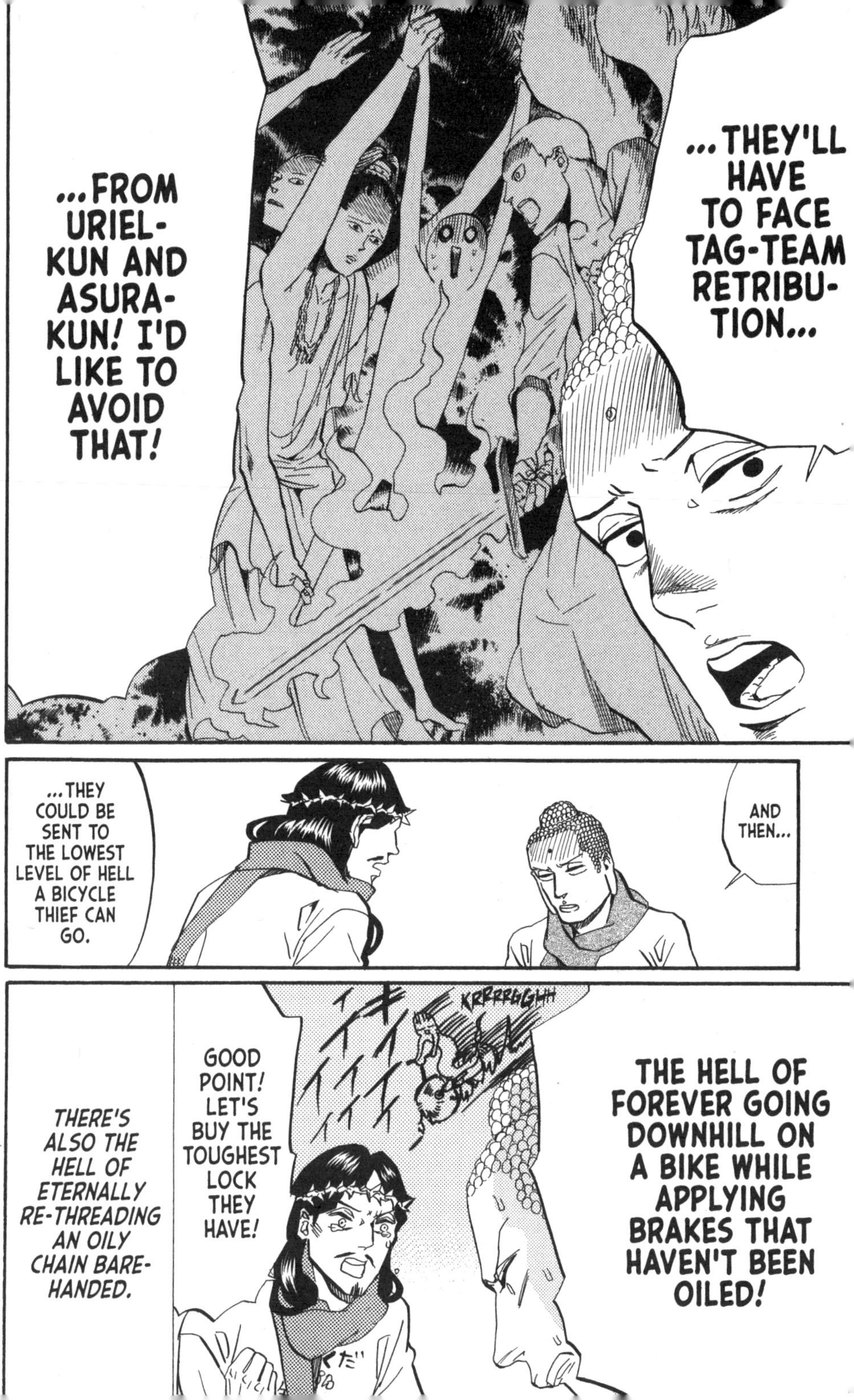
...THEY'LL HAVE TO FACE TAG-TEAM RETRIBUTION...
...FROM URIEL-KUN AND ASURA-KUN! I'D LIKE TO AVOID THAT!
AND THEN...
...THEY COULD BE SENT TO THE LOWEST LEVEL OF HELL A BICYCLE THIEF CAN GO.
THE HELL OF FOREVER GOING DOWNHILL ON A BIKE WHILE APPLYING BRAKES THAT HAVEN'T BEEN OILED!
KRRRRGGHH
GOOD POINT! LET'S BUY THE TOUGHEST LOCK THEY HAVE!
THERE'S ALSO THE HELL OF ETERNALLY RE-THREADING AN OILY CHAIN BARE-HANDED.

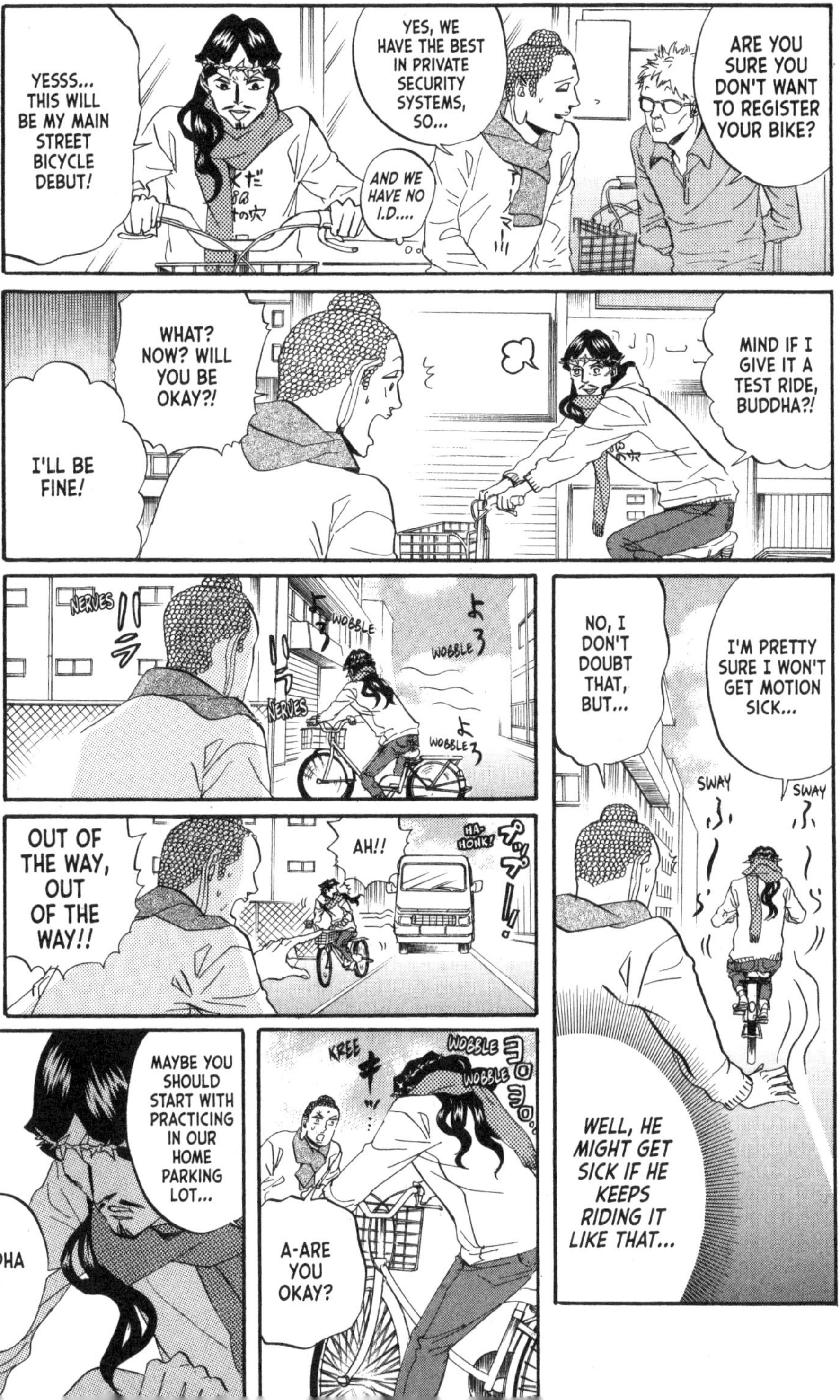
ARE YOU SURE YOU DON'T WANT TO REGISTER YOUR BIKE?
YES, WE HAVE THE BEST IN PRIVATE SECURITY SYSTEMS, SO...
AND WE HAVE NO I.D....
YESSS... THIS WILL BE MY MAIN STREET BICYCLE DEBUT!
MIND IF I GIVE IT A TEST RIDE, BUDDHA?!
WHAT? NOW? WILL YOU BE OKAY?!
I'LL BE FINE!
I'M PRETTY SURE I WON'T GET MOTION SICK...
NO, I DON'T DOUBT THAT, BUT...
SWAY
SWAY
WELL, HE MIGHT GET SICK IF HE KEEPS RIDING IT LIKE THAT...
NERVES
WOBBLE
WOBBLE
NERVES
WOBBLE
HA-HONK!
AH!!
OUT OF THE WAY, OUT OF THE WAY!!
WOBBLE
WOBBLE
KREE
A-ARE YOU OKAY?
MAYBE YOU SHOULD START WITH PRACTICING IN OUR HOME PARKING LOT...
BUDDHA ...

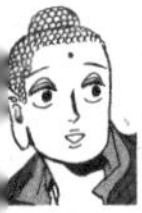

BUDDHA: WAS STARTLED WHEN HE SAW A GIANT FLOCK OF SPARROWS.

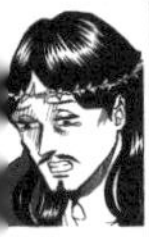

JESUS: WAS STARTLED WHEN HE SAW A GIANT FLOCK OF CUCKOOS.

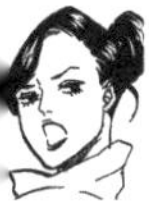

SHIZUKO: WIFE OF THEIR YAKUZA FRIEND. ONCE SAW A FLOCK OF YAKUZA, BUT WAS NOT STARTLED.

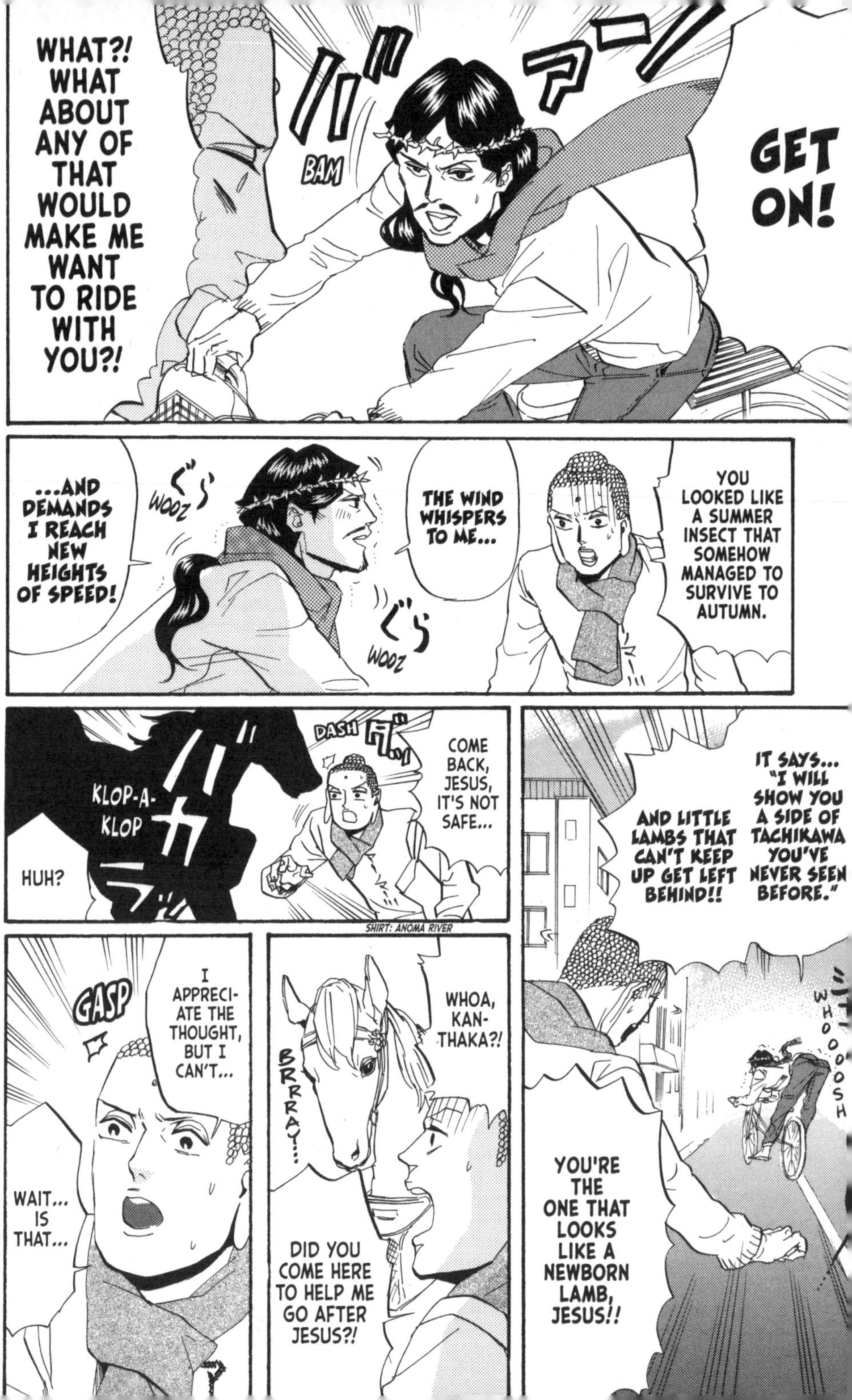
GET ON!
BAM
WHAT?! WHAT ABOUT ANY OF THAT WOULD MAKE ME WANT TO RIDE WITH YOU?!
YOU LOOKED LIKE A SUMMER INSECT THAT SOMEHOW MANAGED TO SURVIVE TO AUTUMN.
THE WIND WHISPERS TO ME...
WOOZ
WOOZ
...AND DEMANDS I REACH NEW HEIGHTS OF SPEED!
IT SAYS... "I WILL SHOW YOU A SIDE OF TACHIKAWA YOU'VE NEVER SEEN BEFORE."
AND LITTLE LAMBS THAT CAN'T KEEP UP GET LEFT BEHIND!!
WHOOOOOSH
YOU'RE THE ONE THAT LOOKS LIKE A NEWBORN LAMB, JESUS!!
DASH
COME BACK, JESUS, IT'S NOT SAFE...
KLOP-A-KLOP
HUH?
SHIRT: ANOMA RIVER
WHOA, KANTHAKA?!
BRRRAY!...
DID YOU COME HERE TO HELP ME GO AFTER JESUS?!
GASP
I APPRECIATE THE THOUGHT, BUT I CAN'T...
WAIT... IS THAT...

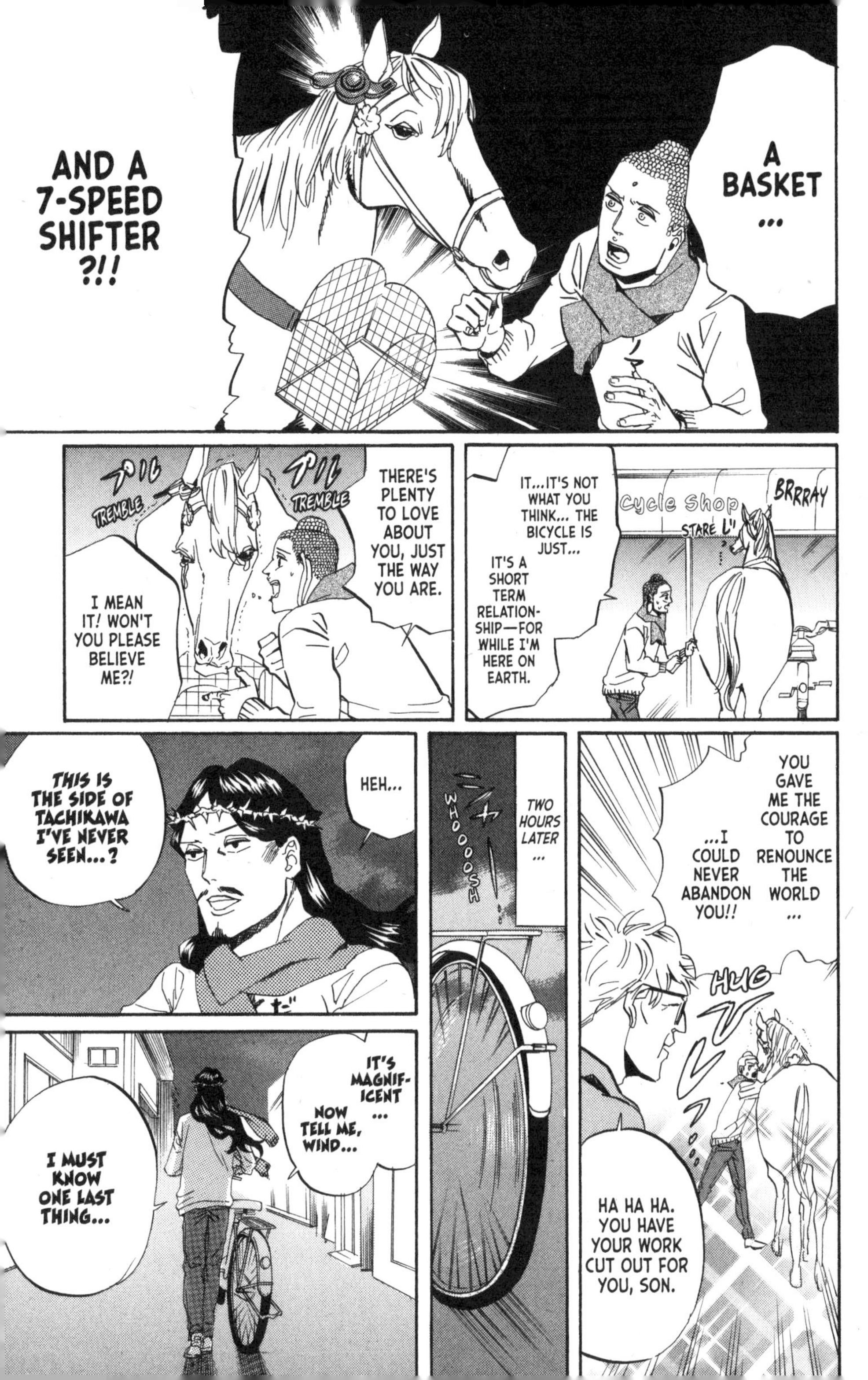
A BASKET...
AND A 7-SPEED SHIFTER?!!
IT...IT'S NOT WHAT YOU THINK... THE BICYCLE IS JUST...
IT'S A SHORT TERM RELATION-SHIP—FOR WHILE I'M HERE ON EARTH.
Cycle Shop
BRRRAY
STARE
TREMBLE
TREMBLE
THERE'S PLENTY TO LOVE ABOUT YOU, JUST THE WAY YOU ARE.
I MEAN IT! WON'T YOU PLEASE BELIEVE ME?!
YOU GAVE ME THE COURAGE TO RENOUNCE THE WORLD...
...I COULD NEVER ABANDON YOU!!
HUG
HA HA HA. YOU HAVE YOUR WORK CUT OUT FOR YOU, SON.
TWO HOURS LATER...
WHOOOOOSH
HEH...
THIS IS THE SIDE OF TACHIKAWA I'VE NEVER SEEN...?
IT'S MAGNIFICENT...
NOW TELL ME, WIND...
I MUST KNOW ONE LAST THING...

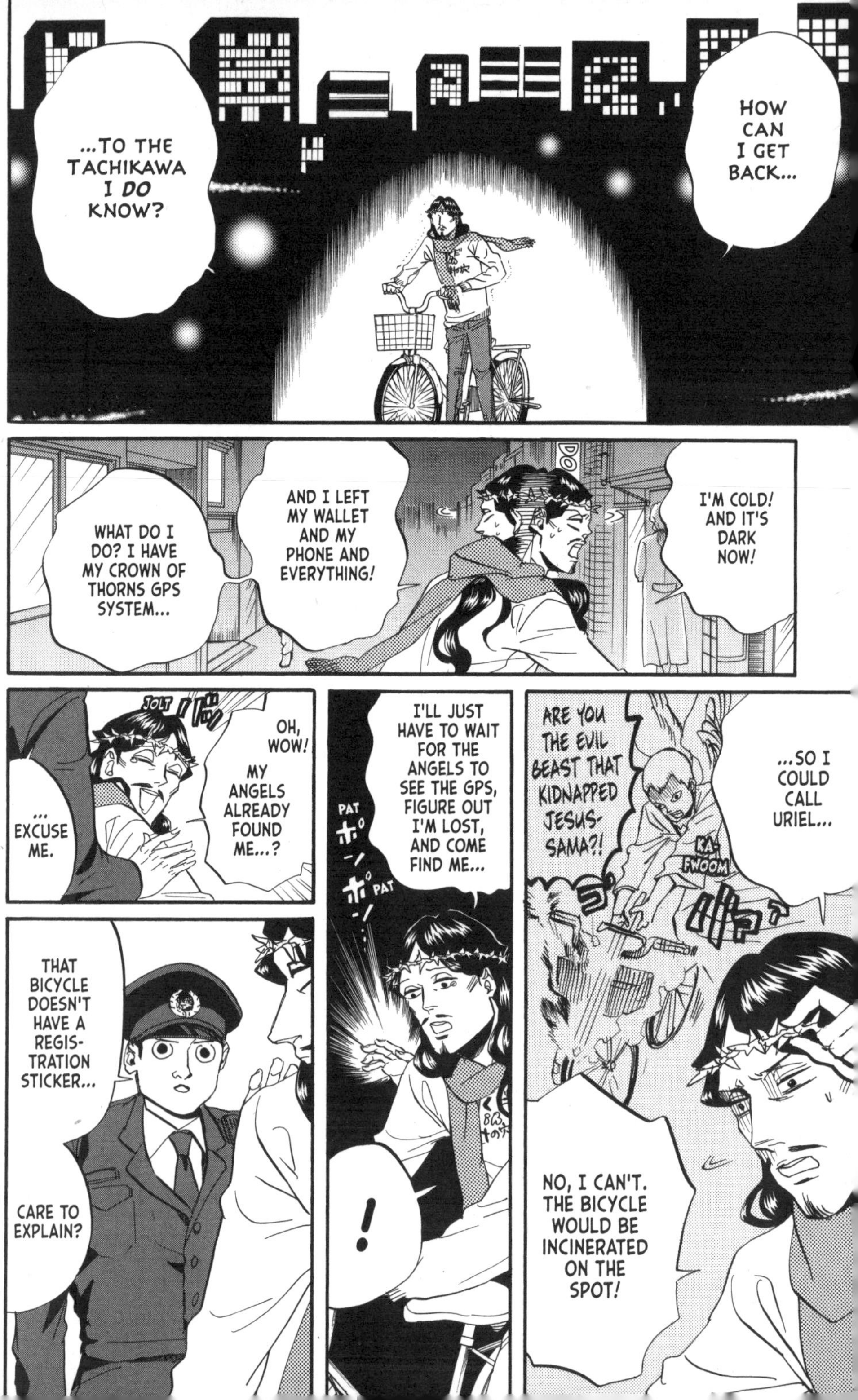
HOW CAN I GET BACK...
...TO THE TACHIKAWA I *DO* KNOW?
I'M COLD! AND IT'S DARK NOW!
AND I LEFT MY WALLET AND MY PHONE AND EVERYTHING!
WHAT DO I DO? I HAVE MY CROWN OF THORNS GPS SYSTEM...
...SO I COULD CALL URIEL...
ARE YOU THE EVIL BEAST THAT KIDNAPPED JESUS-SAMA?!
KA-FWOOM
NO, I CAN'T. THE BICYCLE WOULD BE INCINERATED ON THE SPOT!
I'LL JUST HAVE TO WAIT FOR THE ANGELS TO SEE THE GPS, FIGURE OUT I'M LOST, AND COME FIND ME...
PAT
PAT
!
JOLT
OH, WOW! MY ANGELS ALREADY FOUND ME...?
... EXCUSE ME.
THAT BICYCLE DOESN'T HAVE A REGIS-TRATION STICKER...
CARE TO EXPLAIN?

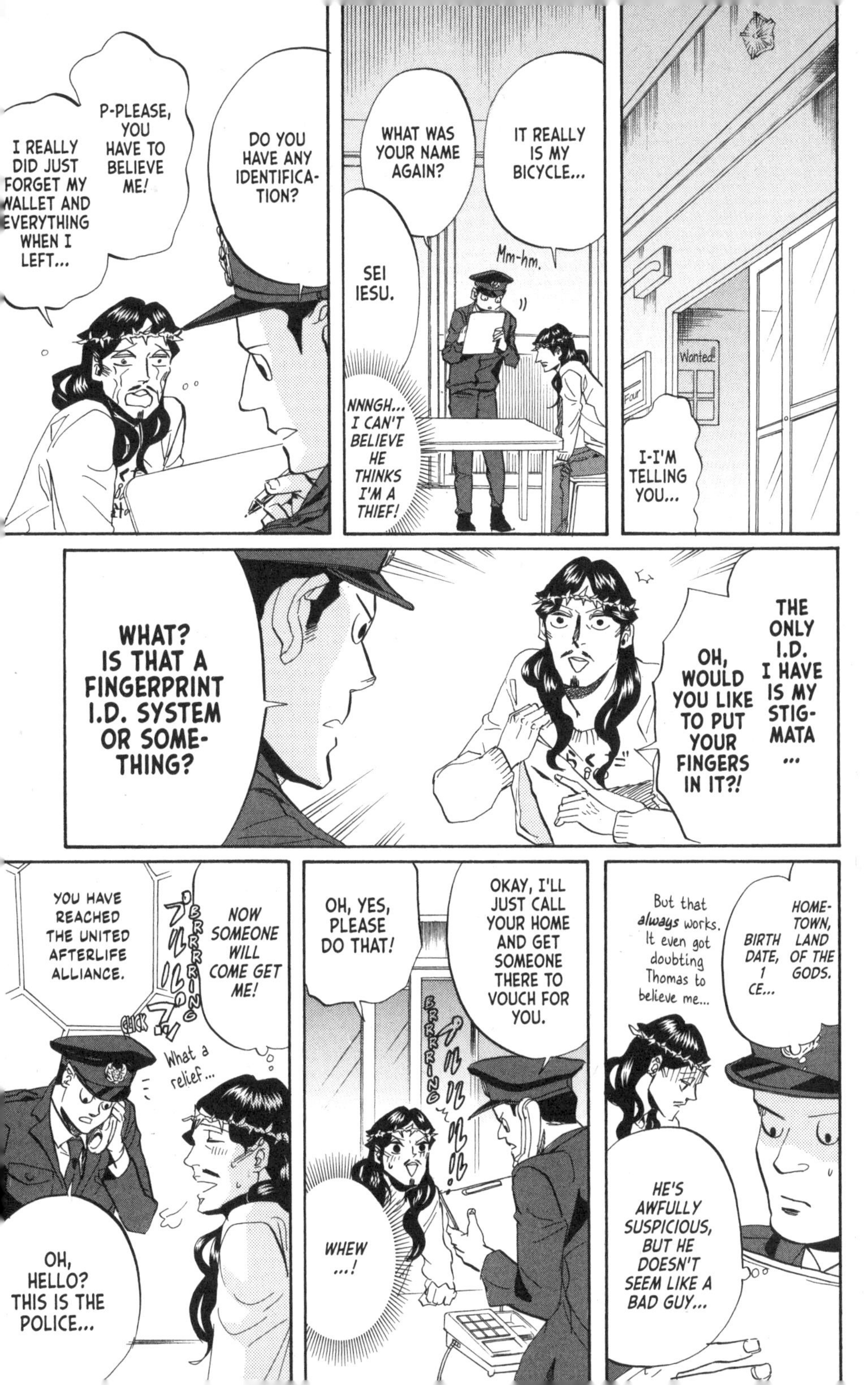

I-I'M TELLING YOU...
IT REALLY IS MY BICYCLE...
WHAT WAS YOUR NAME AGAIN?
Mm-hm.
SEI IESU.
NNNGH... I CAN'T BELIEVE HE THINKS I'M A THIEF!
DO YOU HAVE ANY IDENTIFICATION?
P-PLEASE, YOU HAVE TO BELIEVE ME!
I REALLY DID JUST FORGET MY WALLET AND EVERYTHING WHEN I LEFT...
THE ONLY I.D. I HAVE IS MY STIGMATA...
OH, WOULD YOU LIKE TO PUT YOUR FINGERS IN IT?!
WHAT? IS THAT A FINGERPRINT I.D. SYSTEM OR SOMETHING?
HOMETOWN, LAND OF THE GODS.
BIRTH DATE, 1 CE...
But that always works. It even got doubting Thomas to believe me...
HE'S AWFULLY SUSPICIOUS, BUT HE DOESN'T SEEM LIKE A BAD GUY...
OKAY, I'LL JUST CALL YOUR HOME AND GET SOMEONE THERE TO VOUCH FOR YOU.
OH, YES, PLEASE DO THAT!
BRRRRING
WHEW...!
NOW SOMEONE WILL COME GET ME!
BRRRRING
YOU HAVE REACHED THE UNITED AFTERLIFE ALLIANCE.
CLICK
What a relief...
OH, HELLO? THIS IS THE POLICE...

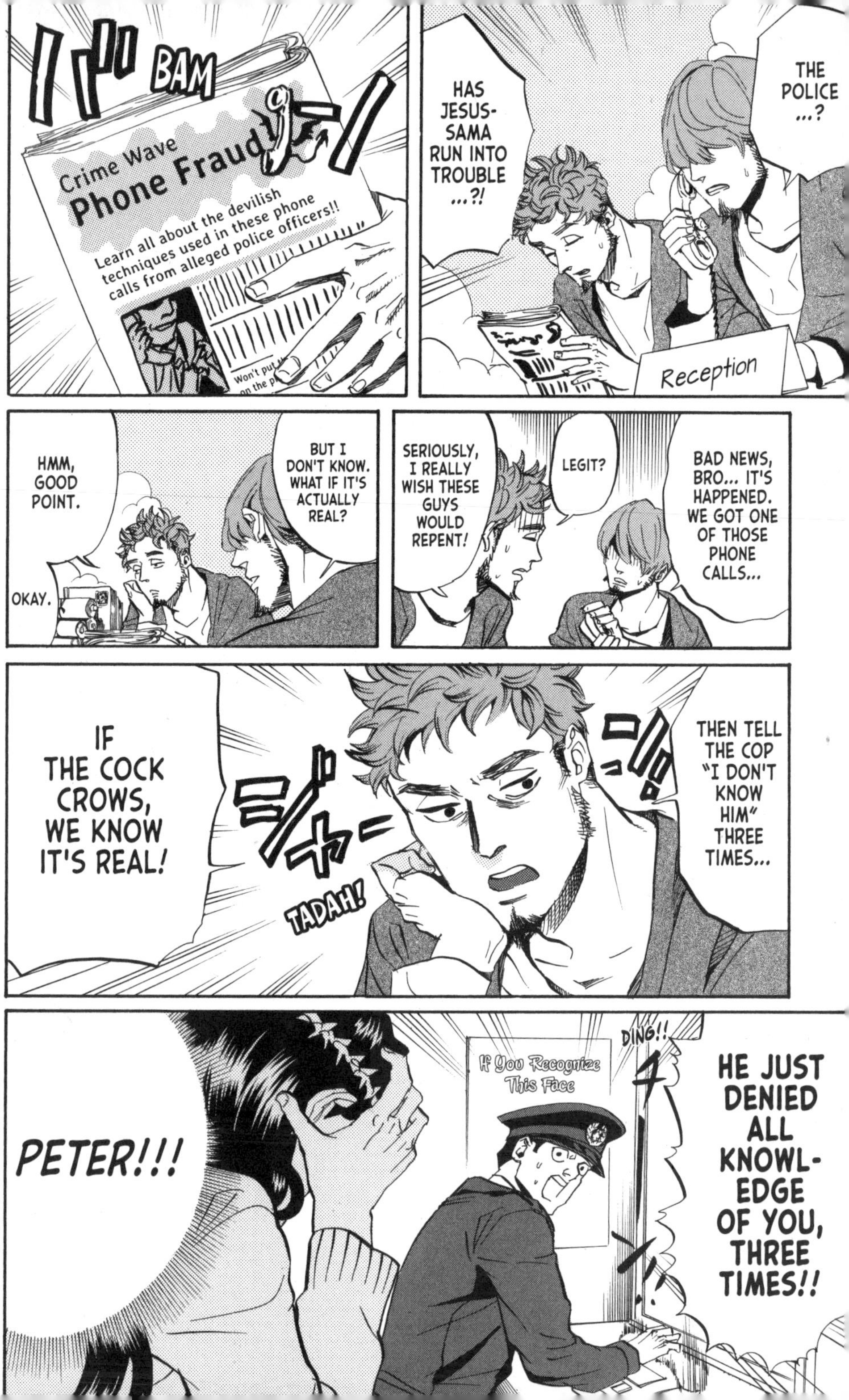
THE POLICE ...?
HAS JESUS-SAMA RUN INTO TROUBLE ...?!
Reception
BAM
Crime Wave
Phone Fraud
Learn all about the devilish techniques used in these phone calls from alleged police officers!!
BAD NEWS, BRO... IT'S HAPPENED. WE GOT ONE OF THOSE PHONE CALLS...
LEGIT?
SERIOUSLY, I REALLY WISH THESE GUYS WOULD REPENT!
BUT I DON'T KNOW. WHAT IF IT'S ACTUALLY REAL?
HMM, GOOD POINT.
OKAY.
THEN TELL THE COP "I DON'T KNOW HIM" THREE TIMES...
TADAH!
IF THE COCK CROWS, WE KNOW IT'S REAL!
HE JUST DENIED ALL KNOWL-EDGE OF YOU, THREE TIMES!!
DING!!
If You Recognize This Face
PETER!!!

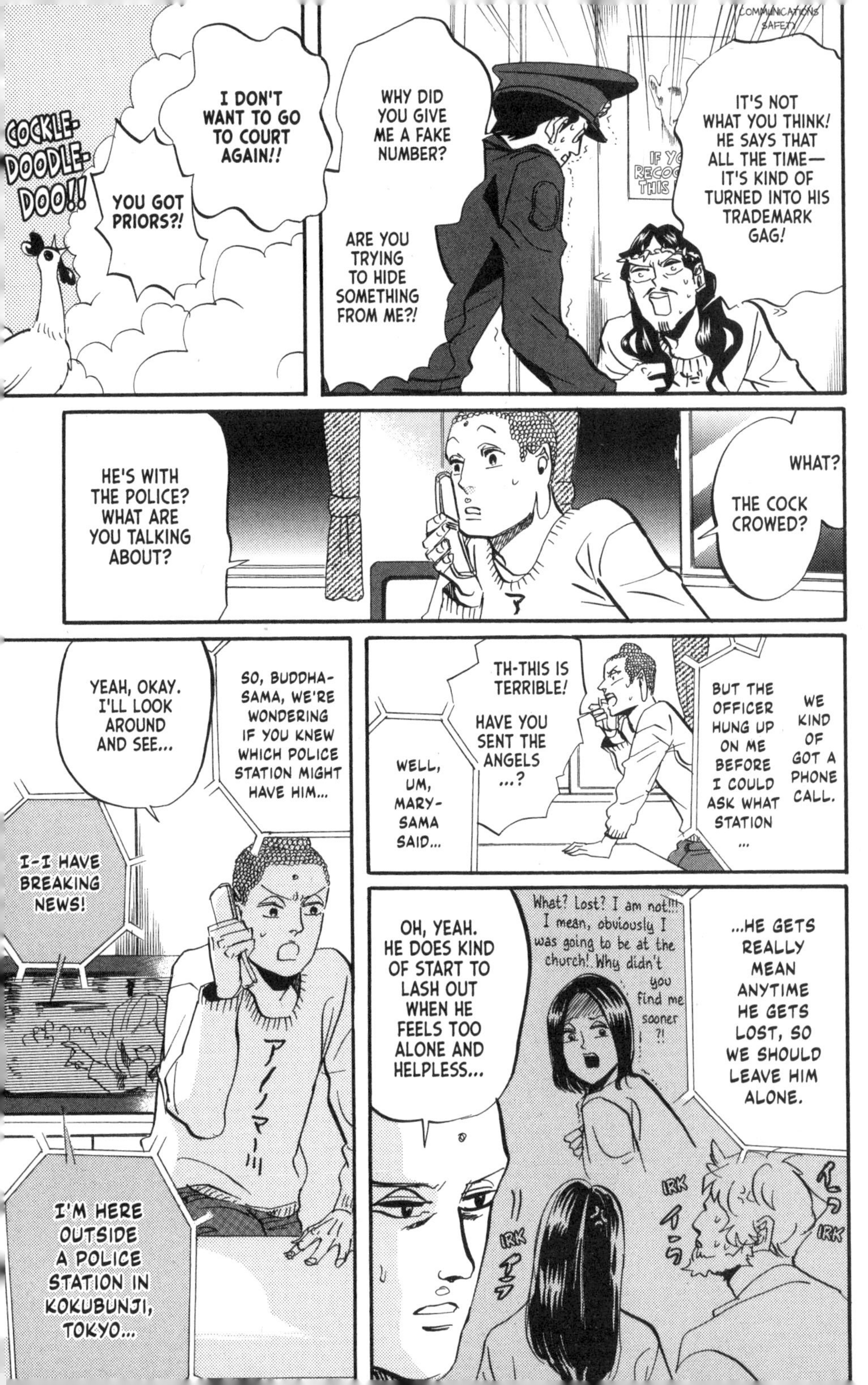
COMMUNICATIONS SAFETY
IF YO RECOG THIS
IT'S NOT WHAT YOU THINK! HE SAYS THAT ALL THE TIME— IT'S KIND OF TURNED INTO HIS TRADEMARK GAG!
WHY DID YOU GIVE ME A FAKE NUMBER?
ARE YOU TRYING TO HIDE SOMETHING FROM ME?!
I DON'T WANT TO GO TO COURT AGAIN!!
YOU GOT PRIORS?!
COCKLE-DOODLE-DOO!!
WHAT?
THE COCK CROWED?
HE'S WITH THE POLICE? WHAT ARE YOU TALKING ABOUT?
WE KIND OF GOT A PHONE CALL.
BUT THE OFFICER HUNG UP ON ME BEFORE I COULD ASK WHAT STATION ...
TH-THIS IS TERRIBLE!
HAVE YOU SENT THE ANGELS ...?
WELL, UM, MARY-SAMA SAID...
...HE GETS REALLY MEAN ANYTIME HE GETS LOST, SO WE SHOULD LEAVE HIM ALONE.
What? Lost? I am not!!! I mean, obviously I was going to be at the church! Why didn't you find me sooner ?!
OH, YEAH. HE DOES KIND OF START TO LASH OUT WHEN HE FEELS TOO ALONE AND HELPLESS...
IRK
IRK
IRK
SO, BUDDHA-SAMA, WE'RE WONDERING IF YOU KNEW WHICH POLICE STATION MIGHT HAVE HIM...
YEAH, OKAY. I'LL LOOK AROUND AND SEE...
I-I HAVE BREAKING NEWS!
I'M HERE OUTSIDE A POLICE STATION IN KOKUBUNJI, TOKYO...

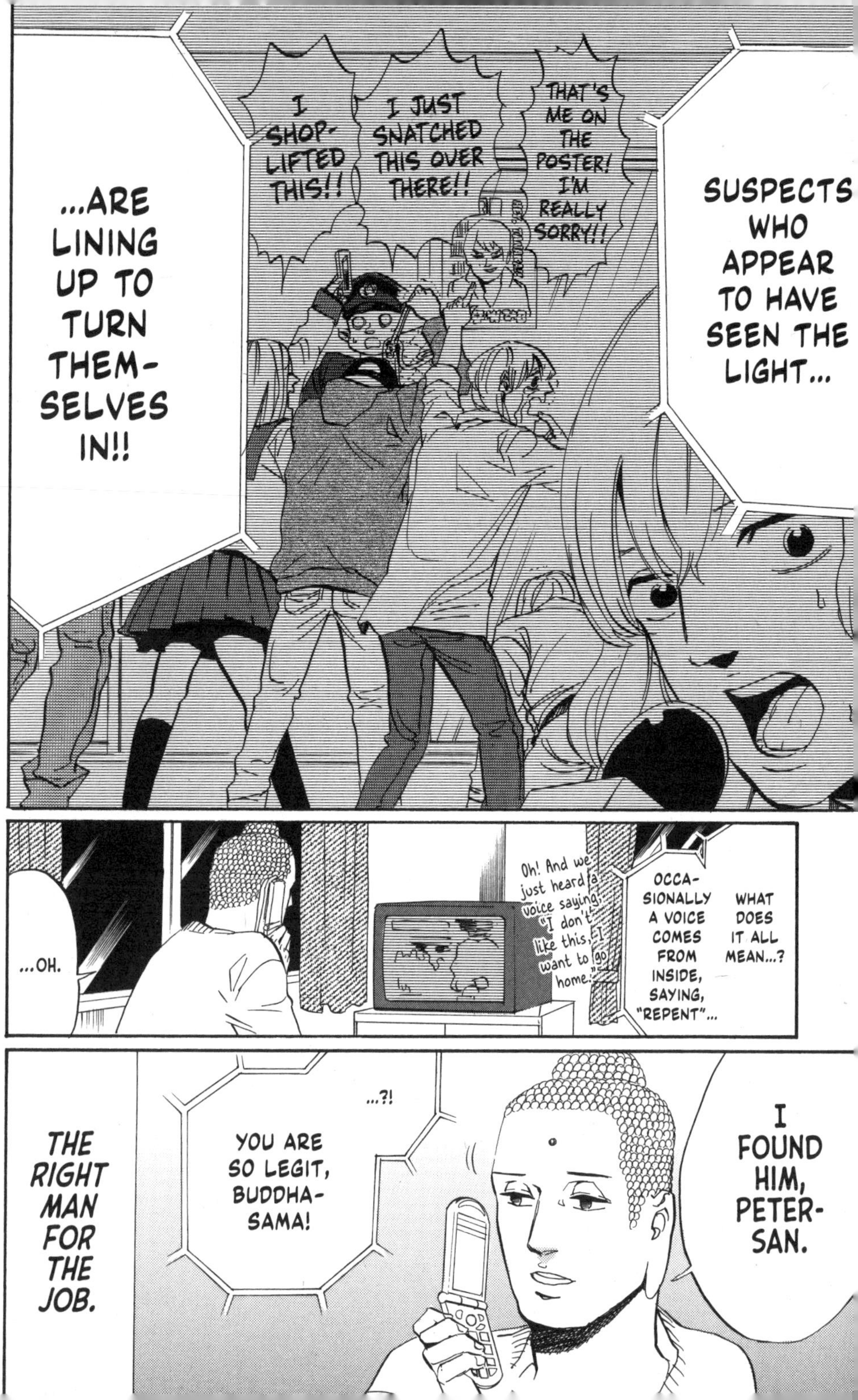
SUSPECTS WHO APPEAR TO HAVE SEEN THE LIGHT...
THAT'S ME ON THE POSTER! I'M REALLY SORRY!!
I JUST SNATCHED THIS OVER THERE!!
I SHOPLIFTED THIS!!
...ARE LINING UP TO TURN THEMSELVES IN!!
WHAT DOES IT ALL MEAN...?
OCCASIONALLY A VOICE COMES FROM INSIDE, SAYING, "REPENT"...
Oh! And we just heard a voice saying, "I don't like this, I want to go home."
...OH.
I FOUND HIM, PETER-SAN.
...?!
YOU ARE SO LEGIT, BUDDHA-SAMA!
THE RIGHT MAN FOR THE JOB.

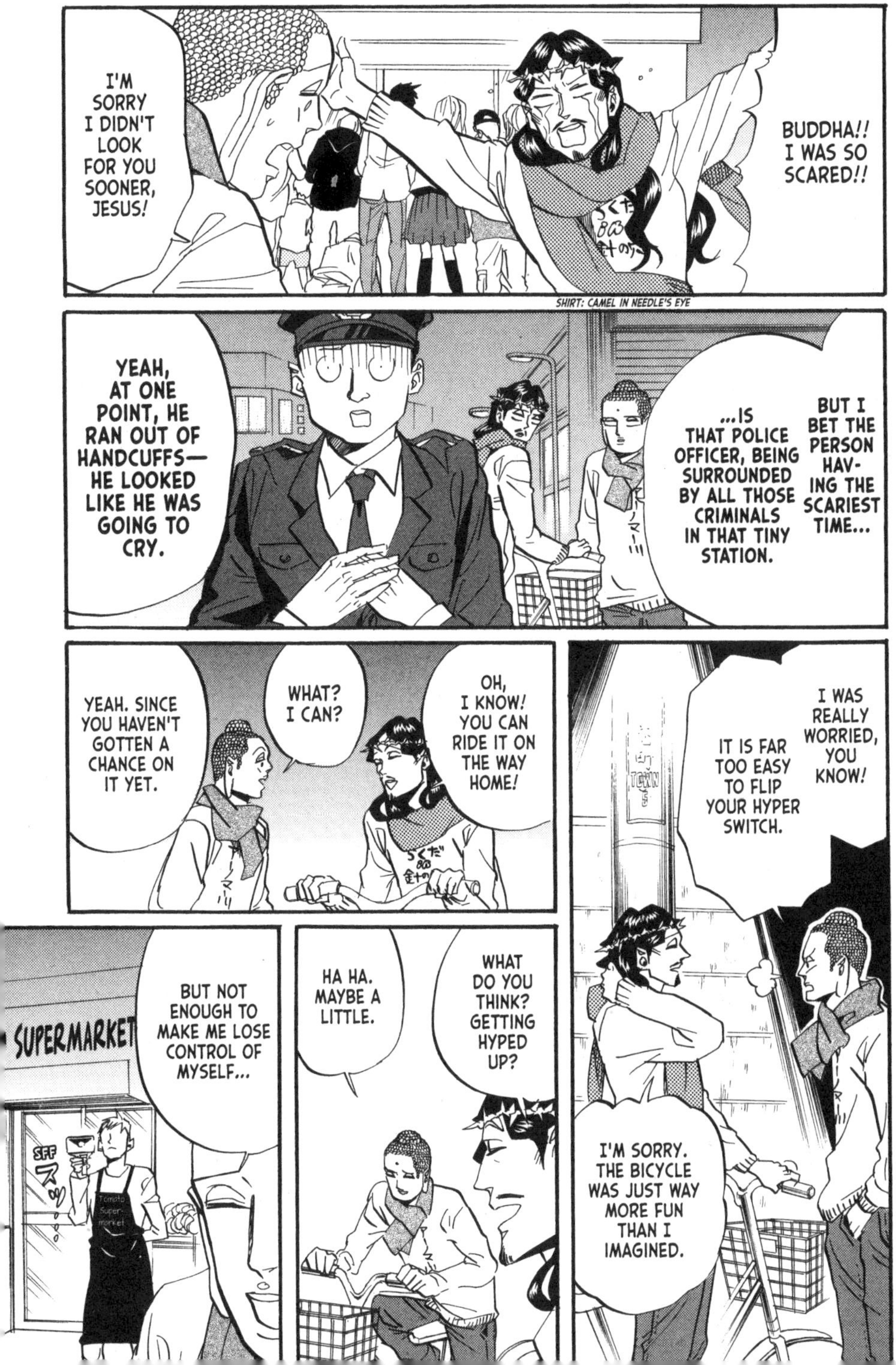
BUDDHA!! I WAS SO SCARED!!
I'M SORRY I DIDN'T LOOK FOR YOU SOONER, JESUS!
SHIRT: CAMEL IN NEEDLE'S EYE
BUT I BET THE PERSON HAV-ING THE SCARIEST TIME...
...IS THAT POLICE OFFICER, BEING SURROUNDED BY ALL THOSE CRIMINALS IN THAT TINY STATION.
YEAH, AT ONE POINT, HE RAN OUT OF HANDCUFFS— HE LOOKED LIKE HE WAS GOING TO CRY.
I WAS REALLY WORRIED, YOU KNOW!
IT IS FAR TOO EASY TO FLIP YOUR HYPER SWITCH.
I'M SORRY. THE BICYCLE WAS JUST WAY MORE FUN THAN I IMAGINED.
OH, I KNOW! YOU CAN RIDE IT ON THE WAY HOME!
WHAT? I CAN?
YEAH. SINCE YOU HAVEN'T GOTTEN A CHANCE ON IT YET.
WHAT DO YOU THINK? GETTING HYPED UP?
HA HA. MAYBE A LITTLE.
BUT NOT ENOUGH TO MAKE ME LOSE CONTROL OF MYSELF...
SUPERMARKET
SFF
Tomato Super-market

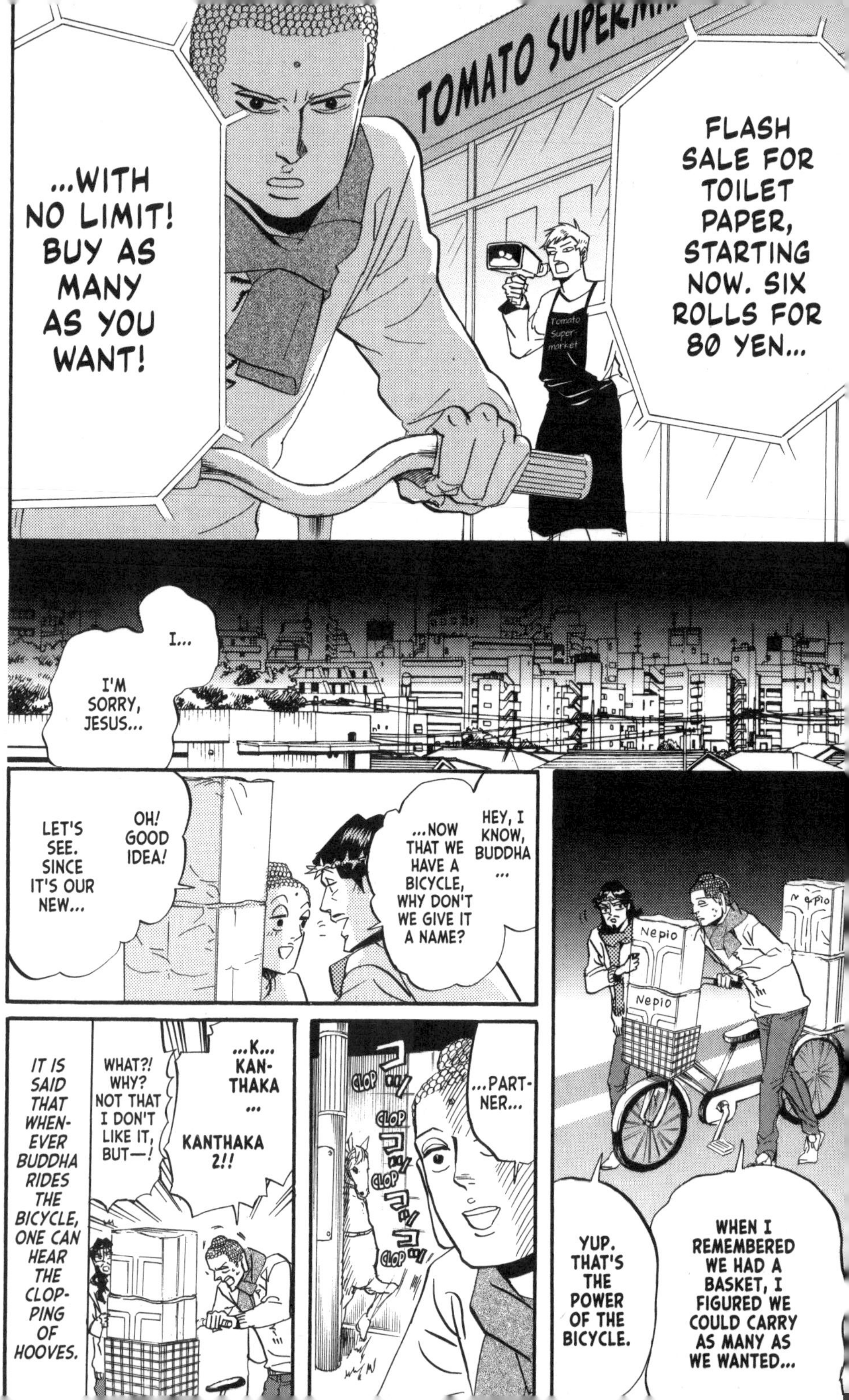
TOMATO SUPERM
FLASH SALE FOR TOILET PAPER, STARTING NOW. SIX ROLLS FOR 80 YEN...
Tomato Super-market
...WITH NO LIMIT! BUY AS MANY AS YOU WANT!
I...
I'M SORRY, JESUS...
WHEN I REMEMBERED WE HAD A BASKET, I FIGURED WE COULD CARRY AS MANY AS WE WANTED...
YUP. THAT'S THE POWER OF THE BICYCLE.
Nepio
Nepio
HEY, I KNOW, BUDDHA...
...NOW THAT WE HAVE A BICYCLE, WHY DON'T WE GIVE IT A NAME?
OH! GOOD IDEA!
LET'S SEE. SINCE IT'S OUR NEW...
...PART-NER...
CLOP
CLOP
CLOP
CLOP
...K... KAN-THAKA ...
KANTHAKA 2!!
WHAT?! WHY? NOT THAT I DON'T LIKE IT, BUT—!
IT IS SAID THAT WHEN-EVER BUDDHA RIDES THE BICYCLE, ONE CAN HEAR THE CLOP-PING OF HOOVES.

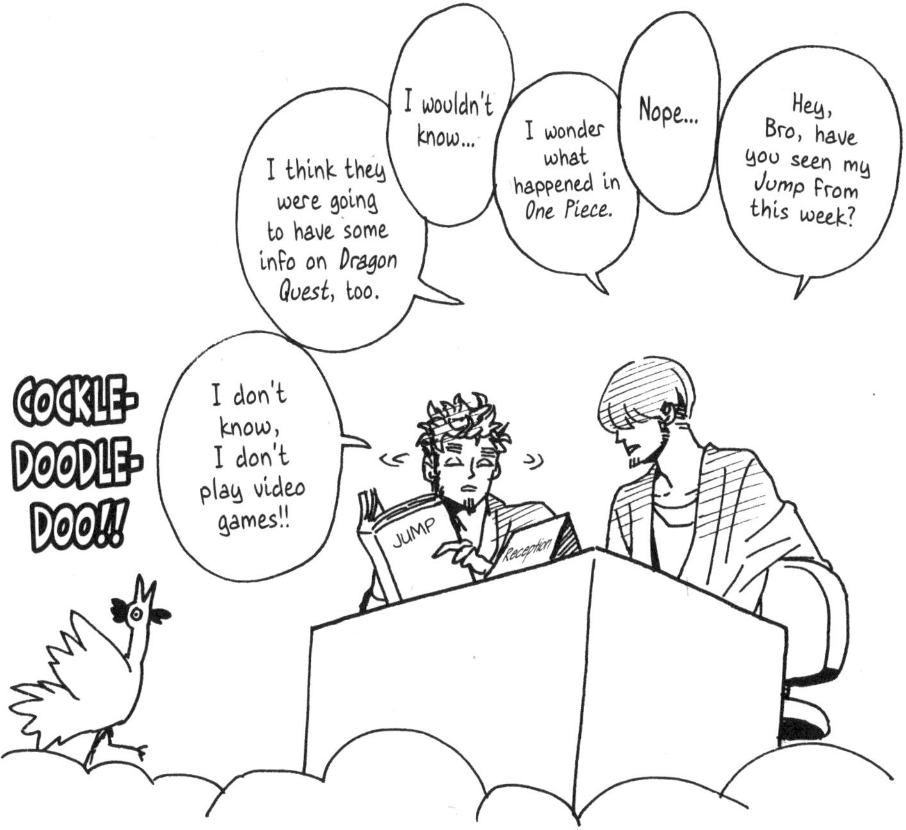
Hey, Bro, have you seen my Jump from this week?
Nope...
I wonder what happened in One Piece.
I wouldn't know...
I think they were going to have some info on Dragon Quest, too.
I don't know, I don't play video games!!
JUMP
Reception
COCKLE-DOODLE-DOO!!

A before-the-cock-crows gag

CHAPTER 31 TRANSLATION NOTES

Horn of a rhinoceros, page 27
This is a reference to the *Rhinoceros Sutra*, a very early Buddhist text. The main theme of the sutra is the virtue of "wandering alone, like a rhinoceros horn," or in other words, seeking enlightenment alone, unattached to the world, as opposed to with or for others.

Anoma River, page 32
The Anoma River is the river in Nepal where Siddhartha Gautama bid a final farewell to his beloved horse Kanthaka before renouncing the world entirely and trading his royal garments for the robes of an ascetic. It is said that after this, Kanthaka died of a broken heart, but was eventually reborn as a human, became a follower of the Buddha, and attained enlightenment.

Doubting Thomas, page 37
After Jesus was resurrected, he appeared to a group of his disciples, but Thomas, one of the Twelve Apostles, was not present then. When the other disciples told him that they knew Jesus had risen from death, Thomas refused to believe until he had seen and felt the stigmata—the wounds in Jesus's hands and side—for himself. By feeling the scars, Thomas could prove to himself that it was really the resurrected Lord, and not a pretender.

If the cock crows, page 38
Before Jesus was arrested at the end of his ministry, although Peter insisted that he would never forsake his lord, Jesus predicted that he would deny him three times before the cock crows (in other words, before dawn). When Jesus was on trial and Peter was watching the proceedings, three times someone recognized him as one of Jesus's disciples, and all three times Peter insisted that Jesus was a stranger to him. When he heard the cock crow, he was reminded of Jesus's prediction and deeply regretted what he had done.

When Jesus gets lost, page 39
When Jesus was twelve years old, Mary and Joseph took him to Jerusalem for Passover. When the feast was over, their caravan had been traveling for about a day when Mary and Joseph discovered that Jesus was not in the group with them. When they returned to Jerusalem to search for him, they found him in the temple conversing with doctors and other highly educated men. Mary asked him, "Son, why hast thou thus dealt with us? Behold, thy father and I have sought thee sorrowing." In response, Jesus asked why they would be searching for him, and pointed out that they should have known that he would be at his father's house—the temple.

Camel in Needle's Eye, page 41
This is a reference to an incident in Jesus's life when a rich young man came to him and asked what more he needed to do to get eternal life. Jesus told him he needed to sell all he had, give the money to the poor, and follow Jesus. The young man didn't want to give away his riches, and so he "went away sorrowful." Seeing him go, Jesus pointed out that it is very difficult for those who put their trust in riches to enter the kingdom of heaven, adding, "It is easier for a camel to go through the eye of a needle, than for a rich man to enter into the kingdom of God."

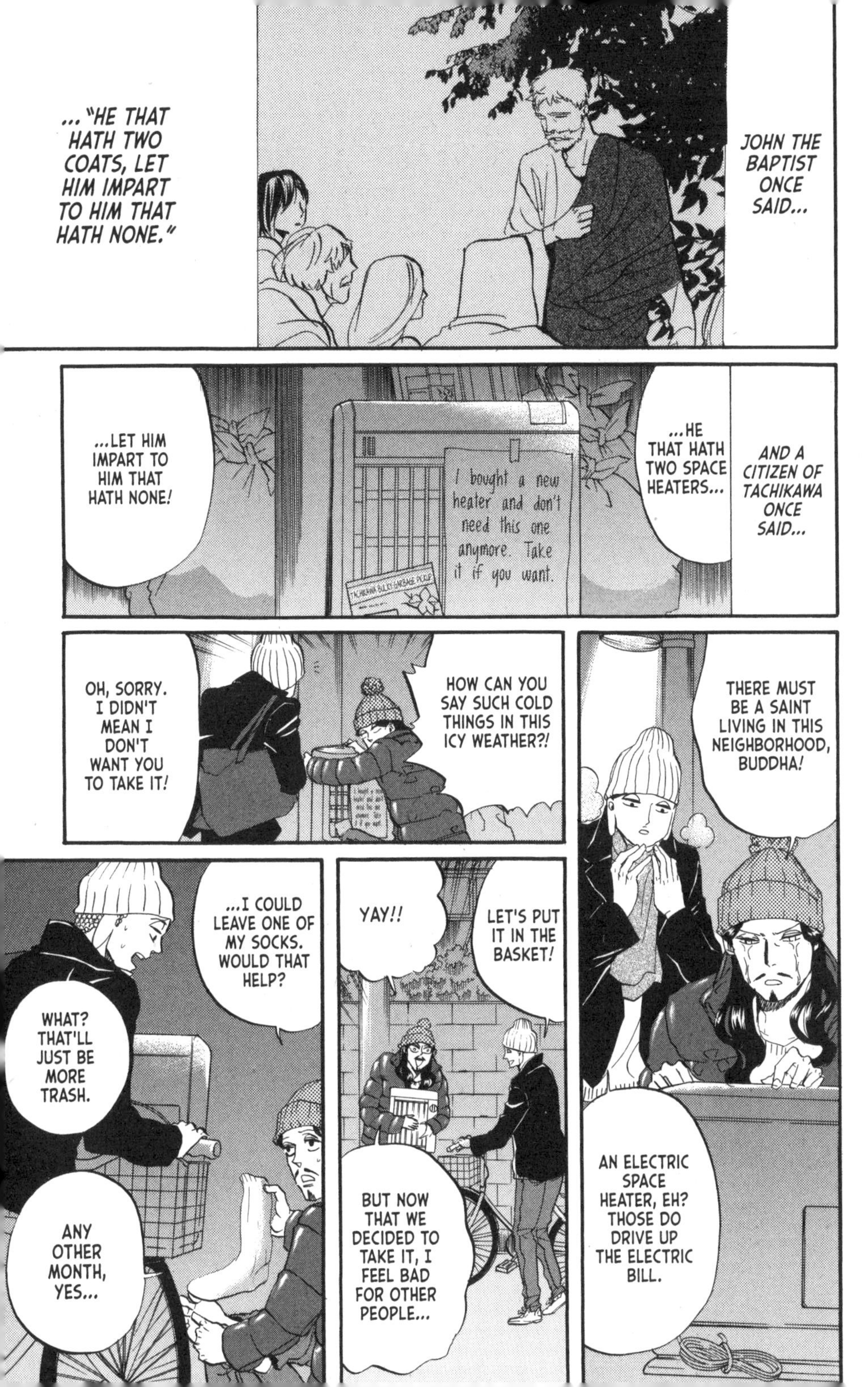
JOHN THE BAPTIST ONCE SAID...
..."HE THAT HATH TWO COATS, LET HIM IMPART TO HIM THAT HATH NONE."
AND A CITIZEN OF TACHIKAWA ONCE SAID...
...HE THAT HATH TWO SPACE HEATERS...
I bought a new heater and don't need this one anymore. Take it if you want.
TACHIKAWA BULKY GARBAGE PICKUP
...LET HIM IMPART TO HIM THAT HATH NONE!
THERE MUST BE A SAINT LIVING IN THIS NEIGHBORHOOD, BUDDHA!
AN ELECTRIC SPACE HEATER, EH? THOSE DO DRIVE UP THE ELECTRIC BILL.
HOW CAN YOU SAY SUCH COLD THINGS IN THIS ICY WEATHER?!
OH, SORRY. I DIDN'T MEAN I DON'T WANT YOU TO TAKE IT!
LET'S PUT IT IN THE BASKET!
YAY!!
BUT NOW THAT WE DECIDED TO TAKE IT, I FEEL BAD FOR OTHER PEOPLE...
...I COULD LEAVE ONE OF MY SOCKS. WOULD THAT HELP?
WHAT? THAT'LL JUST BE MORE TRASH.
ANY OTHER MONTH, YES...

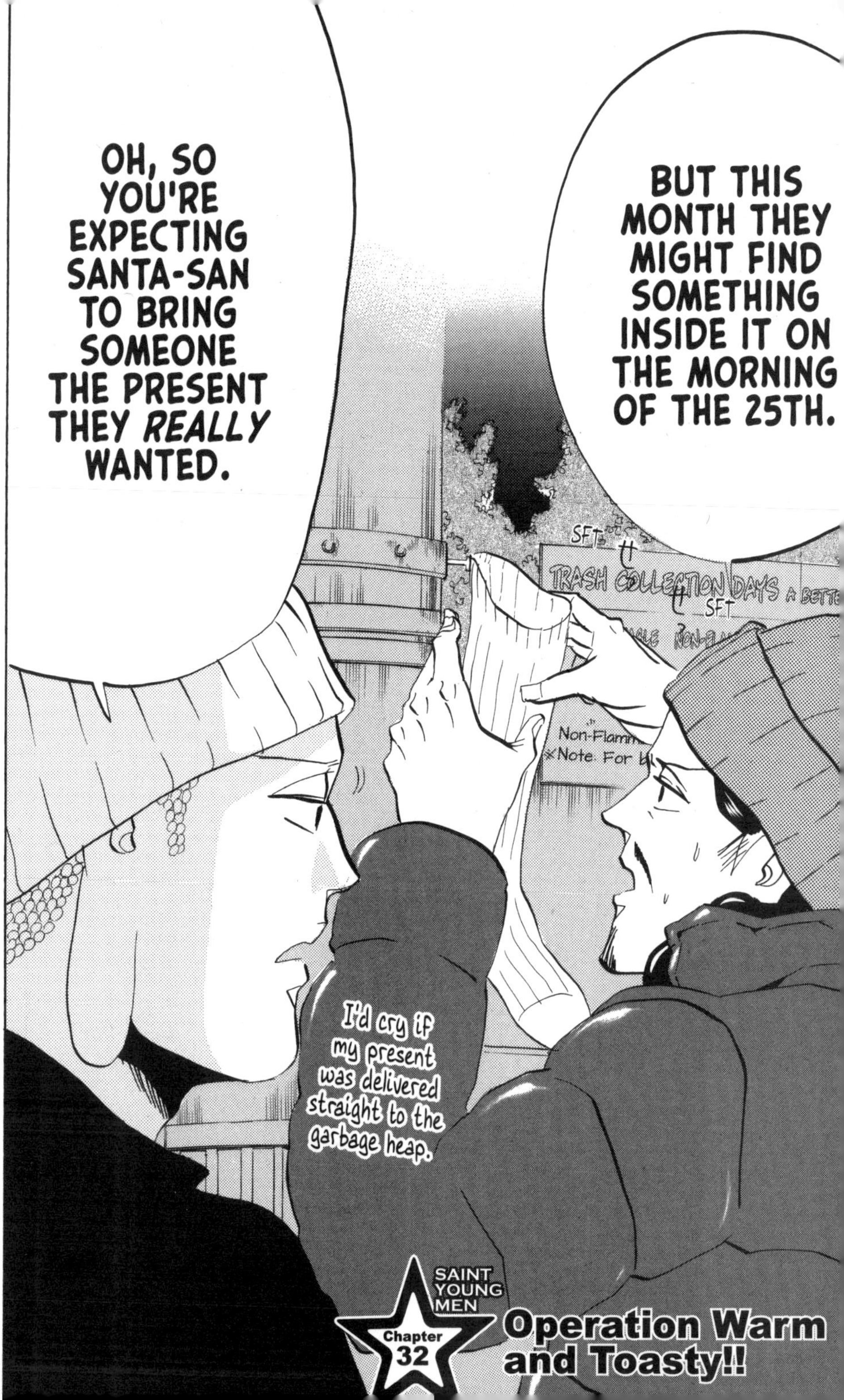
BUT THIS MONTH THEY MIGHT FIND SOMETHING INSIDE IT ON THE MORNING OF THE 25TH.
OH, SO YOU'RE EXPECTING SANTA-SAN TO BRING SOMEONE THE PRESENT THEY *REALLY* WANTED.
TRASH COLLECTION DAYS
I'd cry if my present was delivered straight to the garbage heap.
SAINT YOUNG MEN
Chapter 32
Operation Warm and Toasty!!

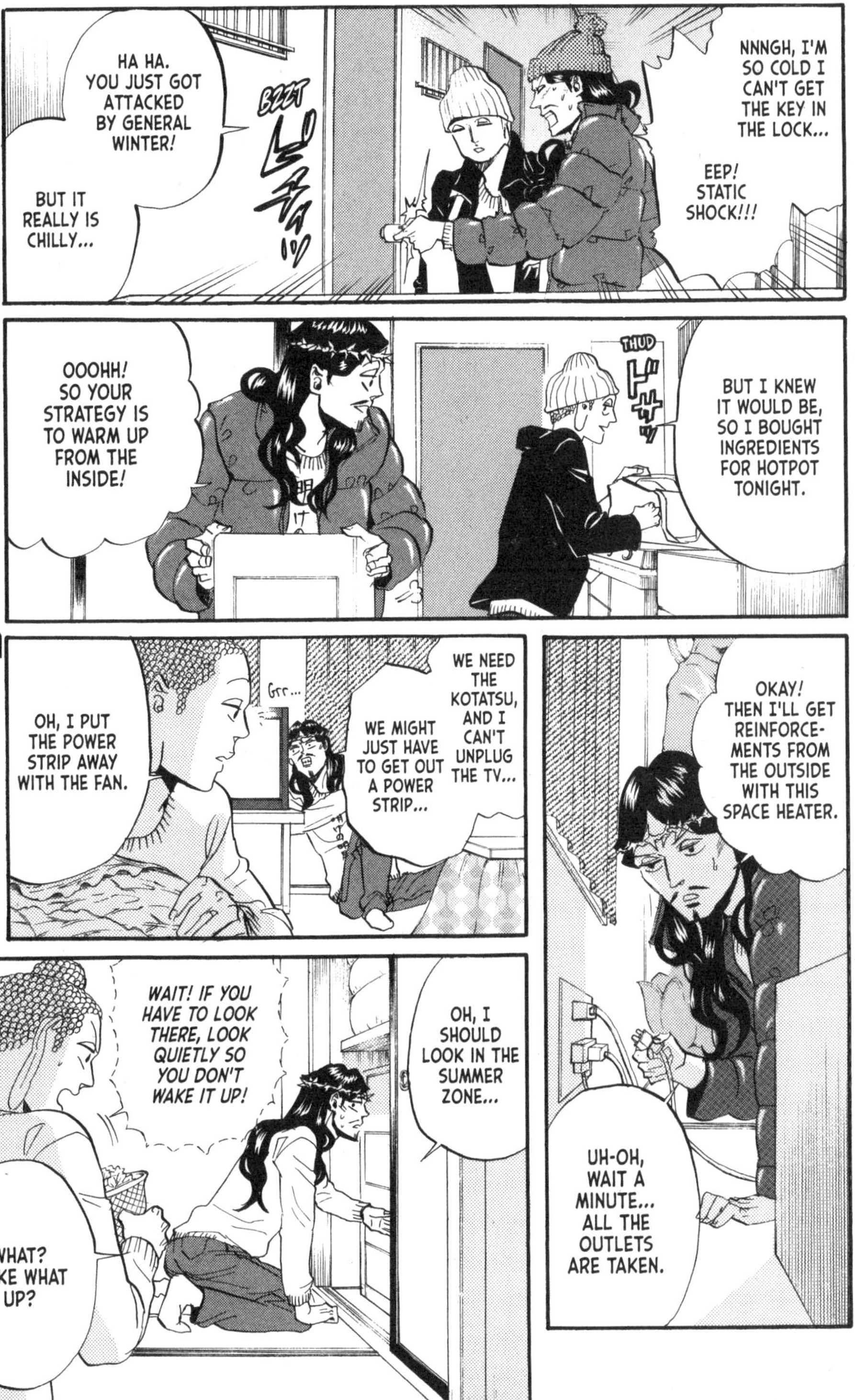
NNNGH, I'M SO COLD I CAN'T GET THE KEY IN THE LOCK...
EEP! STATIC SHOCK!!!
BZZT
HA HA. YOU JUST GOT ATTACKED BY GENERAL WINTER!
BUT IT REALLY IS CHILLY...
THUD
BUT I KNEW IT WOULD BE, SO I BOUGHT INGREDIENTS FOR HOTPOT TONIGHT.
OOOHH! SO YOUR STRATEGY IS TO WARM UP FROM THE INSIDE!
OKAY! THEN I'LL GET REINFORCEMENTS FROM THE OUTSIDE WITH THIS SPACE HEATER.
UH-OH, WAIT A MINUTE... ALL THE OUTLETS ARE TAKEN.
WE NEED THE KOTATSU, AND I CAN'T UNPLUG THE TV...
WE MIGHT JUST HAVE TO GET OUT A POWER STRIP...
Grr...
OH, I PUT THE POWER STRIP AWAY WITH THE FAN.
OH, I SHOULD LOOK IN THE SUMMER ZONE...
WAIT! IF YOU HAVE TO LOOK THERE, LOOK QUIETLY SO YOU DON'T WAKE IT UP!
WHAT? WAKE WHAT UP?

BUDDHA: LATELY HOOKED ON THE WORD *BANKARA* (SCRUFFY).

JESUS: LATELY HOOKED ON THE WORD *HEBEREKE* (BLIND DRUNK).

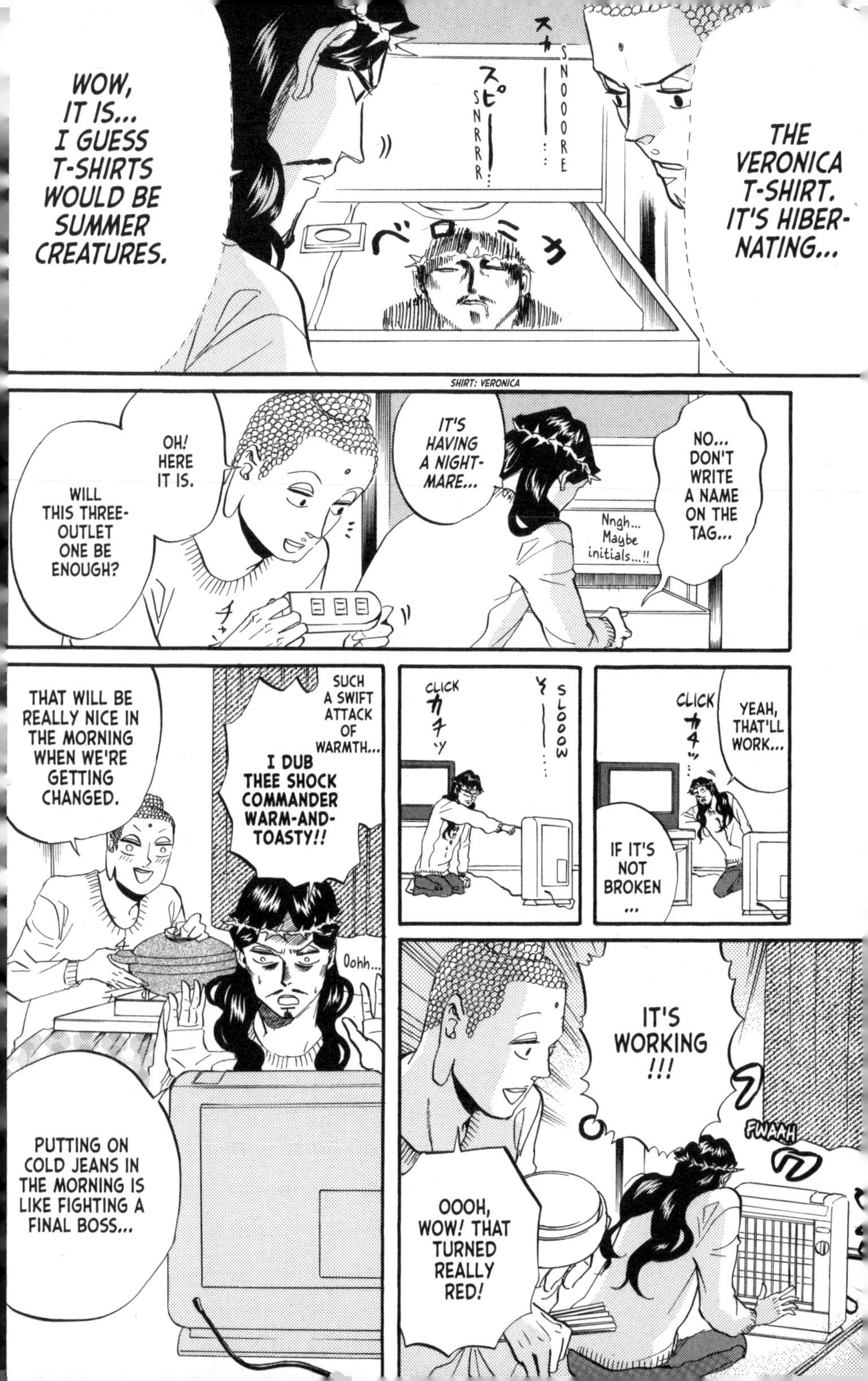
THE VERONICA T-SHIRT. IT'S HIBERNATING...
SNOOORE
SNRRR
WOW, IT IS... I GUESS T-SHIRTS WOULD BE SUMMER CREATURES.
SHIRT: VERONICA
NO... DON'T WRITE A NAME ON THE TAG...
Nngh... Maybe initials...!!
IT'S HAVING A NIGHTMARE...
OH! HERE IT IS.
WILL THIS THREE-OUTLET ONE BE ENOUGH?
YEAH, THAT'LL WORK...
CLICK
IF IT'S NOT BROKEN ...
SLOOOW
CLICK
IT'S WORKING!!!
FWAAH
OOOH, WOW! THAT TURNED REALLY RED!
SUCH A SWIFT ATTACK OF WARMTH...
I DUB THEE SHOCK COMMANDER WARM-AND-TOASTY!!
THAT WILL BE REALLY NICE IN THE MORNING WHEN WE'RE GETTING CHANGED.
Oohh...
PUTTING ON COLD JEANS IN THE MORNING IS LIKE FIGHTING A FINAL BOSS...

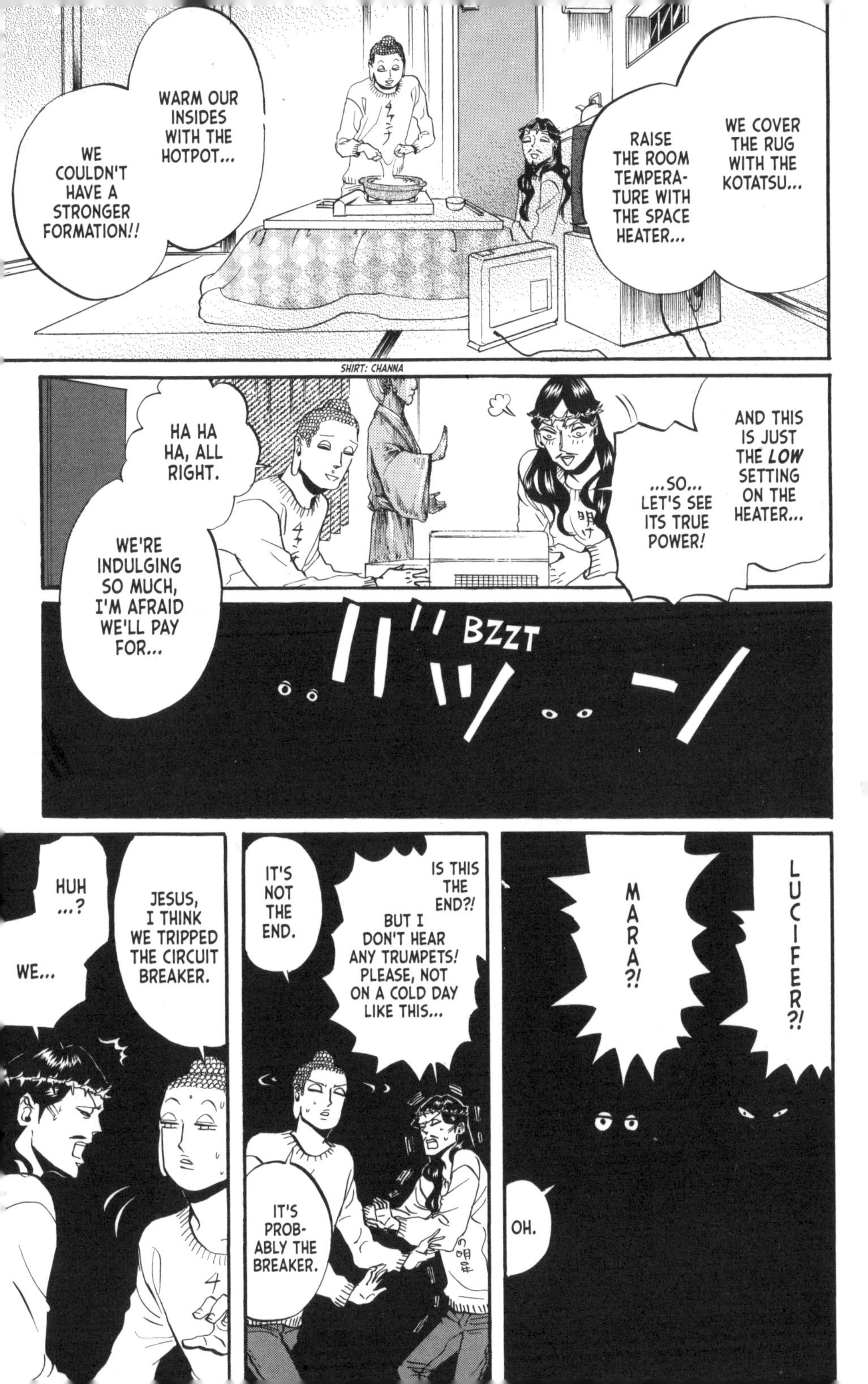
WE COVER THE RUG WITH THE KOTATSU...
RAISE THE ROOM TEMPERA-TURE WITH THE SPACE HEATER...
WARM OUR INSIDES WITH THE HOTPOT...
WE COULDN'T HAVE A STRONGER FORMATION!!
SHIRT: CHANNA
AND THIS IS JUST THE *LOW* SETTING ON THE HEATER...
...SO... LET'S SEE ITS TRUE POWER!
HA HA HA, ALL RIGHT.
WE'RE INDULGING SO MUCH, I'M AFRAID WE'LL PAY FOR...
BZZT
LUCIFER?!
MARA?!
OH.
IS THIS THE END?!
BUT I DON'T HEAR ANY TRUMPETS! PLEASE, NOT ON A COLD DAY LIKE THIS...
IT'S NOT THE END.
IT'S PROBABLY THE BREAKER.
JESUS, I THINK WE TRIPPED THE CIRCUIT BREAKER.
HUH ...?
WE...

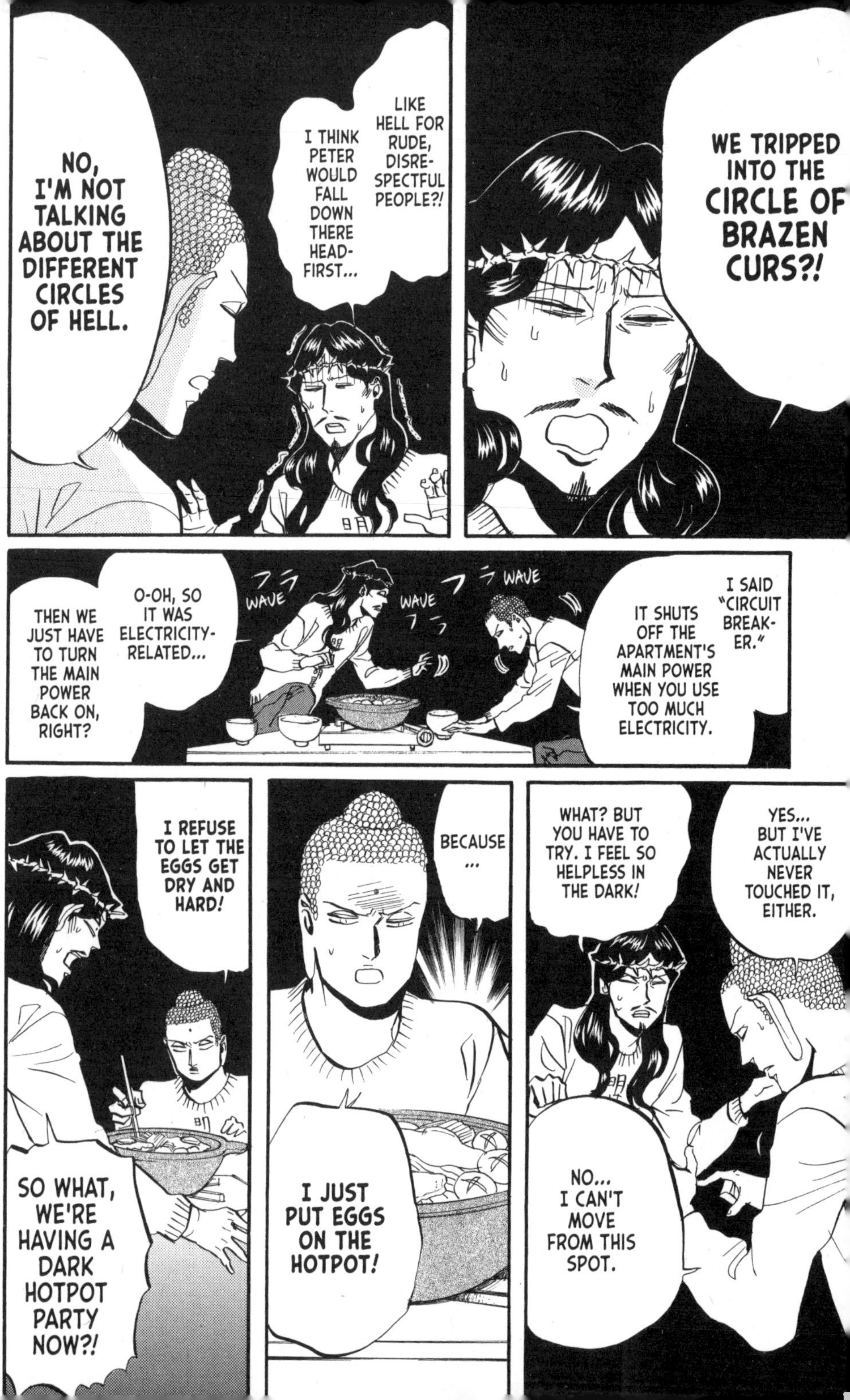
WE TRIPPED INTO THE CIRCLE OF BRAZEN CURS?!
LIKE HELL FOR RUDE, DISRE-SPECTFUL PEOPLE?!
I THINK PETER WOULD FALL DOWN THERE HEAD-FIRST...
NO, I'M NOT TALKING ABOUT THE DIFFERENT CIRCLES OF HELL.
I SAID "CIRCUIT BREAK-ER."
IT SHUTS OFF THE APARTMENT'S MAIN POWER WHEN YOU USE TOO MUCH ELECTRICITY.
WAVE
WAVE
WAVE
O-OH, SO IT WAS ELECTRICITY-RELATED...
THEN WE JUST HAVE TO TURN THE MAIN POWER BACK ON, RIGHT?
YES... BUT I'VE ACTUALLY NEVER TOUCHED IT, EITHER.
WHAT? BUT YOU HAVE TO TRY. I FEEL SO HELPLESS IN THE DARK!
NO... I CAN'T MOVE FROM THIS SPOT.
BECAUSE ...
I JUST PUT EGGS ON THE HOTPOT!
I REFUSE TO LET THE EGGS GET DRY AND HARD!
SO WHAT, WE'RE HAVING A DARK HOTPOT PARTY NOW?!

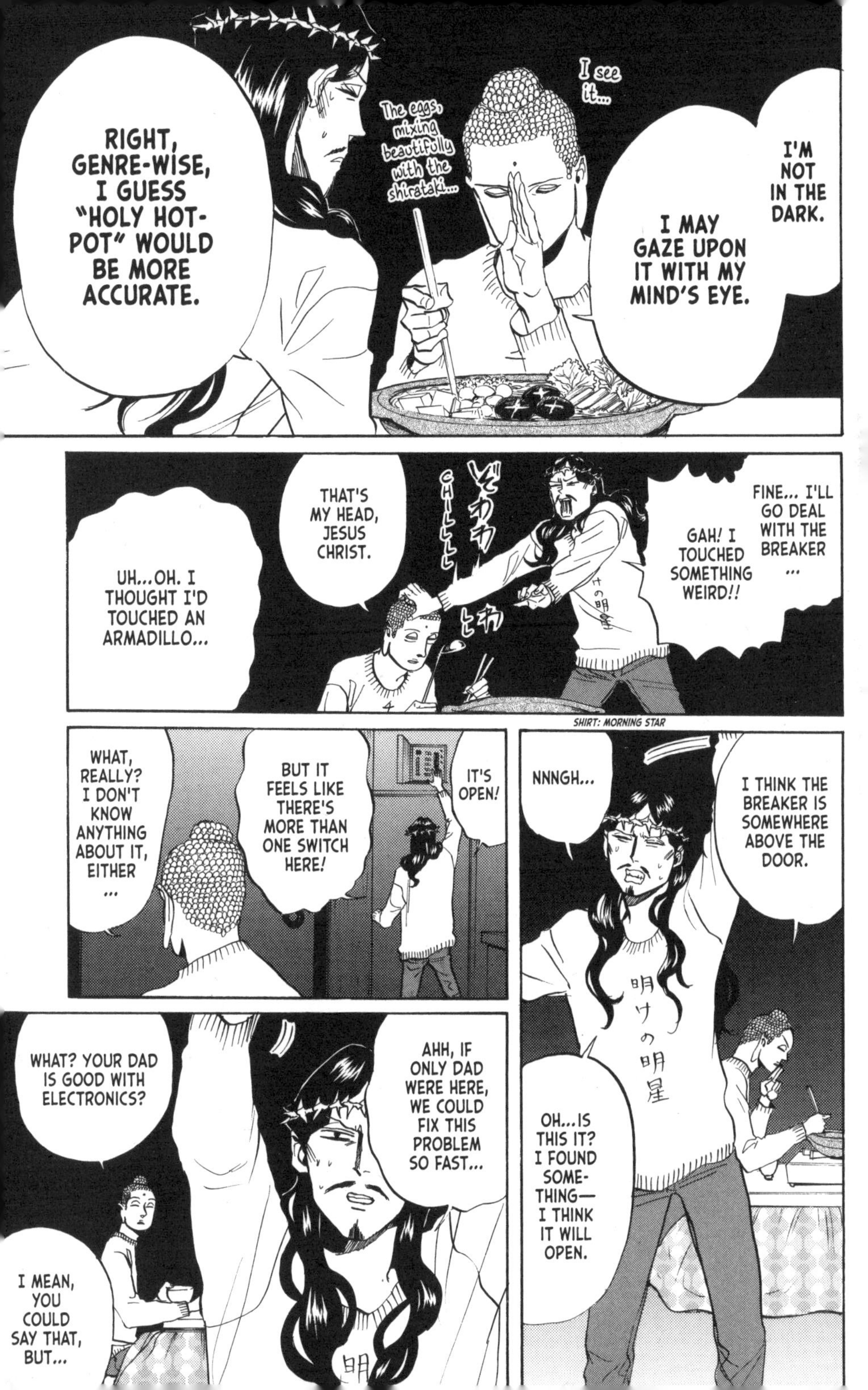
I'M NOT IN THE DARK.
I MAY GAZE UPON IT WITH MY MIND'S EYE.
I see it...
The eggs, mixing beautifully with the shirataki...
RIGHT, GENRE-WISE, I GUESS "HOLY HOT-POT" WOULD BE MORE ACCURATE.
FINE... I'LL GO DEAL WITH THE BREAKER ...
GAH! I TOUCHED SOMETHING WEIRD!!
ぞわわ
CHILLLL
THAT'S MY HEAD, JESUS CHRIST.
UH...OH. I THOUGHT I'D TOUCHED AN ARMADILLO...
けの明星
SHIRT: MORNING STAR
I THINK THE BREAKER IS SOMEWHERE ABOVE THE DOOR.
NNNGH...
明けの明星
OH...IS THIS IT? I FOUND SOME-THING— I THINK IT WILL OPEN.
IT'S OPEN!
BUT IT FEELS LIKE THERE'S MORE THAN ONE SWITCH HERE!
WHAT, REALLY? I DON'T KNOW ANYTHING ABOUT IT, EITHER ...
AHH, IF ONLY DAD WERE HERE, WE COULD FIX THIS PROBLEM SO FAST...
WHAT? YOUR DAD IS GOOD WITH ELECTRONICS?
I MEAN, YOU COULD SAY THAT, BUT...
明

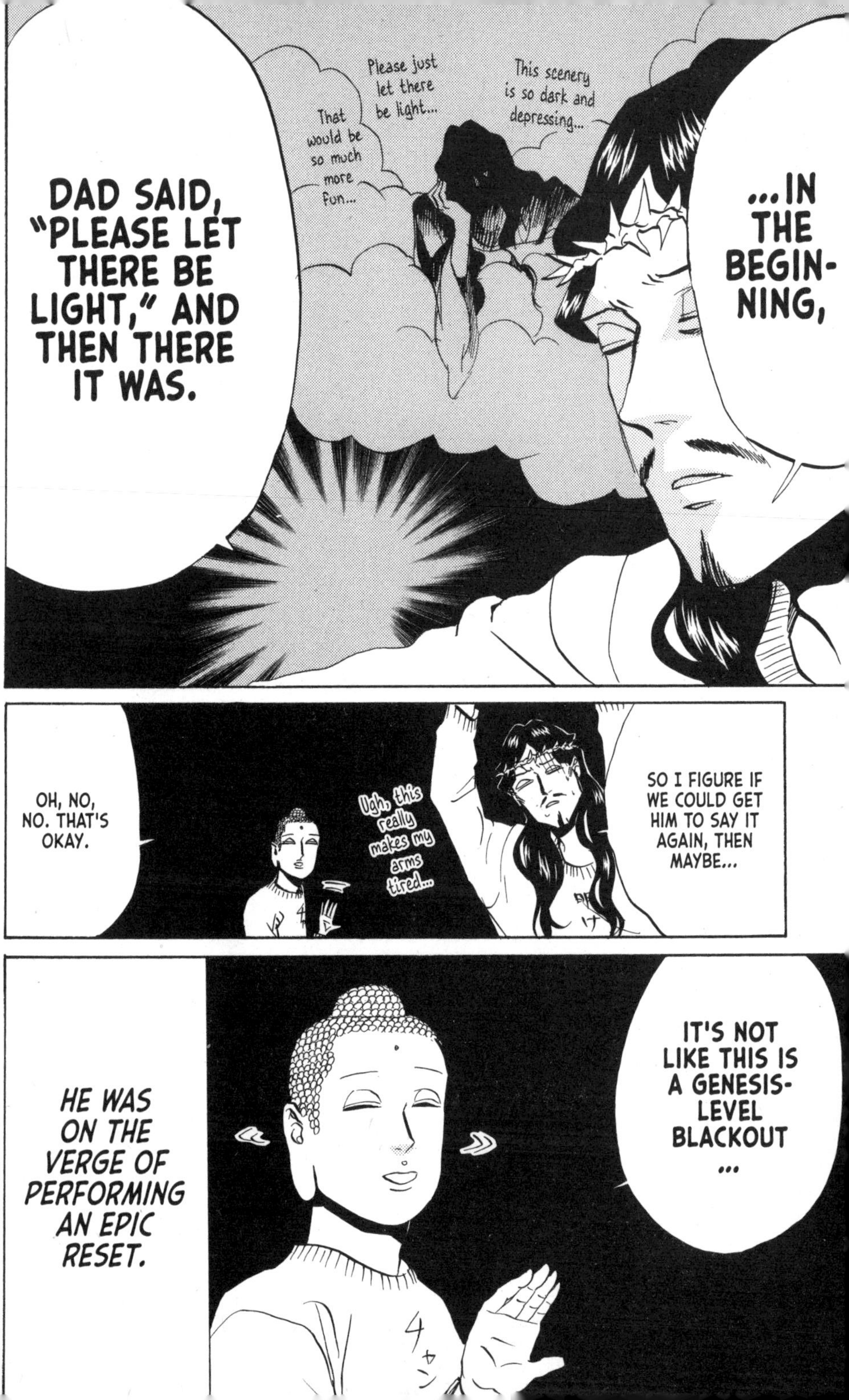

...IN THE BEGINNING,
This scenery is so dark and depressing...
Please just let there be light...
That would be so much more fun...
DAD SAID, "PLEASE LET THERE BE LIGHT," AND THEN THERE IT WAS.
SO I FIGURE IF WE COULD GET HIM TO SAY IT AGAIN, THEN MAYBE...
Ugh, this really makes my arms tired...
OH, NO, NO. THAT'S OKAY.
IT'S NOT LIKE THIS IS A GENESIS-LEVEL BLACKOUT...
HE WAS ON THE VERGE OF PERFORMING AN EPIC RESET.

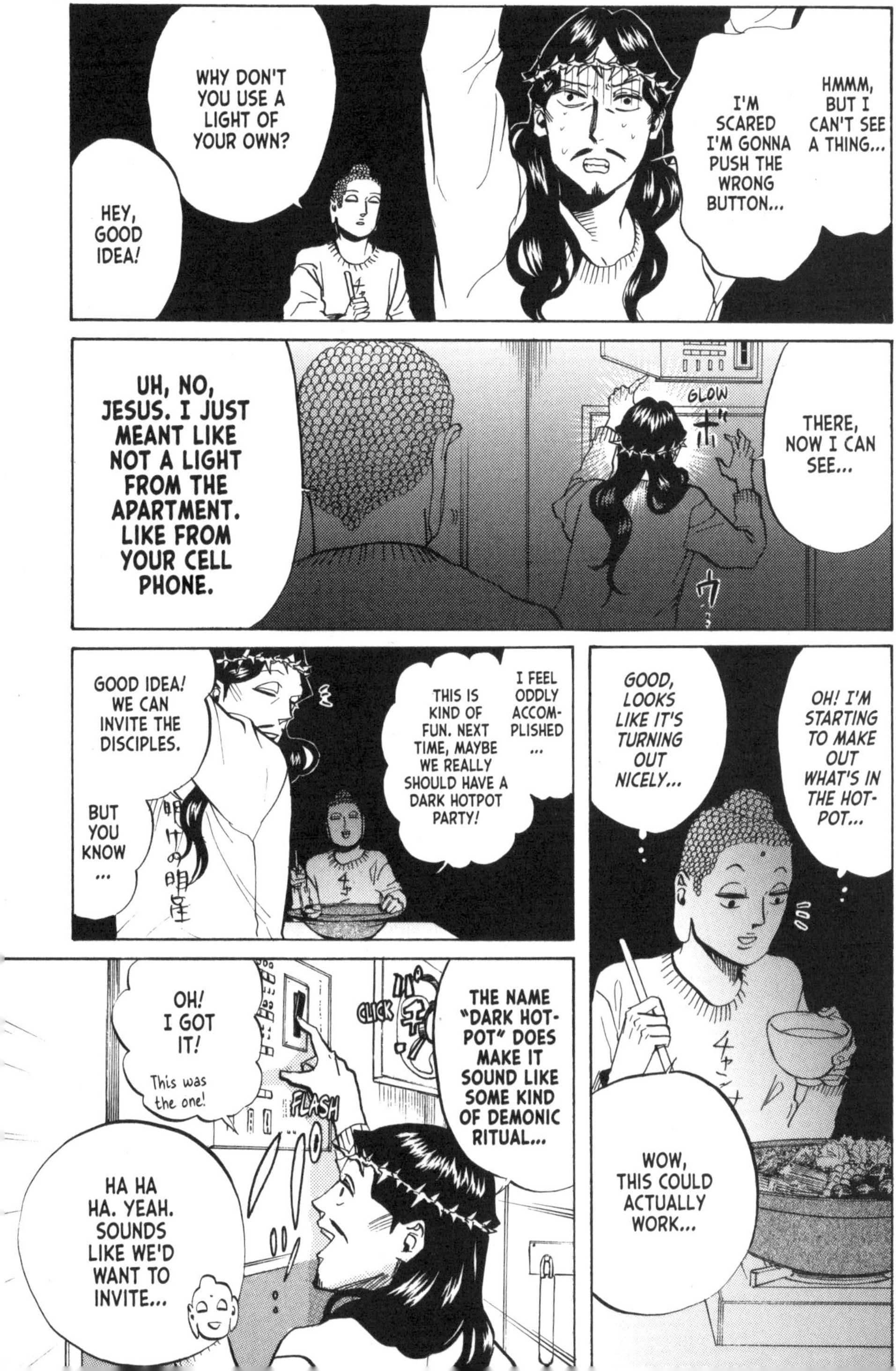
HMMM, BUT I CAN'T SEE A THING...
I'M SCARED I'M GONNA PUSH THE WRONG BUTTON...
WHY DON'T YOU USE A LIGHT OF YOUR OWN?
HEY, GOOD IDEA!
THERE, NOW I CAN SEE...
GLOW
UH, NO, JESUS. I JUST MEANT LIKE NOT A LIGHT FROM THE APARTMENT. LIKE FROM YOUR CELL PHONE.
OH! I'M STARTING TO MAKE OUT WHAT'S IN THE HOT-POT...
GOOD, LOOKS LIKE IT'S TURNING OUT NICELY...
WOW, THIS COULD ACTUALLY WORK...
I FEEL ODDLY ACCOMPLISHED...
THIS IS KIND OF FUN. NEXT TIME, MAYBE WE REALLY SHOULD HAVE A DARK HOTPOT PARTY!
GOOD IDEA! WE CAN INVITE THE DISCIPLES.
BUT YOU KNOW...
THE NAME "DARK HOT-POT" DOES MAKE IT SOUND LIKE SOME KIND OF DEMONIC RITUAL...
CLICK
OH! I GOT IT!
This was the one!
FLASH
HA HA HA. YEAH. SOUNDS LIKE WE'D WANT TO INVITE...

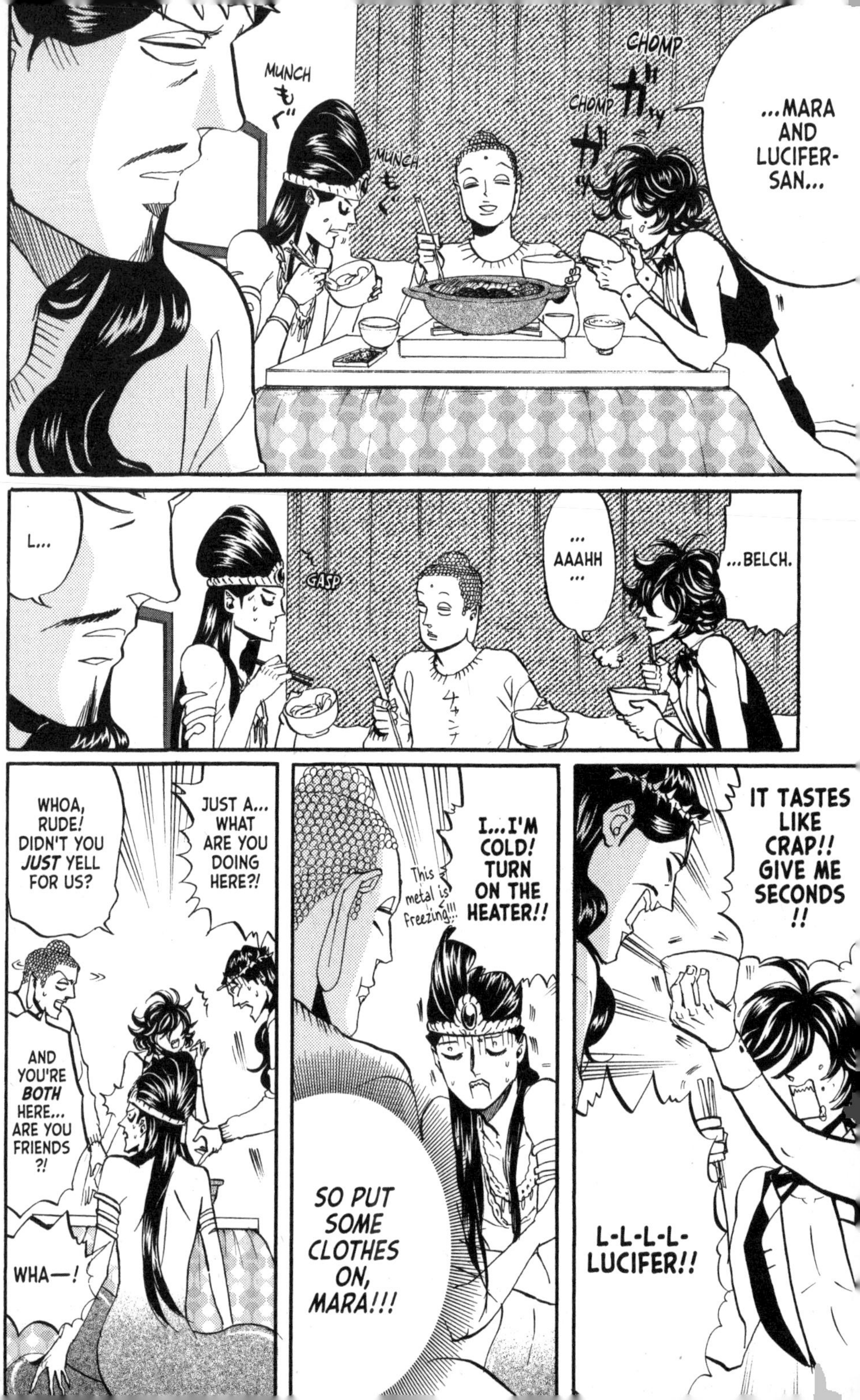
...MARA AND LUCIFER-SAN...
CHOMP ガッ
CHOMP ガッ
MUNCH もぐ
MUNCH もぐ
...BELCH.
... AAAHH ...
GASP
L...
IT TASTES LIKE CRAP!! GIVE ME SECONDS !!
L-L-L-L-LUCIFER!!
I...I'M COLD! TURN ON THE HEATER!!
This metal is freezing!!!
SO PUT SOME CLOTHES ON, MARA!!!
JUST A... WHAT ARE YOU DOING HERE?!
WHOA, RUDE! DIDN'T YOU *JUST* YELL FOR US?
AND YOU'RE *BOTH* HERE... ARE YOU FRIENDS ?!
WHA—!

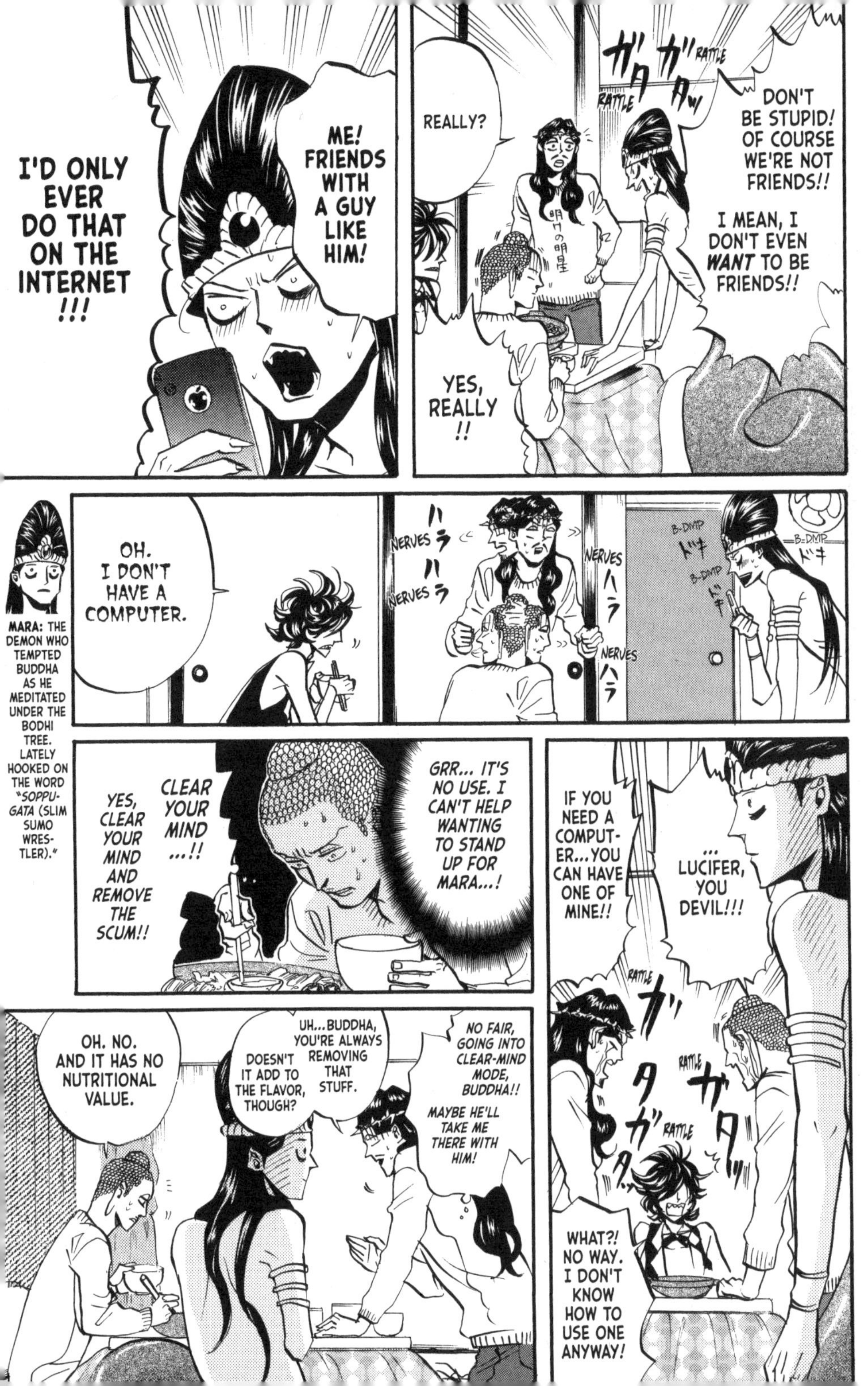

RATTLE
RATTLE
DON'T BE STUPID! OF COURSE WE'RE NOT FRIENDS!!
REALLY?
I MEAN, I DON'T EVEN *WANT* TO BE FRIENDS!!
YES, REALLY!!
ME! FRIENDS WITH A GUY LIKE HIM!
I'D ONLY EVER DO THAT ON THE INTERNET!!!
B-DMP
B-DMP
B-DMP
NERVES
NERVES
NERVES
NERVES
OH. I DON'T HAVE A COMPUTER.
IF YOU NEED A COMPUTER...YOU CAN HAVE ONE OF MINE!!
...LUCIFER, YOU DEVIL!!!
RATTLE
RATTLE
RATTLE
WHAT?! NO WAY. I DON'T KNOW HOW TO USE ONE ANYWAY!
GRR... IT'S NO USE. I CAN'T HELP WANTING TO STAND UP FOR MARA...!
CLEAR YOUR MIND...!!
YES, CLEAR YOUR MIND AND REMOVE THE SCUM!!
NO FAIR, GOING INTO CLEAR-MIND MODE, BUDDHA!!
MAYBE HE'LL TAKE ME THERE WITH HIM!
UH...BUDDHA, YOU'RE ALWAYS REMOVING THAT STUFF.
DOESN'T IT ADD TO THE FLAVOR, THOUGH?
OH. NO. AND IT HAS NO NUTRITIONAL VALUE.
MARA: THE DEMON WHO TEMPTED BUDDHA AS HE MEDITATED UNDER THE BODHI TREE. LATELY HOOKED ON THE WORD "SOPPUGATA (SLIM SUMO WRESTLER)."

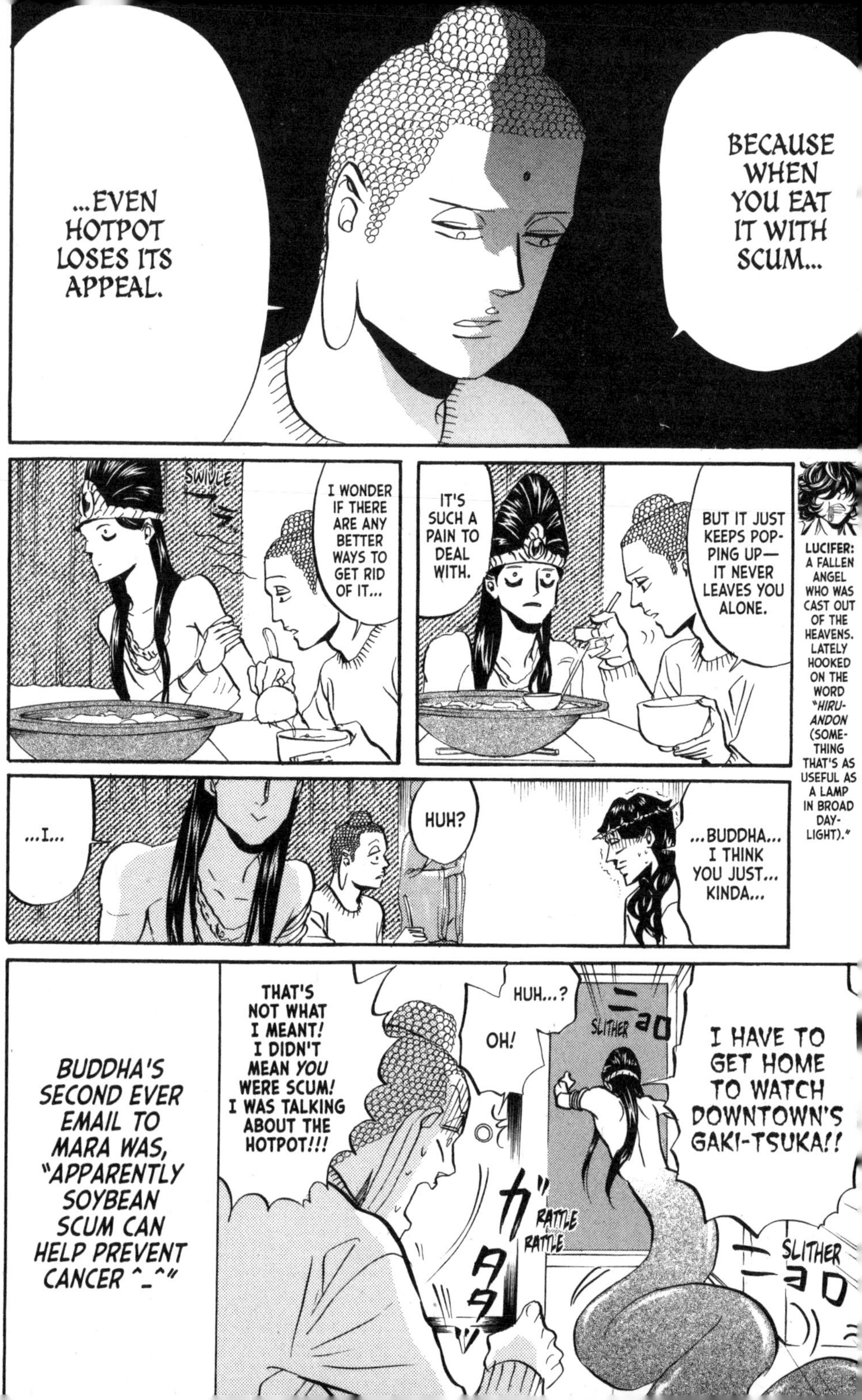
BECAUSE WHEN YOU EAT IT WITH SCUM...
...EVEN HOTPOT LOSES ITS APPEAL.
LUCIFER: A FALLEN ANGEL WHO WAS CAST OUT OF THE HEAVENS. LATELY HOOKED ON THE WORD "HIRU-ANDON (SOMETHING THAT'S AS USEFUL AS A LAMP IN BROAD DAYLIGHT)."
BUT IT JUST KEEPS POPPING UP— IT NEVER LEAVES YOU ALONE.
IT'S SUCH A PAIN TO DEAL WITH.
I WONDER IF THERE ARE ANY BETTER WAYS TO GET RID OF IT...
SWIVLE
...BUDDHA... I THINK YOU JUST... KINDA...
HUH?
...I...
I HAVE TO GET HOME TO WATCH DOWNTOWN'S GAKI-TSUKA!!
SLITHER
HUH...?
OH!
THAT'S NOT WHAT I MEANT! I DIDN'T MEAN YOU WERE SCUM! I WAS TALKING ABOUT THE HOTPOT!!!
RATTLE RATTLE
SLITHER
BUDDHA'S SECOND EVER EMAIL TO MARA WAS, "APPARENTLY SOYBEAN SCUM CAN HELP PREVENT CANCER ^_^"

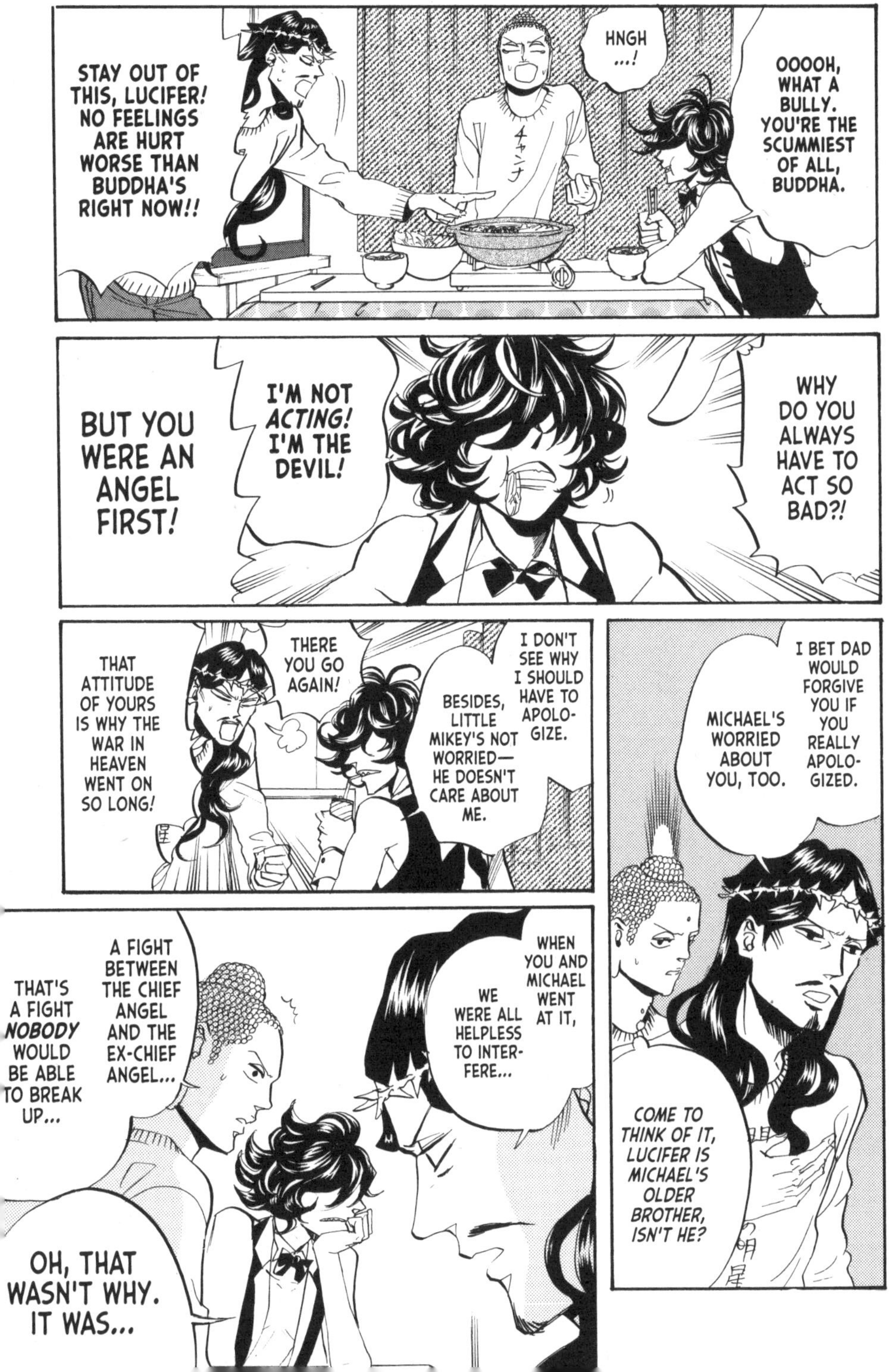
OOOOH, WHAT A BULLY. YOU'RE THE SCUMMIEST OF ALL, BUDDHA.
HNGH ...!
STAY OUT OF THIS, LUCIFER! NO FEELINGS ARE HURT WORSE THAN BUDDHA'S RIGHT NOW!!
WHY DO YOU ALWAYS HAVE TO ACT SO BAD?!
I'M NOT *ACTING!* I'M THE DEVIL!
BUT YOU WERE AN ANGEL FIRST!
I BET DAD WOULD FORGIVE YOU IF YOU REALLY APOLOGIZED.
MICHAEL'S WORRIED ABOUT YOU, TOO.
COME TO THINK OF IT, LUCIFER IS MICHAEL'S OLDER BROTHER, ISN'T HE?
I DON'T SEE WHY I SHOULD HAVE TO APOLOGIZE.
BESIDES, LITTLE MIKEY'S NOT WORRIED— HE DOESN'T CARE ABOUT ME.
THERE YOU GO AGAIN!
THAT ATTITUDE OF YOURS IS WHY THE WAR IN HEAVEN WENT ON SO LONG!
WHEN YOU AND MICHAEL WENT AT IT,
WE WERE ALL HELPLESS TO INTERFERE...
A FIGHT BETWEEN THE CHIEF ANGEL AND THE EX-CHIEF ANGEL...
THAT'S A FIGHT *NOBODY* WOULD BE ABLE TO BREAK UP...
OH, THAT WASN'T WHY. IT WAS...

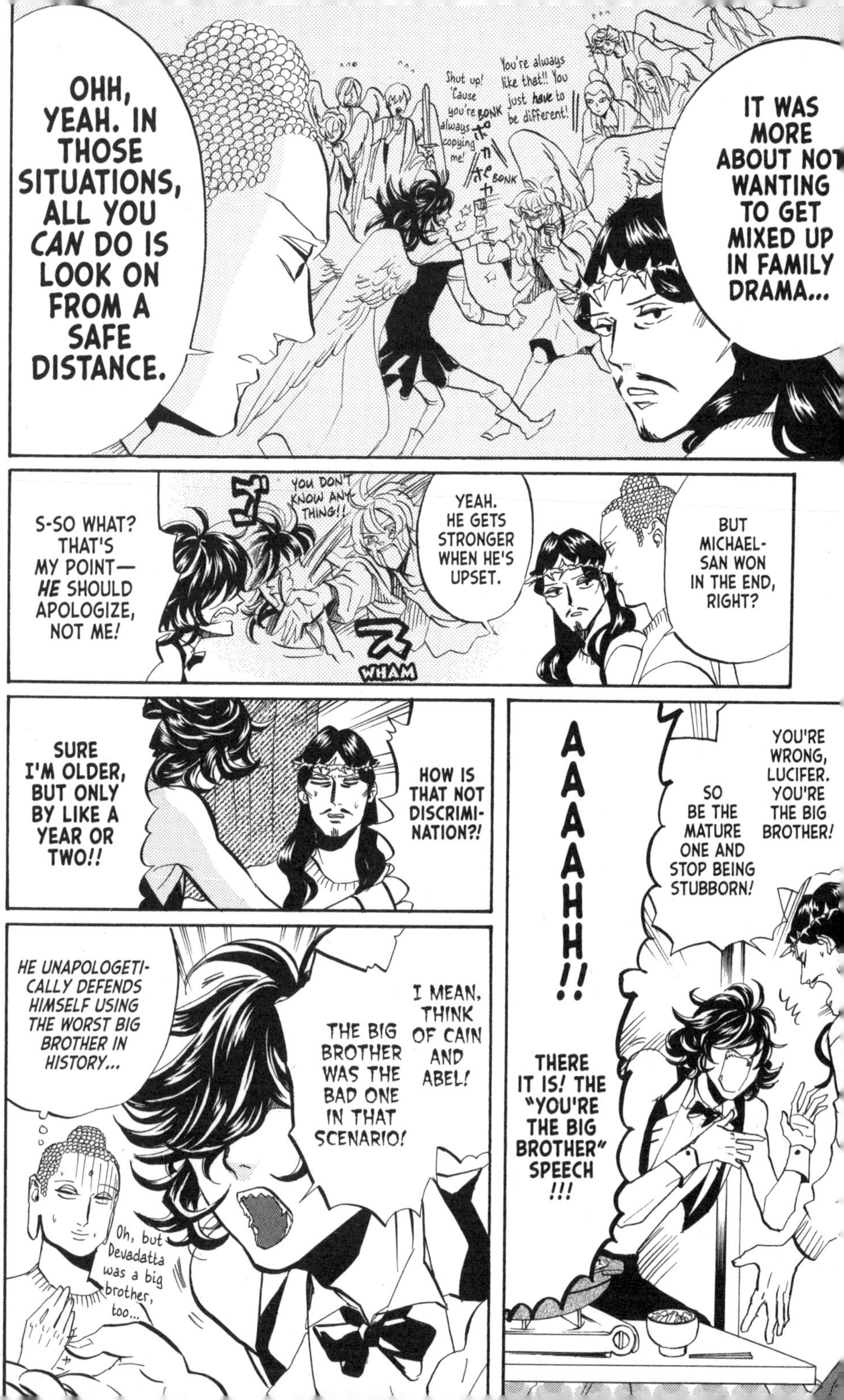
IT WAS MORE ABOUT NOT WANTING TO GET MIXED UP IN FAMILY DRAMA...
You're always like that!! You just have to be different!
Shut up! 'Cause you're always copying me!
BONK
BONK
OHH, YEAH. IN THOSE SITUATIONS, ALL YOU CAN DO IS LOOK ON FROM A SAFE DISTANCE.
BUT MICHAEL-SAN WON IN THE END, RIGHT?
YEAH. HE GETS STRONGER WHEN HE'S UPSET.
YOU DON'T KNOW ANYTHING!!
WHAM
S-SO WHAT? THAT'S MY POINT—HE SHOULD APOLOGIZE, NOT ME!
YOU'RE WRONG, LUCIFER. YOU'RE THE BIG BROTHER!
SO BE THE MATURE ONE AND STOP BEING STUBBORN!
AAAAAHH!!
THERE IT IS! THE "YOU'RE THE BIG BROTHER" SPEECH!!!
HOW IS THAT NOT DISCRIMINATION?!
SURE I'M OLDER, BUT ONLY BY LIKE A YEAR OR TWO!!
I MEAN, THINK OF CAIN AND ABEL!
THE BIG BROTHER WAS THE BAD ONE IN THAT SCENARIO!
HE UNAPOLOGETICALLY DEFENDS HIMSELF USING THE WORST BIG BROTHER IN HISTORY...
Oh, but Devadatta was a big brother, too...

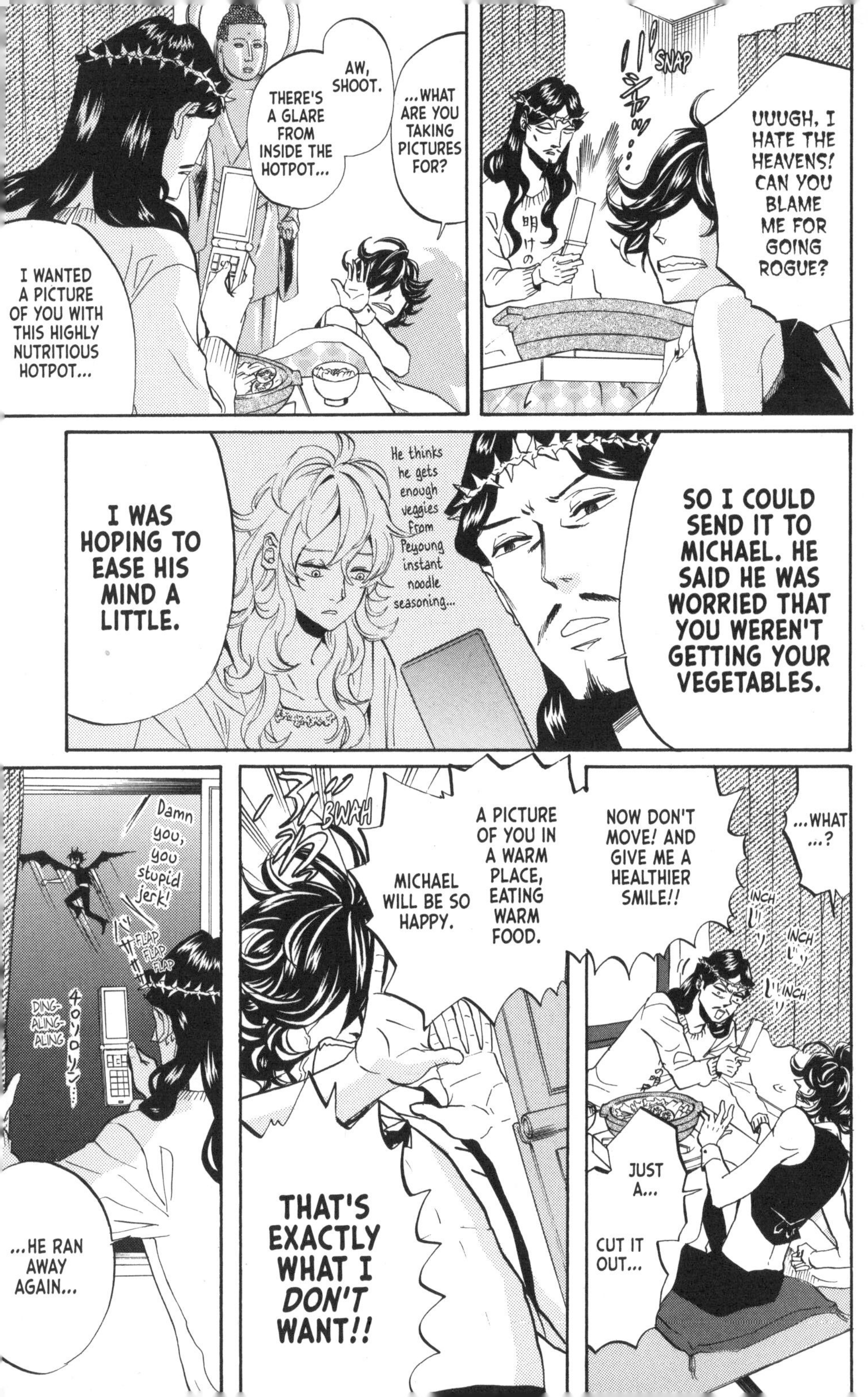
SNAP
UUUGH, I HATE THE HEAVENS! CAN YOU BLAME ME FOR GOING ROGUE?
...WHAT ARE YOU TAKING PICTURES FOR?
AW, SHOOT.
THERE'S A GLARE FROM INSIDE THE HOTPOT...
I WANTED A PICTURE OF YOU WITH THIS HIGHLY NUTRITIOUS HOTPOT...
SO I COULD SEND IT TO MICHAEL. HE SAID HE WAS WORRIED THAT YOU WEREN'T GETTING YOUR VEGETABLES.
He thinks he gets enough veggies from Peyoung instant noodle seasoning...
I WAS HOPING TO EASE HIS MIND A LITTLE.
...WHAT ...?
NOW DON'T MOVE! AND GIVE ME A HEALTHIER SMILE!!
INCH
INCH
INCH
JUST A...
CUT IT OUT...
A PICTURE OF YOU IN A WARM PLACE, EATING WARM FOOD.
MICHAEL WILL BE SO HAPPY.
BWAH
THAT'S EXACTLY WHAT I DON'T WANT!!
Damn you, you stupid jerk!
FLAP FLAP FLAP
DING-ALING-ALING
...HE RAN AWAY AGAIN...

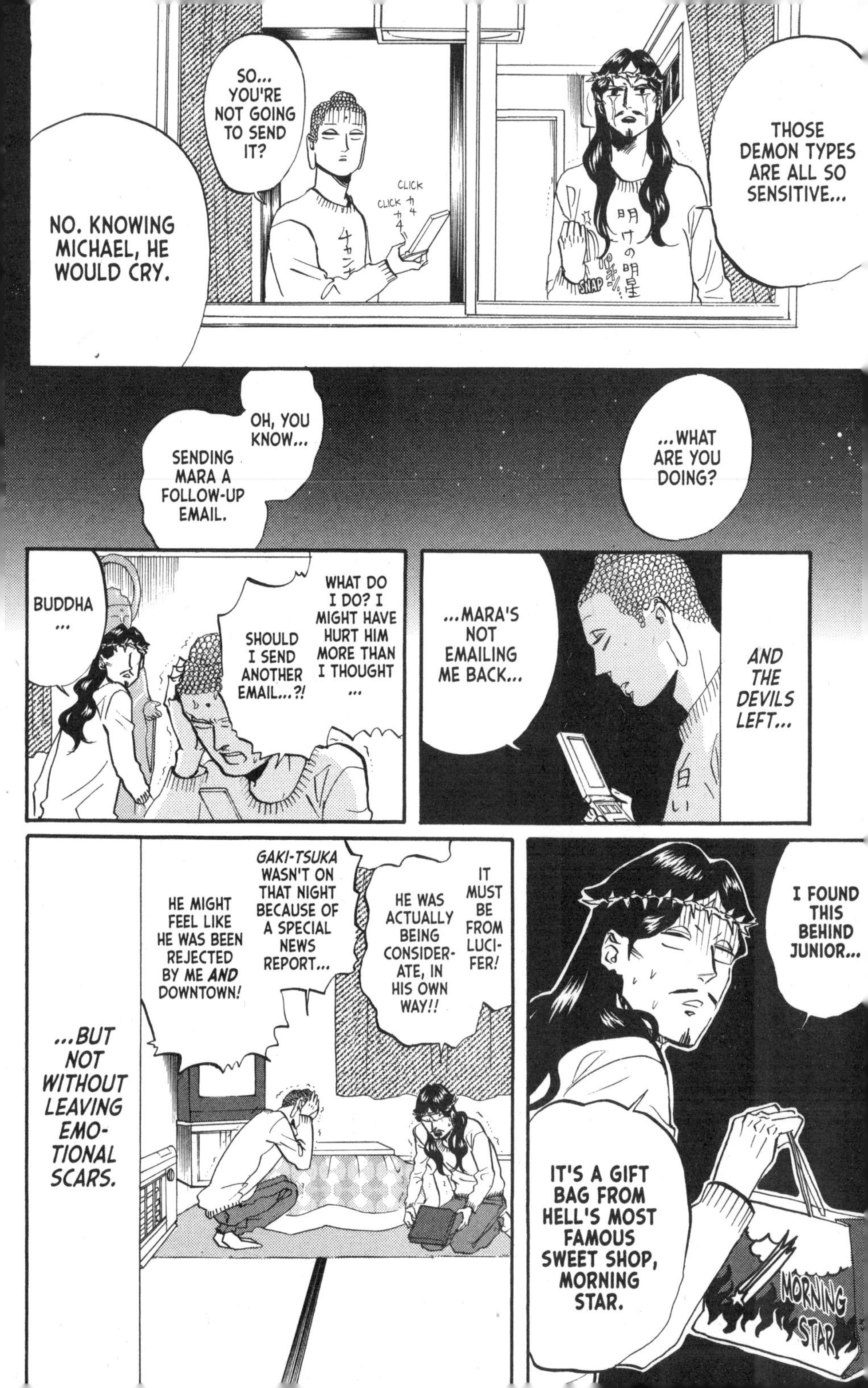
THOSE DEMON TYPES ARE ALL SO SENSITIVE...
SNAP
SO... YOU'RE NOT GOING TO SEND IT?
CLICK CLICK
NO. KNOWING MICHAEL, HE WOULD CRY.
...WHAT ARE YOU DOING?
OH, YOU KNOW...
SENDING MARA A FOLLOW-UP EMAIL.
AND THE DEVILS LEFT...
...MARA'S NOT EMAILING ME BACK...
WHAT DO I DO? I MIGHT HAVE HURT HIM MORE THAN I THOUGHT...
SHOULD I SEND ANOTHER EMAIL...?!
BUDDHA...
I FOUND THIS BEHIND JUNIOR...
IT'S A GIFT BAG FROM HELL'S MOST FAMOUS SWEET SHOP, MORNING STAR.
MORNING STAR
IT MUST BE FROM LUCIFER!
HE WAS ACTUALLY BEING CONSIDERATE, IN HIS OWN WAY!!
GAKI-TSUKA WASN'T ON THAT NIGHT BECAUSE OF A SPECIAL NEWS REPORT...
HE MIGHT FEEL LIKE HE WAS BEEN REJECTED BY ME *AND* DOWNTOWN!
...BUT NOT WITHOUT LEAVING EMOTIONAL SCARS.

Spent a full three days deciding which emoji to use at the end.

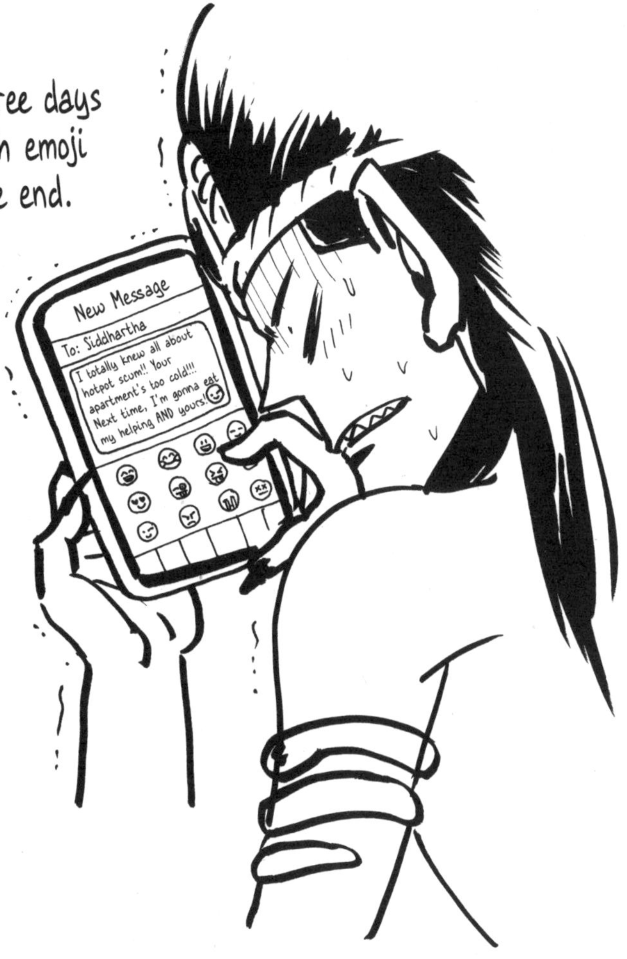
New Message
To: Siddhartha
I totally knew all about hotpot scum!! Your apartment's too cold!!! Next time, I'm gonna eat my helping AND yours!

CHAPTER 32 TRANSLATION NOTES

He that hath two coats, page 45
Many English translations of the Bible use the word "coat" to translate the Greek word *chiton*, which specifically refers to a type of tunic worn over the torso referenced here, but can also simply mean "covering" or "clothes." The Japanese translation of the Bible uses the word *shitagi*, meaning "undergarment." This may be because a chiton was often worn as part of a set, under a himation, which served as a cloak. Other English translations of the Bible use the word "shirt," which, like chiton, refers to a basic piece of clothing that may also be worn as underwear.

Bulky Garbage Pickup, page 45
To dispose of garbage that won't fit in a standard trash can in Japan, there is a very particular process to prevent piles of over-sized garbage from flooding the streets. First, you must call a special number to make an appointment for pickup. To pay for this service, you buy *sodai gomi shori-ken*, or "bulky garbage pickup tickets," which can usually be purchased at a local convenience store. On the morning of the appointment, you place the stickers on the large item you wish to dispose of, and leave it out for pickup. The stickers tell everyone else that the item is scheduled for a pickup, and therefore they are not to take it, as the trash collectors will have to call around to make sure it hasn't been stolen.

Attacked by General Winter, page 47
General Winter, or the *Fuyu Shōgun*, is the personification of severe winter weather. Buddha here suggests that General Winter has done a *tsujigiri* on Jesus, resulting in Jesus getting zapped with static electricity. *Tsujigiri* literally means "crossroads slaying," and refers to a practice of testing a new sword by using it to cut down random passersby.

Channa, page 49
Channa was Prince Siddhartha's royal servant and head charioteer. It was he who saddled Kanthaka and guided Siddhartha out of the city when he ran away from home.

Circle of brazen curs, page 50
When Buddha uses the unfamiliar word *bureekaa*, his roommate tries to put it into a context he understands and interprets it as *burei-kai*, which literally means "rudeness realm."

Dark hotpot party, page 50
Yami nabe, literally "dark pot," is a potluck in the truest sense. People bring ingredients to include in a hot pot stew, without telling anyone else what they have brought.

Morning Star, page 51
The "morning star" is another name for the planet Venus, which appears as a bright star in the early hours of the day, but is not seen in the night sky because of its orbit in relation to the Earth's. Another name for the morning star in Latin is "Lucifer."

Please let there be light, page 52
The Japanese version of the famous quote from Genesis, "Let the be light," is *"hikari are,"* which means "let there be light." By itself, are is the command form of the Japanese verb aru, "to be." Here, the author of the manga added a continuation, and made the word *areba*, which means "if there was." She further added *ii noni,* which roughly means "that would be nice." So altogether, it means, "If only we had some light."

A light of your own, page 53
In the original text, Buddha suggests using a backlight, using the English word backlight, which refers to the light used to light up liquid crystal displays on things like cell phones. When translated literally into Japanese, the word becomes *gokō*, which is the word for "halo." Hence, in the original Japanese, after Jesus turns on his halo, Buddha comments, "I didn't mean it as a literal translation of 'halo.'"

Eating with scum, page 56

The Japanese word for scum, as found in hotpots and other brothy dishes, is *aku*. This *aku* contains the bitterness of the vegetables and the stink of the meat and fish that are being cooked in the pot. However, *aku* is also the word for "evil," as in the first syllable of *akuma*, demon or devil.

Gaki-Tsuka, page 56

Short for *Downtown no Gaki no Tsukai ya Arahen de!!*, roughly translated to *"Downtown's 'This is no job for kids!'"*, a variety show hosted by the famous comedy duo Downtown.

Lucifer is Michael's older brother, isn't he?, page 57

While there are debates about whether the word "lucifer" as it appears in the Bible was meant as a proper name or simply as a mention of the morning star, since the King James Version was translated, it has come to be understood as another name for the devil or Satan—specifically the name he had before he was cast out of heaven for rebellion. He was an archangel, like Michael, however there are no canonical sources that definitively identify him as Michael's brother in any sense that wouldn't make all of the angels brothers. The idea may have come from the Bogomil sect, who taught that God had two sons—Satanail and Michael. In their cosmology, Satanail plays a role similar to Lucifer, and Michael plays a role similar to that of Jesus Christ. The concept of Lucifer and Michael being brothers is alive and well in modern pop culture, including but not limited to the DC Comics series *Lucifer* and the popular '90s manga *Angel Sanctuary*.

The War in Heaven, page 57

As the name suggests, the War in Heaven was a war fought in Heaven. Lucifer rebelled against God and convinced several of the residents of Heaven to join his army. They fought Michael and his armies, lost, and were cast out of Heaven.

Cain and Abel, page 58

Cain and Abel were sons of Adam and Eve, the first man and woman. Cain, the older brother, was the first murderer, killing Abel out of jealousy and to take over Abel's flocks.

SAINT☆YOUNG MEN

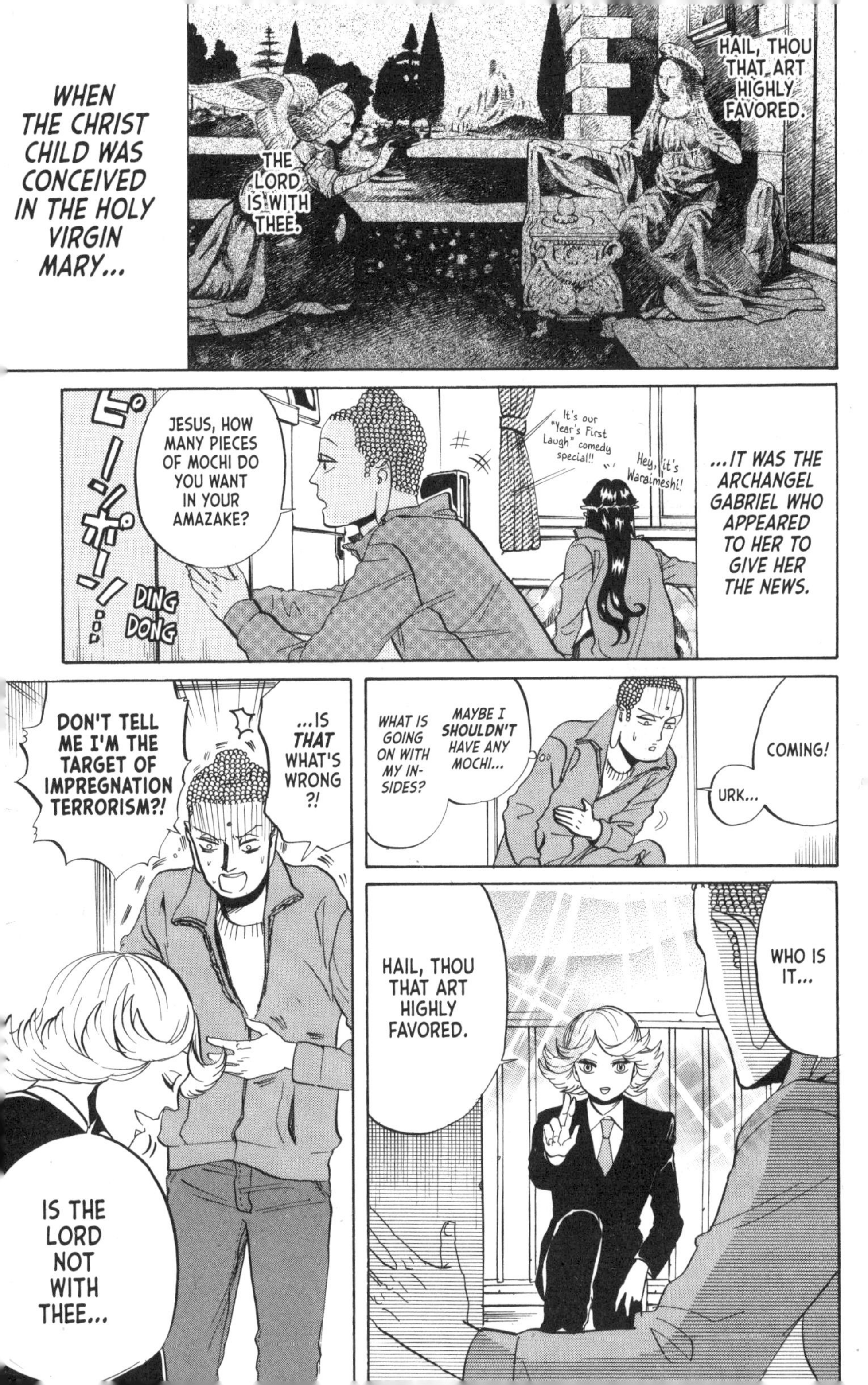
HAIL, THOU THAT ART HIGHLY FAVORED.
THE LORD IS WITH THEE.
WHEN THE CHRIST CHILD WAS CONCEIVED IN THE HOLY VIRGIN MARY...
...IT WAS THE ARCHANGEL GABRIEL WHO APPEARED TO HER TO GIVE HER THE NEWS.
Hey, it's Waraimeshi!
It's our "Year's First Laugh" comedy special!!
JESUS, HOW MANY PIECES OF MOCHI DO YOU WANT IN YOUR AMAZAKE?
DING DONG
COMING!
URK...
MAYBE I SHOULDN'T HAVE ANY MOCHI...
WHAT IS GOING ON WITH MY INSIDES?
WHO IS IT...
HAIL, THOU THAT ART HIGHLY FAVORED.
...IS *THAT* WHAT'S WRONG?!
DON'T TELL ME I'M THE TARGET OF IMPREGNATION TERRORISM?!
IS THE LORD NOT WITH THEE...

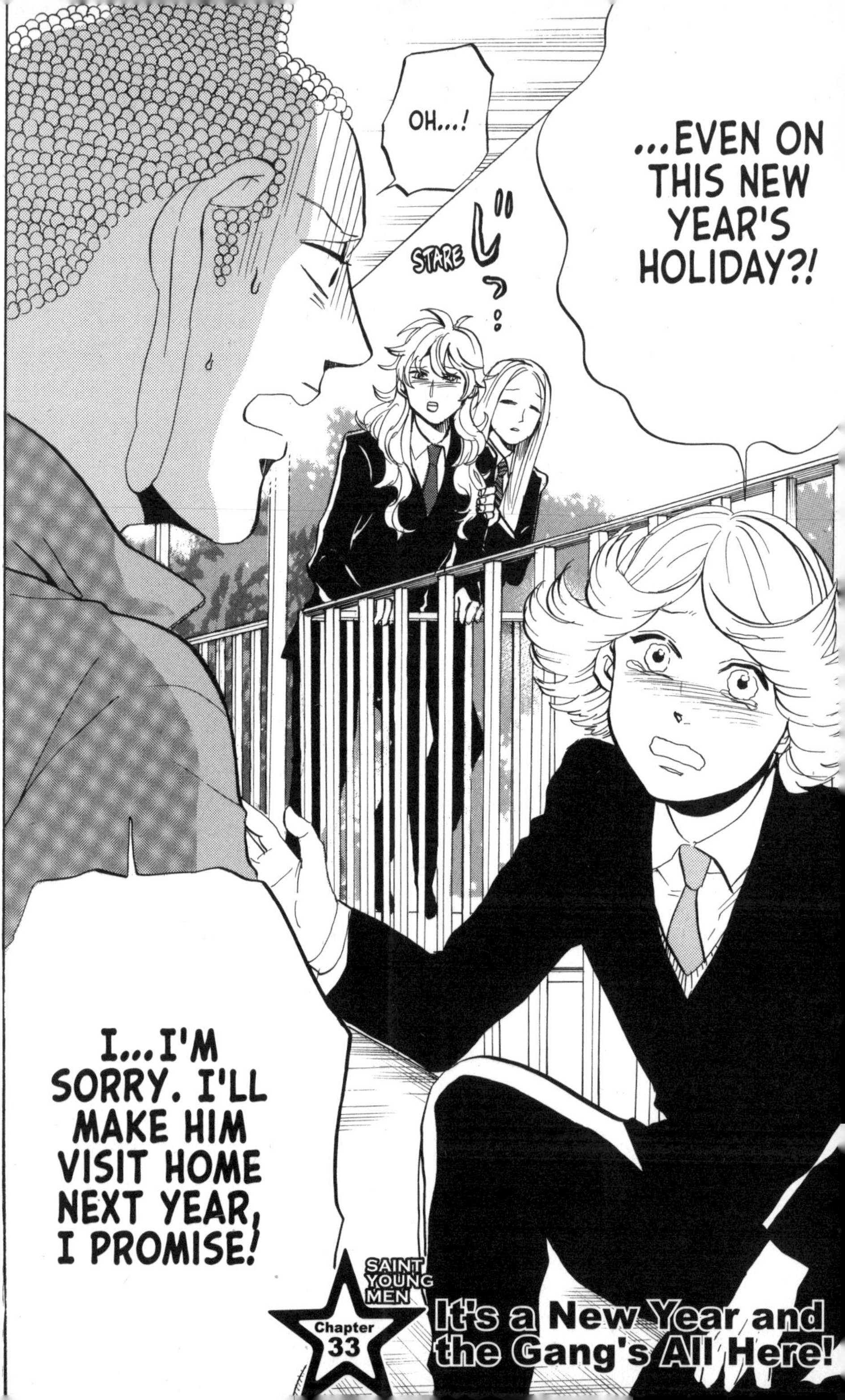
...EVEN ON THIS NEW YEAR'S HOLIDAY?!
OH...!
STARE
じー っ
I...I'M SORRY. I'LL MAKE HIM VISIT HOME NEXT YEAR, I PROMISE!
SAINT YOUNG MEN
Chapter 33
It's a New Year and the Gang's All Here!

BUDDHA: WINTER SPORT HE MOST WANTS TO TRY: CURLING. SWEEPING THE ICE WITH BROOMS LOOKS LIKE FUN.

JESUS: WINTER SPORT HE MOST WANTS TO TRY: THE SKI JUMP. HE FEELS LIKE HE COULD JUMP ALL THE WAY TO THE HEAVENS.

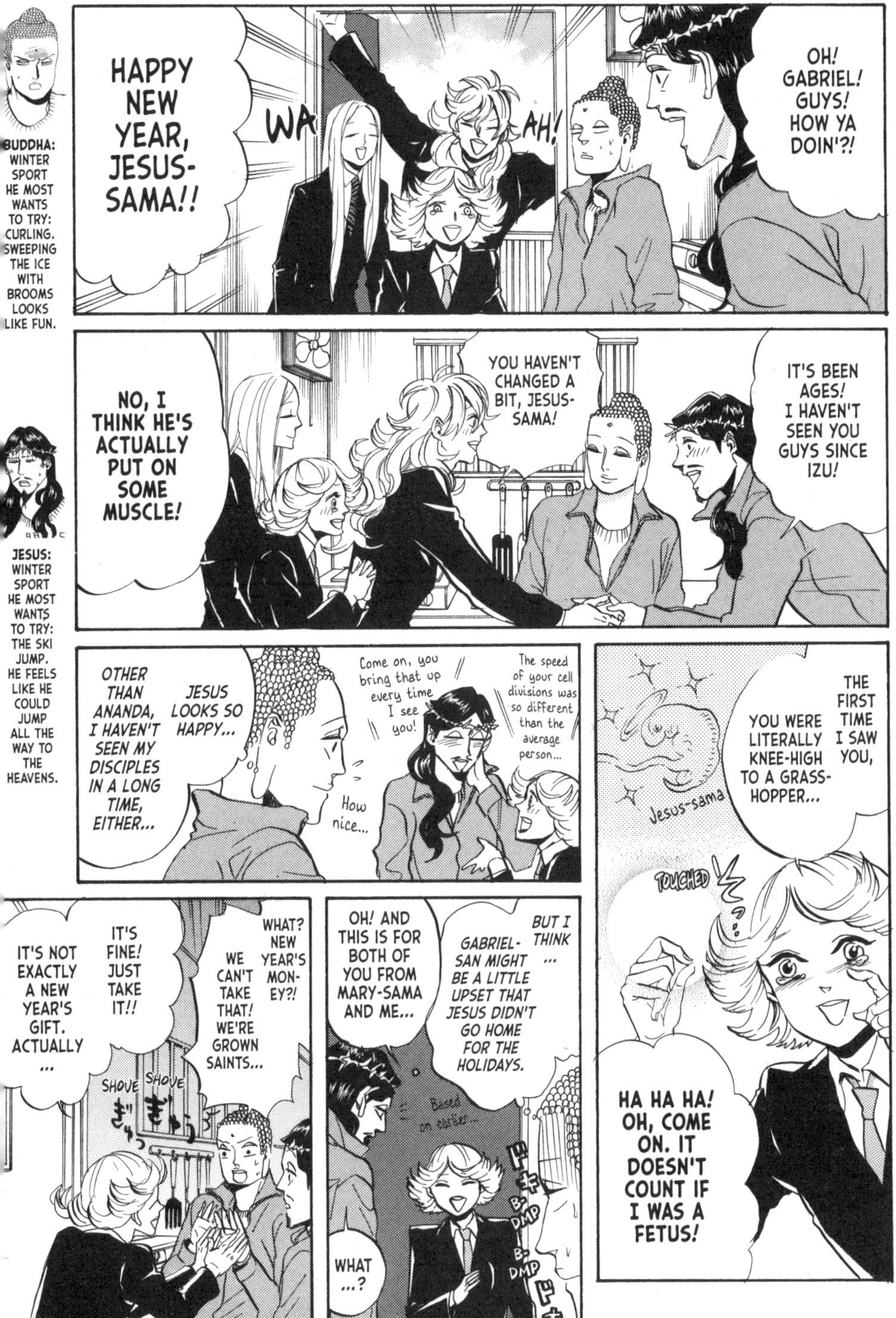
OH! GABRIEL! GUYS! HOW YA DOIN'?!
WA AH!
HAPPY NEW YEAR, JESUS-SAMA!!
IT'S BEEN AGES! I HAVEN'T SEEN YOU GUYS SINCE IZU!
YOU HAVEN'T CHANGED A BIT, JESUS-SAMA!
NO, I THINK HE'S ACTUALLY PUT ON SOME MUSCLE!
THE FIRST TIME I SAW YOU,
YOU WERE LITERALLY KNEE-HIGH TO A GRASS-HOPPER...
Jesus-sama
TOUCHED
HA HA HA! OH, COME ON. IT DOESN'T COUNT IF I WAS A FETUS!
The speed of your cell divisions was so different than the average person...
Come on, you bring that up every time I see you!
How nice...
JESUS LOOKS SO HAPPY...
OTHER THAN ANANDA, I HAVEN'T SEEN MY DISCIPLES IN A LONG TIME, EITHER...
BUT I THINK ...
GABRIEL-SAN MIGHT BE A LITTLE UPSET THAT JESUS DIDN'T GO HOME FOR THE HOLIDAYS.
OH! AND THIS IS FOR BOTH OF YOU FROM MARY-SAMA AND ME...
Based on earlier...
B-DMP
B-DMP
WHAT ...?
WHAT? NEW YEAR'S MON-EY?!
WE CAN'T TAKE THAT! WE'RE GROWN SAINTS...
IT'S FINE! JUST TAKE IT!!
IT'S NOT EXACTLY A NEW YEAR'S GIFT. ACTUALLY ...
SHOVE SHOVE

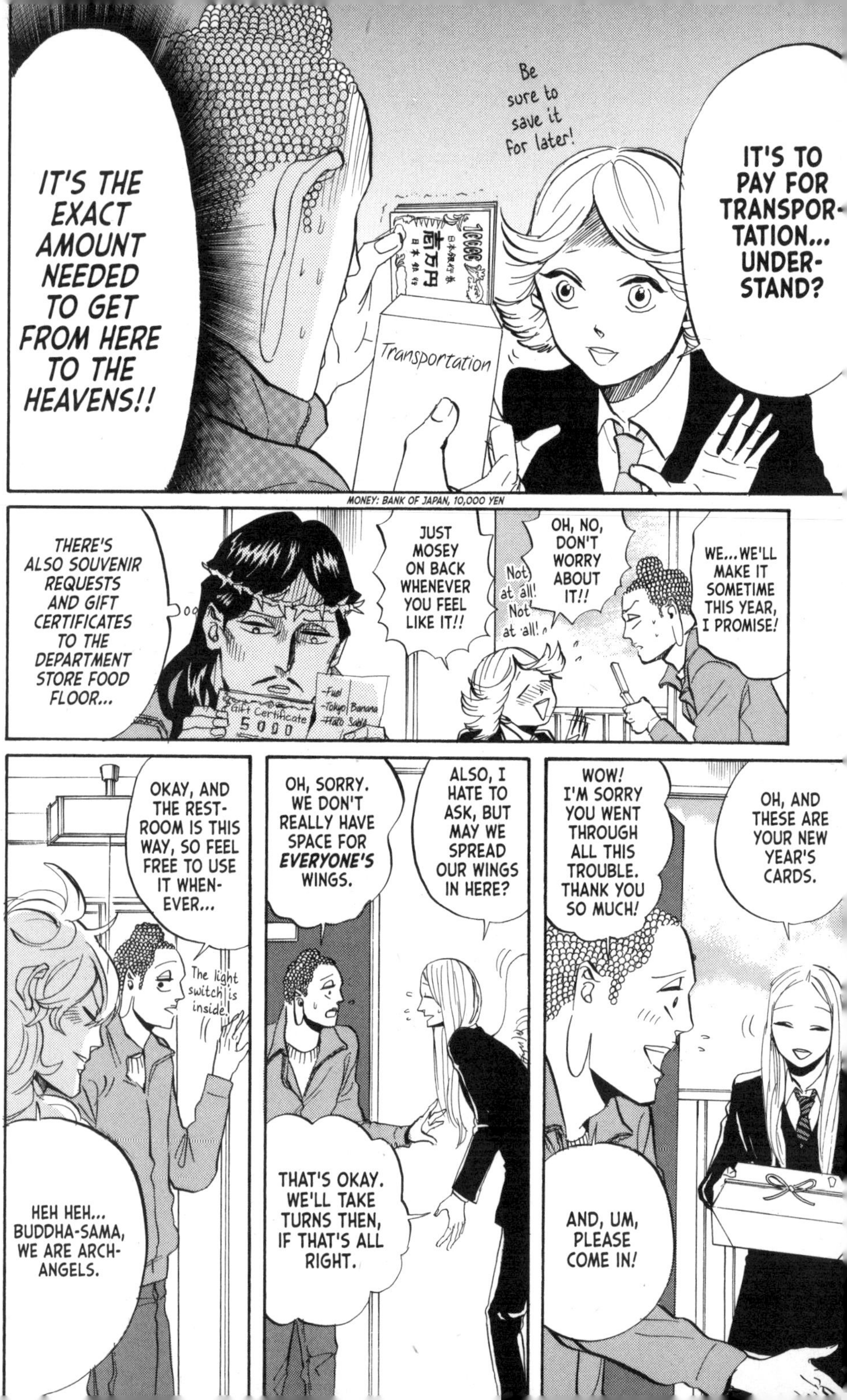
IT'S TO PAY FOR TRANSPORTATION... UNDERSTAND?
Be sure to save it for later!
Transportation
IT'S THE EXACT AMOUNT NEEDED TO GET FROM HERE TO THE HEAVENS!!
MONEY: BANK OF JAPAN, 10,000 YEN
WE...WE'LL MAKE IT SOMETIME THIS YEAR, I PROMISE!
OH, NO, DON'T WORRY ABOUT IT!!
Not at all! Not at all!
JUST MOSEY ON BACK WHENEVER YOU FEEL LIKE IT!!
THERE'S ALSO SOUVENIR REQUESTS AND GIFT CERTIFICATES TO THE DEPARTMENT STORE FOOD FLOOR...
Gift Certificate 5000
-Fuji -Tokyo Banana -Hato Sable
OH, AND THESE ARE YOUR NEW YEAR'S CARDS.
WOW! I'M SORRY YOU WENT THROUGH ALL THIS TROUBLE. THANK YOU SO MUCH!
AND, UM, PLEASE COME IN!
ALSO, I HATE TO ASK, BUT MAY WE SPREAD OUR WINGS IN HERE?
OH, SORRY. WE DON'T REALLY HAVE SPACE FOR EVERYONE'S WINGS.
THAT'S OKAY. WE'LL TAKE TURNS THEN, IF THAT'S ALL RIGHT.
OKAY, AND THE RESTROOM IS THIS WAY, SO FEEL FREE TO USE IT WHENEVER...
The light switch is inside.
HEH HEH... BUDDHA-SAMA, WE ARE ARCHANGELS.

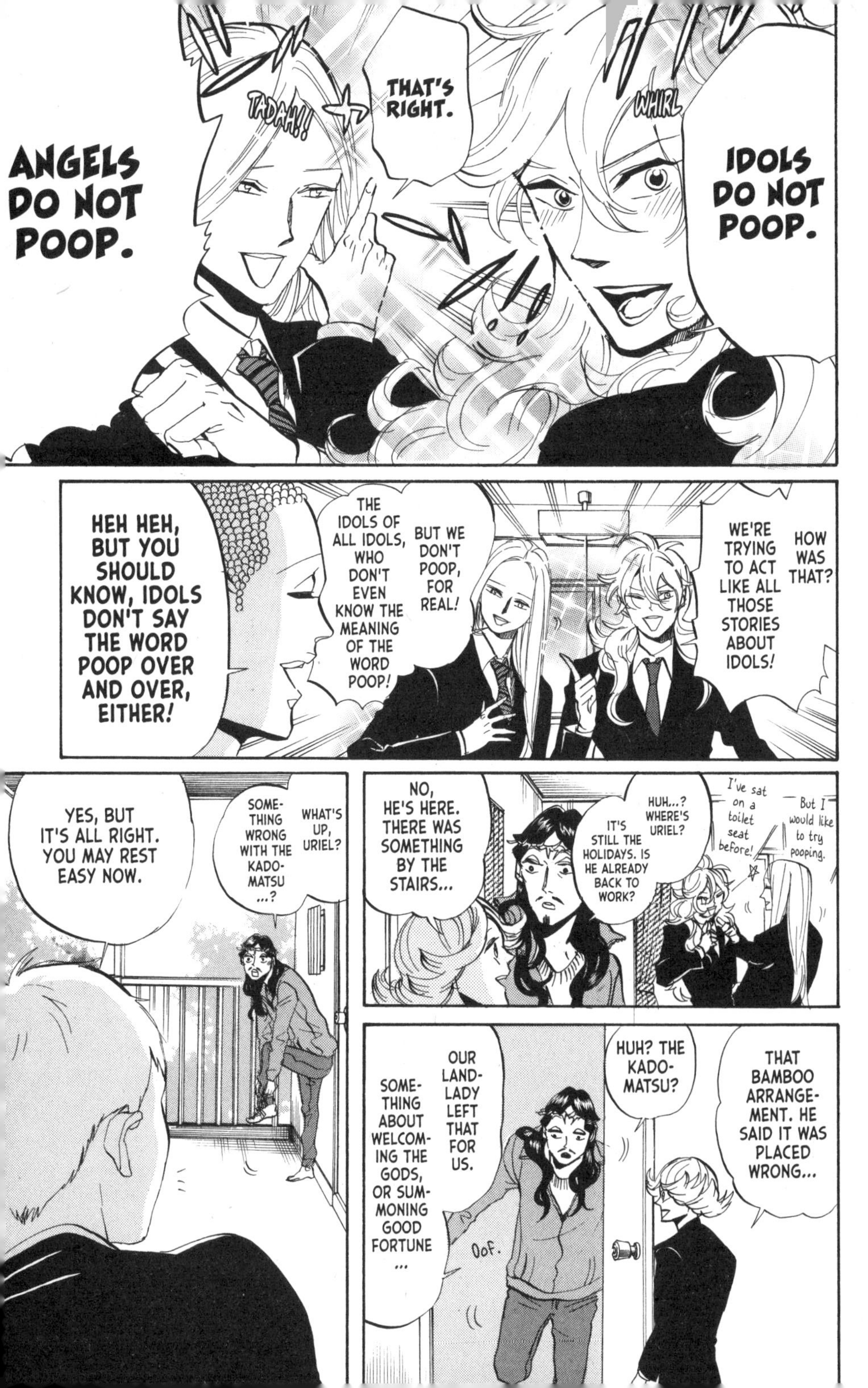
IDOLS DO NOT POOP.
WHIRL
THAT'S RIGHT.
TADAH!!
ANGELS DO NOT POOP.
HOW WAS THAT?
WE'RE TRYING TO ACT LIKE ALL THOSE STORIES ABOUT IDOLS!
BUT WE DON'T POOP, FOR REAL!
THE IDOLS OF ALL IDOLS, WHO DON'T EVEN KNOW THE MEANING OF THE WORD POOP!
HEH HEH, BUT YOU SHOULD KNOW, IDOLS DON'T SAY THE WORD POOP OVER AND OVER, EITHER!
But I would like to try pooping.
I've sat on a toilet seat before!
HUH...? WHERE'S URIEL?
IT'S STILL THE HOLIDAYS. IS HE ALREADY BACK TO WORK?
NO, HE'S HERE. THERE WAS SOMETHING BY THE STAIRS...
THAT BAMBOO ARRANGE-MENT. HE SAID IT WAS PLACED WRONG...
HUH? THE KADO-MATSU?
OUR LAND-LADY LEFT THAT FOR US.
SOME-THING ABOUT WELCOM-ING THE GODS, OR SUM-MONING GOOD FORTUNE ...
Oof.
WHAT'S UP, URIEL?
SOME-THING WRONG WITH THE KADO-MATSU ...?
YES, BUT IT'S ALL RIGHT. YOU MAY REST EASY NOW.

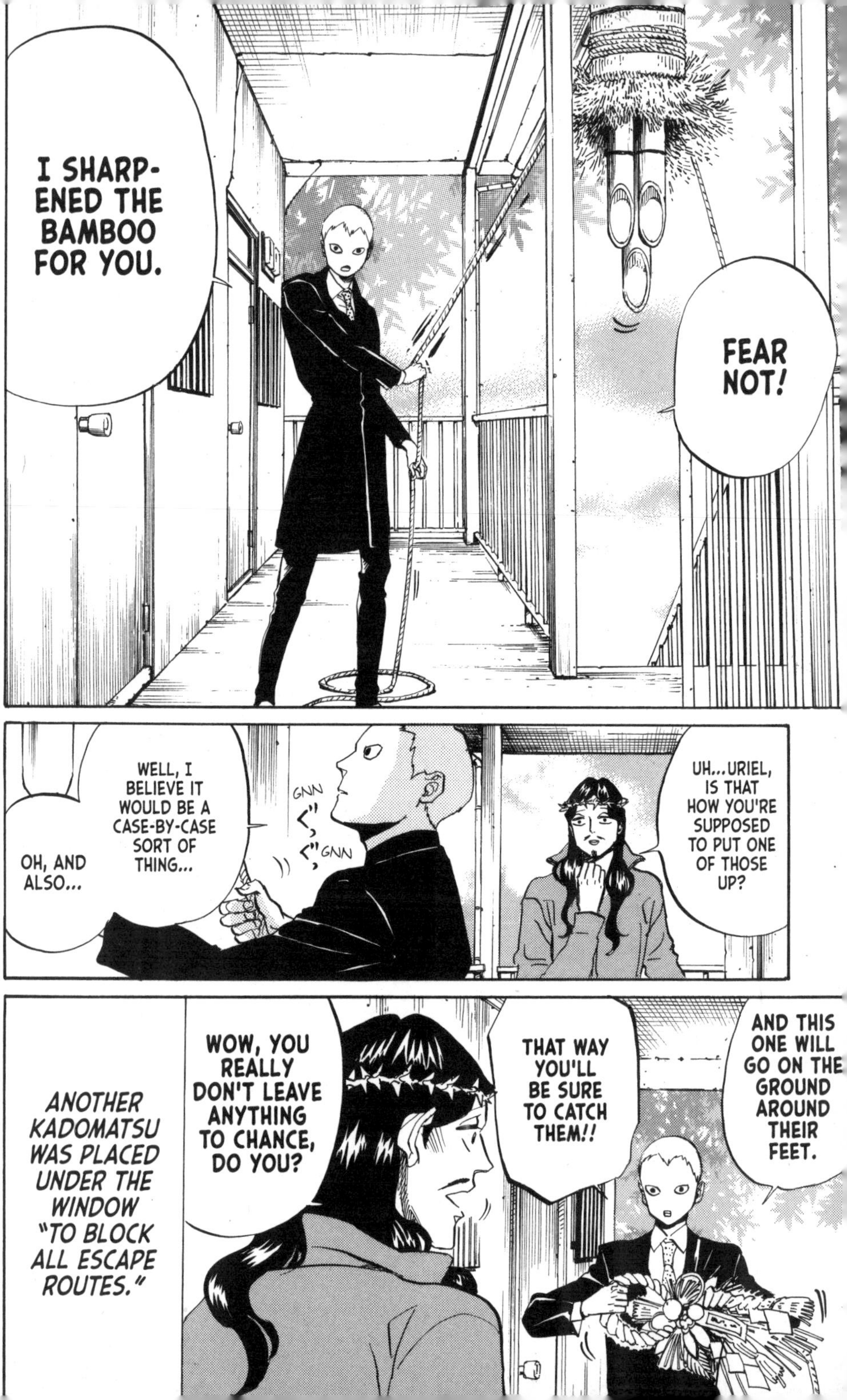
FEAR NOT!
I SHARPENED THE BAMBOO FOR YOU.
UH...URIEL, IS THAT HOW YOU'RE SUPPOSED TO PUT ONE OF THOSE UP?
WELL, I BELIEVE IT WOULD BE A CASE-BY-CASE SORT OF THING...
GNN
GNN
OH, AND ALSO...
AND THIS ONE WILL GO ON THE GROUND AROUND THEIR FEET.
THAT WAY YOU'LL BE SURE TO CATCH THEM!!
WOW, YOU REALLY DON'T LEAVE ANYTHING TO CHANCE, DO YOU?
ANOTHER KADOMATSU WAS PLACED UNDER THE WINDOW "TO BLOCK ALL ESCAPE ROUTES."

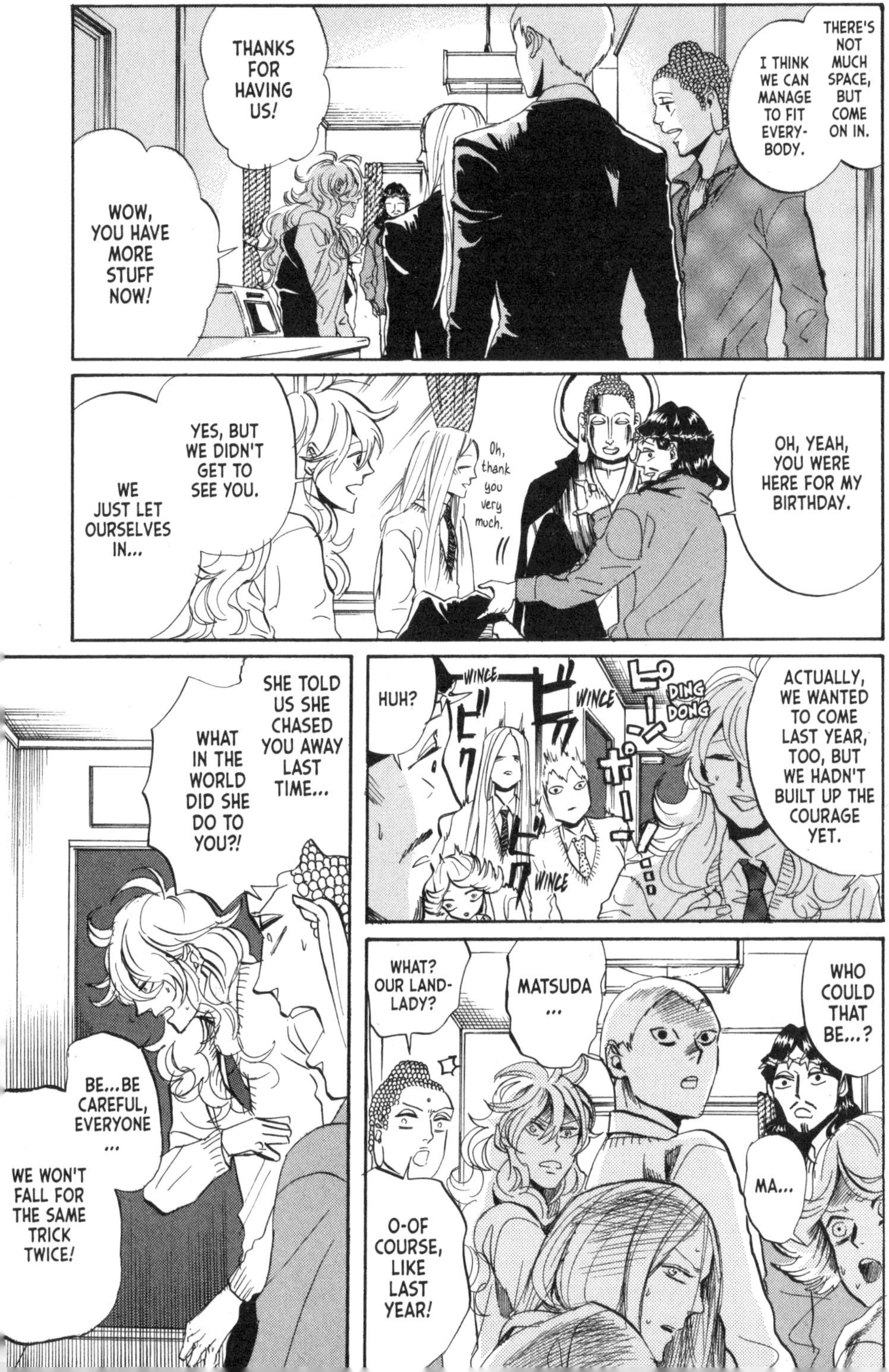

THERE'S NOT MUCH SPACE, BUT COME ON IN.
I THINK WE CAN MANAGE TO FIT EVERYBODY.
THANKS FOR HAVING US!
WOW, YOU HAVE MORE STUFF NOW!
OH, YEAH, YOU WERE HERE FOR MY BIRTHDAY.
Oh, thank you very much.
YES, BUT WE DIDN'T GET TO SEE YOU.
WE JUST LET OURSELVES IN...
ACTUALLY, WE WANTED TO COME LAST YEAR, TOO, BUT WE HADN'T BUILT UP THE COURAGE YET.
DING DONG
WINCE
WINCE
HUH?
WINCE
WHO COULD THAT BE...?
MATSUDA...
WHAT? OUR LAND-LADY?
MA...
O-OF COURSE, LIKE LAST YEAR!
SHE TOLD US SHE CHASED YOU AWAY LAST TIME...
WHAT IN THE WORLD DID SHE DO TO YOU?!
BE...BE CAREFUL, EVERYONE...
WE WON'T FALL FOR THE SAME TRICK TWICE!

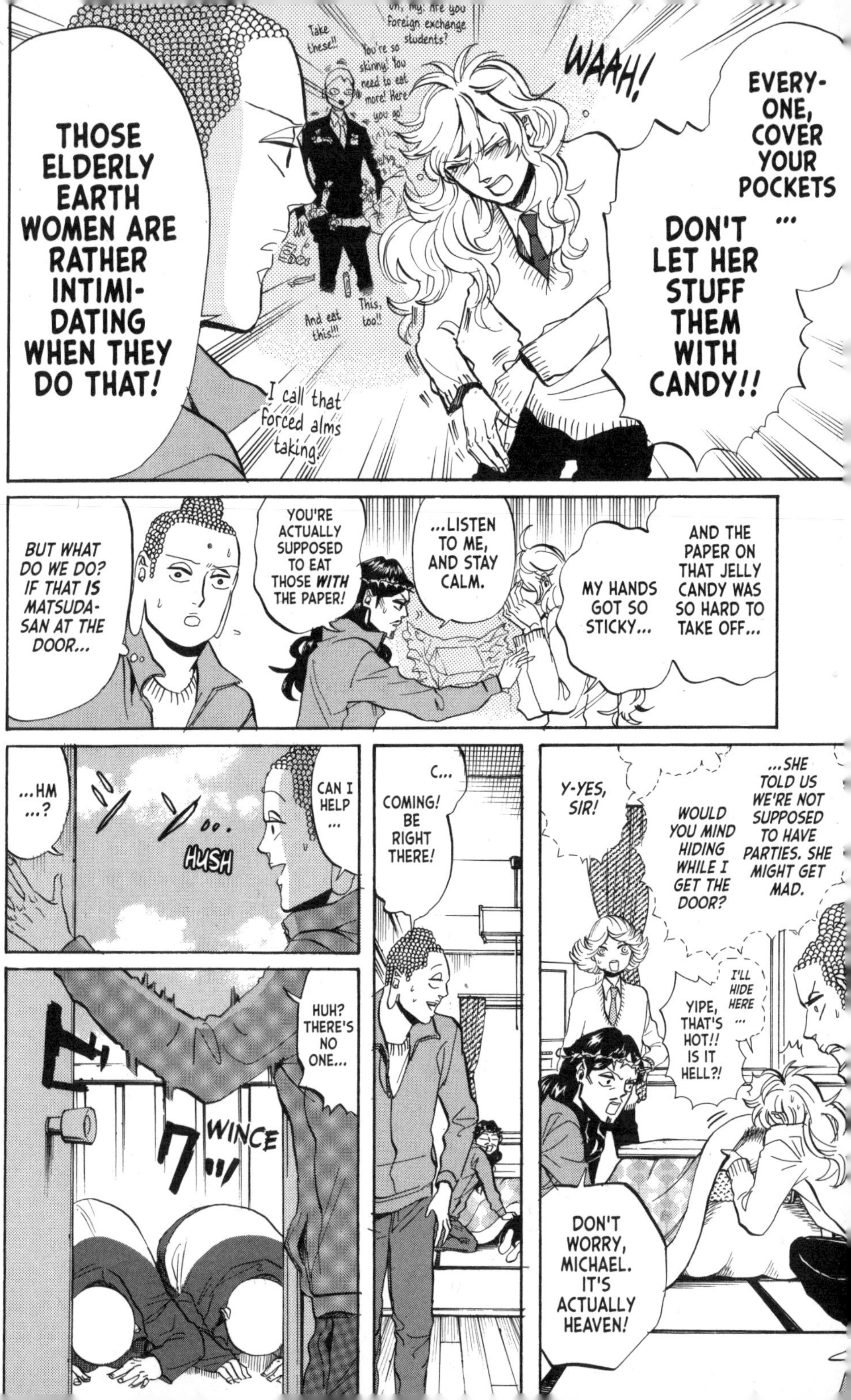
EVERY-ONE, COVER YOUR POCKETS...
DON'T LET HER STUFF THEM WITH CANDY!!
WAAH!
Oh, my! Are you foreign exchange students?
You're so skinny! You need to eat more! Here you go!
Take these!!
This, too!!
And eat this!!!
I call that forced alms taking.
THOSE ELDERLY EARTH WOMEN ARE RATHER INTIMI-DATING WHEN THEY DO THAT!
AND THE PAPER ON THAT JELLY CANDY WAS SO HARD TO TAKE OFF...
MY HANDS GOT SO STICKY...
...LISTEN TO ME, AND STAY CALM.
YOU'RE ACTUALLY SUPPOSED TO EAT THOSE WITH THE PAPER!
BUT WHAT DO WE DO? IF THAT IS MATSUDA-SAN AT THE DOOR...
...SHE TOLD US WE'RE NOT SUPPOSED TO HAVE PARTIES. SHE MIGHT GET MAD.
WOULD YOU MIND HIDING WHILE I GET THE DOOR?
Y-YES, SIR!
I'LL HIDE HERE...
YIPE, THAT'S HOT!! IS IT HELL?!
DON'T WORRY, MICHAEL. IT'S ACTUALLY HEAVEN!
C...
COMING! BE RIGHT THERE!
CAN I HELP...
HUSH
...HM...?
HUH? THERE'S NO ONE...
WINCE

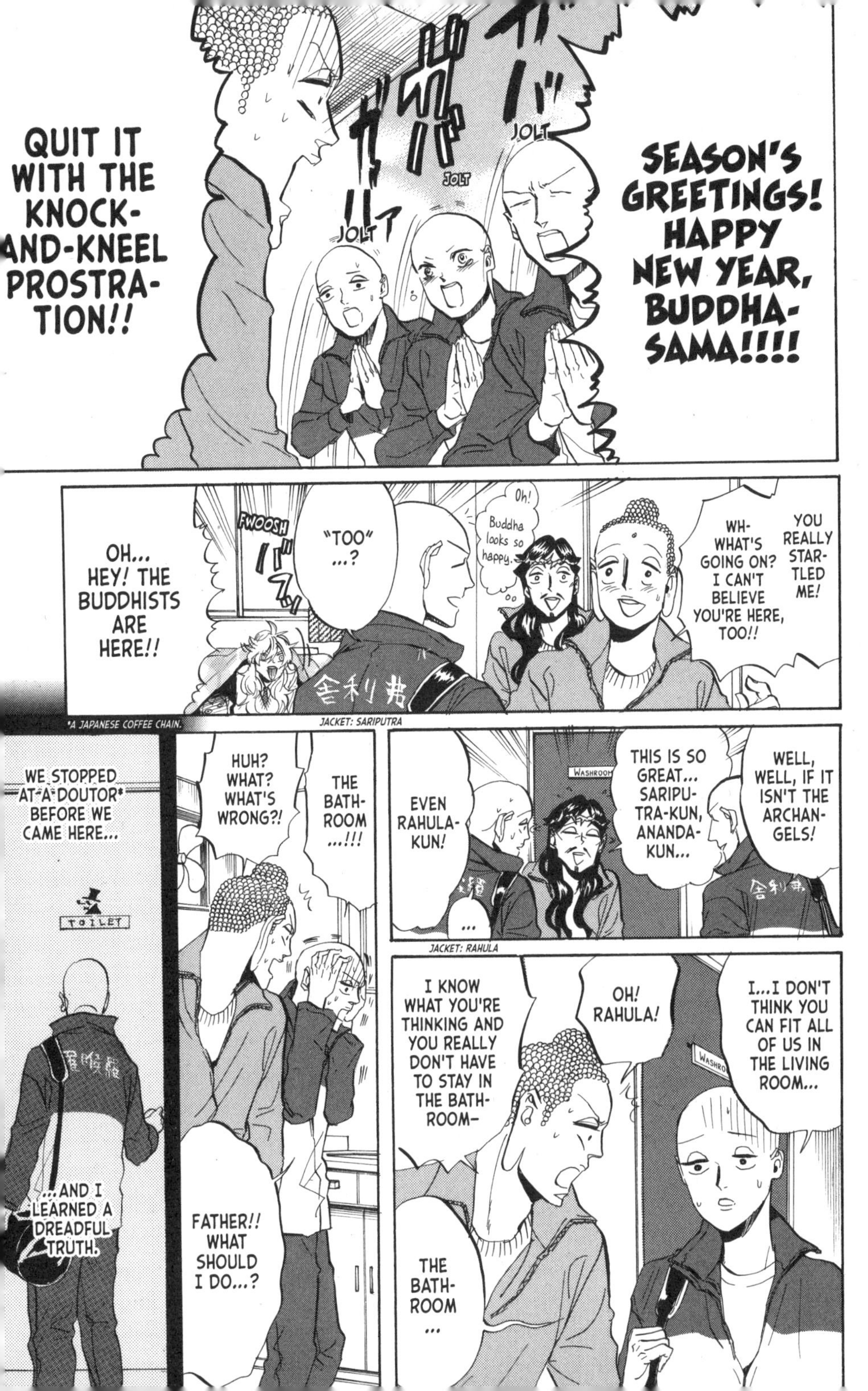
SEASON'S GREETINGS! HAPPY NEW YEAR, BUDDHA-SAMA!!!!
JOLT
JOLT
JOLT
QUIT IT WITH THE KNOCK-AND-KNEEL PROSTRATION!!
YOU REALLY STARTLED ME!
WH-WHAT'S GOING ON? I CAN'T BELIEVE YOU'RE HERE, TOO!!
Oh! Buddha looks so happy.
"TOO" ...?
FWOOSH
OH... HEY! THE BUDDHISTS ARE HERE!!
JACKET: SARIPUTRA
*A JAPANESE COFFEE CHAIN.
WELL, WELL, IF IT ISN'T THE ARCHANGELS!
THIS IS SO GREAT... SARIPUTRA-KUN, ANANDA-KUN...
WASHROOM
EVEN RAHULA-KUN!
...
JACKET: RAHULA
I...I DON'T THINK YOU CAN FIT ALL OF US IN THE LIVING ROOM...
OH! RAHULA!
WASHRO
I KNOW WHAT YOU'RE THINKING AND YOU REALLY DON'T HAVE TO STAY IN THE BATHROOM-
THE BATHROOM ...
THE BATHROOM ...!!!
HUH? WHAT? WHAT'S WRONG?!
FATHER!! WHAT SHOULD I DO...?
WE STOPPED AT A DOUTOR* BEFORE WE CAME HERE...
TOILET
...AND I LEARNED A DREADFUL TRUTH.

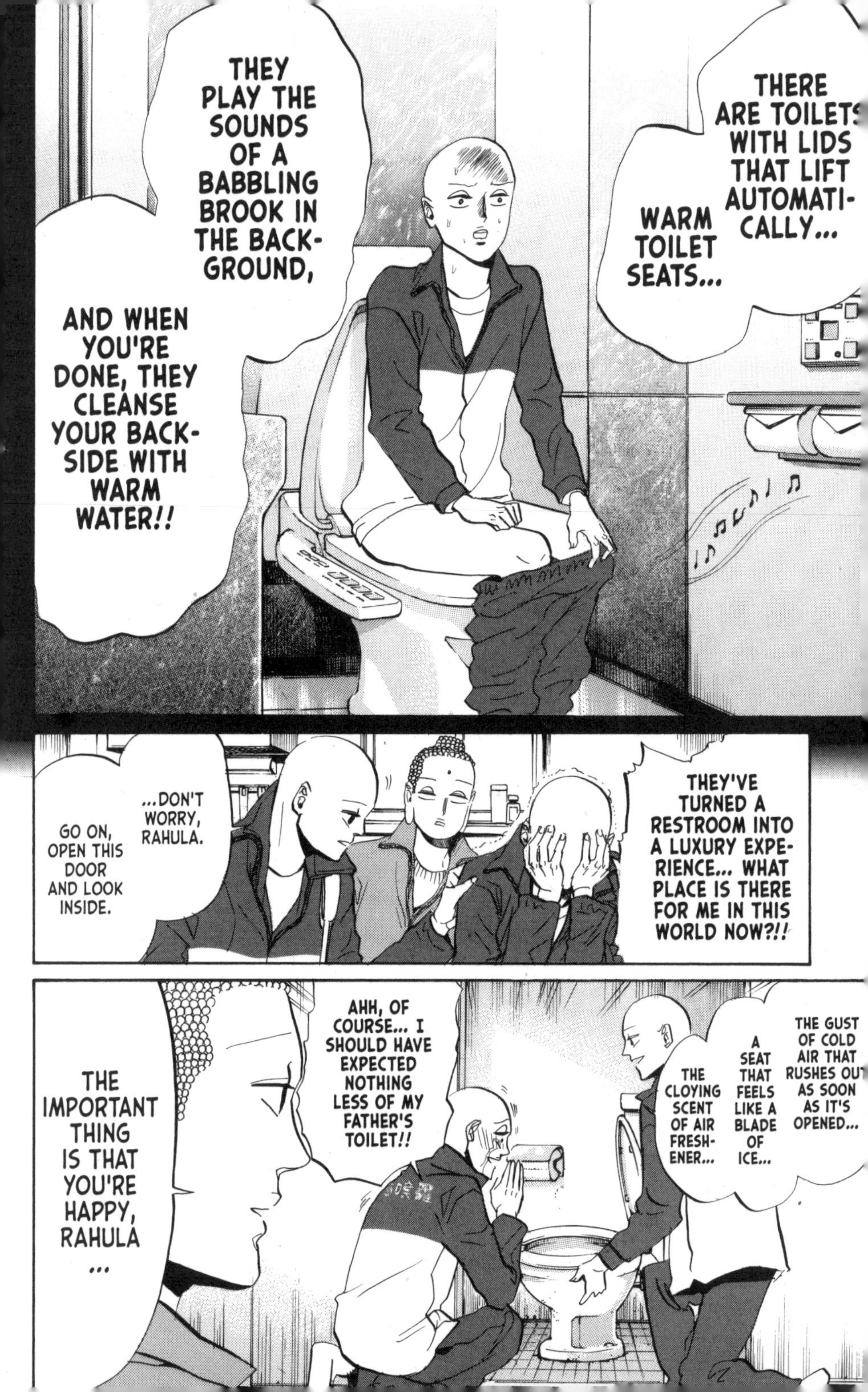
THERE ARE TOILETS WITH LIDS THAT LIFT AUTOMATICALLY...
WARM TOILET SEATS...
THEY PLAY THE SOUNDS OF A BABBLING BROOK IN THE BACKGROUND,
AND WHEN YOU'RE DONE, THEY CLEANSE YOUR BACKSIDE WITH WARM WATER!!
THEY'VE TURNED A RESTROOM INTO A LUXURY EXPERIENCE... WHAT PLACE IS THERE FOR ME IN THIS WORLD NOW?!!
...DON'T WORRY, RAHULA.
GO ON, OPEN THIS DOOR AND LOOK INSIDE.
THE GUST OF COLD AIR THAT RUSHES OUT AS SOON AS IT'S OPENED...
A SEAT THAT FEELS LIKE A BLADE OF ICE...
THE CLOYING SCENT OF AIR FRESHENER...
AHH, OF COURSE... I SHOULD HAVE EXPECTED NOTHING LESS OF MY FATHER'S TOILET!!
THE IMPORTANT THING IS THAT YOU'RE HAPPY, RAHULA...

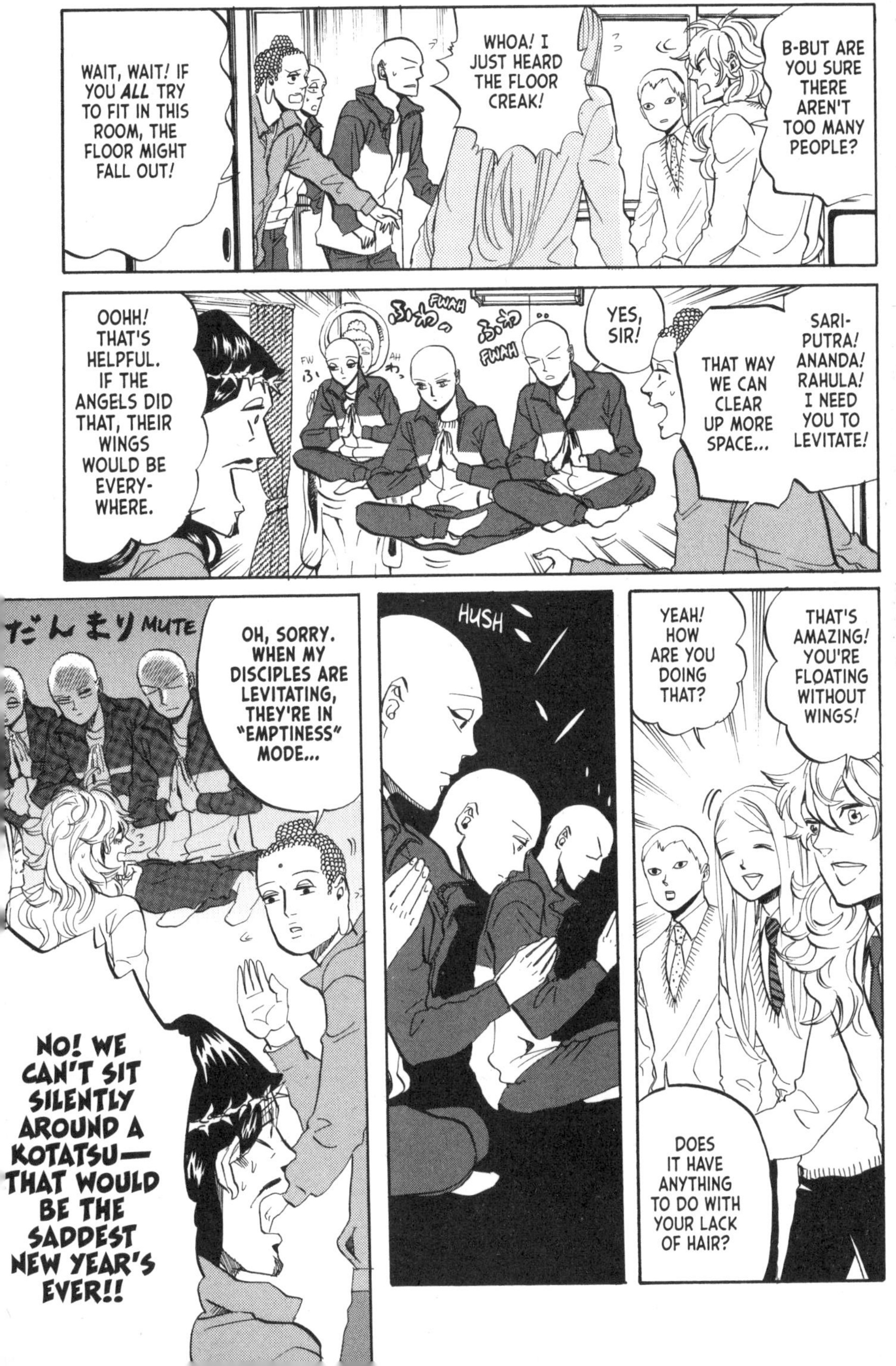
B-BUT ARE YOU SURE THERE AREN'T TOO MANY PEOPLE?
WHOA! I JUST HEARD THE FLOOR CREAK!
WAIT, WAIT! IF YOU ALL TRY TO FIT IN THIS ROOM, THE FLOOR MIGHT FALL OUT!
SARI-PUTRA! ANANDA! RAHULA! I NEED YOU TO LEVITATE!
THAT WAY WE CAN CLEAR UP MORE SPACE...
YES, SIR!
ふわ FWAH
ふわ FWAH
わっ AH
ふ FW
OOHH! THAT'S HELPFUL. IF THE ANGELS DID THAT, THEIR WINGS WOULD BE EVERY-WHERE.
THAT'S AMAZING! YOU'RE FLOATING WITHOUT WINGS!
YEAH! HOW ARE YOU DOING THAT?
DOES IT HAVE ANYTHING TO DO WITH YOUR LACK OF HAIR?
HUSH
だんまり MUTE
OH, SORRY. WHEN MY DISCIPLES ARE LEVITATING, THEY'RE IN "EMPTINESS" MODE...
NO! WE CAN'T SIT SILENTLY AROUND A KOTATSU—THAT WOULD BE THE SADDEST NEW YEAR'S EVER!!

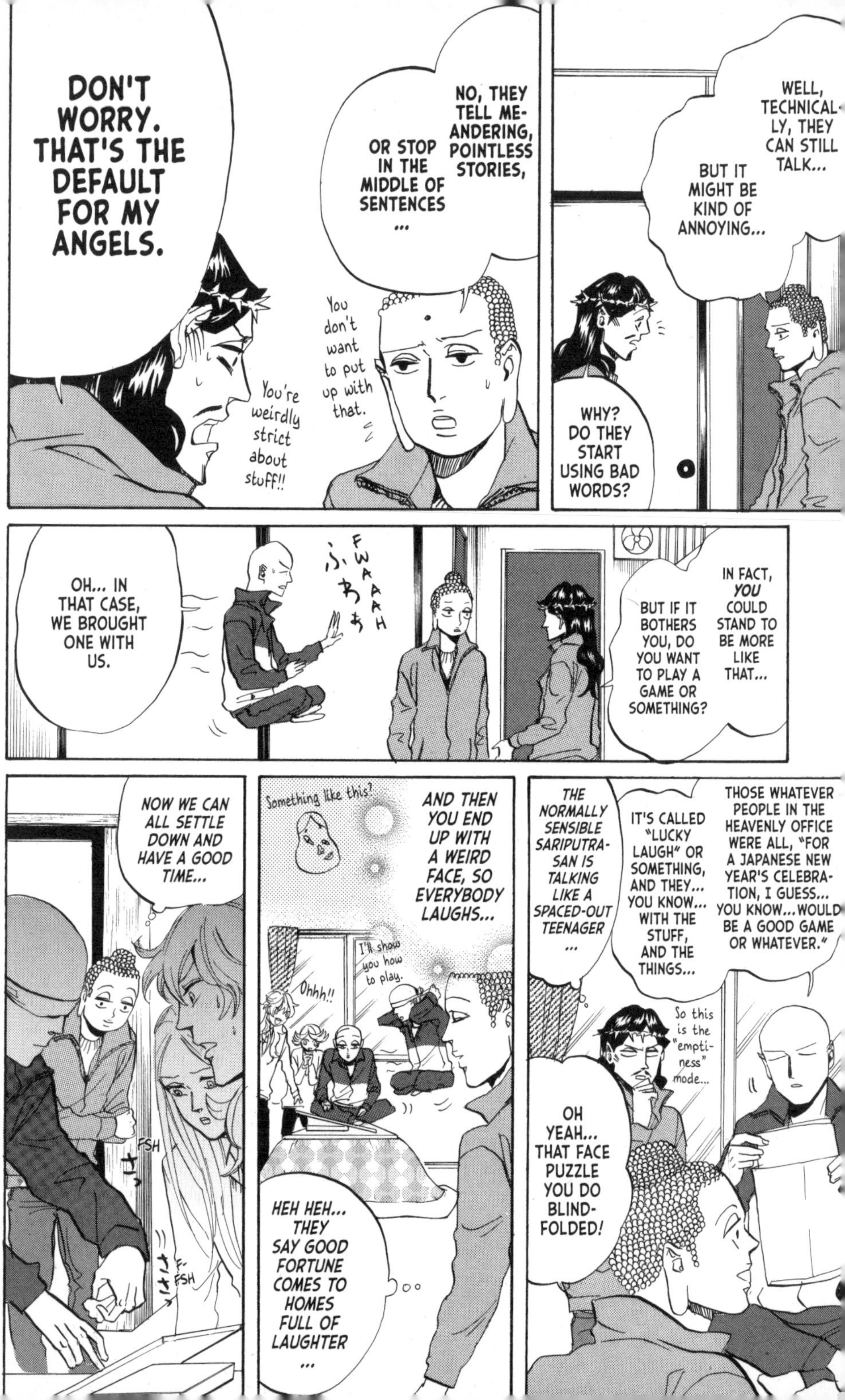
WELL, TECHNICALLY, THEY CAN STILL TALK...
BUT IT MIGHT BE KIND OF ANNOYING...
WHY? DO THEY START USING BAD WORDS?
NO, THEY TELL MEANDERING, POINTLESS STORIES,
OR STOP IN THE MIDDLE OF SENTENCES...
You don't want to put up with that.
DON'T WORRY. THAT'S THE DEFAULT FOR MY ANGELS.
You're weirdly strict about stuff!!
IN FACT, YOU COULD STAND TO BE MORE LIKE THAT...
BUT IF IT BOTHERS YOU, DO YOU WANT TO PLAY A GAME OR SOMETHING?
FWAAAAH
ふわあ
OH... IN THAT CASE, WE BROUGHT ONE WITH US.
THOSE WHATEVER PEOPLE IN THE HEAVENLY OFFICE WERE ALL, "FOR A JAPANESE NEW YEAR'S CELEBRATION, I GUESS... YOU KNOW...WOULD BE A GOOD GAME OR WHATEVER."
IT'S CALLED "LUCKY LAUGH" OR SOMETHING, AND THEY... YOU KNOW... WITH THE STUFF, AND THE THINGS...
THE NORMALLY SENSIBLE SARIPUTRA-SAN IS TALKING LIKE A SPACED-OUT TEENAGER...
So this is the "emptiness" mode...
OH YEAH... THAT FACE PUZZLE YOU DO BLINDFOLDED!
AND THEN YOU END UP WITH A WEIRD FACE, SO EVERYBODY LAUGHS...
Something like this?
I'll show you how to play.
Ohhh!!
HEH HEH... THEY SAY GOOD FORTUNE COMES TO HOMES FULL OF LAUGHTER...
NOW WE CAN ALL SETTLE DOWN AND HAVE A GOOD TIME...
FSH
さっ
FSH
ささ

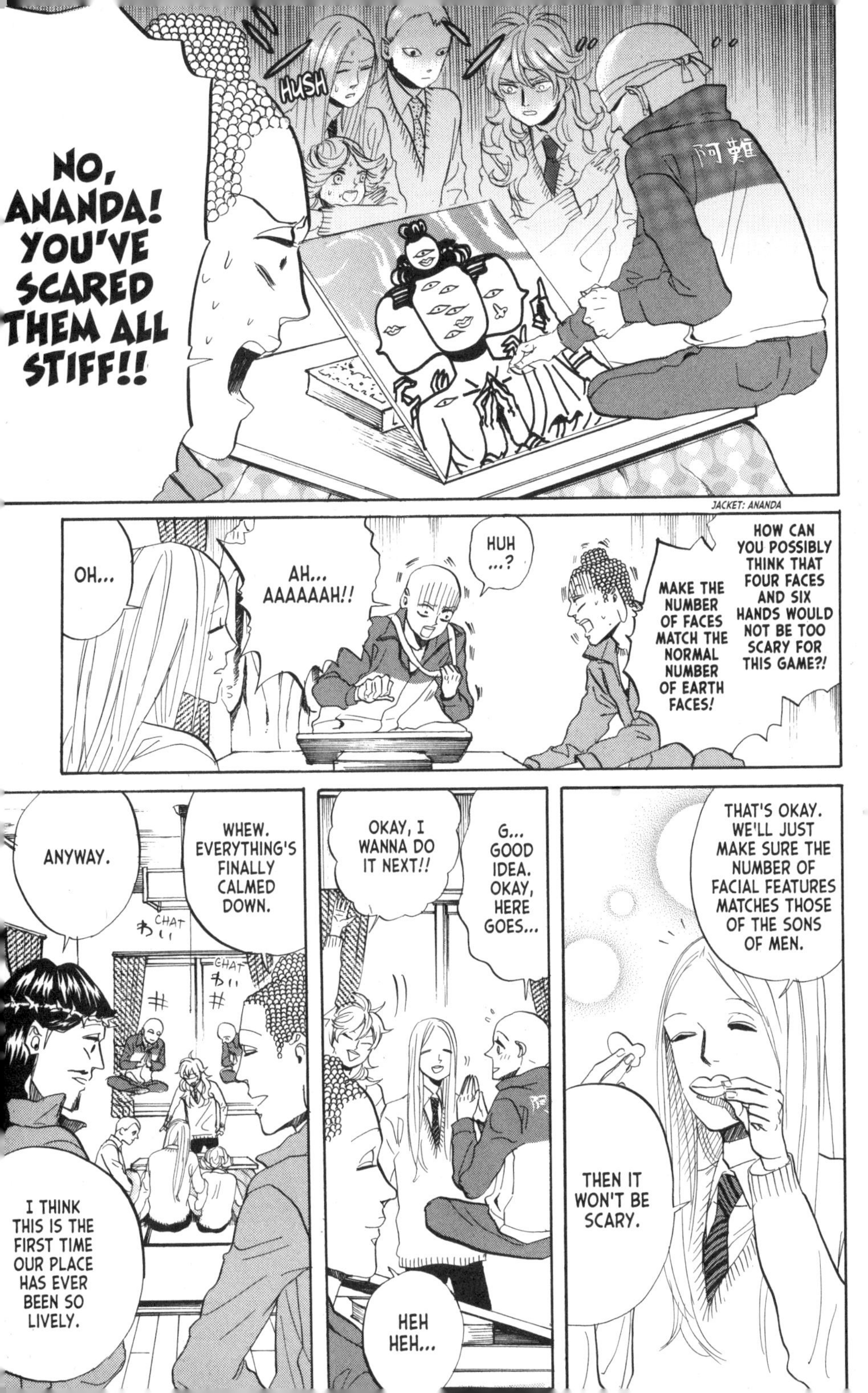
HUSH
NO, ANANDA! YOU'VE SCARED THEM ALL STIFF!!
阿難
JACKET: ANANDA
HOW CAN YOU POSSIBLY THINK THAT FOUR FACES AND SIX HANDS WOULD NOT BE TOO SCARY FOR THIS GAME?!
MAKE THE NUMBER OF FACES MATCH THE NORMAL NUMBER OF EARTH FACES!
HUH ...?
AH... AAAAAAH!!
OH...
THAT'S OKAY. WE'LL JUST MAKE SURE THE NUMBER OF FACIAL FEATURES MATCHES THOSE OF THE SONS OF MEN.
THEN IT WON'T BE SCARY.
G... GOOD IDEA. OKAY, HERE GOES...
OKAY, I WANNA DO IT NEXT!!
HEH HEH...
WHEW. EVERYTHING'S FINALLY CALMED DOWN.
ANYWAY.
CHAT
CHAT
I THINK THIS IS THE FIRST TIME OUR PLACE HAS EVER BEEN SO LIVELY.

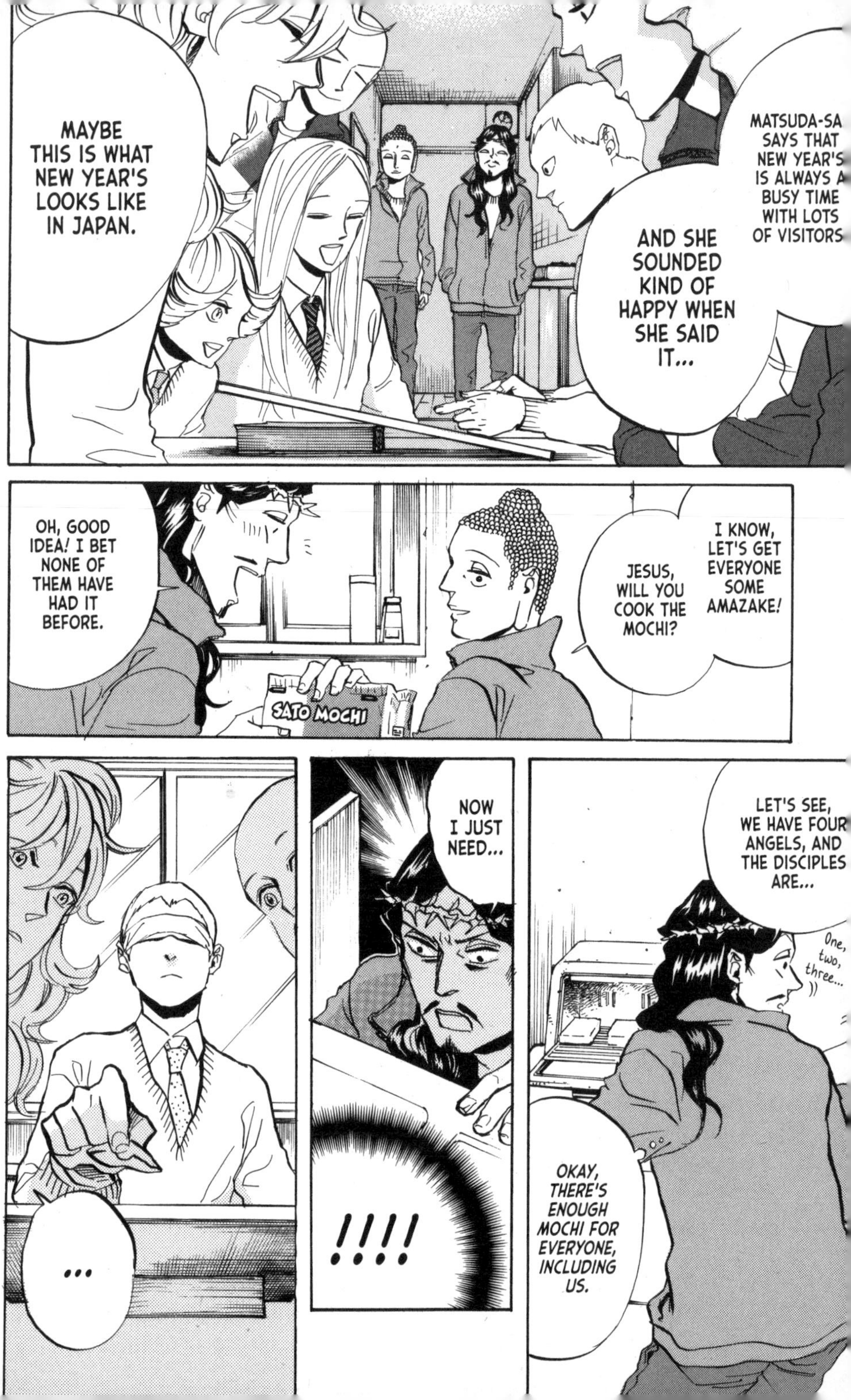
MATSUDA-SA SAYS THAT NEW YEAR'S IS ALWAYS A BUSY TIME WITH LOTS OF VISITORS
AND SHE SOUNDED KIND OF HAPPY WHEN SHE SAID IT...
MAYBE THIS IS WHAT NEW YEAR'S LOOKS LIKE IN JAPAN.
I KNOW, LET'S GET EVERYONE SOME AMAZAKE!
JESUS, WILL YOU COOK THE MOCHI?
OH, GOOD IDEA! I BET NONE OF THEM HAVE HAD IT BEFORE.
SATO MOCHI
LET'S SEE, WE HAVE FOUR ANGELS, AND THE DISCIPLES ARE...
One, two, three...
OKAY, THERE'S ENOUGH MOCHI FOR EVERYONE, INCLUDING US.
NOW I JUST NEED...
!!!!
...

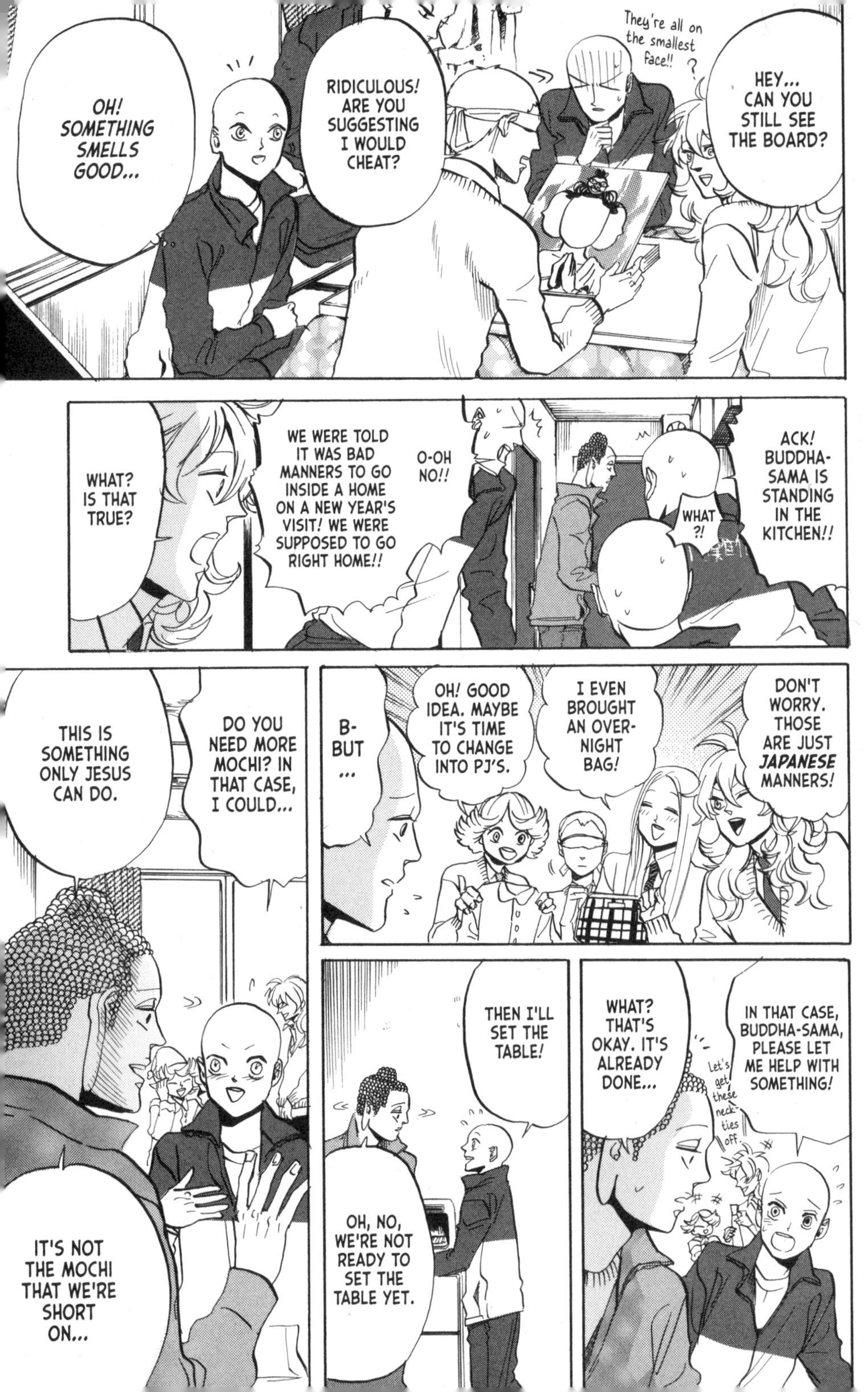
HEY... CAN YOU STILL SEE THE BOARD?
They're all on the smallest face!!
?
RIDICULOUS! ARE YOU SUGGESTING I WOULD CHEAT?
OH! SOMETHING SMELLS GOOD...
ACK! BUDDHA-SAMA IS STANDING IN THE KITCHEN!!
WHAT?!
O-OH NO!!
WE WERE TOLD IT WAS BAD MANNERS TO GO INSIDE A HOME ON A NEW YEAR'S VISIT! WE WERE SUPPOSED TO GO RIGHT HOME!!
WHAT? IS THAT TRUE?
DON'T WORRY. THOSE ARE JUST *JAPANESE* MANNERS!
I EVEN BROUGHT AN OVER-NIGHT BAG!
OH! GOOD IDEA. MAYBE IT'S TIME TO CHANGE INTO PJ'S.
B-BUT ...
IN THAT CASE, BUDDHA-SAMA, PLEASE LET ME HELP WITH SOMETHING!
Let's get these neck-ties off.
WHAT? THAT'S OKAY. IT'S ALREADY DONE...
THEN I'LL SET THE TABLE!
OH, NO, WE'RE NOT READY TO SET THE TABLE YET.
DO YOU NEED MORE MOCHI? IN THAT CASE, I COULD...
THIS IS SOMETHING ONLY JESUS CAN DO.
IT'S NOT THE MOCHI THAT WE'RE SHORT ON...

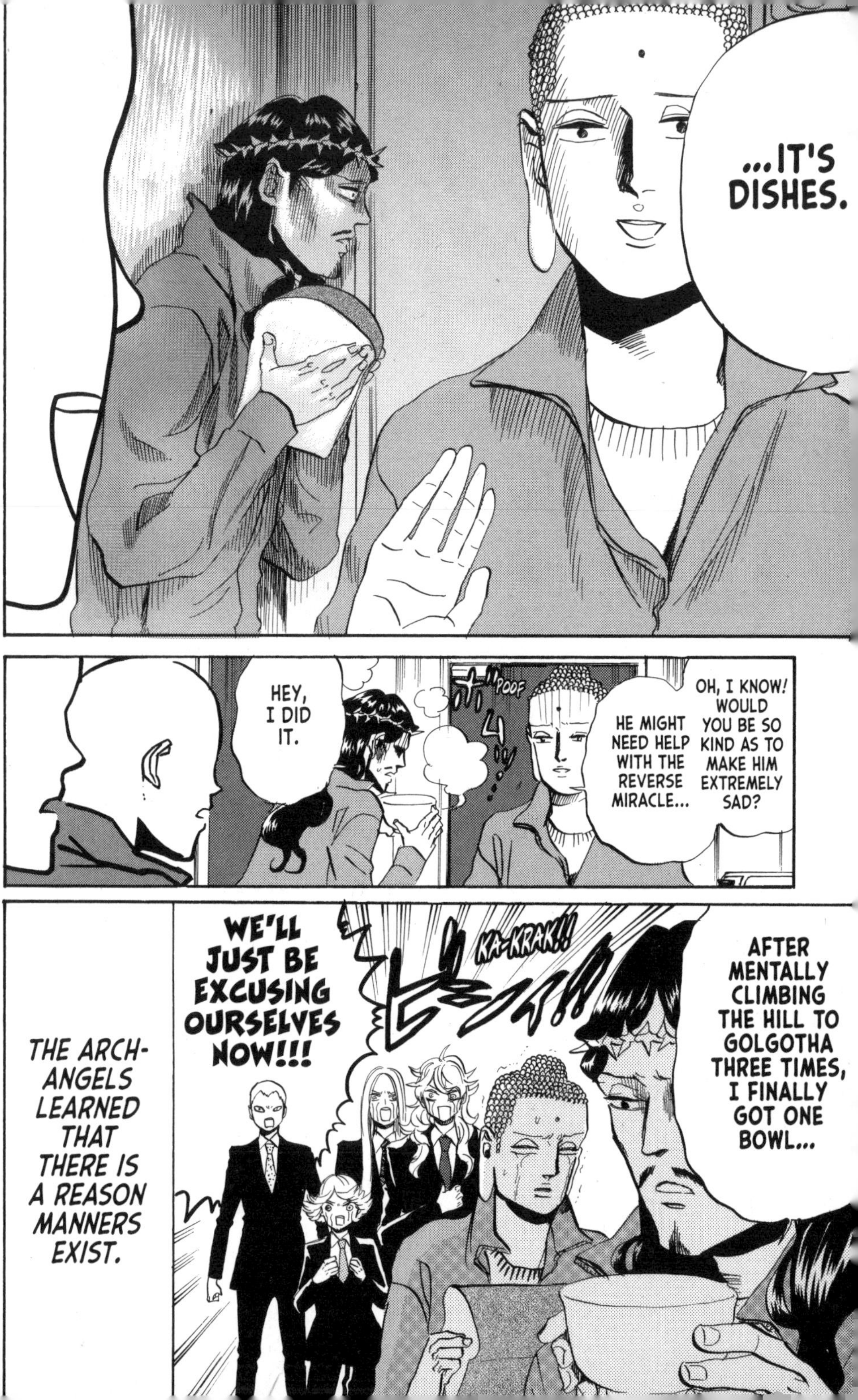
...IT'S DISHES.
OH, I KNOW! WOULD YOU BE SO KIND AS TO MAKE HIM EXTREMELY SAD?
HE MIGHT NEED HELP WITH THE REVERSE MIRACLE...
POOF
HEY, I DID IT.
AFTER MENTALLY CLIMBING THE HILL TO GOLGOTHA THREE TIMES, I FINALLY GOT ONE BOWL...
KA-KRAK!!
WE'LL JUST BE EXCUSING OURSELVES NOW!!!
THE ARCH-ANGELS LEARNED THAT THERE IS A REASON MANNERS EXIST.

Matsuda-san found them on their way home.

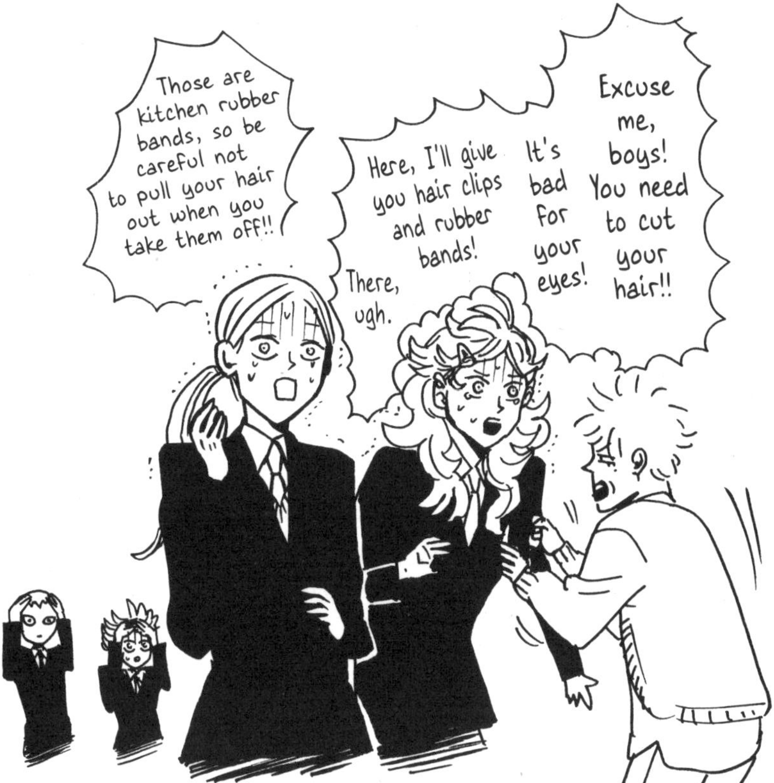

Excuse me, boys! You need to cut your hair!!
It's bad for your eyes!
Here, I'll give you hair clips and rubber bands!
There, ugh.
Those are kitchen rubber bands, so be careful not to pull your hair out when you take them off!!

CHAPTER 33 TRANSLATION NOTES

Waraimeshi, page 65
Waraimeshi is a Japanese comedy duo consisting of Tetsuo Nakanishi and Kōji Nishida. They won the M-1 Grand Prix in 2010.

Amazake, page 65
Literally "sweet sake," or "sweet rice wine," *amazake* is a popular New Year's drink that is very low in alcohol content—often low enough to be considered non-alcoholic.

New Year's money, page 67
In Japan, it is customary for adults to give children gifts of money, called *otoshidama*, at the New Year.

Kadomatsu, page 69
Literally "corner pine," a *kadomatsu* is a traditional decoration placed in front of the home at New Year's. It's usually made of pine, bamboo, and plum blossoms, and is set outside of homes to welcome gods and spirits that will bring blessings for the new year.

Jelly candies, page 72
The candy in question is Botan Rice Candy—a chewy candy wrapped in edible rice paper.

Jackets, page 73
Buddha's disciples are all wearing jackets that have their names written on them in Chinese characters. In Japan, their names are represented by these same characters, but pronounced slightly differently. Sharihotsu is Sariputra, Anan is Ananda, and Ragora is Rahula.

New Year's visit, page 79
Another Japanese New Year's tradition is to do a *nenshi mawari*, or start-of-the-year rounds, in which you visit friends, family, and neighbors to wish them a happy new year. With all the New Year's traditions to observe, it's a busy time of year, and so it would be rude to stay at one house for too long.

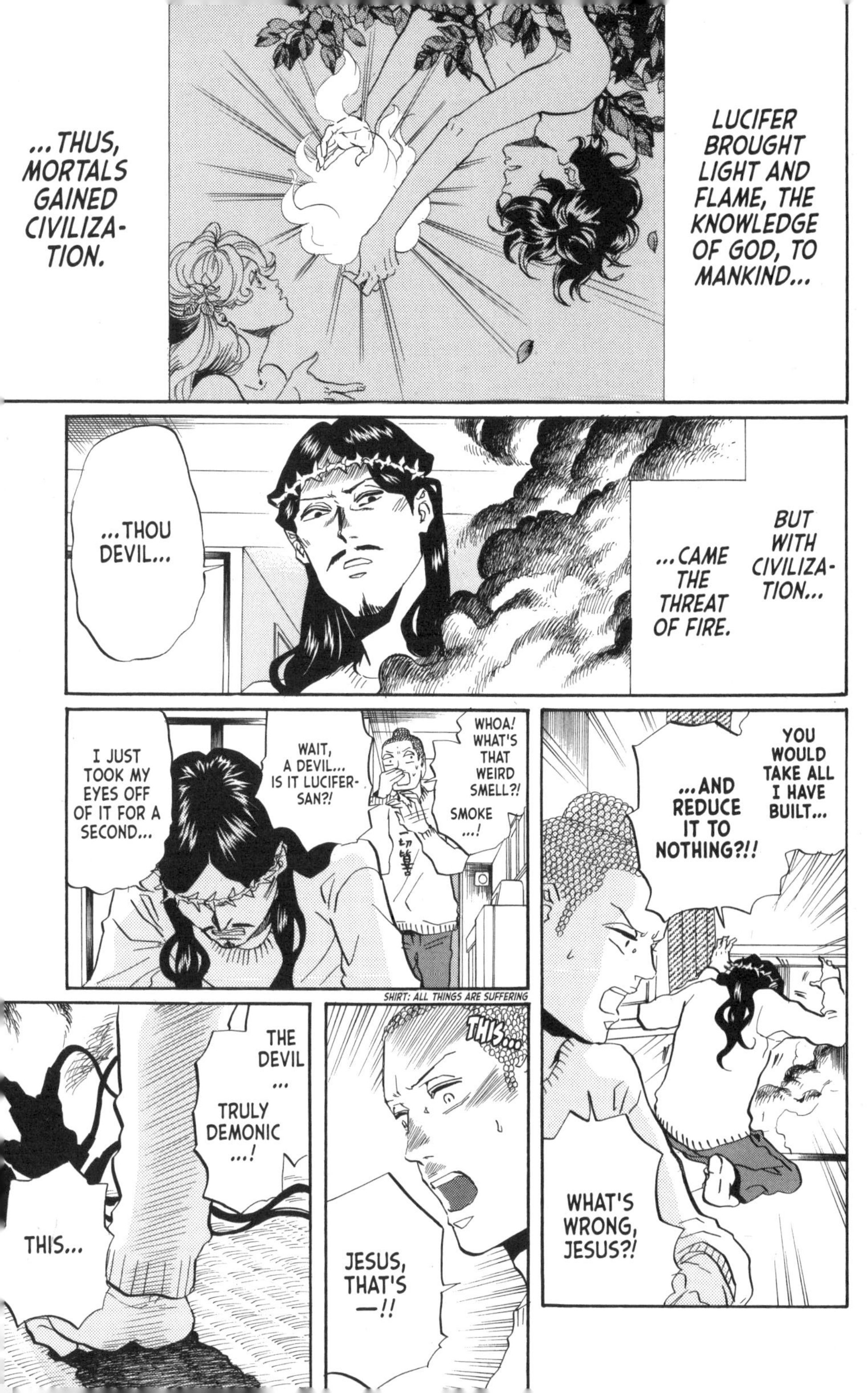
LUCIFER BROUGHT LIGHT AND FLAME, THE KNOWLEDGE OF GOD, TO MANKIND...
...THUS, MORTALS GAINED CIVILIZA-TION.
BUT WITH CIVILIZA-TION...
...CAME THE THREAT OF FIRE.
...THOU DEVIL...
YOU WOULD TAKE ALL I HAVE BUILT...
...AND REDUCE IT TO NOTHING?!!
WHAT'S WRONG, JESUS?!
WHOA! WHAT'S THAT WEIRD SMELL?!
SMOKE ...!
WAIT, A DEVIL... IS IT LUCIFER-SAN?!
I JUST TOOK MY EYES OFF OF IT FOR A SECOND...
SHIRT: ALL THINGS ARE SUFFERING
THIS...
JESUS, THAT'S —!!
THE DEVIL ...
TRULY DEMONIC ...!
THIS...

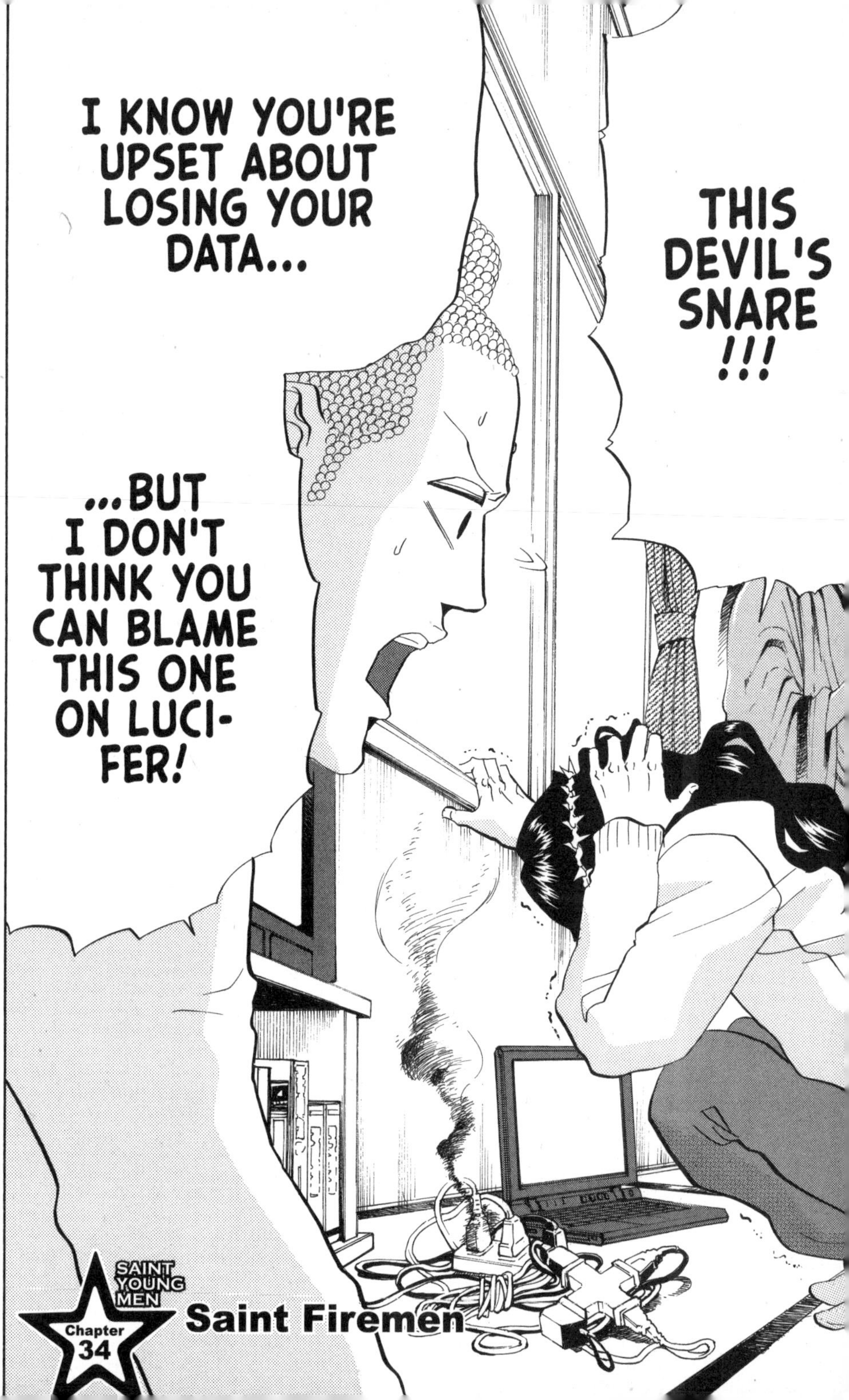
THIS DEVIL'S SNARE !!!
I KNOW YOU'RE UPSET ABOUT LOSING YOUR DATA...
...BUT I DON'T THINK YOU CAN BLAME THIS ONE ON LUCI- FER!
SAINT YOUNG MEN
Chapter 34
Saint Firemen

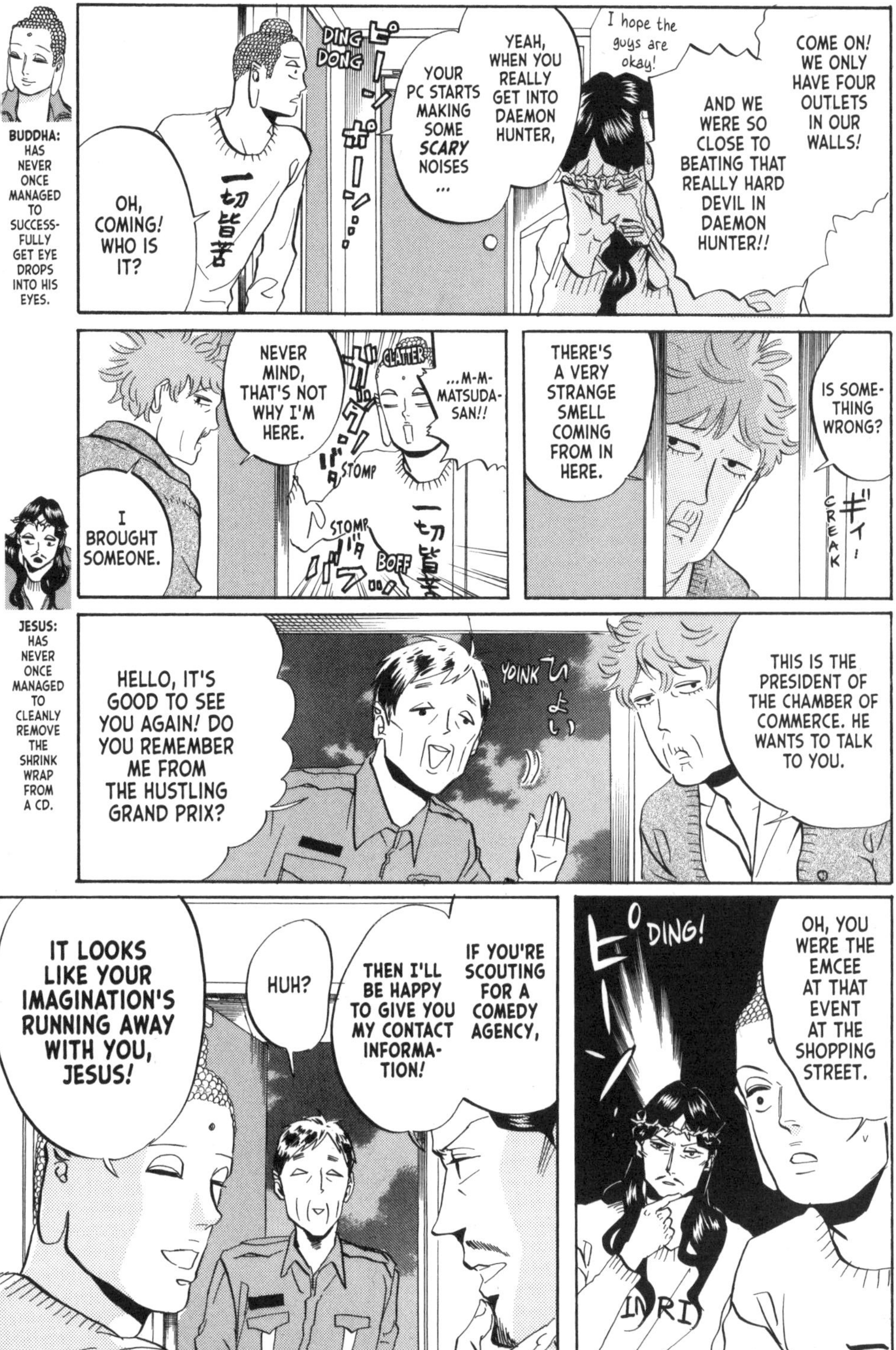
BUDDHA: HAS NEVER ONCE MANAGED TO SUCCESSFULLY GET EYE DROPS INTO HIS EYES.
COME ON! WE ONLY HAVE FOUR OUTLETS IN OUR WALLS!
AND WE WERE SO CLOSE TO BEATING THAT REALLY HARD DEVIL IN DAEMON HUNTER!!
I hope the guys are okay!
YEAH, WHEN YOU REALLY GET INTO DAEMON HUNTER,
YOUR PC STARTS MAKING SOME *SCARY* NOISES...
DING DONG
OH, COMING! WHO IS IT?
IS SOMETHING WRONG?
CREAK
THERE'S A VERY STRANGE SMELL COMING FROM IN HERE.
...M-M-MATSUDA-SAN!!
CLATTER
NEVER MIND, THAT'S NOT WHY I'M HERE.
STOMP
STOMP
BOFF
I BROUGHT SOMEONE.
JESUS: HAS NEVER ONCE MANAGED TO CLEANLY REMOVE THE SHRINK WRAP FROM A CD.
THIS IS THE PRESIDENT OF THE CHAMBER OF COMMERCE. HE WANTS TO TALK TO YOU.
YOINK
HELLO, IT'S GOOD TO SEE YOU AGAIN! DO YOU REMEMBER ME FROM THE HUSTLING GRAND PRIX?
DING!
OH, YOU WERE THE EMCEE AT THAT EVENT AT THE SHOPPING STREET.
IF YOU'RE SCOUTING FOR A COMEDY AGENCY,
THEN I'LL BE HAPPY TO GIVE YOU MY CONTACT INFORMATION!
HUH?
IT LOOKS LIKE YOUR IMAGINATION'S RUNNING AWAY WITH YOU, JESUS!

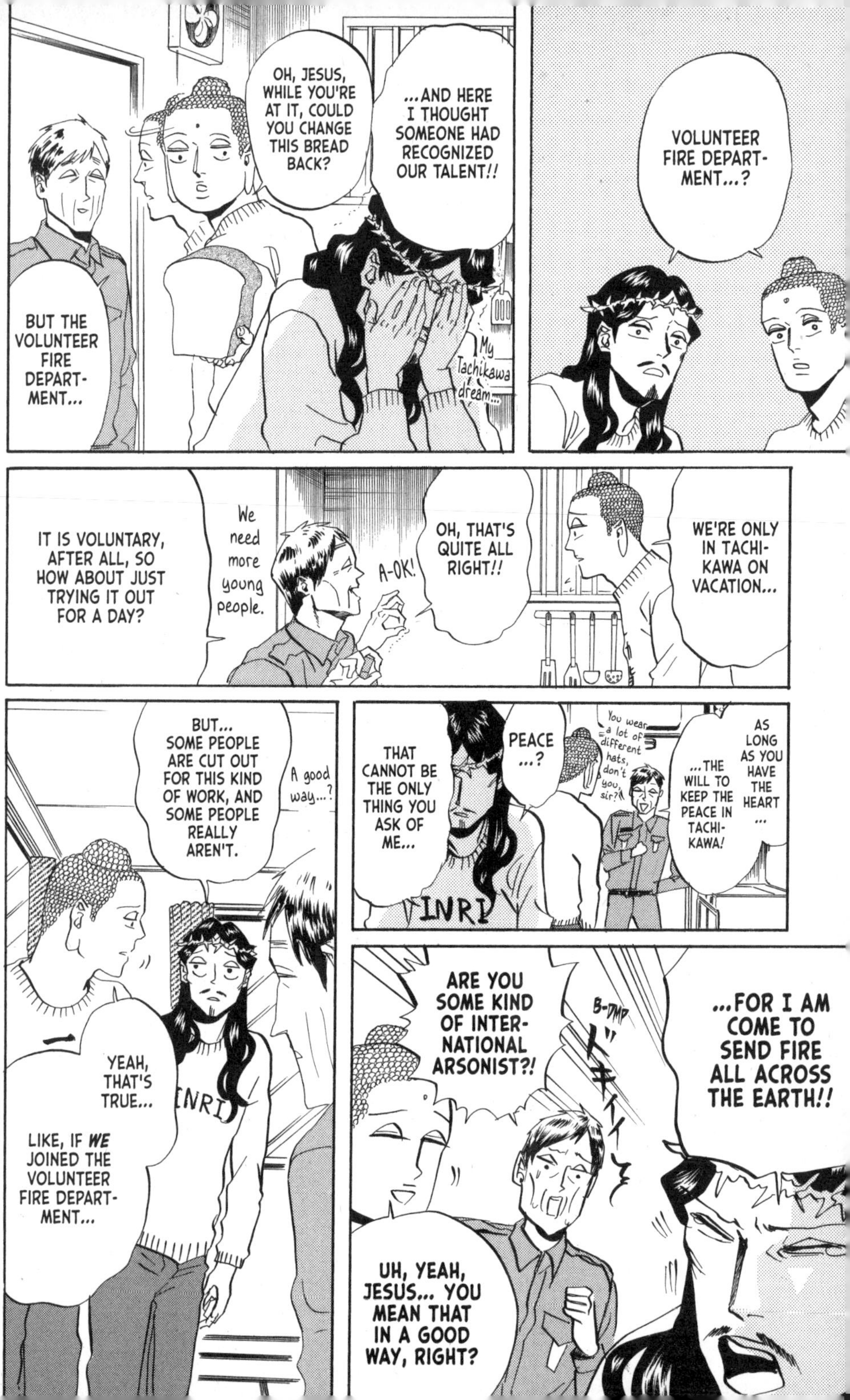
VOLUNTEER FIRE DEPARTMENT...?
...AND HERE I THOUGHT SOMEONE HAD RECOGNIZED OUR TALENT!!
OH, JESUS, WHILE YOU'RE AT IT, COULD YOU CHANGE THIS BREAD BACK?
My Tachikawa dream...
BUT THE VOLUNTEER FIRE DEPARTMENT...
WE'RE ONLY IN TACHIKAWA ON VACATION...
OH, THAT'S QUITE ALL RIGHT!!
A-OK!
We need more young people.
IT IS VOLUNTARY, AFTER ALL, SO HOW ABOUT JUST TRYING IT OUT FOR A DAY?
AS LONG AS YOU HAVE THE HEART...
...THE WILL TO KEEP THE PEACE IN TACHIKAWA!
You wear a lot of different hats, don't you, sir?
PEACE...?
THAT CANNOT BE THE ONLY THING YOU ASK OF ME...
INRI
...FOR I AM COME TO SEND FIRE ALL ACROSS THE EARTH!!
B-DMP
ARE YOU SOME KIND OF INTERNATIONAL ARSONIST?!
UH, YEAH, JESUS... YOU MEAN THAT IN A GOOD WAY, RIGHT?
BUT... SOME PEOPLE ARE CUT OUT FOR THIS KIND OF WORK, AND SOME PEOPLE REALLY AREN'T.
A good way...?
INRI
YEAH, THAT'S TRUE...
LIKE, IF *WE* JOINED THE VOLUNTEER FIRE DEPARTMENT...

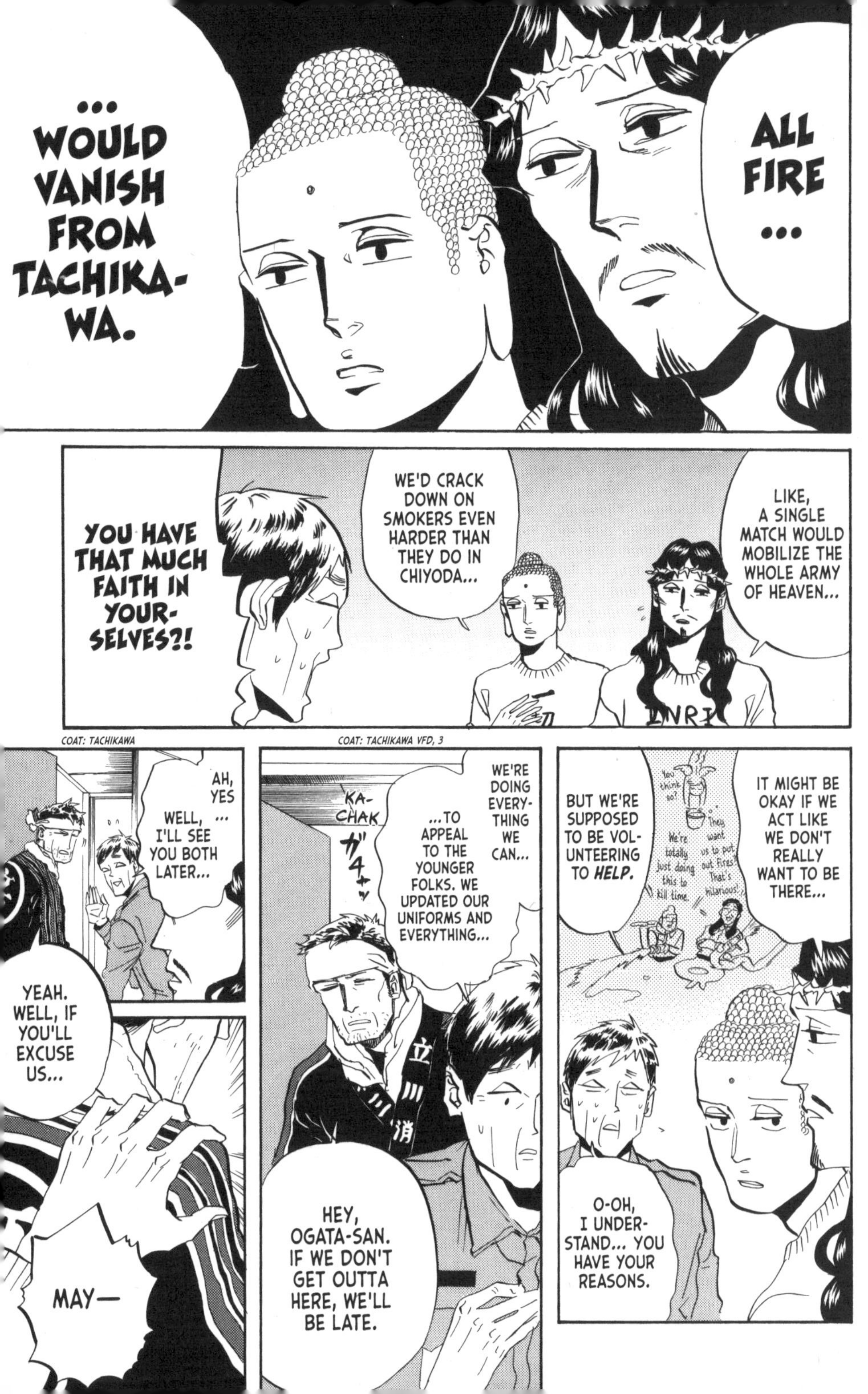
ALL FIRE...
...WOULD VANISH FROM TACHIKAWA.
LIKE, A SINGLE MATCH WOULD MOBILIZE THE WHOLE ARMY OF HEAVEN...
WE'D CRACK DOWN ON SMOKERS EVEN HARDER THAN THEY DO IN CHIYODA...
YOU HAVE THAT MUCH FAITH IN YOURSELVES?!
COAT: TACHIKAWA
COAT: TACHIKAWA VFD, 3
IT MIGHT BE OKAY IF WE ACT LIKE WE DON'T REALLY WANT TO BE THERE...
You think so?
They want us to put out fires? That's hilarious!
We're totally just doing this to kill time.
BUT WE'RE SUPPOSED TO BE VOLUNTEERING TO HELP.
O-OH, I UNDERSTAND... YOU HAVE YOUR REASONS.
WE'RE DOING EVERYTHING WE CAN...
...TO APPEAL TO THE YOUNGER FOLKS. WE UPDATED OUR UNIFORMS AND EVERYTHING...
KA-CHAK
HEY, OGATA-SAN. IF WE DON'T GET OUTTA HERE, WE'LL BE LATE.
AH, YES... WELL, I'LL SEE YOU BOTH LATER...
YEAH. WELL, IF YOU'LL EXCUSE US...
MAY—

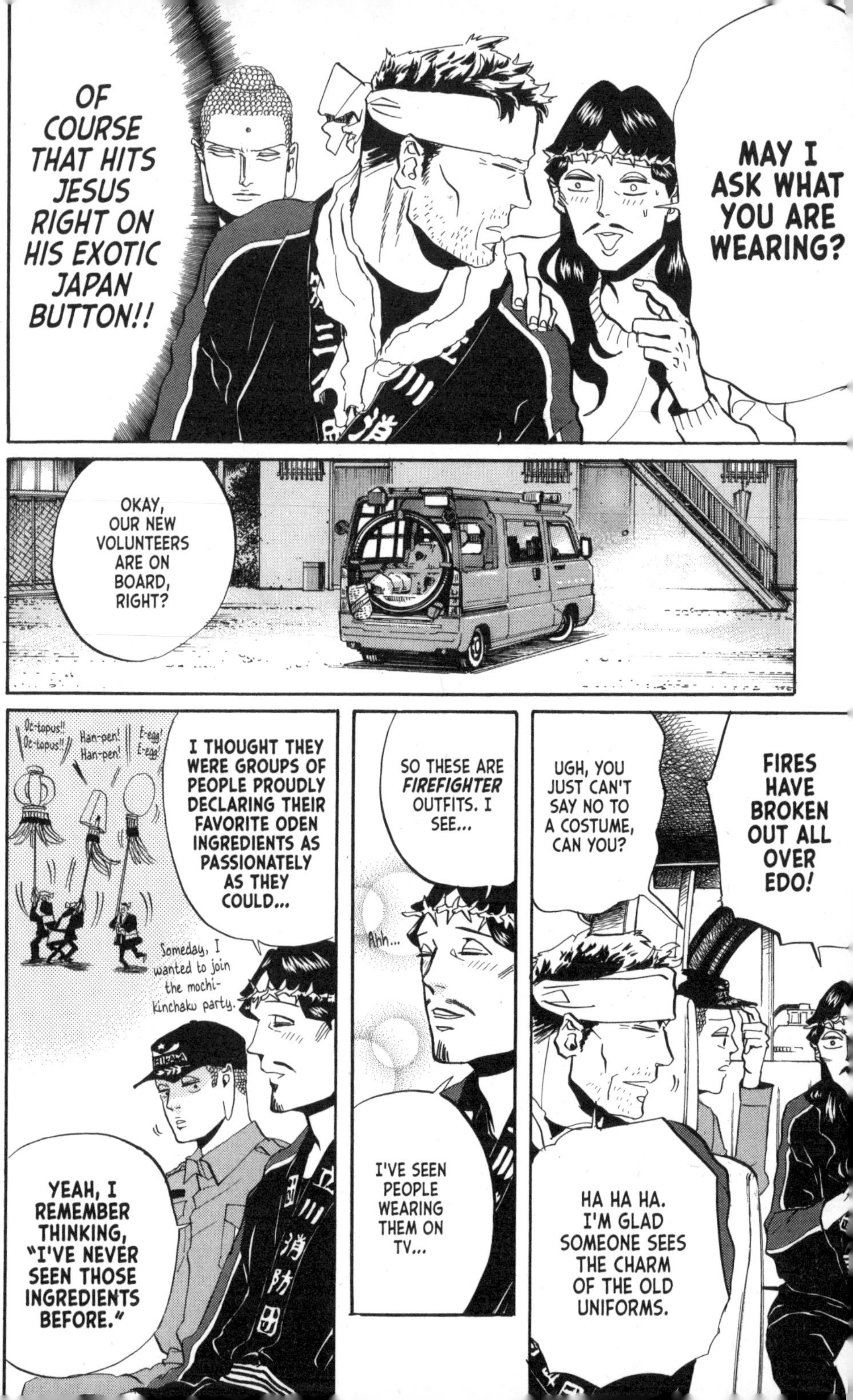
MAY I ASK WHAT YOU ARE WEARING?
OF COURSE THAT HITS JESUS RIGHT ON HIS EXOTIC JAPAN BUTTON!!
OKAY, OUR NEW VOLUNTEERS ARE ON BOARD, RIGHT?
FIRES HAVE BROKEN OUT ALL OVER EDO!
UGH, YOU JUST CAN'T SAY NO TO A COSTUME, CAN YOU?
HA HA HA. I'M GLAD SOMEONE SEES THE CHARM OF THE OLD UNIFORMS.
SO THESE ARE FIREFIGHTER OUTFITS. I SEE...
Ahh...
I'VE SEEN PEOPLE WEARING THEM ON TV...
I THOUGHT THEY WERE GROUPS OF PEOPLE PROUDLY DECLARING THEIR FAVORITE ODEN INGREDIENTS AS PASSIONATELY AS THEY COULD...
E-egg! E-egg!
Han-pen! Han-pen!
Oc-topus!! Oc-topus!!
Someday, I wanted to join the mochi-kinchaku party.
YEAH, I REMEMBER THINKING, "I'VE NEVER SEEN THOSE INGREDIENTS BEFORE."

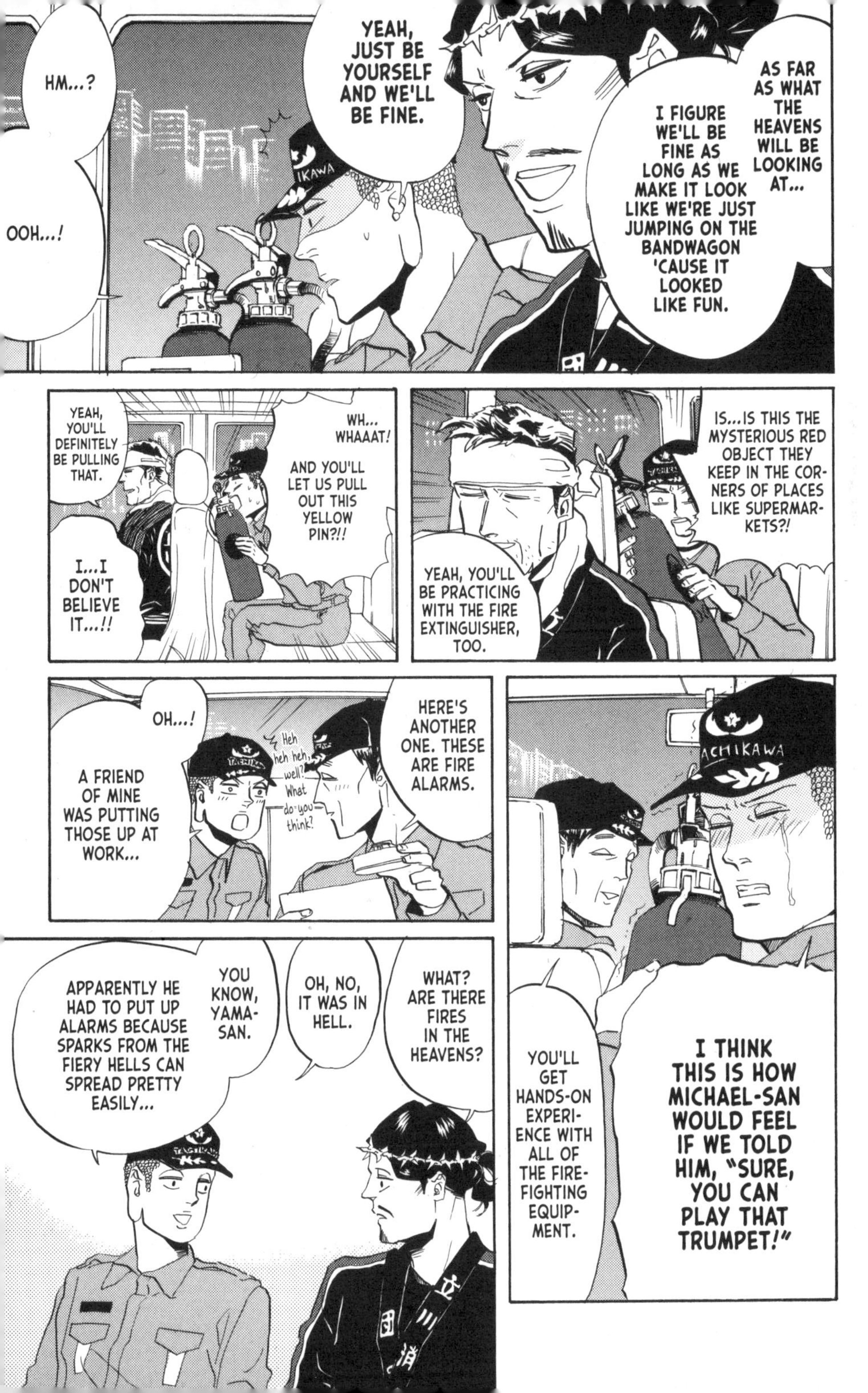

AS FAR AS WHAT THE HEAVENS WILL BE LOOKING AT...
I FIGURE WE'LL BE FINE AS LONG AS WE MAKE IT LOOK LIKE WE'RE JUST JUMPING ON THE BANDWAGON 'CAUSE IT LOOKED LIKE FUN.
YEAH, JUST BE YOURSELF AND WE'LL BE FINE.
HM...?
OOH...!
IS...IS THIS THE MYSTERIOUS RED OBJECT THEY KEEP IN THE CORNERS OF PLACES LIKE SUPERMARKETS?!
YEAH, YOU'LL BE PRACTICING WITH THE FIRE EXTINGUISHER, TOO.
WH... WHAAAT!
AND YOU'LL LET US PULL OUT THIS YELLOW PIN?!!
YEAH, YOU'LL DEFINITELY BE PULLING THAT.
I...I DON'T BELIEVE IT...!!
I THINK THIS IS HOW MICHAEL-SAN WOULD FEEL IF WE TOLD HIM, "SURE, YOU CAN PLAY THAT TRUMPET!"
YOU'LL GET HANDS-ON EXPERIENCE WITH ALL OF THE FIRE-FIGHTING EQUIPMENT.
HERE'S ANOTHER ONE. THESE ARE FIRE ALARMS.
Heh heh heh, well? What do you think?
OH...!
A FRIEND OF MINE WAS PUTTING THOSE UP AT WORK...
WHAT? ARE THERE FIRES IN THE HEAVENS?
OH, NO, IT WAS IN HELL.
YOU KNOW, YAMA-SAN.
APPARENTLY HE HAD TO PUT UP ALARMS BECAUSE SPARKS FROM THE FIERY HELLS CAN SPREAD PRETTY EASILY...

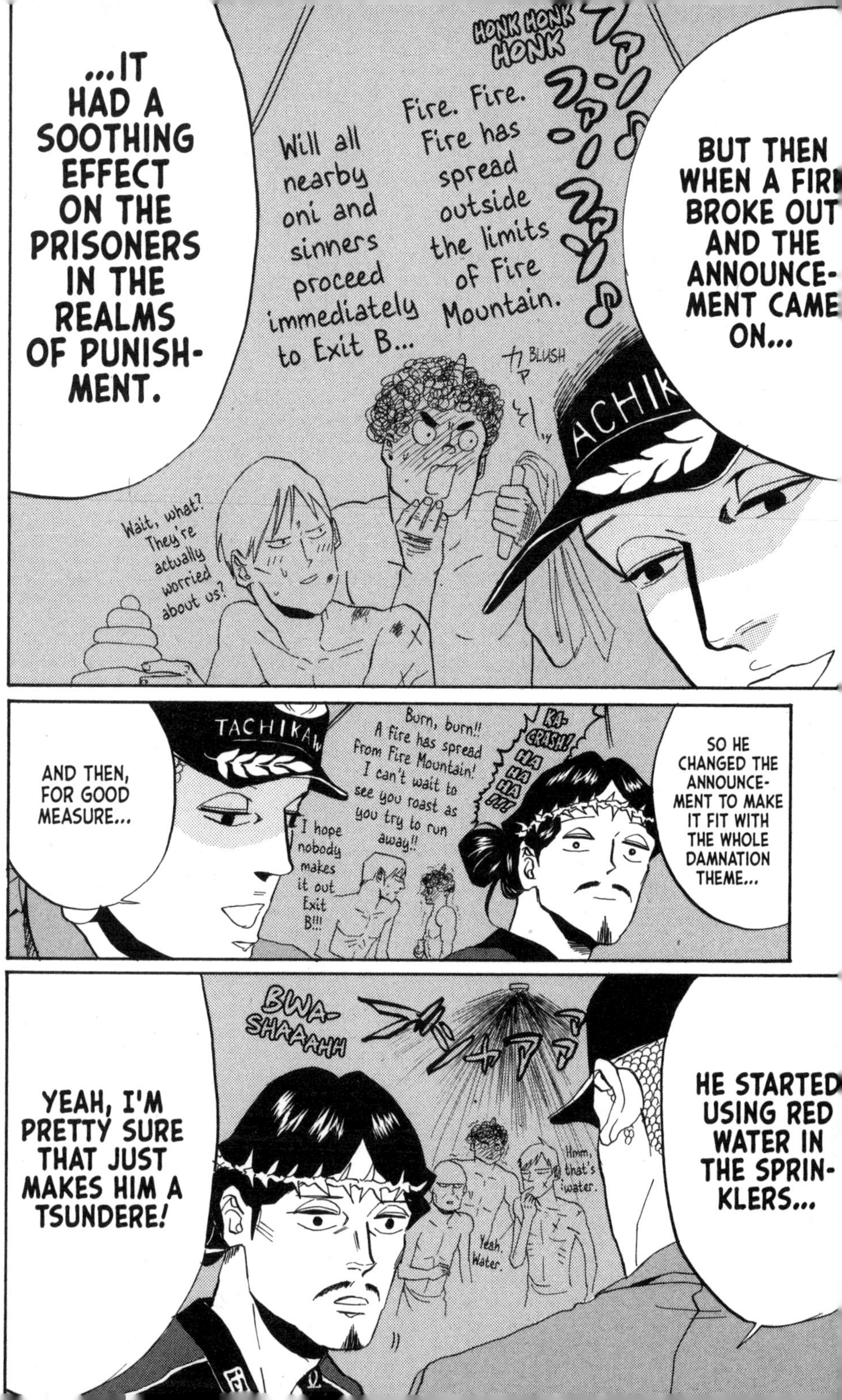

BUT THEN WHEN A FIR BROKE OUT AND THE ANNOUNCE-MENT CAME ON...
HONK HONK HONK
Fire. Fire. Fire has spread outside the limits of Fire Mountain.
Will all nearby oni and sinners proceed immediately to Exit B...
BLUSH
Wait, what? They're actually worried about us?
...IT HAD A SOOTHING EFFECT ON THE PRISONERS IN THE REALMS OF PUNISH-MENT.
SO HE CHANGED THE ANNOUNCE-MENT TO MAKE IT FIT WITH THE WHOLE DAMNATION THEME...
KA-CRASH! HA HA HA
Burn, burn!! A fire has spread from Fire Mountain! I can't wait to see you roast as you try to run away!!
I hope nobody makes it out Exit B!!!
TACHIKAW
AND THEN, FOR GOOD MEASURE...
HE STARTED USING RED WATER IN THE SPRIN-KLERS...
Hmm, that's water.
Yeah. Water.
BWA-SHAAAAHH
YEAH, I'M PRETTY SURE THAT JUST MAKES HIM A TSUNDERE!

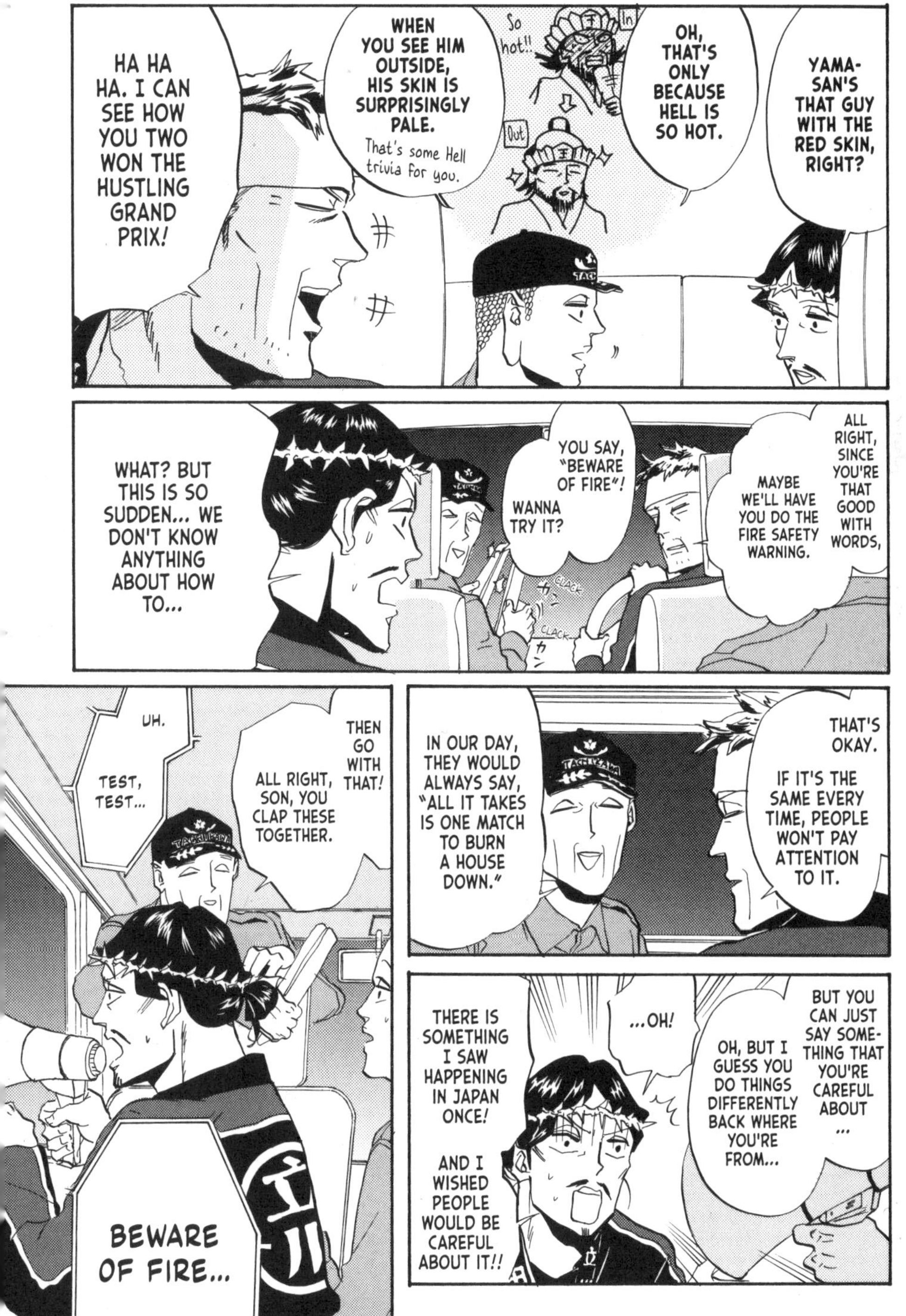
YAMA-SAN'S THAT GUY WITH THE RED SKIN, RIGHT?
OH, THAT'S ONLY BECAUSE HELL IS SO HOT.
In
So hot!!
Out
WHEN YOU SEE HIM OUTSIDE, HIS SKIN IS SURPRISINGLY PALE.
That's some Hell trivia for you.
HA HA HA. I CAN SEE HOW YOU TWO WON THE HUSTLING GRAND PRIX!
ALL RIGHT, SINCE YOU'RE THAT GOOD WITH WORDS,
MAYBE WE'LL HAVE YOU DO THE FIRE SAFETY WARNING.
YOU SAY, "BEWARE OF FIRE"!
WANNA TRY IT?
CLACK
CLACK
WHAT? BUT THIS IS SO SUDDEN... WE DON'T KNOW ANYTHING ABOUT HOW TO...
THAT'S OKAY.
IF IT'S THE SAME EVERY TIME, PEOPLE WON'T PAY ATTENTION TO IT.
IN OUR DAY, THEY WOULD ALWAYS SAY, "ALL IT TAKES IS ONE MATCH TO BURN A HOUSE DOWN."
BUT YOU CAN JUST SAY SOMETHING THAT YOU'RE CAREFUL ABOUT...
OH, BUT I GUESS YOU DO THINGS DIFFERENTLY BACK WHERE YOU'RE FROM...
...OH!
THERE IS SOMETHING I SAW HAPPENING IN JAPAN ONCE!
AND I WISHED PEOPLE WOULD BE CAREFUL ABOUT IT!!
THEN GO WITH THAT!
ALL RIGHT, SON, YOU CLAP THESE TOGETHER.
UH.
TEST, TEST...
BEWARE OF FIRE...

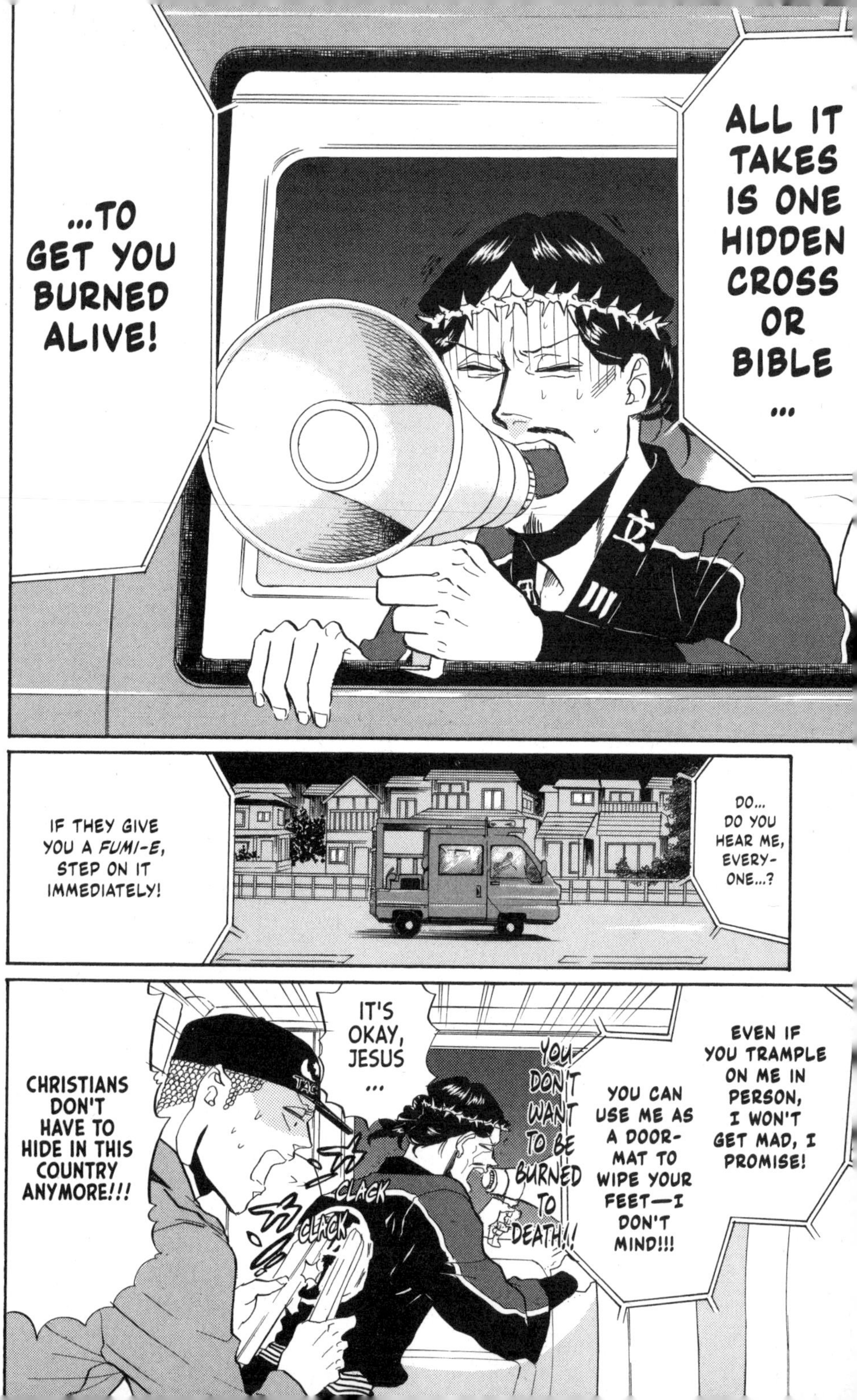
ALL IT TAKES IS ONE HIDDEN CROSS OR BIBLE ...
...TO GET YOU BURNED ALIVE!
DO... DO YOU HEAR ME, EVERY-ONE...?
IF THEY GIVE YOU A *FUMI-E*, STEP ON IT IMMEDIATELY!
EVEN IF YOU TRAMPLE ON ME IN PERSON, I WON'T GET MAD, I PROMISE!
YOU CAN USE ME AS A DOOR-MAT TO WIPE YOUR FEET—I DON'T MIND!!!
YOU DON'T WANT TO BE BURNED TO DEATH!!!
IT'S OKAY, JESUS ...
CLACK
CLACK
CHRISTIANS DON'T HAVE TO HIDE IN THIS COUNTRY ANYMORE!!!

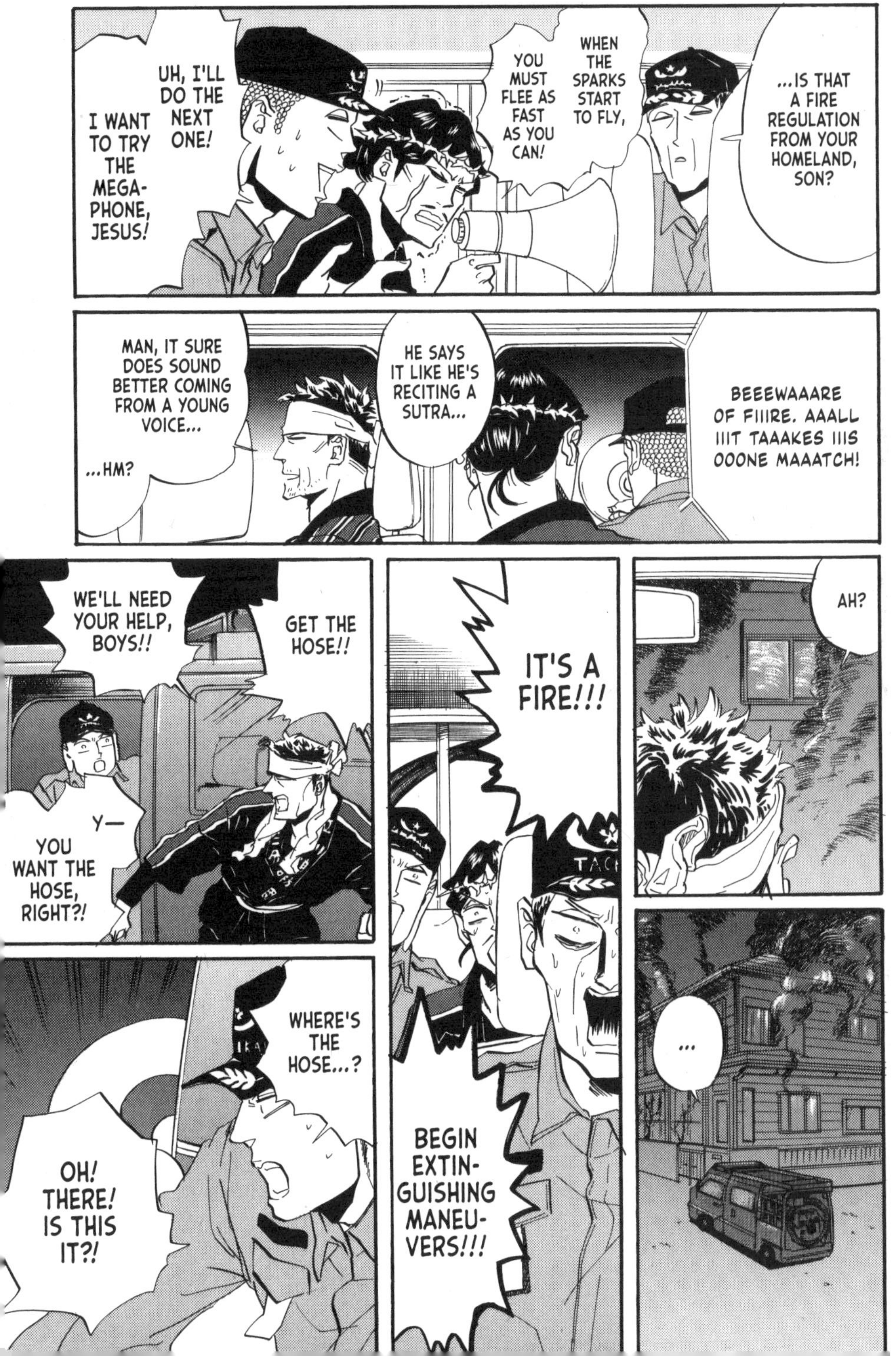
...IS THAT A FIRE REGULATION FROM YOUR HOMELAND, SON?
WHEN THE SPARKS START TO FLY,
YOU MUST FLEE AS FAST AS YOU CAN!
UH, I'LL DO THE NEXT ONE!
I WANT TO TRY THE MEGA-PHONE, JESUS!
BEEEWAAARE OF FIIIRE. AAALL IIIT TAAAKES IIIS OOONE MAAATCH!
HE SAYS IT LIKE HE'S RECITING A SUTRA...
MAN, IT SURE DOES SOUND BETTER COMING FROM A YOUNG VOICE...
...HM?
AH?
...
IT'S A FIRE!!!
BEGIN EXTIN-GUISHING MANEU-VERS!!!
GET THE HOSE!!
WE'LL NEED YOUR HELP, BOYS!!
Y—
YOU WANT THE HOSE, RIGHT?!
WHERE'S THE HOSE...?
OH! THERE! IS THIS IT?!

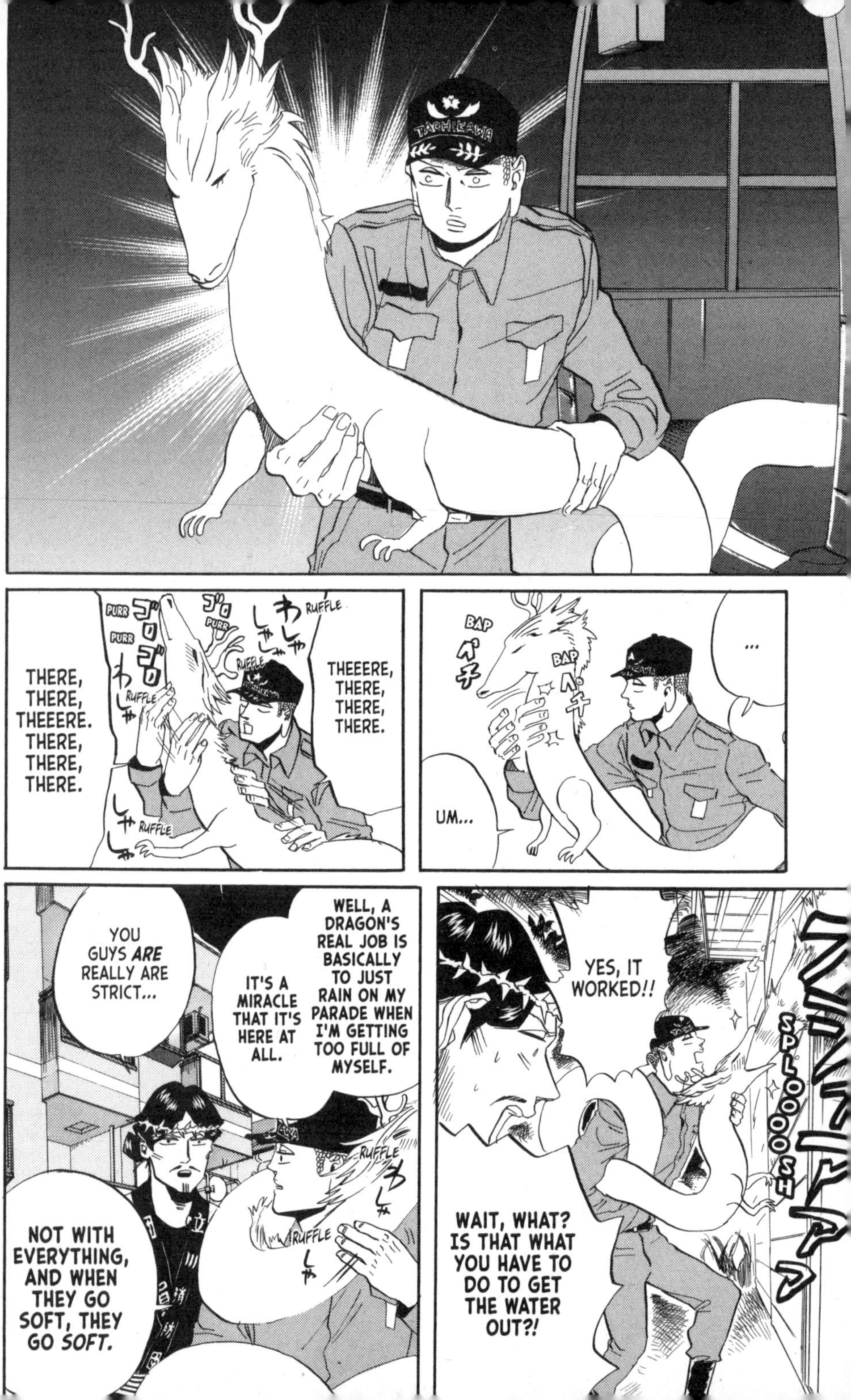
TACHIKAWA
...
UM...
BAP
BAP
THEEERE, THERE, THERE, THERE.
RUFFLE
PURR
PURR
PURR
THERE, THERE, THEEERE. THERE, THERE, THERE.
RUFFLE
RUFFLE
RUFFLE
SPLOOOOSH
YES, IT WORKED!!
WAIT, WHAT? IS THAT WHAT YOU HAVE TO DO TO GET THE WATER OUT?!
WELL, A DRAGON'S REAL JOB IS BASICALLY TO JUST RAIN ON MY PARADE WHEN I'M GETTING TOO FULL OF MYSELF.
IT'S A MIRACLE THAT IT'S HERE AT ALL.
YOU GUYS *ARE* REALLY ARE STRICT...
RUFFLE
RUFFLE
NOT WITH EVERYTHING, AND WHEN THEY GO SOFT, THEY GO *SOFT*.

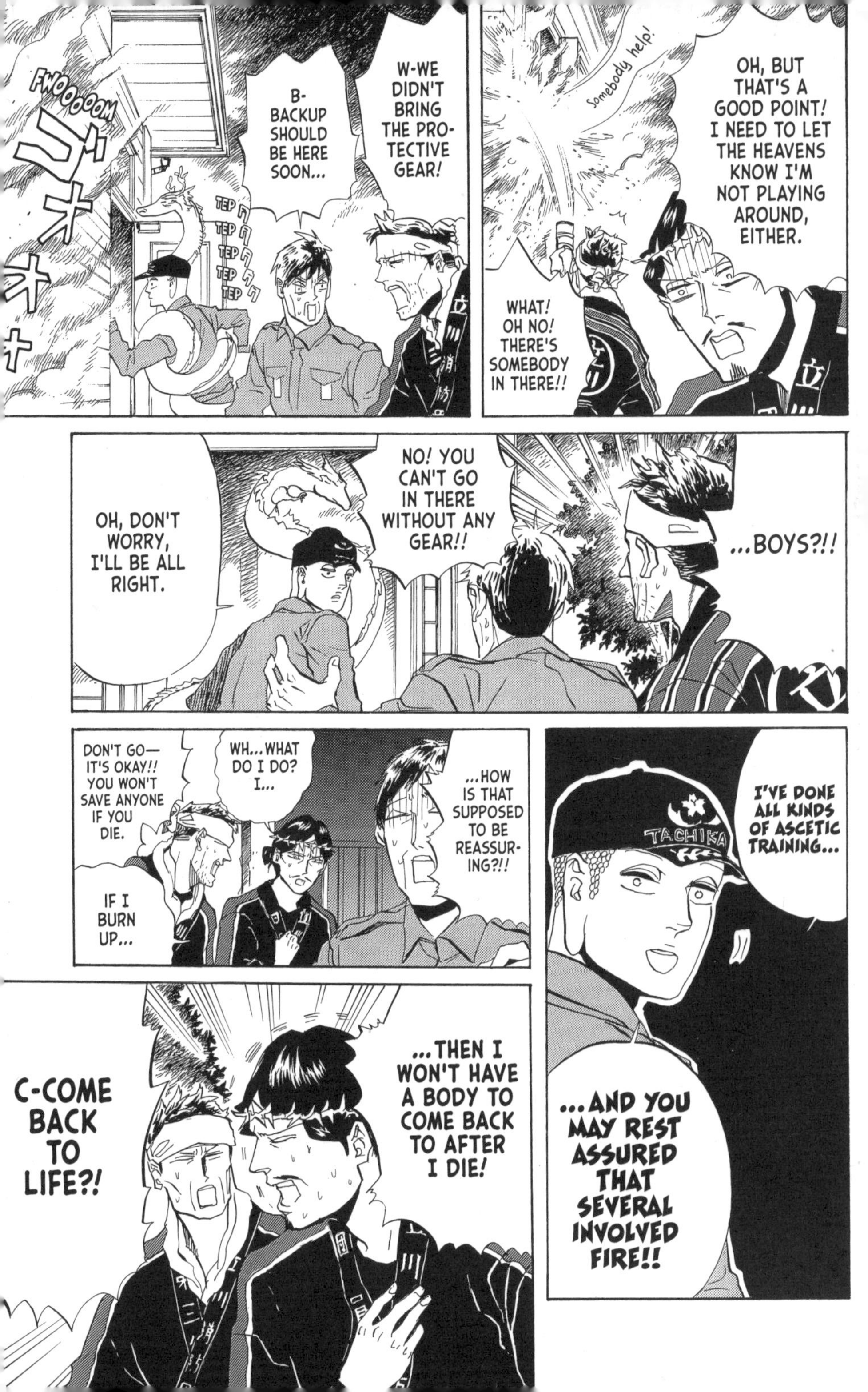

Somebody help!
OH, BUT THAT'S A GOOD POINT! I NEED TO LET THE HEAVENS KNOW I'M NOT PLAYING AROUND, EITHER.
WHAT! OH NO! THERE'S SOMEBODY IN THERE!!
W-WE DIDN'T BRING THE PROTECTIVE GEAR!
B-BACKUP SHOULD BE HERE SOON...
FWOOOOOM
ゴオオオ
TEP TEP TEP TEP TEP
...BOYS?!!
NO! YOU CAN'T GO IN THERE WITHOUT ANY GEAR!!
OH, DON'T WORRY, I'LL BE ALL RIGHT.
I'VE DONE ALL KINDS OF ASCETIC TRAINING...
TACHIKA
...AND YOU MAY REST ASSURED THAT SEVERAL INVOLVED FIRE!!
...HOW IS THAT SUPPOSED TO BE REASSURING?!!
WH...WHAT DO I DO? I...
DON'T GO— IT'S OKAY!! YOU WON'T SAVE ANYONE IF YOU DIE.
IF I BURN UP...
...THEN I WON'T HAVE A BODY TO COME BACK TO AFTER I DIE!
C-COME BACK TO LIFE?!

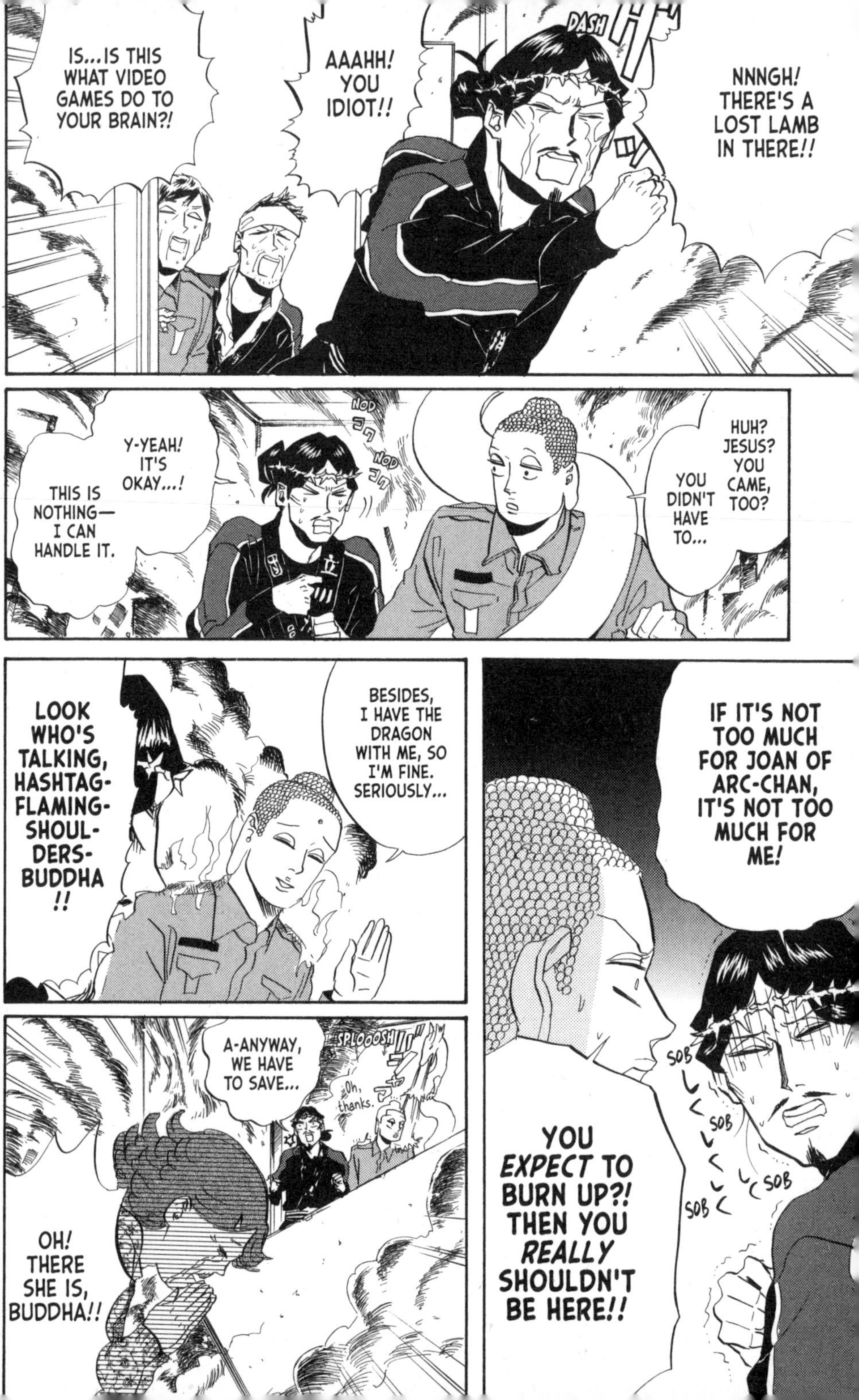
DASH
NNNGH! THERE'S A LOST LAMB IN THERE!!
AAAHH! YOU IDIOT!!
IS...IS THIS WHAT VIDEO GAMES DO TO YOUR BRAIN?!
HUH? JESUS? YOU CAME, TOO?
YOU DIDN'T HAVE TO...
NOD
NOD
Y-YEAH! IT'S OKAY...!
THIS IS NOTHING— I CAN HANDLE IT.
IF IT'S NOT TOO MUCH FOR JOAN OF ARC-CHAN, IT'S NOT TOO MUCH FOR ME!
SOB
SOB
SOB
SOB
YOU EXPECT TO BURN UP?! THEN YOU REALLY SHOULDN'T BE HERE!!
BESIDES, I HAVE THE DRAGON WITH ME, SO I'M FINE. SERIOUSLY...
LOOK WHO'S TALKING, HASHTAG-FLAMING-SHOULDERS-BUDDHA!!
SPLOOOSH
A-ANYWAY, WE HAVE TO SAVE...
Oh, thanks.
OH! THERE SHE IS, BUDDHA!!

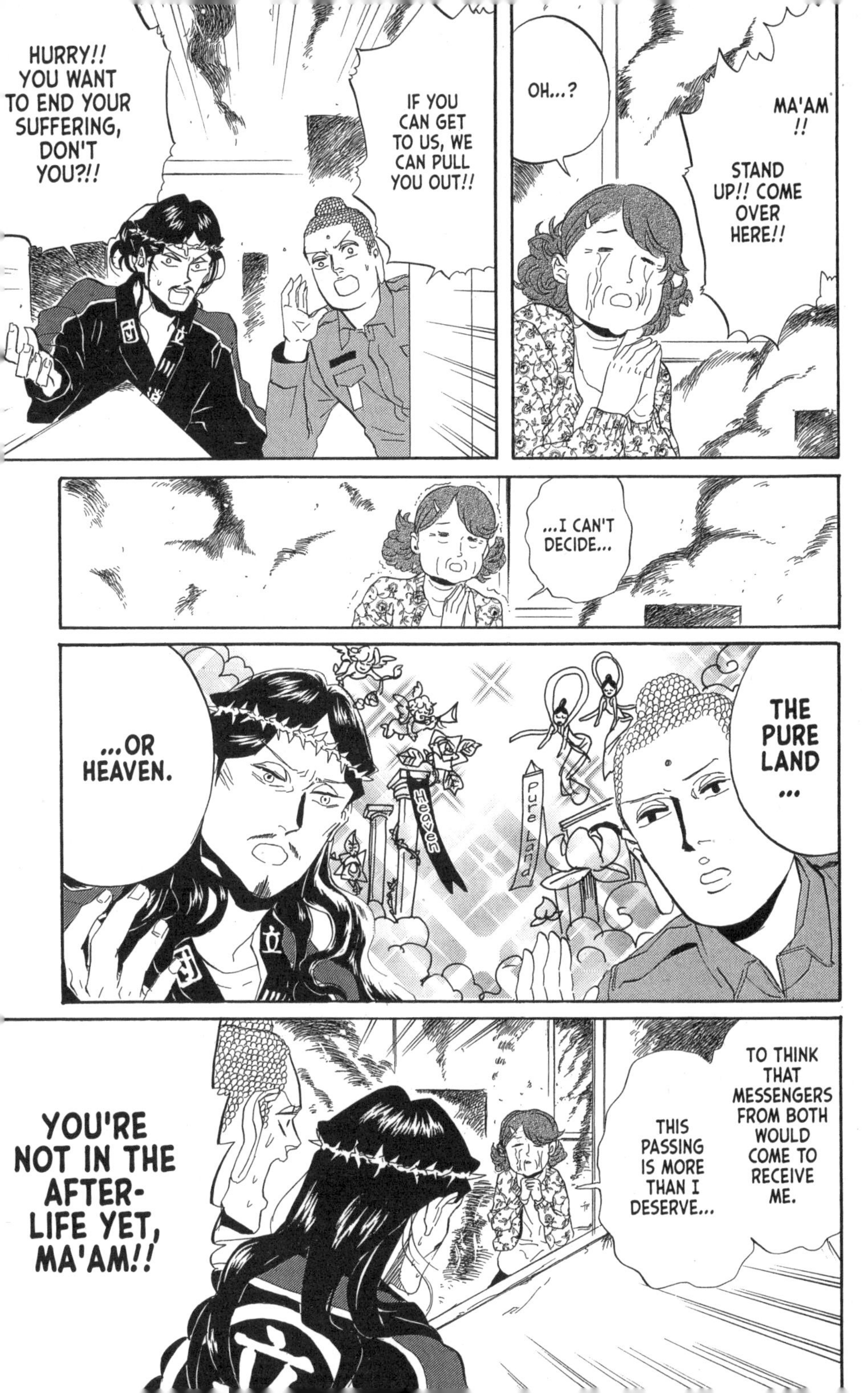
MA'AM!!
STAND UP!! COME OVER HERE!!
OH...?
IF YOU CAN GET TO US, WE CAN PULL YOU OUT!!
HURRY!! YOU WANT TO END YOUR SUFFERING, DON'T YOU?!!
...I CAN'T DECIDE...
THE PURE LAND...
Pure Land
Heaven
...OR HEAVEN.
TO THINK THAT MESSENGERS FROM BOTH WOULD COME TO RECEIVE ME.
THIS PASSING IS MORE THAN I DESERVE...
YOU'RE NOT IN THE AFTER-LIFE YET, MA'AM!!

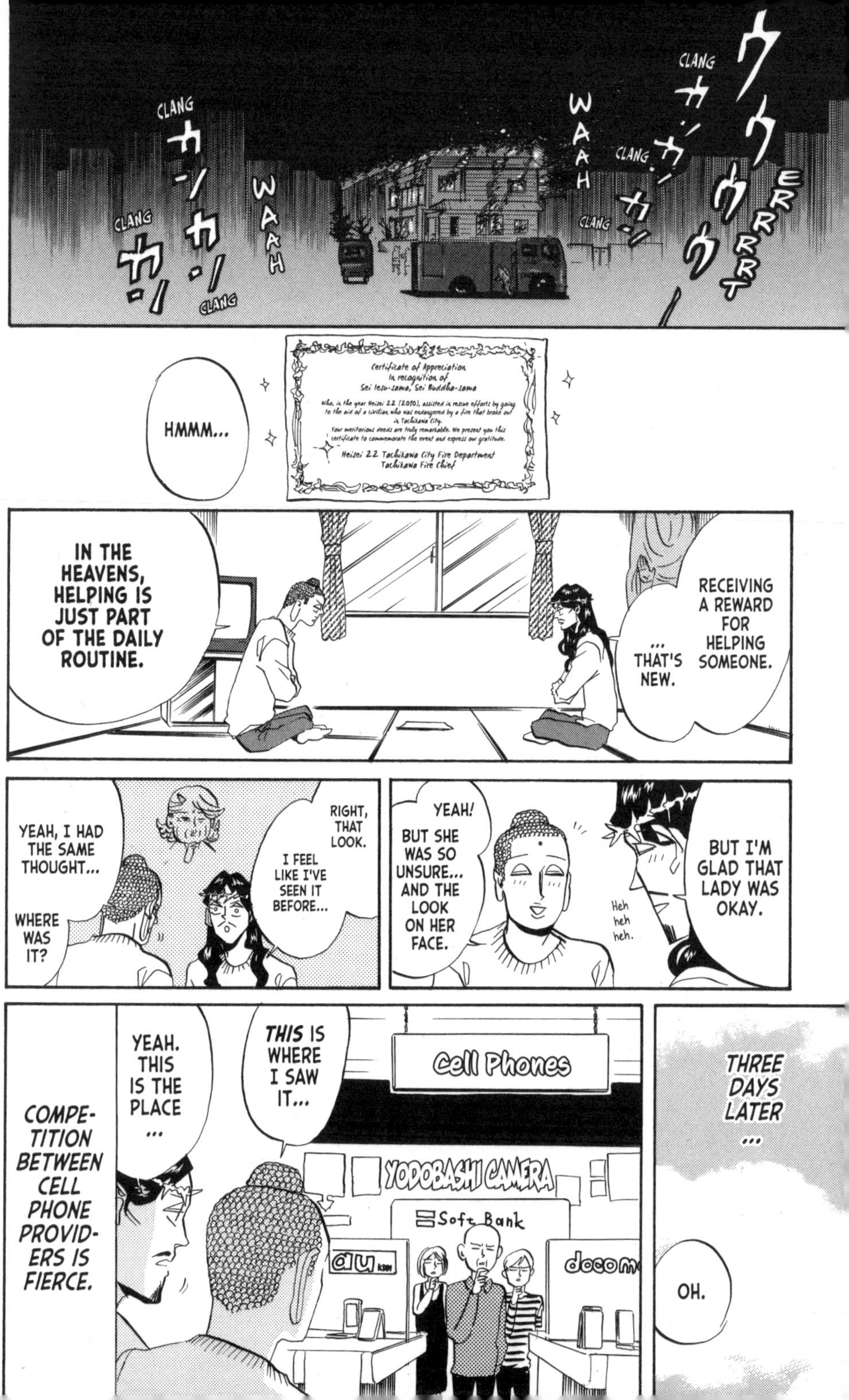
ERRRRRT
CLANG
WAAH
CLANG
CLANG
CLANG
WAAH
CLANG
CLANG
Certificate of Appreciation
In recognition of
Sei Iesu-sama, Sei Buddha-sama
Who, in the year Heisei 22 (2010), assisted in rescue efforts by going to the aid of a civilian who was endangered by a fire that broke out in Tachikawa City.
Your meritorious deeds are truly remarkable. We present you this certificate to commemorate the event and express our gratitude.
Heisei 22 Tachikawa City Fire Department
Tachikawa Fire Chief
HMMM...
RECEIVING A REWARD FOR HELPING SOMEONE.
... THAT'S NEW.
IN THE HEAVENS, HELPING IS JUST PART OF THE DAILY ROUTINE.
BUT I'M GLAD THAT LADY WAS OKAY.
Heh heh heh.
YEAH! BUT SHE WAS SO UNSURE... AND THE LOOK ON HER FACE.
RIGHT, THAT LOOK.
I FEEL LIKE I'VE SEEN IT BEFORE...
YEAH, I HAD THE SAME THOUGHT...
WHERE WAS IT?
THREE DAYS LATER...
OH.
Cell Phones
THIS IS WHERE I SAW IT...
YEAH. THIS IS THE PLACE...
YODOBASHI CAMERA
Soft Bank
au
COMPETITION BETWEEN CELL PHONE PROVIDERS IS FIERCE.

Eventually selected the Pure Land, because he looks a little like the enka singer Kiyoshi.
Sorry about this.
Just because I have an Asian face...

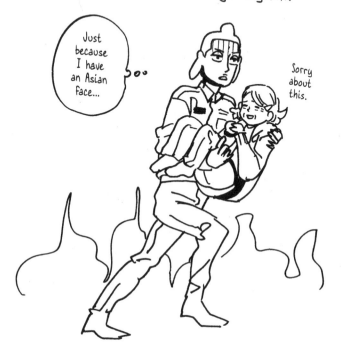

CHAPTER 34 TRANSLATION NOTES

Lucifer the light-bringer, page 83
Because the name means "light-bringer," and because it was Lucifer who beguiled Eve into partaking of the fruit of the Tree of Knowledge of Good and Evil, there are some schools of thought that see Lucifer not as an evil devil, but as a symbol of enlightenment. In that sense, he can be compared to Prometheus, who is known in Greek mythology for stealing fire (another symbol of enlightenment) from the heavens and giving it to mankind.

All things are suffering, page 83
This is one of the three marks of existence in Buddhism, which state that all things are impermanent, and attachment to them would lead to suffering.

Devil's snare, page 84
In Japanese, the power splitter that allows you to plug more appliances into one wall outlet is called a *tako-ashi*, which literally means "octopus foot," presumably because the wall begins to look like an octopus with various cable tentacles. In keeping with that, when the numbers of wires gets to be unruly, it is named after a specific kind of octopus—the devilfish.

INRI, page 86
These letters are the initials for *Iesus Nazarenus, Rex Iudaeorum*, which is Latin for "Jesus of Nazareth, King of the Jews." Pontius Pilate had the phrase written on a board and placed over Jesus's cross in accordance with a practice of informing passersby the identity of a crucified criminal, as well as the nature of their crime. The leaders of the Jewish people demanded that Pilate change the inscription to indicate that Jesus had only claimed the title of King, but Pilate refused. In alchemy, the acronym is also used to stand for *Igne Natura Renovatur Integra*, which means "by fire, nature renews itself."

Come to send fire on the earth, page 86
In Luke 12:49, Jesus says, "I am come to send fire on the earth; and what will I, if it be already kindled?"

Cracking down on smokers in Chiyoda, page 87
Chiyoda Ward in Tokyo was the first municipality in Japan to enact a smoking ban, imposing a fine of 2,000 yen (about $20) on anyone caught smoking in non-designated areas.

The oden party, page 88
The food-shaped beacons being waved by these firefighters are *matoi*—a kind of banner used during the Edo era to signal to the other firefighters which building or area is on fire. The *matoi-mochi*, or standard-bearer, would take the *matoi* to the roof of the building and wave it to catch the attention of the others. Each brigade had its own *matoi*, and often there would be a race to see who could get to the fire first. Unaware of this history, our protagonists see the resemblance to ingredients in the Japanese hot pot dish called *oden*.

Yama, page 90
Known as Enma in Japanese, Yama is the king of hell, and it's his job to make sure sinners are appropriately punished for the wrongs they committed in life.

Fire safety warning, page 91
One of the precautions taken in Japan against fire is to remind the citizens to be careful. Volunteers walk (or drive) around town and get people's attention with the clappers seen in Ogata's hands, then say, "*Hi no yoooojin*," meaning "beware of fire." Sometimes additional messages or tips will be given as well. The method may seem old fashioned because it dates back to the Edo period (1603 - 1868).

All it takes is one cross, page 92
As mentioned in the notes to volume two, Christians in Japan were persecuted during the Edo Era, and sometimes identified by their reluctance to step on a *fumi-e* "trample picture" representing Jesus Christ or the Virgin Mary. Eventually Christians did start stepping on them, believing that they could pray for forgiveness. While many think that the hidden Christians (or *Kakure Kirishitan*) either died out or joined mainstream Christianity when the religion was again legalized in Japan, the faith still has some communities in Nagasaki.

Joan of Arc, page 96
Joan of Arc is a national hero of France who received divine revelation that helped her lead her homeland to a series of important military victories in the Hundred Years War. She was burned at the stake for heresy and later sainted.

Flaming shoulders Buddha, page 96
The *Amida Sutra* contains a list of many buddhas, including one named Arciskandha, which means "flaming shoulders." Additionally, the Buddha is often depicted with flaming shoulders as a symbol of his powers.

SAINT☆YOUNG MEN

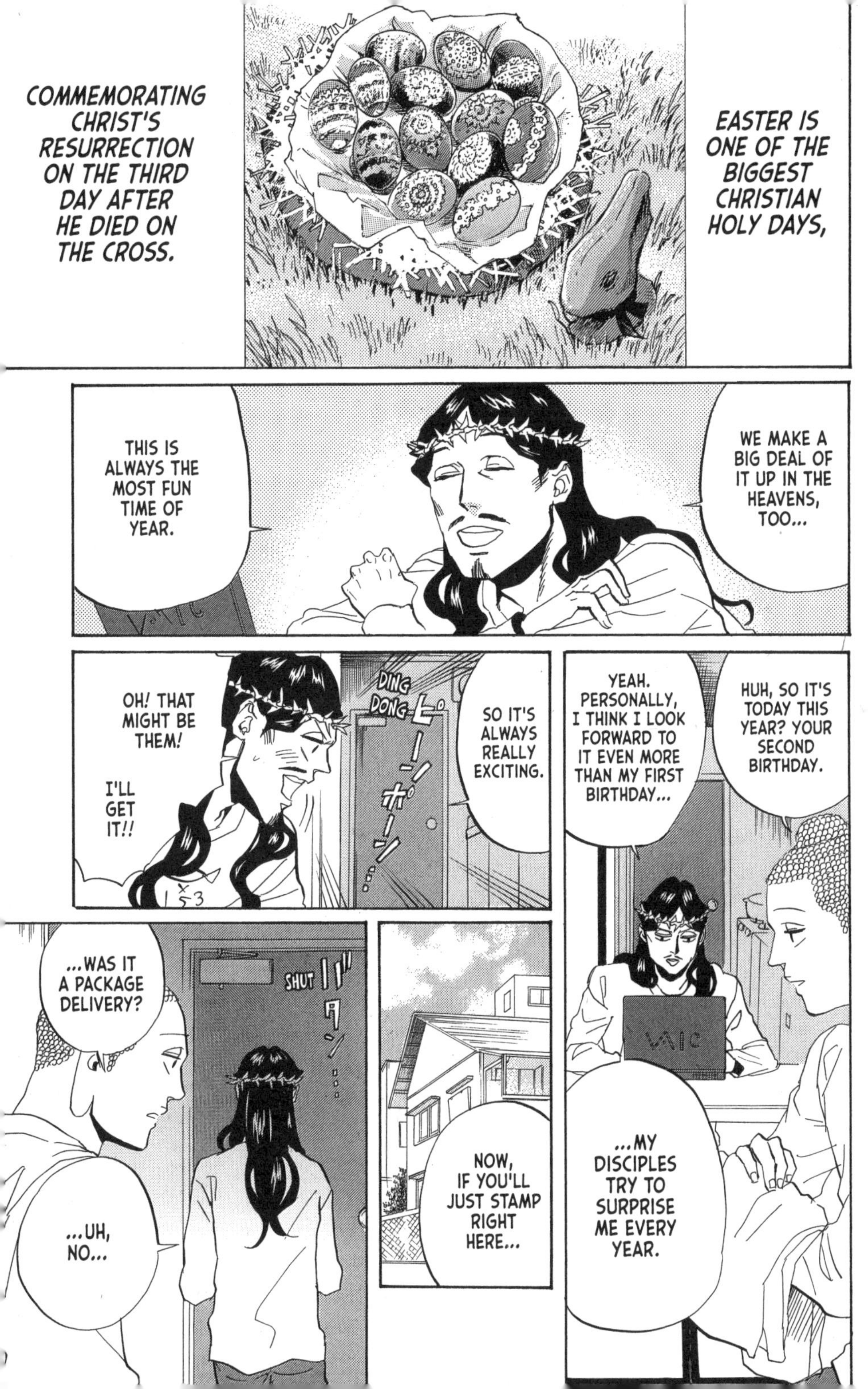
EASTER IS ONE OF THE BIGGEST CHRISTIAN HOLY DAYS,
COMMEMORATING CHRIST'S RESURRECTION ON THE THIRD DAY AFTER HE DIED ON THE CROSS.
WE MAKE A BIG DEAL OF IT UP IN THE HEAVENS, TOO...
THIS IS ALWAYS THE MOST FUN TIME OF YEAR.
HUH, SO IT'S TODAY THIS YEAR? YOUR SECOND BIRTHDAY.
YEAH. PERSONALLY, I THINK I LOOK FORWARD TO IT EVEN MORE THAN MY FIRST BIRTHDAY...
...MY DISCIPLES TRY TO SURPRISE ME EVERY YEAR.
SO IT'S ALWAYS REALLY EXCITING.
DING DONG
OH! THAT MIGHT BE THEM!
I'LL GET IT!!
NOW, IF YOU'LL JUST STAMP RIGHT HERE...
SHUT
...WAS IT A PACKAGE DELIVERY?
...UH, NO...

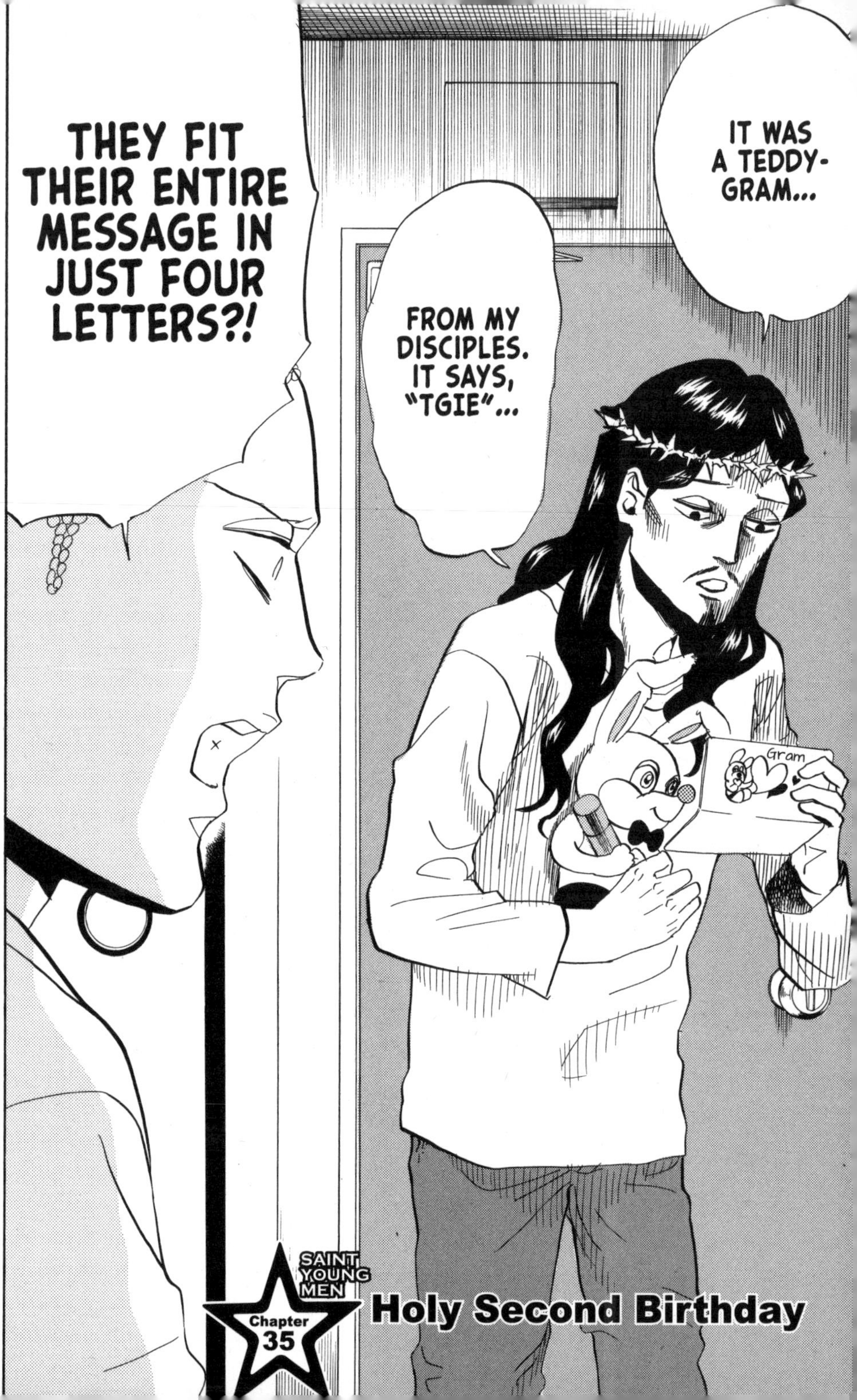
IT WAS A TEDDY-GRAM...
FROM MY DISCIPLES. IT SAYS, "TGIE"...
Gram
THEY FIT THEIR ENTIRE MESSAGE IN JUST FOUR LETTERS?!
SAINT YOUNG MEN
Chapter 35
Holy Second Birthday

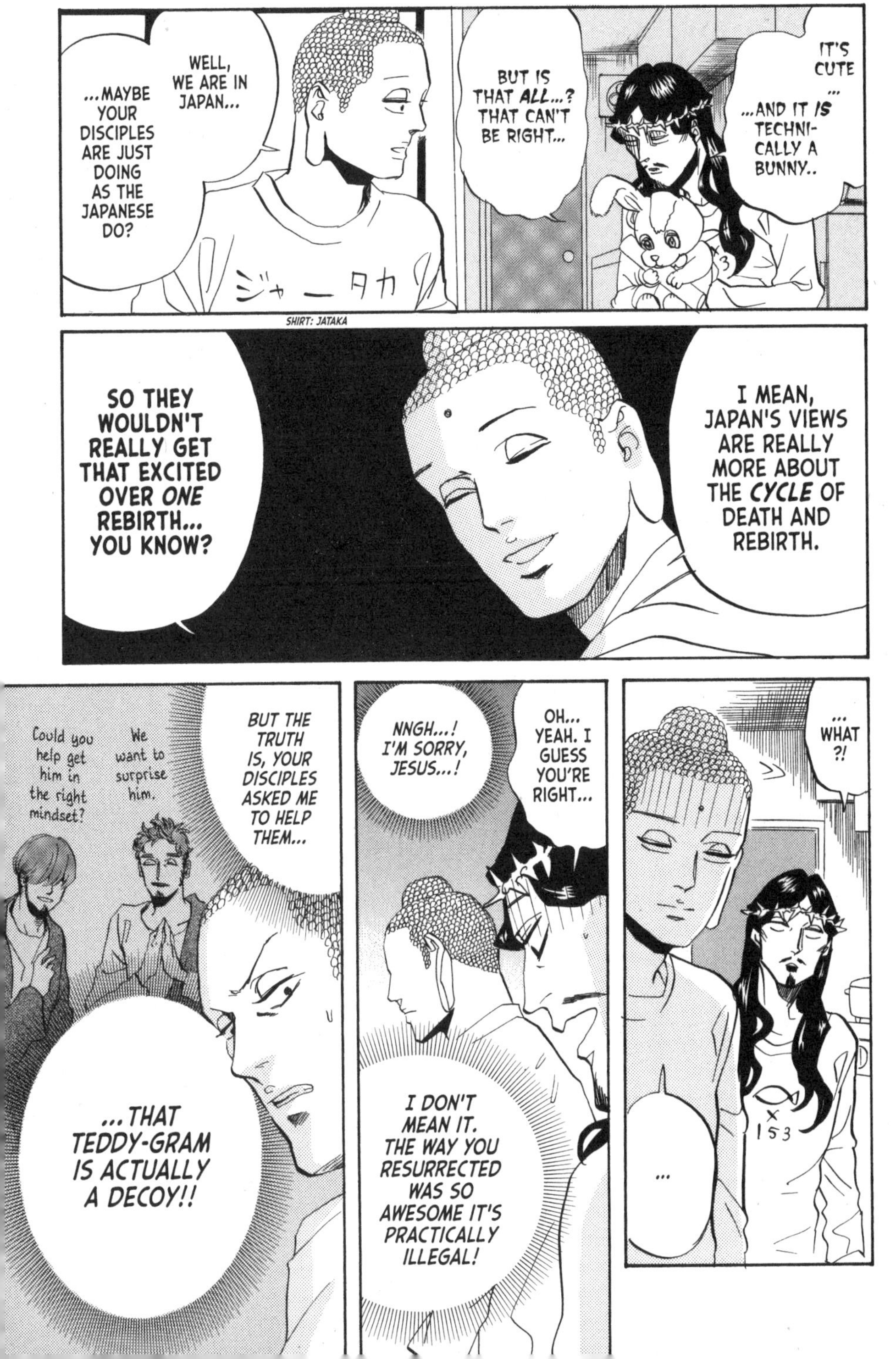
IT'S CUTE ...
...AND IT *IS* TECHNICALLY A BUNNY..
BUT IS THAT *ALL*...? THAT CAN'T BE RIGHT...
WELL, WE ARE IN JAPAN...
...MAYBE YOUR DISCIPLES ARE JUST DOING AS THE JAPANESE DO?
ジャータカ
SHIRT: JATAKA
I MEAN, JAPAN'S VIEWS ARE REALLY MORE ABOUT THE *CYCLE* OF DEATH AND REBIRTH.
SO THEY WOULDN'T REALLY GET THAT EXCITED OVER *ONE* REBIRTH... YOU KNOW?
... WHAT ?!
...
OH... YEAH. I GUESS YOU'RE RIGHT...
NNGH...! I'M SORRY, JESUS...!
I DON'T MEAN IT. THE WAY YOU RESURRECTED WAS SO AWESOME IT'S PRACTICALLY ILLEGAL!
BUT THE TRUTH IS, YOUR DISCIPLES ASKED ME TO HELP THEM...
We want to surprise him.
Could you help get him in the right mindset?
...THAT TEDDY-GRAM IS ACTUALLY A DECOY!!

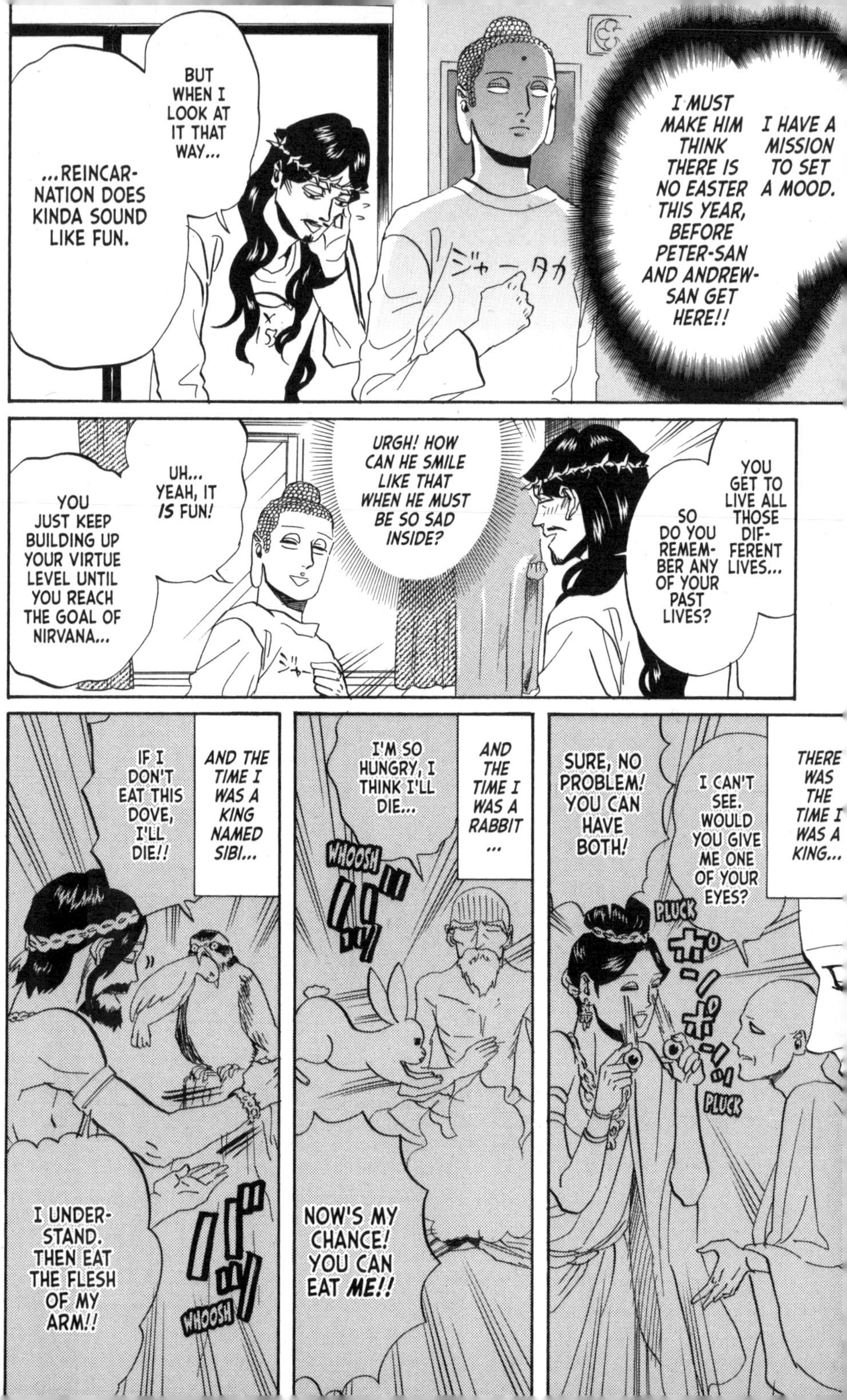
I HAVE A MISSION TO SET A MOOD.
I MUST MAKE HIM THINK THERE IS NO EASTER THIS YEAR, BEFORE PETER-SAN AND ANDREW-SAN GET HERE!!
ジャータカ
BUT WHEN I LOOK AT IT THAT WAY...
...REINCARNATION DOES KINDA SOUND LIKE FUN.
YOU GET TO LIVE ALL THOSE DIFFERENT LIVES...
SO DO YOU REMEMBER ANY OF YOUR PAST LIVES?
URGH! HOW CAN HE SMILE LIKE THAT WHEN HE MUST BE SO SAD INSIDE?
UH... YEAH, IT IS FUN!
YOU JUST KEEP BUILDING UP YOUR VIRTUE LEVEL UNTIL YOU REACH THE GOAL OF NIRVANA...
THERE WAS THE TIME I WAS A KING...
I CAN'T SEE. WOULD YOU GIVE ME ONE OF YOUR EYES?
SURE, NO PROBLEM! YOU CAN HAVE BOTH!
PLUCK
PLUCK
AND THE TIME I WAS A RABBIT...
I'M SO HUNGRY, I THINK I'LL DIE...
WHOOSH
NOW'S MY CHANCE! YOU CAN EAT ME!!
AND THE TIME I WAS A KING NAMED SIBI...
IF I DON'T EAT THIS DOVE, I'LL DIE!!
I UNDERSTAND. THEN EAT THE FLESH OF MY ARM!!
WHOOSH

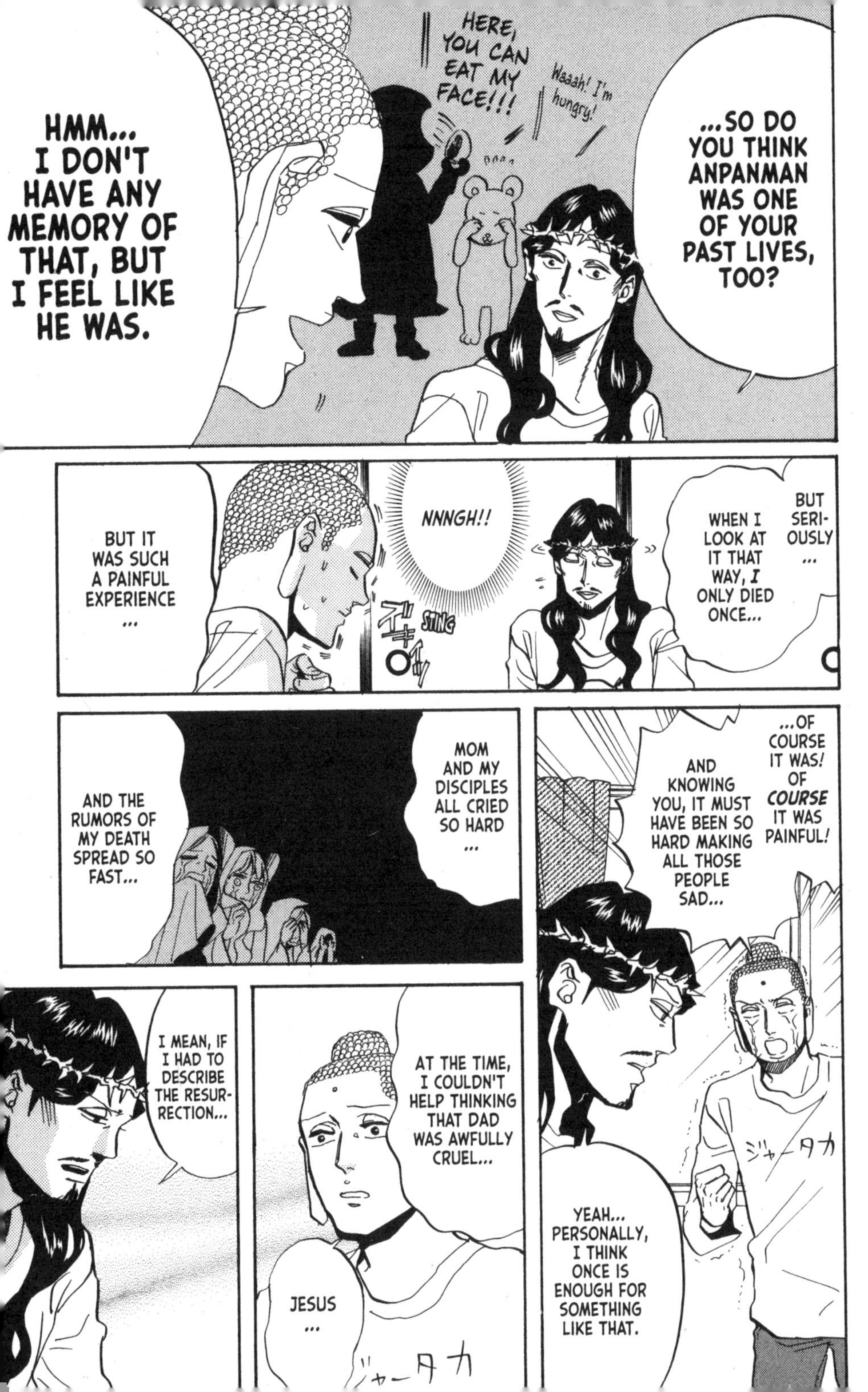
...SO DO YOU THINK ANPANMAN WAS ONE OF YOUR PAST LIVES, TOO?
HERE, YOU CAN EAT MY FACE!!!
Waaah! I'm hungry!
HMM... I DON'T HAVE ANY MEMORY OF THAT, BUT I FEEL LIKE HE WAS.
BUT SERIOUSLY...
WHEN I LOOK AT IT THAT WAY, *I* ONLY DIED ONCE...
NNNGH!!
STING
BUT IT WAS SUCH A PAINFUL EXPERIENCE...
...OF COURSE IT WAS! OF *COURSE* IT WAS PAINFUL!
AND KNOWING YOU, IT MUST HAVE BEEN SO HARD MAKING ALL THOSE PEOPLE SAD...
ジャータカ
YEAH... PERSONALLY, I THINK ONCE IS ENOUGH FOR SOMETHING LIKE THAT.
MOM AND MY DISCIPLES ALL CRIED SO HARD...
AND THE RUMORS OF MY DEATH SPREAD SO FAST...
AT THE TIME, I COULDN'T HELP THINKING THAT DAD WAS AWFULLY CRUEL...
JESUS...
ジャータカ
I MEAN, IF I HAD TO DESCRIBE THE RESURRECTION...

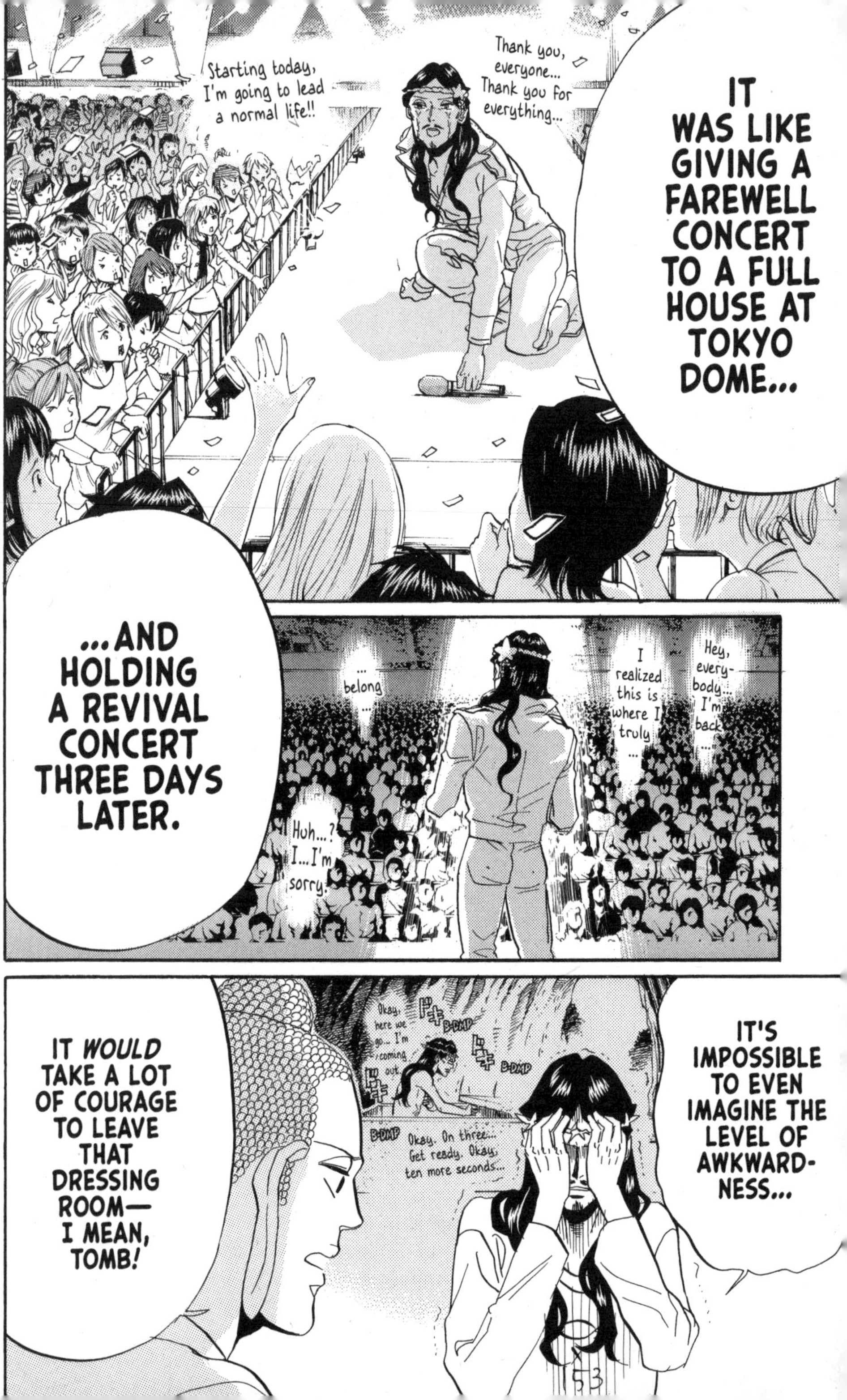
IT WAS LIKE GIVING A FAREWELL CONCERT TO A FULL HOUSE AT TOKYO DOME...
Thank you, everyone... Thank you for everything...
Starting today, I'm going to lead a normal life!!
...AND HOLDING A REVIVAL CONCERT THREE DAYS LATER.
Hey, every-body... I'm back...
I realized this is where I truly...
...belong...
Huh...? I...I'm sorry.
IT'S IMPOSSIBLE TO EVEN IMAGINE THE LEVEL OF AWKWARD-NESS...
Okay, here we go... I'm coming out.
B-DMP
B-DMP
B-DMP
Okay. On three... Get ready. Okay, ten more seconds...
IT *WOULD* TAKE A LOT OF COURAGE TO LEAVE THAT DRESSING ROOM— I MEAN, TOMB!

BUDDHA: HAS NEVER SEEN ANYONE FLY ON A FLIGHT OF STAIRS.

JESUS: CAN SEE THAT JAMES BOND WOULD SEEM PRETTY WEAK IF DOUBLE-O SEVEN WERE PRONOUNCED ZERO-ZERO-SEVEN.

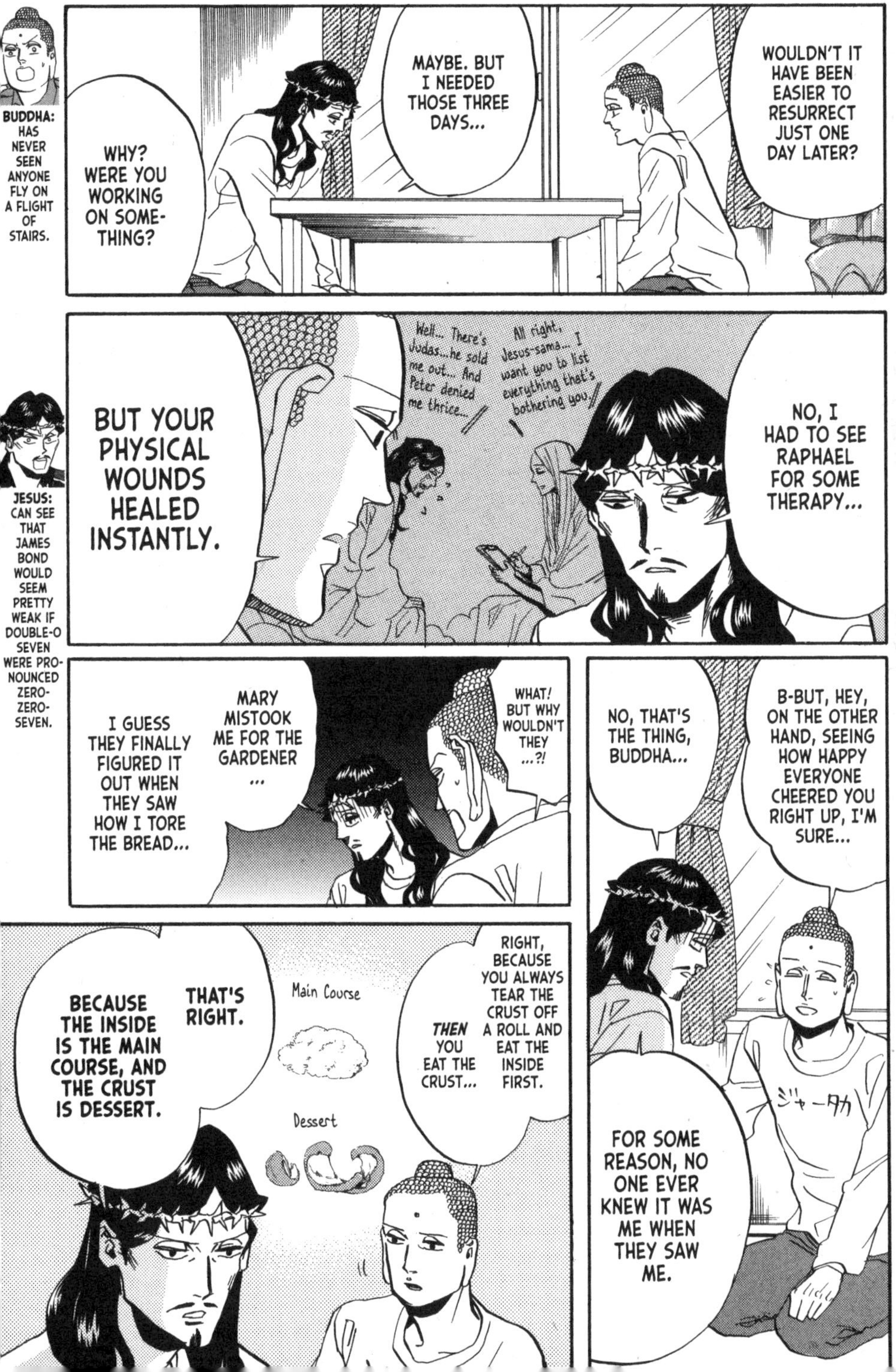
WOULDN'T IT HAVE BEEN EASIER TO RESURRECT JUST ONE DAY LATER?
MAYBE. BUT I NEEDED THOSE THREE DAYS...
WHY? WERE YOU WORKING ON SOME-THING?
NO, I HAD TO SEE RAPHAEL FOR SOME THERAPY...
All right, Jesus-sama... I want you to list everything that's bothering you.
Well... There's Judas...he sold me out... And Peter denied me thrice...
BUT YOUR PHYSICAL WOUNDS HEALED INSTANTLY.
B-BUT, HEY, ON THE OTHER HAND, SEEING HOW HAPPY EVERYONE CHEERED YOU RIGHT UP, I'M SURE...
NO, THAT'S THE THING, BUDDHA...
ジャータカ
FOR SOME REASON, NO ONE EVER KNEW IT WAS ME WHEN THEY SAW ME.
WHAT! BUT WHY WOULDN'T THEY ...?!
MARY MISTOOK ME FOR THE GARDENER ...
I GUESS THEY FINALLY FIGURED IT OUT WHEN THEY SAW HOW I TORE THE BREAD...
RIGHT, BECAUSE YOU ALWAYS TEAR THE CRUST OFF A ROLL AND EAT THE INSIDE FIRST.
THEN YOU EAT THE CRUST...
Main Course
Dessert
THAT'S RIGHT.
BECAUSE THE INSIDE IS THE MAIN COURSE, AND THE CRUST IS DESSERT.

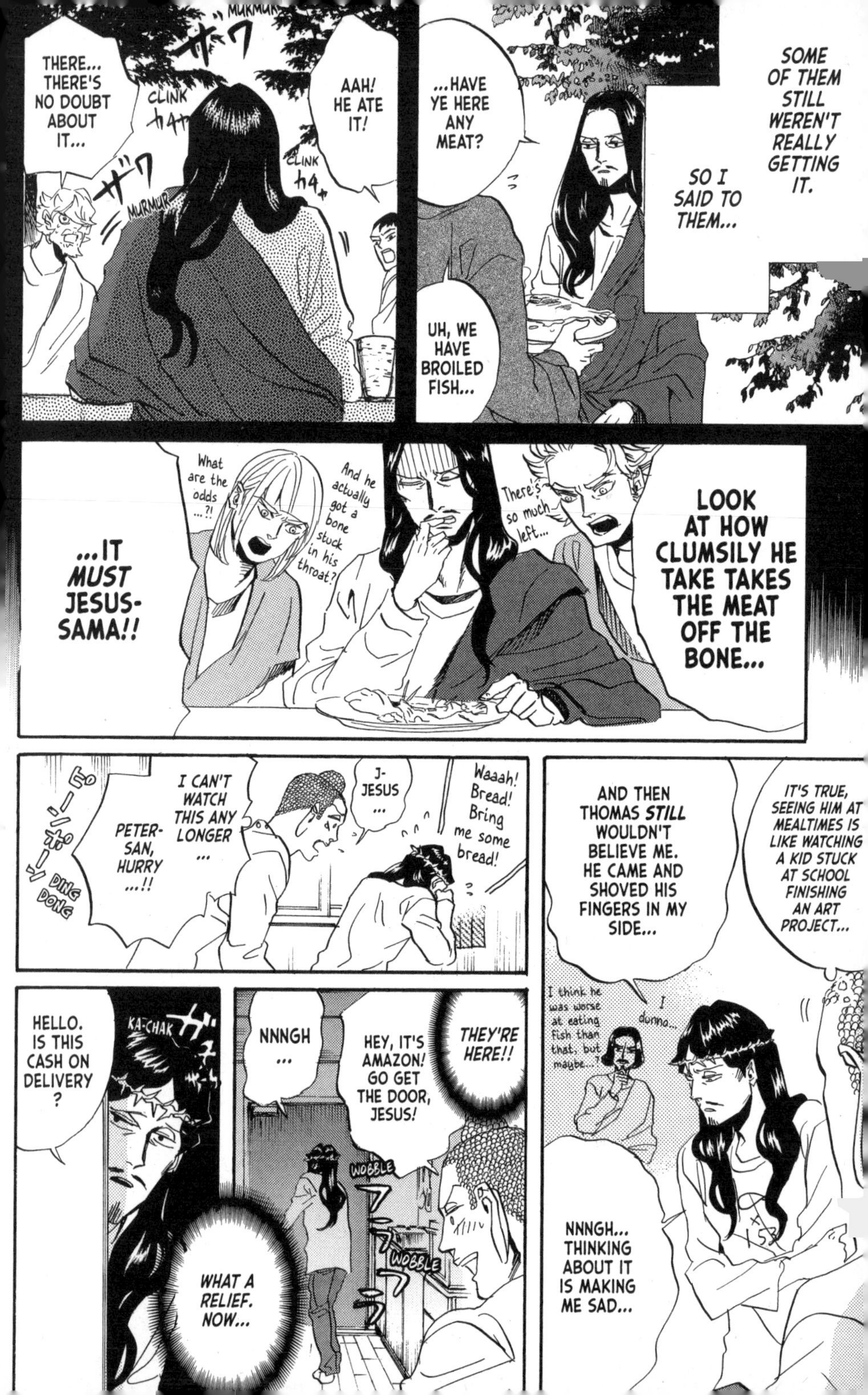
SOME OF THEM STILL WEREN'T REALLY GETTING IT.
SO I SAID TO THEM...
...HAVE YE HERE ANY MEAT?
UH, WE HAVE BROILED FISH...
AAH! HE ATE IT!
MURMUR
CLINK
CLINK
MURMUR
THERE... THERE'S NO DOUBT ABOUT IT...
LOOK AT HOW CLUMSILY HE TAKE TAKES THE MEAT OFF THE BONE...
There's so much left...
And he actually got a bone stuck in his throat?
What are the odds...?!
...IT MUST JESUS-SAMA!!
IT'S TRUE, SEEING HIM AT MEALTIMES IS LIKE WATCHING A KID STUCK AT SCHOOL FINISHING AN ART PROJECT...
AND THEN THOMAS STILL WOULDN'T BELIEVE ME. HE CAME AND SHOVED HIS FINGERS IN MY SIDE...
I dunno...
I think he was worse at eating fish than that, but maybe...?
NNNGH... THINKING ABOUT IT IS MAKING ME SAD...
Waaah! Bread! Bring me some bread!
J-JESUS...
I CAN'T WATCH THIS ANY LONGER...
PETER-SAN, HURRY...!!
DING DONG
THEY'RE HERE!!
HEY, IT'S AMAZON! GO GET THE DOOR, JESUS!
NNNGH...
WOBBLE
WOBBLE
KA-CHAK
HELLO. IS THIS CASH ON DELIVERY?
WHAT A RELIEF. NOW...

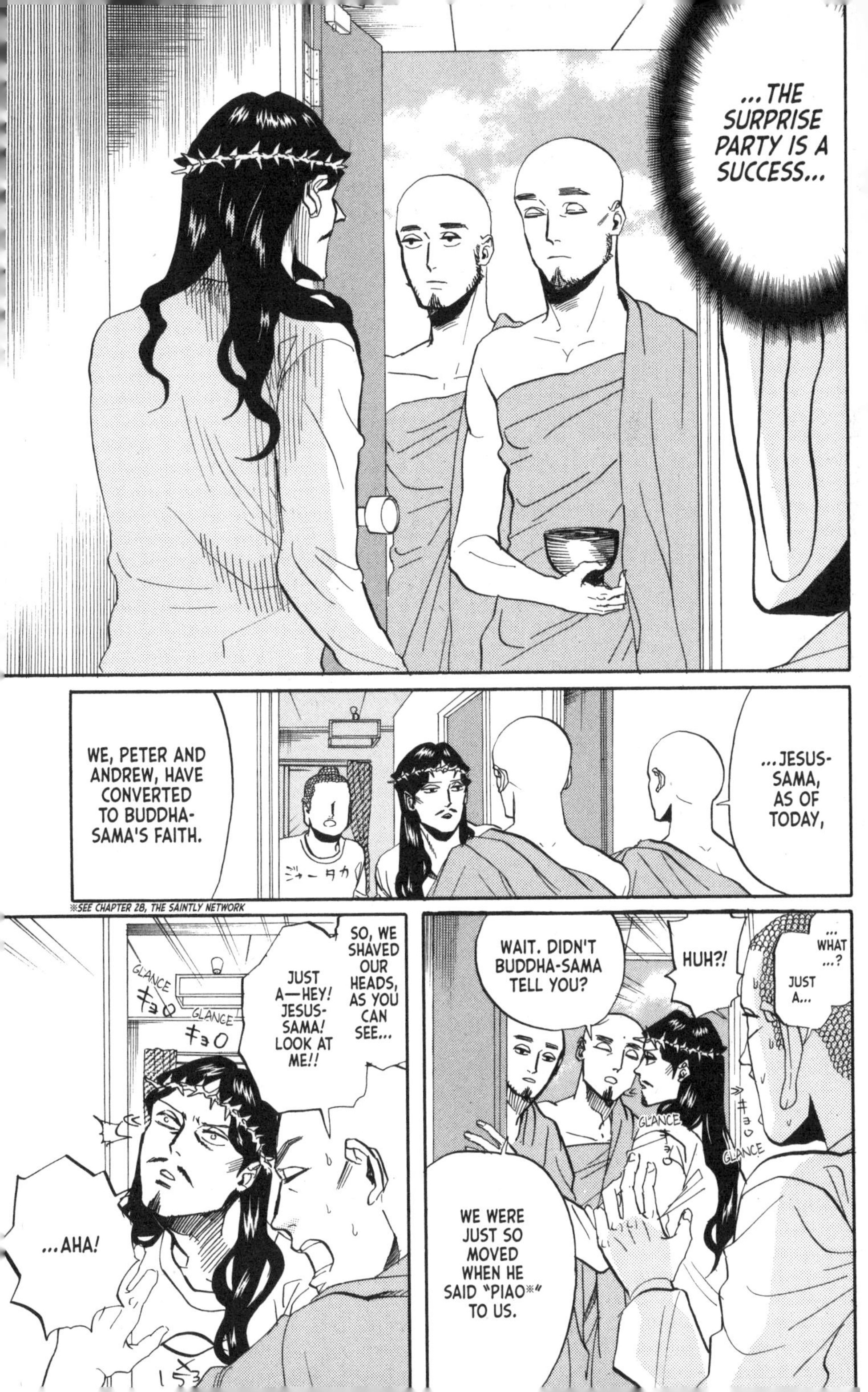
...THE SURPRISE PARTY IS A SUCCESS...
...JESUS-SAMA, AS OF TODAY,
WE, PETER AND ANDREW, HAVE CONVERTED TO BUDDHA-SAMA'S FAITH.
ジャータカ
※SEE CHAPTER 28, THE SAINTLY NETWORK
...WHAT...?
JUST A...
HUH?!
WAIT. DIDN'T BUDDHA-SAMA TELL YOU?
GLANCE キョロ
GLANCE キョロ
WE WERE JUST SO MOVED WHEN HE SAID "PIAO※" TO US.
SO, WE SHAVED OUR HEADS, AS YOU CAN SEE...
JUST A—HEY! JESUS-SAMA! LOOK AT ME!!
GLANCE キョロ
GLANCE キョロ
...AHA!

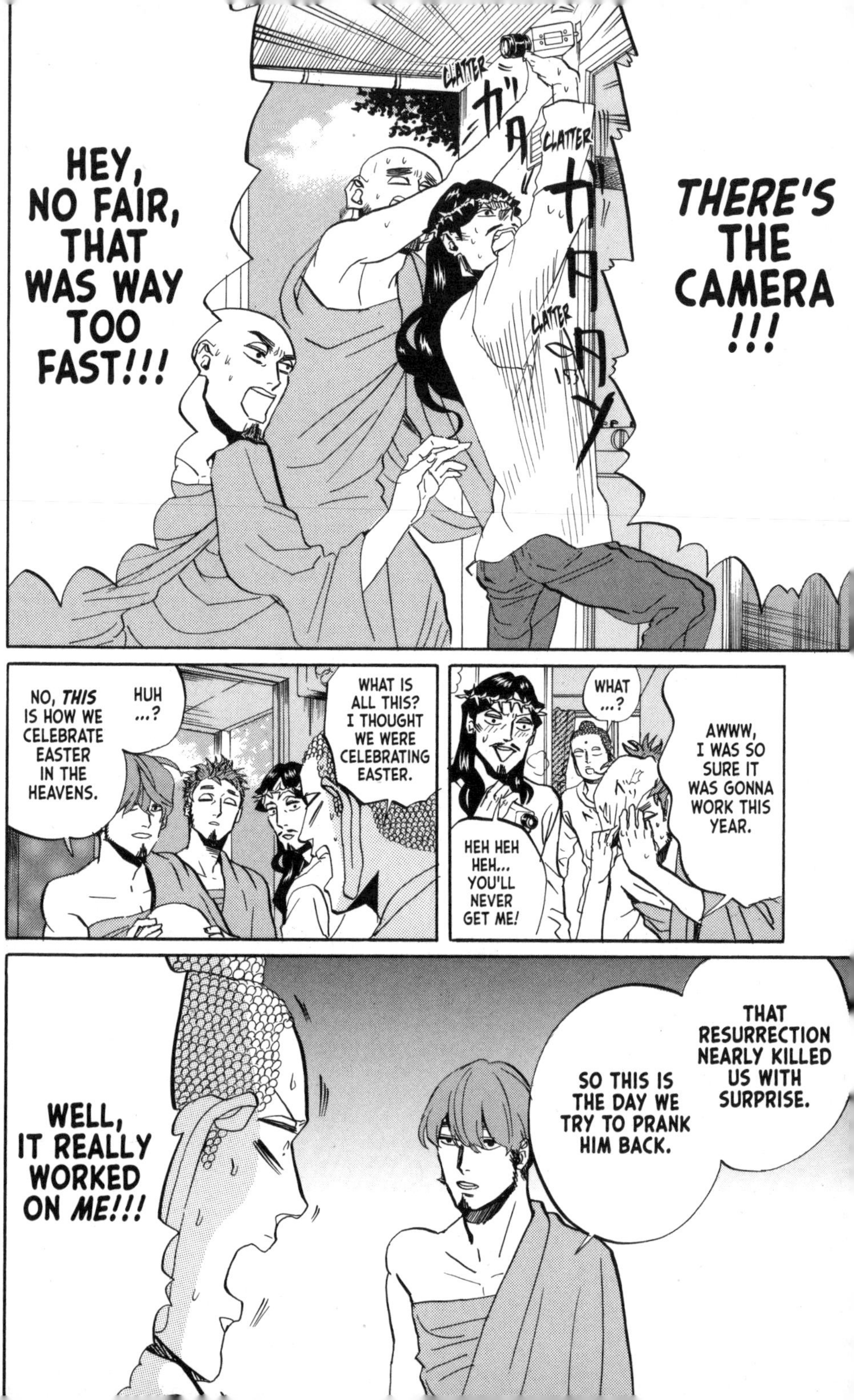
THERE'S THE CAMERA!!!
CLATTER
CLATTER
CLATTER
HEY, NO FAIR, THAT WAS WAY TOO FAST!!!
WHAT ...?
AWWW, I WAS SO SURE IT WAS GONNA WORK THIS YEAR.
HEH HEH HEH... YOU'LL NEVER GET ME!
WHAT IS ALL THIS? I THOUGHT WE WERE CELEBRATING EASTER.
HUH ...?
NO, THIS IS HOW WE CELEBRATE EASTER IN THE HEAVENS.
THAT RESURRECTION NEARLY KILLED US WITH SURPRISE.
SO THIS IS THE DAY WE TRY TO PRANK HIM BACK.
WELL, IT REALLY WORKED ON ME!!!

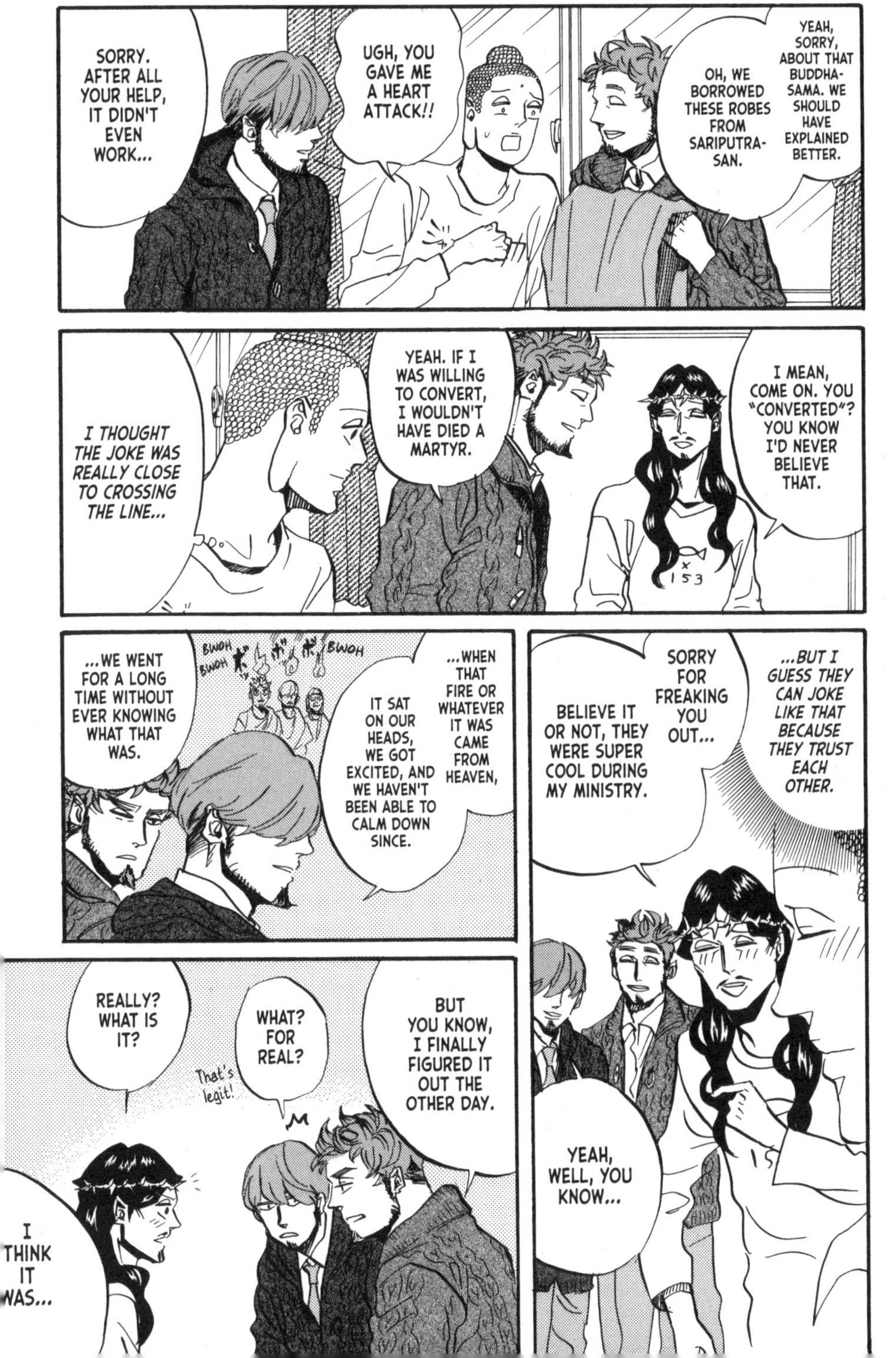
YEAH, SORRY, ABOUT THAT BUDDHA-SAMA. WE SHOULD HAVE EXPLAINED BETTER.
OH, WE BORROWED THESE ROBES FROM SARIPUTRA-SAN.
UGH, YOU GAVE ME A HEART ATTACK!!
SORRY. AFTER ALL YOUR HELP, IT DIDN'T EVEN WORK...
I MEAN, COME ON. YOU "CONVERTED"? YOU KNOW I'D NEVER BELIEVE THAT.
YEAH. IF I WAS WILLING TO CONVERT, I WOULDN'T HAVE DIED A MARTYR.
I THOUGHT THE JOKE WAS REALLY CLOSE TO CROSSING THE LINE...
...BUT I GUESS THEY CAN JOKE LIKE THAT BECAUSE THEY TRUST EACH OTHER.
SORRY FOR FREAKING YOU OUT...
BELIEVE IT OR NOT, THEY WERE SUPER COOL DURING MY MINISTRY.
YEAH, WELL, YOU KNOW...
...WHEN THAT FIRE OR WHATEVER IT WAS CAME FROM HEAVEN,
IT SAT ON OUR HEADS, WE GOT EXCITED, AND WE HAVEN'T BEEN ABLE TO CALM DOWN SINCE.
BWOH
BWOH BWOH
...WE WENT FOR A LONG TIME WITHOUT EVER KNOWING WHAT THAT WAS.
BUT YOU KNOW, I FINALLY FIGURED IT OUT THE OTHER DAY.
WHAT? FOR REAL?
That's legit!
REALLY? WHAT IS IT?
I THINK IT WAS...

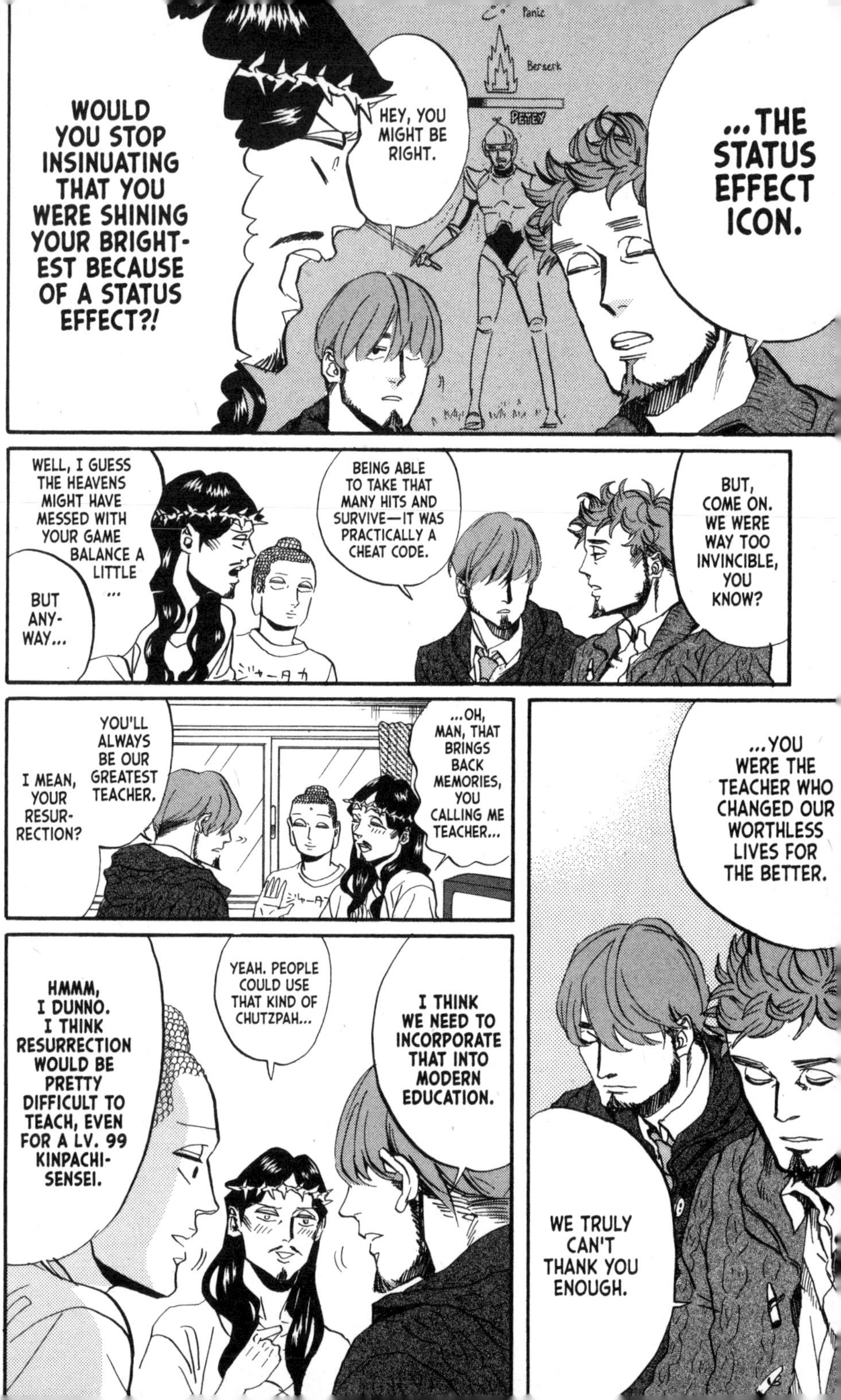
...THE STATUS EFFECT ICON.
Panic
Berserk
PETEY
HEY, YOU MIGHT BE RIGHT.
WOULD YOU STOP INSINUATING THAT YOU WERE SHINING YOUR BRIGHT-EST BECAUSE OF A STATUS EFFECT?!
BUT, COME ON. WE WERE WAY TOO INVINCIBLE, YOU KNOW?
BEING ABLE TO TAKE THAT MANY HITS AND SURVIVE—IT WAS PRACTICALLY A CHEAT CODE.
WELL, I GUESS THE HEAVENS MIGHT HAVE MESSED WITH YOUR GAME BALANCE A LITTLE ...
BUT ANY-WAY...
...YOU WERE THE TEACHER WHO CHANGED OUR WORTHLESS LIVES FOR THE BETTER.
WE TRULY CAN'T THANK YOU ENOUGH.
...OH, MAN, THAT BRINGS BACK MEMORIES, YOU CALLING ME TEACHER...
YOU'LL ALWAYS BE OUR GREATEST TEACHER.
I MEAN, YOUR RESUR-RECTION?
I THINK WE NEED TO INCORPORATE THAT INTO MODERN EDUCATION.
YEAH. PEOPLE COULD USE THAT KIND OF CHUTZPAH...
HMMM, I DUNNO. I THINK RESURRECTION WOULD BE PRETTY DIFFICULT TO TEACH, EVEN FOR A LV. 99 KINPACHI-SENSEI.

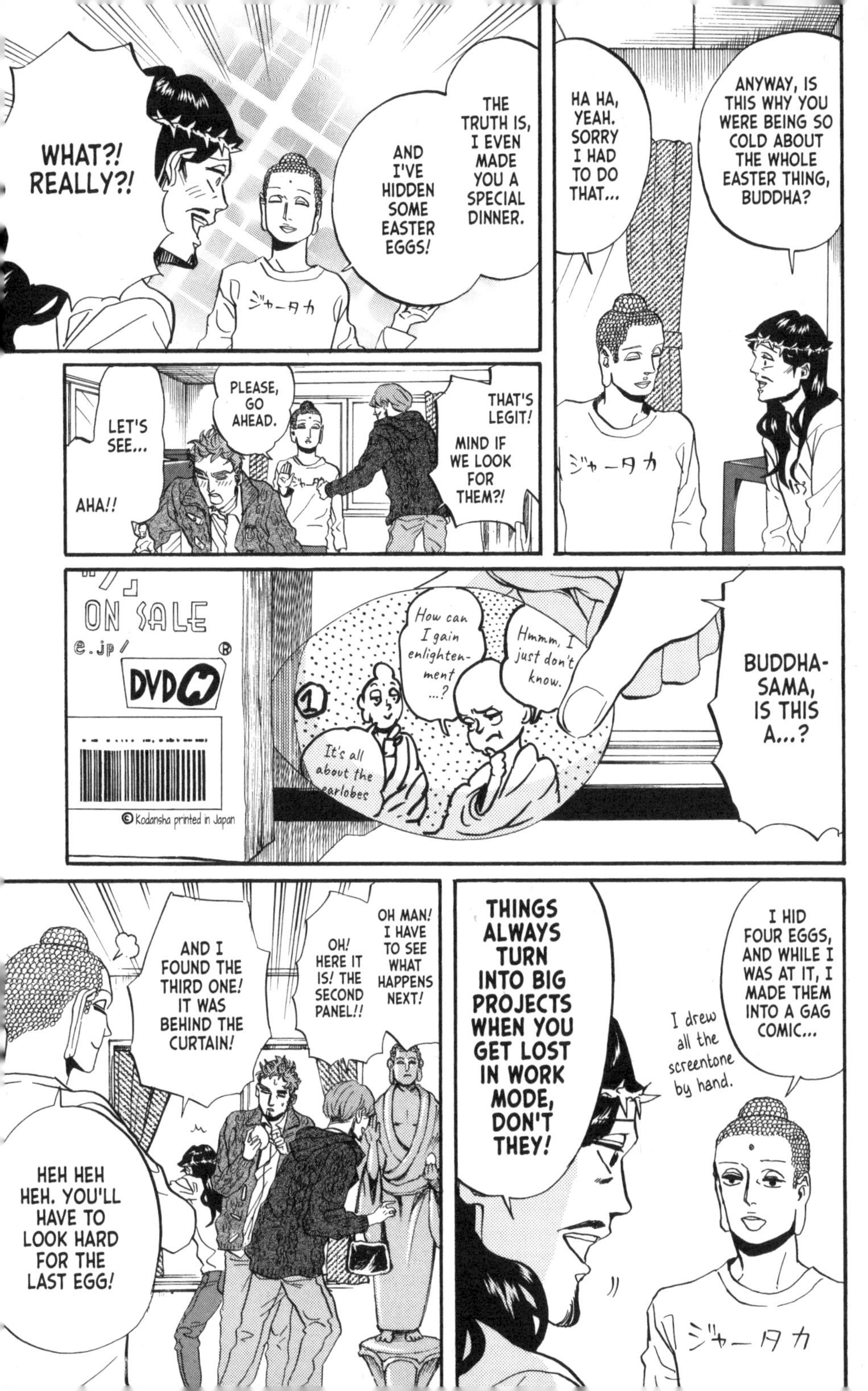
ANYWAY, IS THIS WHY YOU WERE BEING SO COLD ABOUT THE WHOLE EASTER THING, BUDDHA?
HA HA, YEAH. SORRY I HAD TO DO THAT...
ジャータカ
THE TRUTH IS, I EVEN MADE YOU A SPECIAL DINNER.
AND I'VE HIDDEN SOME EASTER EGGS!
WHAT?! REALLY?!
ジャータカ
THAT'S LEGIT!
MIND IF WE LOOK FOR THEM?!
PLEASE, GO AHEAD.
LET'S SEE...
AHA!!
BUDDHA-SAMA, IS THIS A...?
Hmmm, I just don't know.
How can I gain enlightenment...?
It's all about the earlobes
ON SALE
e.jp/
DVD
© Kodansha printed in Japan
I HID FOUR EGGS, AND WHILE I WAS AT IT, I MADE THEM INTO A GAG COMIC...
I drew all the screentone by hand.
ジャータカ
THINGS ALWAYS TURN INTO BIG PROJECTS WHEN YOU GET LOST IN WORK MODE, DON'T THEY!
OH MAN! I HAVE TO SEE WHAT HAPPENS NEXT!
OH! HERE IT IS! THE SECOND PANEL!!
AND I FOUND THE THIRD ONE! IT WAS BEHIND THE CURTAIN!
HEH HEH HEH. YOU'LL HAVE TO LOOK HARD FOR THE LAST EGG!

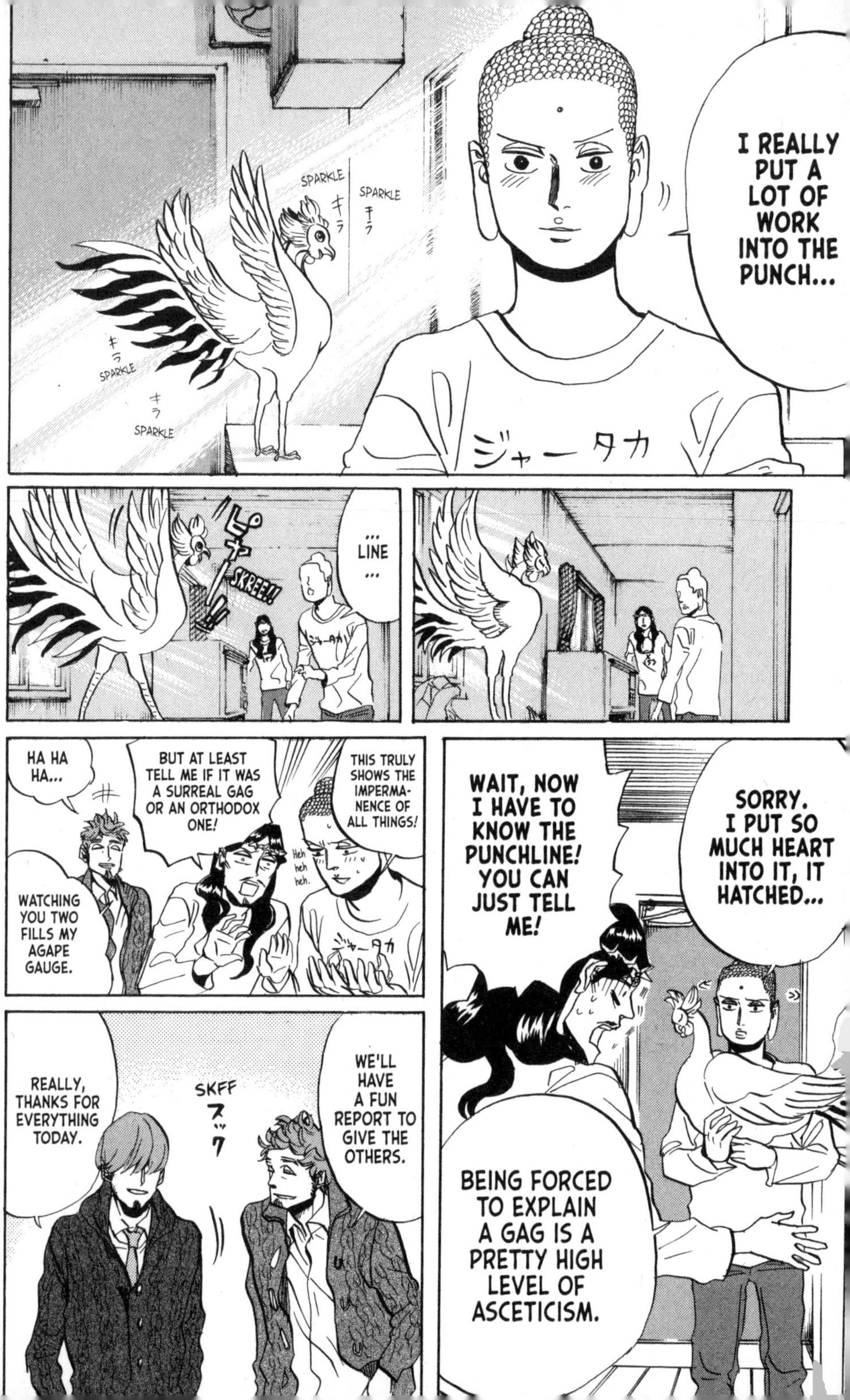
I REALLY PUT A LOT OF WORK INTO THE PUNCH...
キラ SPARKLE
キラ SPARKLE
キラ SPARKLE
キラ SPARKLE
ジャータカ
...LINE...
ピャ SKREE!!
SORRY. I PUT SO MUCH HEART INTO IT, IT HATCHED...
WAIT, NOW I HAVE TO KNOW THE PUNCHLINE! YOU CAN JUST TELL ME!
BEING FORCED TO EXPLAIN A GAG IS A PRETTY HIGH LEVEL OF ASCETICISM.
THIS TRULY SHOWS THE IMPERMANENCE OF ALL THINGS!
Heh heh heh.
BUT AT LEAST TELL ME IF IT WAS A SURREAL GAG OR AN ORTHODOX ONE!
HA HA HA...
WATCHING YOU TWO FILLS MY AGAPE GAUGE.
WE'LL HAVE A FUN REPORT TO GIVE THE OTHERS.
SKFF スッ
REALLY, THANKS FOR EVERYTHING TODAY.

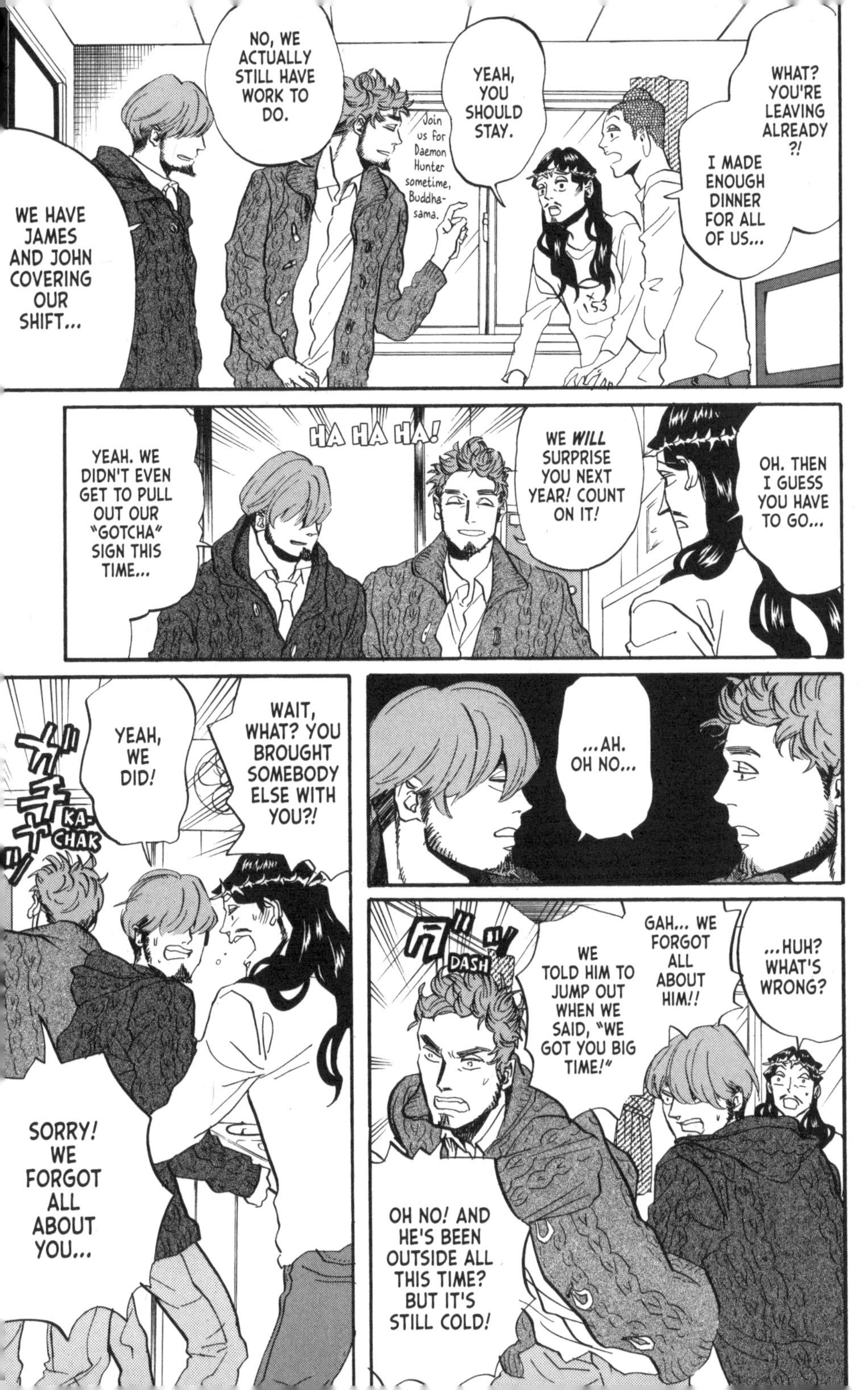

WHAT? YOU'RE LEAVING ALREADY?!
I MADE ENOUGH DINNER FOR ALL OF US...
YEAH, YOU SHOULD STAY.
Join us for Daemon Hunter sometime, Buddha-sama.
NO, WE ACTUALLY STILL HAVE WORK TO DO.
WE HAVE JAMES AND JOHN COVERING OUR SHIFT...
OH. THEN I GUESS YOU HAVE TO GO...
WE *WILL* SURPRISE YOU NEXT YEAR! COUNT ON IT!
HA HA HA!
YEAH. WE DIDN'T EVEN GET TO PULL OUT OUR "GOTCHA" SIGN THIS TIME...
...AH. OH NO...
...HUH? WHAT'S WRONG?
GAH... WE FORGOT ALL ABOUT HIM!!
WE TOLD HIM TO JUMP OUT WHEN WE SAID, "WE GOT YOU BIG TIME!"
DASH
OH NO! AND HE'S BEEN OUTSIDE ALL THIS TIME? BUT IT'S STILL COLD!
WAIT, WHAT? YOU BROUGHT SOMEBODY ELSE WITH YOU?!
YEAH, WE DID!
KA-CHAK
SORRY! WE FORGOT ALL ABOUT YOU...

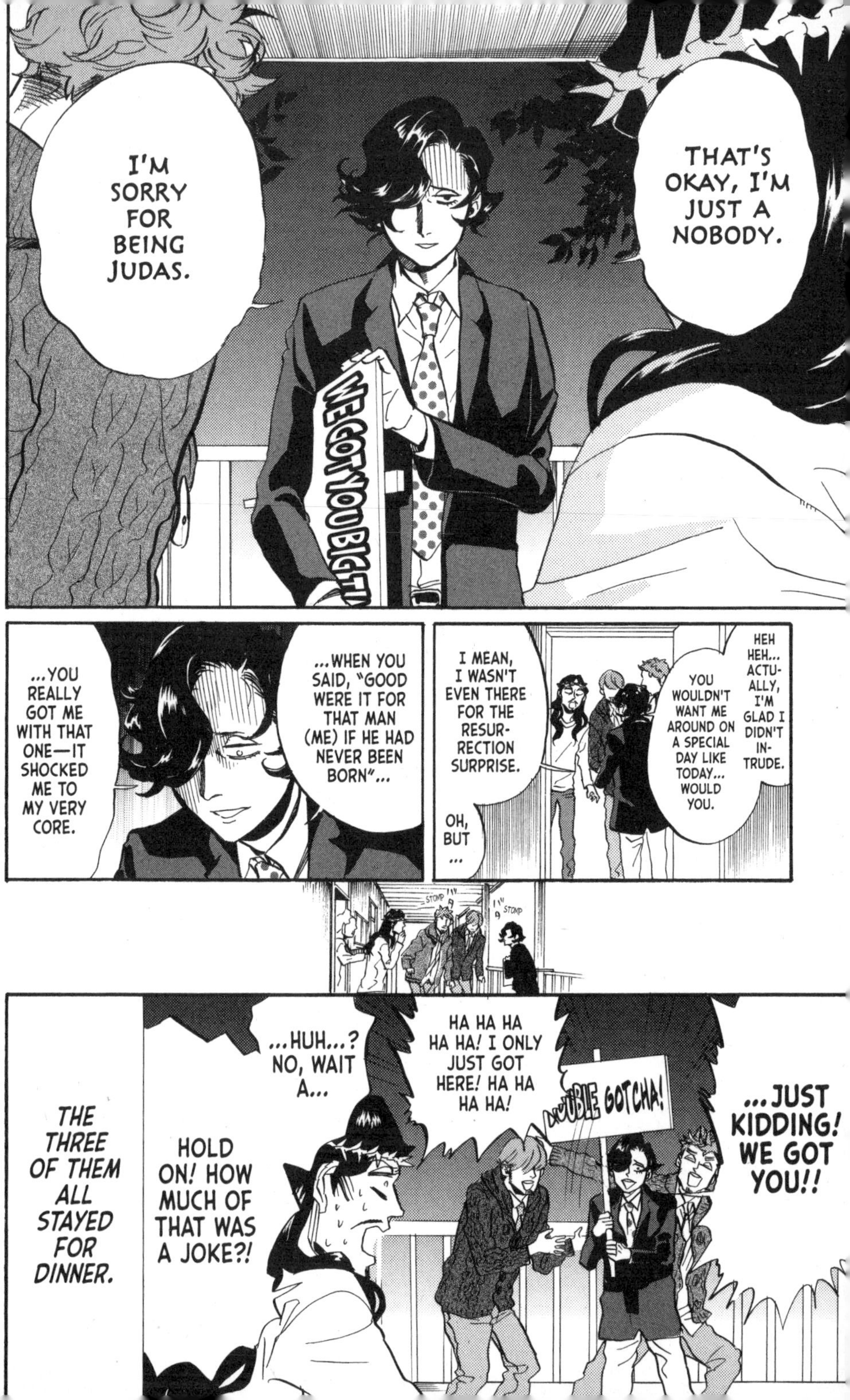

THAT'S OKAY, I'M JUST A NOBODY.
I'M SORRY FOR BEING JUDAS.
HEH HEH... ACTUALLY, I'M GLAD I DIDN'T INTRUDE.
YOU WOULDN'T WANT ME AROUND ON A SPECIAL DAY LIKE TODAY... WOULD YOU.
I MEAN, I WASN'T EVEN THERE FOR THE RESURRECTION SURPRISE.
OH, BUT ...
...WHEN YOU SAID, "GOOD WERE IT FOR THAT MAN (ME) IF HE HAD NEVER BEEN BORN"...
...YOU REALLY GOT ME WITH THAT ONE—IT SHOCKED ME TO MY VERY CORE.
STOMP
STOMP
...JUST KIDDING! WE GOT YOU!!
DOUBLE GOTCHA!
HA HA HA HA HA! I ONLY JUST GOT HERE! HA HA HA HA!
...HUH...? NO, WAIT A...
HOLD ON! HOW MUCH OF THAT WAS A JOKE?!
THE THREE OF THEM ALL STAYED FOR DINNER.

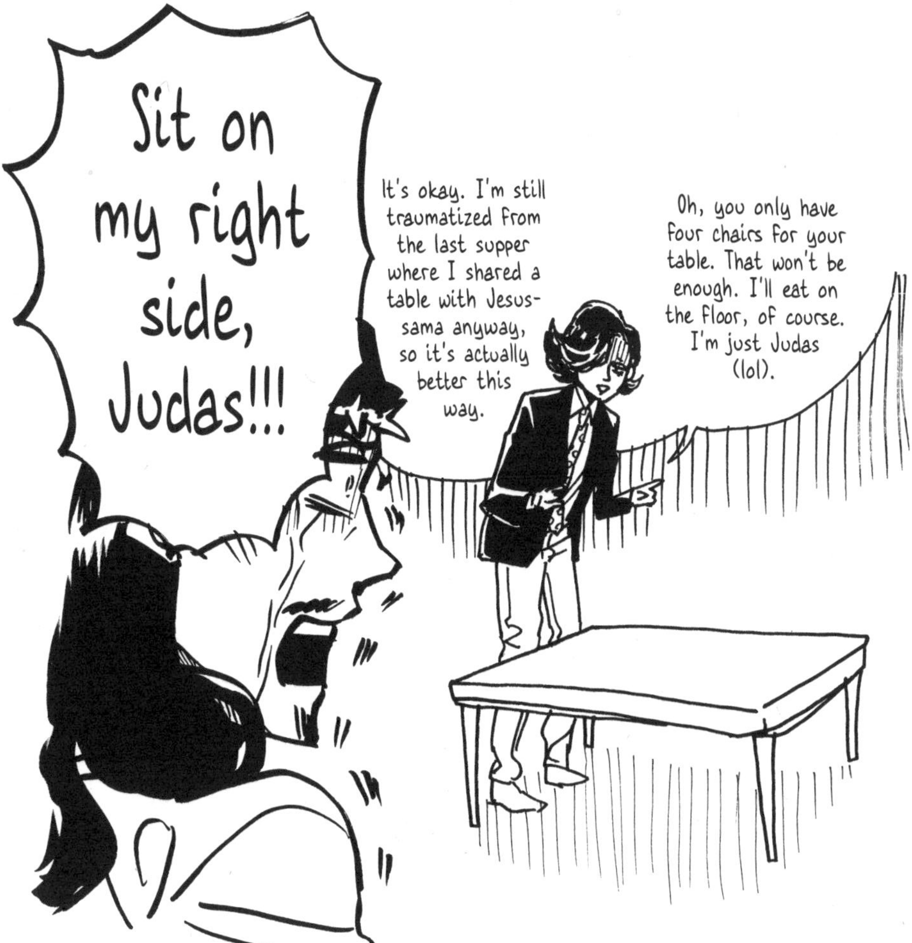
Oh, you only have four chairs for your table. That won't be enough. I'll eat on the floor, of course. I'm just Judas (lol).
It's okay. I'm still traumatized from the last supper where I shared a table with Jesus-sama anyway, so it's actually better this way.
Sit on my right side, Judas!!!

CHAPTER 35 TRANSLATION NOTES

It's today this year, page 103
Christ's Resurrection took place at the time of Passover, which was celebrated on the first full moon after the first day of spring. Because full moons do not occur on the same dates every year, the date for the Passover, as well as the date for Easter, vary from year to year.

Jataka, page 105
The Jataka tales are stories of the various past lives of Gautama Buddha before becoming enlightened.

153 fishes, page 105
After Christ's death, Peter thought he would give up the ministry and go back to his life as a fisherman. While he was having a particularly difficult time fishing, the Resurrected Lord appeared and told him to cast his nets on the right side of the boat, which he did and promptly caught several large fish. When they were brought to shore and counted, the number came out to 153. The number is believed to be symbolic, but no definitive evidence has been found to explain what the symbol may be.

Buddha's past lives, page 106
These are all references to the Jataka tales. The stories are as shown, although there are different variations in each of the tales. For example, the king mentioned in the first story is King Vessantara in some versions and King Sibi in others. King Vessantara was known for his generosity in giving away everything he had. King Sibi is definitely the king in the tale of the falcon and dove (or sparrow), in which he offers up his own flesh to protect both of his subjects, the birds. More details on the story of the rabbit can be found in the notes to volume one (Chapter 5, "cat barbecue").

Anpanman, page 107
Anpanman is a Japanese superhero who has a head made of anpan—bread (pan) filled with sweet red bean paste (anko). When he comes across a starving creature, he will help them by generously offering a piece of his own head. This weakens him, but he regains energy when Uncle Jam bakes him a new head.

Why? Were you working on something?, page 109
According to the First Epistle of Peter, "For Christ also hath once suffered for sins, the just for the unjust, that he might bring us to God, being put to death in the flesh, but quickened by the Spirit: By which also he went and preached unto the spirits in prison."

No one ever knew it was me, page 109
After Jesus had risen, Mary Magdalene stood outside his empty tomb, crying and wondering what had become of his body. Jesus appeared and asked her why she was crying. She believed he was the gardener and asked if he had taken the body, and only recognized him after he called her by her name. Additionally, there is a story of two disciples who met Jesus as they traveled to Emmaus, discussing the recent crucifixion of the master teacher. The account says that "their eyes were holden," or prevented, from recognizing him. They eventually had dinner with him, and when he broke bread with them, "their eyes were opened" and they finally realized it was him.

Have ye here any meat, page 110
When the disciples from the road to Emmaus told the Apostles about their experience, Jesus appeared to all of them. This frightened them, because they thought he might be a ghost. To prove that he was indeed alive, not only in spirit but in body as well, he asked for food.

Fire from heaven, page 113

This is a reference to what is known as the Day of Pentecost. The apostles had gathered to celebrate the Feast of Weeks, seven weeks (50 days) after Passover. "And suddenly there came a sound from heaven as of a rushing mighty wind, and it filled all the house where they were sitting. And there appeared unto them cloven tongues like as of fire, and it sat upon each of them. And they were all filled with the Holy Ghost, and began to speak with other tongues, as the Spirit gave them utterance," (Acts 2:2-4).

Kinpachi-sensei, page 114

Kinpachi-sensei is the hero of the 1979 TV drama, *San-nen B-gumi Kinpachi-sensei,* or *Mr. Kinpachi of Class 3B*. He was a middle-school teacher who helped his students deal with difficult issues such as teenage pregnancy, suicide, etc.

Good were it for that man, page 118

For context, the whole quote is as follows: "The Son of man indeed goeth, as it is written of him: but woe to that man by whom the Son of man is betrayed! Good were it for that man if he had never been born." (Mark 14:21) It was spoken by Jesus to his Apostles before Judas's betrayal.

SAINT☆YOUNG MEN

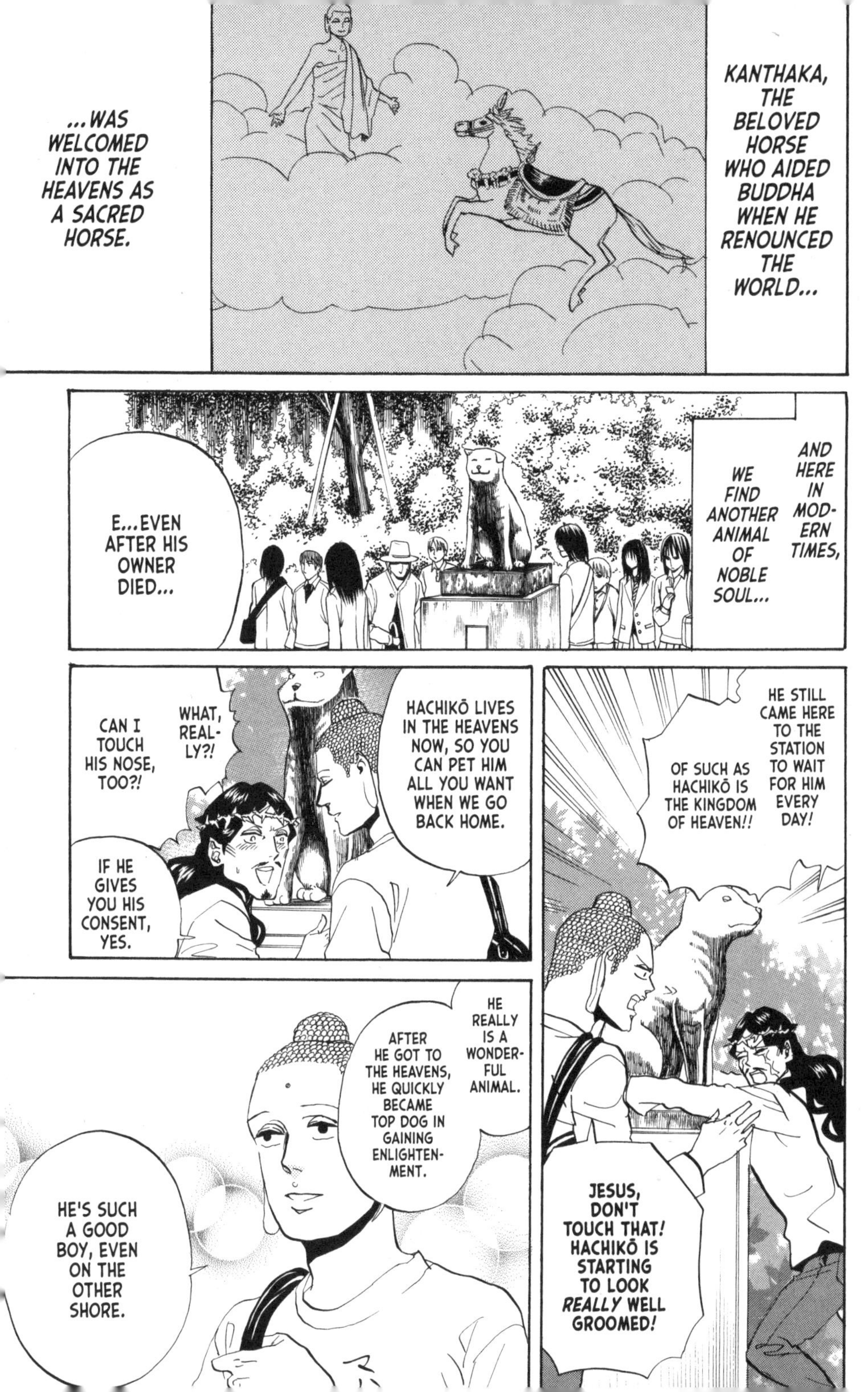
KANTHAKA, THE BELOVED HORSE WHO AIDED BUDDHA WHEN HE RENOUNCED THE WORLD...
...WAS WELCOMED INTO THE HEAVENS AS A SACRED HORSE.
AND HERE IN MODERN TIMES,
WE FIND ANOTHER ANIMAL OF NOBLE SOUL...
E...EVEN AFTER HIS OWNER DIED...
HE STILL CAME HERE TO THE STATION TO WAIT FOR HIM EVERY DAY!
OF SUCH AS HACHIKŌ IS THE KINGDOM OF HEAVEN!!
JESUS, DON'T TOUCH THAT! HACHIKŌ IS STARTING TO LOOK *REALLY* WELL GROOMED!
HACHIKŌ LIVES IN THE HEAVENS NOW, SO YOU CAN PET HIM ALL YOU WANT WHEN WE GO BACK HOME.
WHAT, REALLY?!
CAN I TOUCH HIS NOSE, TOO?!
IF HE GIVES YOU HIS CONSENT, YES.
HE REALLY IS A WONDERFUL ANIMAL.
AFTER HE GOT TO THE HEAVENS, HE QUICKLY BECAME TOP DOG IN GAINING ENLIGHTENMENT.
HE'S SUCH A GOOD BOY, EVEN ON THE OTHER SHORE.

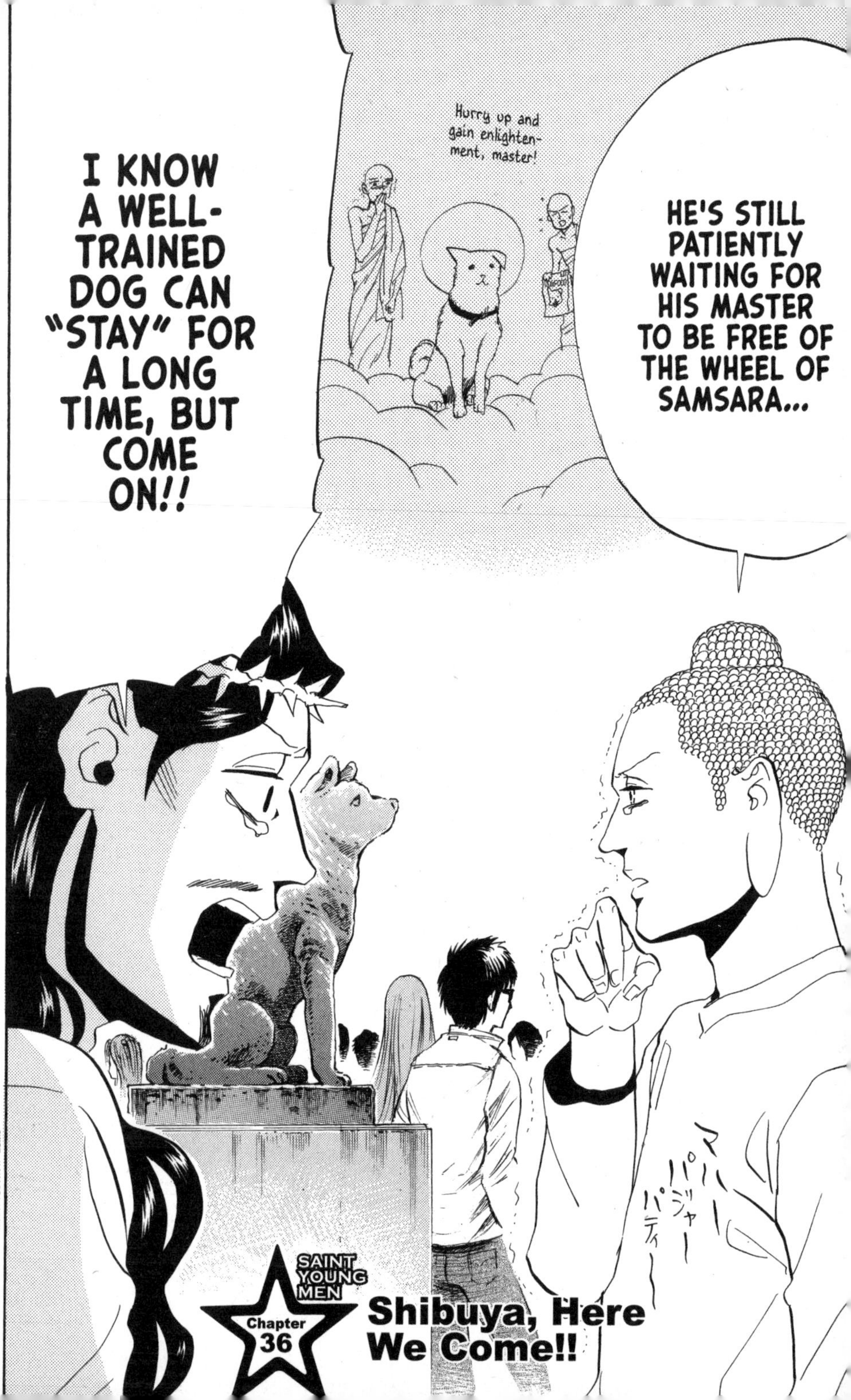
HE'S STILL PATIENTLY WAITING FOR HIS MASTER TO BE FREE OF THE WHEEL OF SAMSARA...
Hurry up and gain enlighten-ment, master!
I KNOW A WELL-TRAINED DOG CAN "STAY" FOR A LONG TIME, BUT COME ON!!
マハーパジャーパティー
SAINT YOUNG MEN
Chapter 36
Shibuya, Here We Come!!

SHIRT: MAHAPRAJAPATI

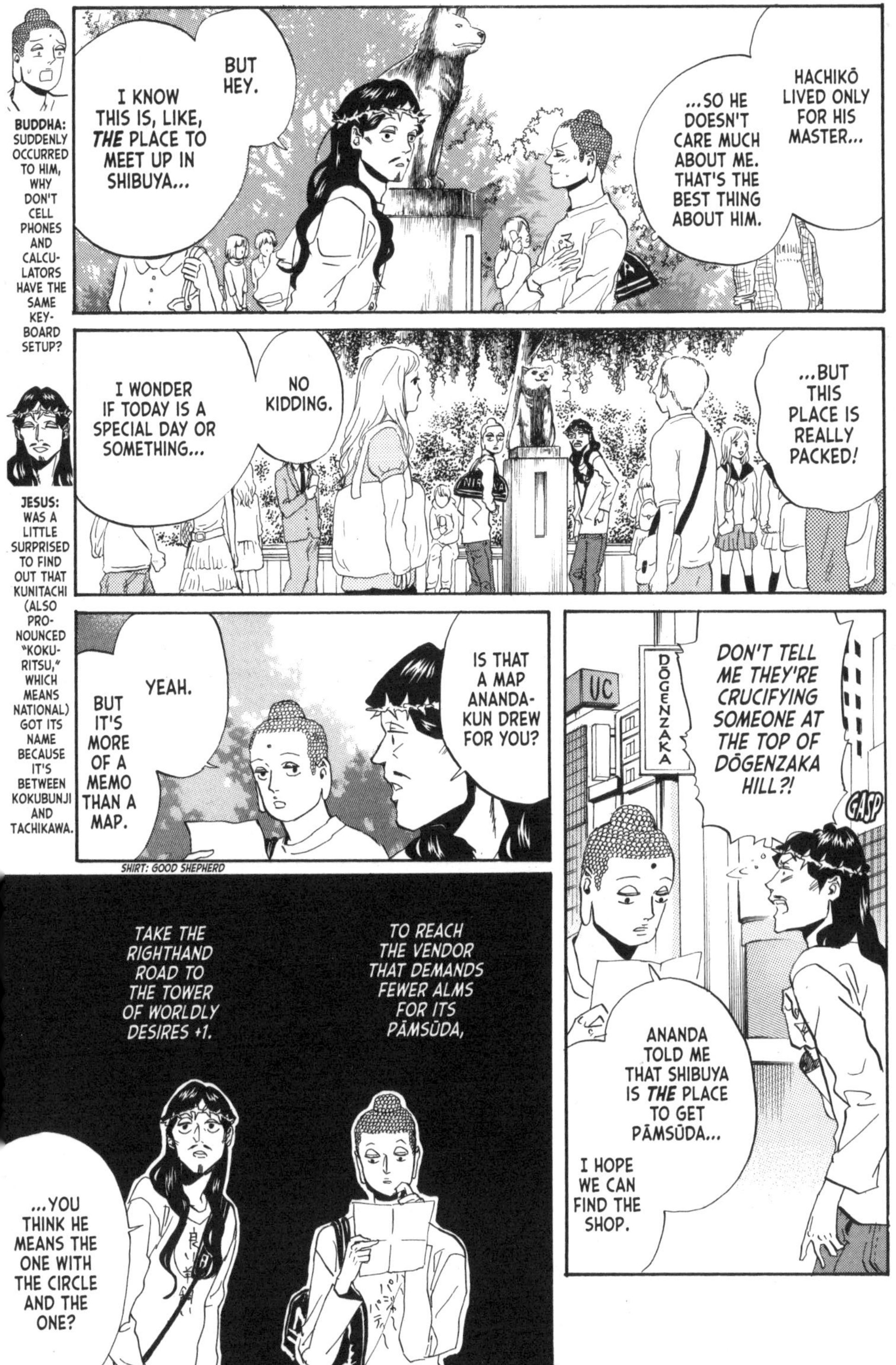
BUDDHA: SUDDENLY OCCURRED TO HIM, WHY DON'T CELL PHONES AND CALCULATORS HAVE THE SAME KEYBOARD SETUP?
JESUS: WAS A LITTLE SURPRISED TO FIND OUT THAT KUNITACHI (ALSO PRONOUNCED "KOKURITSU," WHICH MEANS NATIONAL) GOT ITS NAME BECAUSE IT'S BETWEEN KOKUBUNJI AND TACHIKAWA.
HACHIKŌ LIVED ONLY FOR HIS MASTER...
...SO HE DOESN'T CARE MUCH ABOUT ME. THAT'S THE BEST THING ABOUT HIM.
BUT HEY.
I KNOW THIS IS, LIKE, *THE* PLACE TO MEET UP IN SHIBUYA...
...BUT THIS PLACE IS REALLY PACKED!
NO KIDDING.
I WONDER IF TODAY IS A SPECIAL DAY OR SOMETHING...
UC
DŌGENZAKA
DON'T TELL ME THEY'RE CRUCIFYING SOMEONE AT THE TOP OF DŌGENZAKA HILL?!
GASP
ANANDA TOLD ME THAT SHIBUYA IS *THE* PLACE TO GET PĀMSŪDA...
I HOPE WE CAN FIND THE SHOP.
IS THAT A MAP ANANDA-KUN DREW FOR YOU?
YEAH.
BUT IT'S MORE OF A MEMO THAN A MAP.
SHIRT: GOOD SHEPHERD
TO REACH THE VENDOR THAT DEMANDS FEWER ALMS FOR ITS PĀMSŪDA,
TAKE THE RIGHTHAND ROAD TO THE TOWER OF WORLDLY DESIRES +1.
...YOU THINK HE MEANS THE ONE WITH THE CIRCLE AND THE ONE?

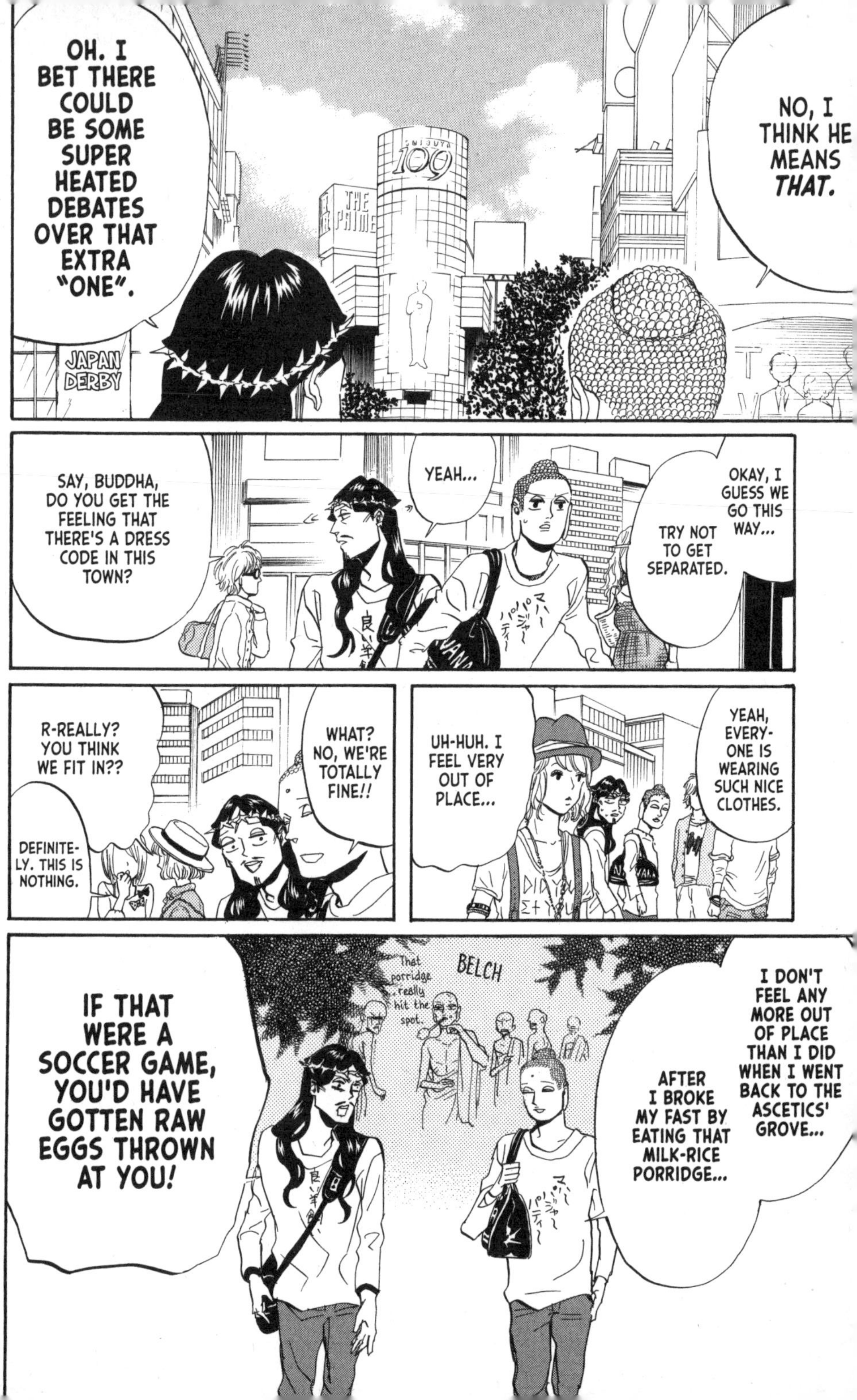
NO, I THINK HE MEANS *THAT.*
OH. I BET THERE COULD BE SOME SUPER HEATED DEBATES OVER THAT EXTRA "ONE".
109
THE PRIME
JAPAN DERBY
OKAY, I GUESS WE GO THIS WAY...
TRY NOT TO GET SEPARATED.
YEAH...
SAY, BUDDHA, DO YOU GET THE FEELING THAT THERE'S A DRESS CODE IN THIS TOWN?
YEAH, EVERYONE IS WEARING SUCH NICE CLOTHES.
UH-HUH. I FEEL VERY OUT OF PLACE...
WHAT? NO, WE'RE TOTALLY FINE!!
R-REALLY? YOU THINK WE FIT IN??
DEFINITELY. THIS IS NOTHING.
I DON'T FEEL ANY MORE OUT OF PLACE THAN I DID WHEN I WENT BACK TO THE ASCETICS' GROVE...
AFTER I BROKE MY FAST BY EATING THAT MILK-RICE PORRIDGE...
BELCH
That porridge really hit the spot.
IF THAT WERE A SOCCER GAME, YOU'D HAVE GOTTEN RAW EGGS THROWN AT YOU!

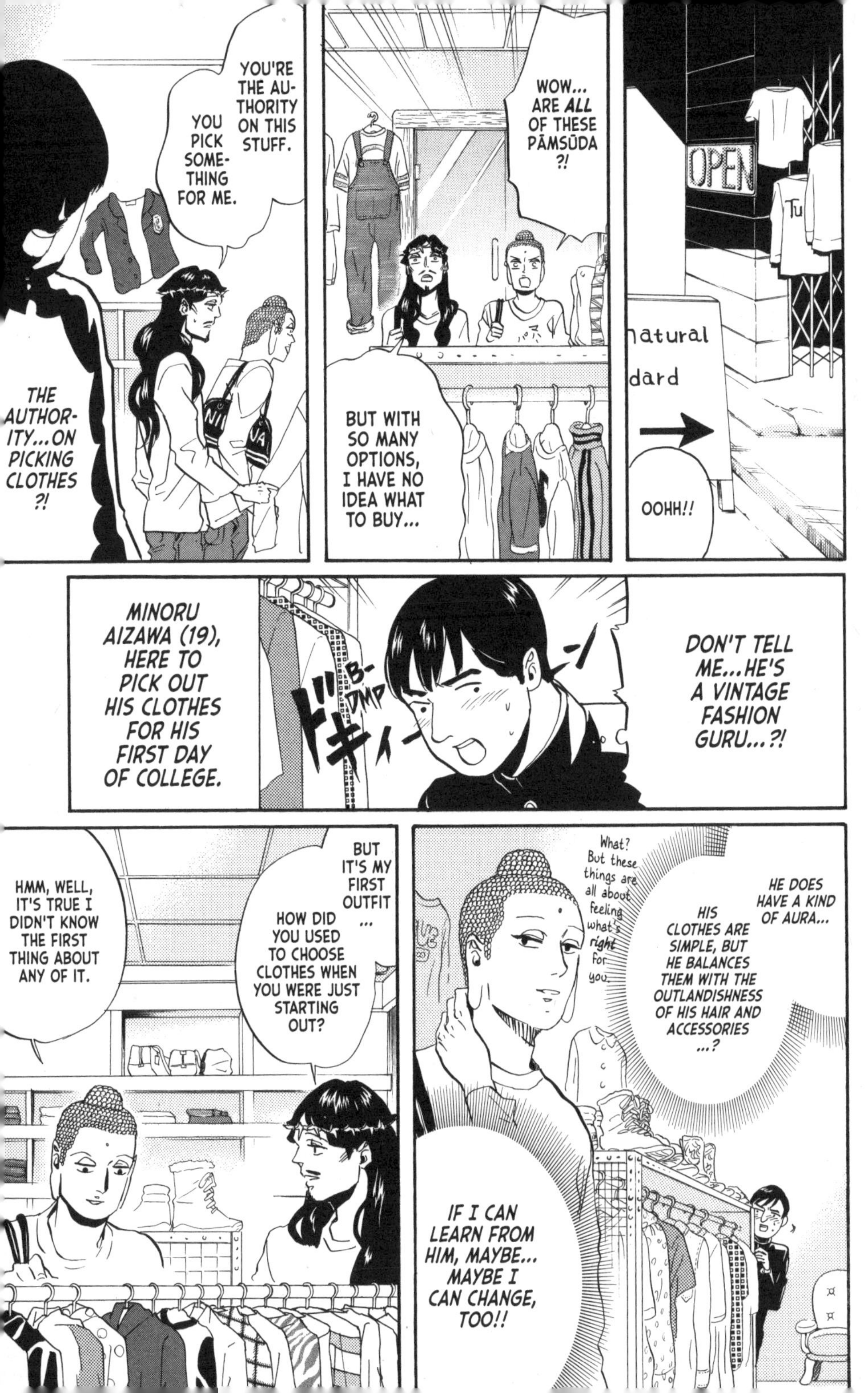
OPEN
natural
dard
OOHH!!
WOW... ARE *ALL* OF THESE PĀMSŪDA ?!
BUT WITH SO MANY OPTIONS, I HAVE NO IDEA WHAT TO BUY...
YOU'RE THE AUTHORITY ON THIS STUFF.
YOU PICK SOMETHING FOR ME.
THE AUTHORITY...ON PICKING CLOTHES ?!
DON'T TELL ME...HE'S A VINTAGE FASHION GURU...?!
B-DMP
MINORU AIZAWA (19), HERE TO PICK OUT HIS CLOTHES FOR HIS FIRST DAY OF COLLEGE.
HE DOES HAVE A KIND OF AURA...
HIS CLOTHES ARE SIMPLE, BUT HE BALANCES THEM WITH THE OUTLANDISHNESS OF HIS HAIR AND ACCESSORIES ...?
What? But these things are all about feeling what's *right* for you.
IF I CAN LEARN FROM HIM, MAYBE... MAYBE I CAN CHANGE, TOO!!
BUT IT'S MY FIRST OUTFIT ...
HOW DID YOU USED TO CHOOSE CLOTHES WHEN YOU WERE JUST STARTING OUT?
HMM, WELL, IT'S TRUE I DIDN'T KNOW THE FIRST THING ABOUT ANY OF IT.

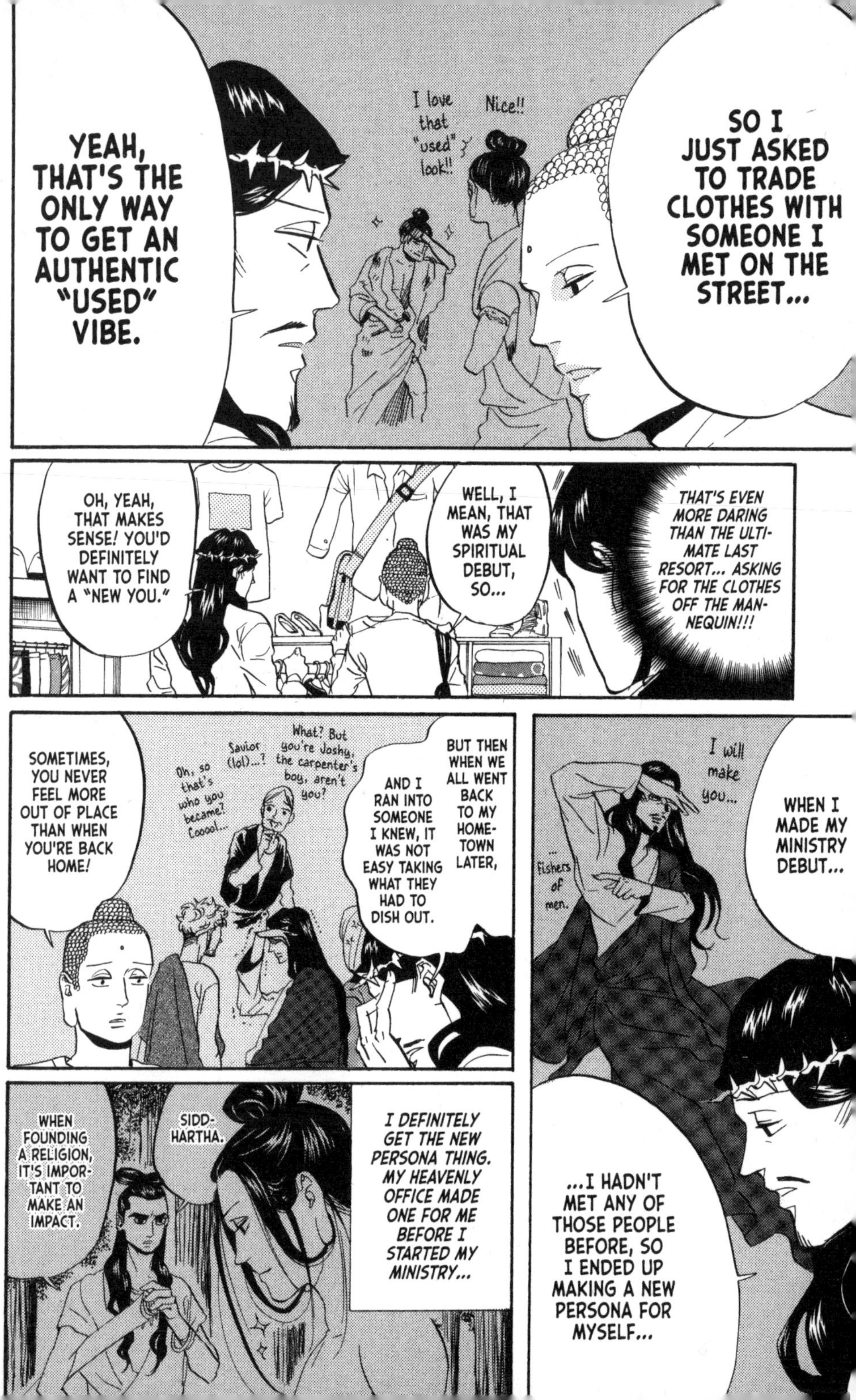
SO I JUST ASKED TO TRADE CLOTHES WITH SOMEONE I MET ON THE STREET...
Nice!!
I love that "used" look!!
YEAH, THAT'S THE ONLY WAY TO GET AN AUTHENTIC "USED" VIBE.
THAT'S EVEN MORE DARING THAN THE ULTI-MATE LAST RESORT... ASKING FOR THE CLOTHES OFF THE MAN-NEQUIN!!!
WELL, I MEAN, THAT WAS MY SPIRITUAL DEBUT, SO...
OH, YEAH, THAT MAKES SENSE! YOU'D DEFINITELY WANT TO FIND A "NEW YOU."
I will make you...
WHEN I MADE MY MINISTRY DEBUT...
... Fishers of men.
...I HADN'T MET ANY OF THOSE PEOPLE BEFORE, SO I ENDED UP MAKING A NEW PERSONA FOR MYSELF...
BUT THEN WHEN WE ALL WENT BACK TO MY HOME-TOWN LATER,
AND I RAN INTO SOMEONE I KNEW, IT WAS NOT EASY TAKING WHAT THEY HAD TO DISH OUT.
What? But you're Joshy, the carpenter's boy, aren't you?
Savior (lol)...?
Oh, so that's who you became? Cooool...
SOMETIMES, YOU NEVER FEEL MORE OUT OF PLACE THAN WHEN YOU'RE BACK HOME!
I DEFINITELY GET THE NEW PERSONA THING. MY HEAVENLY OFFICE MADE ONE FOR ME BEFORE I STARTED MY MINISTRY...
SIDD-HARTHA.
WHEN FOUNDING A RELIGION, IT'S IMPOR-TANT TO MAKE AN IMPACT.

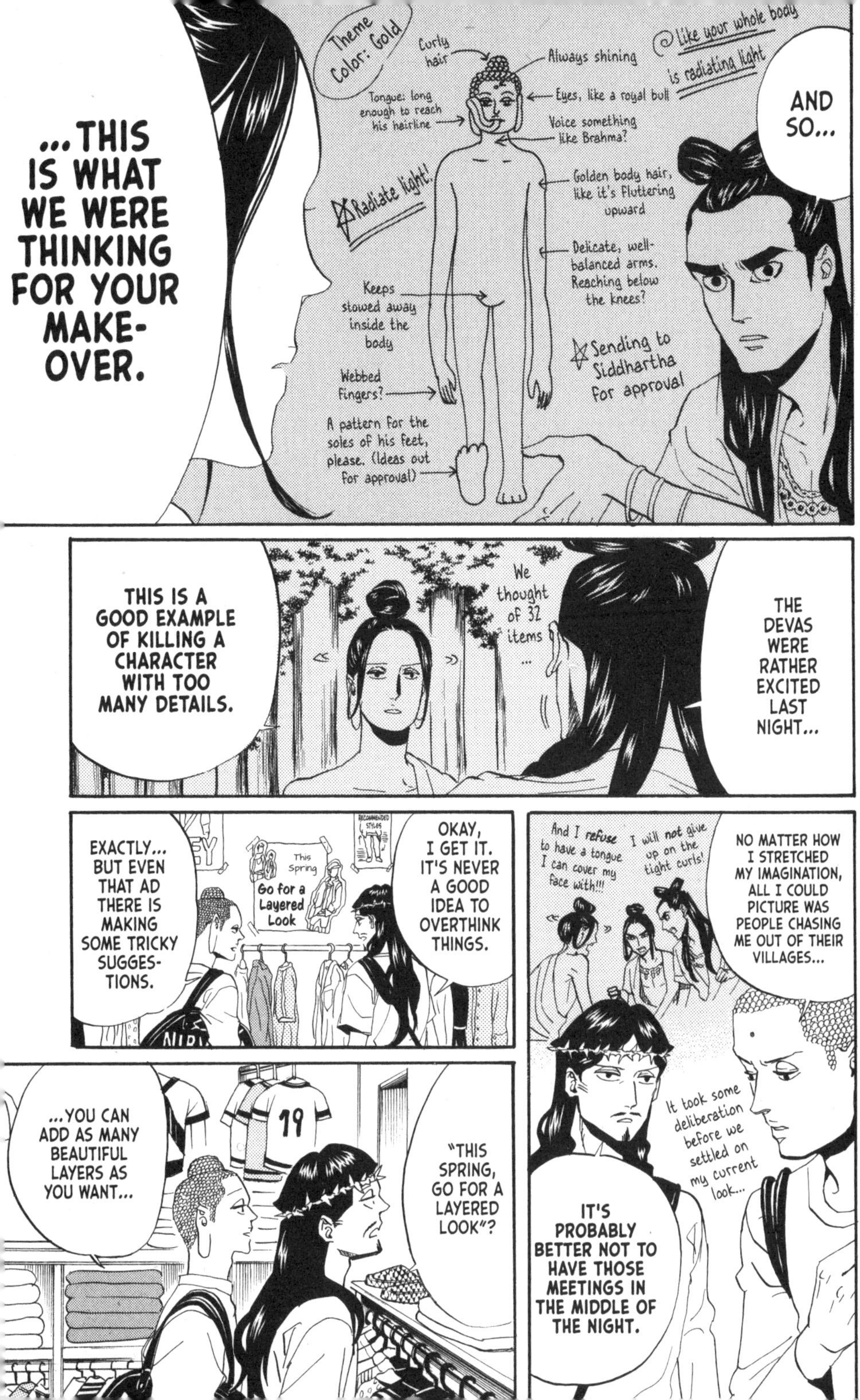
AND SO...
Theme Color: Gold
Curly hair
Always shining
@ Like your whole body is radiating light
Tongue: long enough to reach his hairline
Eyes, like a royal bull
Voice something like Brahma?
Radiate light!
Golden body hair, like it's fluttering upward
Delicate, well-balanced arms. Reaching below the knees?
Keeps stowed away inside the body
Sending to Siddhartha for approval
Webbed fingers?
A pattern for the soles of his feet, please. (Ideas out for approval)
...THIS IS WHAT WE WERE THINKING FOR YOUR MAKE-OVER.
THE DEVAS WERE RATHER EXCITED LAST NIGHT...
We thought of 32 items ...
THIS IS A GOOD EXAMPLE OF KILLING A CHARACTER WITH TOO MANY DETAILS.
NO MATTER HOW I STRETCHED MY IMAGINATION, ALL I COULD PICTURE WAS PEOPLE CHASING ME OUT OF THEIR VILLAGES...
I will not give up on the tight curls!
And I refuse to have a tongue I can cover my face with!!!
It took some deliberation before we settled on my current look...
IT'S PROBABLY BETTER NOT TO HAVE THOSE MEETINGS IN THE MIDDLE OF THE NIGHT.
OKAY, I GET IT. IT'S NEVER A GOOD IDEA TO OVERTHINK THINGS.
This Spring Go for a Layered Look
EXACTLY... BUT EVEN THAT AD THERE IS MAKING SOME TRICKY SUGGES-TIONS.
"THIS SPRING, GO FOR A LAYERED LOOK"?
...YOU CAN ADD AS MANY BEAUTIFUL LAYERS AS YOU WANT...

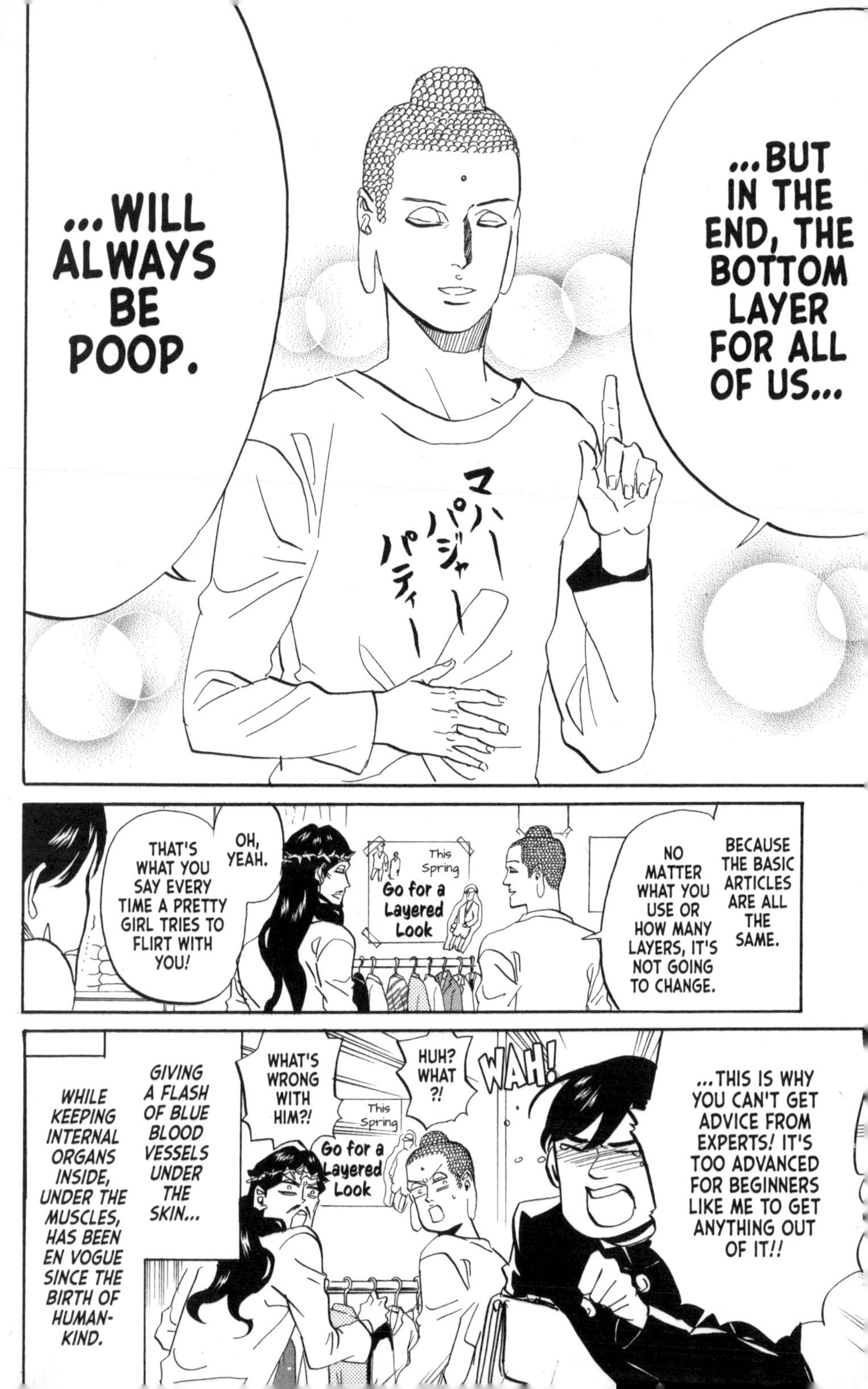
...BUT IN THE END, THE BOTTOM LAYER FOR ALL OF US...
...WILL ALWAYS BE POOP.
マハーパジャーパティー
BECAUSE THE BASIC ARTICLES ARE ALL THE SAME.
NO MATTER WHAT YOU USE OR HOW MANY LAYERS, IT'S NOT GOING TO CHANGE.
This Spring Go for a Layered Look
OH, YEAH.
THAT'S WHAT YOU SAY EVERY TIME A PRETTY GIRL TRIES TO FLIRT WITH YOU!
...THIS IS WHY YOU CAN'T GET ADVICE FROM EXPERTS! IT'S TOO ADVANCED FOR BEGINNERS LIKE ME TO GET ANYTHING OUT OF IT!!
WAH!
HUH? WHAT?!
WHAT'S WRONG WITH HIM?!
This Spring Go for a Layered Look
GIVING A FLASH OF BLUE BLOOD VESSELS UNDER THE SKIN...
WHILE KEEPING INTERNAL ORGANS INSIDE, UNDER THE MUSCLES, HAS BEEN EN VOGUE SINCE THE BIRTH OF HUMAN-KIND.

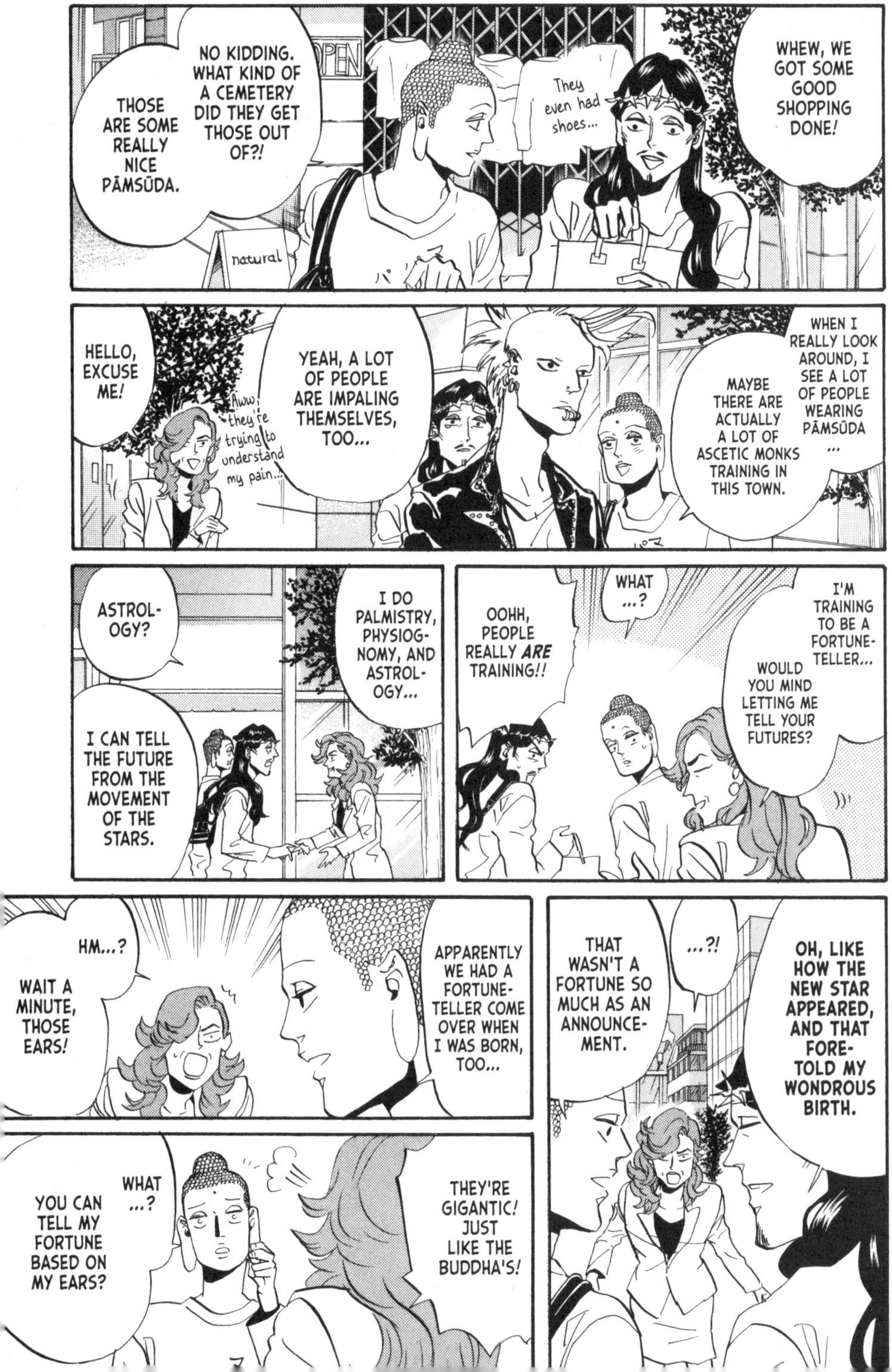
WHEW, WE GOT SOME GOOD SHOPPING DONE!
They even had shoes...
OPEN
NO KIDDING. WHAT KIND OF A CEMETERY DID THEY GET THOSE OUT OF?!
THOSE ARE SOME REALLY NICE PĀMSŪDA.
natural
WHEN I REALLY LOOK AROUND, I SEE A LOT OF PEOPLE WEARING PĀMSŪDA ...
MAYBE THERE ARE ACTUALLY A LOT OF ASCETIC MONKS TRAINING IN THIS TOWN.
YEAH, A LOT OF PEOPLE ARE IMPALING THEMSELVES, TOO...
Aww, they're trying to understand my pain...
HELLO, EXCUSE ME!
I'M TRAINING TO BE A FORTUNE-TELLER...
WOULD YOU MIND LETTING ME TELL YOUR FUTURES?
WHAT ...?
OOHH, PEOPLE REALLY *ARE* TRAINING!!
I DO PALMISTRY, PHYSIOGNOMY, AND ASTROLOGY...
ASTROLOGY?
I CAN TELL THE FUTURE FROM THE MOVEMENT OF THE STARS.
OH, LIKE HOW THE NEW STAR APPEARED, AND THAT FORETOLD MY WONDROUS BIRTH.
...?!
THAT WASN'T A FORTUNE SO MUCH AS AN ANNOUNCEMENT.
APPARENTLY WE HAD A FORTUNE-TELLER COME OVER WHEN I WAS BORN, TOO...
HM...?
WAIT A MINUTE, THOSE EARS!
THEY'RE GIGANTIC! JUST LIKE THE BUDDHA'S!
WHAT ...?
YOU CAN TELL MY FORTUNE BASED ON MY EARS?

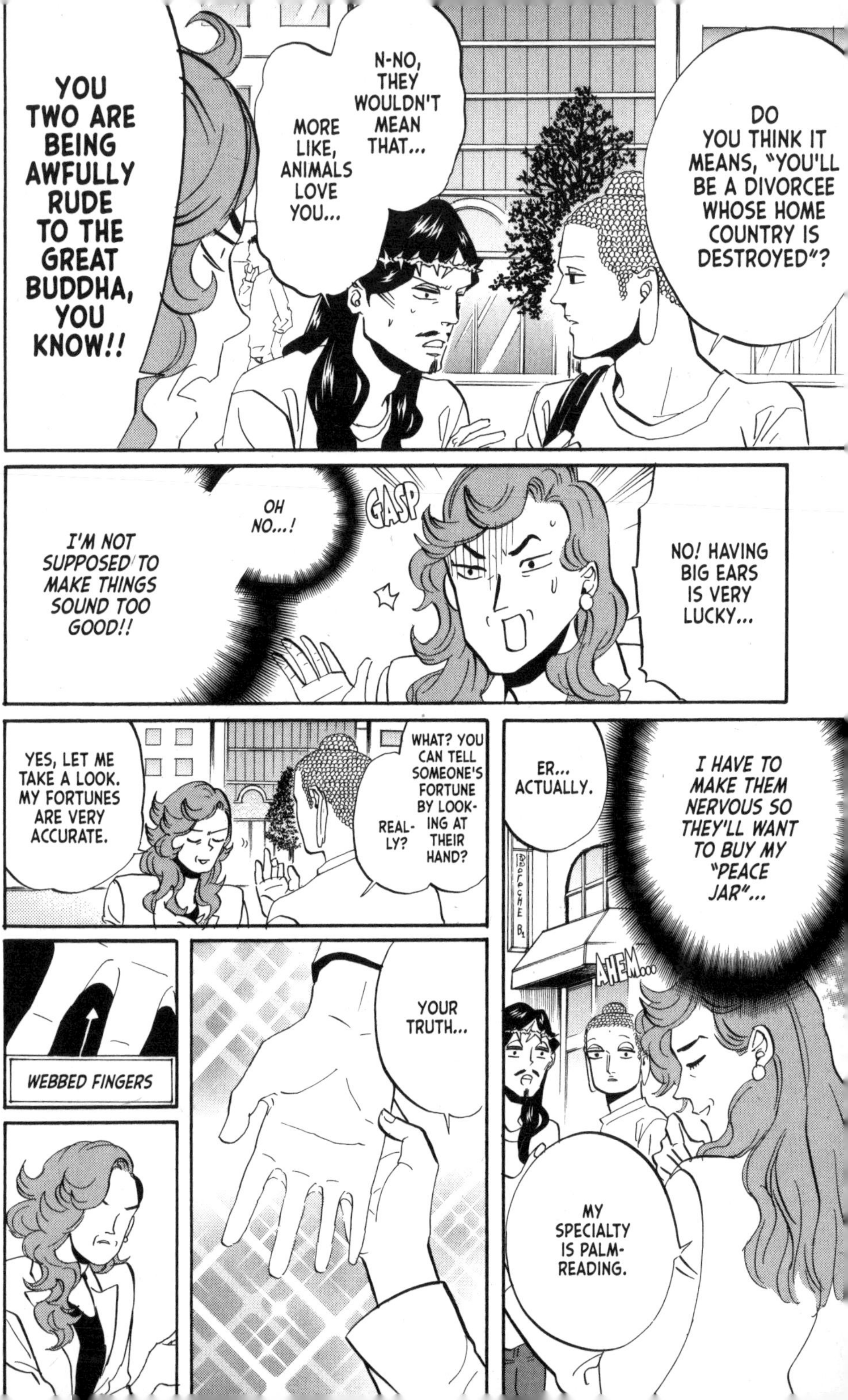
DO YOU THINK IT MEANS, "YOU'LL BE A DIVORCEE WHOSE HOME COUNTRY IS DESTROYED"?
N-NO, THEY WOULDN'T MEAN THAT...
MORE LIKE, ANIMALS LOVE YOU...
YOU TWO ARE BEING AWFULLY RUDE TO THE GREAT BUDDHA, YOU KNOW!!
NO! HAVING BIG EARS IS VERY LUCKY...
GASP
OH NO...!
I'M NOT SUPPOSED TO MAKE THINGS SOUND TOO GOOD!!
I HAVE TO MAKE THEM NERVOUS SO THEY'LL WANT TO BUY MY "PEACE JAR"...
ER... ACTUALLY.
AHEM...
MY SPECIALTY IS PALM-READING.
WHAT? YOU CAN TELL SOMEONE'S FORTUNE BY LOOKING AT THEIR HAND?
REALLY?
YES, LET ME TAKE A LOOK. MY FORTUNES ARE VERY ACCURATE.
YOUR TRUTH...
WEBBED FINGERS

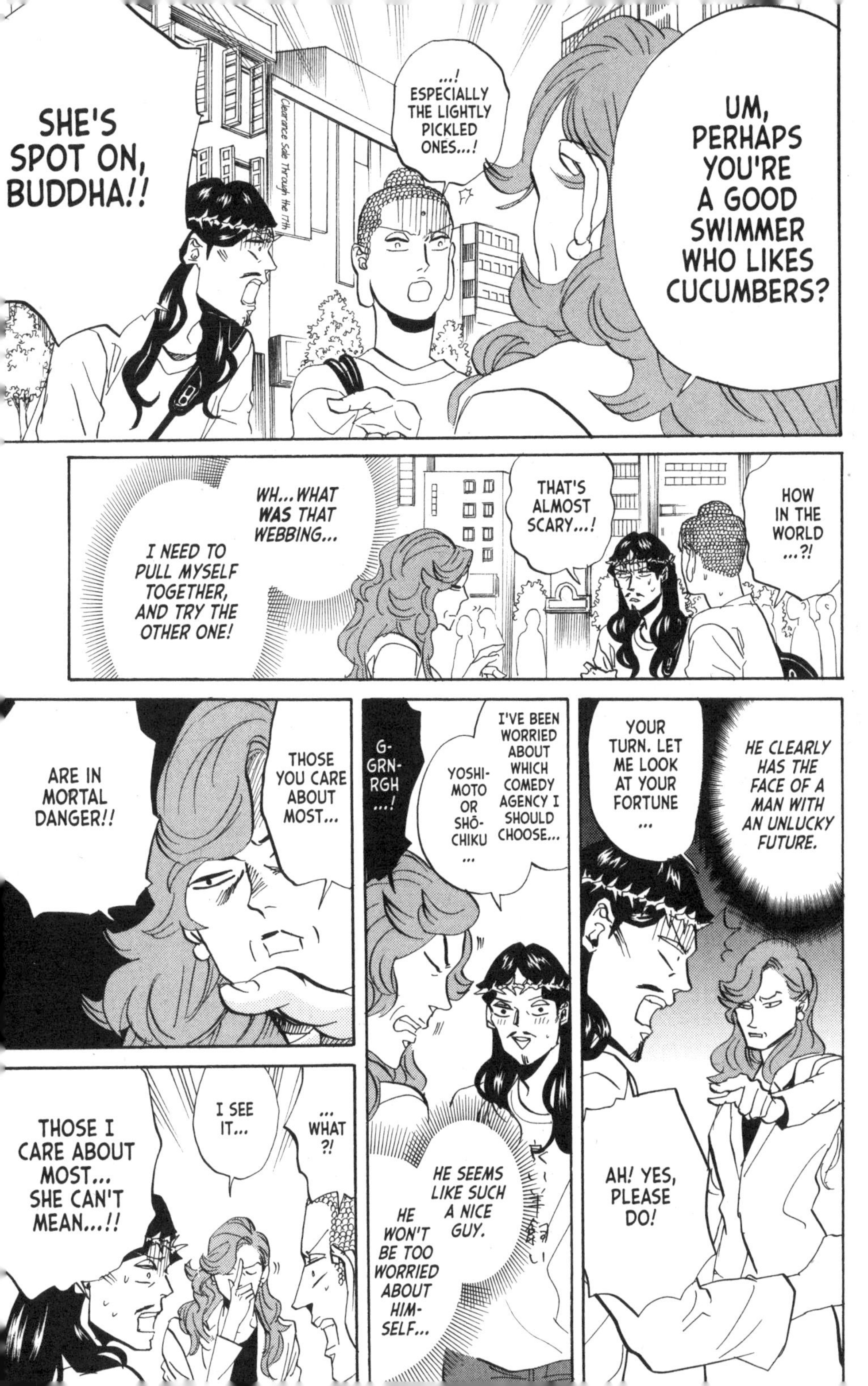
UM, PERHAPS YOU'RE A GOOD SWIMMER WHO LIKES CUCUMBERS?
...! ESPECIALLY THE LIGHTLY PICKLED ONES...!
Clearance Sale Through the 17th
SHE'S SPOT ON, BUDDHA!!
HOW IN THE WORLD ...?!
THAT'S ALMOST SCARY...!
WH...WHAT WAS THAT WEBBING...
I NEED TO PULL MYSELF TOGETHER, AND TRY THE OTHER ONE!
HE CLEARLY HAS THE FACE OF A MAN WITH AN UNLUCKY FUTURE.
YOUR TURN. LET ME LOOK AT YOUR FORTUNE ...
AH! YES, PLEASE DO!
I'VE BEEN WORRIED ABOUT WHICH COMEDY AGENCY I SHOULD CHOOSE...
YOSHIMOTO OR SHŌCHIKU ...
G-GRN-RGH ...!
HE SEEMS LIKE SUCH A NICE GUY.
HE WON'T BE TOO WORRIED ABOUT HIMSELF...
THOSE YOU CARE ABOUT MOST...
ARE IN MORTAL DANGER!!
...WHAT ?!
I SEE IT...
THOSE I CARE ABOUT MOST... SHE CAN'T MEAN...!!

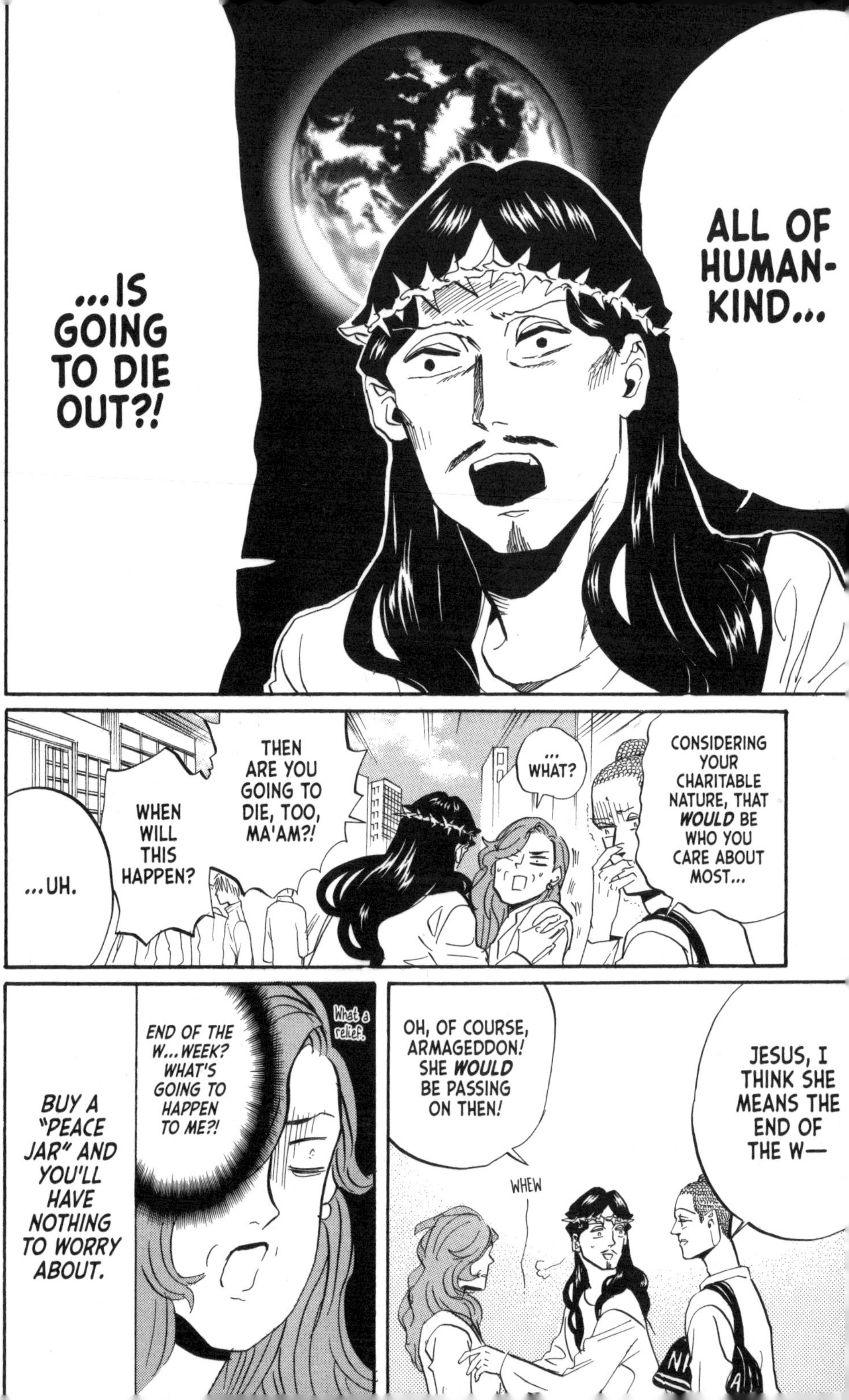
ALL OF HUMAN-KIND...
...IS GOING TO DIE OUT?!
CONSIDERING YOUR CHARITABLE NATURE, THAT WOULD BE WHO YOU CARE ABOUT MOST...
... WHAT?
THEN ARE YOU GOING TO DIE, TOO, MA'AM?!
WHEN WILL THIS HAPPEN?
...UH.
JESUS, I THINK SHE MEANS THE END OF THE W—
OH, OF COURSE, ARMAGEDDON! SHE WOULD BE PASSING ON THEN!
WHEW
What a relief.
END OF THE W...WEEK? WHAT'S GOING TO HAPPEN TO ME?!
BUY A "PEACE JAR" AND YOU'LL HAVE NOTHING TO WORRY ABOUT.

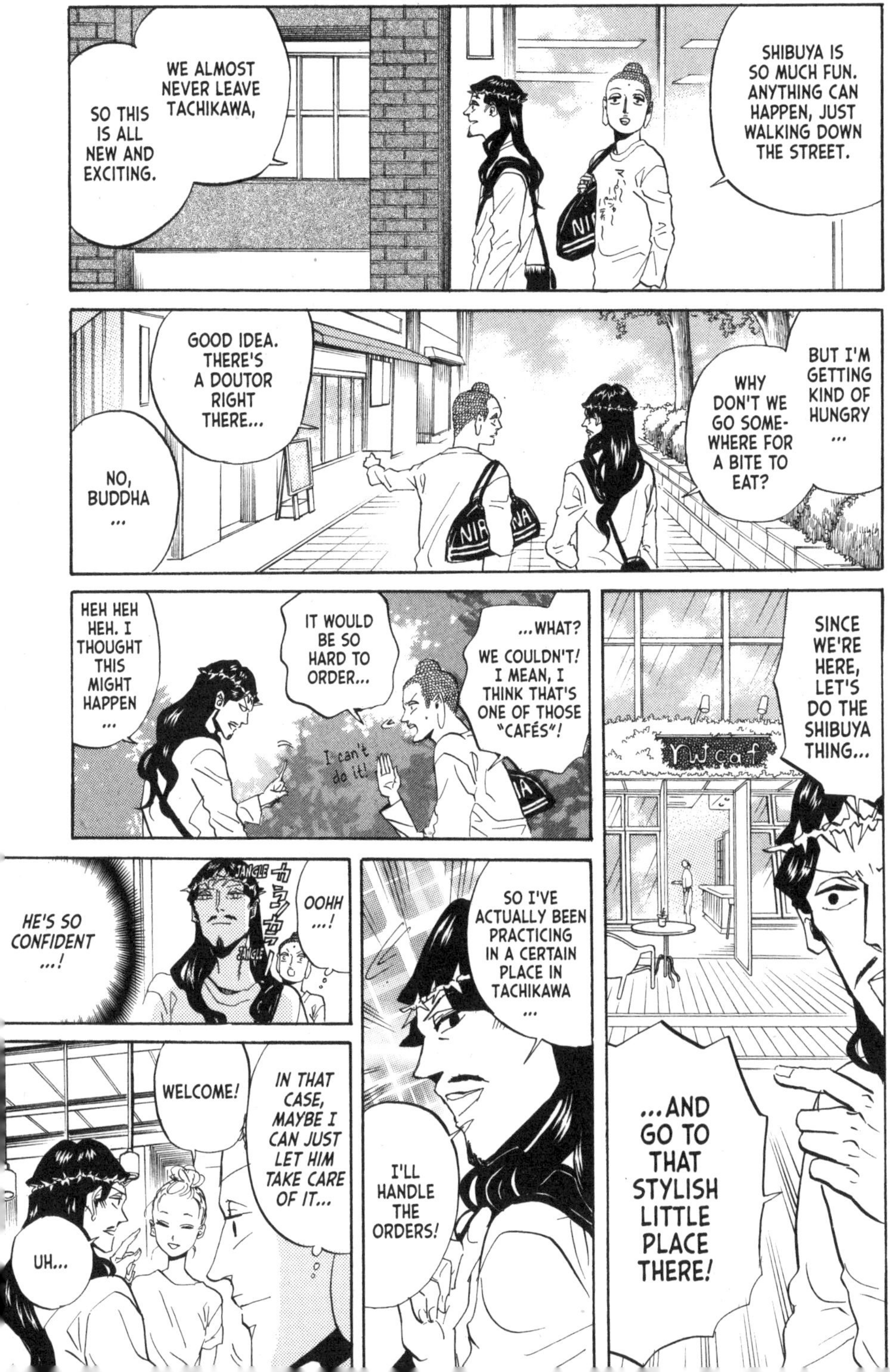
SHIBUYA IS SO MUCH FUN. ANYTHING CAN HAPPEN, JUST WALKING DOWN THE STREET.
WE ALMOST NEVER LEAVE TACHIKAWA,
SO THIS IS ALL NEW AND EXCITING.
BUT I'M GETTING KIND OF HUNGRY...
WHY DON'T WE GO SOME-WHERE FOR A BITE TO EAT?
GOOD IDEA. THERE'S A DOUTOR RIGHT THERE...
NO, BUDDHA...
SINCE WE'RE HERE, LET'S DO THE SHIBUYA THING...
...AND GO TO THAT STYLISH LITTLE PLACE THERE!
...WHAT?
WE COULDN'T! I MEAN, I THINK THAT'S ONE OF THOSE "CAFÉS"!
IT WOULD BE SO HARD TO ORDER...
I can't do it!
HEH HEH HEH. I THOUGHT THIS MIGHT HAPPEN...
SO I'VE ACTUALLY BEEN PRACTICING IN A CERTAIN PLACE IN TACHIKAWA...
I'LL HANDLE THE ORDERS!
OOHH...!
JANGLE
JANGLE
HE'S SO CONFIDENT...!
IN THAT CASE, MAYBE I CAN JUST LET HIM TAKE CARE OF IT...
WELCOME!
UH...

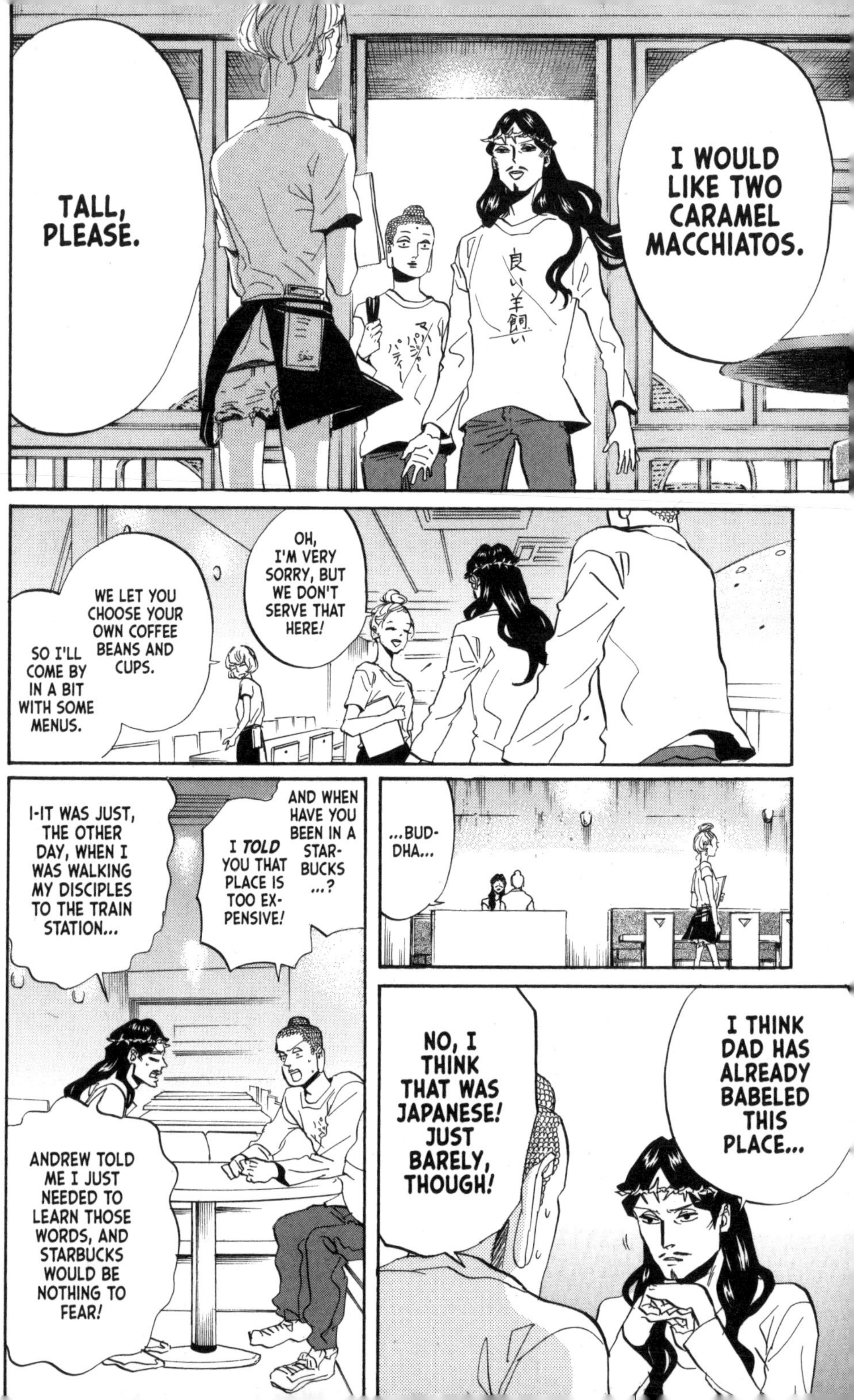
I WOULD LIKE TWO CARAMEL MACCHIATOS.
TALL, PLEASE.
良い羊飼い
OH, I'M VERY SORRY, BUT WE DON'T SERVE THAT HERE!
WE LET YOU CHOOSE YOUR OWN COFFEE BEANS AND CUPS.
SO I'LL COME BY IN A BIT WITH SOME MENUS.
...BUD-DHA...
I THINK DAD HAS ALREADY BABELED THIS PLACE...
NO, I THINK THAT WAS JAPANESE! JUST BARELY, THOUGH!
AND WHEN HAVE YOU BEEN IN A STAR-BUCKS ...?
I *TOLD* YOU THAT PLACE IS TOO EX-PENSIVE!
I-IT WAS JUST, THE OTHER DAY, WHEN I WAS WALKING MY DISCIPLES TO THE TRAIN STATION...
ANDREW TOLD ME I JUST NEEDED TO LEARN THOSE WORDS, AND STARBUCKS WOULD BE NOTHING TO FEAR!

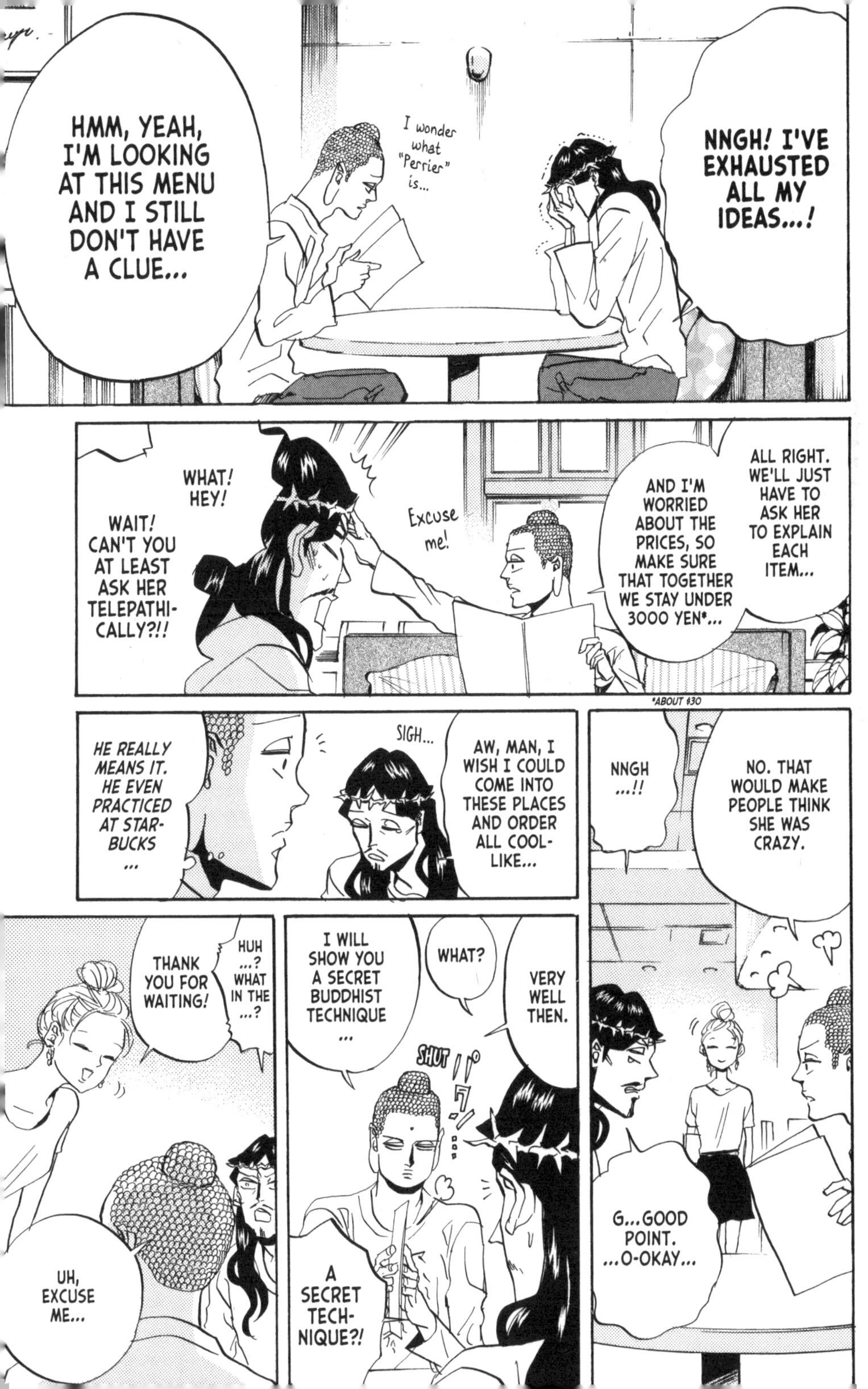
NNGH! I'VE EXHAUSTED ALL MY IDEAS...!
I wonder what "Perrier" is...
HMM, YEAH, I'M LOOKING AT THIS MENU AND I STILL DON'T HAVE A CLUE...
ALL RIGHT. WE'LL JUST HAVE TO ASK HER TO EXPLAIN EACH ITEM...
AND I'M WORRIED ABOUT THE PRICES, SO MAKE SURE THAT TOGETHER WE STAY UNDER 3000 YEN*...
Excuse me!
WHAT! HEY!
WAIT! CAN'T YOU AT LEAST ASK HER TELEPATHICALLY?!!
*ABOUT $30
NO. THAT WOULD MAKE PEOPLE THINK SHE WAS CRAZY.
NNGH ...!!
G...GOOD POINT. ...O-OKAY...
SIGH...
AW, MAN, I WISH I COULD COME INTO THESE PLACES AND ORDER ALL COOL-LIKE...
HE REALLY MEANS IT. HE EVEN PRACTICED AT STARBUCKS ...
VERY WELL THEN.
WHAT?
I WILL SHOW YOU A SECRET BUDDHIST TECHNIQUE ...
SHUT
A SECRET TECHNIQUE?!
HUH ...? WHAT IN THE ...?
THANK YOU FOR WAITING!
UH, EXCUSE ME...

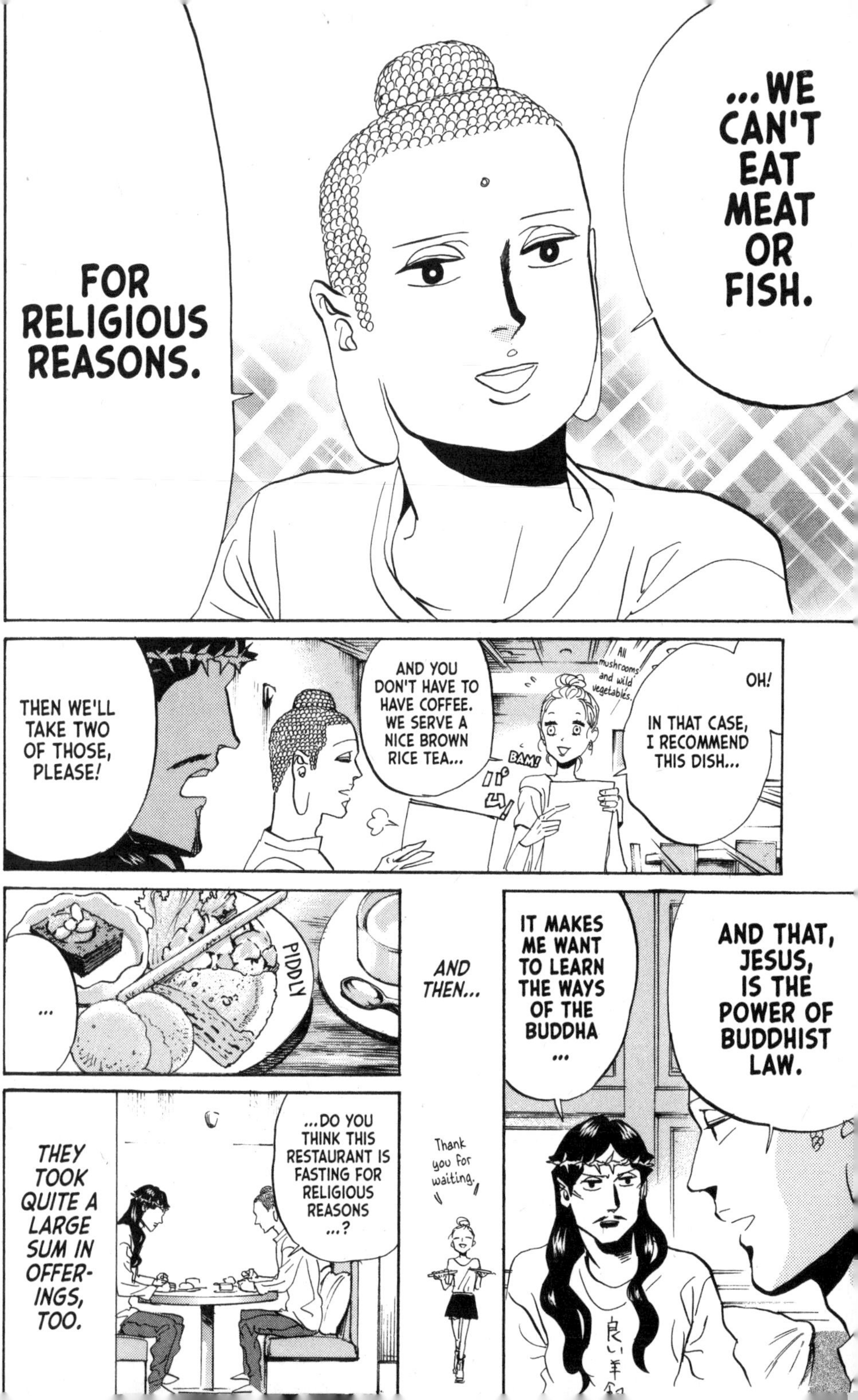
...WE CAN'T EAT MEAT OR FISH.
FOR RELIGIOUS REASONS.
All mushrooms and wild vegetables.
OH! IN THAT CASE, I RECOMMEND THIS DISH...
BAM!
AND YOU DON'T HAVE TO HAVE COFFEE. WE SERVE A NICE BROWN RICE TEA...
THEN WE'LL TAKE TWO OF THOSE, PLEASE!
AND THAT, JESUS, IS THE POWER OF BUDDHIST LAW.
IT MAKES ME WANT TO LEARN THE WAYS OF THE BUDDHA ...
AND THEN...
PIDDLY
...
Thank you for waiting.
...DO YOU THINK THIS RESTAURANT IS FASTING FOR RELIGIOUS REASONS ...?
THEY TOOK QUITE A LARGE SUM IN OFFERINGS, TOO.

A short break at the
Tachikawa Doutor before
returning home.

CHAPTER 36 TRANSLATION NOTES

Hachikō, page 123
This famous statue in Shibuya is dedicated to the loyal dog Hachikō, who came to the train station to wait for his master's arrival every day. When his master passed away while at work, and failed to arrive at the station, Hachikō waited, and returned to the station every day at the same time for nine years until his own death. In honor of his faithfulness, he has been immortalized as a bronze statue, which has become a popular spot to meet up with friends for a day in Shibuya.

Mahaprajapati, page 124
This is the name of Siddhartha's maternal aunt, who raised him after Maya (his mother) died. She was also the first Buddhist nun.

The tower of worldly desires +1, page 125
As previously mentioned (see volume 2), the number of worldly desires that exist in the world is 108. Add one to that, and you get 109, which is a number proudly emblazoned on a prominent department store in Shibuya. Jesus's guess is that maybe the note is referring to a different Japanese retail chain, Marui, whose name is written with a circle and a vertical line, followed by another circle and vertical line, represented in their website url with numbers: 0101.

Trading clothes, page 128
After Siddhartha Gautama renounced the world and fled the palace, one of the first things he did was trade away his fine silk robes to a beggar in exchange for the beggar's simple ensemble.

The carpenter's boy, page 128
On a visit back to his hometown, Jesus taught in the synagogue, but the people there wouldn't listen to him, as it stated in Mark 6: Is not this the carpenter, the son of Mary, the brother of James, and Joses, and of Juda, and Simon? And are not his sisters here with us? And they were offended at him. To this Jesus replied, "A prophet is not without honour, but in his own country, and among his own kin, and in his own house."

A good swimmer who likes cucumbers, page 133
Cucumbers are the favorite food of a Japanese folkloric creature known as the kappa. Kappa look something like duck-billed monkeys, and are often depicted with webbed hands and feet because they live in rivers.

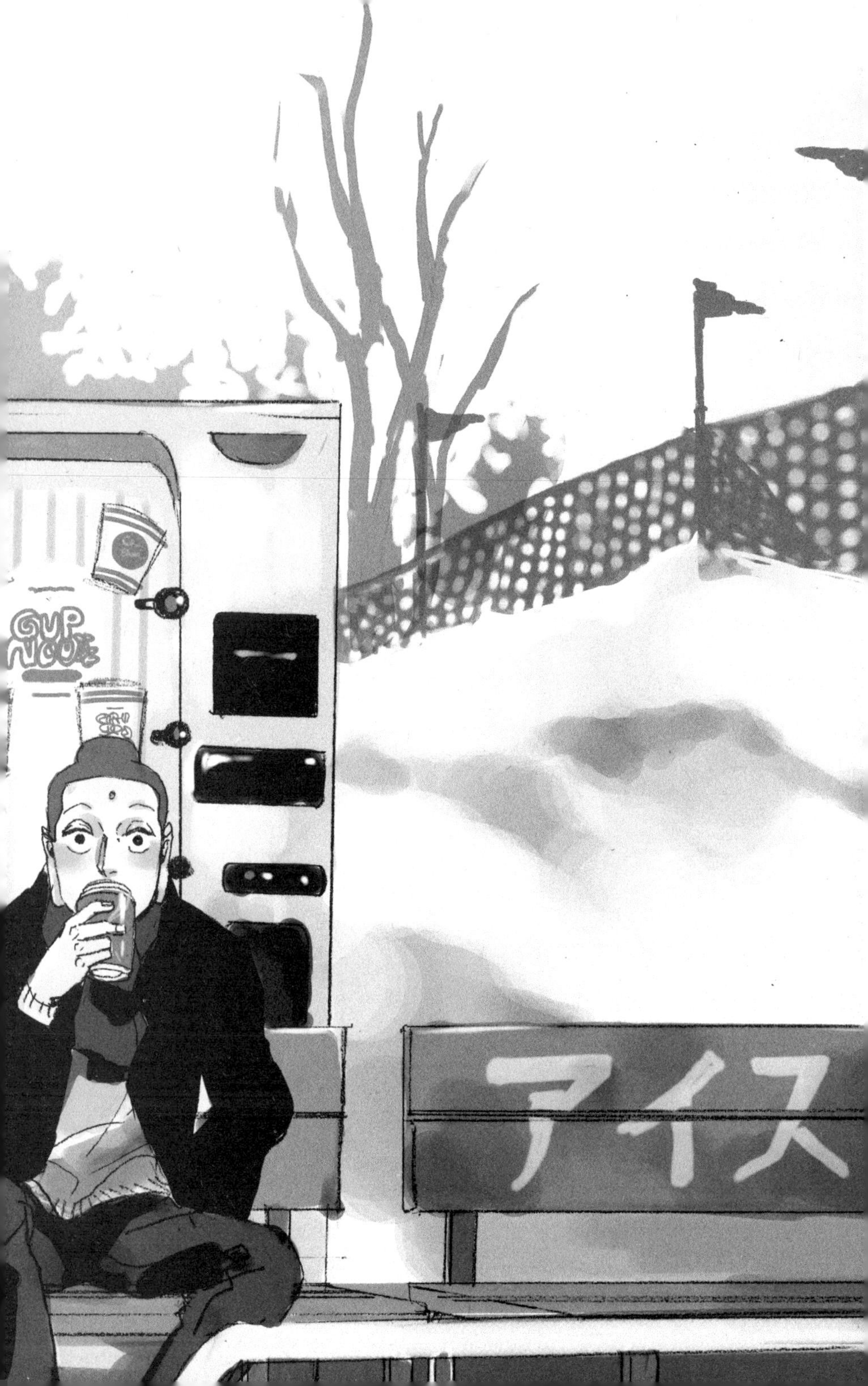
アイス

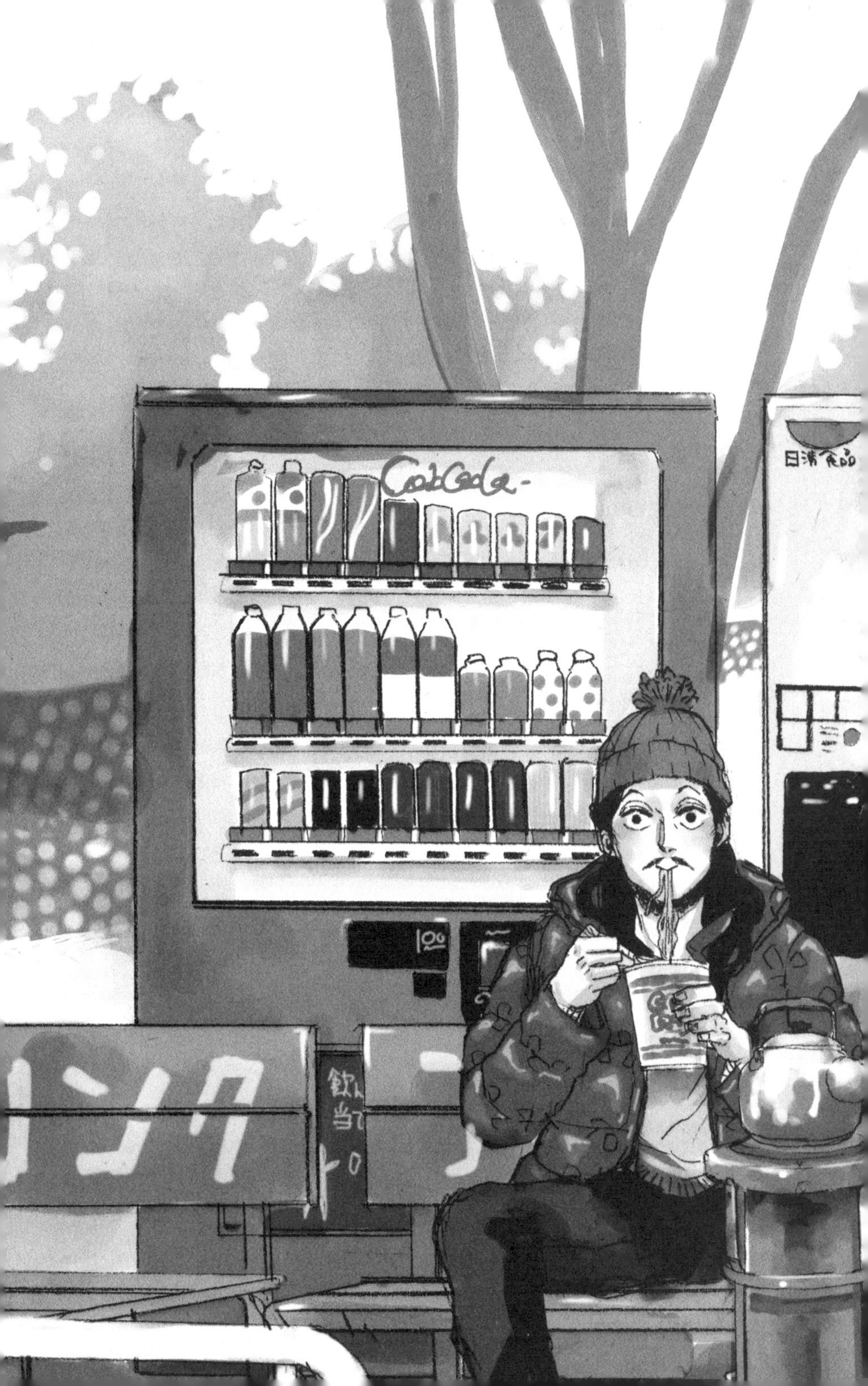
日清食品

SAINT☆YOUNG MEN

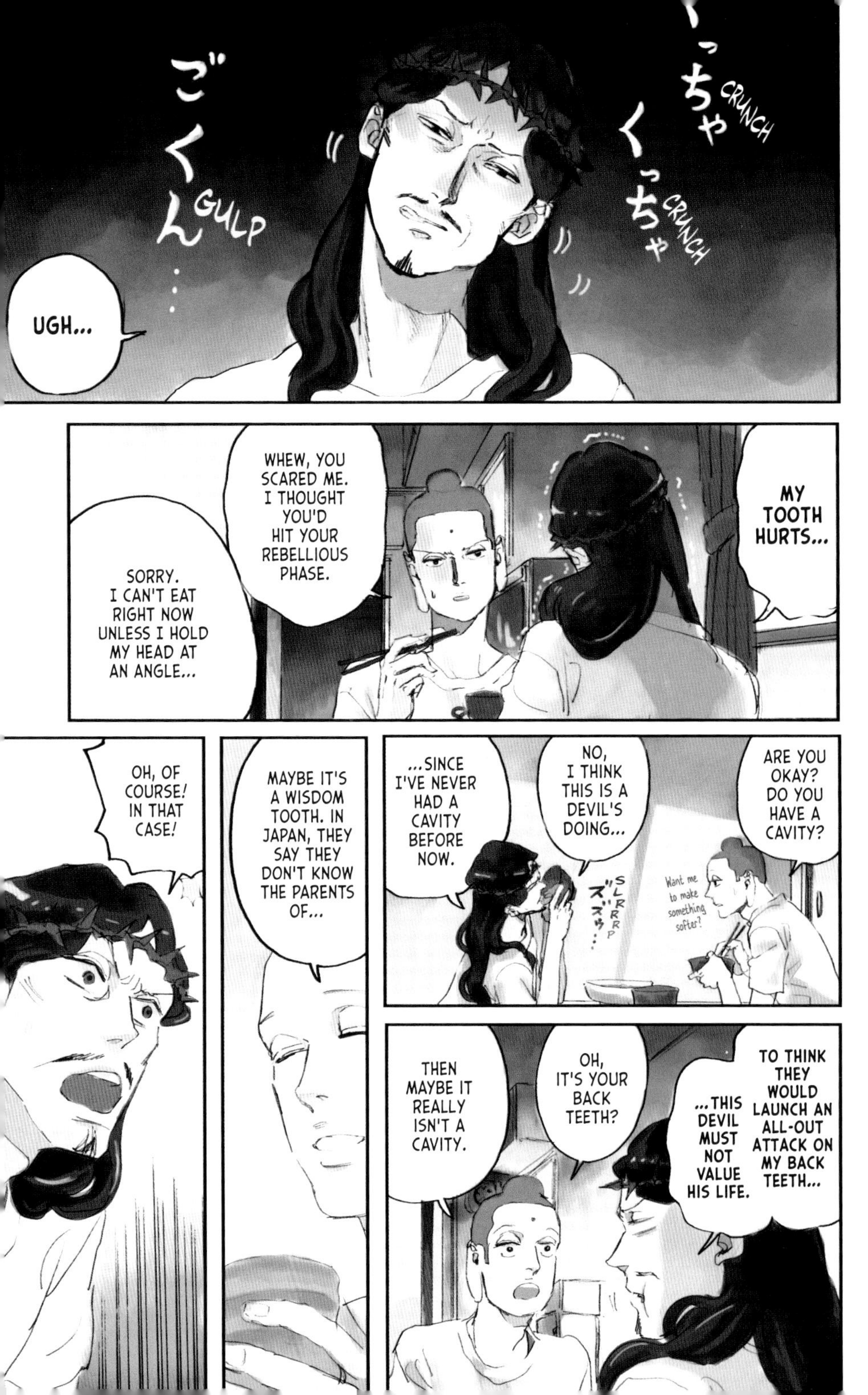

くっちゃ CRUNCH
くっちゃ CRUNCH
ごくん GULP
UGH...
MY TOOTH HURTS...
WHEW, YOU SCARED ME. I THOUGHT YOU'D HIT YOUR REBELLIOUS PHASE.
SORRY. I CAN'T EAT RIGHT NOW UNLESS I HOLD MY HEAD AT AN ANGLE...
ARE YOU OKAY? DO YOU HAVE A CAVITY?
Want me to make something softer?
NO, I THINK THIS IS A DEVIL'S DOING...
ズズッ... SLRRRP
...SINCE I'VE NEVER HAD A CAVITY BEFORE NOW.
TO THINK THEY WOULD LAUNCH AN ALL-OUT ATTACK ON MY BACK TEETH...
...THIS DEVIL MUST NOT VALUE HIS LIFE.
OH, IT'S YOUR BACK TEETH?
THEN MAYBE IT REALLY ISN'T A CAVITY.
MAYBE IT'S A WISDOM TOOTH. IN JAPAN, THEY SAY THEY DON'T KNOW THE PARENTS OF...
OH, OF COURSE! IN THAT CASE!

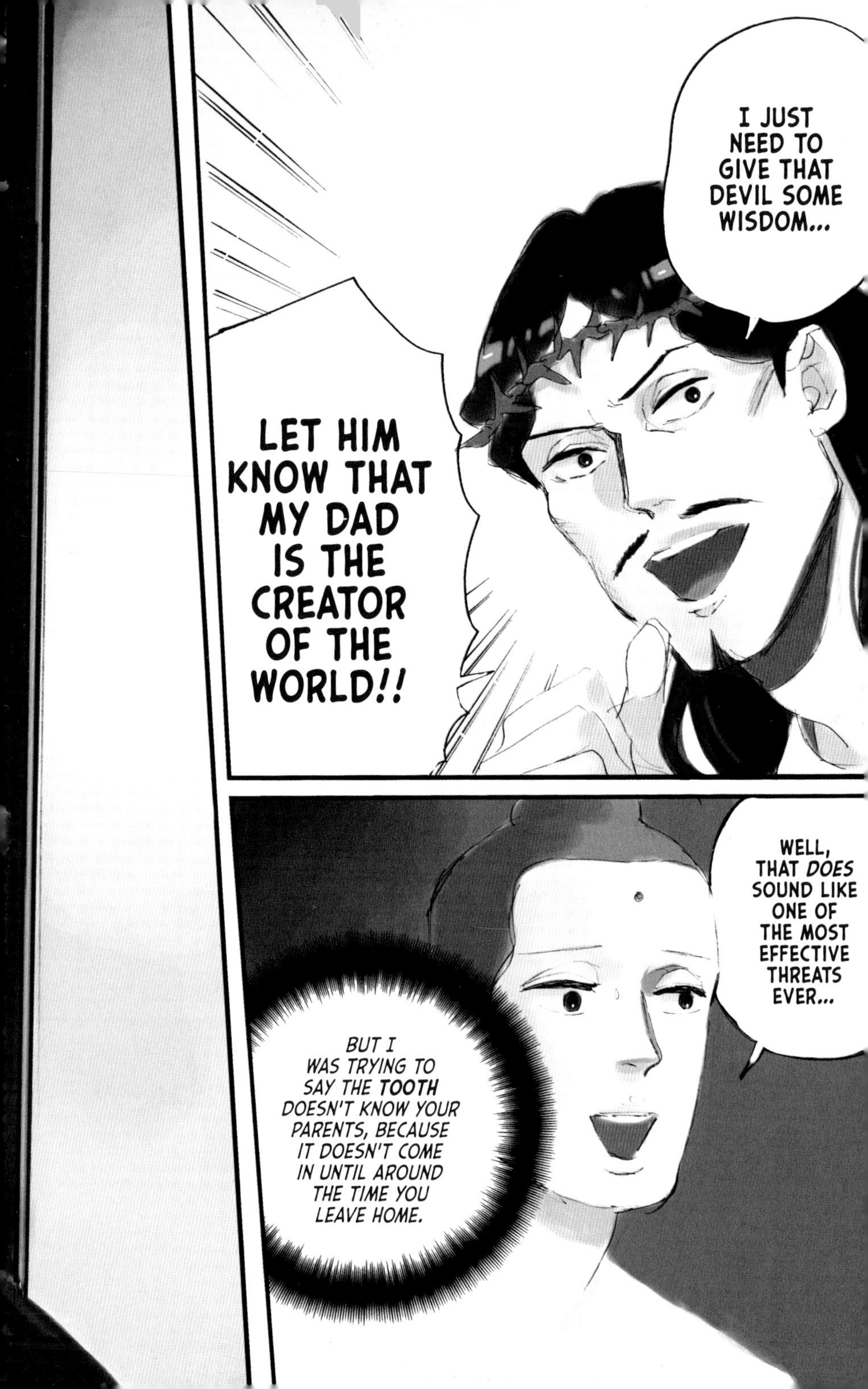
I JUST NEED TO GIVE THAT DEVIL SOME WISDOM...
LET HIM KNOW THAT MY DAD IS THE CREATOR OF THE WORLD!!
WELL, THAT *DOES* SOUND LIKE ONE OF THE MOST EFFECTIVE THREATS EVER...
BUT I WAS TRYING TO SAY THE **TOOTH** DOESN'T KNOW YOUR PARENTS, BECAUSE IT DOESN'T COME IN UNTIL AROUND THE TIME YOU LEAVE HOME.

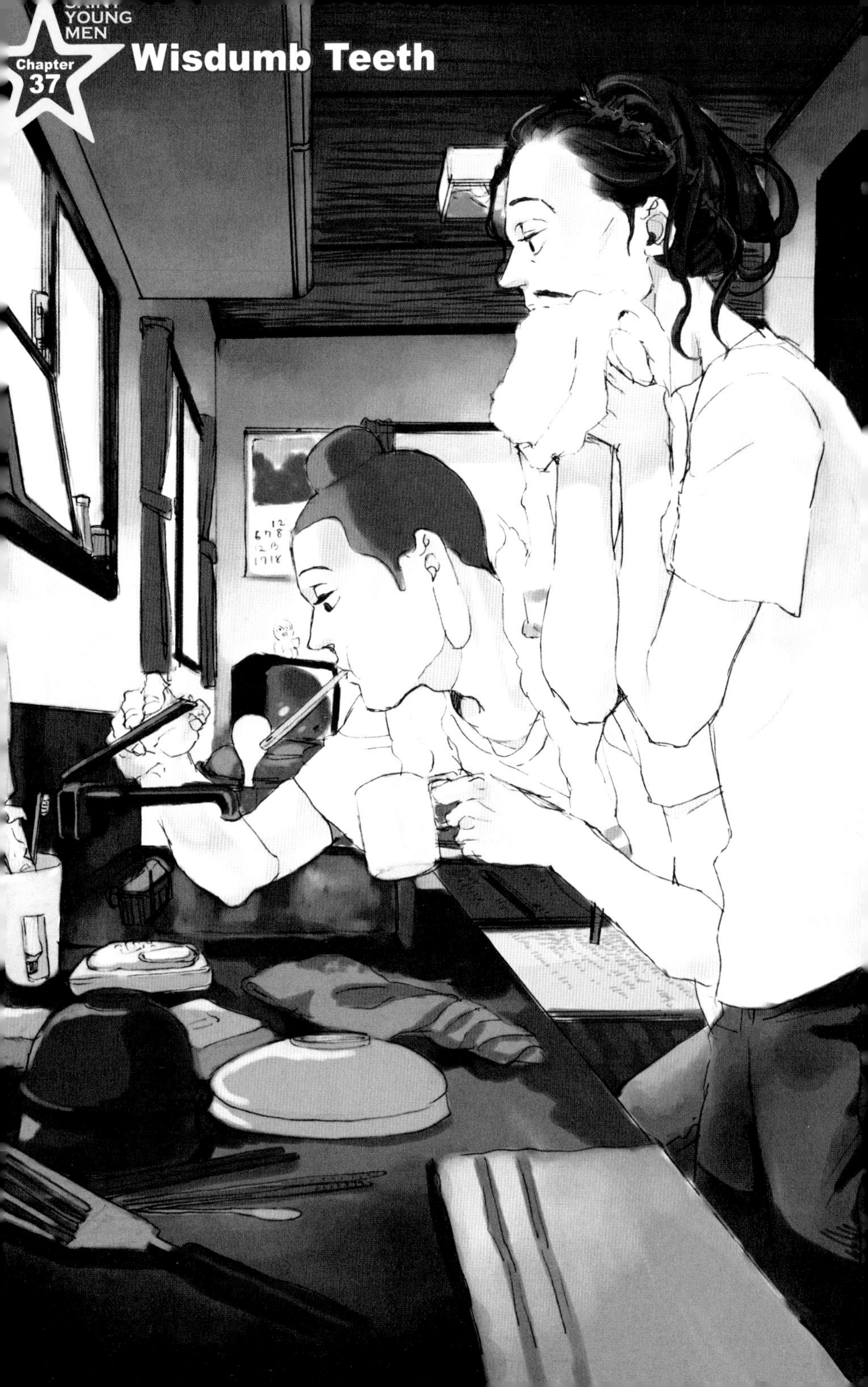
SAINT YOUNG MEN
Chapter 37
Wisdumb Teeth

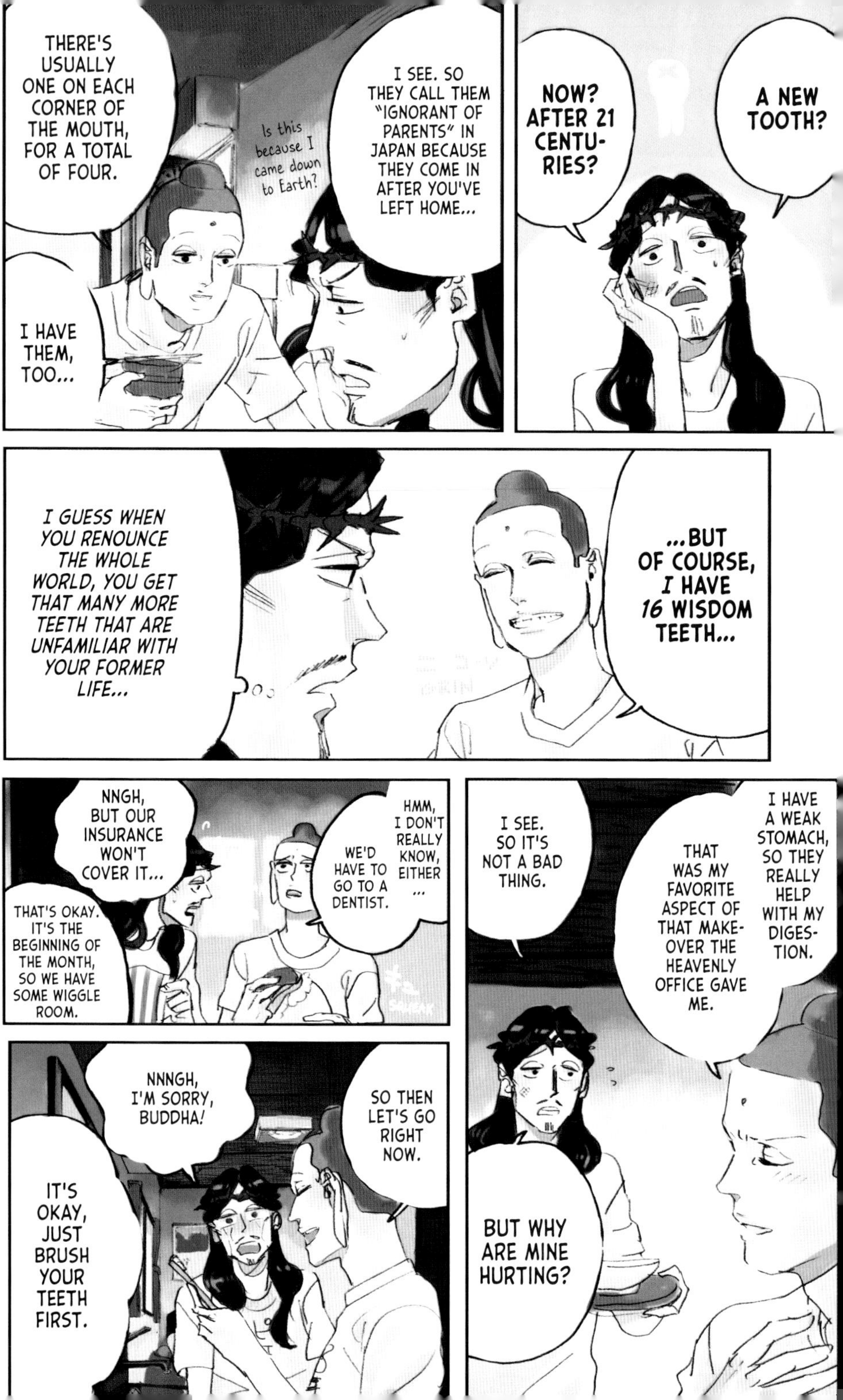
A NEW TOOTH?
NOW? AFTER 21 CENTURIES?
I SEE. SO THEY CALL THEM "IGNORANT OF PARENTS" IN JAPAN BECAUSE THEY COME IN AFTER YOU'VE LEFT HOME...
Is this because I came down to Earth?
THERE'S USUALLY ONE ON EACH CORNER OF THE MOUTH, FOR A TOTAL OF FOUR.
I HAVE THEM, TOO...
...BUT OF COURSE, I HAVE 16 WISDOM TEETH...
I GUESS WHEN YOU RENOUNCE THE WHOLE WORLD, YOU GET THAT MANY MORE TEETH THAT ARE UNFAMILIAR WITH YOUR FORMER LIFE...
I HAVE A WEAK STOMACH, SO THEY REALLY HELP WITH MY DIGESTION.
THAT WAS MY FAVORITE ASPECT OF THAT MAKEOVER THE HEAVENLY OFFICE GAVE ME.
I SEE. SO IT'S NOT A BAD THING.
BUT WHY ARE MINE HURTING?
HMM, I DON'T REALLY KNOW, EITHER...
WE'D HAVE TO GO TO A DENTIST.
NNGH, BUT OUR INSURANCE WON'T COVER IT...
THAT'S OKAY. IT'S THE BEGINNING OF THE MONTH, SO WE HAVE SOME WIGGLE ROOM.
SO THEN LET'S GO RIGHT NOW.
NNNGH, I'M SORRY, BUDDHA!
IT'S OKAY, JUST BRUSH YOUR TEETH FIRST.

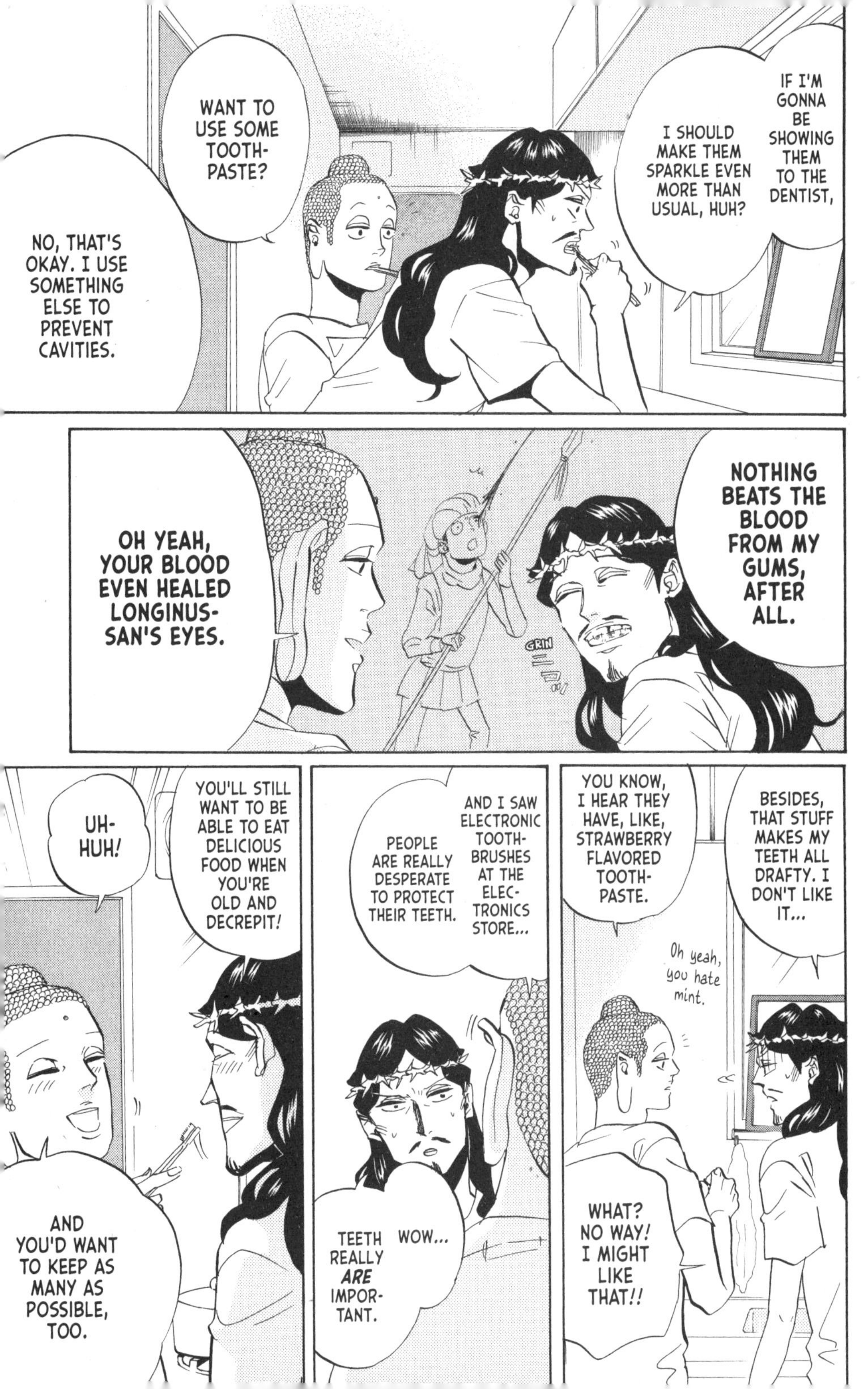
IF I'M GONNA BE SHOWING THEM TO THE DENTIST,
I SHOULD MAKE THEM SPARKLE EVEN MORE THAN USUAL, HUH?
WANT TO USE SOME TOOTHPASTE?
NO, THAT'S OKAY. I USE SOMETHING ELSE TO PREVENT CAVITIES.
NOTHING BEATS THE BLOOD FROM MY GUMS, AFTER ALL.
GRIN
OH YEAH, YOUR BLOOD EVEN HEALED LONGINUS-SAN'S EYES.
BESIDES, THAT STUFF MAKES MY TEETH ALL DRAFTY. I DON'T LIKE IT...
YOU KNOW, I HEAR THEY HAVE, LIKE, STRAWBERRY FLAVORED TOOTHPASTE.
Oh yeah, you hate mint.
WHAT? NO WAY! I MIGHT LIKE THAT!!
AND I SAW ELECTRONIC TOOTHBRUSHES AT THE ELECTRONICS STORE...
PEOPLE ARE REALLY DESPERATE TO PROTECT THEIR TEETH.
WOW...
TEETH REALLY *ARE* IMPORTANT.
YOU'LL STILL WANT TO BE ABLE TO EAT DELICIOUS FOOD WHEN YOU'RE OLD AND DECREPIT!
UH-HUH!
AND YOU'D WANT TO KEEP AS MANY AS POSSIBLE, TOO.

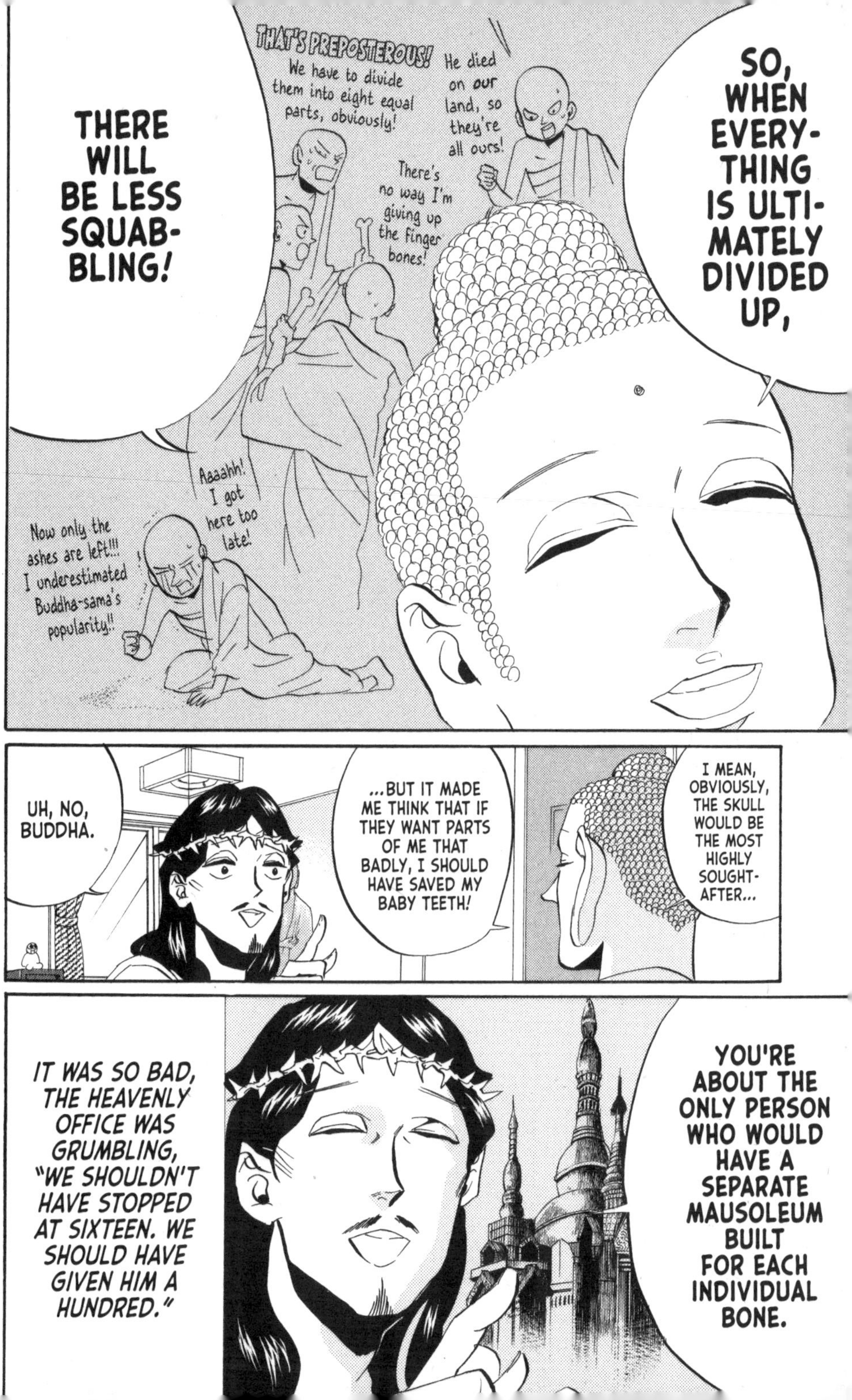
SO, WHEN EVERYTHING IS ULTIMATELY DIVIDED UP,
THERE WILL BE LESS SQUABBLING!
He died on our land, so they're all ours!
THAT'S PREPOSTEROUS!
We have to divide them into eight equal parts, obviously!
There's no way I'm giving up the finger bones!
Aaaahh! I got here too late!
Now only the ashes are left!!! I underestimated Buddha-sama's popularity!!
I MEAN, OBVIOUSLY, THE SKULL WOULD BE THE MOST HIGHLY SOUGHT-AFTER...
UH, NO, BUDDHA.
...BUT IT MADE ME THINK THAT IF THEY WANT PARTS OF ME THAT BADLY, I SHOULD HAVE SAVED MY BABY TEETH!
YOU'RE ABOUT THE ONLY PERSON WHO WOULD HAVE A SEPARATE MAUSOLEUM BUILT FOR EACH INDIVIDUAL BONE.
IT WAS SO BAD, THE HEAVENLY OFFICE WAS GRUMBLING, "WE SHOULDN'T HAVE STOPPED AT SIXTEEN. WE SHOULD HAVE GIVEN HIM A HUNDRED."

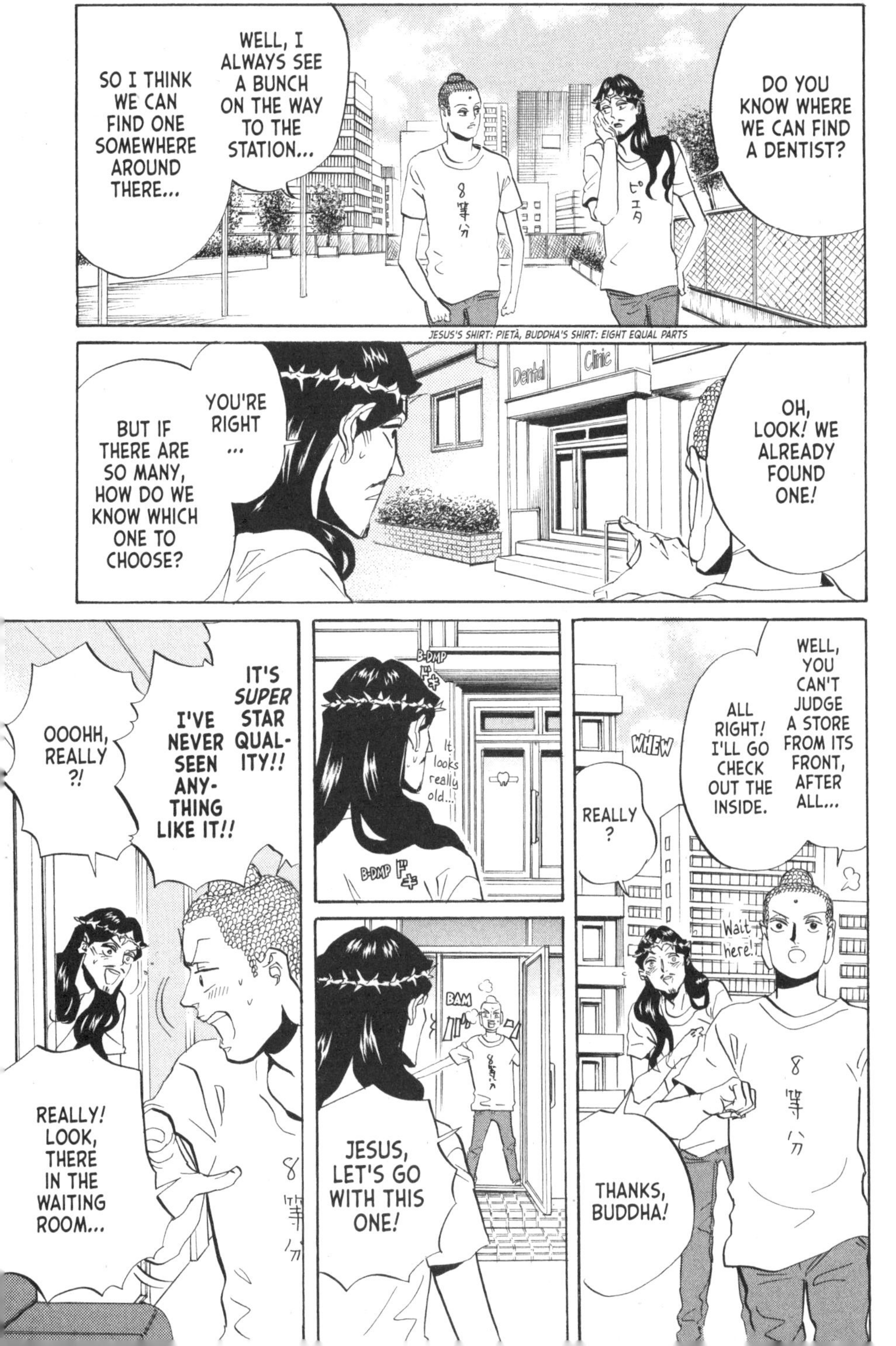
DO YOU KNOW WHERE WE CAN FIND A DENTIST?
WELL, I ALWAYS SEE A BUNCH ON THE WAY TO THE STATION...
SO I THINK WE CAN FIND ONE SOMEWHERE AROUND THERE...
ピエタ
8等分
JESUS'S SHIRT: PIETÀ, BUDDHA'S SHIRT: EIGHT EQUAL PARTS
Dental Clinic
OH, LOOK! WE ALREADY FOUND ONE!
YOU'RE RIGHT ...
BUT IF THERE ARE SO MANY, HOW DO WE KNOW WHICH ONE TO CHOOSE?
WELL, YOU CAN'T JUDGE A STORE FROM ITS FRONT, AFTER ALL...
ALL RIGHT! I'LL GO CHECK OUT THE INSIDE.
WHEW
REALLY?
Wait here!
THANKS, BUDDHA!
B-DMP ドキ
It looks really old...
B-DMP ドキ
BAM
JESUS, LET'S GO WITH THIS ONE!
IT'S SUPER STAR QUALITY!!
I'VE NEVER SEEN ANYTHING LIKE IT!!
OOOHH, REALLY?!
REALLY! LOOK, THERE IN THE WAITING ROOM...

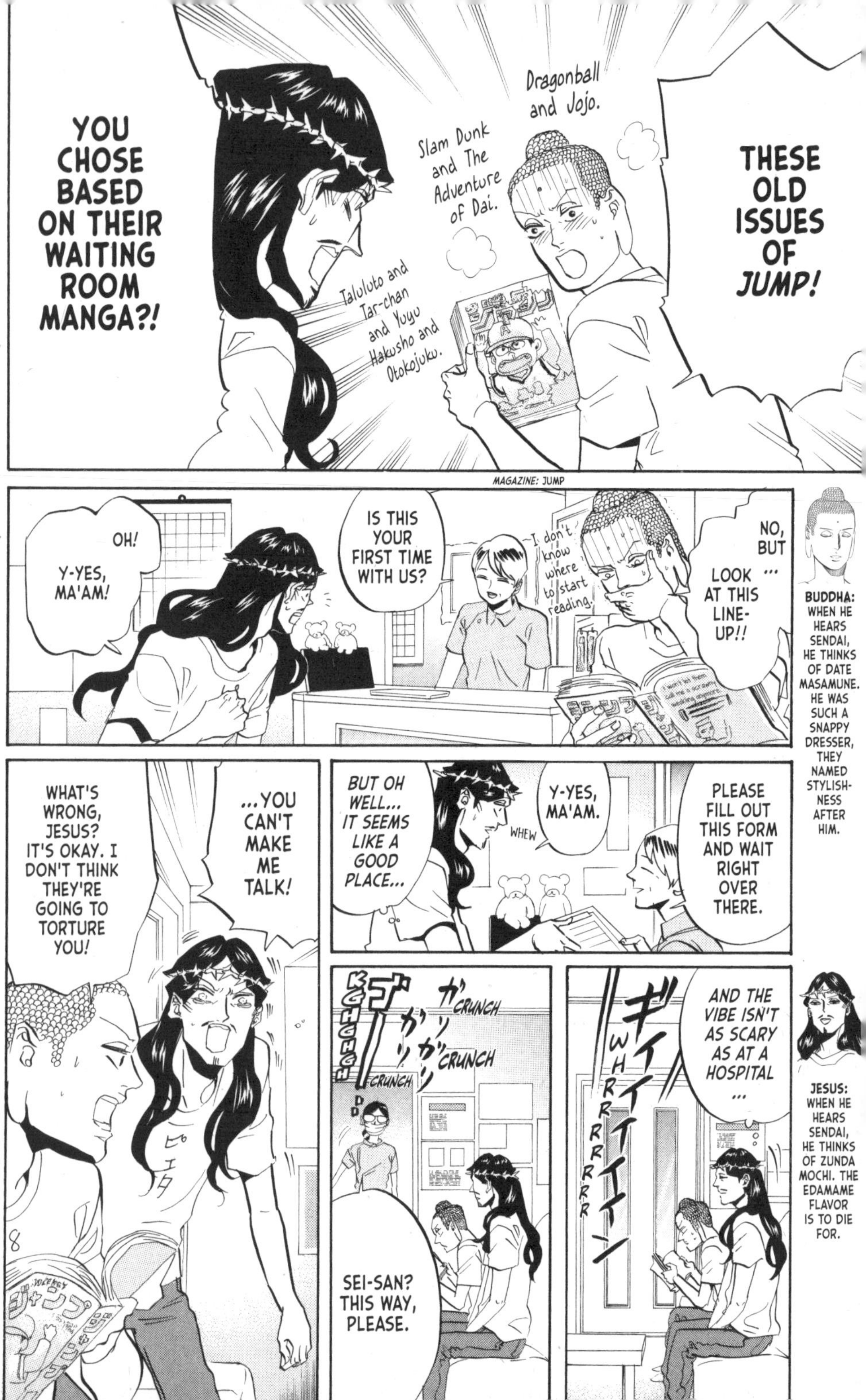
THESE OLD ISSUES OF JUMP!
Dragonball and Jojo.
Slam Dunk and The Adventure of Dai.
Taluluto and Tar-chan and Yuyu Hakusho and Otokojuku.
YOU CHOSE BASED ON THEIR WAITING ROOM MANGA?!
MAGAZINE: JUMP
NO, BUT ... LOOK AT THIS LINE-UP!!
I don't know where to start reading.
IS THIS YOUR FIRST TIME WITH US?
OH!
Y-YES, MA'AM!
BUDDHA: WHEN HE HEARS SENDAI, HE THINKS OF DATE MASAMUNE. HE WAS SUCH A SNAPPY DRESSER, THEY NAMED STYLISH-NESS AFTER HIM.
PLEASE FILL OUT THIS FORM AND WAIT RIGHT OVER THERE.
Y-YES, MA'AM.
WHEW
BUT OH WELL... IT SEEMS LIKE A GOOD PLACE...
AND THE VIBE ISN'T AS SCARY AS AT A HOSPITAL ...
WHRRRRRRR
CRUNCH
CRUNCH
KGHGHGH
CRUNCH
SEI-SAN? THIS WAY, PLEASE.
...YOU CAN'T MAKE ME TALK!
WHAT'S WRONG, JESUS? IT'S OKAY. I DON'T THINK THEY'RE GOING TO TORTURE YOU!
JESUS: WHEN HE HEARS SENDAI, HE THINKS OF ZUNDA MOCHI. THE EDAMAME FLAVOR IS TO DIE FOR.

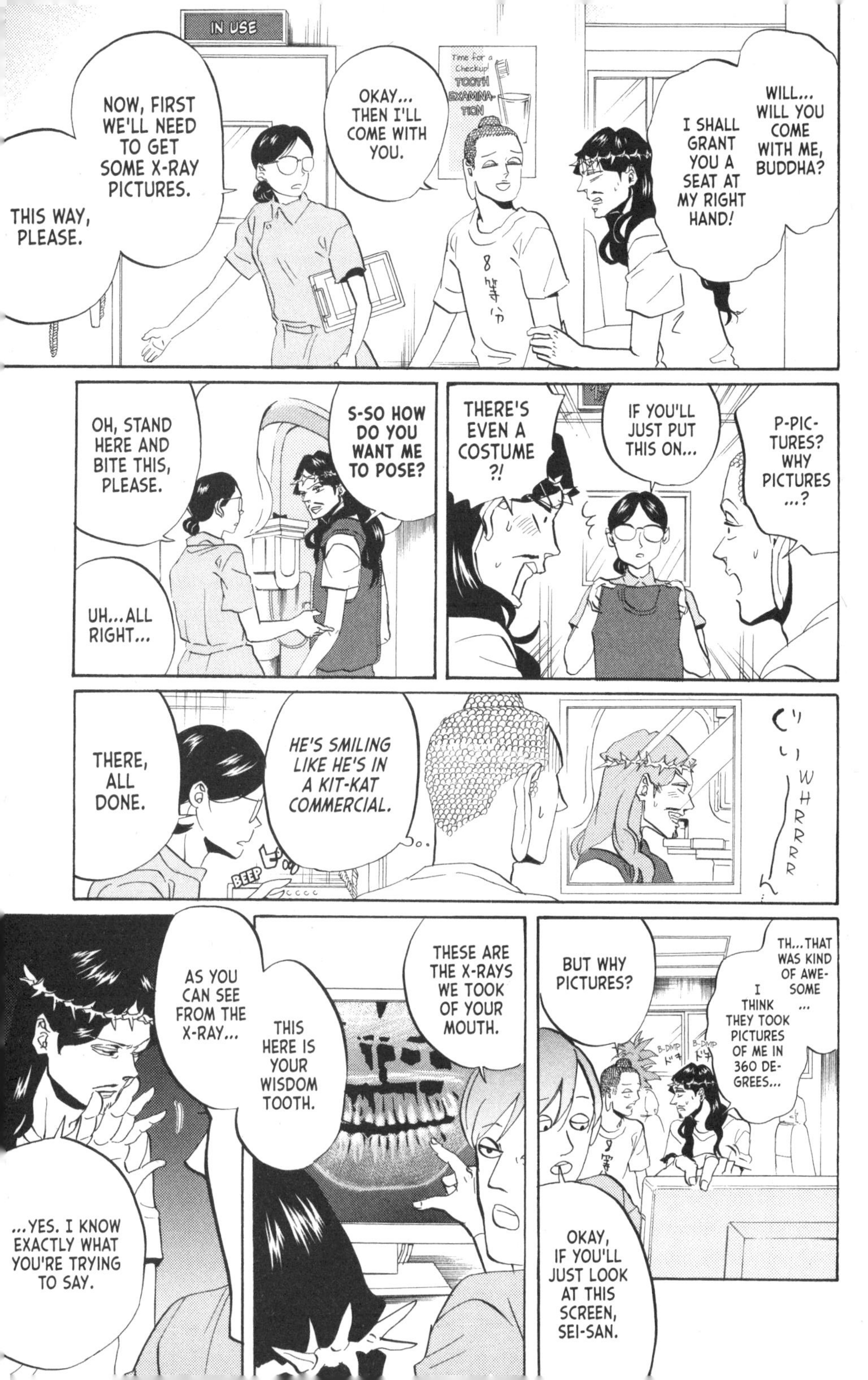
IN USE
Time for a Checkup! TOOTH EXAMINATION
WILL... WILL YOU COME WITH ME, BUDDHA?
I SHALL GRANT YOU A SEAT AT MY RIGHT HAND!
OKAY... THEN I'LL COME WITH YOU.
NOW, FIRST WE'LL NEED TO GET SOME X-RAY PICTURES.
THIS WAY, PLEASE.
P-PICTURES? WHY PICTURES...?
IF YOU'LL JUST PUT THIS ON...
THERE'S EVEN A COSTUME?!
S-SO HOW DO YOU WANT ME TO POSE?
OH, STAND HERE AND BITE THIS, PLEASE.
UH...ALL RIGHT...
WHHRRRR
HE'S SMILING LIKE HE'S IN A KIT-KAT COMMERCIAL.
BEEP
THERE, ALL DONE.
TH...THAT WAS KIND OF AWESOME...
I THINK THEY TOOK PICTURES OF ME IN 360 DEGREES...
B-DMP
B-DMP
BUT WHY PICTURES?
OKAY, IF YOU'LL JUST LOOK AT THIS SCREEN, SEI-SAN.
THESE ARE THE X-RAYS WE TOOK OF YOUR MOUTH.
THIS HERE IS YOUR WISDOM TOOTH.
AS YOU CAN SEE FROM THE X-RAY...
...YES. I KNOW EXACTLY WHAT YOU'RE TRYING TO SAY.

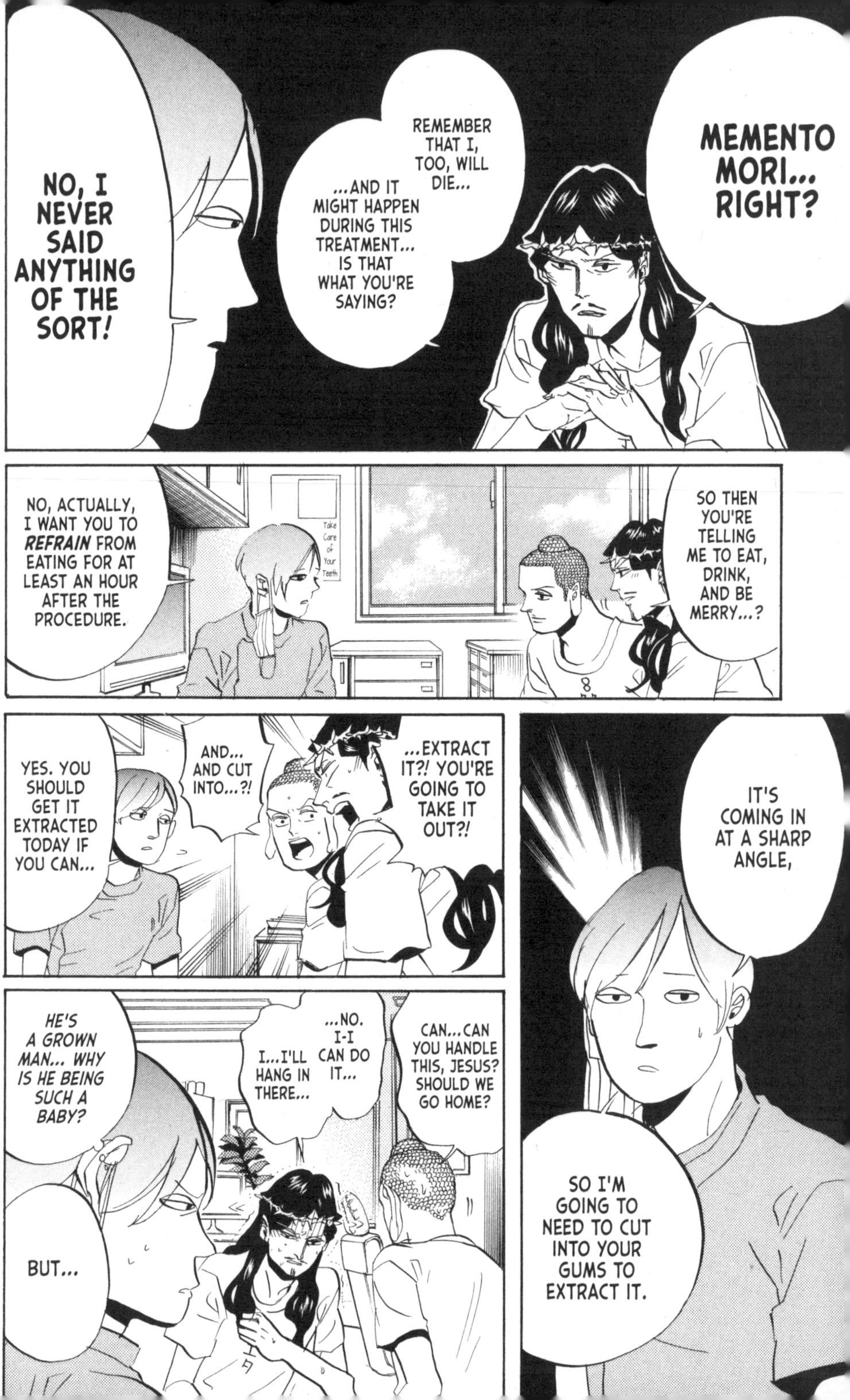
MEMENTO MORI... RIGHT?
REMEMBER THAT I, TOO, WILL DIE...
...AND IT MIGHT HAPPEN DURING THIS TREATMENT... IS THAT WHAT YOU'RE SAYING?
NO, I NEVER SAID ANYTHING OF THE SORT!
SO THEN YOU'RE TELLING ME TO EAT, DRINK, AND BE MERRY...?
Take Care of Your Teeth
NO, ACTUALLY, I WANT YOU TO *REFRAIN* FROM EATING FOR AT LEAST AN HOUR AFTER THE PROCEDURE.
IT'S COMING IN AT A SHARP ANGLE,
SO I'M GOING TO NEED TO CUT INTO YOUR GUMS TO EXTRACT IT.
...EXTRACT IT?! YOU'RE GOING TO TAKE IT OUT?!
AND... AND CUT INTO...?!
YES. YOU SHOULD GET IT EXTRACTED TODAY IF YOU CAN...
CAN...CAN YOU HANDLE THIS, JESUS? SHOULD WE GO HOME?
...NO. I-I CAN DO IT...
I...I'LL HANG IN THERE...
HE'S A GROWN MAN... WHY IS HE BEING SUCH A BABY?
BUT...

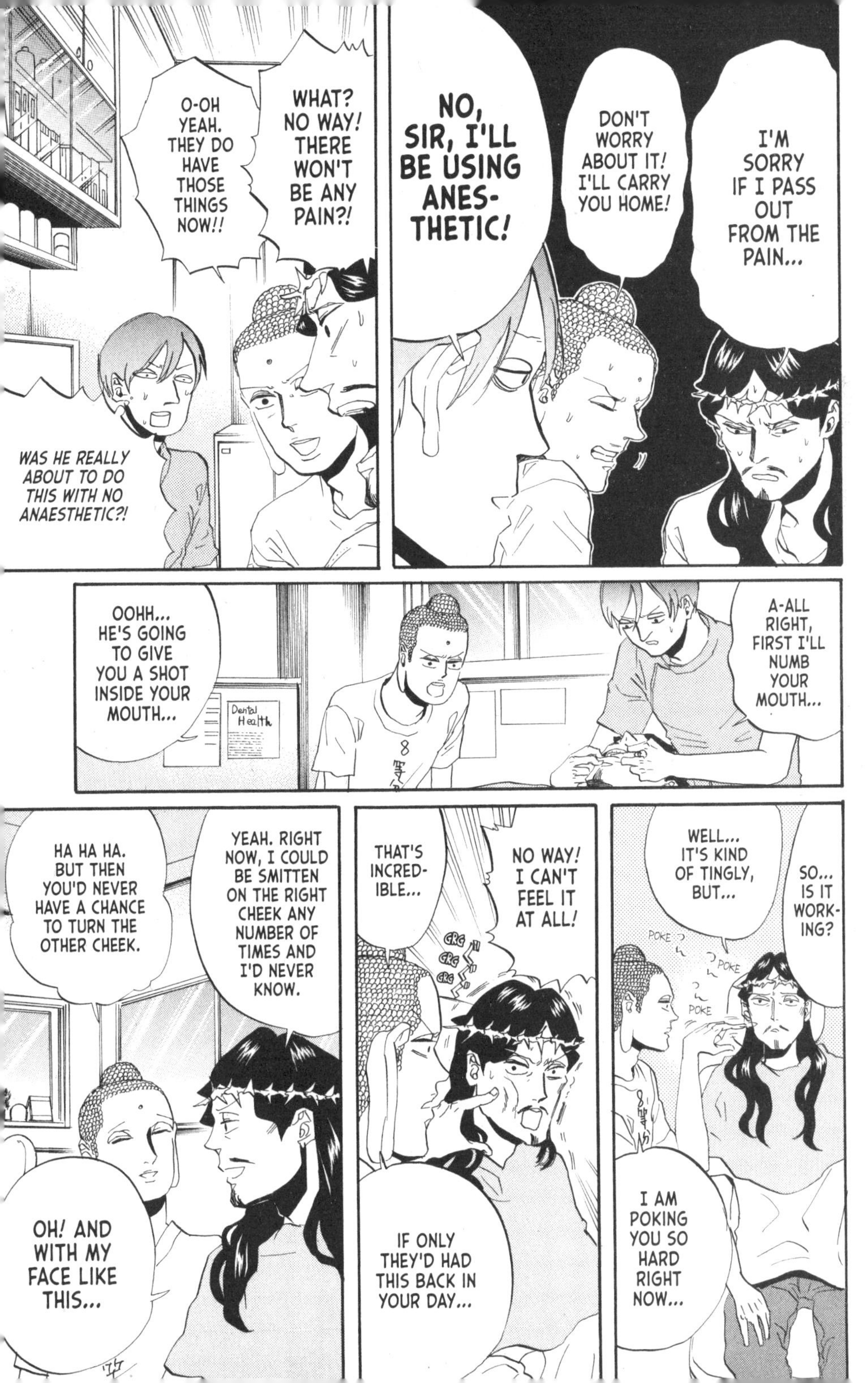
I'M SORRY IF I PASS OUT FROM THE PAIN...
DON'T WORRY ABOUT IT! I'LL CARRY YOU HOME!
NO, SIR, I'LL BE USING ANES-THETIC!
WHAT? NO WAY! THERE WON'T BE ANY PAIN?!
O-OH YEAH. THEY DO HAVE THOSE THINGS NOW!!
WAS HE REALLY ABOUT TO DO THIS WITH NO ANAESTHETIC?!
A-ALL RIGHT, FIRST I'LL NUMB YOUR MOUTH...
OOHH... HE'S GOING TO GIVE YOU A SHOT INSIDE YOUR MOUTH...
Dental Health
SO... IS IT WORKING?
WELL... IT'S KIND OF TINGLY, BUT...
POKE
POKE
POKE
I AM POKING YOU SO HARD RIGHT NOW...
NO WAY! I CAN'T FEEL IT AT ALL!
THAT'S INCRED-IBLE...
GRG
GRG
GRG
IF ONLY THEY'D HAD THIS BACK IN YOUR DAY...
YEAH. RIGHT NOW, I COULD BE SMITTEN ON THE RIGHT CHEEK ANY NUMBER OF TIMES AND I'D NEVER KNOW.
HA HA HA. BUT THEN YOU'D NEVER HAVE A CHANCE TO TURN THE OTHER CHEEK.
OH! AND WITH MY FACE LIKE THIS...

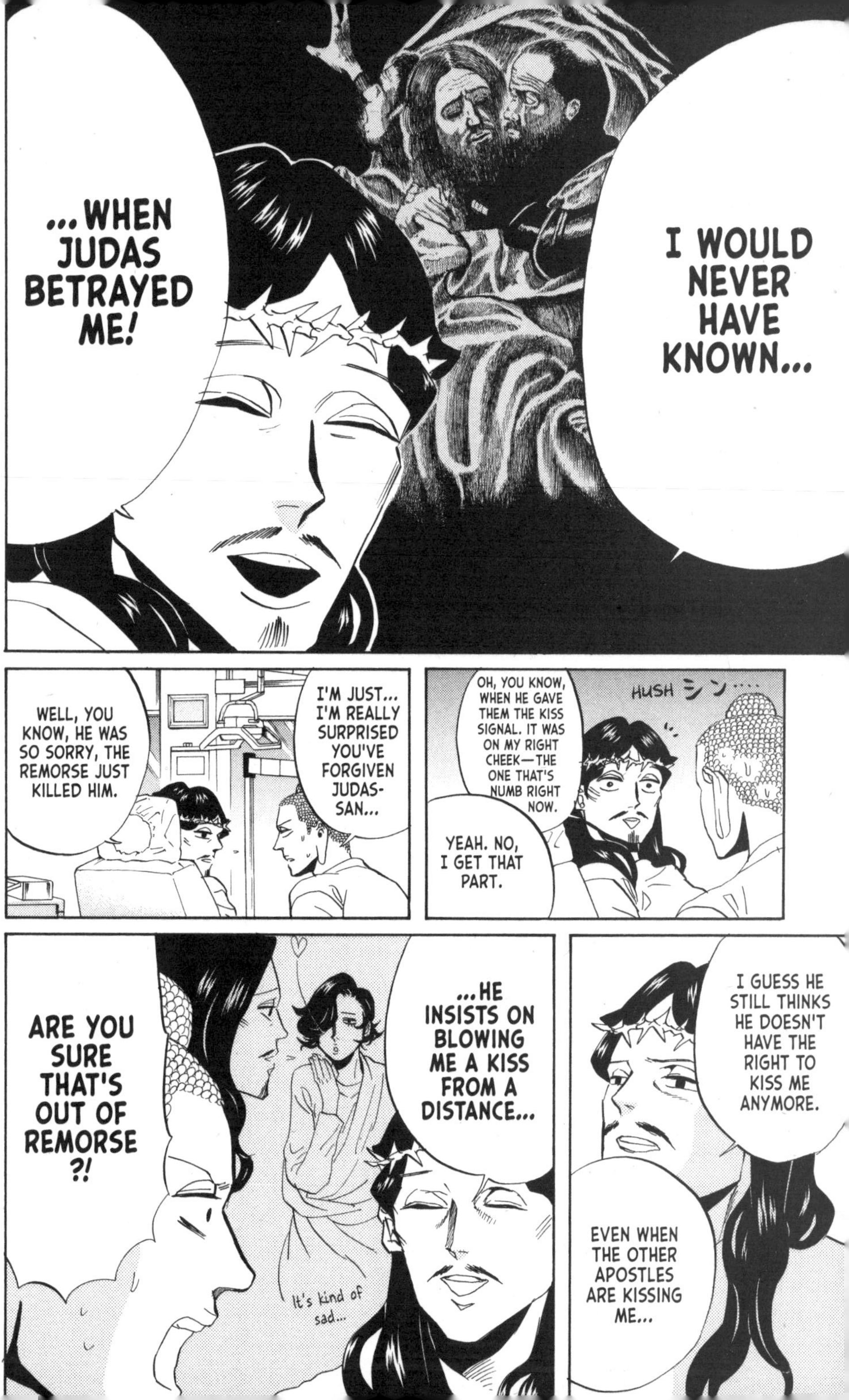
I WOULD NEVER HAVE KNOWN...
...WHEN JUDAS BETRAYED ME!
OH, YOU KNOW, WHEN HE GAVE THEM THE KISS SIGNAL. IT WAS ON MY RIGHT CHEEK—THE ONE THAT'S NUMB RIGHT NOW.
HUSH シン…
YEAH. NO, I GET THAT PART.
I'M JUST... I'M REALLY SURPRISED YOU'VE FORGIVEN JUDAS-SAN...
WELL, YOU KNOW, HE WAS SO SORRY, THE REMORSE JUST KILLED HIM.
I GUESS HE STILL THINKS HE DOESN'T HAVE THE RIGHT TO KISS ME ANYMORE.
EVEN WHEN THE OTHER APOSTLES ARE KISSING ME...
...HE INSISTS ON BLOWING ME A KISS FROM A DISTANCE...
It's kind of sad...
ARE YOU SURE THAT'S OUT OF REMORSE?!

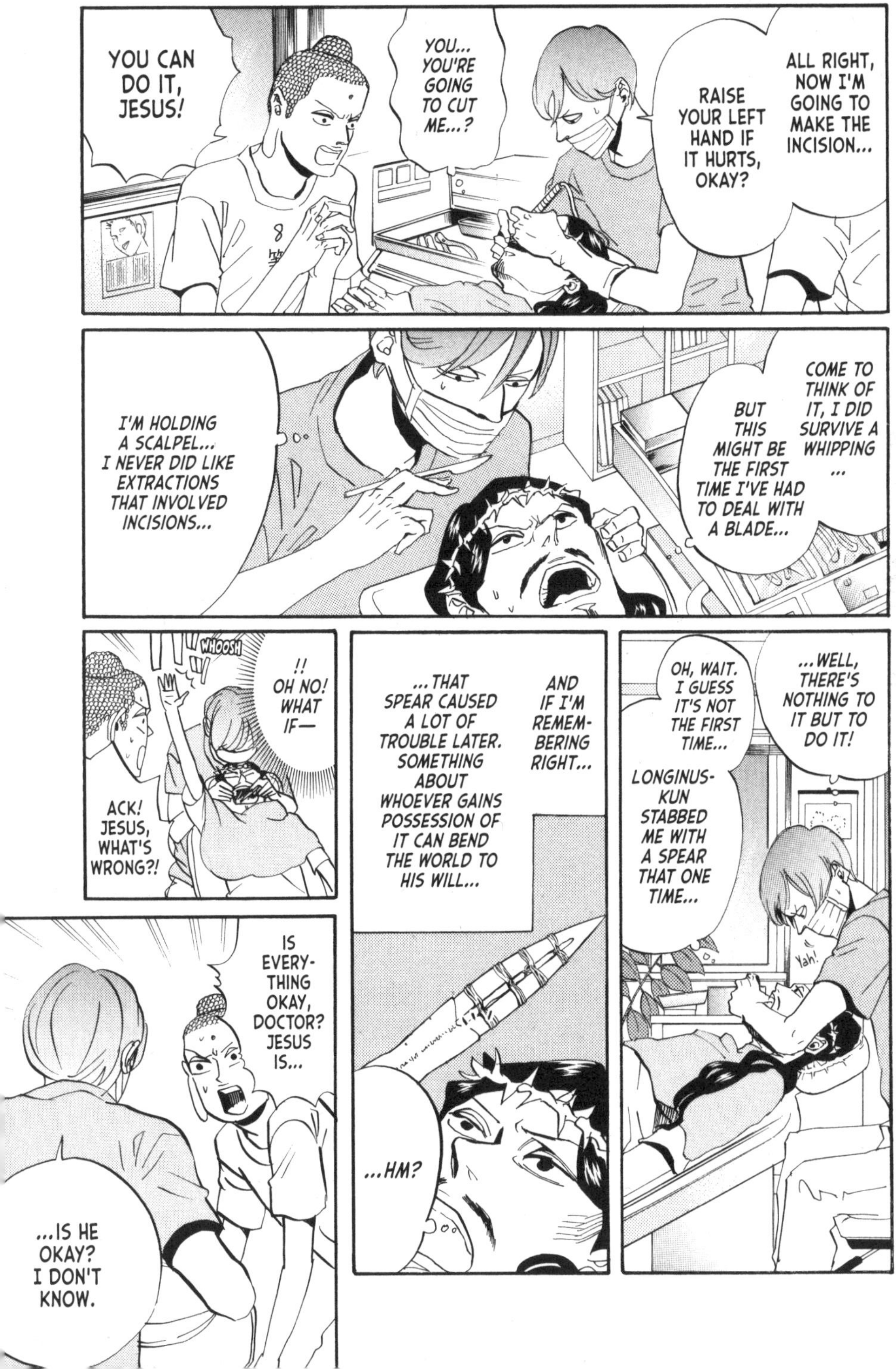
ALL RIGHT, NOW I'M GOING TO MAKE THE INCISION...
RAISE YOUR LEFT HAND IF IT HURTS, OKAY?
YOU... YOU'RE GOING TO CUT ME...?
YOU CAN DO IT, JESUS!
COME TO THINK OF IT, I DID SURVIVE A WHIPPING...
BUT THIS MIGHT BE THE FIRST TIME I'VE HAD TO DEAL WITH A BLADE...
I'M HOLDING A SCALPEL... I NEVER DID LIKE EXTRACTIONS THAT INVOLVED INCISIONS...
...WELL, THERE'S NOTHING TO IT BUT TO DO IT!
OH, WAIT. I GUESS IT'S NOT THE FIRST TIME...
LONGINUS-KUN STABBED ME WITH A SPEAR THAT ONE TIME...
Yah!
AND IF I'M REMEMBERING RIGHT...
...THAT SPEAR CAUSED A LOT OF TROUBLE LATER. SOMETHING ABOUT WHOEVER GAINS POSSESSION OF IT CAN BEND THE WORLD TO HIS WILL...
...HM?
!! OH NO! WHAT IF—
WHOOSH
ACK! JESUS, WHAT'S WRONG?!
IS EVERYTHING OKAY, DOCTOR? JESUS IS...
...IS HE OKAY? I DON'T KNOW.

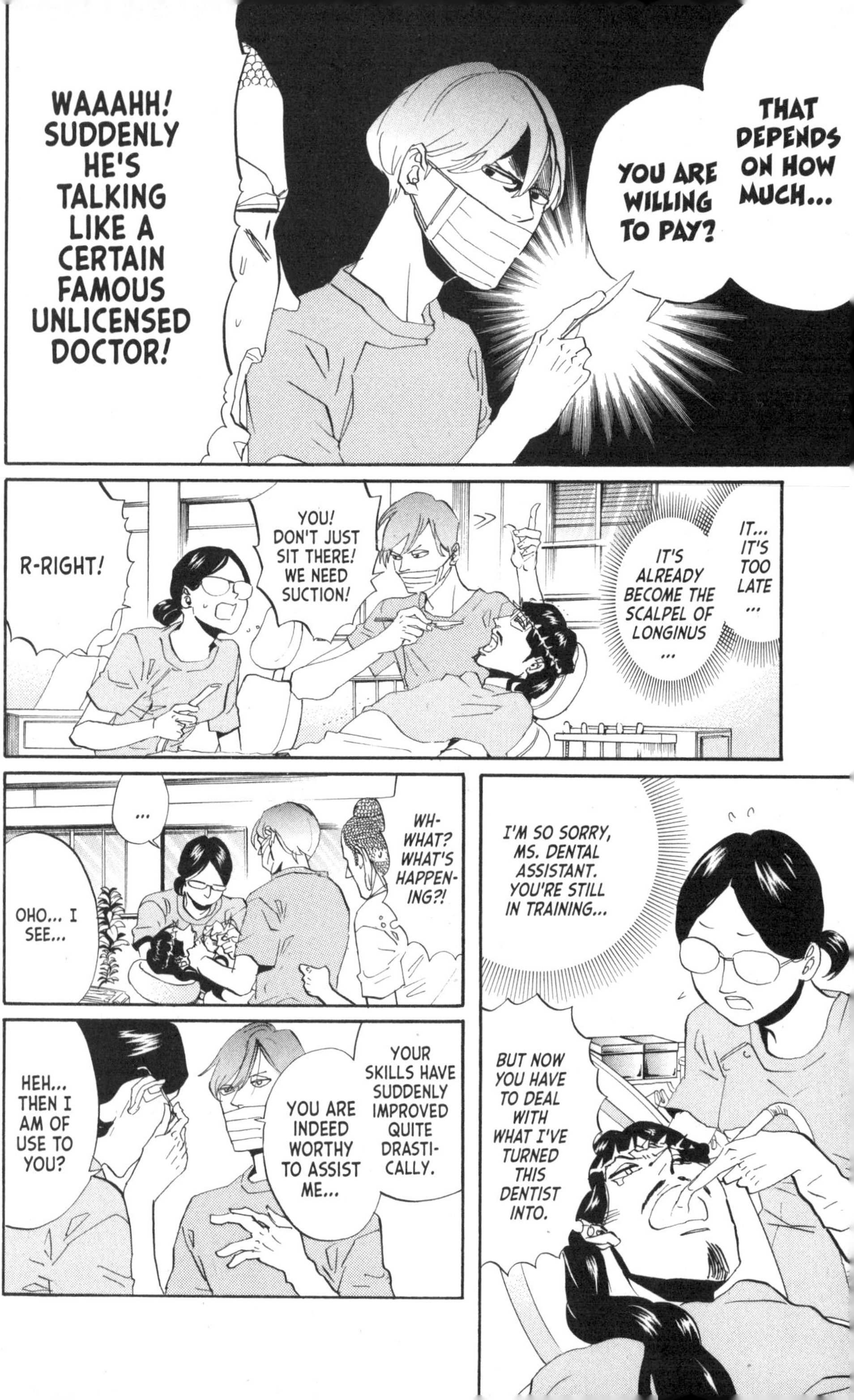
THAT DEPENDS ON HOW MUCH...
YOU ARE WILLING TO PAY?
WAAAHH! SUDDENLY HE'S TALKING LIKE A CERTAIN FAMOUS UNLICENSED DOCTOR!
IT... IT'S TOO LATE ...
IT'S ALREADY BECOME THE SCALPEL OF LONGINUS ...
YOU! DON'T JUST SIT THERE! WE NEED SUCTION!
R-RIGHT!
I'M SO SORRY, MS. DENTAL ASSISTANT. YOU'RE STILL IN TRAINING...
BUT NOW YOU HAVE TO DEAL WITH WHAT I'VE TURNED THIS DENTIST INTO.
WH-WHAT? WHAT'S HAPPEN-ING?!
...
OHO... I SEE...
YOUR SKILLS HAVE SUDDENLY IMPROVED QUITE DRASTI-CALLY.
YOU ARE INDEED WORTHY TO ASSIST ME...
HEH... THEN I AM OF USE TO YOU?

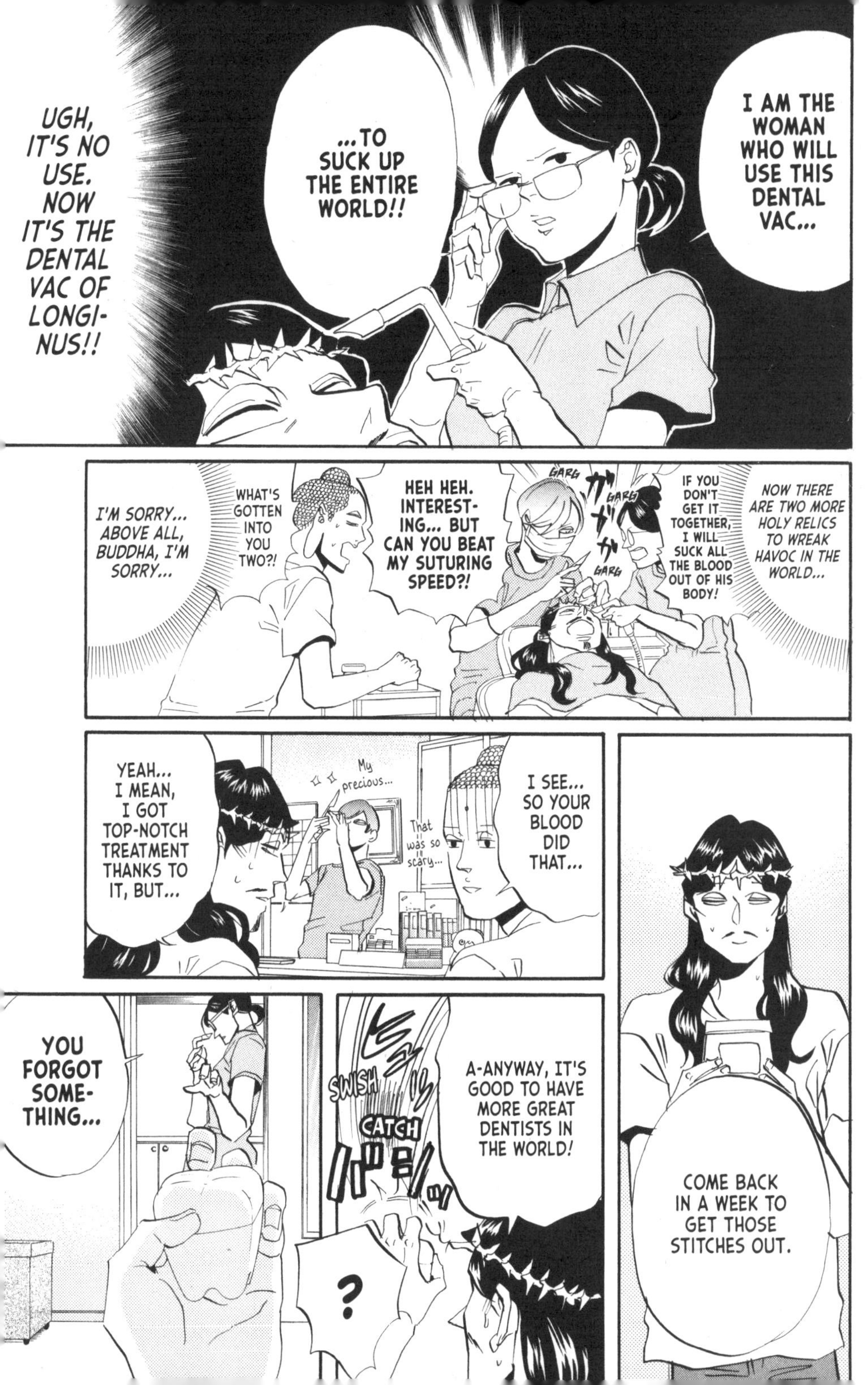
I AM THE WOMAN WHO WILL USE THIS DENTAL VAC...
...TO SUCK UP THE ENTIRE WORLD!!
UGH, IT'S NO USE. NOW IT'S THE DENTAL VAC OF LONGI-NUS!!
NOW THERE ARE TWO MORE HOLY RELICS TO WREAK HAVOC IN THE WORLD...
GARG
GARG
GARG
IF YOU DON'T GET IT TOGETHER, I WILL SUCK ALL THE BLOOD OUT OF HIS BODY!
HEH HEH. INTEREST-ING... BUT CAN YOU BEAT MY SUTURING SPEED?!
WHAT'S GOTTEN INTO YOU TWO?!
I'M SORRY... ABOVE ALL, BUDDHA, I'M SORRY...
COME BACK IN A WEEK TO GET THOSE STITCHES OUT.
I SEE... SO YOUR BLOOD DID THAT...
That was so scary...
My precious...
YEAH... I MEAN, I GOT TOP-NOTCH TREATMENT THANKS TO IT, BUT...
A-ANYWAY, IT'S GOOD TO HAVE MORE GREAT DENTISTS IN THE WORLD!
SWISH
CATCH
?
YOU FORGOT SOME-THING...

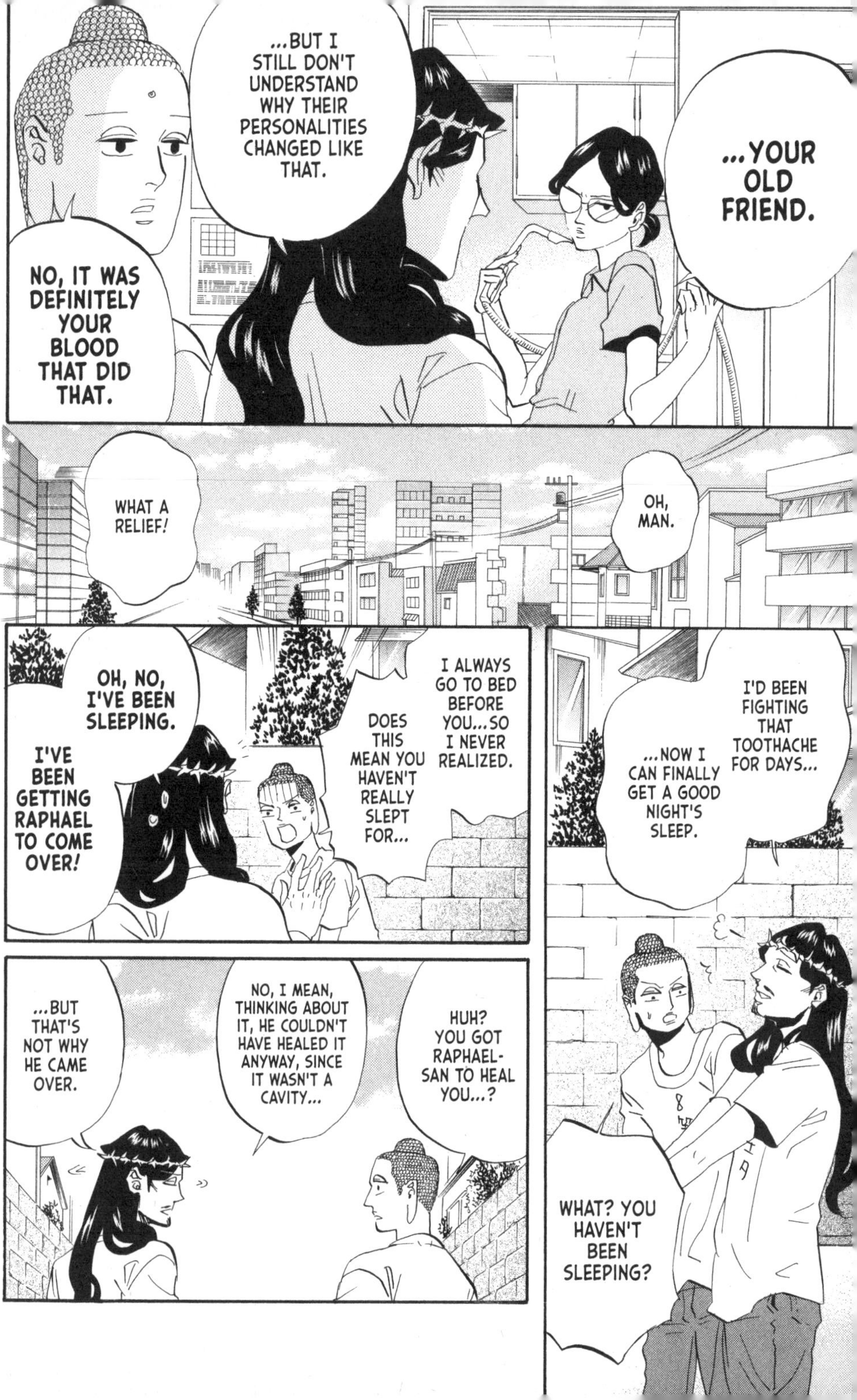
...YOUR OLD FRIEND.
...BUT I STILL DON'T UNDERSTAND WHY THEIR PERSONALITIES CHANGED LIKE THAT.
NO, IT WAS DEFINITELY YOUR BLOOD THAT DID THAT.
OH, MAN.
WHAT A RELIEF!
I'D BEEN FIGHTING THAT TOOTHACHE FOR DAYS...
...NOW I CAN FINALLY GET A GOOD NIGHT'S SLEEP.
WHAT? YOU HAVEN'T BEEN SLEEPING?
I ALWAYS GO TO BED BEFORE YOU...SO I NEVER REALIZED.
DOES THIS MEAN YOU HAVEN'T REALLY SLEPT FOR...
OH, NO, I'VE BEEN SLEEPING.
I'VE BEEN GETTING RAPHAEL TO COME OVER!
HUH? YOU GOT RAPHAEL-SAN TO HEAL YOU...?
NO, I MEAN, THINKING ABOUT IT, HE COULDN'T HAVE HEALED IT ANYWAY, SINCE IT WASN'T A CAVITY...
...BUT THAT'S NOT WHY HE CAME OVER.

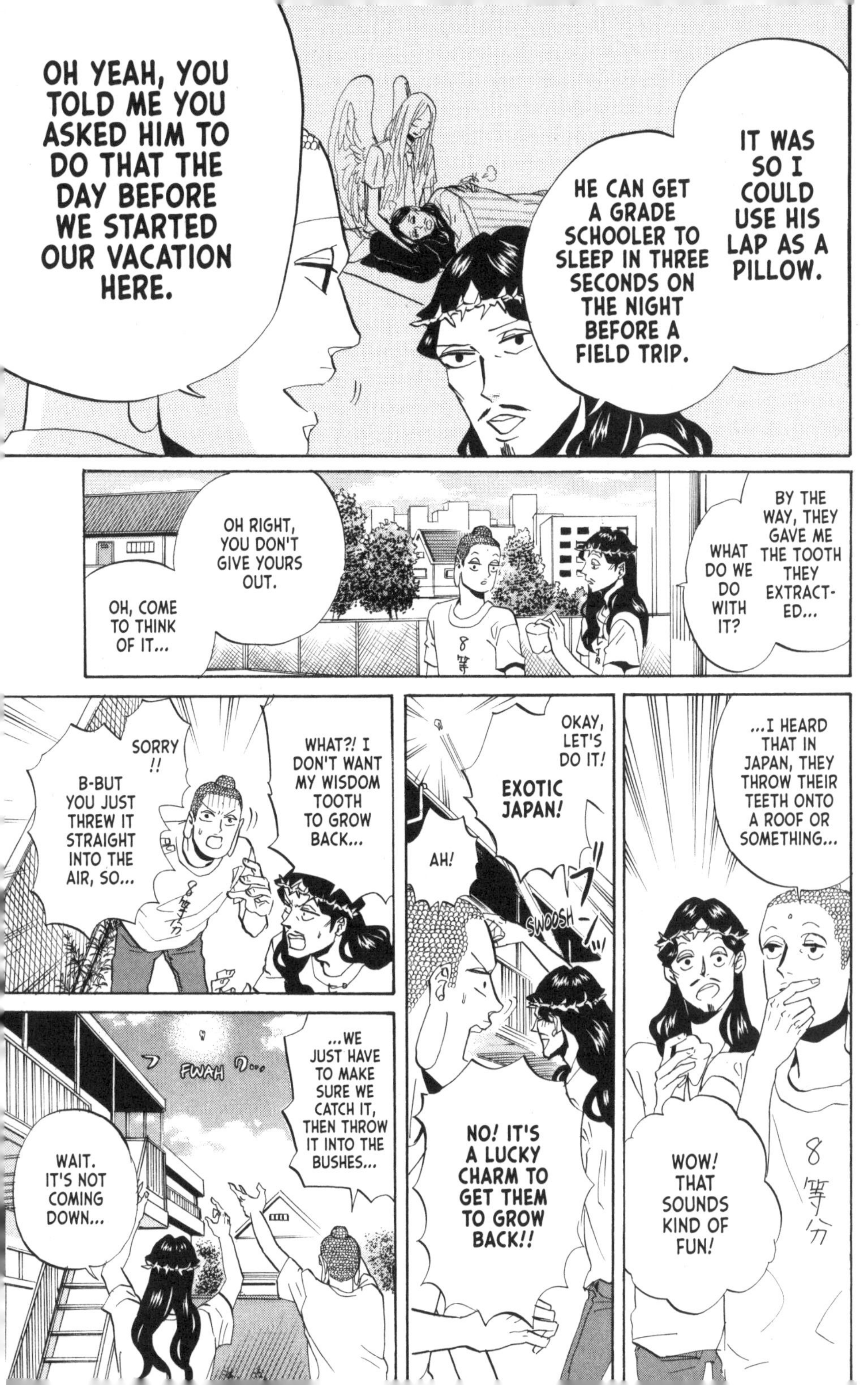
OH YEAH, YOU TOLD ME YOU ASKED HIM TO DO THAT THE DAY BEFORE WE STARTED OUR VACATION HERE.
IT WAS SO I COULD USE HIS LAP AS A PILLOW.
HE CAN GET A GRADE SCHOOLER TO SLEEP IN THREE SECONDS ON THE NIGHT BEFORE A FIELD TRIP.
BY THE WAY, THEY GAVE ME THE TOOTH THEY EXTRACTED...
WHAT DO WE DO WITH IT?
OH, COME TO THINK OF IT...
OH RIGHT, YOU DON'T GIVE YOURS OUT.
...I HEARD THAT IN JAPAN, THEY THROW THEIR TEETH ONTO A ROOF OR SOMETHING...
WOW! THAT SOUNDS KIND OF FUN!
8等分
OKAY, LET'S DO IT!
EXOTIC JAPAN!
AH!
SWOOSH
NO! IT'S A LUCKY CHARM TO GET THEM TO GROW BACK!!
WHAT?! I DON'T WANT MY WISDOM TOOTH TO GROW BACK...
SORRY!!
B-BUT YOU JUST THREW IT STRAIGHT INTO THE AIR, SO...
...WE JUST HAVE TO MAKE SURE WE CATCH IT, THEN THROW IT INTO THE BUSHES...
FWAH
WAIT. IT'S NOT COMING DOWN...

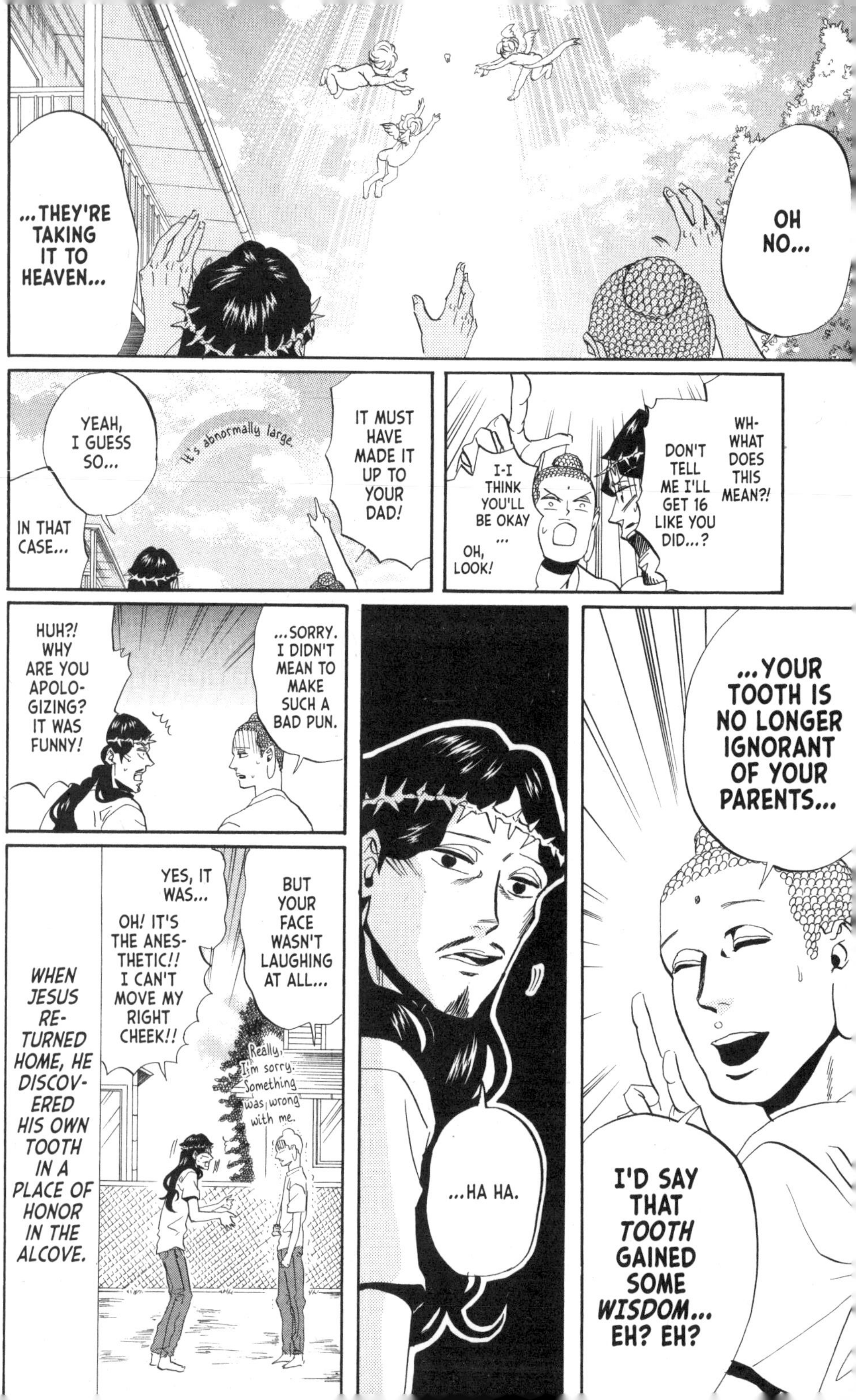
OH NO...
...THEY'RE TAKING IT TO HEAVEN...
WH-WHAT DOES THIS MEAN?!
DON'T TELL ME I'LL GET 16 LIKE YOU DID...?
I-I THINK YOU'LL BE OKAY...
OH, LOOK!
IT MUST HAVE MADE IT UP TO YOUR DAD!
It's abnormally large.
YEAH, I GUESS SO...
IN THAT CASE...
...YOUR TOOTH IS NO LONGER IGNORANT OF YOUR PARENTS...
I'D SAY THAT *TOOTH* GAINED SOME *WISDOM*... EH? EH?
...HA HA.
...SORRY. I DIDN'T MEAN TO MAKE SUCH A BAD PUN.
HUH?! WHY ARE YOU APOLOGIZING? IT WAS FUNNY!
BUT YOUR FACE WASN'T LAUGHING AT ALL...
YES, IT WAS...
OH! IT'S THE ANES-THETIC!! I CAN'T MOVE MY RIGHT CHEEK!!
Really, I'm sorry. Something was wrong with me.
WHEN JESUS RE-TURNED HOME, HE DISCOV-ERED HIS OWN TOOTH IN A PLACE OF HONOR IN THE ALCOVE.

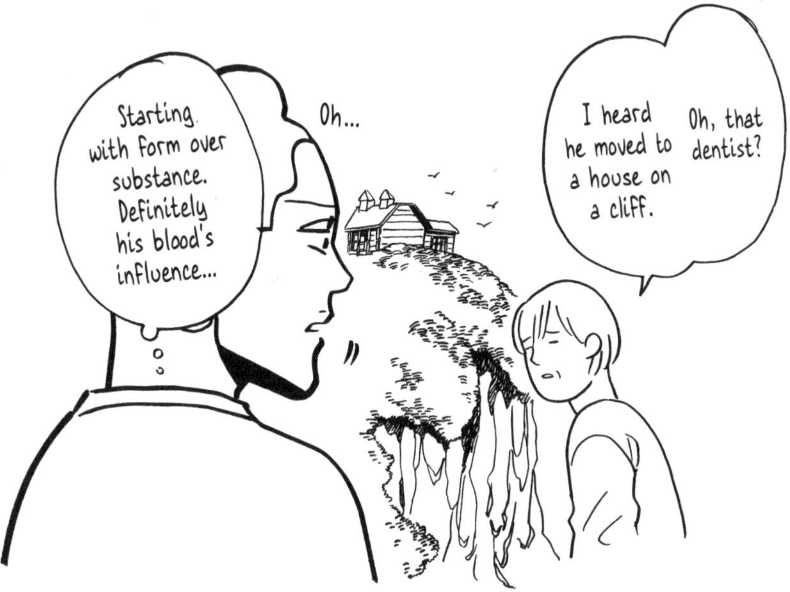
Oh, that dentist?
I heard he moved to a house on a cliff.
Oh...
Starting with form over substance. Definitely his blood's influence...

CHAPTER 37 TRANSLATION NOTES

Healed Longinus-san's eyes, page 147
Sometimes the Romans would help victims of a crucifixion to die sooner by breaking their legs—the shock of which, combined with the exhaustion and pain already experienced, would usually be enough to kill them. They were about to do this to Jesus's legs, but the executioners saw that he appeared to be already dead. To make doubly sure this was the case, a centurion thrust a spear into his side. This centurion's name was not recorded in the Bible, but he later came to be known as Longinus, a name derived from *lonchi*, the Greek word for "spear." Legend has it that Longinus had weak eyesight, and when Jesus's blood fell upon his eyes, he was able to see again.

When everything is divided, page 148
After the Buddha died, there was a dispute over which clan would receive his remains. To appease them all, one Brahmin priest divided the body relics into eight equal portions, and added the Buddha's ashes and the urn that contained them, and distributed them as ten shares. This is also what the "eight equal parts" on Buddha's t-shirt is referring to.

Pietà, page 149
This is an Italian art term referring to a sculpture or other work of art depicting the Virgin Mary cradling the dead body of Jesus.

Date Masamune and zunda mochi, page 150
Date Masamune was a regional ruler in Sendai (northern Japan) from the late 16th to early 17th centuries. He was known for being well dressed, and a man who dresses to impress in Japan is sometimes called a *Datesha*, or "Date person." *Zunda mochi* is *mochi* made with *edamame*.

Memento mori, page 152
This Latin phrase meaning, "Remember death," or, "Remember, you will die," served to help Christians focus on heavenly rewards by reminding them that earthly pleasures and achievements are fleeting.

When Judas betrayed me, page 154
As depicted in this painting by Caravaggio, when Judas led a group armed men to arrest Jesus, he identified their target by giving him a kiss: "Now he that betrayed him gave them a sign, saying, Whomsoever I shall kiss, that same is he: hold him fast." (Matthew 26:48).

The remorse killed him, page 154
After Jesus was condemned, Judas felt sorry about what he had done and tried to return the money he took as payment for betraying his master, and then hanged himself.

When the apostles are kissing me, page 154
In Biblical times, and to this day in some parts of Europe, kissing is used as a greeting.

I did survive a whipping, page 155
According to Roman law, before a criminal was crucified, they were whipped with a scourge—a type of whip consisting of multiple leather thongs attached to a handle.

The Spear of Destiny, page 155
Tradition has it that the Lance of Longinus, or Spear of Destiny, gives its owner the power to bend the world's destiny to his or her will. The spear pictured here is specifically the Vienna Lance, or the Holy Lance in Vienna, and is one of a few that claim to be the actual Lance of Longinus.

A certain famous unlicensed doctor, page 156
The doctor in question is Dr. Kurō Hazama, more commonly known as Black Jack. He is the protagonist of the the Osamu Tezuka manga *Black Jack*. His skills as a surgeon are unmatched, but because he has no medical license, his patients mostly come from the dark underbelly of society. He can save any patient from death, but is extremely expensive to hire.

In the alcove, page 160
"Alcove" is a translation of *tokonoma*, which is a kind of nook built into Japanese rooms to display art and other treasures to be admired.

SAINT☆YOUNG MEN

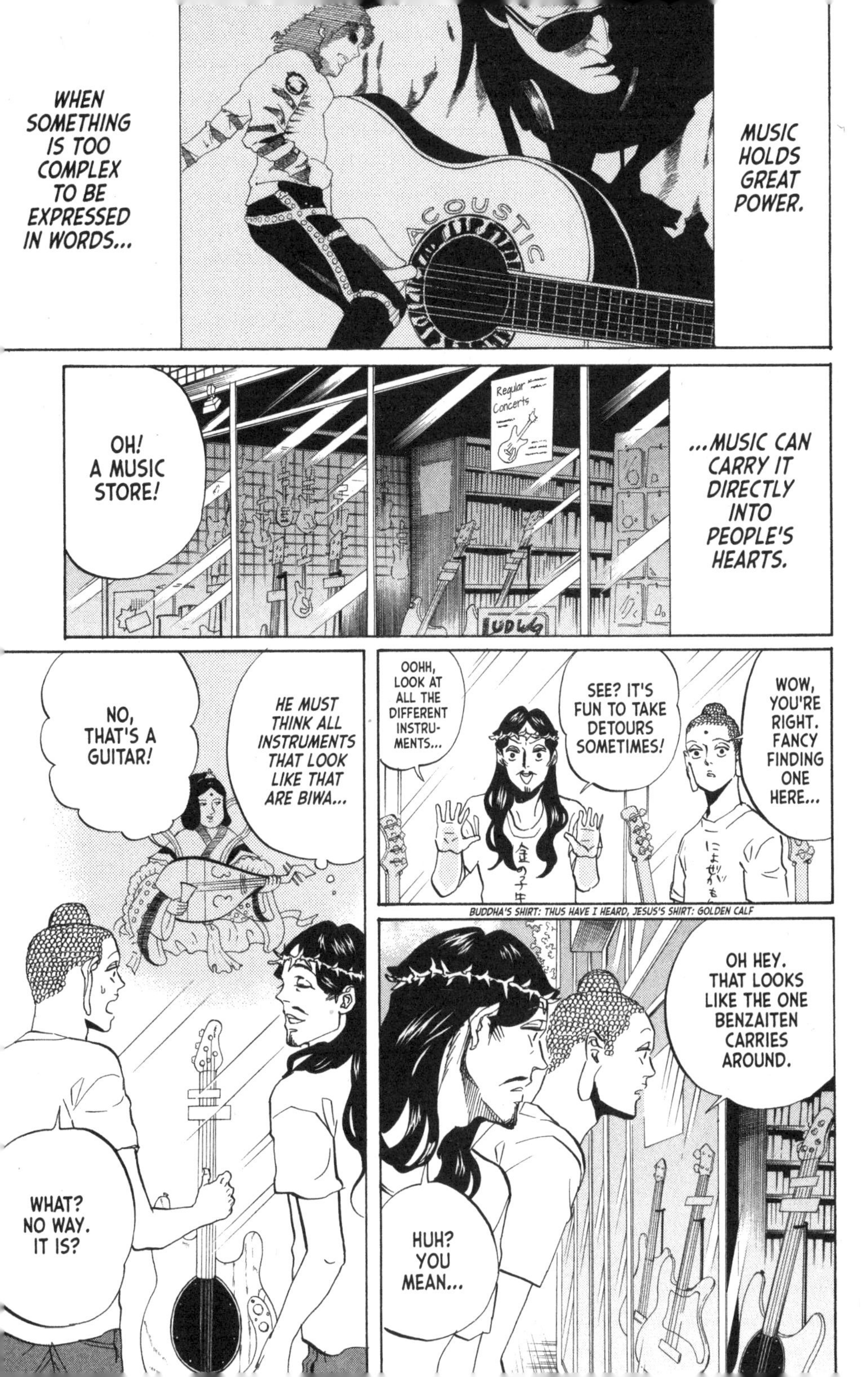

MUSIC HOLDS GREAT POWER.
WHEN SOMETHING IS TOO COMPLEX TO BE EXPRESSED IN WORDS...
ACOUSTIC
...MUSIC CAN CARRY IT DIRECTLY INTO PEOPLE'S HEARTS.
Regular Concerts
OH! A MUSIC STORE!
WOW, YOU'RE RIGHT. FANCY FINDING ONE HERE...
SEE? IT'S FUN TO TAKE DETOURS SOMETIMES!
OOHH, LOOK AT ALL THE DIFFERENT INSTRU-MENTS...
BUDDHA'S SHIRT: THUS HAVE I HEARD, JESUS'S SHIRT: GOLDEN CALF
OH HEY. THAT LOOKS LIKE THE ONE BENZAITEN CARRIES AROUND.
HUH? YOU MEAN...
HE MUST THINK ALL INSTRUMENTS THAT LOOK LIKE THAT ARE BIWA...
NO, THAT'S A GUITAR!
WHAT? NO WAY. IT IS?

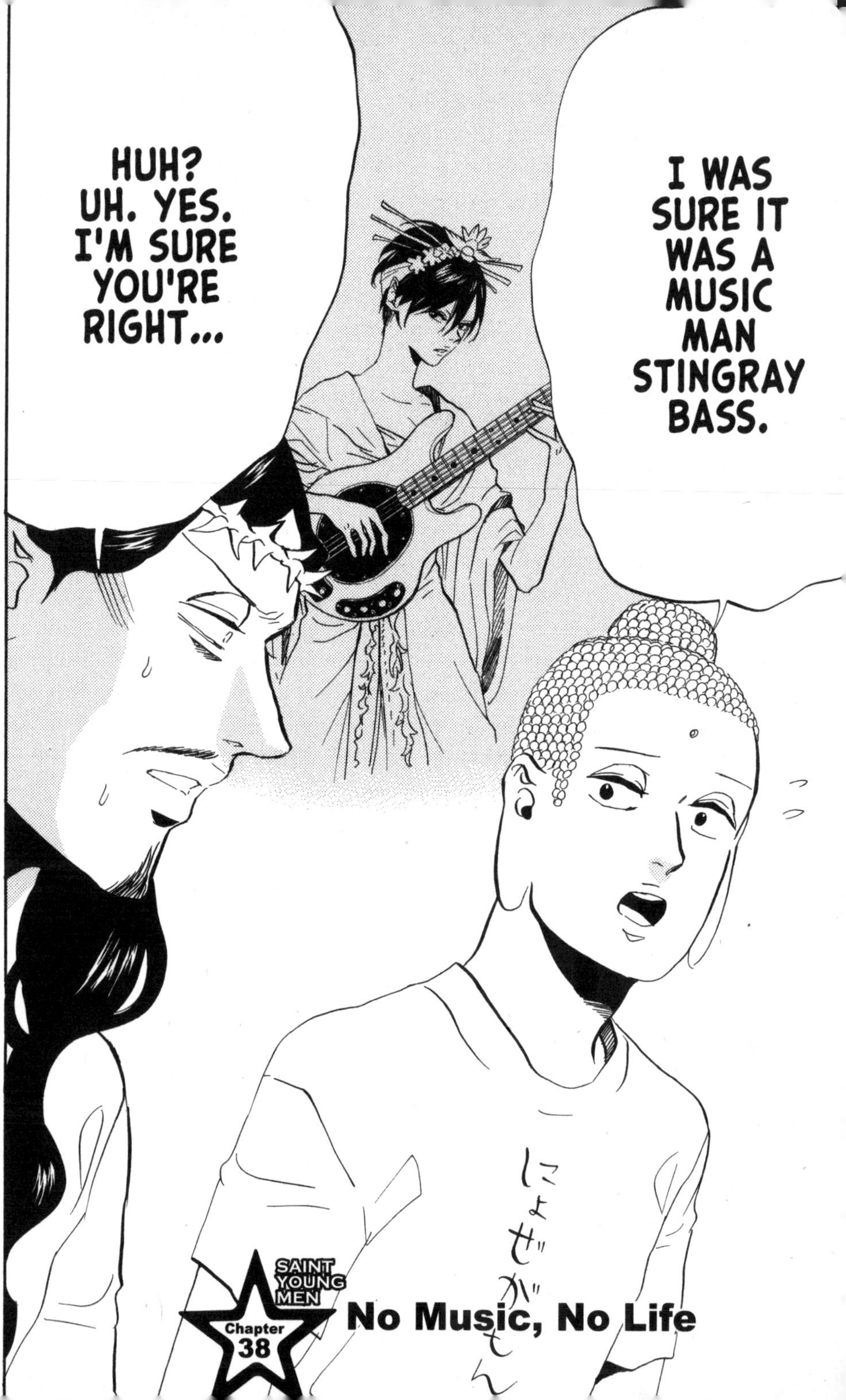
I WAS SURE IT WAS A MUSIC MAN STINGRAY BASS.
HUH? UH. YES. I'M SURE YOU'RE RIGHT...
にょぜがもん
SAINT YOUNG MEN
Chapter 38
No Music, No Life

BUDDHA: WANTS TO SEE AN OUTDOOR MUSIC FESTIVAL. IT WOULD BE LIKE GOING TO A PICNIC, AND HE'D GET TO HEAR UNFAMILIAR BANDS, SO IT HAS DOUBLE THE VALUE.

JESUS: WANTS TO SEE A LIVE MUSIC CLUB. FEELS LIKE IT WOULD BE REALLY EXCITING TO HAVE THE STAGE SO CLOSE TO EVERYONE.

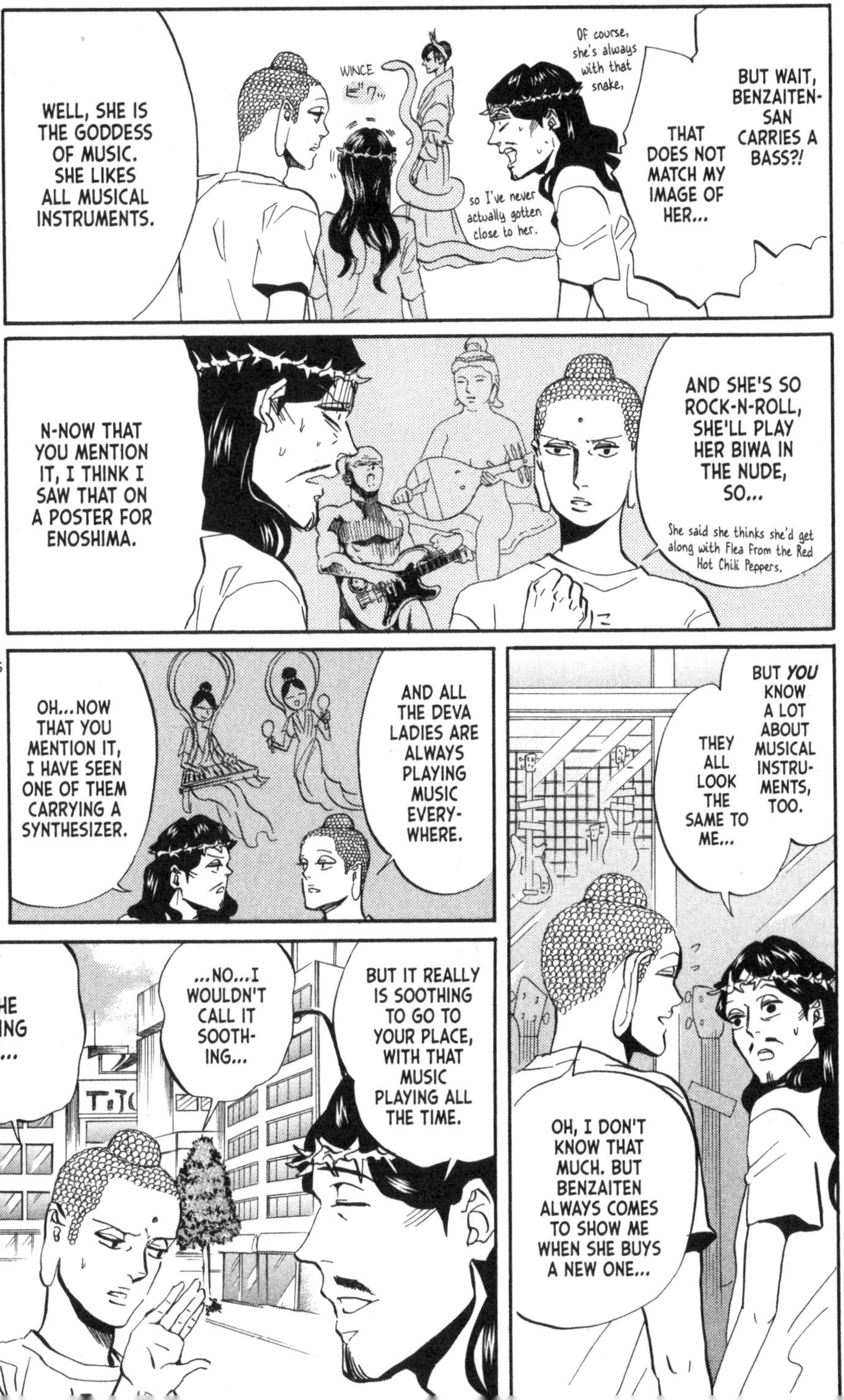

BUT WAIT, BENZAITEN-SAN CARRIES A BASS?!
THAT DOES NOT MATCH MY IMAGE OF HER...
Of course, she's always with that snake,
so I've never actually gotten close to her.
WINCE
ビクッ
WELL, SHE IS THE GODDESS OF MUSIC. SHE LIKES ALL MUSICAL INSTRUMENTS.
AND SHE'S SO ROCK-N-ROLL, SHE'LL PLAY HER BIWA IN THE NUDE, SO...
She said she thinks she'd get along with Flea from the Red Hot Chili Peppers.
N-NOW THAT YOU MENTION IT, I THINK I SAW THAT ON A POSTER FOR ENOSHIMA.
BUT *YOU* KNOW A LOT ABOUT MUSICAL INSTRUMENTS, TOO.
THEY ALL LOOK THE SAME TO ME...
OH, I DON'T KNOW THAT MUCH. BUT BENZAITEN ALWAYS COMES TO SHOW ME WHEN SHE BUYS A NEW ONE...
AND ALL THE DEVA LADIES ARE ALWAYS PLAYING MUSIC EVERYWHERE.
OH...NOW THAT YOU MENTION IT, I HAVE SEEN ONE OF THEM CARRYING A SYNTHESIZER.
BUT IT REALLY IS SOOTHING TO GO TO YOUR PLACE, WITH THAT MUSIC PLAYING ALL THE TIME.
...NO...I WOULDN'T CALL IT SOOTHING...
THE THING IS...

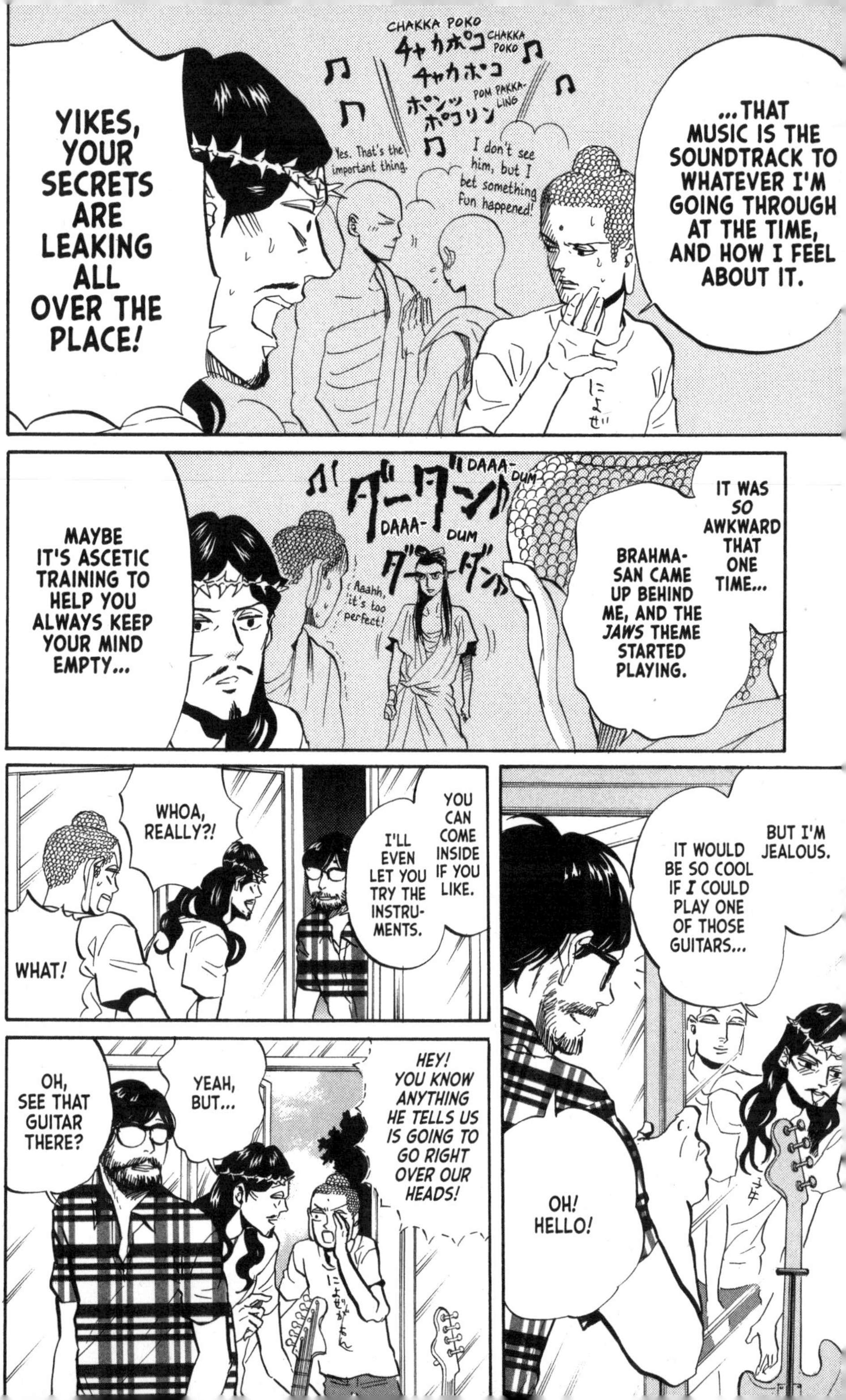
...THAT MUSIC IS THE SOUNDTRACK TO WHATEVER I'M GOING THROUGH AT THE TIME, AND HOW I FEEL ABOUT IT.
CHAKKA POKO チャカポコ
CHAKKA POKO チャカポコ
POM PAKKA-LING ポンッ ポコリン
I don't see him, but I bet something fun happened!
Yes. That's the important thing.
YIKES, YOUR SECRETS ARE LEAKING ALL OVER THE PLACE!
IT WAS SO AWKWARD THAT ONE TIME...
BRAHMA-SAN CAME UP BEHIND ME, AND THE JAWS THEME STARTED PLAYING.
DAAA-DUM ダーダン
DAAA-DUM ダーダン
Aaahh, it's too perfect!
MAYBE IT'S ASCETIC TRAINING TO HELP YOU ALWAYS KEEP YOUR MIND EMPTY...
BUT I'M JEALOUS.
IT WOULD BE SO COOL IF I COULD PLAY ONE OF THOSE GUITARS...
OH! HELLO!
YOU CAN COME INSIDE IF YOU LIKE.
I'LL EVEN LET YOU TRY THE INSTRUMENTS.
WHOA, REALLY?!
WHAT!
HEY! YOU KNOW ANYTHING HE TELLS US IS GOING TO GO RIGHT OVER OUR HEADS!
YEAH, BUT...
OH, SEE THAT GUITAR THERE?

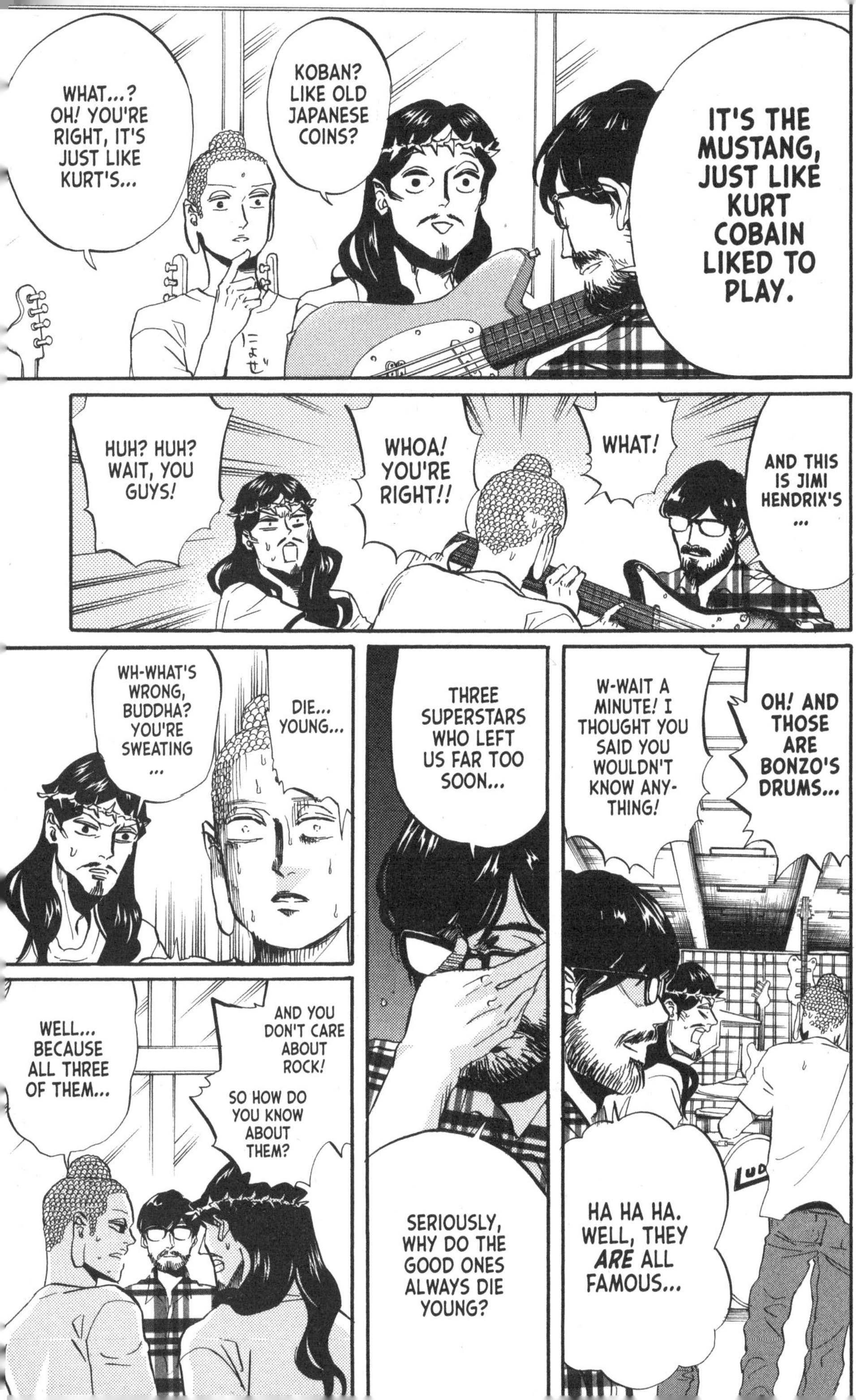
IT'S THE MUSTANG, JUST LIKE KURT COBAIN LIKED TO PLAY.
KOBAN? LIKE OLD JAPANESE COINS?
WHAT...? OH! YOU'RE RIGHT, IT'S JUST LIKE KURT'S...
AND THIS IS JIMI HENDRIX'S ...
WHAT!
WHOA! YOU'RE RIGHT!!
HUH? HUH? WAIT, YOU GUYS!
OH! AND THOSE ARE BONZO'S DRUMS...
W-WAIT A MINUTE! I THOUGHT YOU SAID YOU WOULDN'T KNOW ANY-THING!
HA HA HA. WELL, THEY *ARE* ALL FAMOUS...
THREE SUPERSTARS WHO LEFT US FAR TOO SOON...
SERIOUSLY, WHY DO THE GOOD ONES ALWAYS DIE YOUNG?
DIE... YOUNG...
WH-WHAT'S WRONG, BUDDHA? YOU'RE SWEATING ...
AND YOU DON'T CARE ABOUT ROCK!
SO HOW DO YOU KNOW ABOUT THEM?
WELL... BECAUSE ALL THREE OF THEM...

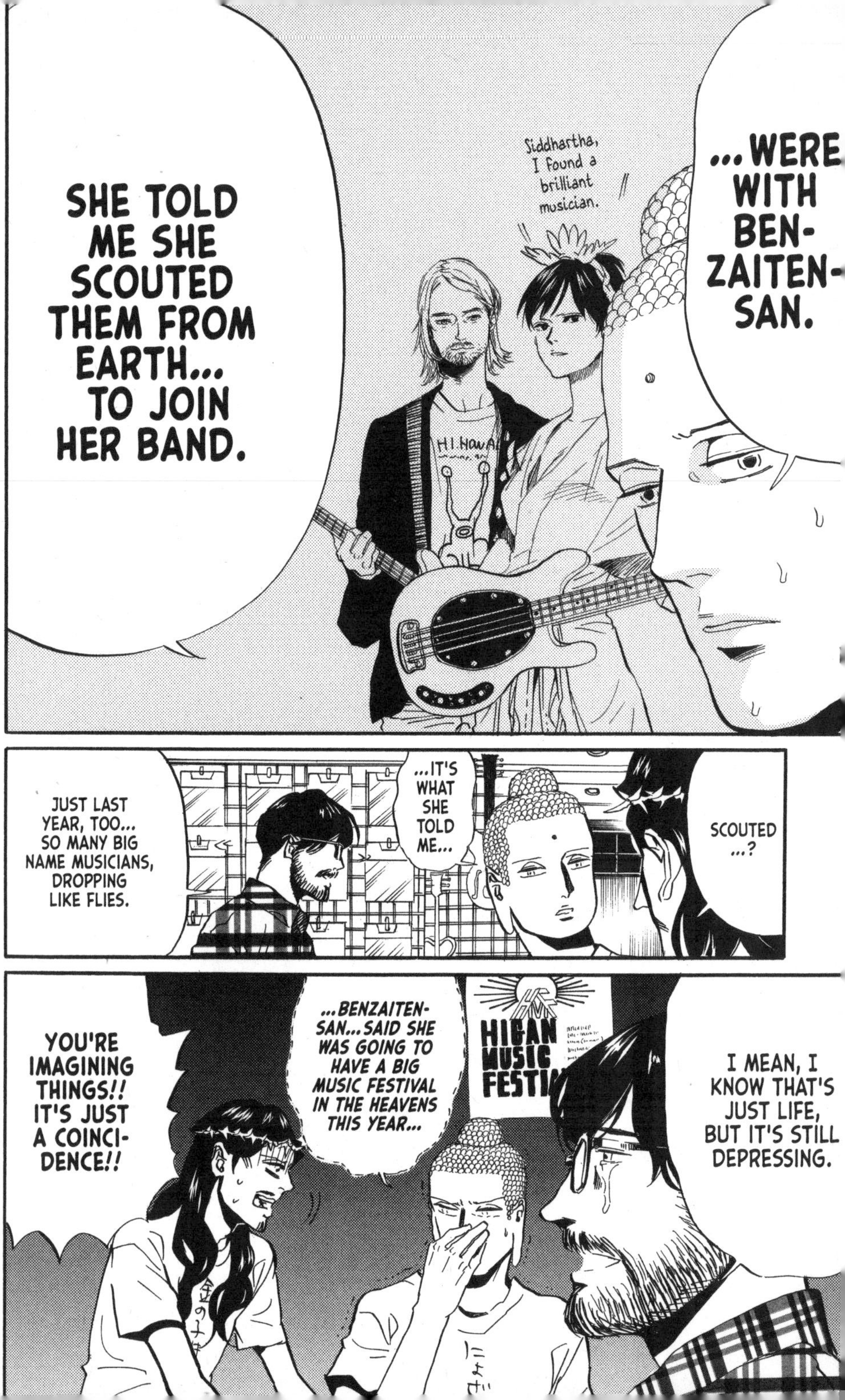
...WERE WITH BEN- ZAITEN- SAN.
Siddhartha, I found a brilliant musician.
SHE TOLD ME SHE SCOUTED THEM FROM EARTH... TO JOIN HER BAND.
SCOUTED ...?
...IT'S WHAT SHE TOLD ME...
JUST LAST YEAR, TOO... SO MANY BIG NAME MUSICIANS, DROPPING LIKE FLIES.
I MEAN, I KNOW THAT'S JUST LIFE, BUT IT'S STILL DEPRESSING.
HIGAN MUSIC FESTI
...BENZAITEN- SAN...SAID SHE WAS GOING TO HAVE A BIG MUSIC FESTIVAL IN THE HEAVENS THIS YEAR...
YOU'RE IMAGINING THINGS!! IT'S JUST A COINCI- DENCE!!

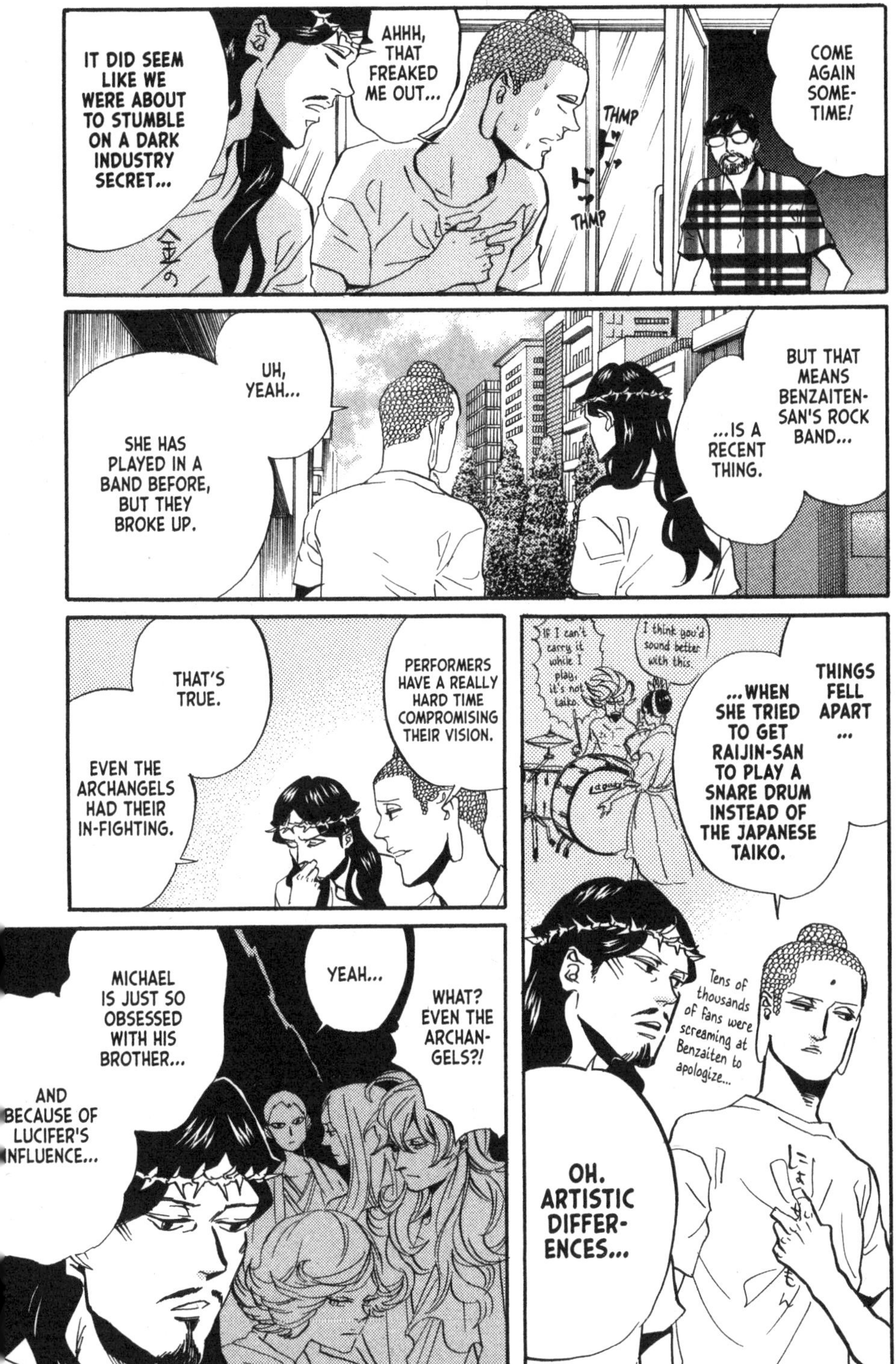

COME AGAIN SOME-TIME!
THMP
THMP
AHHH, THAT FREAKED ME OUT...
IT DID SEEM LIKE WE WERE ABOUT TO STUMBLE ON A DARK INDUSTRY SECRET...
BUT THAT MEANS BENZAITEN-SAN'S ROCK BAND...
...IS A RECENT THING.
UH, YEAH...
SHE HAS PLAYED IN A BAND BEFORE, BUT THEY BROKE UP.
THINGS FELL APART ...
...WHEN SHE TRIED TO GET RAIJIN-SAN TO PLAY A SNARE DRUM INSTEAD OF THE JAPANESE TAIKO.
I think you'd sound better with this.
If I can't carry it while I play, it's not taiko.
Tens of thousands of fans were screaming at Benzaiten to apologize...
OH. ARTISTIC DIFFER-ENCES...
PERFORMERS HAVE A REALLY HARD TIME COMPROMISING THEIR VISION.
THAT'S TRUE.
EVEN THE ARCHANGELS HAD THEIR IN-FIGHTING.
WHAT? EVEN THE ARCHAN-GELS?!
YEAH...
MICHAEL IS JUST SO OBSESSED WITH HIS BROTHER...
AND BECAUSE OF LUCIFER'S INFLUENCE...

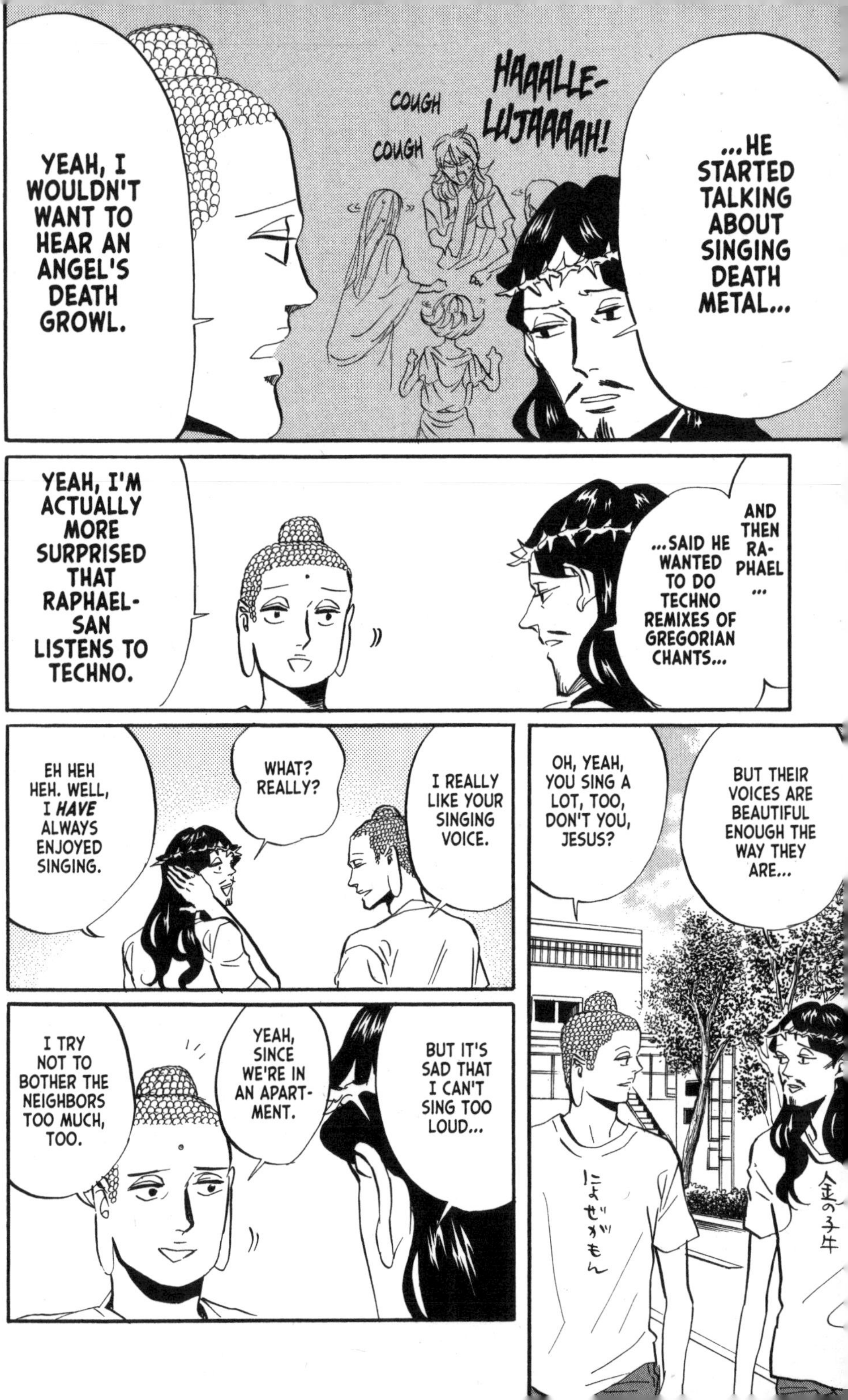
...HE STARTED TALKING ABOUT SINGING DEATH METAL...
HAAALLE-LUJAAAAH!
COUGH
COUGH
YEAH, I WOULDN'T WANT TO HEAR AN ANGEL'S DEATH GROWL.
AND THEN RA-PHAEL...
...SAID HE WANTED TO DO TECHNO REMIXES OF GREGORIAN CHANTS...
YEAH, I'M ACTUALLY MORE SURPRISED THAT RAPHAEL-SAN LISTENS TO TECHNO.
BUT THEIR VOICES ARE BEAUTIFUL ENOUGH THE WAY THEY ARE...
OH, YEAH, YOU SING A LOT, TOO, DON'T YOU, JESUS?
金の子牛
にょぜがもん
I REALLY LIKE YOUR SINGING VOICE.
WHAT? REALLY?
EH HEH HEH. WELL, I *HAVE* ALWAYS ENJOYED SINGING.
BUT IT'S SAD THAT I CAN'T SING TOO LOUD...
YEAH, SINCE WE'RE IN AN APART-MENT.
I TRY NOT TO BOTHER THE NEIGHBORS TOO MUCH, TOO.

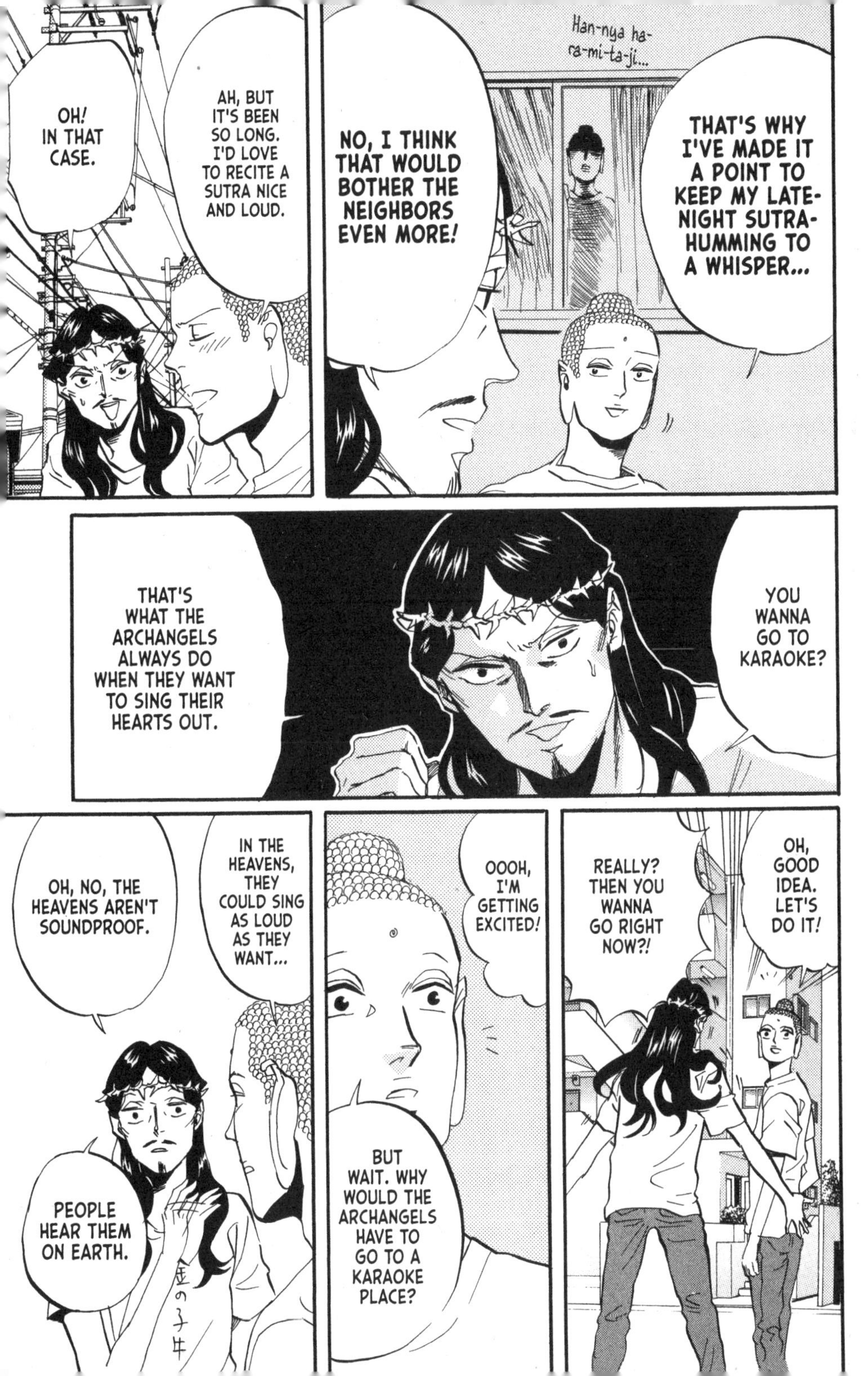
Han-nya ha-ra-mi-ta-ji...
THAT'S WHY I'VE MADE IT A POINT TO KEEP MY LATE-NIGHT SUTRA-HUMMING TO A WHISPER...
NO, I THINK THAT WOULD BOTHER THE NEIGHBORS EVEN MORE!
AH, BUT IT'S BEEN SO LONG. I'D LOVE TO RECITE A SUTRA NICE AND LOUD.
OH! IN THAT CASE.
YOU WANNA GO TO KARAOKE?
THAT'S WHAT THE ARCHANGELS ALWAYS DO WHEN THEY WANT TO SING THEIR HEARTS OUT.
OH, GOOD IDEA. LET'S DO IT!
REALLY? THEN YOU WANNA GO RIGHT NOW?!
OOOH, I'M GETTING EXCITED!
BUT WAIT. WHY WOULD THE ARCHANGELS HAVE TO GO TO A KARAOKE PLACE?
IN THE HEAVENS, THEY COULD SING AS LOUD AS THEY WANT...
OH, NO, THE HEAVENS AREN'T SOUNDPROOF.
PEOPLE HEAR THEM ON EARTH.

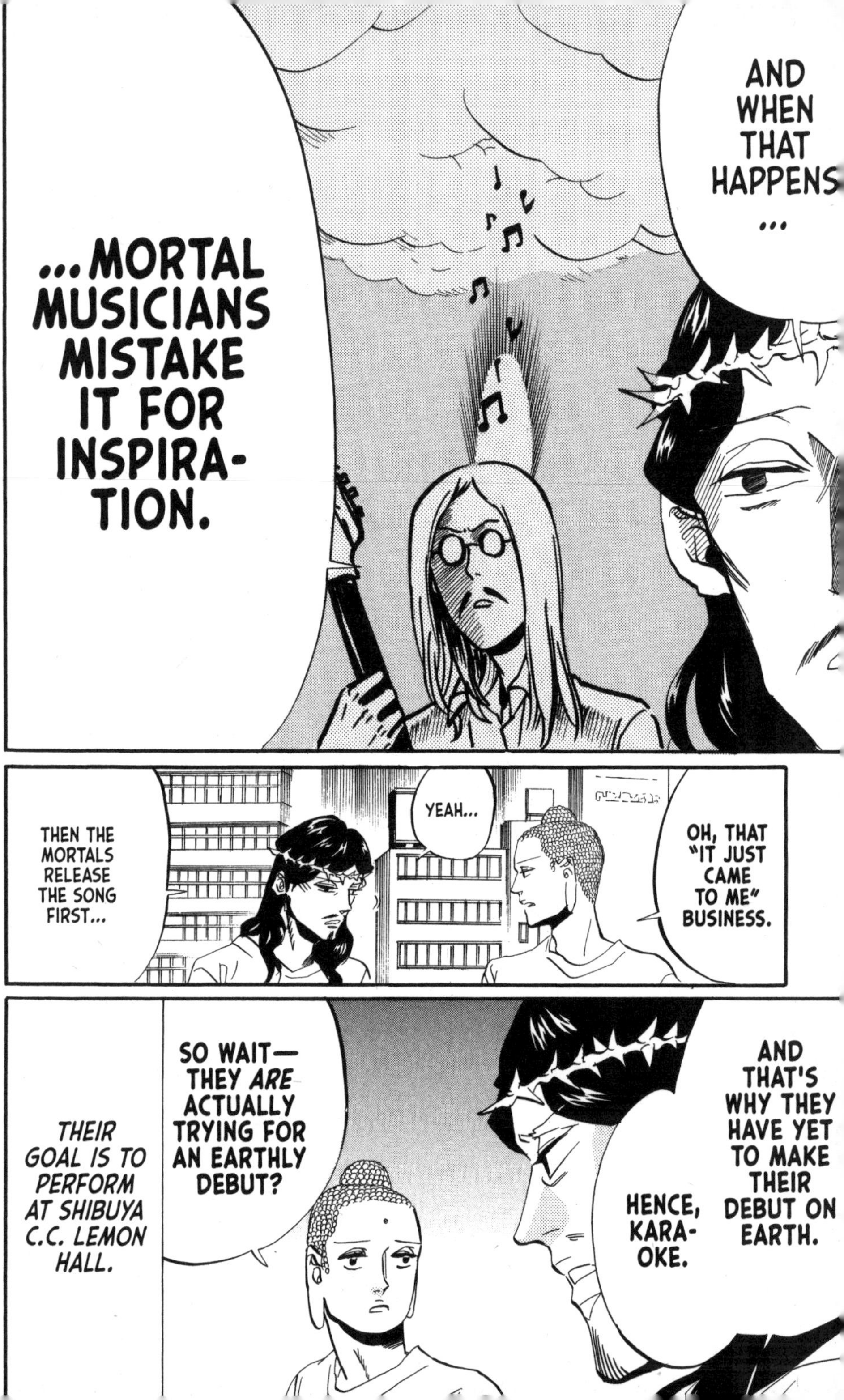
AND WHEN THAT HAPPENS...
...MORTAL MUSICIANS MISTAKE IT FOR INSPIRA-TION.
OH, THAT "IT JUST CAME TO ME" BUSINESS.
YEAH...
THEN THE MORTALS RELEASE THE SONG FIRST...
AND THAT'S WHY THEY HAVE YET TO MAKE THEIR DEBUT ON EARTH.
HENCE, KARA-OKE.
SO WAIT— THEY *ARE* ACTUALLY TRYING FOR AN EARTHLY DEBUT?
THEIR GOAL IS TO PERFORM AT SHIBUYA C.C. LEMON HALL.

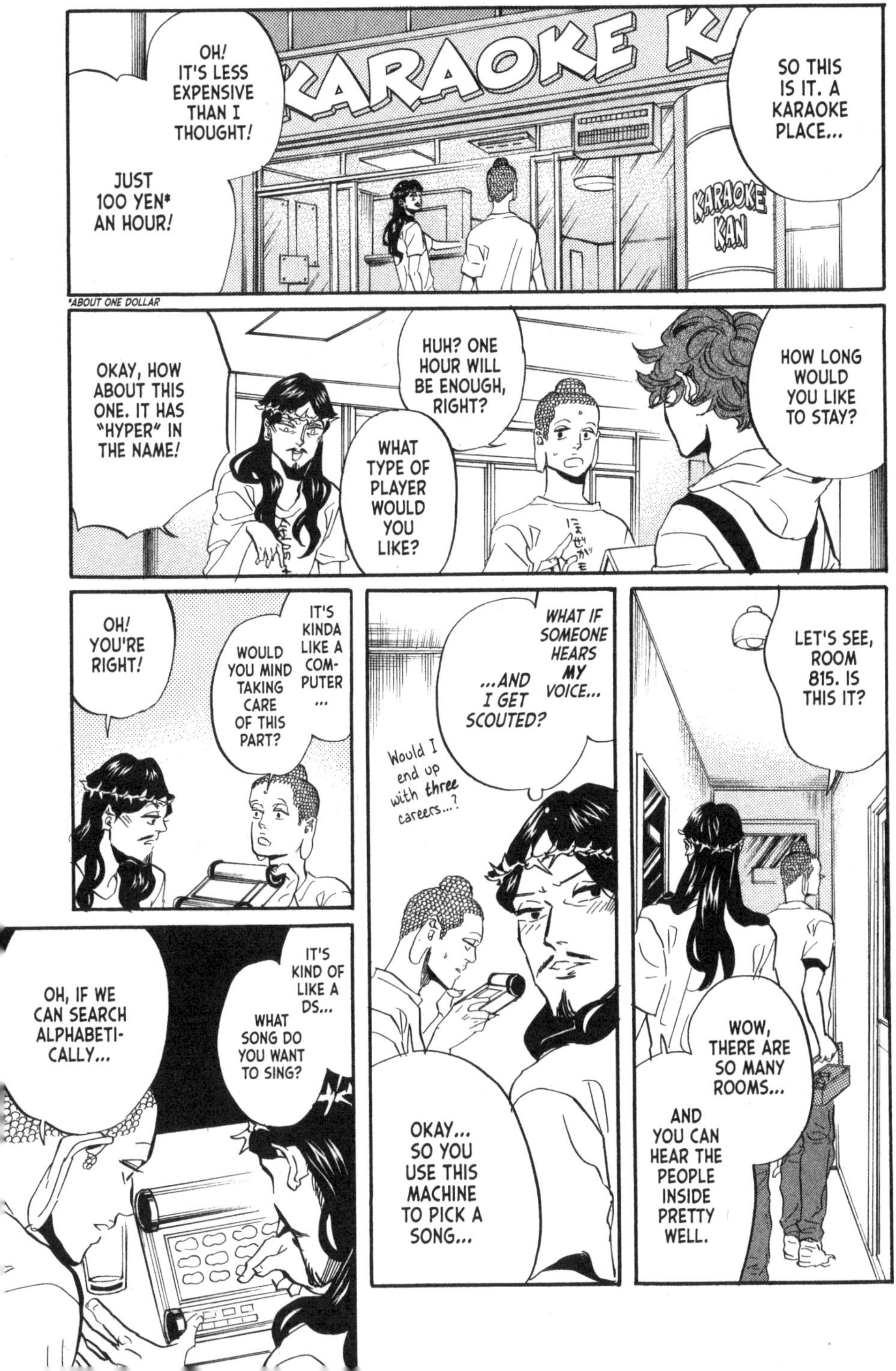
SO THIS IS IT. A KARAOKE PLACE...
KARAOKE KAN
KARAOKE K
OH! IT'S LESS EXPENSIVE THAN I THOUGHT!
JUST 100 YEN* AN HOUR!
HOW LONG WOULD YOU LIKE TO STAY?
HUH? ONE HOUR WILL BE ENOUGH, RIGHT?
WHAT TYPE OF PLAYER WOULD YOU LIKE?
OKAY, HOW ABOUT THIS ONE. IT HAS "HYPER" IN THE NAME!
LET'S SEE, ROOM 815. IS THIS IT?
WOW, THERE ARE SO MANY ROOMS...
AND YOU CAN HEAR THE PEOPLE INSIDE PRETTY WELL.
WHAT IF SOMEONE HEARS MY VOICE...
...AND I GET SCOUTED?
Would I end up with three careers...?
OKAY... SO YOU USE THIS MACHINE TO PICK A SONG...
IT'S KINDA LIKE A COM-PUTER...
WOULD YOU MIND TAKING CARE OF THIS PART?
OH! YOU'RE RIGHT!
IT'S KIND OF LIKE A DS...
WHAT SONG DO YOU WANT TO SING?
OH, IF WE CAN SEARCH ALPHABETI-CALLY...

*ABOUT ONE DOLLAR

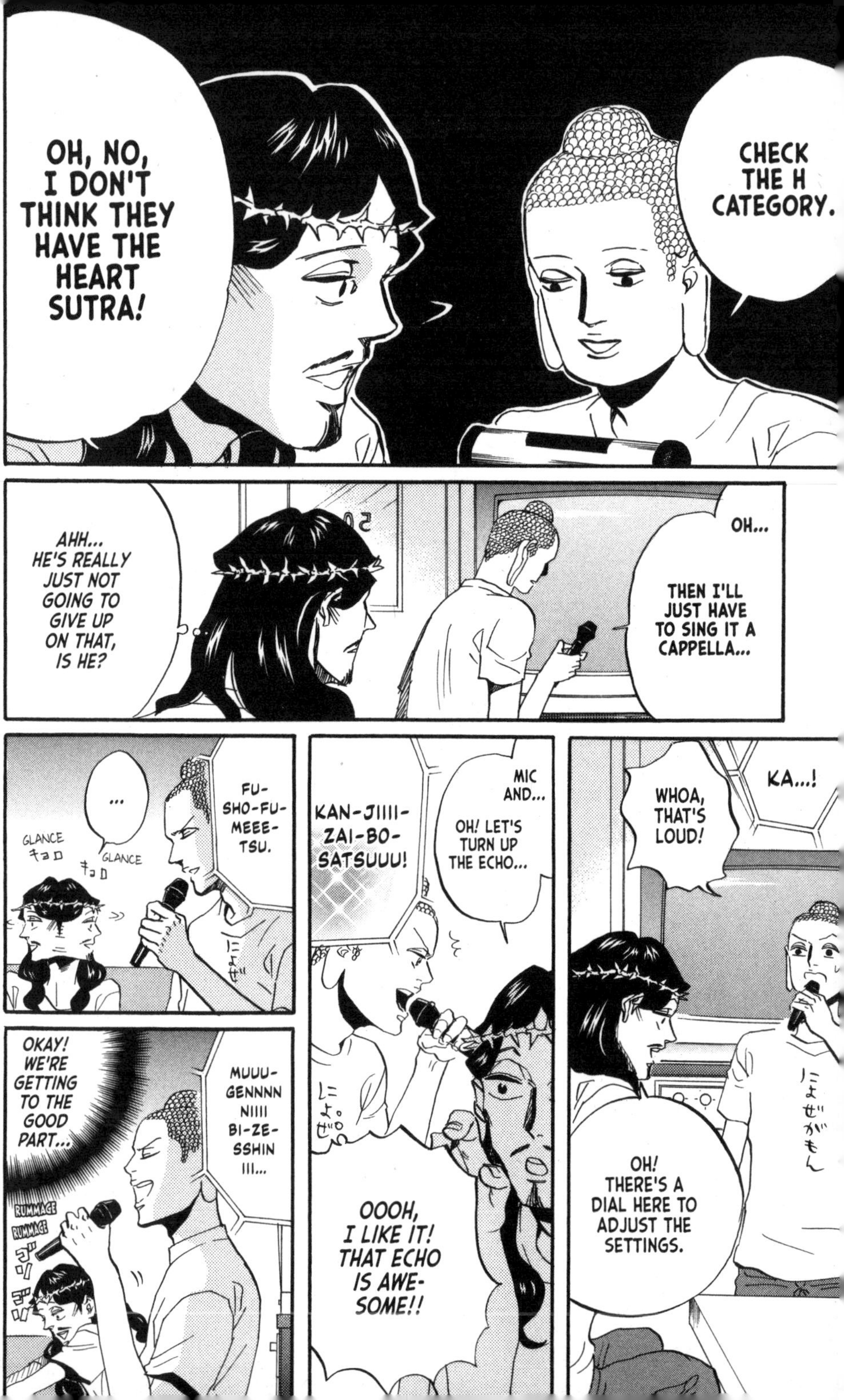
CHECK THE H CATEGORY.
OH, NO, I DON'T THINK THEY HAVE THE HEART SUTRA!
OH...
THEN I'LL JUST HAVE TO SING IT A CAPPELLA...
AHH... HE'S REALLY JUST NOT GOING TO GIVE UP ON THAT, IS HE?
KA...!
WHOA, THAT'S LOUD!
にょぜがもん
OH! THERE'S A DIAL HERE TO ADJUST THE SETTINGS.
MIC AND...
OH! LET'S TURN UP THE ECHO...
KAN-JIIII-ZAI-BO-SATSUUU!
にょ。ぜ
OOOH, I LIKE IT! THAT ECHO IS AWE-SOME!!
FU-SHO-FU-MEEE-TSU.
...
GLANCE キョロ
GLANCE キョロ
にょぜ
MUUU-GENNNN NIIII BI-ZE-SSHIN III...
OKAY! WE'RE GETTING TO THE GOOD PART...
RUMMAGE
RUMMAGE
ゴソ
ゴソ

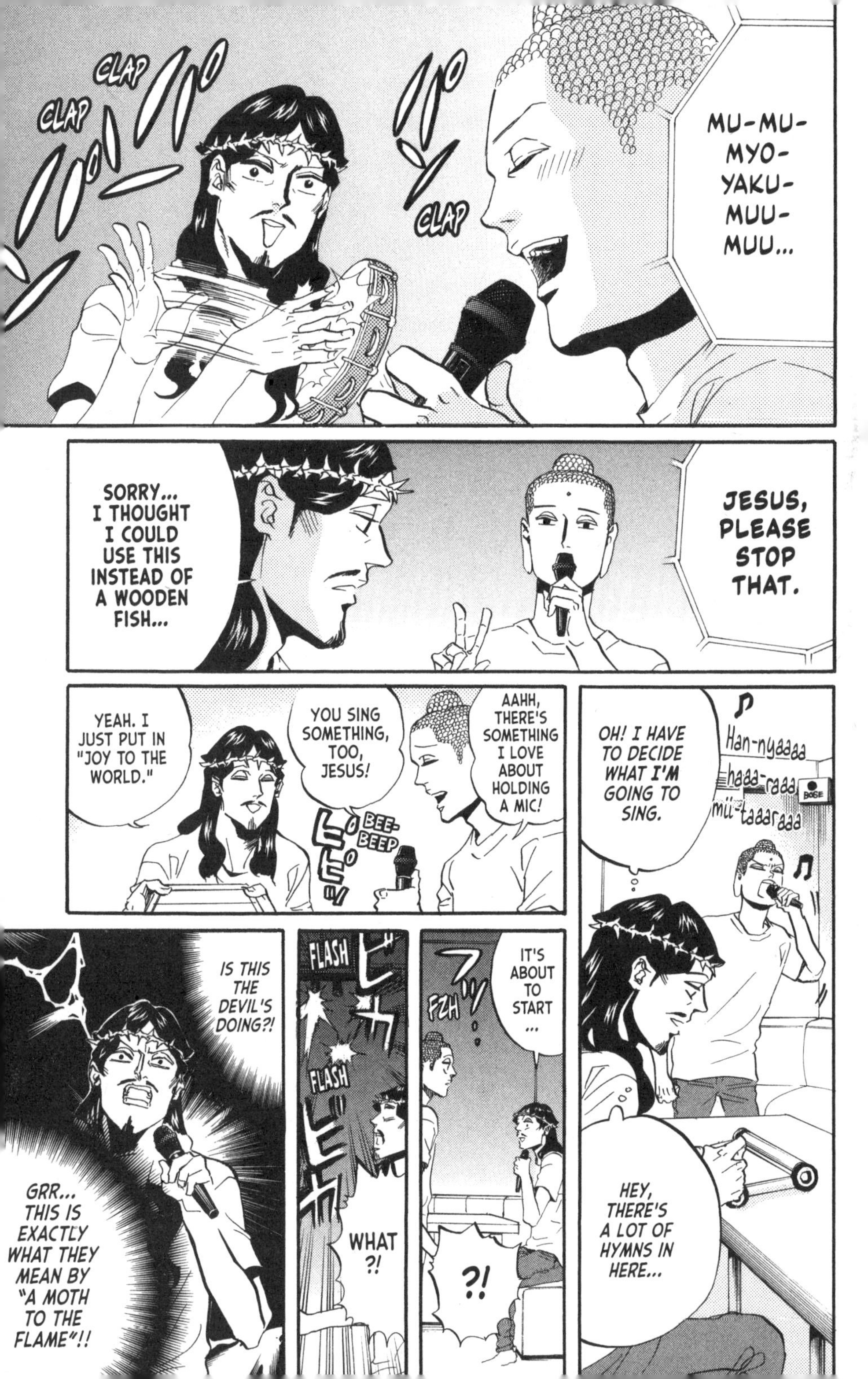
MU-MU-MYO-YAKU-MUU-MUU...
CLAP
CLAP
CLAP
JESUS, PLEASE STOP THAT.
SORRY... I THOUGHT I COULD USE THIS INSTEAD OF A WOODEN FISH...
Han-nyaaaa haaa-raaa mii-taaaraaa
OH! I HAVE TO DECIDE WHAT I'M GOING TO SING.
HEY, THERE'S A LOT OF HYMNS IN HERE...
AAHH, THERE'S SOMETHING I LOVE ABOUT HOLDING A MIC!
YOU SING SOMETHING, TOO, JESUS!
BEE-BEEP
YEAH. I JUST PUT IN "JOY TO THE WORLD."
IT'S ABOUT TO START...
FZH
?!
FLASH
FLASH
WHAT ?!
IS THIS THE DEVIL'S DOING?!
GRR... THIS IS EXACTLY WHAT THEY MEAN BY "A MOTH TO THE FLAME"!!

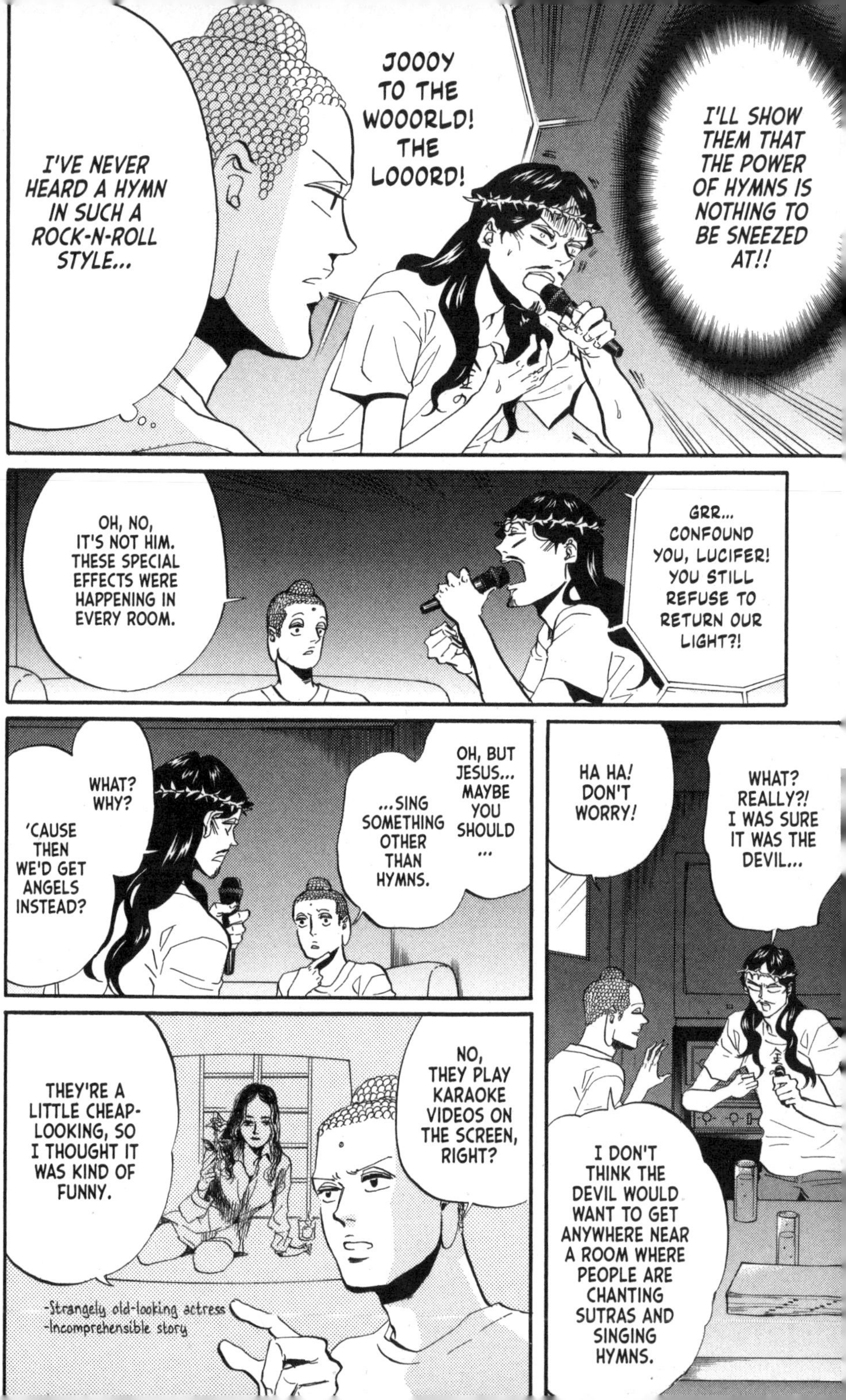
I'LL SHOW THEM THAT THE POWER OF HYMNS IS NOTHING TO BE SNEEZED AT!!
JOOOY TO THE WOOORLD! THE LOOORD!
I'VE NEVER HEARD A HYMN IN SUCH A ROCK-N-ROLL STYLE...
GRR... CONFOUND YOU, LUCIFER! YOU STILL REFUSE TO RETURN OUR LIGHT?!
OH, NO, IT'S NOT HIM. THESE SPECIAL EFFECTS WERE HAPPENING IN EVERY ROOM.
WHAT? REALLY?! I WAS SURE IT WAS THE DEVIL...
HA HA! DON'T WORRY!
I DON'T THINK THE DEVIL WOULD WANT TO GET ANYWHERE NEAR A ROOM WHERE PEOPLE ARE CHANTING SUTRAS AND SINGING HYMNS.
OH, BUT JESUS... MAYBE YOU SHOULD ...
...SING SOMETHING OTHER THAN HYMNS.
WHAT? WHY?
'CAUSE THEN WE'D GET ANGELS INSTEAD?
NO, THEY PLAY KARAOKE VIDEOS ON THE SCREEN, RIGHT?
THEY'RE A LITTLE CHEAP-LOOKING, SO I THOUGHT IT WAS KIND OF FUNNY.
-Strangely old-looking actress
-Incomprehensible story

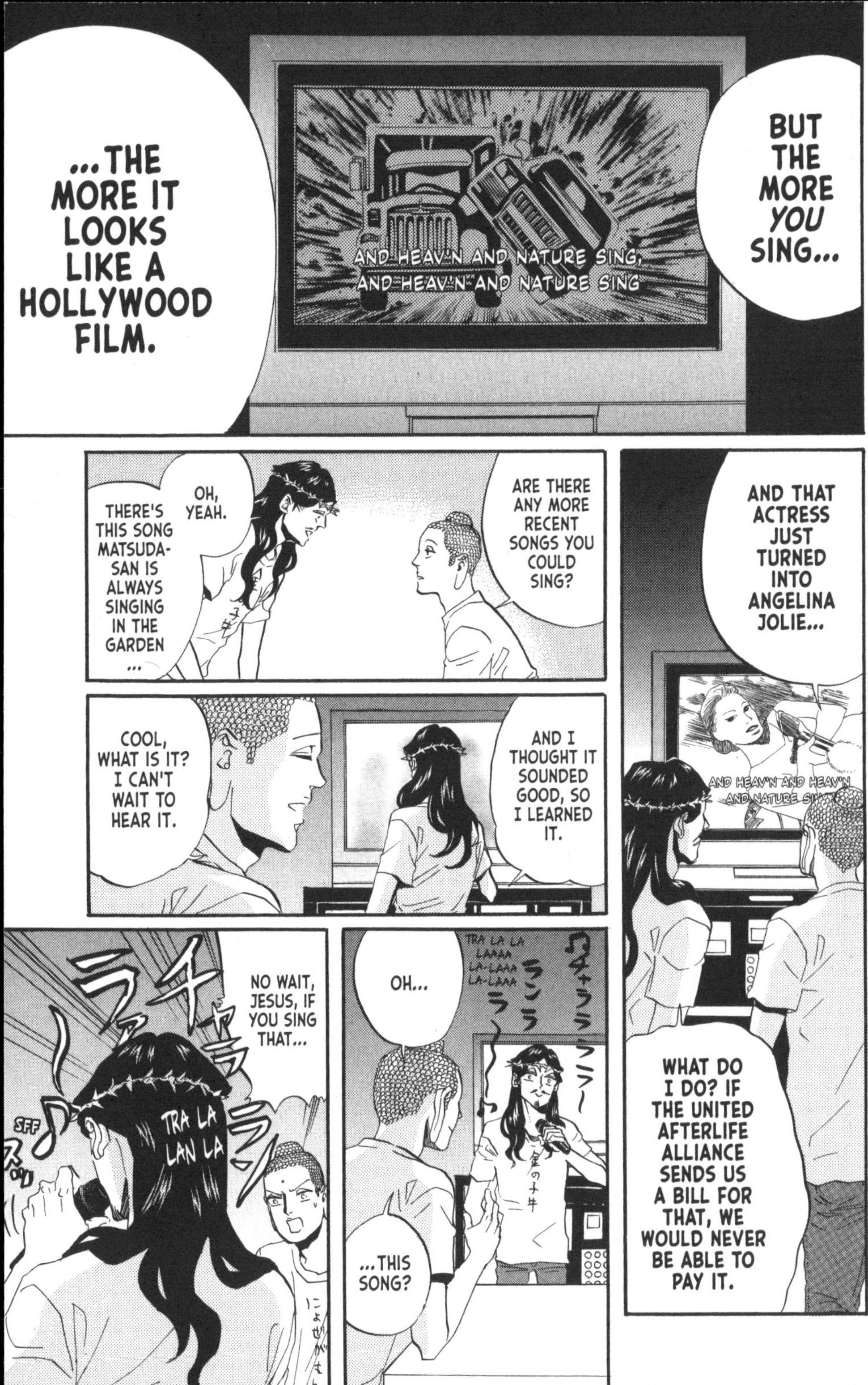
BUT THE MORE *YOU* SING...
AND HEAV'N AND NATURE SING,
AND HEAV'N AND NATURE SING
...THE MORE IT LOOKS LIKE A HOLLYWOOD FILM.
AND THAT ACTRESS JUST TURNED INTO ANGELINA JOLIE...
AND HEAV'N AND HEAV'N AND NATURE SI
WHAT DO I DO? IF THE UNITED AFTERLIFE ALLIANCE SENDS US A BILL FOR THAT, WE WOULD NEVER BE ABLE TO PAY IT.
ARE THERE ANY MORE RECENT SONGS YOU COULD SING?
OH, YEAH.
THERE'S THIS SONG MATSUDA-SAN IS ALWAYS SINGING IN THE GARDEN ...
AND I THOUGHT IT SOUNDED GOOD, SO I LEARNED IT.
COOL, WHAT IS IT? I CAN'T WAIT TO HEAR IT.
OH...
TRA LA LA LAAAA LA-LAAA LA-LAAA
金の子牛
...THIS SONG?
NO WAIT, JESUS, IF YOU SING THAT...
TRA LA LAN LA
SFF

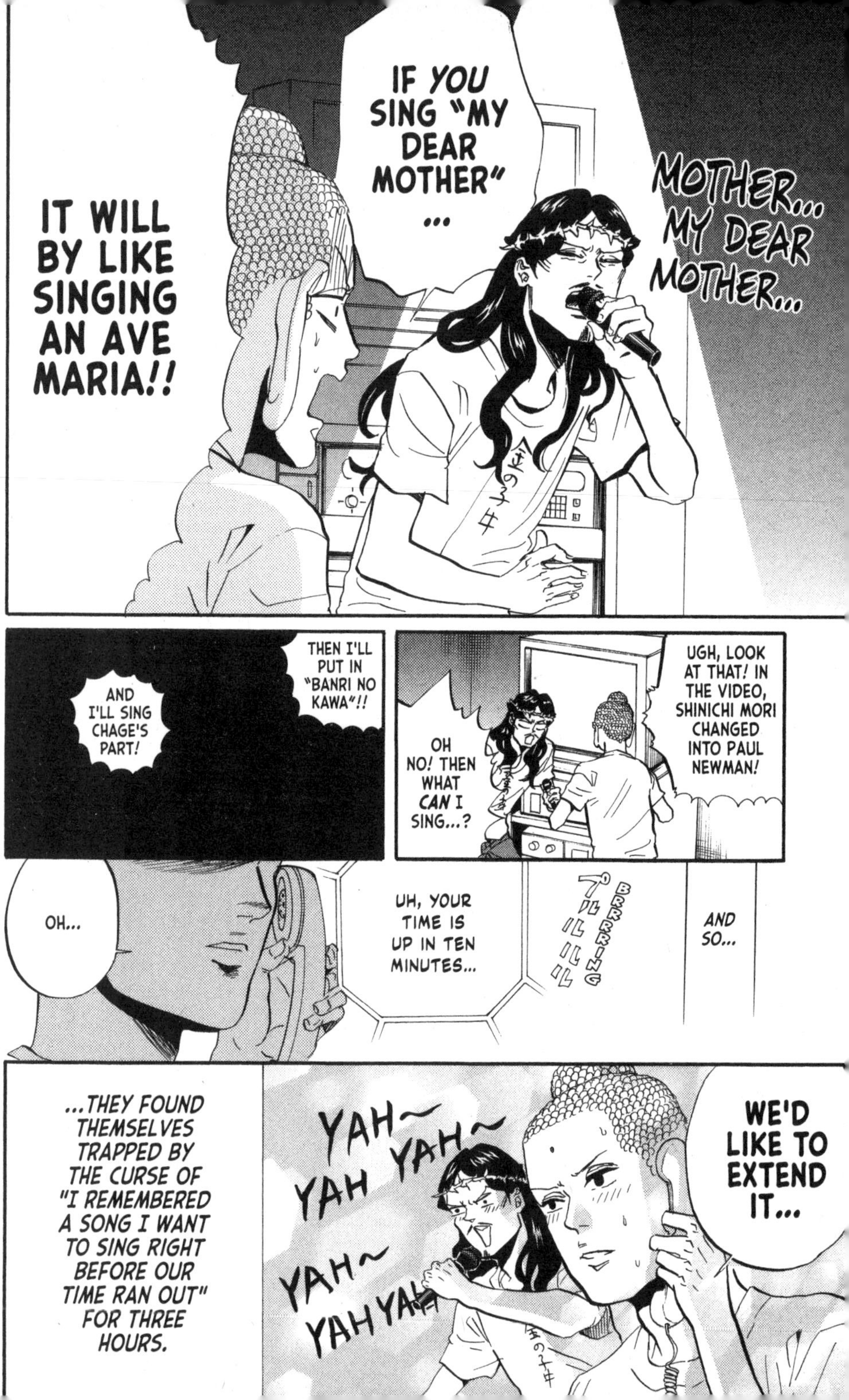
MOTHER... MY DEAR MOTHER...
IF *YOU* SING "MY DEAR MOTHER"...
IT WILL BY LIKE SINGING AN AVE MARIA!!
UGH, LOOK AT THAT! IN THE VIDEO, SHINICHI MORI CHANGED INTO PAUL NEWMAN!
OH NO! THEN WHAT *CAN* I SING...?
THEN I'LL PUT IN "BANRI NO KAWA"!!
AND I'LL SING CHAGE'S PART!
AND SO...
BRRRRING
プルルルル
UH, YOUR TIME IS UP IN TEN MINUTES...
OH...
WE'D LIKE TO EXTEND IT...
YAH~ YAH YAH~
YAH~ YAH YAH
...THEY FOUND THEMSELVES TRAPPED BY THE CURSE OF "I REMEMBERED A SONG I WANT TO SING RIGHT BEFORE OUR TIME RAN OUT" FOR THREE HOURS.

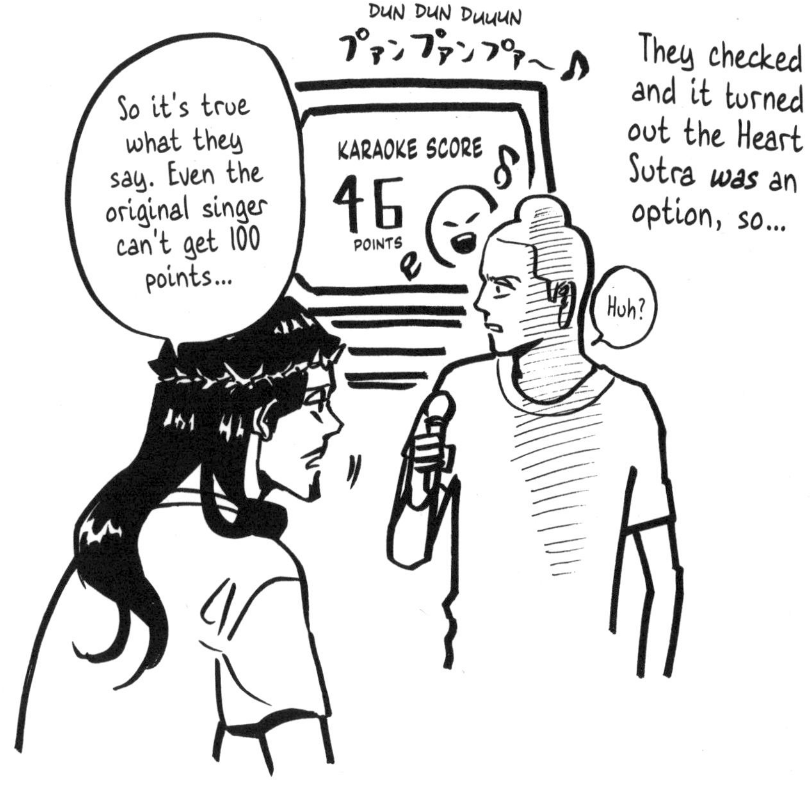
They checked and it turned out the Heart Sutra *was* an option, so...
DUN DUN DUUUN
プァンプァンプァ〜♪
Huh?
KARAOKE SCORE
46
POINTS
So it's true what they say. Even the original singer can't get 100 points...

CHAPTER 38 TRANSLATION NOTES

Thus have I heard, page 165
This is a common translation of the phrase that appears at the beginning of all Buddhist sutras.

Golden Calf, page 165
Soon after Moses led the Jewish people out of Egypt, he went into Mt. Sinai to commune with God and receive the law. Because he was gone so long, the Israelites, desiring a god to follow, convinced the prophet's brother Aaron to make an idol for them to worship. He melted down all their golden earrings and made a statue of a young cow.

Benzaiten, page 165
Benzaiten originated as the goddess Saraswati in South Asia, however evolved over time to be part of the Buddhist pantheon in East Asia as the goddess of everything that flows, including water, time, and music. She is often depicted holding a *biwa* (a traditional Japanese lute), and her messenger is a snake.

Biwa in the nude, page 167
During the Kamakura Period, Benzaiten was often sculpted in the nude. Shown here is the *Hadaka Benzaiten* (Naked Benzaiten) found in Enoshima. Flea is the bassist of the Red Hot Chili Peppers, who famously performed at Woodstock 1999 in the nude.

Higan Music Festival, page 170
Higan literally means "the other shore" or "the far shore" specifically referring to the Far Shore of the Sanzu River—the river that separates the living from the dead.

Raijin, page 171
Raijin is the Japanese god of thunder, lightning, and storms. As such, he is often depicted making thunder by beating on the Japanese taiko drum.

Gregorian chants, page 172
Gregorian chant is religious music used in the Catholic Church, named after Pope Gregory I. It is sung in unison, without accompaniment.

Shibuya C.C. Lemon Hall, page 174
Shibuya C.C. Lemon Hall, originally known as Shibuya Public Hall, is a theater that was first opened during the 1964 Tokyo Olympics and has since hosted concerts for several famous performers. It was renamed to Shibuya C.C. Lemon Hall in 2006 to promote the C.C. Lemon beverage produced by the hall's sponsor, Suntory. It is now under new management from Amuse, Inc. and the LINE Corporation, and has been renamed again to LINE CUBE SHIBUYA.

Karaoke Kan, page 175
Karaoke Kan is a chain of karaoke shops, also known as karaoke boxes, which is building consisting of several private rooms, in which one can sing karaoke without having to perform for complete strangers. While renting one of these rooms, it is also possible to rent costumes and props, and to order food and drinks. The different rooms will be equipped with different karaoke players, which will have different song selections. The machines will also grade the singer's performance, giving them a score when the song is done.

Wooden fish, page 177
A wooden fish, or Chinese wooden temple block, is a wooden percussion instrument that is used in to keep rhythm while chanting sutras. It is a hollow instrument that is struck with a mallet and can either be round, or shaped like a fish.

My Dear Mother, page 178

This is the English translation of the title of the song "Ofukuro-san," by the Japanese musician Shinichi Mori (born 1947), about how he will never forget his mother. "Ave Maria" is Latin for "Hail Mary," and is a prayer to the Virgin Mary. The prayer has been put to music by many different composers. Paul Newman is a legendary actor who lived from 1925 to 2008.

Banri no Kawa, page 178

"*Banri no Kawa* (Thousand-Mile River)" is the first hit by pop duo Chage & Aska.

SAINT☆YOUNG MEN

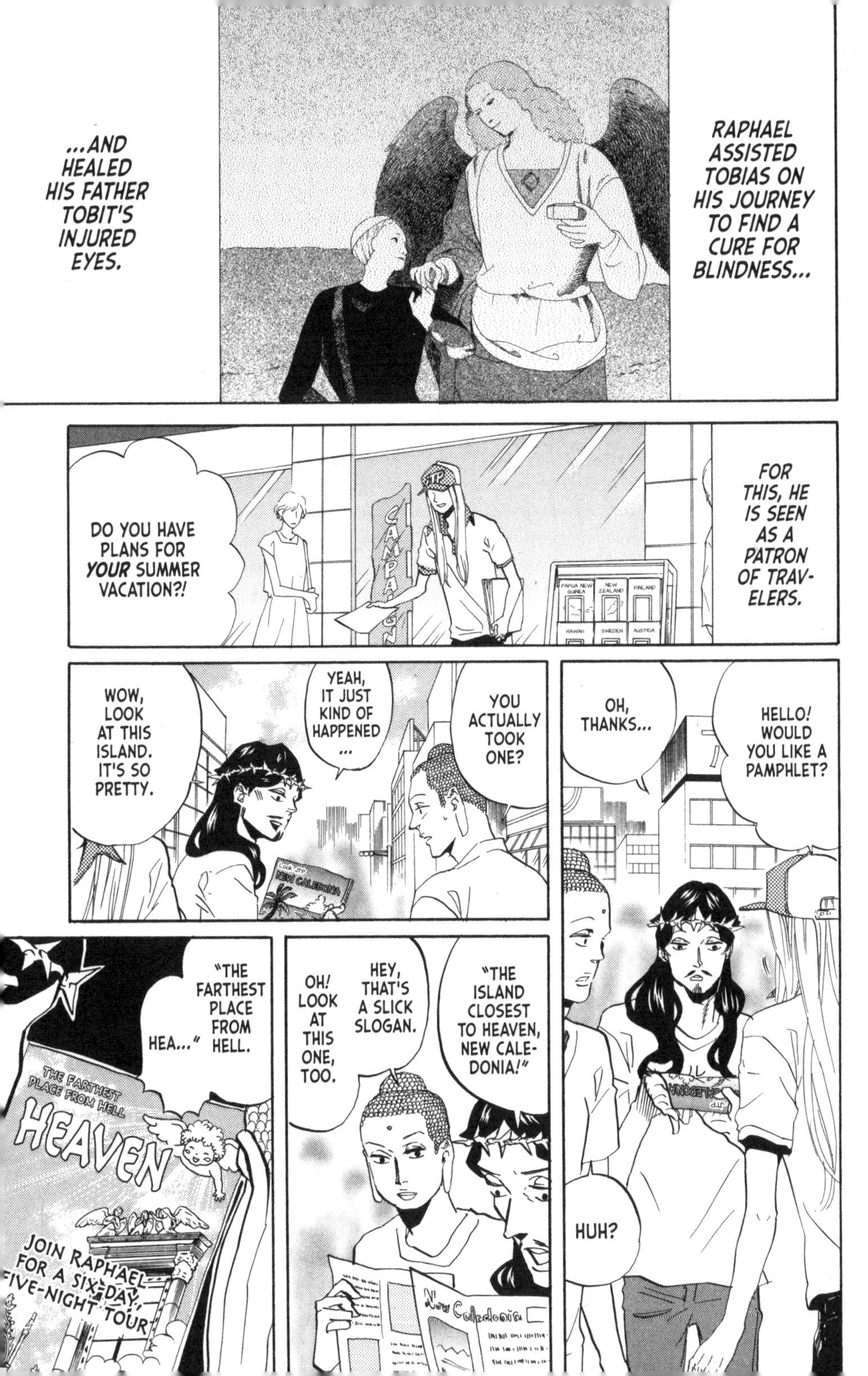
RAPHAEL ASSISTED TOBIAS ON HIS JOURNEY TO FIND A CURE FOR BLINDNESS...
...AND HEALED HIS FATHER TOBIT'S INJURED EYES.
FOR THIS, HE IS SEEN AS A PATRON OF TRAVELERS.
DO YOU HAVE PLANS FOR *YOUR* SUMMER VACATION?!
PAPUA NEW GUINEA
NEW ZEALAND
FINLAND
HAWAII
SWEDEN
AUSTRIA
HELLO! WOULD YOU LIKE A PAMPHLET?
OH, THANKS...
HUH?
YOU ACTUALLY TOOK ONE?
YEAH, IT JUST KIND OF HAPPENED...
WOW, LOOK AT THIS ISLAND. IT'S SO PRETTY.
NEW CALEDONIA
"THE ISLAND CLOSEST TO HEAVEN, NEW CALEDONIA!"
HEY, THAT'S A SLICK SLOGAN.
OH! LOOK AT THIS ONE, TOO.
New Caledonia
"THE FARTHEST PLACE FROM HELL. HEA..."
THE FARTHEST PLACE FROM HELL
HEAVEN
JOIN RAPHAEL FOR A SIX-DAY, FIVE-NIGHT TOUR

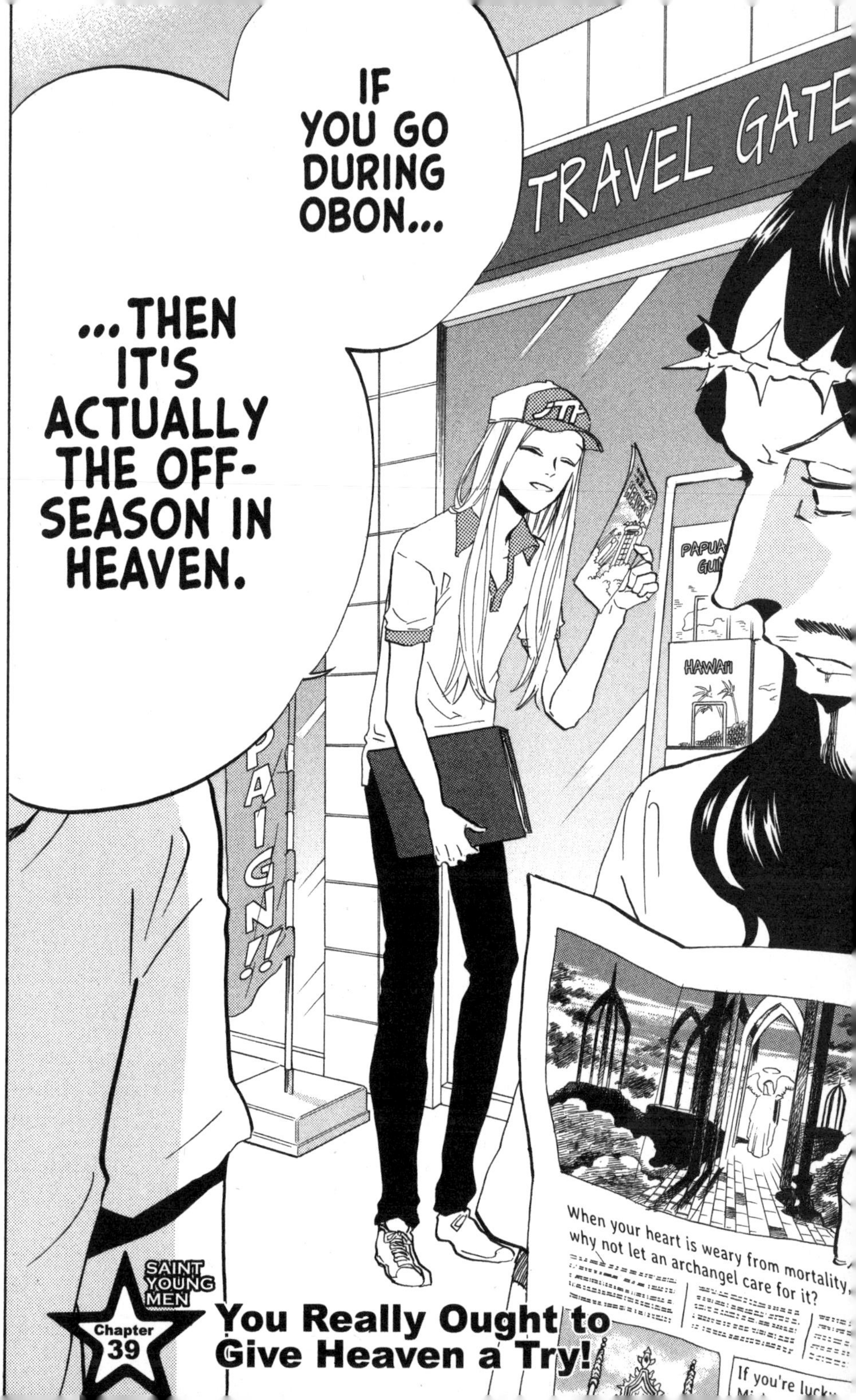
IF YOU GO DURING OBON...
...THEN IT'S ACTUALLY THE OFF-SEASON IN HEAVEN.
TRAVEL GATE
HAWAII
PAIGN!!
When your heart is weary from mortality, why not let an archangel care for it?
SAINT YOUNG MEN
Chapter 39
You Really Ought to Give Heaven a Try!

BUDDHA: SUMMER IS ALL ABOUT FIREWORKS. LAUNCHING FIREWORKS IS NICE, TOO, BUT SPARKLERS ARE HARD TO PASS UP.

JESUS: SUMMER IS ALL ABOUT SHAVED ICE. HIS FAVORITE FLAVOR IS WATER-MELON, BUT THEY DON'T SELL IT MANY PLACES.

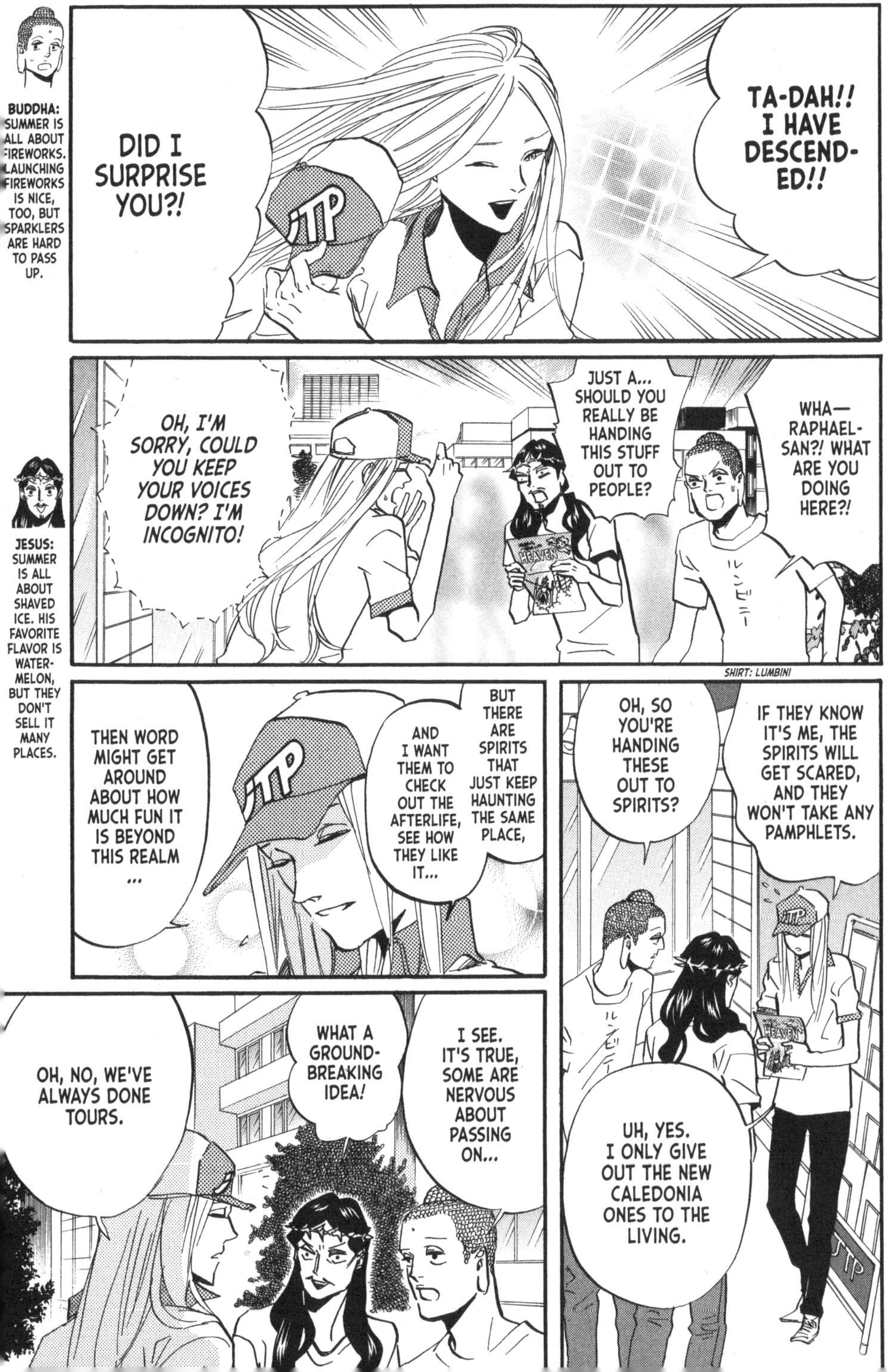
TA-DAH!! I HAVE DESCEND-ED!!
DID I SURPRISE YOU?!
WHA— RAPHAEL-SAN?! WHAT ARE YOU DOING HERE?!
JUST A... SHOULD YOU REALLY BE HANDING THIS STUFF OUT TO PEOPLE?
OH, I'M SORRY, COULD YOU KEEP YOUR VOICES DOWN? I'M INCOGNITO!
HEAVEN
SHIRT: LUMBINI
IF THEY KNOW IT'S ME, THE SPIRITS WILL GET SCARED, AND THEY WON'T TAKE ANY PAMPHLETS.
OH, SO YOU'RE HANDING THESE OUT TO SPIRITS?
UH, YES. I ONLY GIVE OUT THE NEW CALEDONIA ONES TO THE LIVING.
BUT THERE ARE SPIRITS THAT JUST KEEP HAUNTING THE SAME PLACE,
AND I WANT THEM TO CHECK OUT THE AFTERLIFE, SEE HOW THEY LIKE IT...
THEN WORD MIGHT GET AROUND ABOUT HOW MUCH FUN IT IS BEYOND THIS REALM ...
I SEE. IT'S TRUE, SOME ARE NERVOUS ABOUT PASSING ON...
WHAT A GROUND-BREAKING IDEA!
OH, NO, WE'VE ALWAYS DONE TOURS.

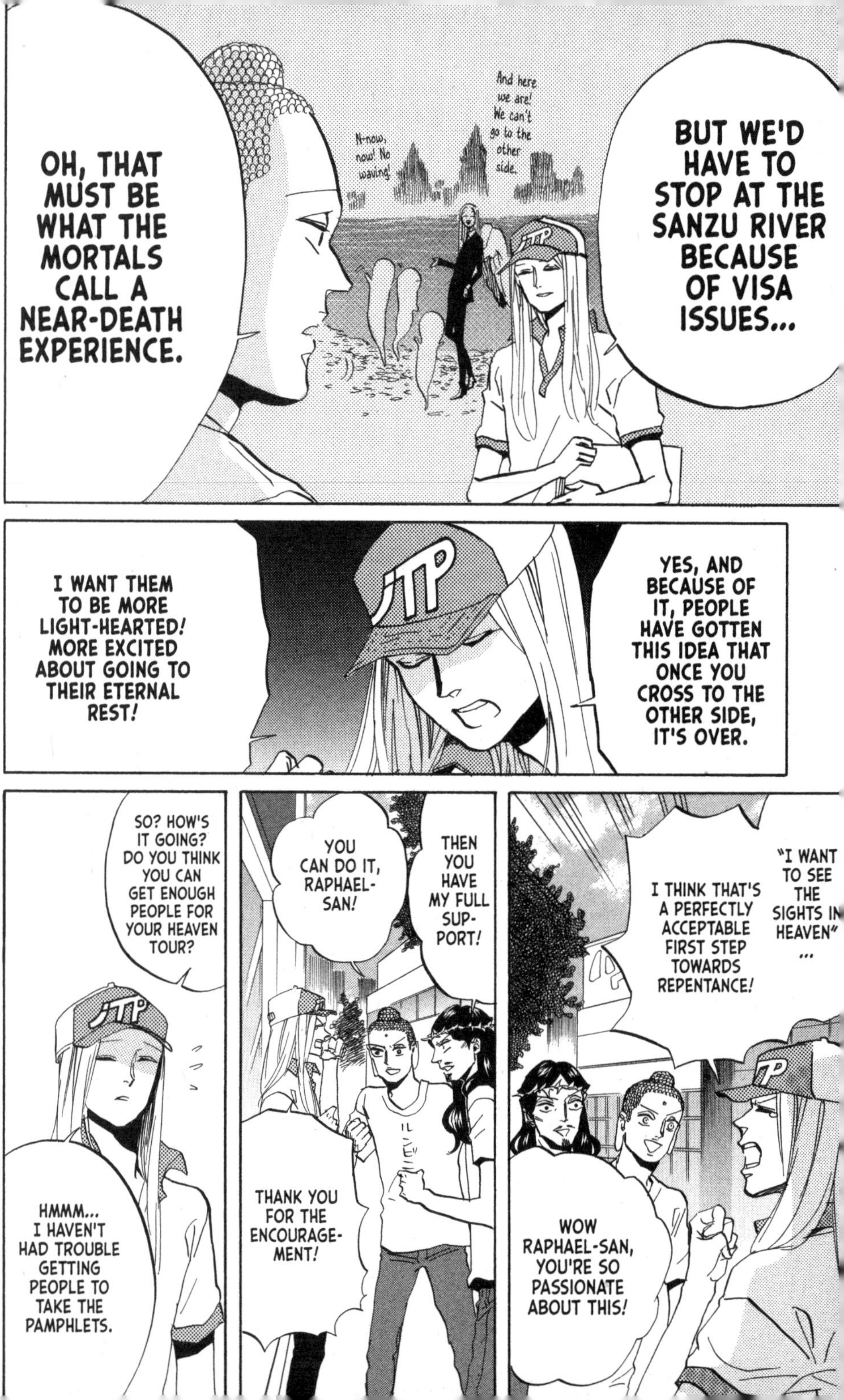
BUT WE'D HAVE TO STOP AT THE SANZU RIVER BECAUSE OF VISA ISSUES...
And here we are! We can't go to the other side.
N-now, now! No waving!
OH, THAT MUST BE WHAT THE MORTALS CALL A NEAR-DEATH EXPERIENCE.
YES, AND BECAUSE OF IT, PEOPLE HAVE GOTTEN THIS IDEA THAT ONCE YOU CROSS TO THE OTHER SIDE, IT'S OVER.
I WANT THEM TO BE MORE LIGHT-HEARTED! MORE EXCITED ABOUT GOING TO THEIR ETERNAL REST!
"I WANT TO SEE THE SIGHTS IN HEAVEN"...
I THINK THAT'S A PERFECTLY ACCEPTABLE FIRST STEP TOWARDS REPENTANCE!
WOW RAPHAEL-SAN, YOU'RE SO PASSIONATE ABOUT THIS!
THEN YOU HAVE MY FULL SUP-PORT!
YOU CAN DO IT, RAPHAEL-SAN!
THANK YOU FOR THE ENCOURAGE-MENT!
SO? HOW'S IT GOING? DO YOU THINK YOU CAN GET ENOUGH PEOPLE FOR YOUR HEAVEN TOUR?
HMMM... I HAVEN'T HAD TROUBLE GETTING PEOPLE TO TAKE THE PAMPHLETS.

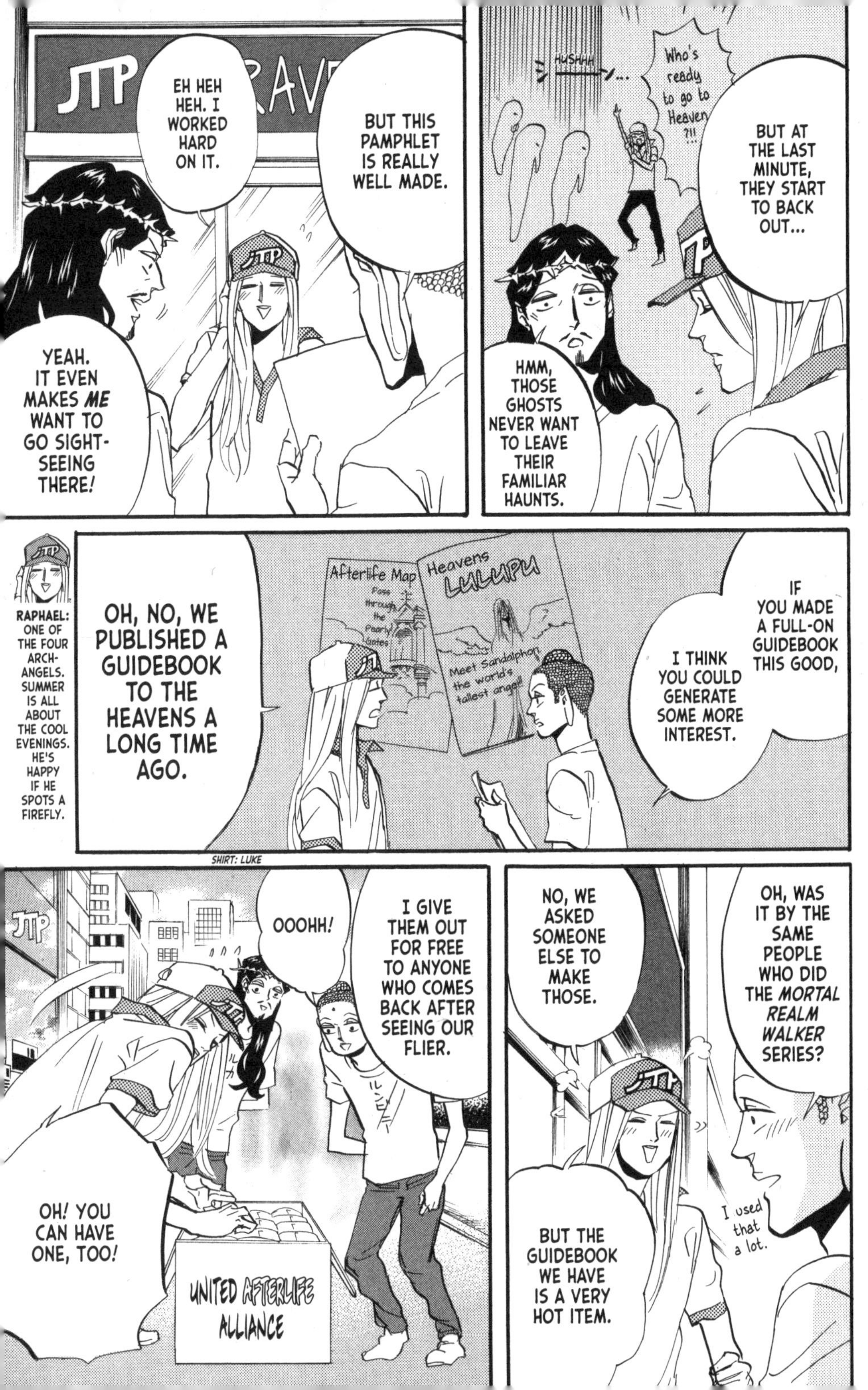
HUSHHH
Who's ready to go to Heaven?!!
BUT AT THE LAST MINUTE, THEY START TO BACK OUT...
HMM, THOSE GHOSTS NEVER WANT TO LEAVE THEIR FAMILIAR HAUNTS.
BUT THIS PAMPHLET IS REALLY WELL MADE.
EH HEH HEH. I WORKED HARD ON IT.
YEAH. IT EVEN MAKES *ME* WANT TO GO SIGHT-SEEING THERE!
IF YOU MADE A FULL-ON GUIDEBOOK THIS GOOD,
I THINK YOU COULD GENERATE SOME MORE INTEREST.
Afterlife Map
Pass through the Pearly Gates
Heavens LULUPU
Meet Sandalphon the world's tallest angel!
OH, NO, WE PUBLISHED A GUIDEBOOK TO THE HEAVENS A LONG TIME AGO.
RAPHAEL: ONE OF THE FOUR ARCH-ANGELS. SUMMER IS ALL ABOUT THE COOL EVENINGS. HE'S HAPPY IF HE SPOTS A FIREFLY.
SHIRT: LUKE
OH, WAS IT BY THE SAME PEOPLE WHO DID THE *MORTAL REALM WALKER* SERIES?
NO, WE ASKED SOMEONE ELSE TO MAKE THOSE.
I used that a lot.
BUT THE GUIDEBOOK WE HAVE IS A VERY HOT ITEM.
I GIVE THEM OUT FOR FREE TO ANYONE WHO COMES BACK AFTER SEEING OUR FLIER.
OOOHH!
OH! YOU CAN HAVE ONE, TOO!
UNITED AFTERLIFE ALLIANCE

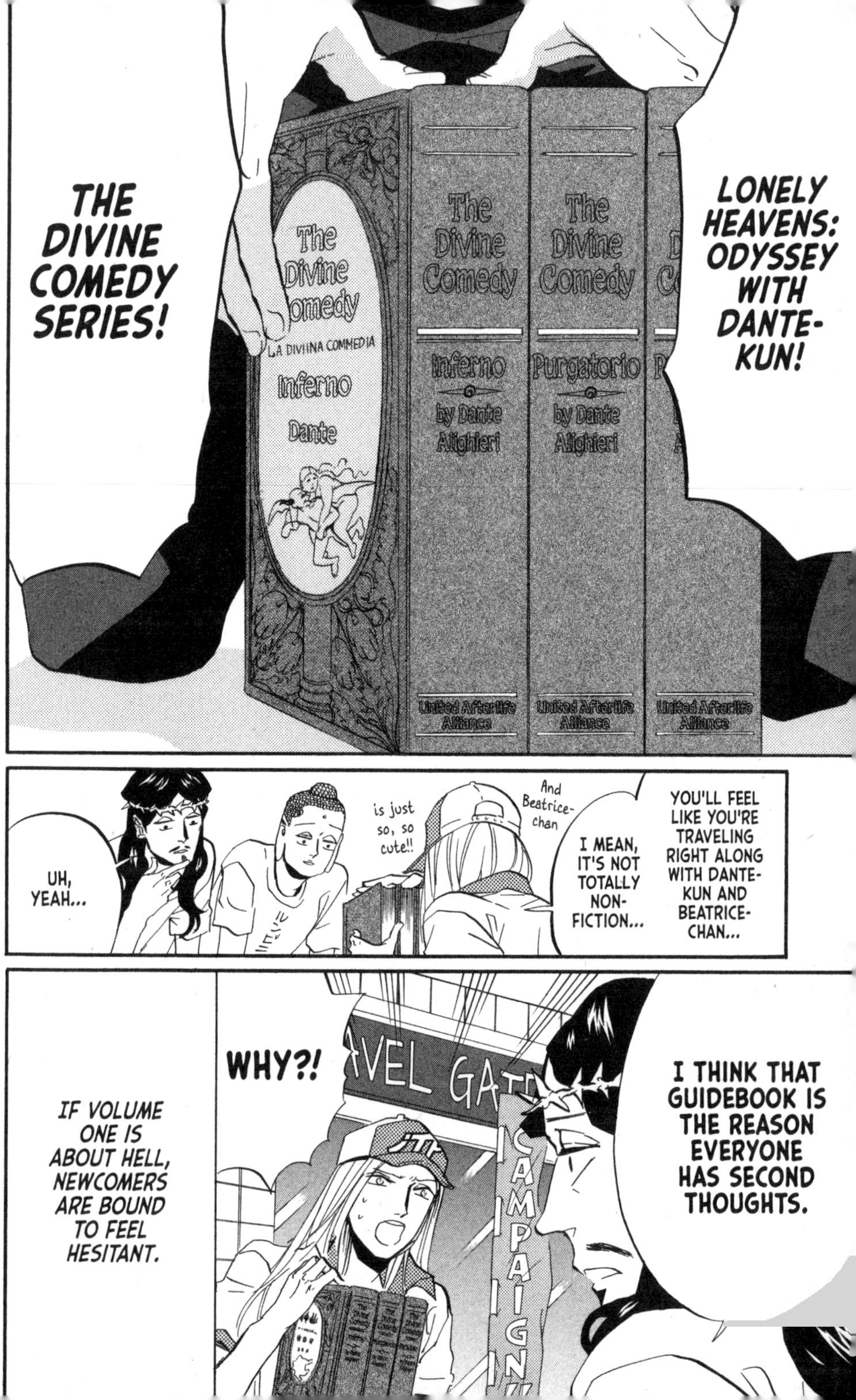
LONELY HEAVENS: ODYSSEY WITH DANTE-KUN!
The Divine Comedy
LA DIVINA COMMEDIA
Inferno
Dante
The Divine Comedy
Inferno
by Dante Alighieri
The Divine Comedy
Purgatorio
by Dante Alighieri
United Afterlife Alliance
United Afterlife Alliance
United Afterlife Alliance
THE DIVINE COMEDY SERIES!
YOU'LL FEEL LIKE YOU'RE TRAVELING RIGHT ALONG WITH DANTE-KUN AND BEATRICE-CHAN...
I MEAN, IT'S NOT TOTALLY NON-FICTION...
And Beatrice-chan is just so, so cute!!
UH, YEAH...
I THINK THAT GUIDEBOOK IS THE REASON EVERYONE HAS SECOND THOUGHTS.
WHY?!
IF VOLUME ONE IS ABOUT HELL, NEWCOMERS ARE BOUND TO FEEL HESITANT.

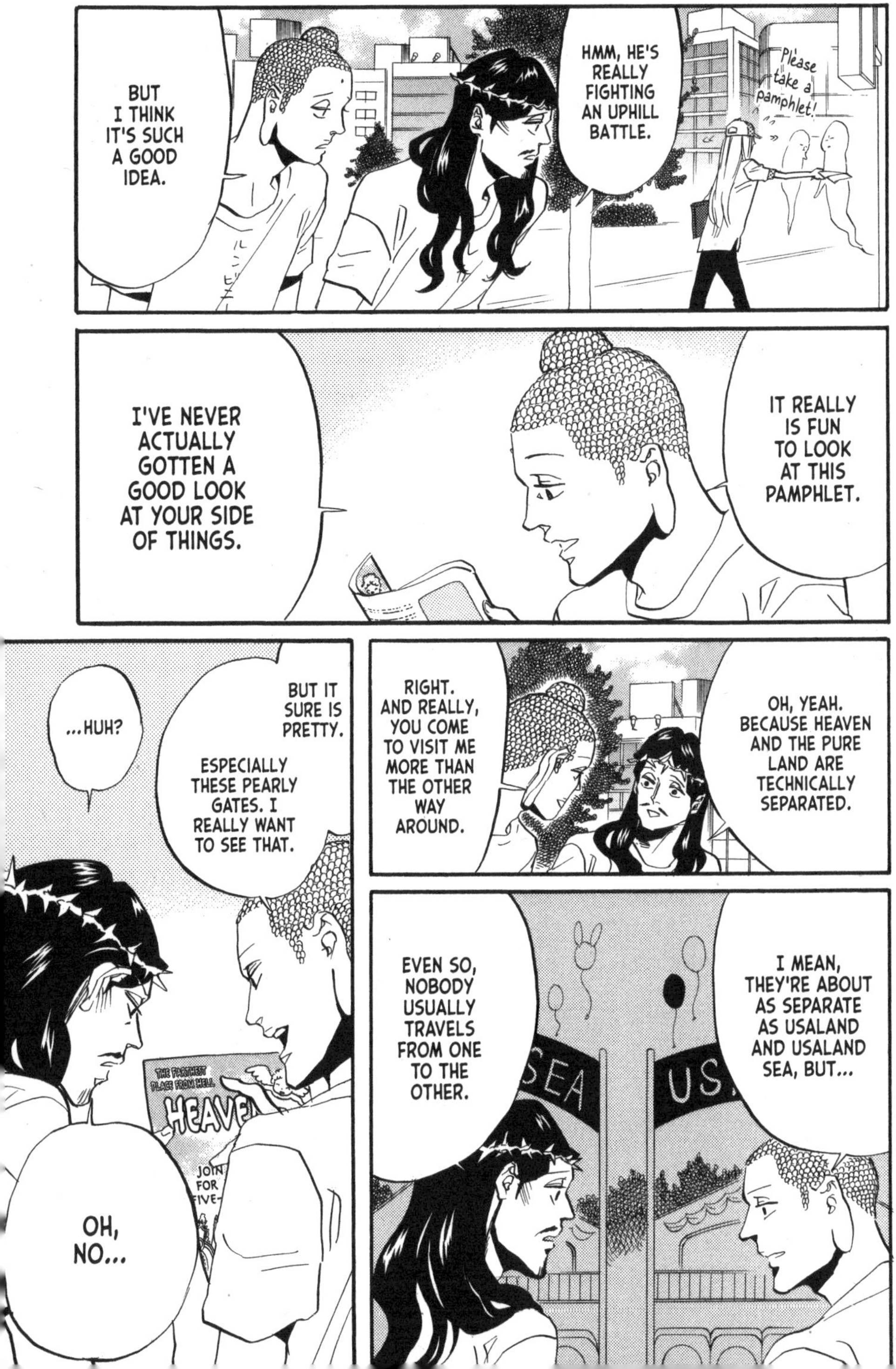

Please take a pamphlet!
HMM, HE'S REALLY FIGHTING AN UPHILL BATTLE.
BUT I THINK IT'S SUCH A GOOD IDEA.
IT REALLY IS FUN TO LOOK AT THIS PAMPHLET.
I'VE NEVER ACTUALLY GOTTEN A GOOD LOOK AT YOUR SIDE OF THINGS.
OH, YEAH. BECAUSE HEAVEN AND THE PURE LAND ARE TECHNICALLY SEPARATED.
RIGHT. AND REALLY, YOU COME TO VISIT ME MORE THAN THE OTHER WAY AROUND.
I MEAN, THEY'RE ABOUT AS SEPARATE AS USALAND AND USALAND SEA, BUT...
EVEN SO, NOBODY USUALLY TRAVELS FROM ONE TO THE OTHER.
SEA
BUT IT SURE IS PRETTY.
ESPECIALLY THESE PEARLY GATES. I REALLY WANT TO SEE THAT.
...HUH?
THE FARTHEST PLACE FROM HELL
OH, NO...

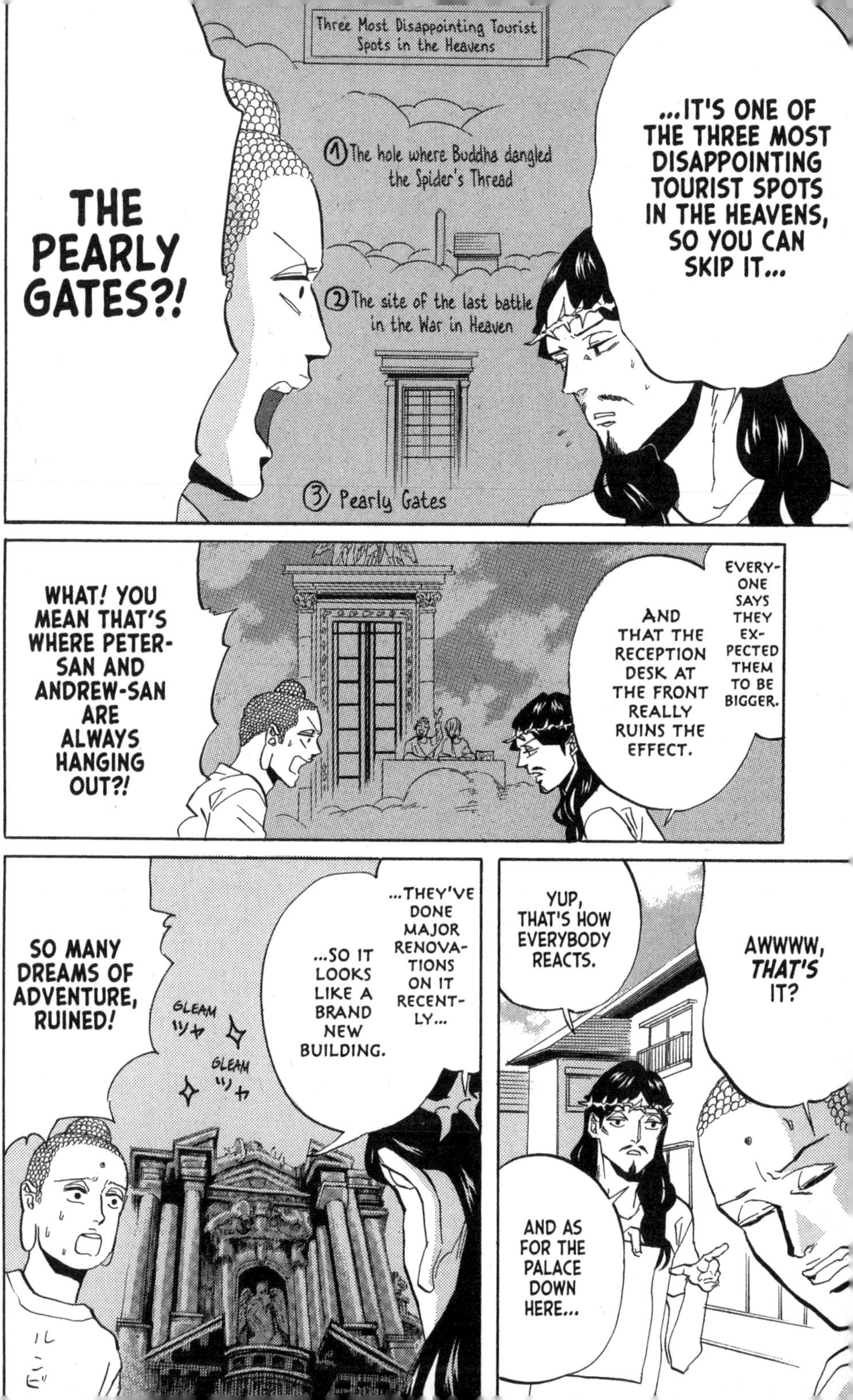
Three Most Disappointing Tourist Spots in the Heavens
① The hole where Buddha dangled the Spider's Thread
② The site of the last battle in the War in Heaven
③ Pearly Gates
...IT'S ONE OF THE THREE MOST DISAPPOINTING TOURIST SPOTS IN THE HEAVENS, SO YOU CAN SKIP IT...
THE PEARLY GATES?!
EVERYONE SAYS THEY EXPECTED THEM TO BE BIGGER.
AND THAT THE RECEPTION DESK AT THE FRONT REALLY RUINS THE EFFECT.
WHAT! YOU MEAN THAT'S WHERE PETER-SAN AND ANDREW-SAN ARE ALWAYS HANGING OUT?!
AWWWW, *THAT'S* IT?
YUP, THAT'S HOW EVERYBODY REACTS.
AND AS FOR THE PALACE DOWN HERE...
...THEY'VE DONE MAJOR RENOVATIONS ON IT RECENTLY...
...SO IT LOOKS LIKE A BRAND NEW BUILDING.
GLEAM ツヤ
GLEAM ツヤ
SO MANY DREAMS OF ADVENTURE, RUINED!

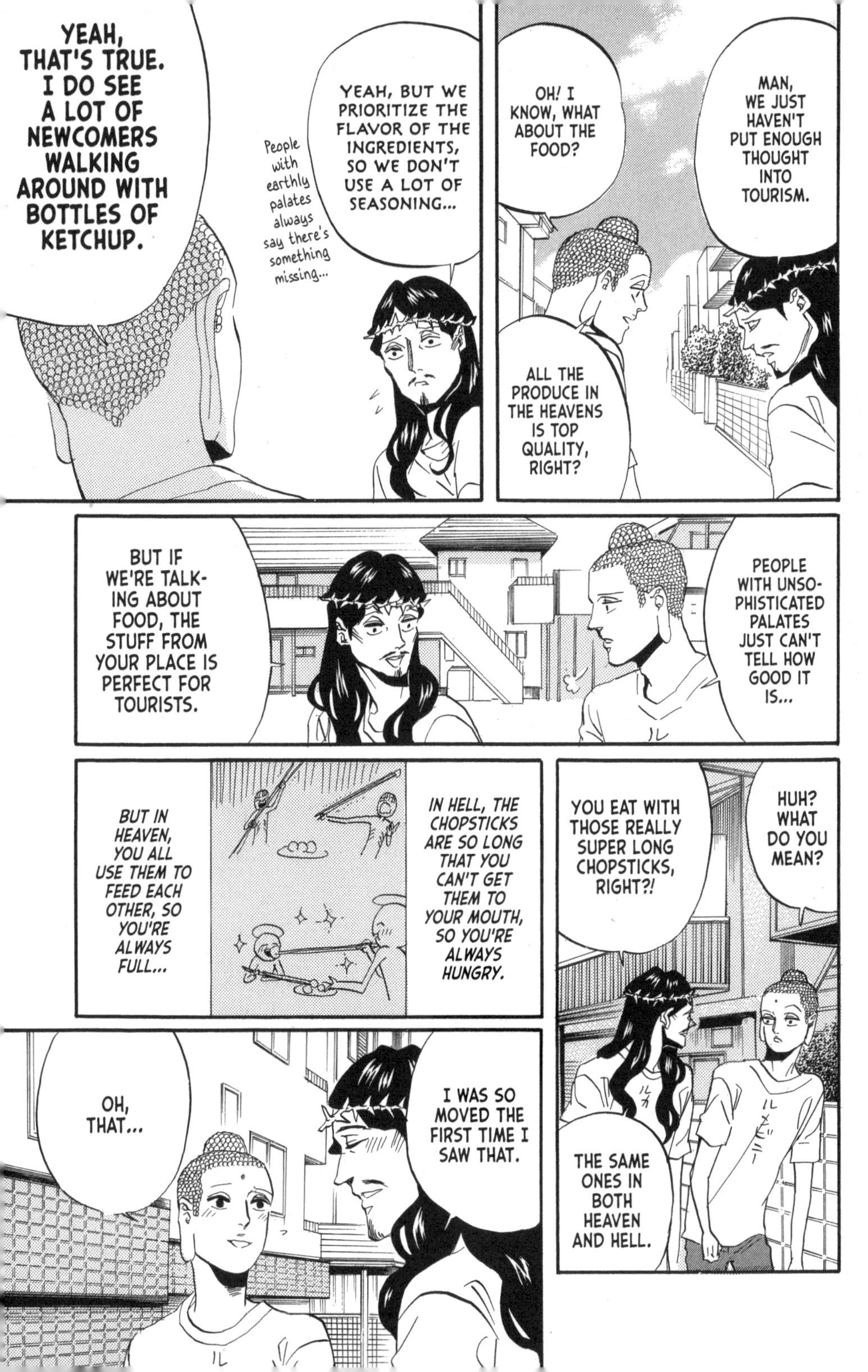
MAN, WE JUST HAVEN'T PUT ENOUGH THOUGHT INTO TOURISM.
OH! I KNOW, WHAT ABOUT THE FOOD?
ALL THE PRODUCE IN THE HEAVENS IS TOP QUALITY, RIGHT?
YEAH, BUT WE PRIORITIZE THE FLAVOR OF THE INGREDIENTS, SO WE DON'T USE A LOT OF SEASONING...
People with earthly palates always say there's something missing...
YEAH, THAT'S TRUE. I DO SEE A LOT OF NEWCOMERS WALKING AROUND WITH BOTTLES OF KETCHUP.
PEOPLE WITH UNSO-PHISTICATED PALATES JUST CAN'T TELL HOW GOOD IT IS...
BUT IF WE'RE TALK-ING ABOUT FOOD, THE STUFF FROM YOUR PLACE IS PERFECT FOR TOURISTS.
HUH? WHAT DO YOU MEAN?
YOU EAT WITH THOSE REALLY SUPER LONG CHOPSTICKS, RIGHT?!
THE SAME ONES IN BOTH HEAVEN AND HELL.
IN HELL, THE CHOPSTICKS ARE SO LONG THAT YOU CAN'T GET THEM TO YOUR MOUTH, SO YOU'RE ALWAYS HUNGRY.
BUT IN HEAVEN, YOU ALL USE THEM TO FEED EACH OTHER, SO YOU'RE ALWAYS FULL...
I WAS SO MOVED THE FIRST TIME I SAW THAT.
OH, THAT...

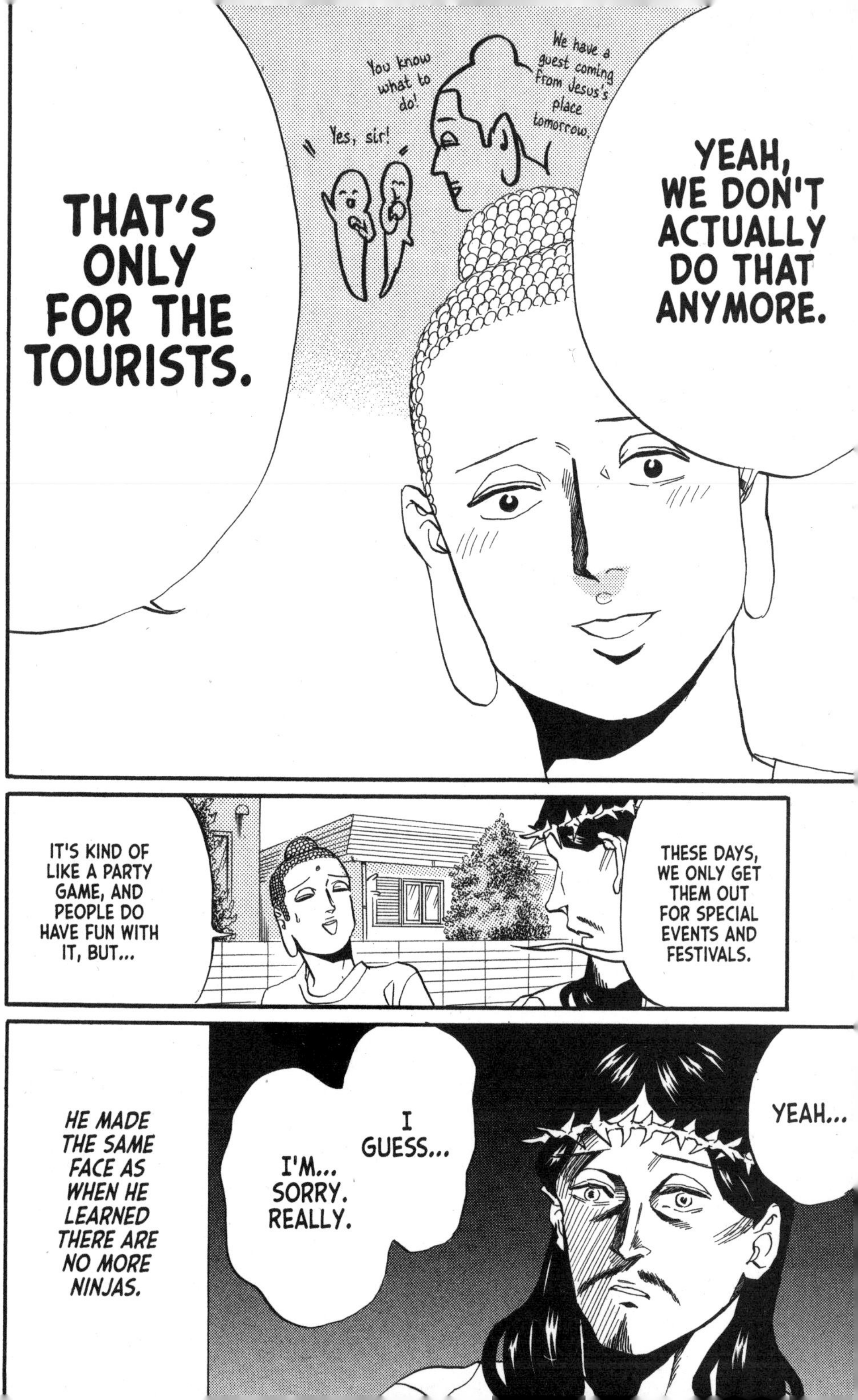
YEAH, WE DON'T ACTUALLY DO THAT ANYMORE.
We have a guest coming from Jesus's place tomorrow.
You know what to do!
Yes, sir!
THAT'S ONLY FOR THE TOURISTS.
THESE DAYS, WE ONLY GET THEM OUT FOR SPECIAL EVENTS AND FESTIVALS.
IT'S KIND OF LIKE A PARTY GAME, AND PEOPLE DO HAVE FUN WITH IT, BUT...
YEAH...
I GUESS...
I'M... SORRY. REALLY.
HE MADE THE SAME FACE AS WHEN HE LEARNED THERE ARE NO MORE NINJAS.

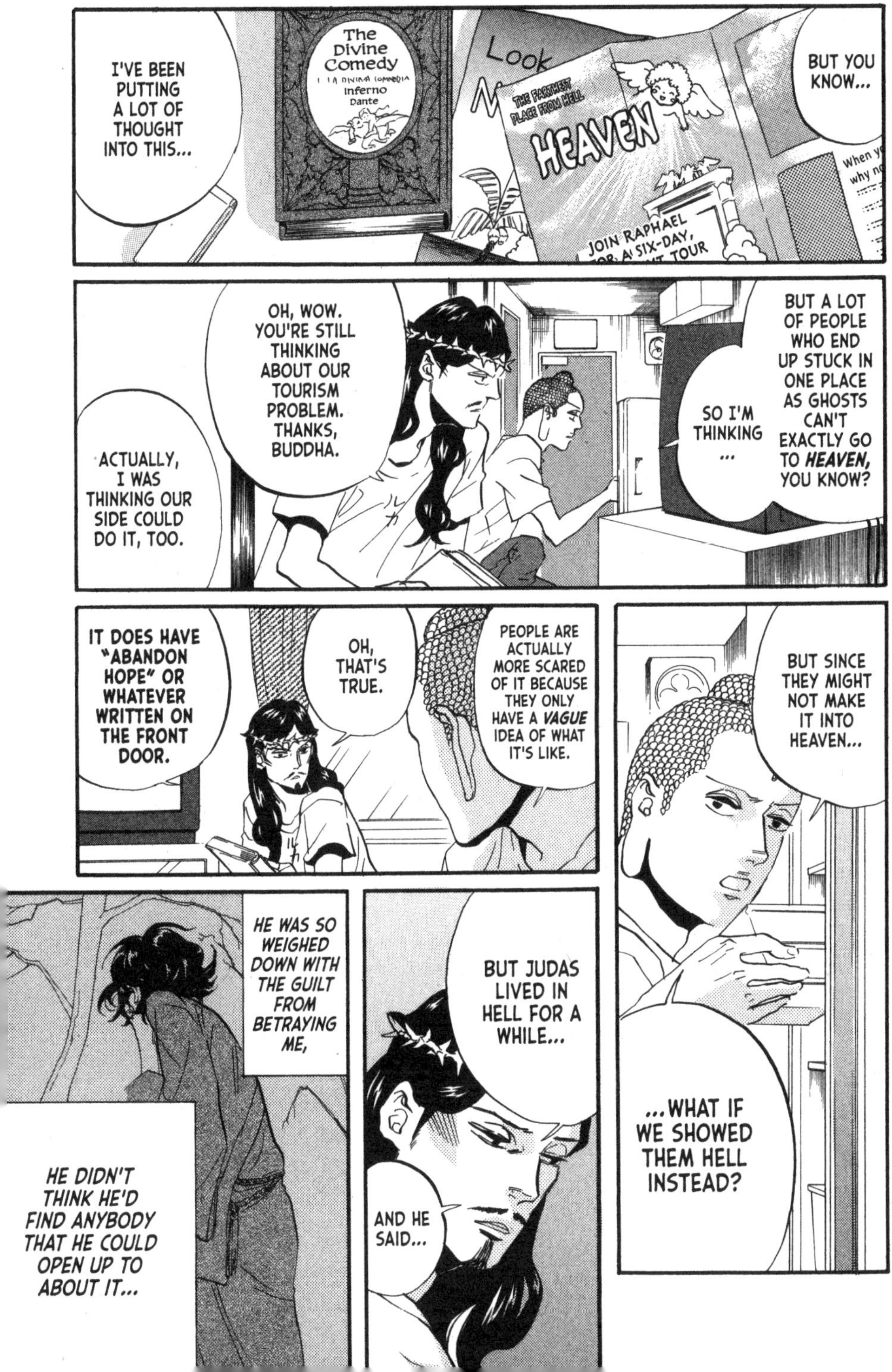
BUT YOU KNOW...
Look
THE FARTHEST PLACE FROM HELL
HEAVEN
JOIN RAPHAEL FOR A SIX-DAY,
The Divine Comedy
LA DIVINA COMMEDIA
Inferno
Dante
I'VE BEEN PUTTING A LOT OF THOUGHT INTO THIS...
BUT A LOT OF PEOPLE WHO END UP STUCK IN ONE PLACE AS GHOSTS CAN'T EXACTLY GO TO *HEAVEN,* YOU KNOW?
SO I'M THINKING ...
OH, WOW. YOU'RE STILL THINKING ABOUT OUR TOURISM PROBLEM. THANKS, BUDDHA.
ACTUALLY, I WAS THINKING OUR SIDE COULD DO IT, TOO.
BUT SINCE THEY MIGHT NOT MAKE IT INTO HEAVEN...
...WHAT IF WE SHOWED THEM HELL INSTEAD?
PEOPLE ARE ACTUALLY MORE SCARED OF IT BECAUSE THEY ONLY HAVE A *VAGUE* IDEA OF WHAT IT'S LIKE.
OH, THAT'S TRUE.
IT DOES HAVE "ABANDON HOPE" OR WHATEVER WRITTEN ON THE FRONT DOOR.
BUT JUDAS LIVED IN HELL FOR A WHILE...
AND HE SAID...
HE WAS SO WEIGHED DOWN WITH THE GUILT FROM BETRAYING ME,
HE DIDN'T THINK HE'D FIND ANYBODY THAT HE COULD OPEN UP TO ABOUT IT...

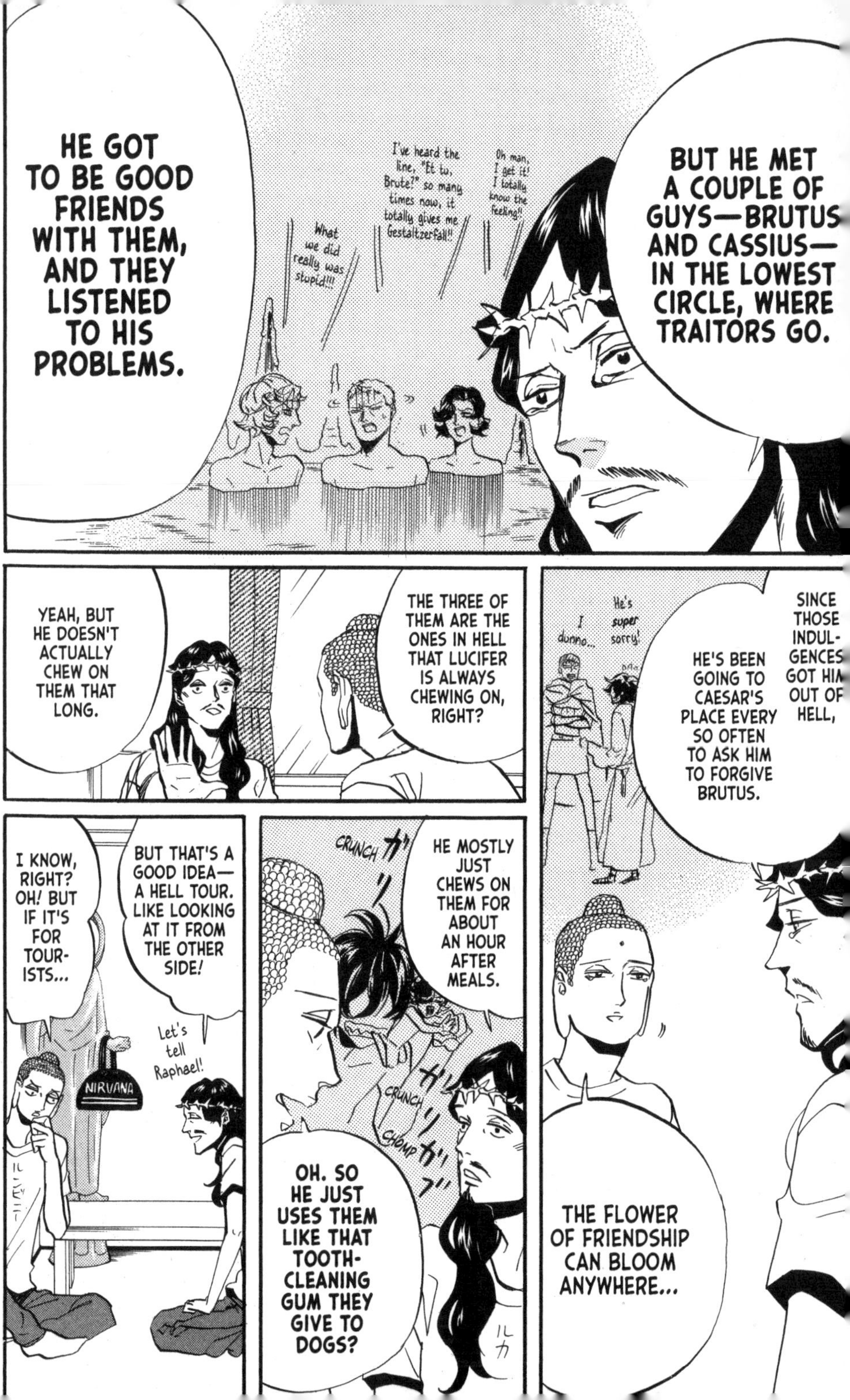
BUT HE MET A COUPLE OF GUYS—BRUTUS AND CASSIUS—IN THE LOWEST CIRCLE, WHERE TRAITORS GO.
Oh man, I get it! I totally know the feeling!!
I've heard the line, "Et tu, Brute?" so many times now, it totally gives me Gestaltzerfall!!
What we did really was stupid!!!
HE GOT TO BE GOOD FRIENDS WITH THEM, AND THEY LISTENED TO HIS PROBLEMS.
SINCE THOSE INDULGENCES GOT HIM OUT OF HELL,
HE'S BEEN GOING TO CAESAR'S PLACE EVERY SO OFTEN TO ASK HIM TO FORGIVE BRUTUS.
He's super sorry!
I dunno...
THE FLOWER OF FRIENDSHIP CAN BLOOM ANYWHERE...
THE THREE OF THEM ARE THE ONES IN HELL THAT LUCIFER IS ALWAYS CHEWING ON, RIGHT?
YEAH, BUT HE DOESN'T ACTUALLY CHEW ON THEM THAT LONG.
HE MOSTLY JUST CHEWS ON THEM FOR ABOUT AN HOUR AFTER MEALS.
CRUNCH
CRUNCH
CHOMP
OH. SO HE JUST USES THEM LIKE THAT TOOTH-CLEANING GUM THEY GIVE TO DOGS?
BUT THAT'S A GOOD IDEA—A HELL TOUR. LIKE LOOKING AT IT FROM THE OTHER SIDE!
I KNOW, RIGHT? OH! BUT IF IT'S FOR TOUR-ISTS...
Let's tell Raphael!
NIRVANA

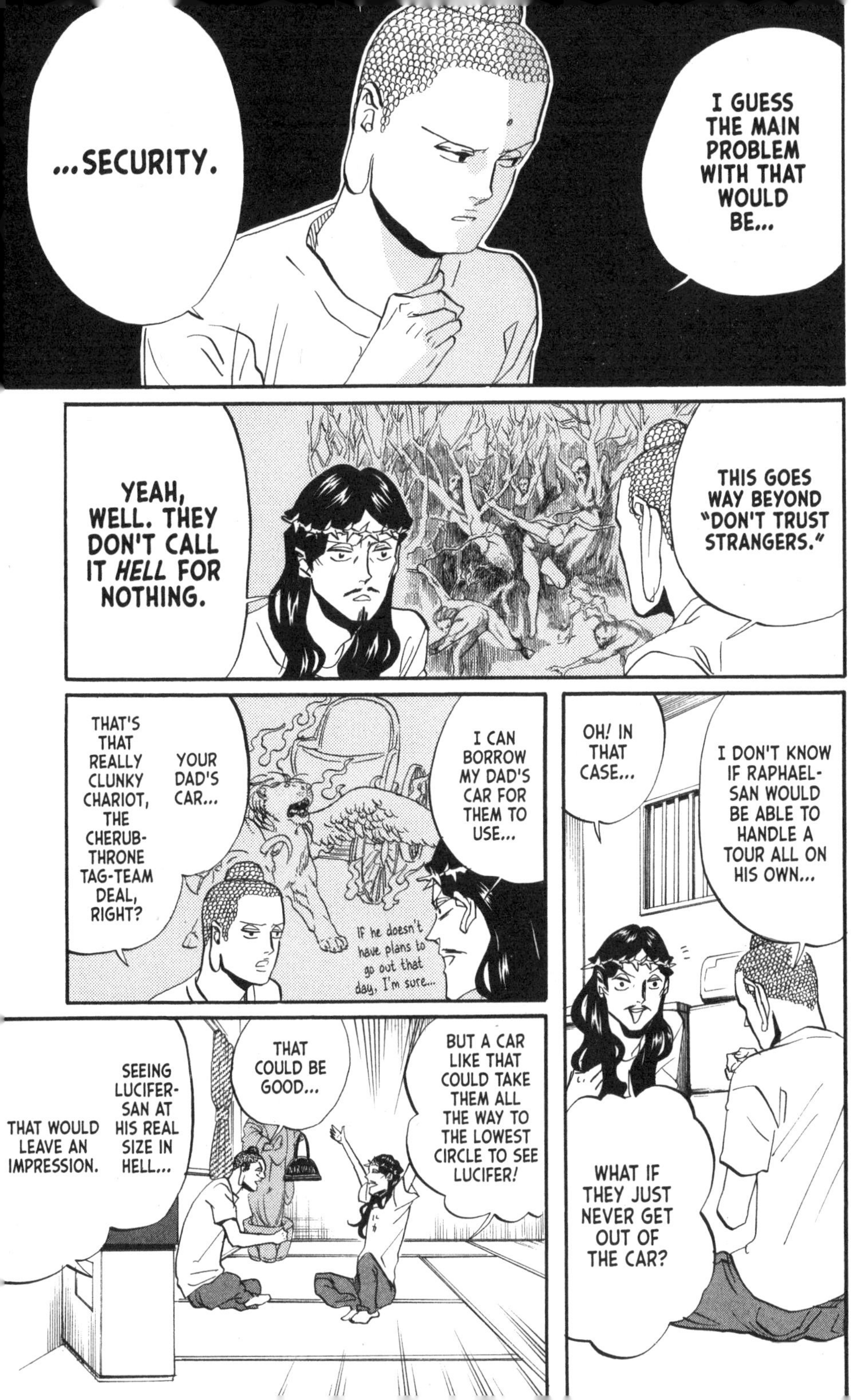
I GUESS THE MAIN PROBLEM WITH THAT WOULD BE...
...SECURITY.
THIS GOES WAY BEYOND "DON'T TRUST STRANGERS."
YEAH, WELL. THEY DON'T CALL IT *HELL* FOR NOTHING.
I DON'T KNOW IF RAPHAEL-SAN WOULD BE ABLE TO HANDLE A TOUR ALL ON HIS OWN...
OH! IN THAT CASE...
WHAT IF THEY JUST NEVER GET OUT OF THE CAR?
I CAN BORROW MY DAD'S CAR FOR THEM TO USE...
If he doesn't have plans to go out that day, I'm sure...
YOUR DAD'S CAR...
THAT'S THAT REALLY CLUNKY CHARIOT, THE CHERUB-THRONE TAG-TEAM DEAL, RIGHT?
BUT A CAR LIKE THAT COULD TAKE THEM ALL THE WAY TO THE LOWEST CIRCLE TO SEE LUCIFER!
THAT COULD BE GOOD...
SEEING LUCIFER-SAN AT HIS REAL SIZE IN HELL...
THAT WOULD LEAVE AN IMPRESSION.

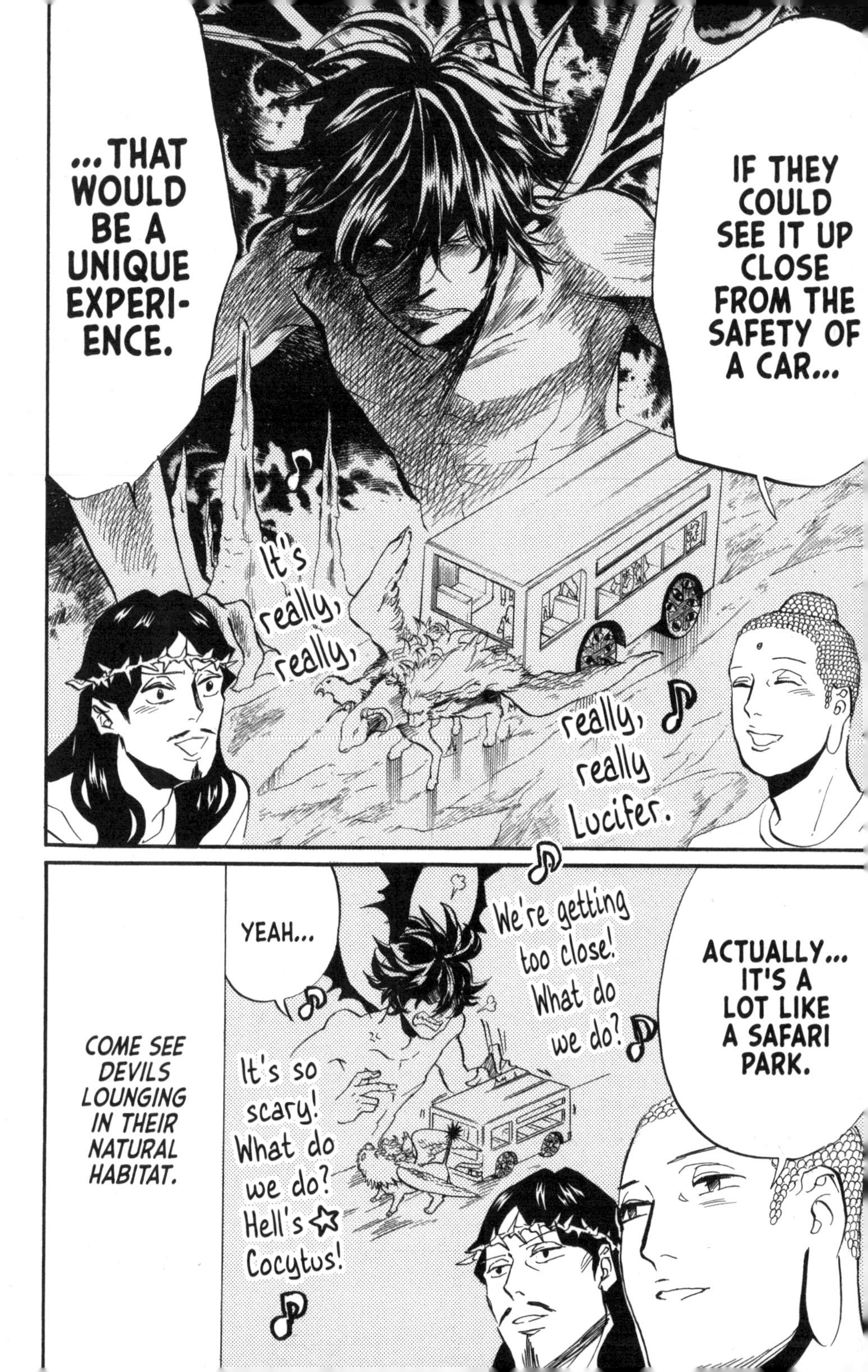
IF THEY COULD SEE IT UP CLOSE FROM THE SAFETY OF A CAR...
...THAT WOULD BE A UNIQUE EXPERI-ENCE.
It's really, really,
really, really Lucifer.
ACTUALLY... IT'S A LOT LIKE A SAFARI PARK.
We're getting too close! What do we do?
YEAH...
It's so scary! What do we do? Hell's ☆ Cocytus!
COME SEE DEVILS LOUNGING IN THEIR NATURAL HABITAT.

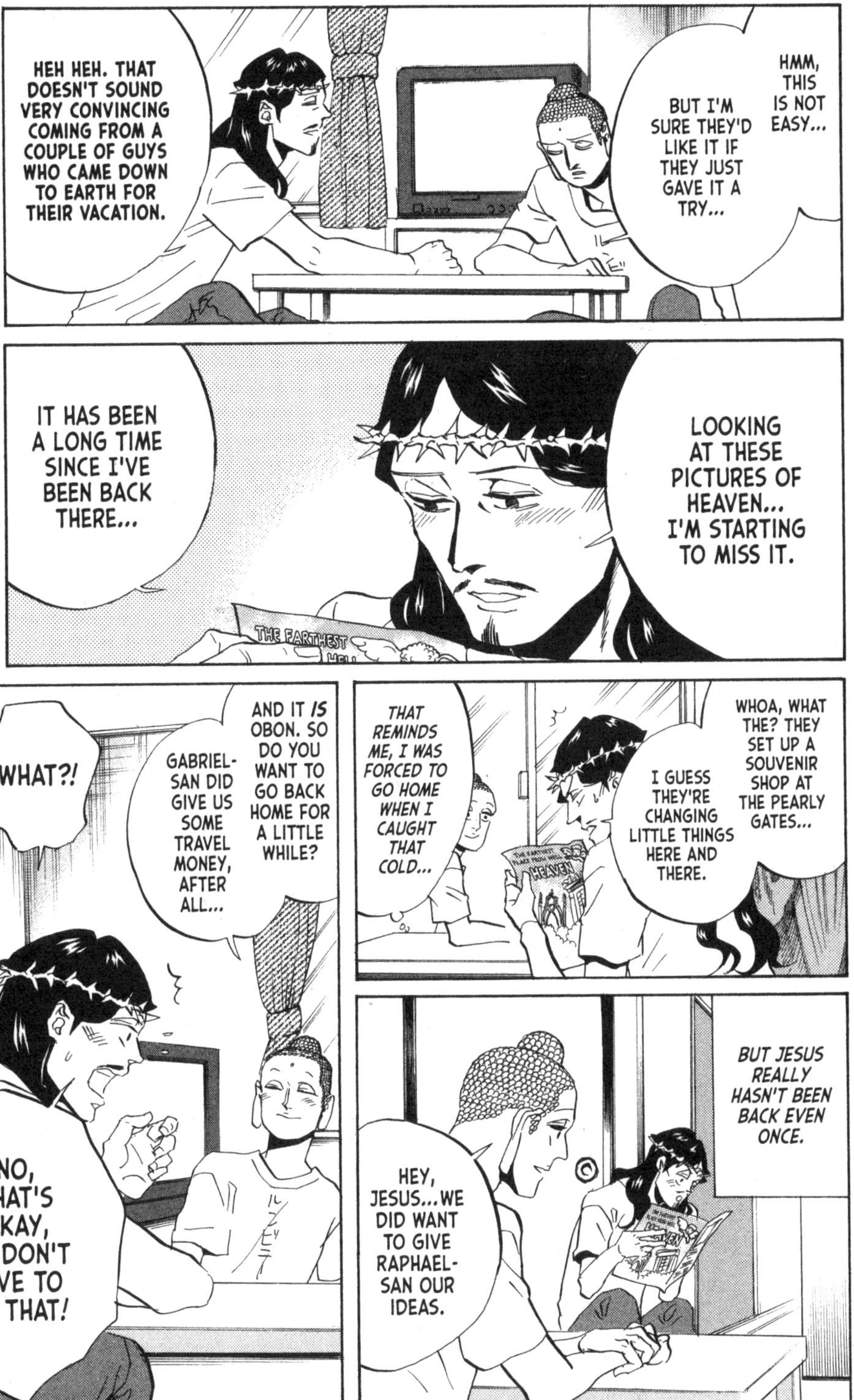
HMM, THIS IS NOT EASY...
BUT I'M SURE THEY'D LIKE IT IF THEY JUST GAVE IT A TRY...
HEH HEH. THAT DOESN'T SOUND VERY CONVINCING COMING FROM A COUPLE OF GUYS WHO CAME DOWN TO EARTH FOR THEIR VACATION.
LOOKING AT THESE PICTURES OF HEAVEN... I'M STARTING TO MISS IT.
IT HAS BEEN A LONG TIME SINCE I'VE BEEN BACK THERE...
THE FARTHEST
WHOA, WHAT THE? THEY SET UP A SOUVENIR SHOP AT THE PEARLY GATES...
I GUESS THEY'RE CHANGING LITTLE THINGS HERE AND THERE.
THAT REMINDS ME, I WAS FORCED TO GO HOME WHEN I CAUGHT THAT COLD...
HEAVEN
BUT JESUS REALLY HASN'T BEEN BACK EVEN ONCE.
HEY, JESUS...WE DID WANT TO GIVE RAPHAEL-SAN OUR IDEAS.
AND IT *IS* OBON. SO DO YOU WANT TO GO BACK HOME FOR A LITTLE WHILE?
GABRIEL-SAN DID GIVE US SOME TRAVEL MONEY, AFTER ALL...
WHAT?!
NO, THAT'S OKAY, WE DON'T HAVE TO DO THAT!

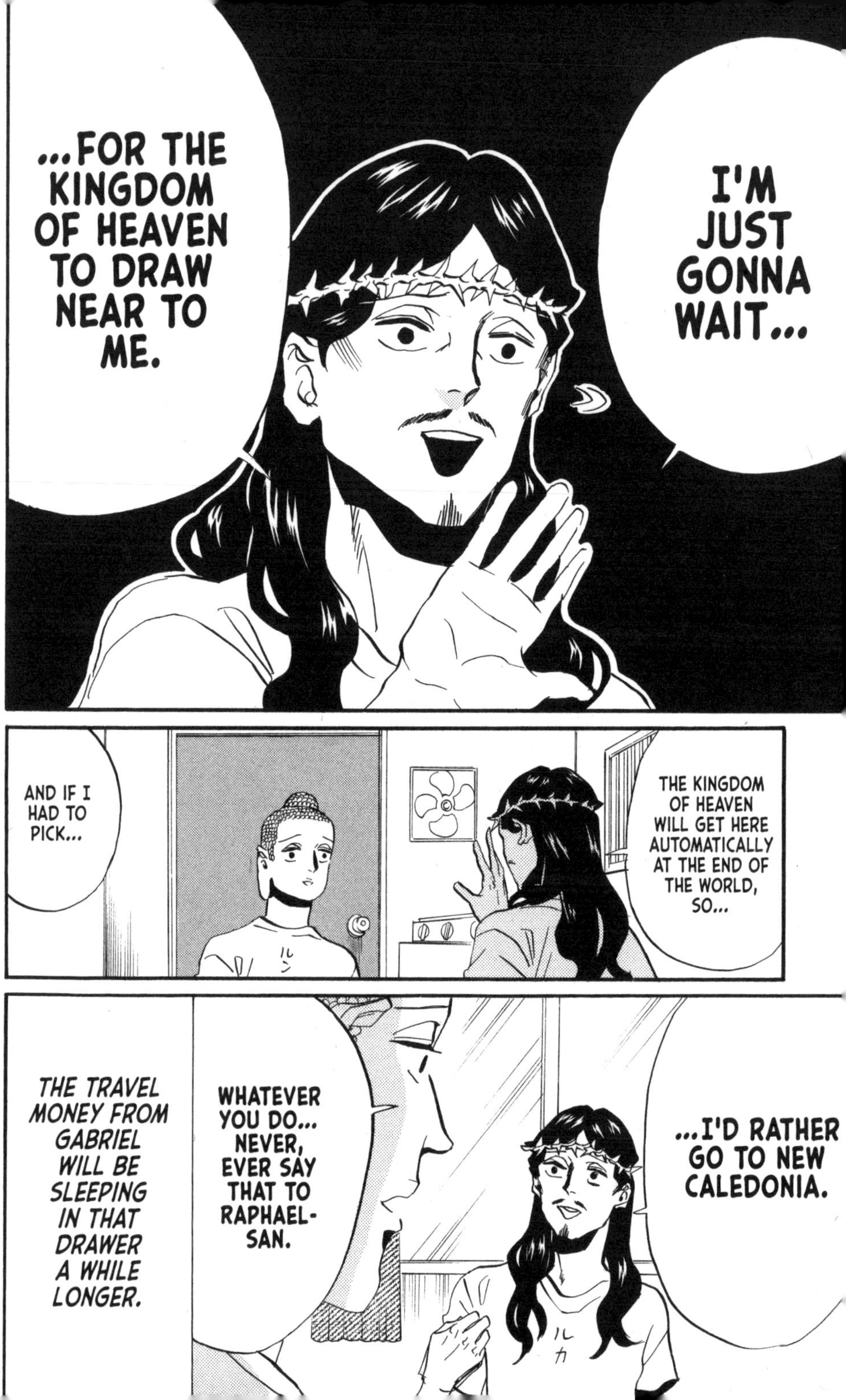
I'M JUST GONNA WAIT...
...FOR THE KINGDOM OF HEAVEN TO DRAW NEAR TO ME.
THE KINGDOM OF HEAVEN WILL GET HERE AUTOMATICALLY AT THE END OF THE WORLD, SO...
AND IF I HAD TO PICK...
...I'D RATHER GO TO NEW CALEDONIA.
WHATEVER YOU DO... NEVER, EVER SAY THAT TO RAPHAEL-SAN.
THE TRAVEL MONEY FROM GABRIEL WILL BE SLEEPING IN THAT DRAWER A WHILE LONGER.

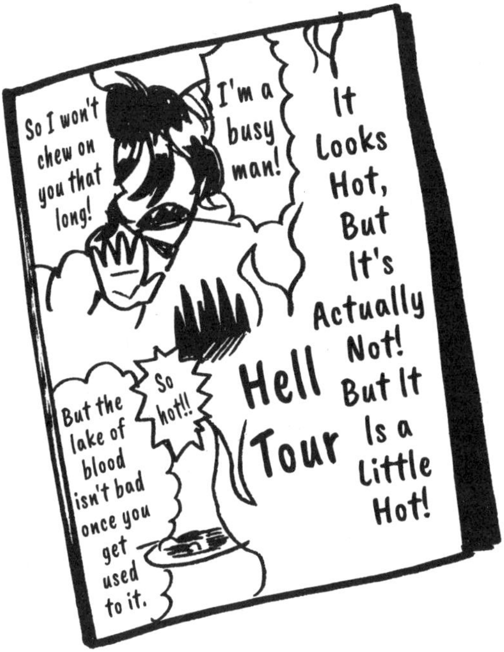
It Looks Hot, But It's Actually Not! But It Is a Little Hot!
I'm a busy man!
So I won't chew on you that long!
Hell Tour
So hot!!
But the lake of blood isn't bad once you get used to it.

CHAPTER 39 TRANSLATION NOTES

Tobias and Tobit, page 185
The Book of Tobit is a book of scripture included in the Catholic Old Testament canon but not the Protestant or Jewish canon. It tells the story of Tobias, or Tobiah, who sets out on a journey to get some money his blind father deposited in Media. He is aided by the angel Raphael in human guise, who helps him accomplish his task, find a cure for his father's blindness, and free his future wife from a demon's curse.

During Obon, page 186
Obon is an important holiday in Japan, so it's a busy time for many domestic tourist attractions.

Lumbini, page 187
Lumbini is a place in Nepal traditionally considered to be where Siddhartha Gautama was born, and as such, it is a Buddhist pilgrimage site.

Luke, page 189
Luke is one of the writers of the Four Gospels of the New Testament, as well as the writer of the Acts of the Apostles.

Lonely Heavens, page 190
The Japanese name Raphael gives his guidebook translates more literally to *Dante-kun's Tear-Jerking Heavenly Travels*. This is a parody of the Japanese documentary show, *Sekai Ururun Teizaiki*, or *"World Tear-Jerking Sojourns."* *The Divine Comedy* is a narrative poem in which the author, Dante Alighieri, recounts his journey through Hell (*Inferno*), Purgatory (*Purgatorio*), and Heaven (*Paradiso*).

Pearly Gates, page 192
In some Christian denominations, the gateway to Heaven is called the Pearly Gates. This name comes from a verse in Revelation that describes the City of God, stating, "And the twelve gates were twelve pearls; every several gate was of one pearl." (Revalations 21:21) The Pearly Gates that Peter and Andrew sit in front of share a design with the golden gates on the Florence Baptistery—the Gates of Paradise, created by Lorenzo Ghiberti. Each panel depicts a scene from the Old Testament.

The palace down here, page 192
This palace is the Cathedral of Syracuse in Sicily, which is a UNESCO World Heritage Site. It has been through many changes, including extensive renovations after the Sicily Earthquake in 1693.

The long chopsticks, page 193
This comes from a parable that is taught in cultures around the world. It basically goes as Jesus describes, although when told in Western cultures, the chopsticks become spoons.

Abandon Hope, page 195
According to Dante's *Inferno*, the entrance to Hell is inscribed with the phrase, "Abandon hope, all ye who enter here."

Et tu, Brute? and *Gestaltzerfall*, page 196
"*Et tu, Brute?*" is Latin for, "You, too, Brutus?", and is famously spoken in William Shakespeare's play, *Julius Caesar*, by the character of the same name. Marcus Junius Brutus and Gaius Cassius Longinus were the leaders of a group of senators who attacked and killed the Roman emperor Julius Caesar, and Brutus was Caesar's friend and protege. In Dante's *Inferno*, the two traitors to the emperor join Judas Iscariot in receiving the worst punishment in all of Hell: to be eternally chewed on by Lucifer. *Gestaltzerfall*, German for "shape decomposition," is a phenomenon in which a shape, word, set of letters, etc. is observed so many times that the observer begins to lose the ability to recognize it as anything with meaning.

Don't trust strangers, page 197
The reader may be interested to note that the art in the background here is based off of Gustave Doré's illustration of "Spendthrifts running through the Forest of Suicide," a scene in Dante's *Inferno*.

Cherub-throne tag-team, page 197
The Old Testament prophet Ezekiel had a vision where he saw the chariot of God. It was made of four angels, of the type called "thrones," who linked together to form a sort of box with wheels. These thrones each have four faces—the face of a man, the face of a lion, the face of an eagle, and the face of an ox.

Cocytus safari park, page 198
Specifically, this experience is likened to Fuji Safari Park, which advertised using a song that goes, "It's really, really, really, really a lion." Cocytus is the ninth and lowest circle of hell in Dante's Inferno.

SAINT☆YOUNG MEN

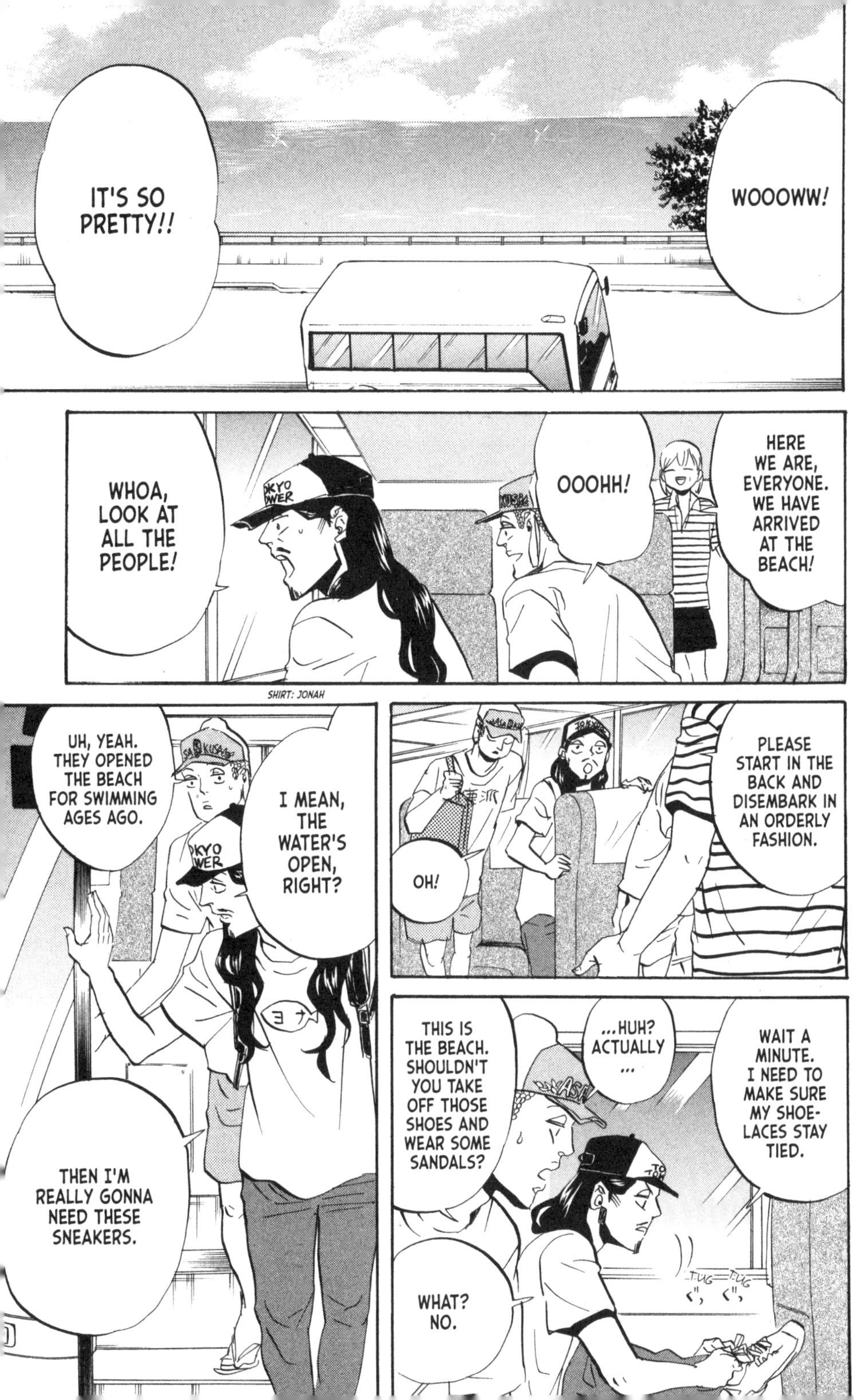
WOOOWW!
IT'S SO PRETTY!!
HERE WE ARE, EVERYONE. WE HAVE ARRIVED AT THE BEACH!
OOOHH!
WHOA, LOOK AT ALL THE PEOPLE!
SHIRT: JONAH
PLEASE START IN THE BACK AND DISEMBARK IN AN ORDERLY FASHION.
OH!
WAIT A MINUTE. I NEED TO MAKE SURE MY SHOE-LACES STAY TIED.
...HUH? ACTUALLY ...
THIS IS THE BEACH. SHOULDN'T YOU TAKE OFF THOSE SHOES AND WEAR SOME SANDALS?
T-UG T-UG
WHAT? NO.
I MEAN, THE WATER'S OPEN, RIGHT?
UH, YEAH. THEY OPENED THE BEACH FOR SWIMMING AGES AGO.
THEN I'M REALLY GONNA NEED THESE SNEAKERS.

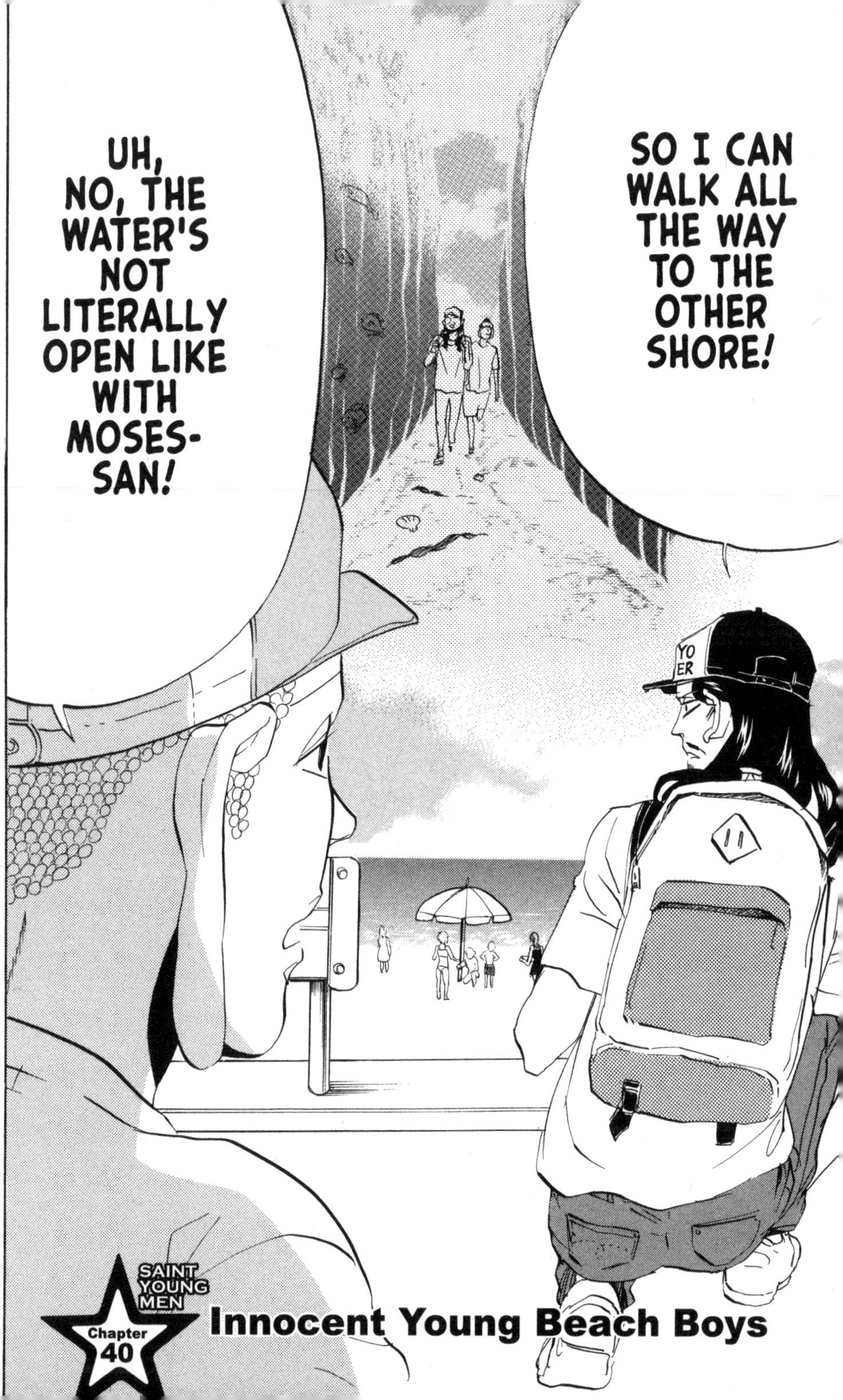
SO I CAN WALK ALL THE WAY TO THE OTHER SHORE!
UH, NO, THE WATER'S NOT LITERALLY OPEN LIKE WITH MOSES-SAN!
SAINT YOUNG MEN
Chapter 40
Innocent Young Beach Boys

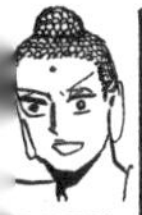

BUDDHA: HIS CURRENT AMBITION IS TO EAT AN ENTIRE HONEYDEW MELON.

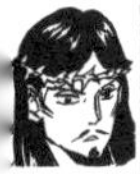

JESUS: HIS CURRENT AMBITION IS TO COLLECT AND EAT AN ENTIRE BOWL'S WORTH OF ONLY THE COLORED SŌMEN AND/OR HIYAMUGI NOODLES.

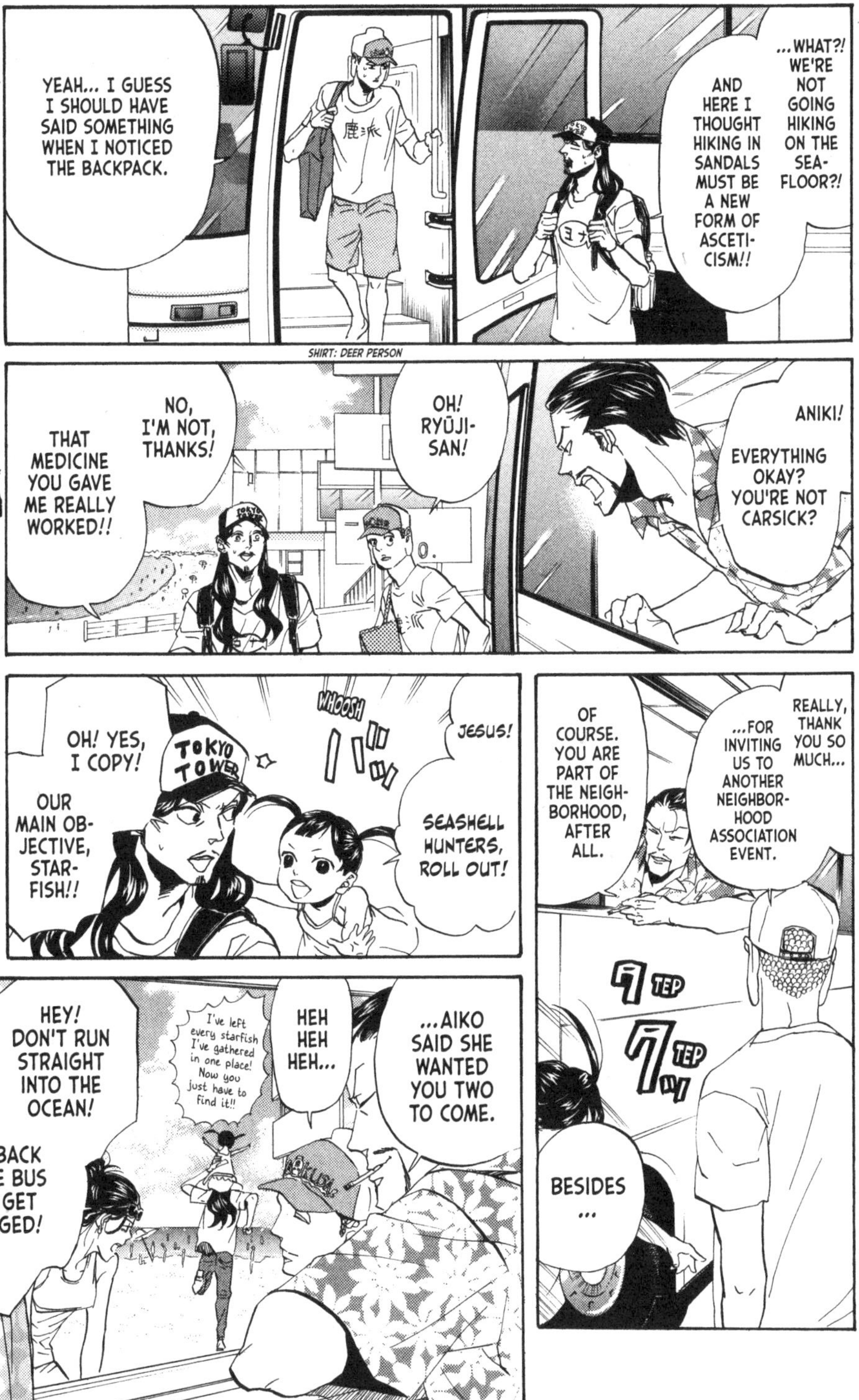

...WHAT?! WE'RE NOT GOING HIKING ON THE SEAFLOOR?!
AND HERE I THOUGHT HIKING IN SANDALS MUST BE A NEW FORM OF ASCETICISM!!
YEAH... I GUESS I SHOULD HAVE SAID SOMETHING WHEN I NOTICED THE BACKPACK.
SHIRT: DEER PERSON
ANIKI!
EVERYTHING OKAY? YOU'RE NOT CARSICK?
OH! RYŪJI-SAN!
NO, I'M NOT, THANKS!
THAT MEDICINE YOU GAVE ME REALLY WORKED!!
REALLY, THANK YOU SO MUCH...
...FOR INVITING US TO ANOTHER NEIGHBORHOOD ASSOCIATION EVENT.
OF COURSE. YOU ARE PART OF THE NEIGHBORHOOD, AFTER ALL.
TEP
TEP
BESIDES...
WHOOSH
JESUS!
SEASHELL HUNTERS, ROLL OUT!
TOKYO TOWER
OH! YES, I COPY!
OUR MAIN OBJECTIVE, STARFISH!!
...AIKO SAID SHE WANTED YOU TWO TO COME.
HEH HEH HEH...
I've left every starfish I've gathered in one place! Now you just have to find it!!
HEY! DON'T RUN STRAIGHT INTO THE OCEAN!
GET BACK IN THE BUS AND GET CHANGED!

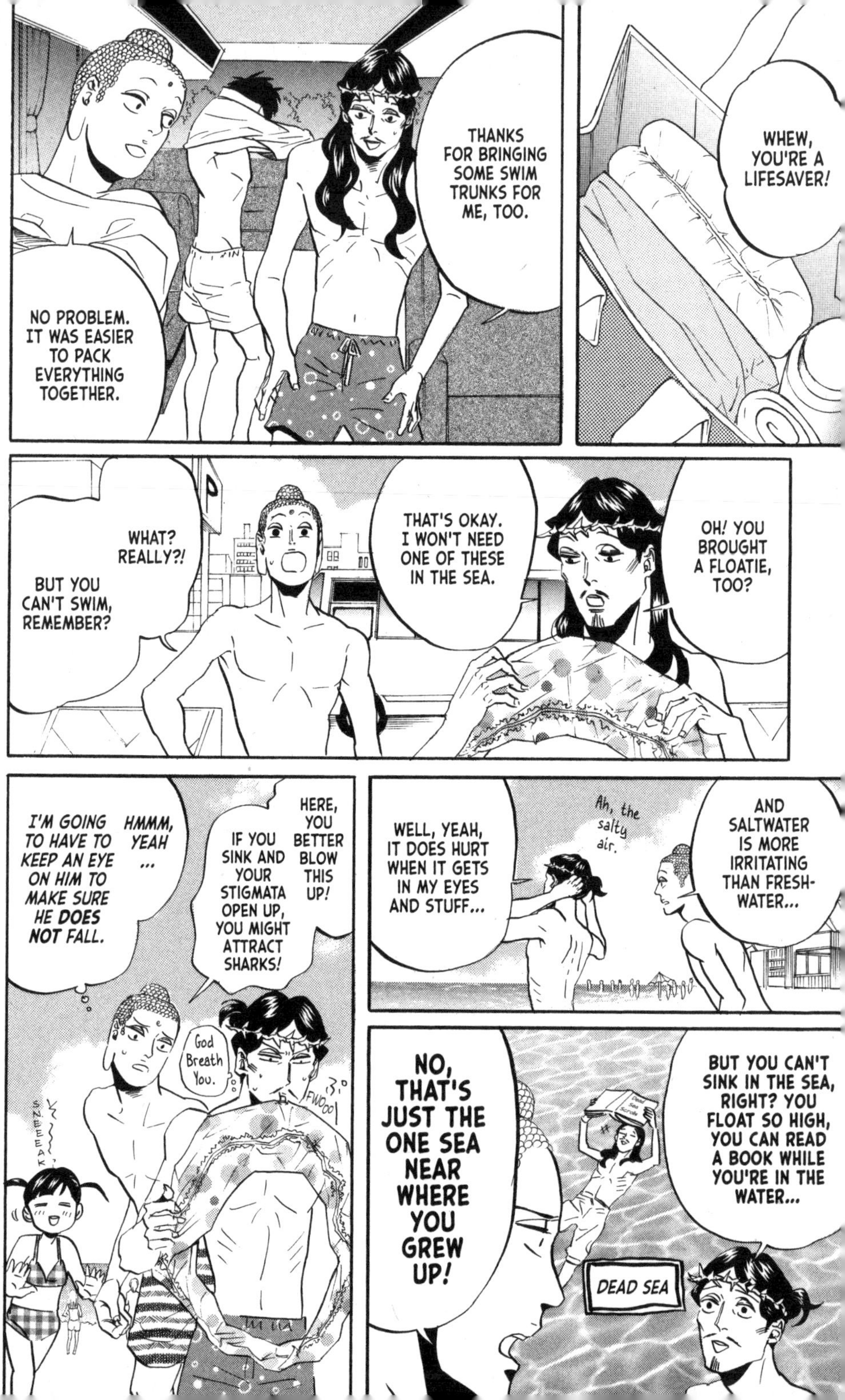
WHEW, YOU'RE A LIFESAVER!
THANKS FOR BRINGING SOME SWIM TRUNKS FOR ME, TOO.
NO PROBLEM. IT WAS EASIER TO PACK EVERYTHING TOGETHER.
OH! YOU BROUGHT A FLOATIE, TOO?
THAT'S OKAY. I WON'T NEED ONE OF THESE IN THE SEA.
WHAT? REALLY?!
BUT YOU CAN'T SWIM, REMEMBER?
AND SALTWATER IS MORE IRRITATING THAN FRESH-WATER...
Ah, the salty air.
WELL, YEAH, IT DOES HURT WHEN IT GETS IN MY EYES AND STUFF...
BUT YOU CAN'T SINK IN THE SEA, RIGHT? YOU FLOAT SO HIGH, YOU CAN READ A BOOK WHILE YOU'RE IN THE WATER...
DEAD SEA
NO, THAT'S JUST THE ONE SEA NEAR WHERE YOU GREW UP!
HERE, YOU BETTER BLOW THIS UP!
IF YOU SINK AND YOUR STIGMATA OPEN UP, YOU MIGHT ATTRACT SHARKS!
HMMM, YEAH ...
I'M GOING TO HAVE TO KEEP AN EYE ON HIM TO MAKE SURE HE DOES NOT FALL.
God Breath You.
FWOOO
SNEEEAK

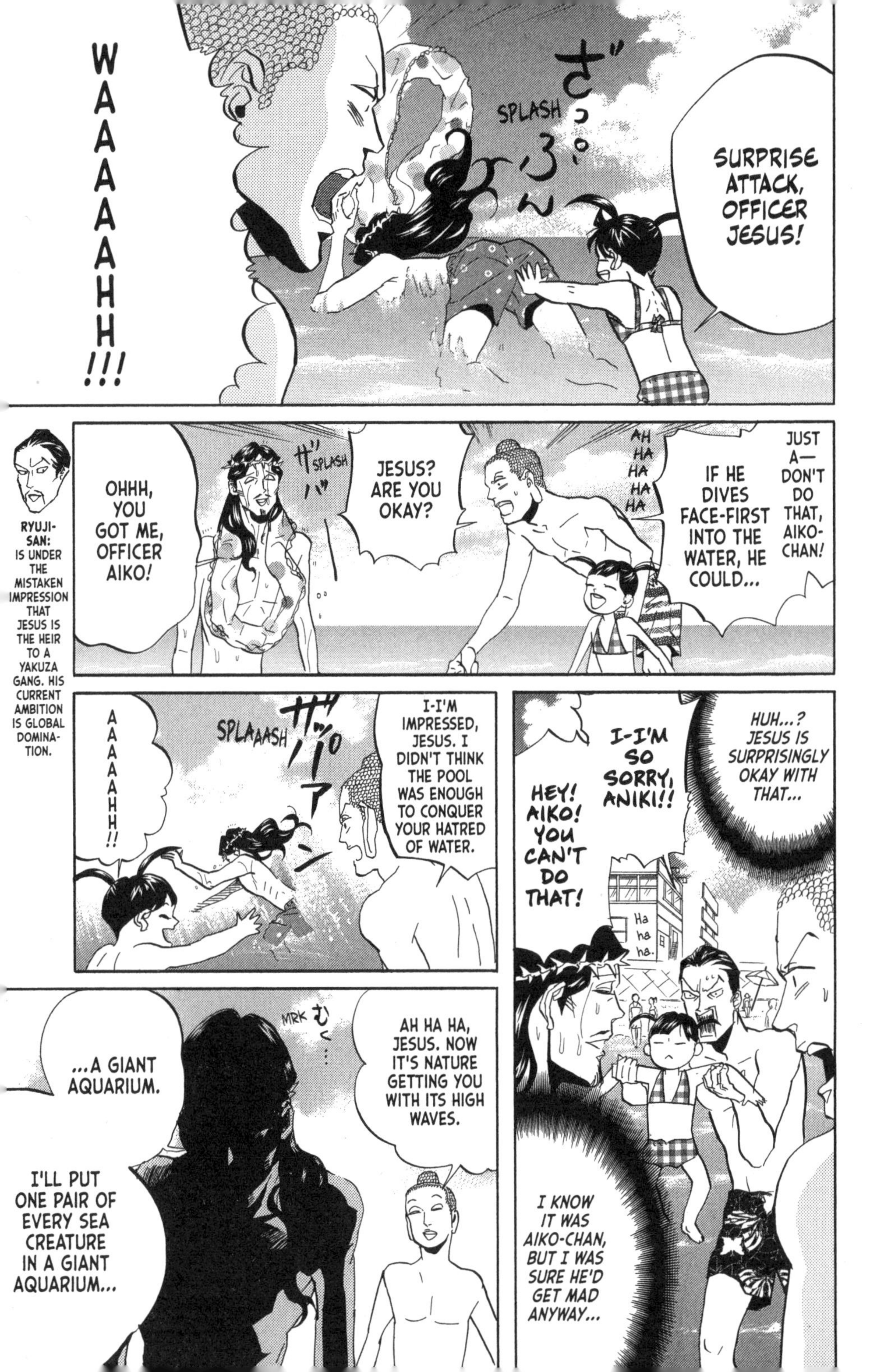
SURPRISE ATTACK, OFFICER JESUS!
SPLASH
WAAAAAHH!!!
JUST A— DON'T DO THAT, AIKO-CHAN!
IF HE DIVES FACE-FIRST INTO THE WATER, HE COULD...
AH HA HA HA HA
JESUS? ARE YOU OKAY?
SPLASH
OHHH, YOU GOT ME, OFFICER AIKO!
RYUJI-SAN: IS UNDER THE MISTAKEN IMPRESSION THAT JESUS IS THE HEIR TO A YAKUZA GANG. HIS CURRENT AMBITION IS GLOBAL DOMINATION.
HUH...? JESUS IS SURPRISINGLY OKAY WITH THAT...
I-I'M SO SORRY, ANIKI!!
HEY! AIKO! YOU CAN'T DO THAT!
Ha ha ha.
I KNOW IT WAS AIKO-CHAN, BUT I WAS SURE HE'D GET MAD ANYWAY...
I-I'M IMPRESSED, JESUS. I DIDN'T THINK THE POOL WAS ENOUGH TO CONQUER YOUR HATRED OF WATER.
SPLAAASH
AAAAAAHH!!
AH HA HA, JESUS. NOW IT'S NATURE GETTING YOU WITH ITS HIGH WAVES.
MRK
...A GIANT AQUARIUM.
I'LL PUT ONE PAIR OF EVERY SEA CREATURE IN A GIANT AQUARIUM...

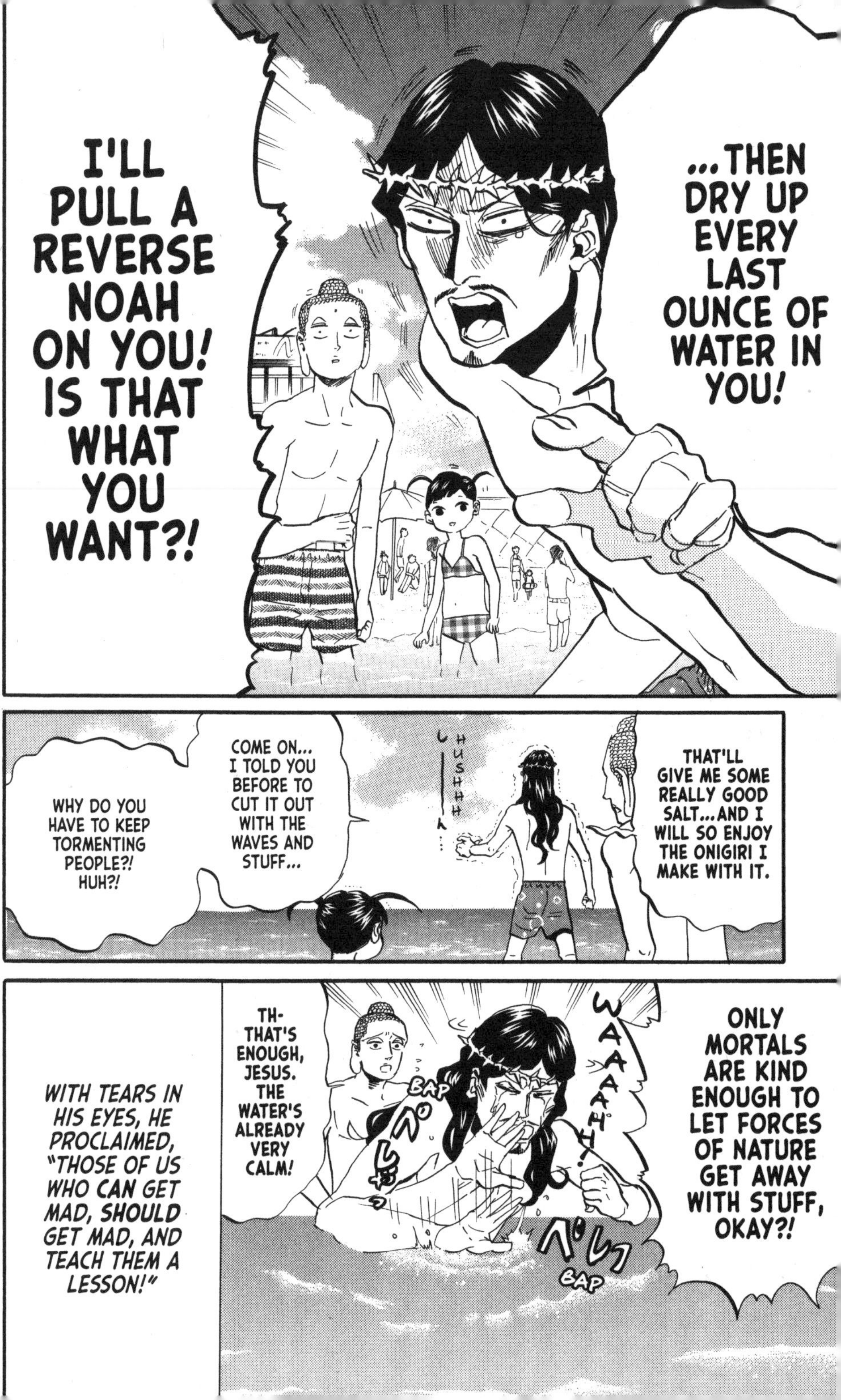
...THEN DRY UP EVERY LAST OUNCE OF WATER IN YOU!
I'LL PULL A REVERSE NOAH ON YOU! IS THAT WHAT YOU WANT?!
THAT'LL GIVE ME SOME REALLY GOOD SALT...AND I WILL SO ENJOY THE ONIGIRI I MAKE WITH IT.
HUSHHH
COME ON... I TOLD YOU BEFORE TO CUT IT OUT WITH THE WAVES AND STUFF...
WHY DO YOU HAVE TO KEEP TORMENTING PEOPLE?! HUH?!
ONLY MORTALS ARE KIND ENOUGH TO LET FORCES OF NATURE GET AWAY WITH STUFF, OKAY?!
WAAAAH!
BAP
TH- THAT'S ENOUGH, JESUS. THE WATER'S ALREADY VERY CALM!
BAP
WITH TEARS IN HIS EYES, HE PROCLAIMED, "THOSE OF US WHO CAN GET MAD, SHOULD GET MAD, AND TEACH THEM A LESSON!"

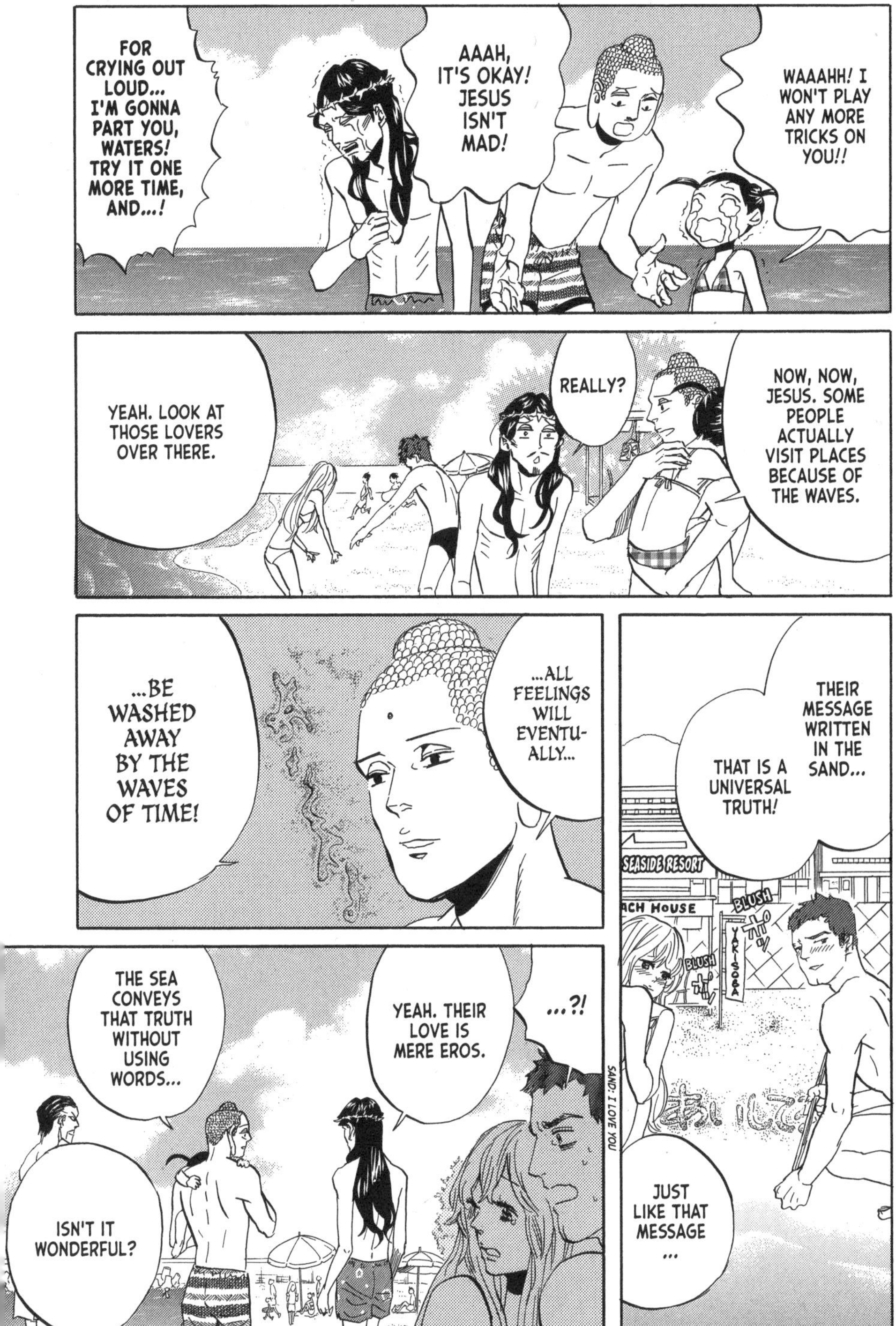
WAAAHH! I WON'T PLAY ANY MORE TRICKS ON YOU!!
AAAH, IT'S OKAY! JESUS ISN'T MAD!
FOR CRYING OUT LOUD... I'M GONNA PART YOU, WATERS! TRY IT ONE MORE TIME, AND...!
NOW, NOW, JESUS. SOME PEOPLE ACTUALLY VISIT PLACES BECAUSE OF THE WAVES.
REALLY?
YEAH. LOOK AT THOSE LOVERS OVER THERE.
THEIR MESSAGE WRITTEN IN THE SAND...
THAT IS A UNIVERSAL TRUTH!
SEASIDE RESORT
ACH HOUSE
YAKISOBA
BLUSH
BLUSH
JUST LIKE THAT MESSAGE ...
...ALL FEELINGS WILL EVENTU-ALLY...
...BE WASHED AWAY BY THE WAVES OF TIME!
SAND: I LOVE YOU
...?!
YEAH. THEIR LOVE IS MERE EROS.
THE SEA CONVEYS THAT TRUTH WITHOUT USING WORDS...
ISN'T IT WONDERFUL?

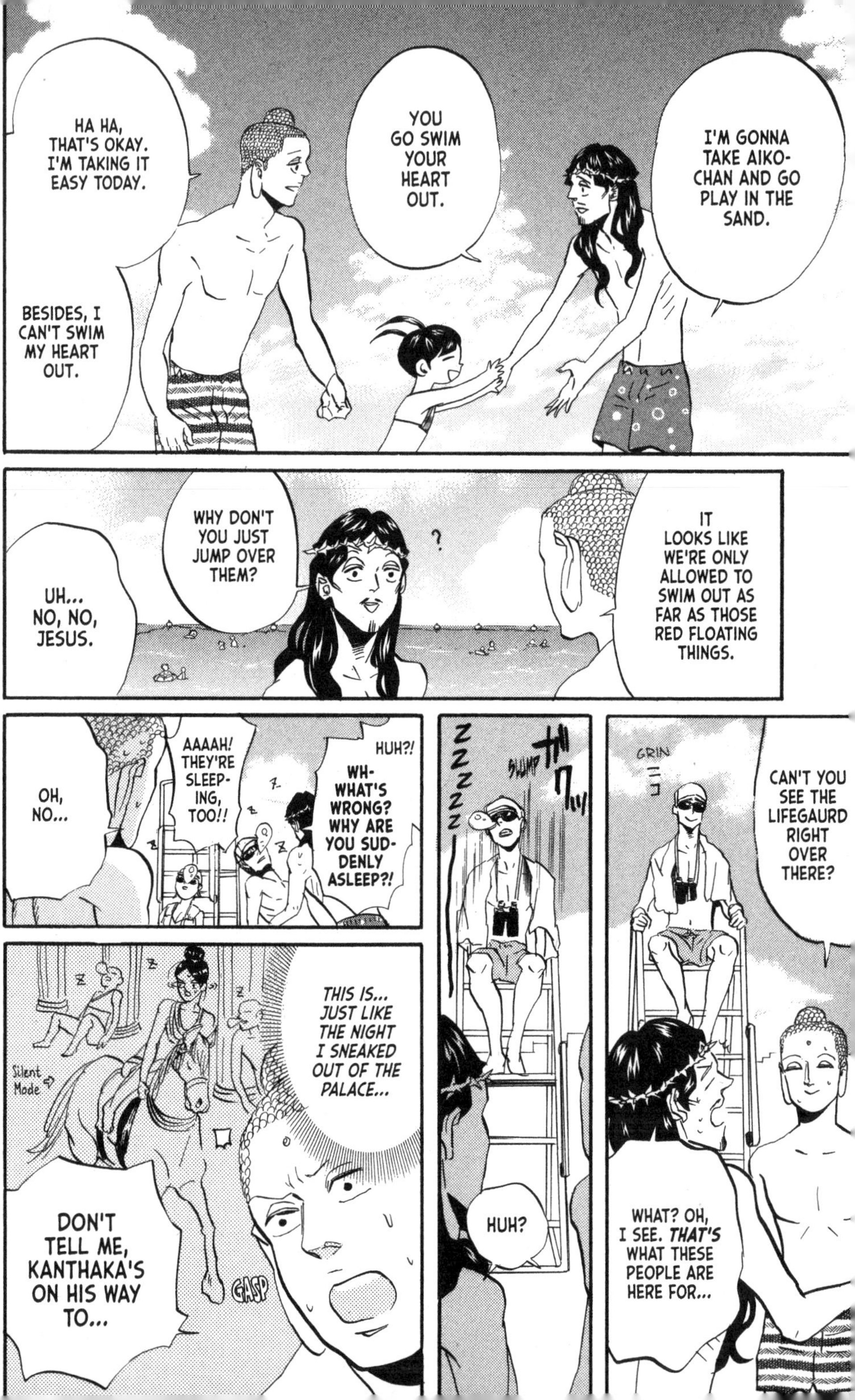
I'M GONNA TAKE AIKO-CHAN AND GO PLAY IN THE SAND.
YOU GO SWIM YOUR HEART OUT.
HA HA, THAT'S OKAY. I'M TAKING IT EASY TODAY.
BESIDES, I CAN'T SWIM MY HEART OUT.
IT LOOKS LIKE WE'RE ONLY ALLOWED TO SWIM OUT AS FAR AS THOSE RED FLOATING THINGS.
?
WHY DON'T YOU JUST JUMP OVER THEM?
UH... NO, NO, JESUS.
GRIN
CAN'T YOU SEE THE LIFEGAURD RIGHT OVER THERE?
WHAT? OH, I SEE. *THAT'S* WHAT THESE PEOPLE ARE HERE FOR...
SLUMP
ZZZZZ
HUH?
HUH?!
WH-WHAT'S WRONG? WHY ARE YOU SUDDENLY ASLEEP?!
AAAAH! THEY'RE SLEEPING, TOO!!
OH, NO...
THIS IS... JUST LIKE THE NIGHT I SNEAKED OUT OF THE PALACE...
Silent Mode
GASP
DON'T TELL ME, KANTHAKA'S ON HIS WAY TO...

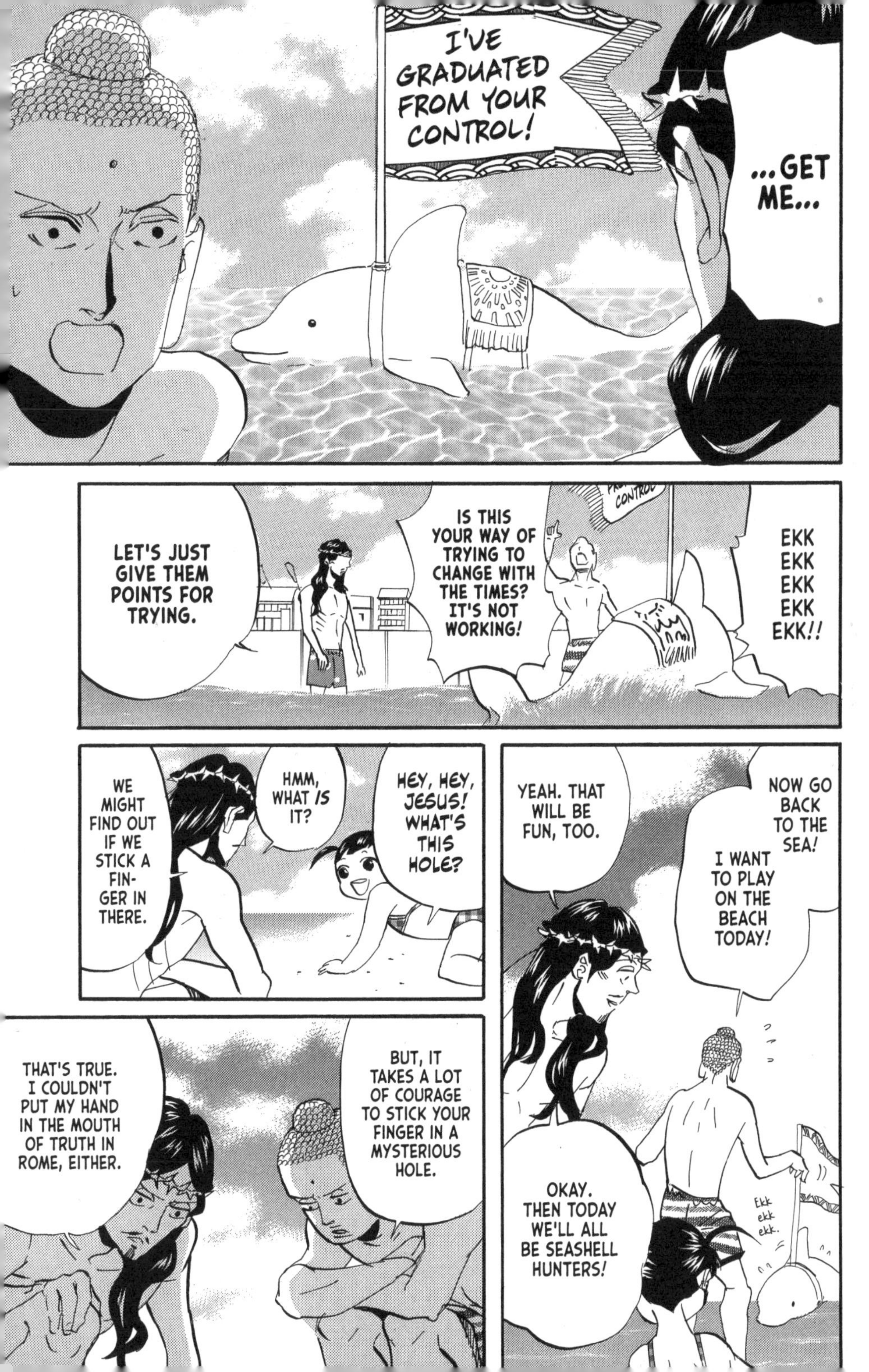
...GET ME...
I'VE GRADUATED FROM YOUR CONTROL!
EKK EKK EKK EKK EKK!!
IS THIS YOUR WAY OF TRYING TO CHANGE WITH THE TIMES? IT'S NOT WORKING!
LET'S JUST GIVE THEM POINTS FOR TRYING.
NOW GO BACK TO THE SEA!
I WANT TO PLAY ON THE BEACH TODAY!
YEAH. THAT WILL BE FUN, TOO.
OKAY. THEN TODAY WE'LL ALL BE SEASHELL HUNTERS!
Ekk ekk ekk.
HEY, HEY, JESUS! WHAT'S THIS HOLE?
HMM, WHAT *IS* IT?
WE MIGHT FIND OUT IF WE STICK A FIN-GER IN THERE.
BUT, IT TAKES A LOT OF COURAGE TO STICK YOUR FINGER IN A MYSTERIOUS HOLE.
THAT'S TRUE. I COULDN'T PUT MY HAND IN THE MOUTH OF TRUTH IN ROME, EITHER.

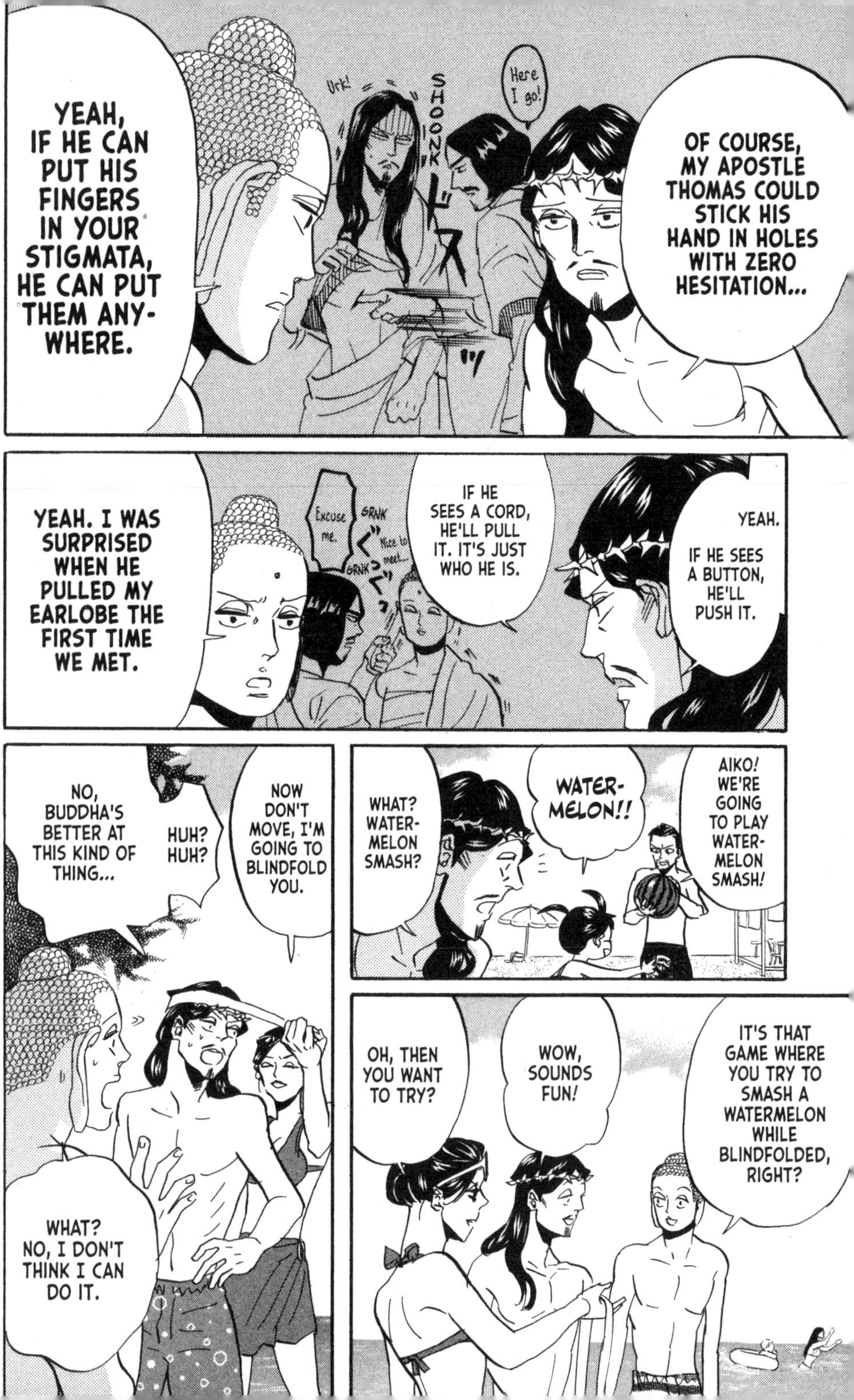
OF COURSE, MY APOSTLE THOMAS COULD STICK HIS HAND IN HOLES WITH ZERO HESITATION...
Here I go!
SHOONK
Urk!
YEAH, IF HE CAN PUT HIS FINGERS IN YOUR STIGMATA, HE CAN PUT THEM ANY-WHERE.
YEAH.
IF HE SEES A BUTTON, HE'LL PUSH IT.
IF HE SEES A CORD, HE'LL PULL IT. IT'S JUST WHO HE IS.
Excuse me.
GRNK
Nice to meet...
GRNK
YEAH. I WAS SURPRISED WHEN HE PULLED MY EARLOBE THE FIRST TIME WE MET.
AIKO! WE'RE GOING TO PLAY WATER-MELON SMASH!
WATER-MELON!!
WHAT? WATER-MELON SMASH?
IT'S THAT GAME WHERE YOU TRY TO SMASH A WATERMELON WHILE BLINDFOLDED, RIGHT?
WOW, SOUNDS FUN!
OH, THEN YOU WANT TO TRY?
NOW DON'T MOVE, I'M GOING TO BLINDFOLD YOU.
HUH? HUH?
NO, BUDDHA'S BETTER AT THIS KIND OF THING...
WHAT? NO, I DON'T THINK I CAN DO IT.

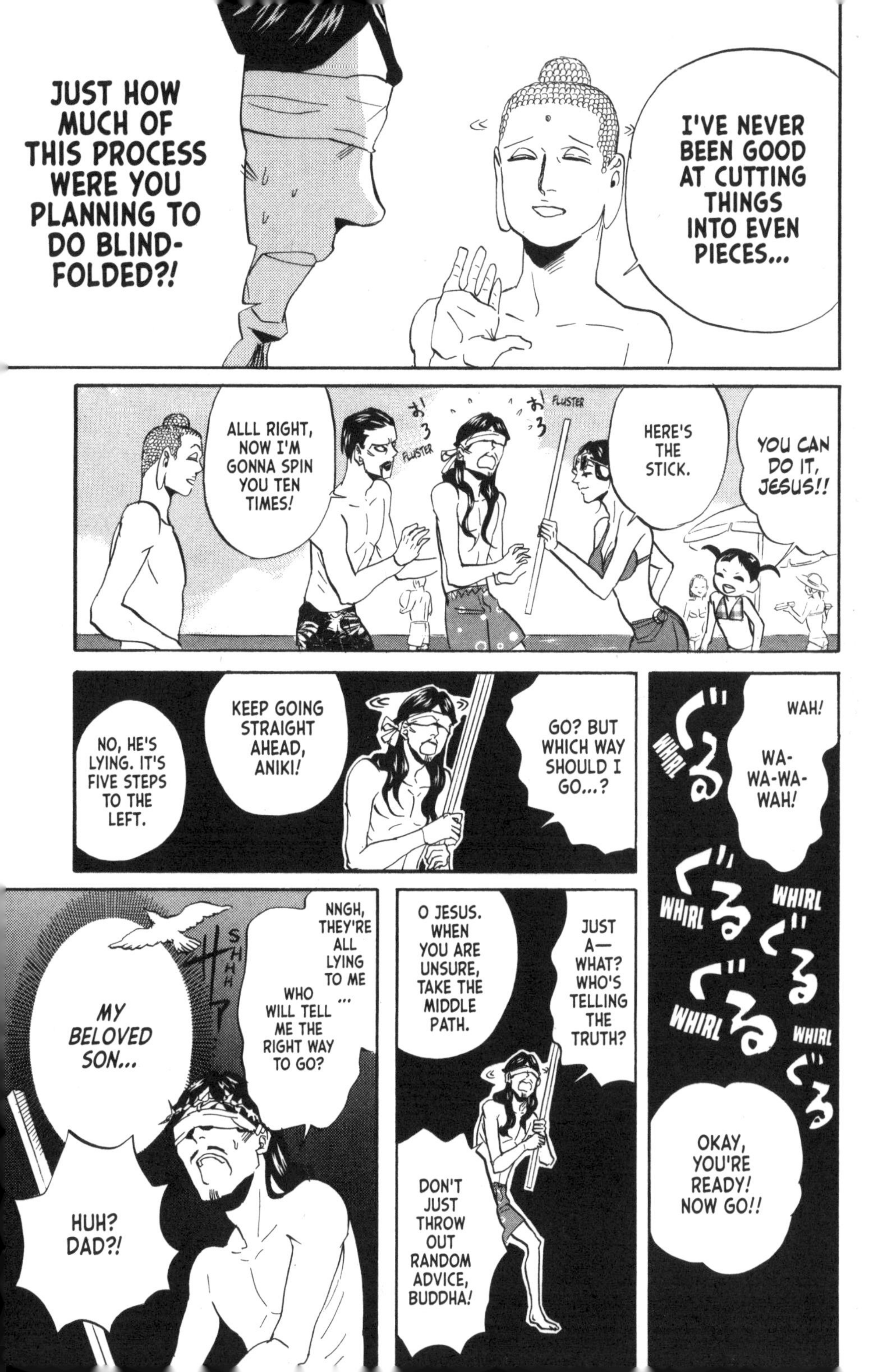
I'VE NEVER BEEN GOOD AT CUTTING THINGS INTO EVEN PIECES...
JUST HOW MUCH OF THIS PROCESS WERE YOU PLANNING TO DO BLIND-FOLDED?!
YOU CAN DO IT, JESUS!!
HERE'S THE STICK.
FLUSTER
FLUSTER
ALLL RIGHT, NOW I'M GONNA SPIN YOU TEN TIMES!
WAH!
WA-WA-WA-WAH!
ぐる WHIRL
ぐる WHIRL
ぐる WHIRL
ぐる WHIRL
ぐる WHIRL
OKAY, YOU'RE READY! NOW GO!!
GO? BUT WHICH WAY SHOULD I GO...?
KEEP GOING STRAIGHT AHEAD, ANIKI!
NO, HE'S LYING. IT'S FIVE STEPS TO THE LEFT.
JUST A— WHAT? WHO'S TELLING THE TRUTH?
O JESUS. WHEN YOU ARE UNSURE, TAKE THE MIDDLE PATH.
DON'T JUST THROW OUT RANDOM ADVICE, BUDDHA!
NNGH, THEY'RE ALL LYING TO ME ...
WHO WILL TELL ME THE RIGHT WAY TO GO?
SHHH
MY BELOVED SON...
HUH? DAD?!

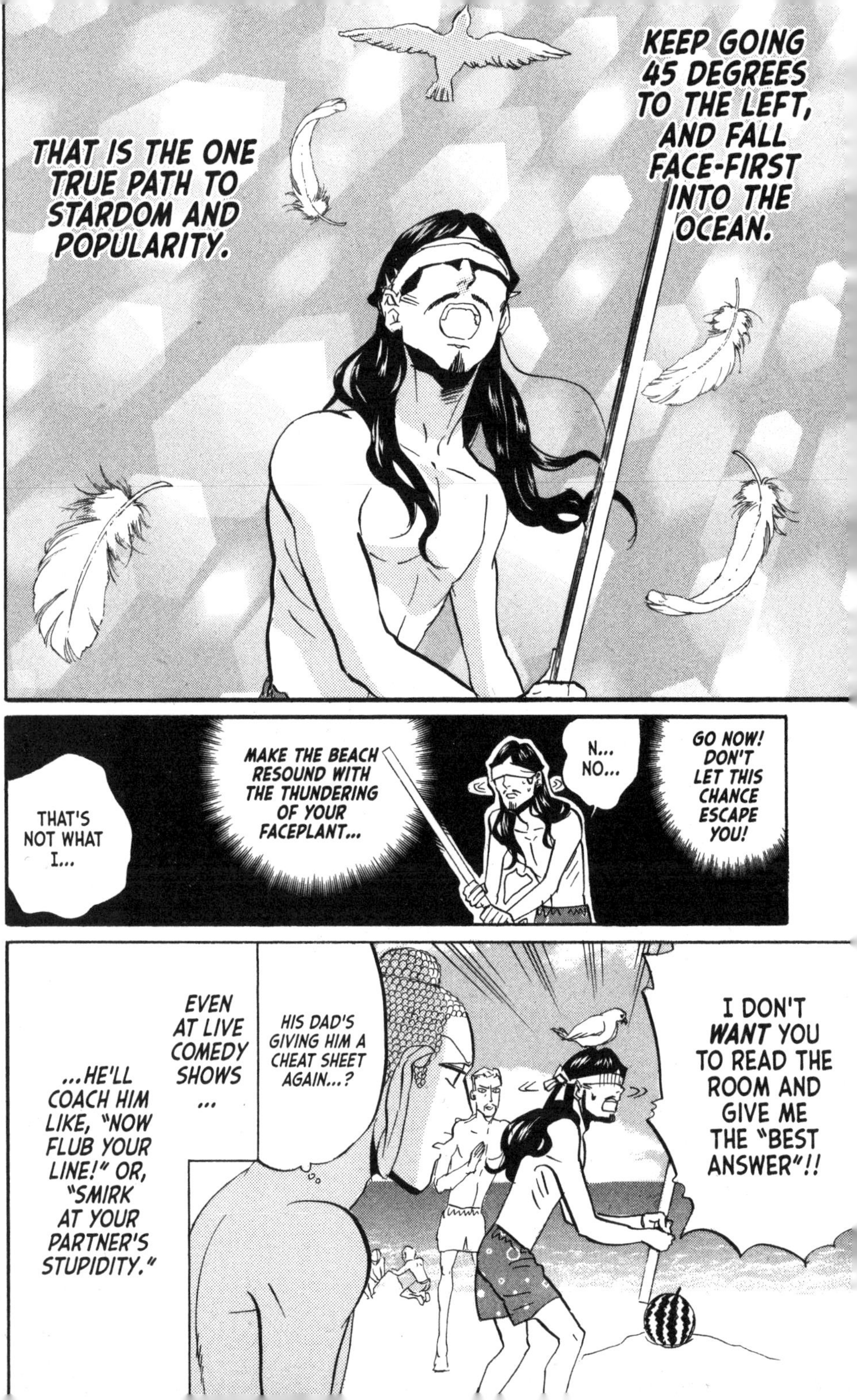
KEEP GOING 45 DEGREES TO THE LEFT, AND FALL FACE-FIRST INTO THE OCEAN.
THAT IS THE ONE TRUE PATH TO STARDOM AND POPULARITY.
GO NOW! DON'T LET THIS CHANCE ESCAPE YOU!
N... NO...
MAKE THE BEACH RESOUND WITH THE THUNDERING OF YOUR FACEPLANT...
THAT'S NOT WHAT I...
I DON'T *WANT* YOU TO READ THE ROOM AND GIVE ME THE "BEST ANSWER"!!
HIS DAD'S GIVING HIM A CHEAT SHEET AGAIN...?
EVEN AT LIVE COMEDY SHOWS ...
...HE'LL COACH HIM LIKE, "NOW FLUB YOUR LINE!" OR, "SMIRK AT YOUR PARTNER'S STUPIDITY."

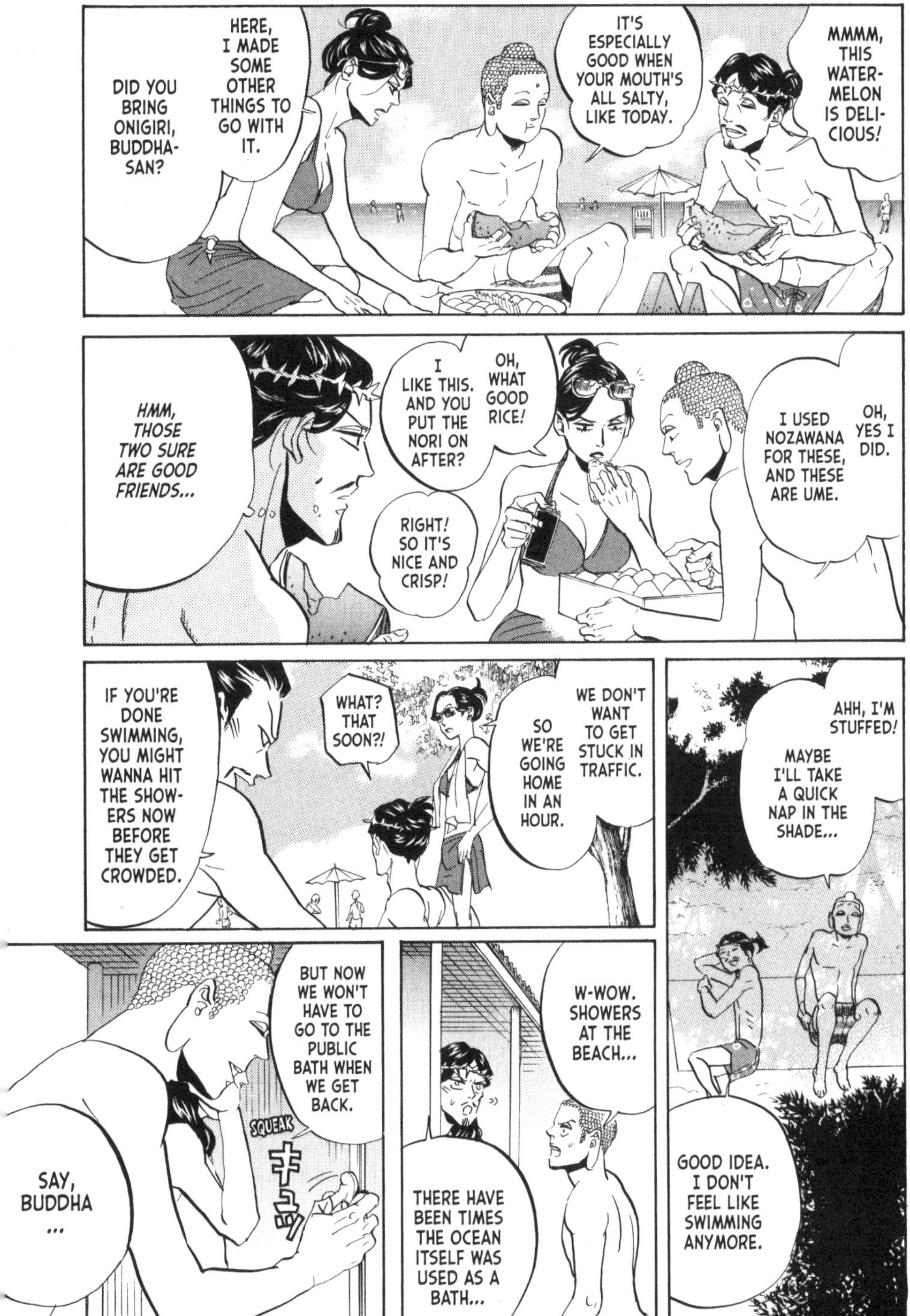
MMMM, THIS WATER-MELON IS DELI-CIOUS!
IT'S ESPECIALLY GOOD WHEN YOUR MOUTH'S ALL SALTY, LIKE TODAY.
HERE, I MADE SOME OTHER THINGS TO GO WITH IT.
DID YOU BRING ONIGIRI, BUDDHA-SAN?
OH, YES I DID.
I USED NOZAWANA FOR THESE, AND THESE ARE UME.
OH, WHAT GOOD RICE!
I LIKE THIS. AND YOU PUT THE NORI ON AFTER?
RIGHT! SO IT'S NICE AND CRISP!
HMM, THOSE TWO SURE ARE GOOD FRIENDS...
AHH, I'M STUFFED!
MAYBE I'LL TAKE A QUICK NAP IN THE SHADE...
GOOD IDEA. I DON'T FEEL LIKE SWIMMING ANYMORE.
WE DON'T WANT TO GET STUCK IN TRAFFIC.
SO WE'RE GOING HOME IN AN HOUR.
WHAT? THAT SOON?!
IF YOU'RE DONE SWIMMING, YOU MIGHT WANNA HIT THE SHOW-ERS NOW BEFORE THEY GET CROWDED.
W-WOW. SHOWERS AT THE BEACH...
THERE HAVE BEEN TIMES THE OCEAN ITSELF WAS USED AS A BATH...
BUT NOW WE WON'T HAVE TO GO TO THE PUBLIC BATH WHEN WE GET BACK.
SQUEAK
キュッ
SAY, BUDDHA...

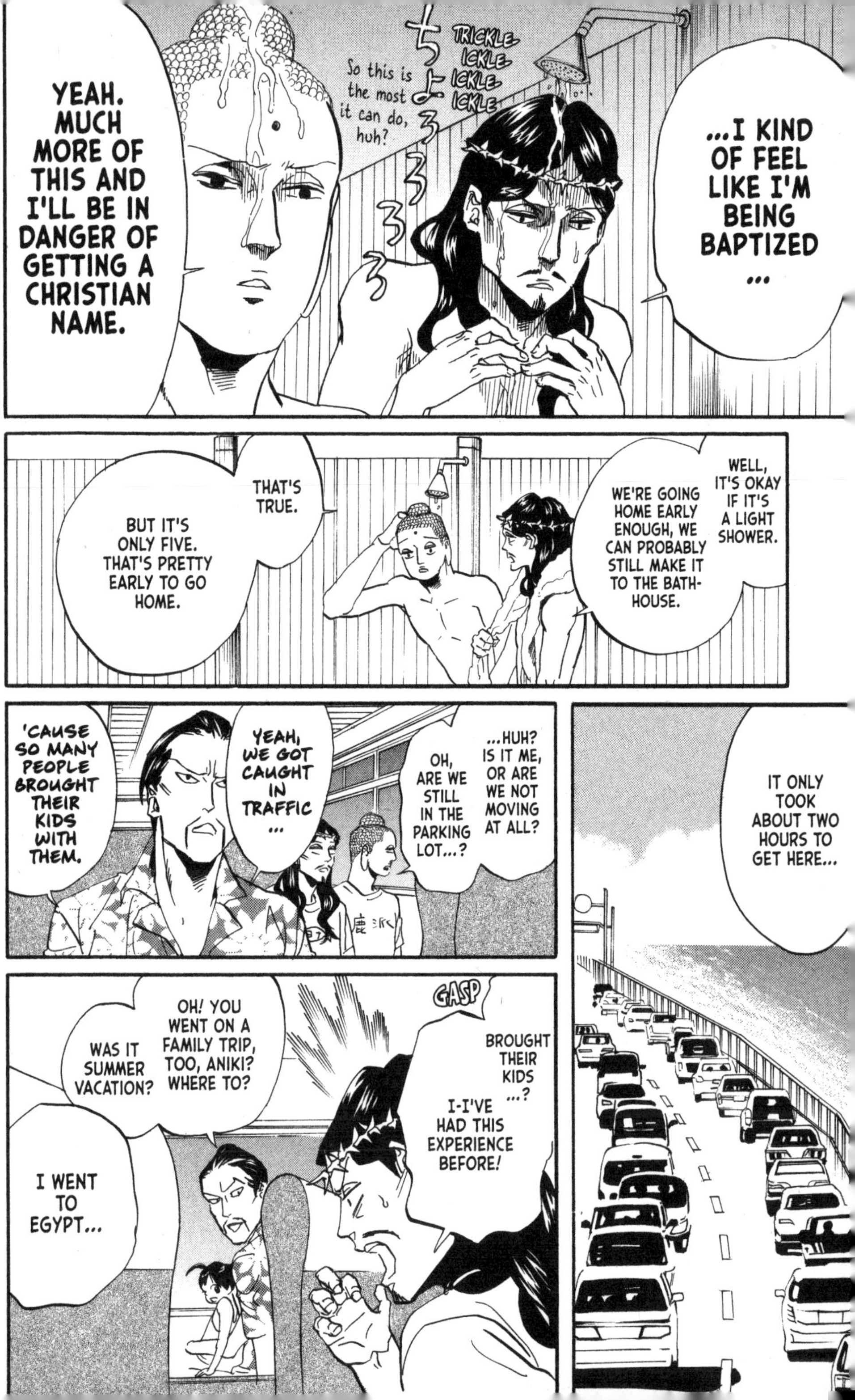
...I KIND OF FEEL LIKE I'M BEING BAPTIZED...
TRICKLE ICKLE ICKLE ICKLE
So this is the most it can do, huh?
YEAH. MUCH MORE OF THIS AND I'LL BE IN DANGER OF GETTING A CHRISTIAN NAME.
WELL, IT'S OKAY IF IT'S A LIGHT SHOWER.
WE'RE GOING HOME EARLY ENOUGH, WE CAN PROBABLY STILL MAKE IT TO THE BATH-HOUSE.
THAT'S TRUE.
BUT IT'S ONLY FIVE. THAT'S PRETTY EARLY TO GO HOME.
IT ONLY TOOK ABOUT TWO HOURS TO GET HERE...
...HUH? IS IT ME, OR ARE WE NOT MOVING AT ALL?
OH, ARE WE STILL IN THE PARKING LOT...?
YEAH, WE GOT CAUGHT IN TRAFFIC...
'CAUSE SO MANY PEOPLE BROUGHT THEIR KIDS WITH THEM.
GASP
BROUGHT THEIR KIDS...?
I-I'VE HAD THIS EXPERIENCE BEFORE!
OH! YOU WENT ON A FAMILY TRIP, TOO, ANIKI? WHERE TO?
WAS IT SUMMER VACATION?
I WENT TO EGYPT...

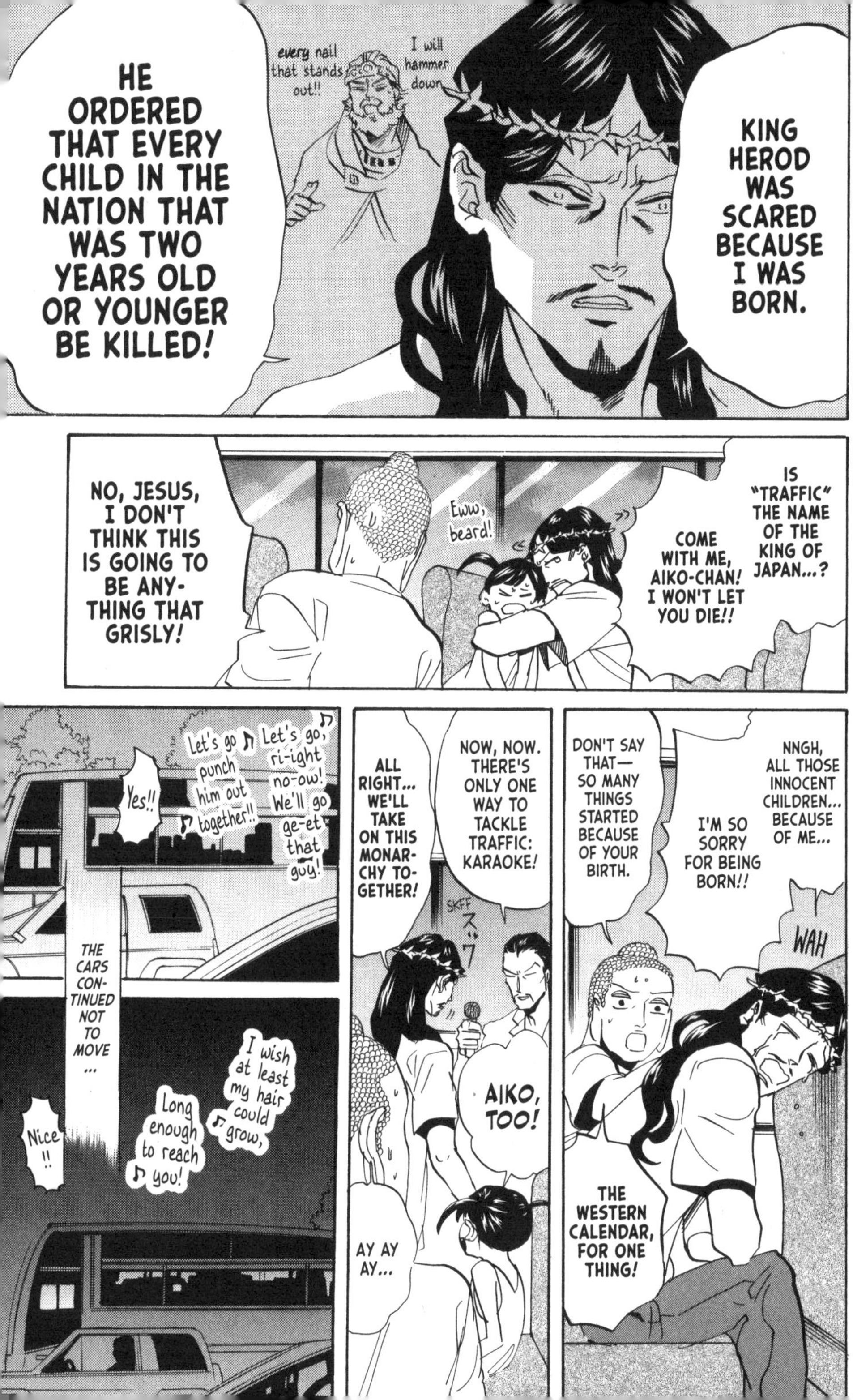
KING HEROD WAS SCARED BECAUSE I WAS BORN.
I will hammer down
every nail that stands out!!
HE ORDERED THAT EVERY CHILD IN THE NATION THAT WAS TWO YEARS OLD OR YOUNGER BE KILLED!
IS "TRAFFIC" THE NAME OF THE KING OF JAPAN...?
COME WITH ME, AIKO-CHAN! I WON'T LET YOU DIE!!
Eww, beard!
NO, JESUS, I DON'T THINK THIS IS GOING TO BE ANYTHING THAT GRISLY!
NNGH, ALL THOSE INNOCENT CHILDREN... BECAUSE OF ME...
I'M SO SORRY FOR BEING BORN!!
WAH
DON'T SAY THAT— SO MANY THINGS STARTED BECAUSE OF YOUR BIRTH.
THE WESTERN CALENDAR, FOR ONE THING!
NOW, NOW. THERE'S ONLY ONE WAY TO TACKLE TRAFFIC: KARAOKE!
ALL RIGHT... WE'LL TAKE ON THIS MONARCHY TOGETHER!
SKFF
AIKO, TOO!
AY AY AY...
Let's go, ri-ight no-ow! We'll go ge-et that guy!
Let's go punch him out together!!
Yes!!
THE CARS CONTINUED NOT TO MOVE...
I wish at least my hair could grow,
Long enough to reach you!
Nice!!

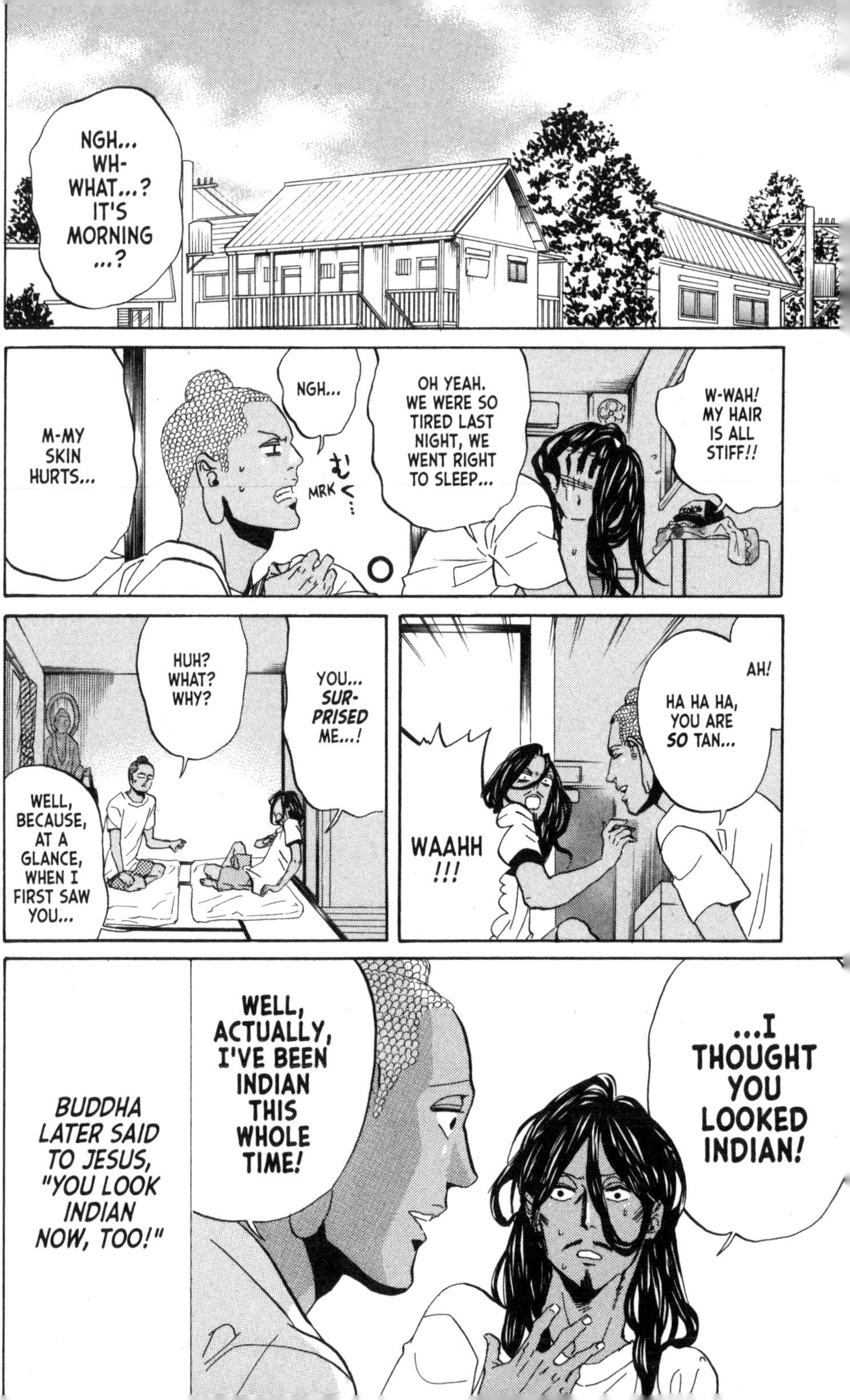
NGH... WH- WHAT...? IT'S MORNING ...?
W-WAH! MY HAIR IS ALL STIFF!!
OH YEAH. WE WERE SO TIRED LAST NIGHT, WE WENT RIGHT TO SLEEP...
NGH...
む
MRK
M-MY SKIN HURTS...
AH!
HA HA HA, YOU ARE *SO* TAN...
WAAHH !!!
YOU... *SURPRISED* ME...!
HUH? WHAT? WHY?
WELL, BECAUSE, AT A GLANCE, WHEN I FIRST SAW YOU...
...I THOUGHT YOU LOOKED INDIAN!
WELL, ACTUALLY, I'VE BEEN INDIAN THIS WHOLE TIME!
BUDDHA LATER SAID TO JESUS, "YOU LOOK INDIAN NOW, TOO!"

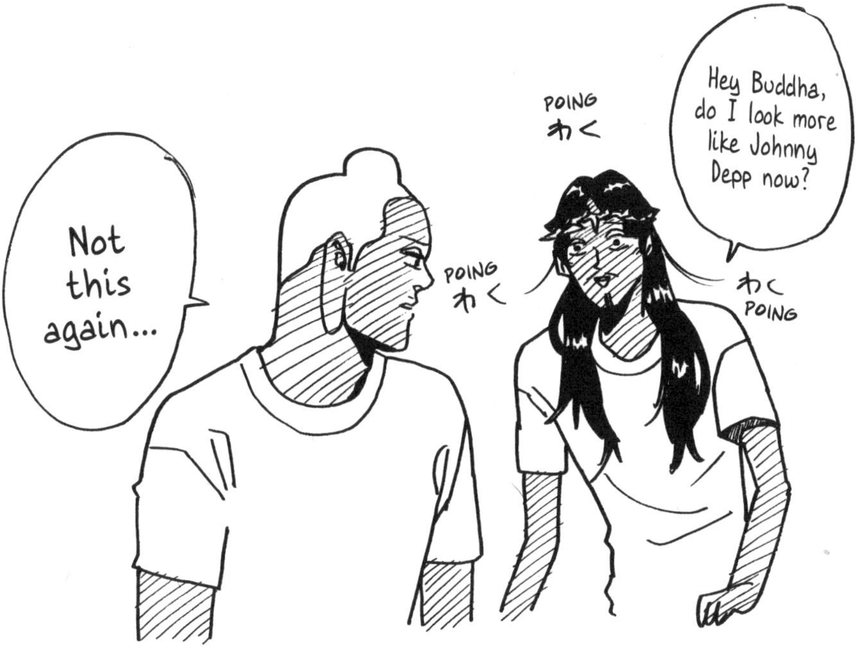
Hey Buddha, do I look more like Johnny Depp now?
POING
わく
わく
POING
POING
わく
Not this again...

CHAPTER 40 TRANSLATION NOTES

Jonah, page 205
Jonah was an Old Testament prophet who ran away from God's assignment to preach to the people in Nineveh. The ship he boarded in his escape was caught in a terrible storm, and Jonah advised the sailors to toss him overboard to appease God's wrath. Reluctantly, they did so, and the storm abated. Meanwhile, Jonah was swallowed by a giant fish, which spit him out after three days.

Deer Person, page 207
This specifically refers to Buddha's preference for deer, perhaps in this case in relation to preaching, as Jesus previously wore a shirt that said "Mountain Person," and was known for preaching his most famous sermon on a mountain, while Buddha first preached in Deer Park.

Eros, page 211
Eros is one of four ancient Greco-Christian terms that can be translated as "love." Readers will already be familiar with *agape*, or "selfless love." *Eros* is "passionate love," or "romantic love." The other two terms are *storge*, which is love for family, and *philia*, which is love for friends.

Graduated from their control, page 213
This is a lyric from Yutaka Ozaki's song, "Graduation," where he sings about breaking free of the societal rules he felt were oppressing him.

The Mouth of Truth, page 213
The Mouth of Truth is a marble mask that can be found at the Santa Maria in Cosmedin Church in Rome. The mouth of the mask is open, and legend has it that if one were to stick a hand into the mouth and tell a lie, the mask would bite that hand off. Tourist will line up to get a picture of themselves with their hand inside the mask's mouth.

Watermelon Smash, page 214
This is a common summer game in Japan with a simple objective: to smash a watermelon. The watermelon will be set on a towel on the ground, and the players will take turns being blindfolded and spun around three times. They will then take a wooden stick and try to find and smash the watermelon. Often those watching will offer advice that will lead the player in the right (or wrong) direction. Whoever breaks the watermelon open wins.

The Middle Path, page 215
The Middle Path, or the Middle Way, is a common description for Buddhist teachings in Mahayana Buddhism. It is often described as the middle path which is neither too ascetic nor indulgent. It can also describe Buddhism's philosophy of the non-self (*anatman*), which holds a position about the self between the existence of an eternal soul, and the mere physical body.

Nozawana and *ume*, page 217
Nozawana is a Japanese leafy green and *ume* is a Japanese plum. Both are often eaten pickled.

King Herod, page 219
When the Wise Men came looking for Jesus, they first went to King Herod and asked him where the child was born that would be King of the Jews. Hearing of a potential rival, Herod hoped that the Wise Men would return after finding Jesus and tell him (Herod) where to find the child. When they failed to reappear, Herod decided not to take any chances, and kill every child that might be the one the Wise Men sought—those two years and younger. An angel warned Joseph, Mary's husband, about the Herod's evil plot, and so the family escaped into Egypt.

Karaoke, page 219

The songs performed in this karaoke party are both by Chage and Aska. The first one is "YAH YAH YAH," which happens to be the same song being sung at the end of "No Music, No Life." The second is *"Banri no Kawa* (Thousand-Mile River)," Chage and Aska's first hit.

SAINT☆YOUNG MEN

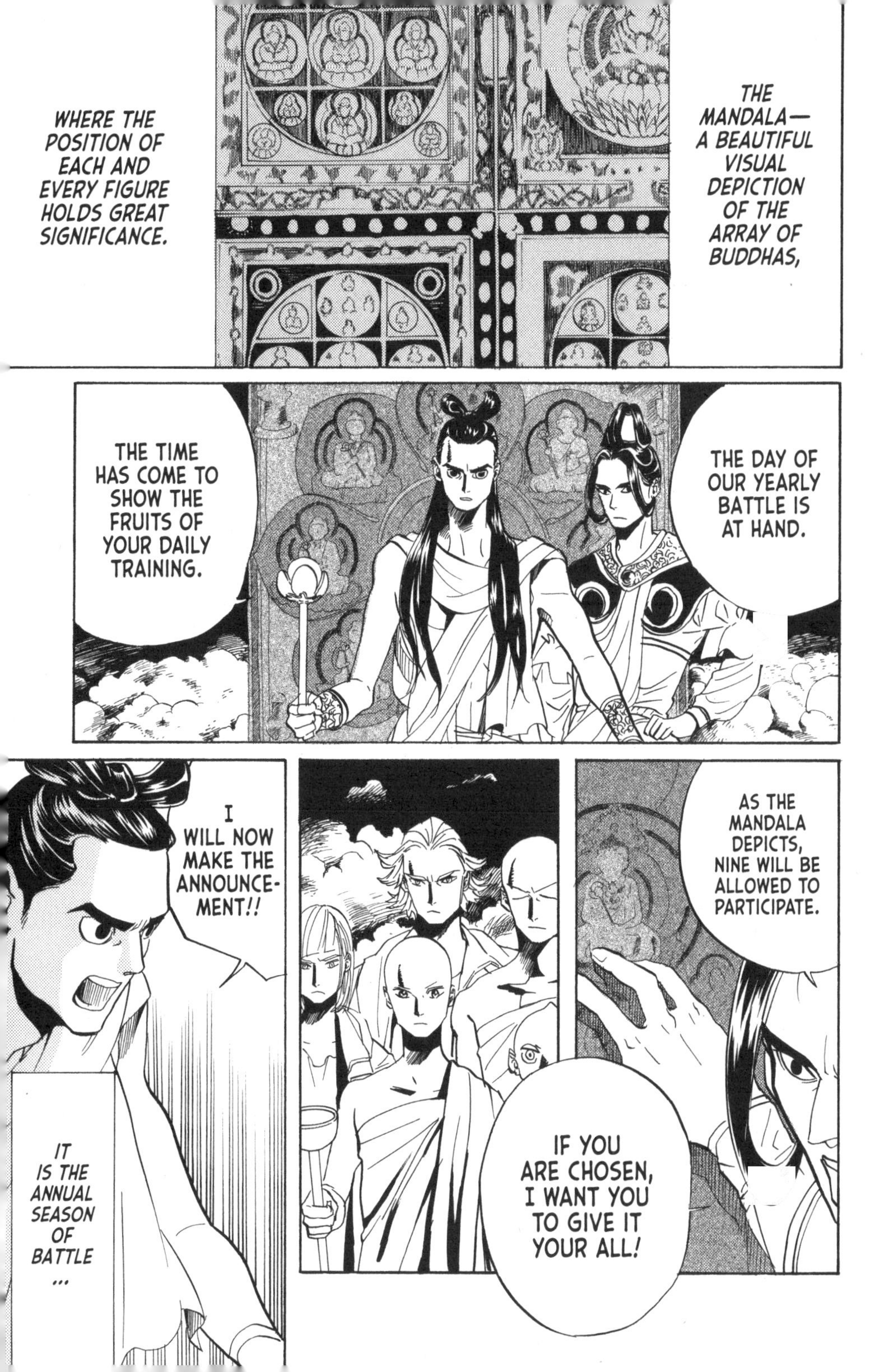
THE MANDALA—A BEAUTIFUL VISUAL DEPICTION OF THE ARRAY OF BUDDHAS,
WHERE THE POSITION OF EACH AND EVERY FIGURE HOLDS GREAT SIGNIFICANCE.
THE DAY OF OUR YEARLY BATTLE IS AT HAND.
THE TIME HAS COME TO SHOW THE FRUITS OF YOUR DAILY TRAINING.
AS THE MANDALA DEPICTS, NINE WILL BE ALLOWED TO PARTICIPATE.
IF YOU ARE CHOSEN, I WANT YOU TO GIVE IT YOUR ALL!
I WILL NOW MAKE THE ANNOUNCE-MENT!!
IT IS THE ANNUAL SEASON OF BATTLE ...

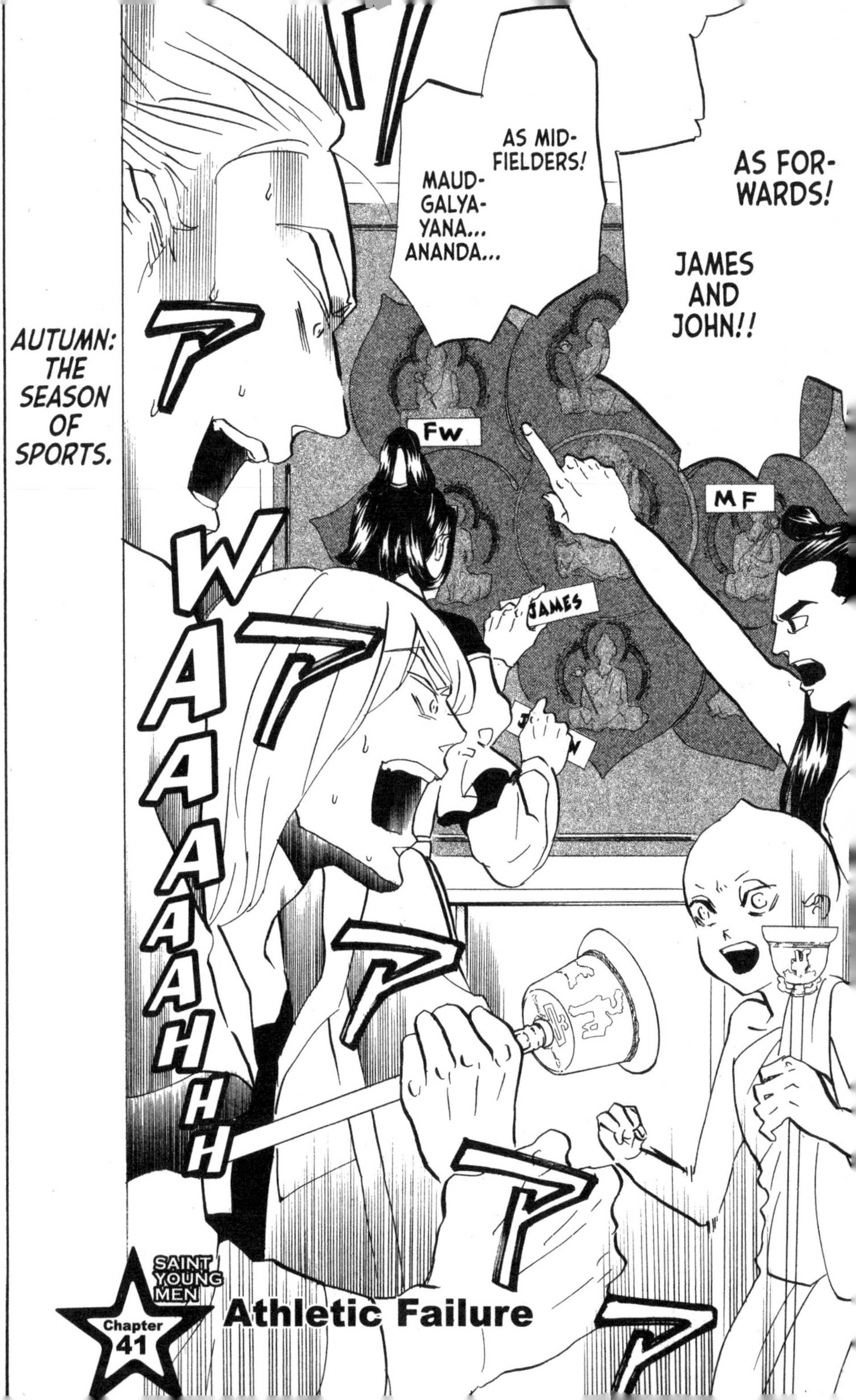
AS FOR-WARDS!
JAMES AND JOHN!!
AS MID-FIELDERS!
MAUD-GALYA-YANA... ANANDA...
MF
FW
JAMES
AUTUMN: THE SEASON OF SPORTS.
WAAAAAAAHHH
SAINT YOUNG MEN
Chapter 41
Athletic Failure

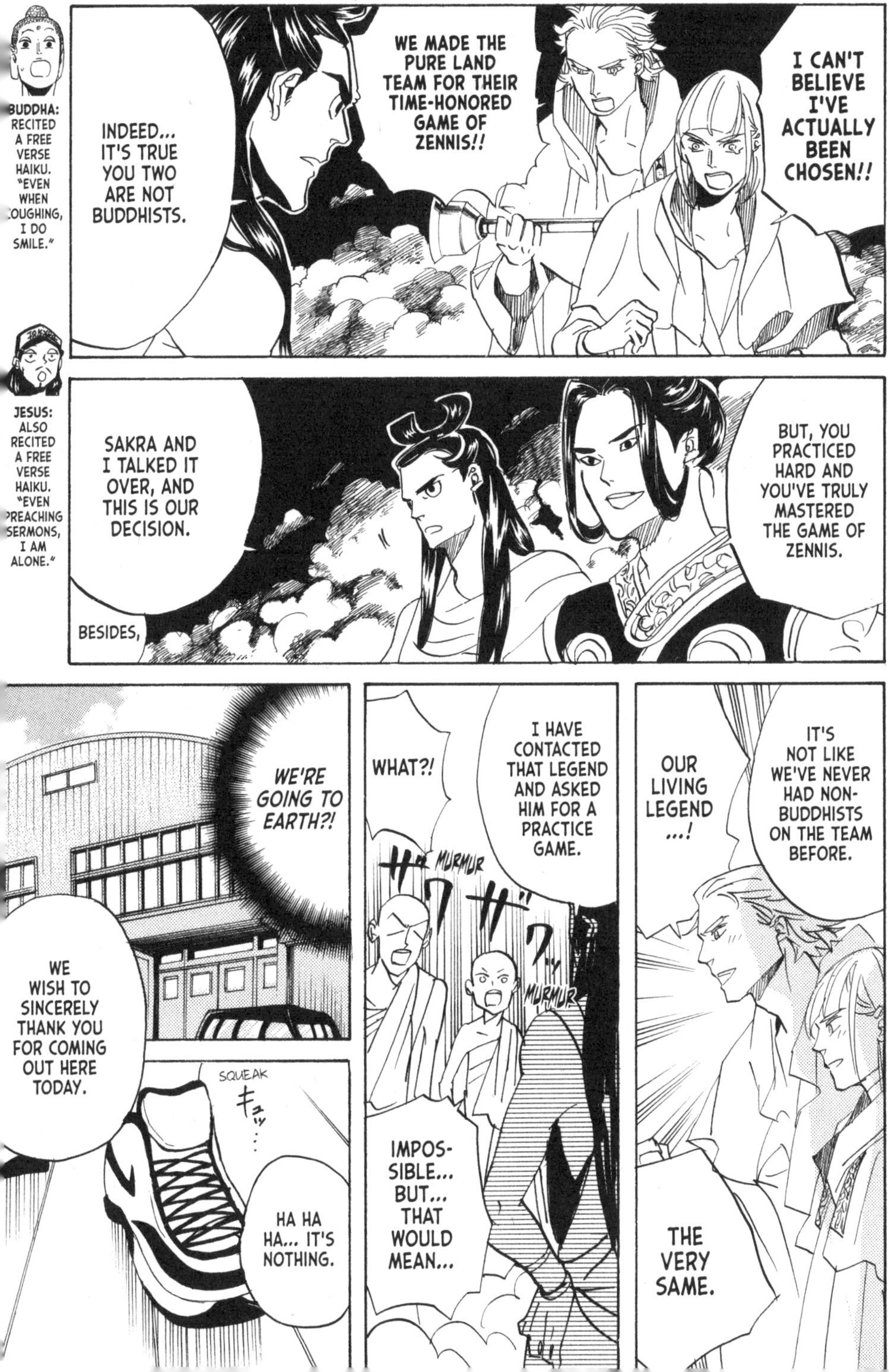
I CAN'T BELIEVE I'VE ACTUALLY BEEN CHOSEN!!
WE MADE THE PURE LAND TEAM FOR THEIR TIME-HONORED GAME OF ZENNIS!!
INDEED... IT'S TRUE YOU TWO ARE NOT BUDDHISTS.
BUT, YOU PRACTICED HARD AND YOU'VE TRULY MASTERED THE GAME OF ZENNIS.
SAKRA AND I TALKED IT OVER, AND THIS IS OUR DECISION.
BESIDES,
IT'S NOT LIKE WE'VE NEVER HAD NON-BUDDHISTS ON THE TEAM BEFORE.
OUR LIVING LEGEND ...!
THE VERY SAME.
I HAVE CONTACTED THAT LEGEND AND ASKED HIM FOR A PRACTICE GAME.
WHAT?!
MURMUR
MURMUR
IMPOSSIBLE... BUT... THAT WOULD MEAN...
WE'RE GOING TO EARTH?!
WE WISH TO SINCERELY THANK YOU FOR COMING OUT HERE TODAY.
SQUEAK
HA HA HA... IT'S NOTHING.
BUDDHA: RECITED A FREE VERSE HAIKU. "EVEN WHEN COUGHING, I DO SMILE."
JESUS: ALSO RECITED A FREE VERSE HAIKU. "EVEN PREACHING SERMONS, I AM ALONE."

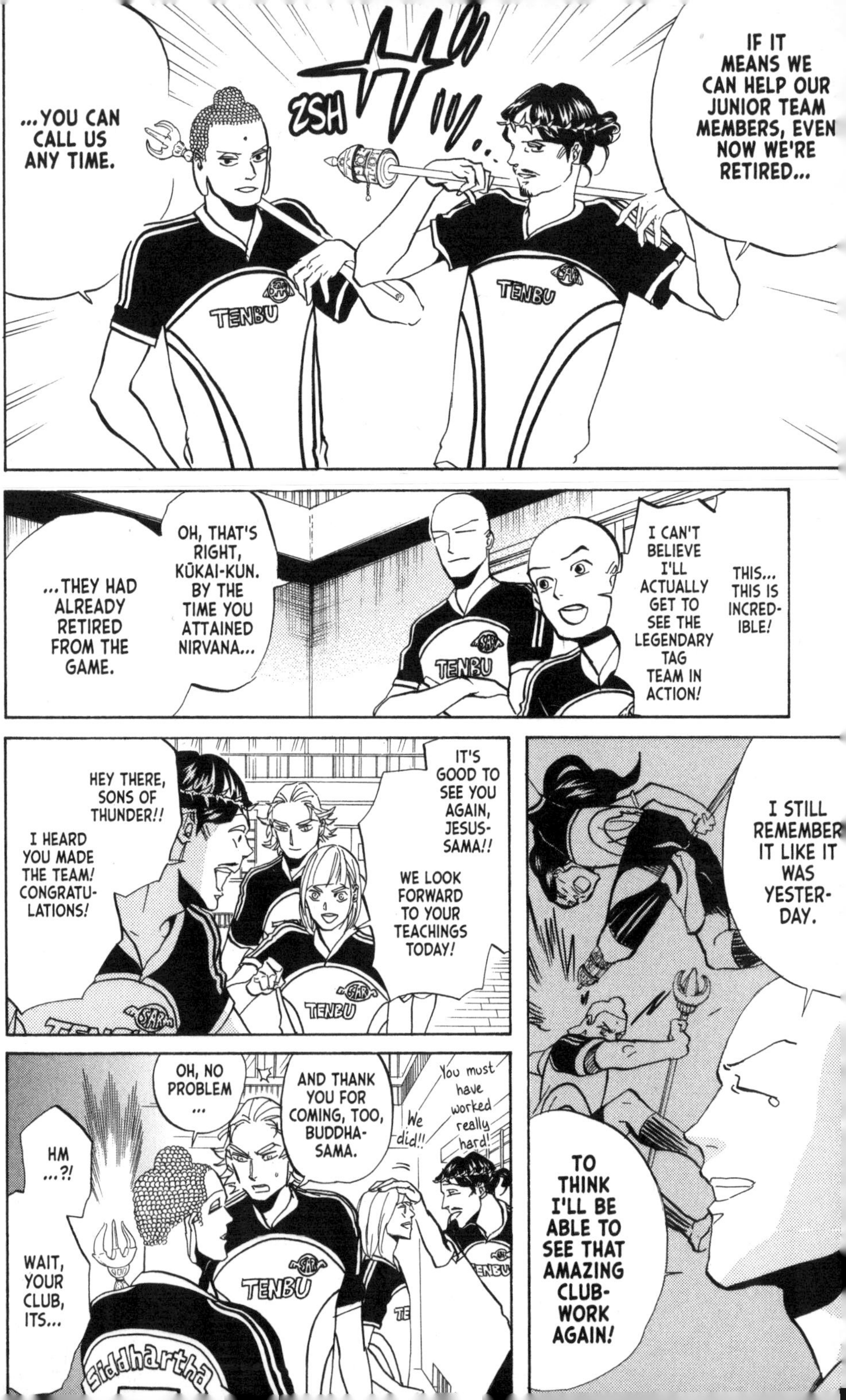
IF IT MEANS WE CAN HELP OUR JUNIOR TEAM MEMBERS, EVEN NOW WE'RE RETIRED...
ZSH
...YOU CAN CALL US ANY TIME.
THIS... THIS IS INCREDIBLE!
I CAN'T BELIEVE I'LL ACTUALLY GET TO SEE THE LEGENDARY TAG TEAM IN ACTION!
OH, THAT'S RIGHT, KŪKAI-KUN. BY THE TIME YOU ATTAINED NIRVANA...
...THEY HAD ALREADY RETIRED FROM THE GAME.
I STILL REMEMBER IT LIKE IT WAS YESTERDAY.
TO THINK I'LL BE ABLE TO SEE THAT AMAZING CLUB-WORK AGAIN!
IT'S GOOD TO SEE YOU AGAIN, JESUS-SAMA!!
WE LOOK FORWARD TO YOUR TEACHINGS TODAY!
HEY THERE, SONS OF THUNDER!!
I HEARD YOU MADE THE TEAM! CONGRATULATIONS!
You must have worked really hard!
We did!!
AND THANK YOU FOR COMING, TOO, BUDDHA-SAMA.
OH, NO PROBLEM ...
HM ...?!
WAIT, YOUR CLUB, ITS...
Siddhartha

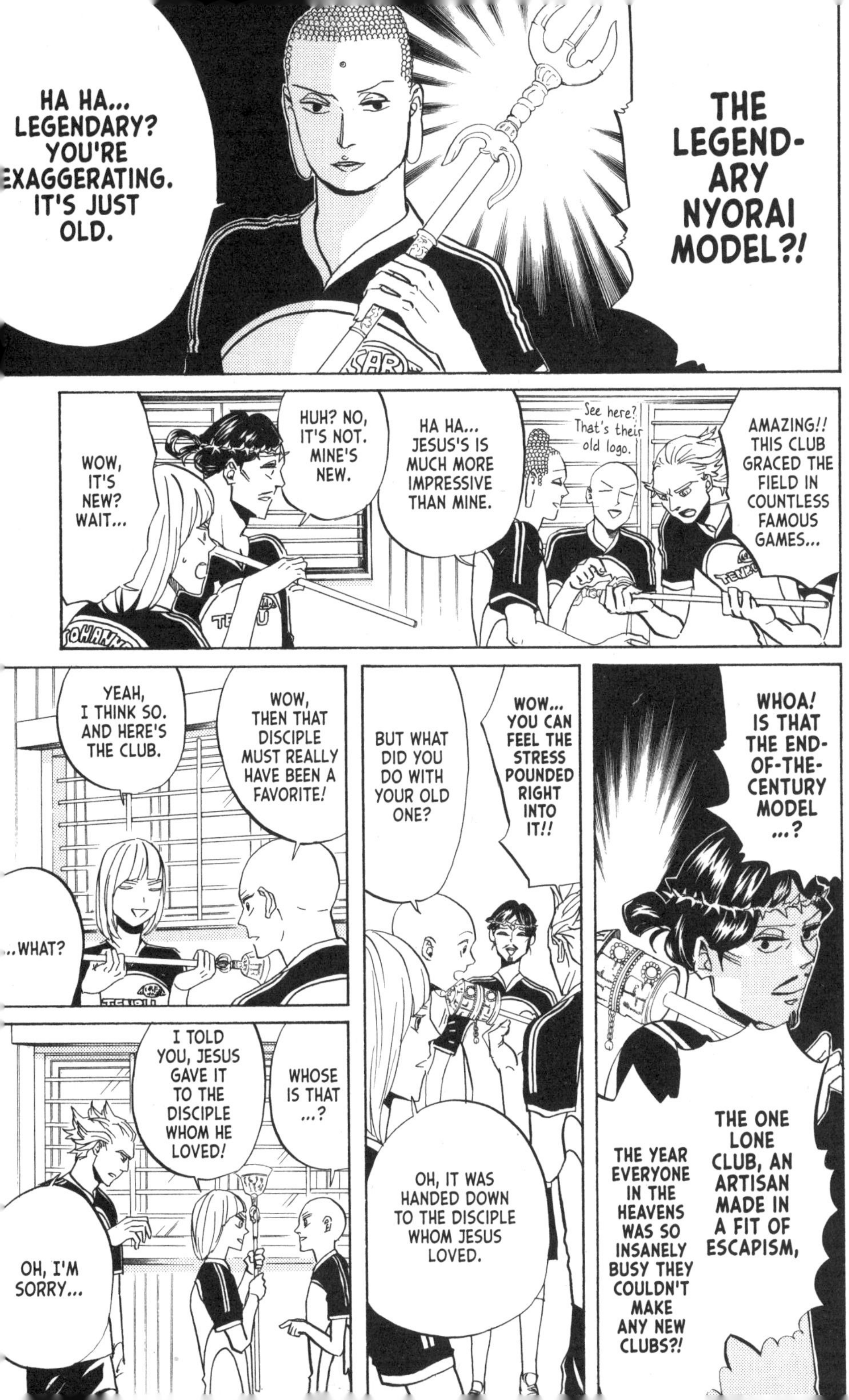
THE LEGENDARY NYORAI MODEL?!
HA HA... LEGENDARY? YOU'RE EXAGGERATING. IT'S JUST OLD.
AMAZING!! THIS CLUB GRACED THE FIELD IN COUNTLESS FAMOUS GAMES...
See here? That's their old logo.
HA HA... JESUS'S IS MUCH MORE IMPRESSIVE THAN MINE.
HUH? NO, IT'S NOT. MINE'S NEW.
WOW, IT'S NEW? WAIT...
WHOA! IS THAT THE END-OF-THE-CENTURY MODEL ...?
THE ONE LONE CLUB, AN ARTISAN MADE IN A FIT OF ESCAPISM,
THE YEAR EVERYONE IN THE HEAVENS WAS SO INSANELY BUSY THEY COULDN'T MAKE ANY NEW CLUBS?!
WOW... YOU CAN FEEL THE STRESS POUNDED RIGHT INTO IT!!
BUT WHAT DID YOU DO WITH YOUR OLD ONE?
OH, IT WAS HANDED DOWN TO THE DISCIPLE WHOM JESUS LOVED.
WOW, THEN THAT DISCIPLE MUST REALLY HAVE BEEN A FAVORITE!
YEAH, I THINK SO. AND HERE'S THE CLUB.
...WHAT?
WHOSE IS THAT ...?
I TOLD YOU, JESUS GAVE IT TO THE DISCIPLE WHOM HE LOVED!
OH, I'M SORRY...

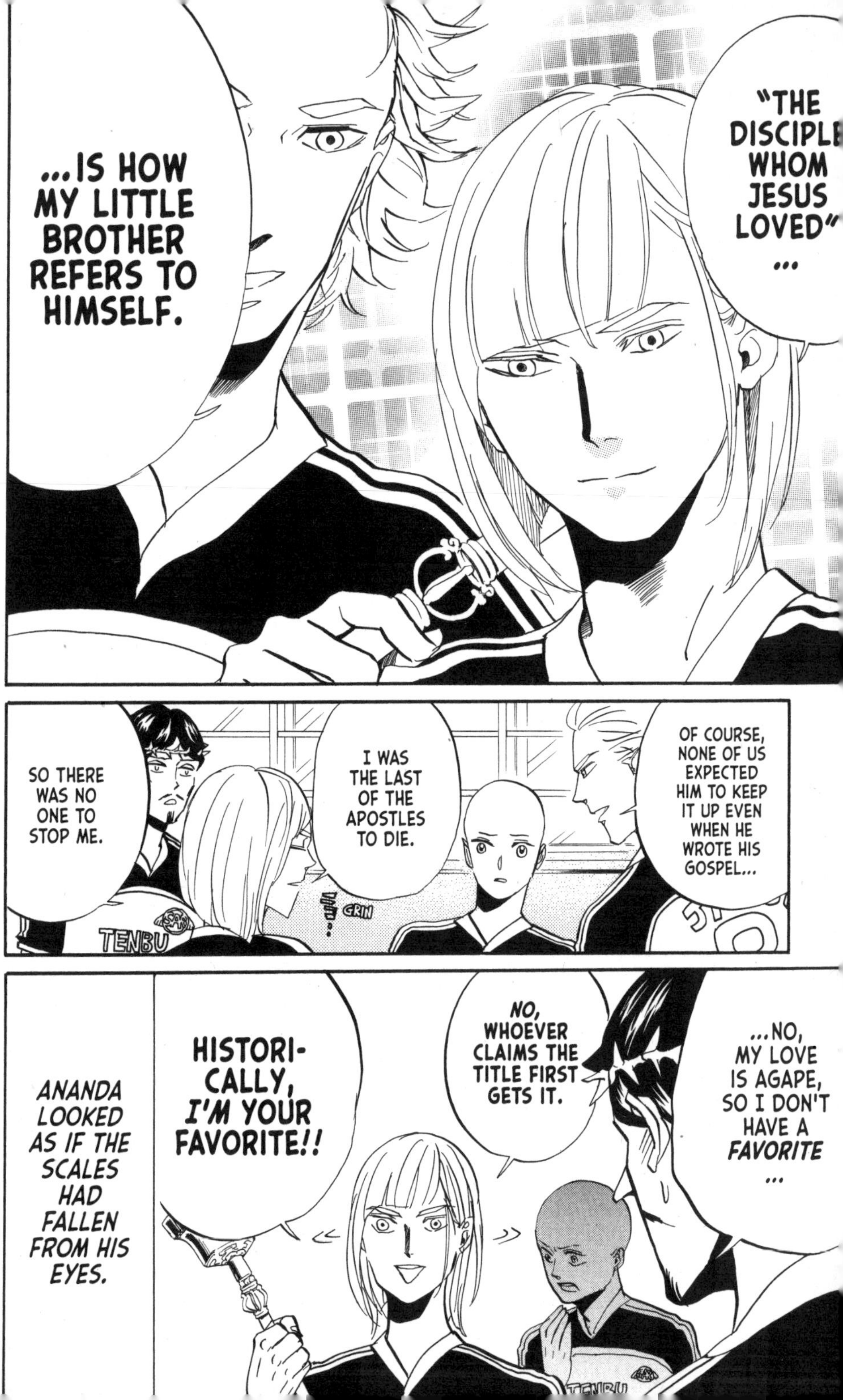
"THE DISCIPL WHOM JESUS LOVED"...
...IS HOW MY LITTLE BROTHER REFERS TO HIMSELF.
OF COURSE, NONE OF US EXPECTED HIM TO KEEP IT UP EVEN WHEN HE WROTE HIS GOSPEL...
I WAS THE LAST OF THE APOSTLES TO DIE.
GRIN
SO THERE WAS NO ONE TO STOP ME.
TENBU
...NO, MY LOVE IS AGAPE, SO I DON'T HAVE A *FAVORITE*...
NO, WHOEVER CLAIMS THE TITLE FIRST GETS IT.
HISTORI-CALLY, *I'M* YOUR FAVORITE!!
ANANDA LOOKED AS IF THE SCALES HAD FALLEN FROM HIS EYES.

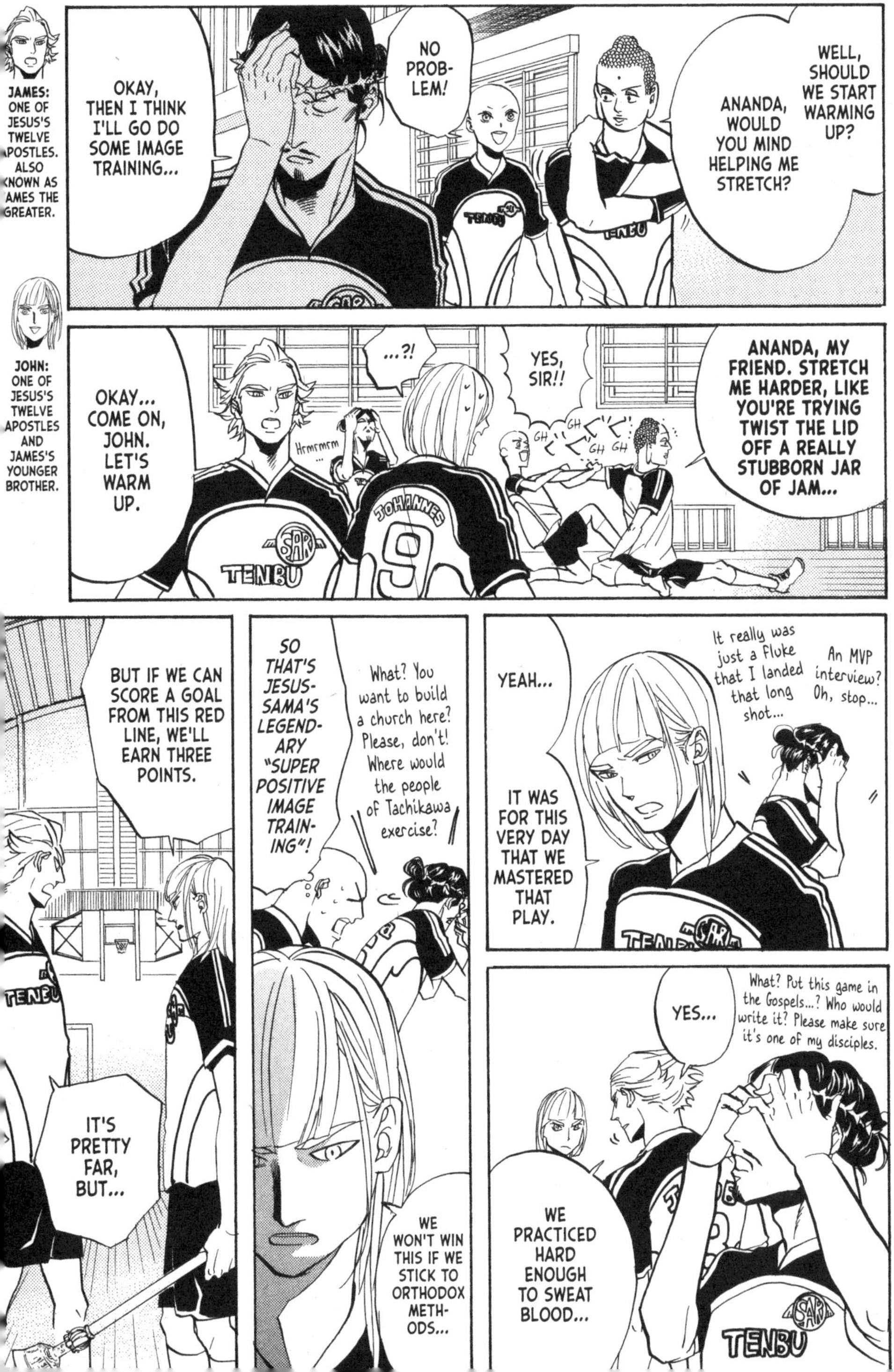
WELL, SHOULD WE START WARMING UP?
ANANDA, WOULD YOU MIND HELPING ME STRETCH?
NO PROB-LEM!
OKAY, THEN I THINK I'LL GO DO SOME IMAGE TRAINING...
JAMES: ONE OF JESUS'S TWELVE APOSTLES. ALSO KNOWN AS JAMES THE GREATER.
ANANDA, MY FRIEND. STRETCH ME HARDER, LIKE YOU'RE TRYING TWIST THE LID OFF A REALLY STUBBORN JAR OF JAM...
GH GH GH GH
YES, SIR!!
...?!
Hrmrmrm...
OKAY... COME ON, JOHN. LET'S WARM UP.
JOHN: ONE OF JESUS'S TWELVE APOSTLES AND JAMES'S YOUNGER BROTHER.
An MVP interview? Oh, stop...
It really was just a fluke that I landed that long shot...
YEAH...
IT WAS FOR THIS VERY DAY THAT WE MASTERED THAT PLAY.
What? Put this game in the Gospels...? Who would write it? Please make sure it's one of my disciples.
YES...
WE PRACTICED HARD ENOUGH TO SWEAT BLOOD...
SO THAT'S JESUS-SAMA'S LEGEND-ARY "SUPER POSITIVE IMAGE TRAIN-ING"!
What? You want to build a church here? Please, don't! Where would the people of Tachikawa exercise?
WE WON'T WIN THIS IF WE STICK TO ORTHODOX METH-ODS...
BUT IF WE CAN SCORE A GOAL FROM THIS RED LINE, WE'LL EARN THREE POINTS.
IT'S PRETTY FAR, BUT...

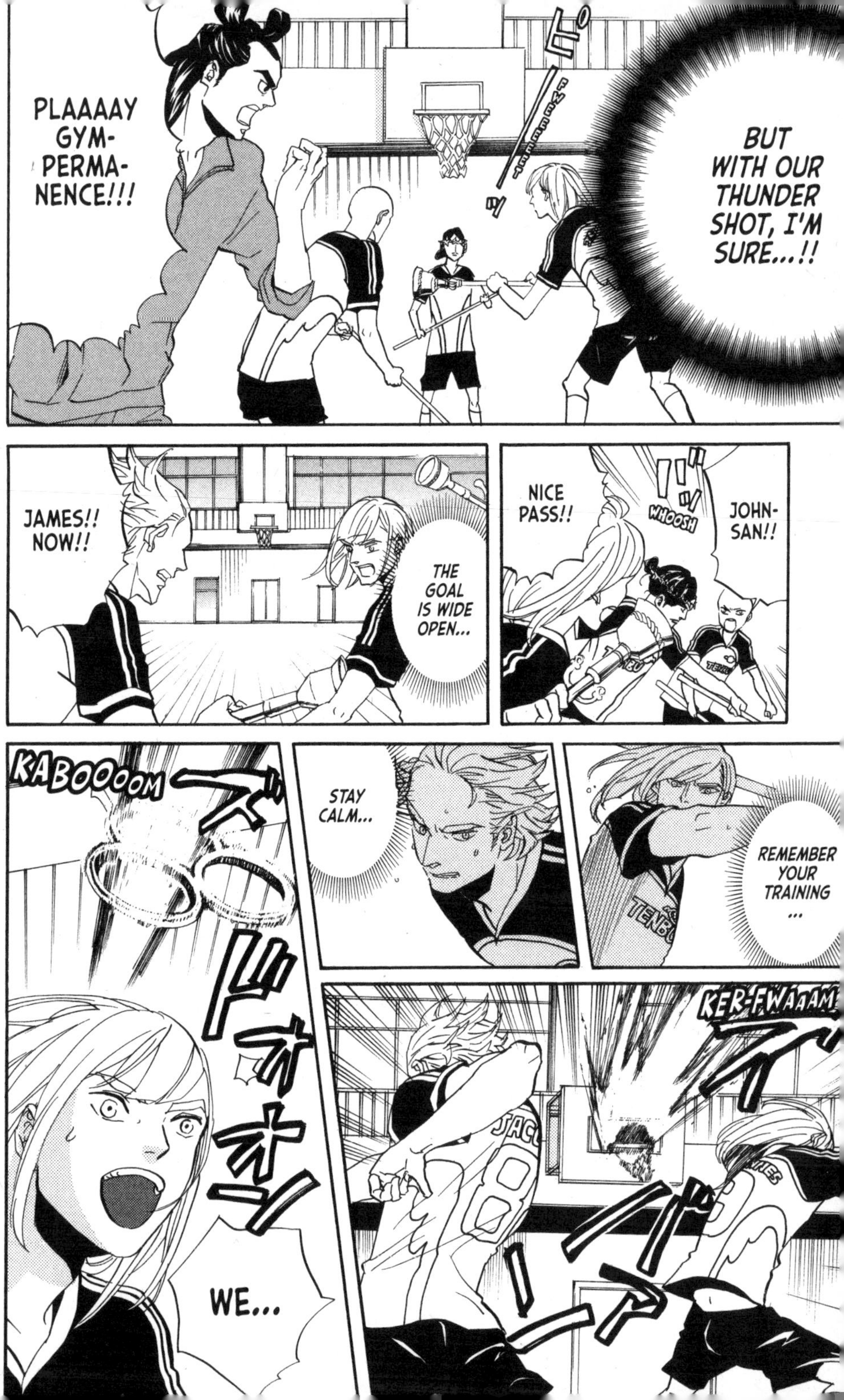
BUT WITH OUR THUNDER SHOT, I'M SURE...!!
PLAAAAY GYM-PERMA-NENCE!!!
JOHN-SAN!!
WHOOSH
NICE PASS!!
THE GOAL IS WIDE OPEN...
JAMES!! NOW!!
REMEMBER YOUR TRAINING ...
STAY CALM...
KER-FWAAAM
KABOOOOM
WE...

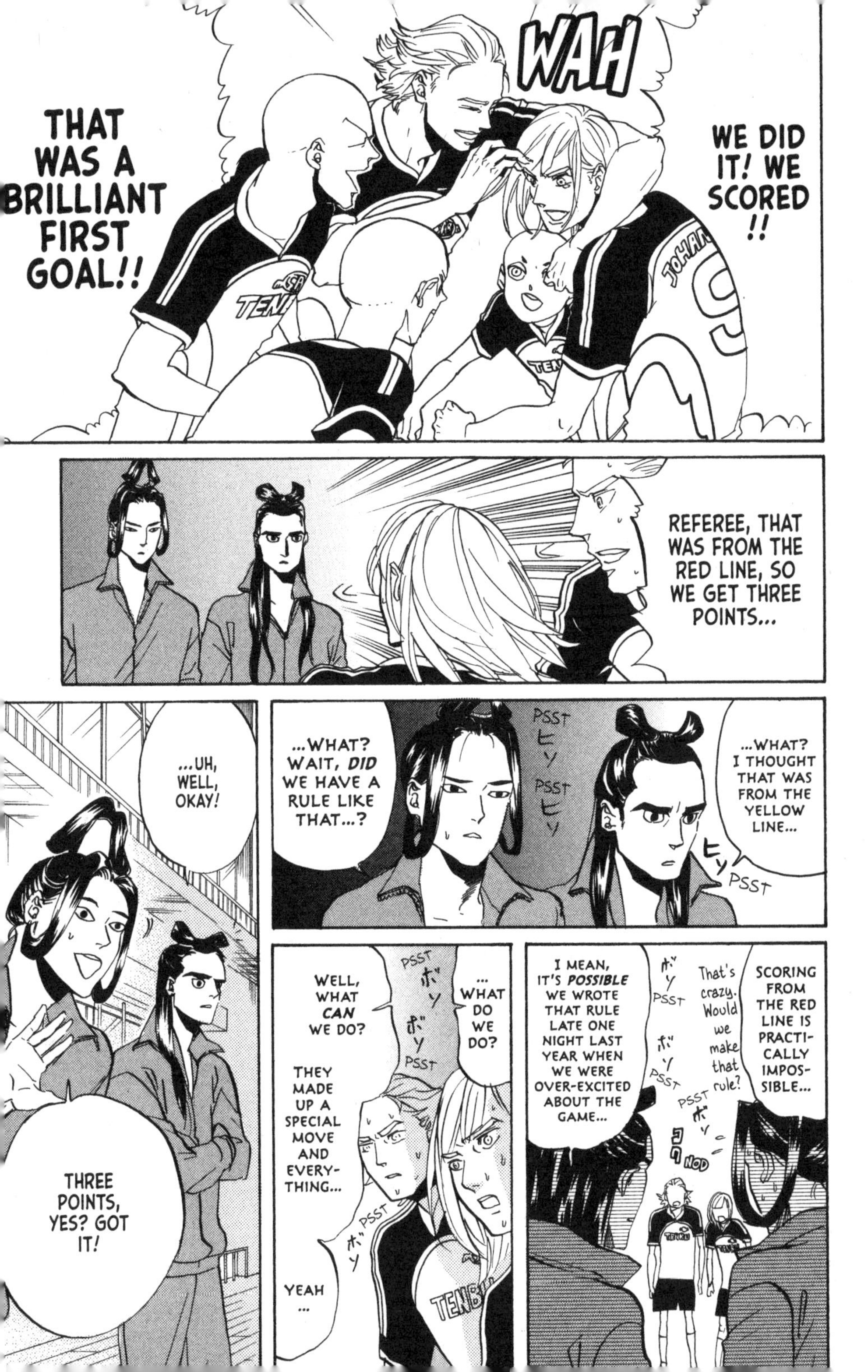
WAH
WE DID IT! WE SCORED!!
THAT WAS A BRILLIANT FIRST GOAL!!
REFEREE, THAT WAS FROM THE RED LINE, SO WE GET THREE POINTS...
...WHAT? I THOUGHT THAT WAS FROM THE YELLOW LINE...
ヒソ PSST
PSST ヒソ
PSST ヒソ
...WHAT? WAIT, *DID* WE HAVE A RULE LIKE THAT...?
SCORING FROM THE RED LINE IS PRACTICALLY IMPOSSIBLE...
That's crazy. Would we make that rule?
ボソ PSST
ボソ PSST
I MEAN, IT'S *POSSIBLE* WE WROTE THAT RULE LATE ONE NIGHT LAST YEAR WHEN WE WERE OVER-EXCITED ABOUT THE GAME...
PSST ボソ
コク NOD
...WHAT DO WE DO?
PSST ボソ
ボソ PSST
WELL, WHAT *CAN* WE DO?
THEY MADE UP A SPECIAL MOVE AND EVERY-THING...
ボソ PSST
YEAH...
...UH, WELL, OKAY!
THREE POINTS, YES? GOT IT!

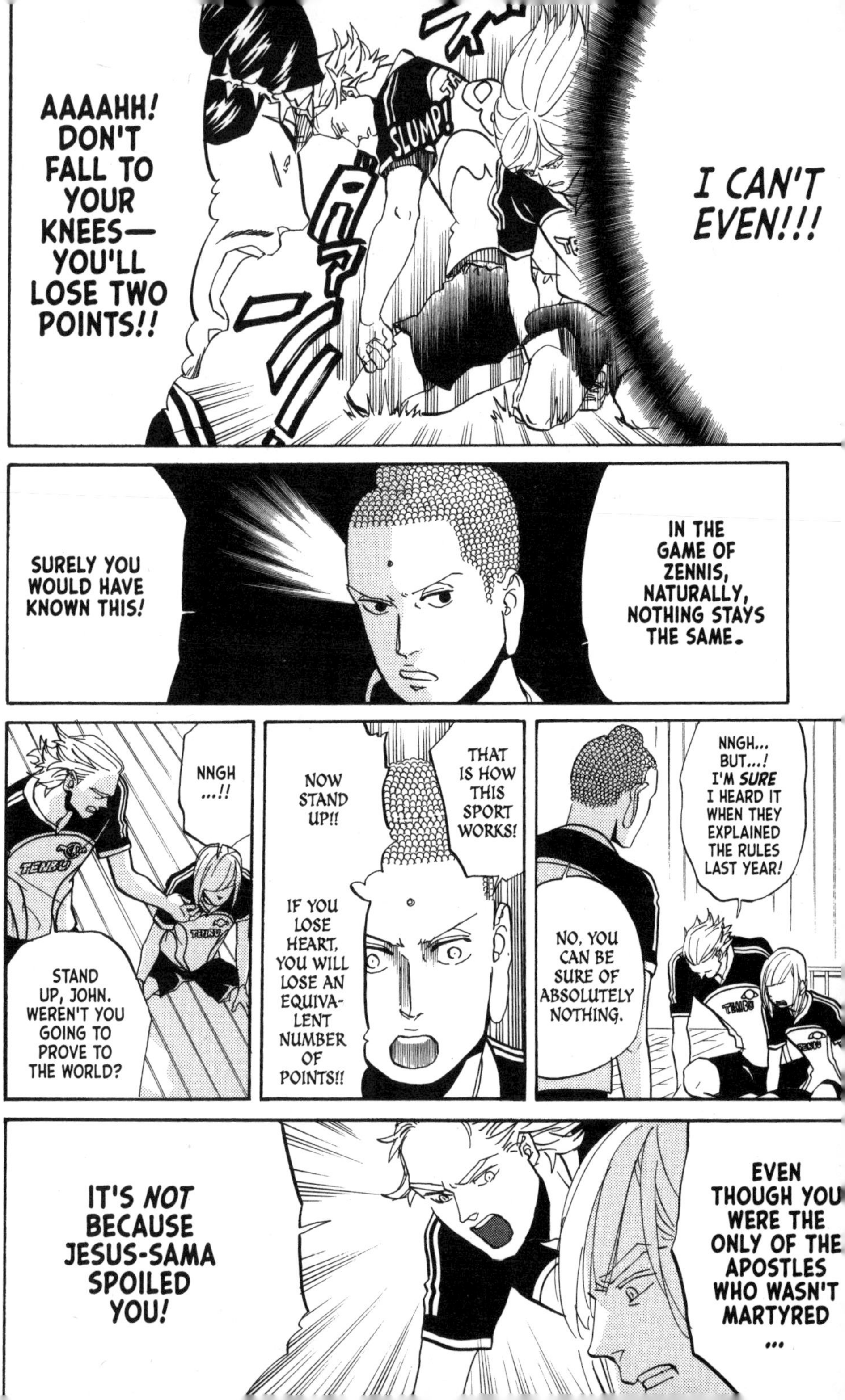
I CAN'T EVEN!!!
SLUMP!
AAAAHH! DON'T FALL TO YOUR KNEES—YOU'LL LOSE TWO POINTS!!
IN THE GAME OF ZENNIS, NATURALLY, NOTHING STAYS THE SAME.
SURELY YOU WOULD HAVE KNOWN THIS!
NNGH... BUT...! I'M SURE I HEARD IT WHEN THEY EXPLAINED THE RULES LAST YEAR!
NO, YOU CAN BE SURE OF ABSOLUTELY NOTHING.
THAT IS HOW THIS SPORT WORKS!
NOW STAND UP!!
IF YOU LOSE HEART, YOU WILL LOSE AN EQUIVALENT NUMBER OF POINTS!!
NNGH ...!!
STAND UP, JOHN. WEREN'T YOU GOING TO PROVE TO THE WORLD?
EVEN THOUGH YOU WERE THE ONLY OF THE APOSTLES WHO WASN'T MARTYRED ...
IT'S NOT BECAUSE JESUS-SAMA SPOILED YOU!

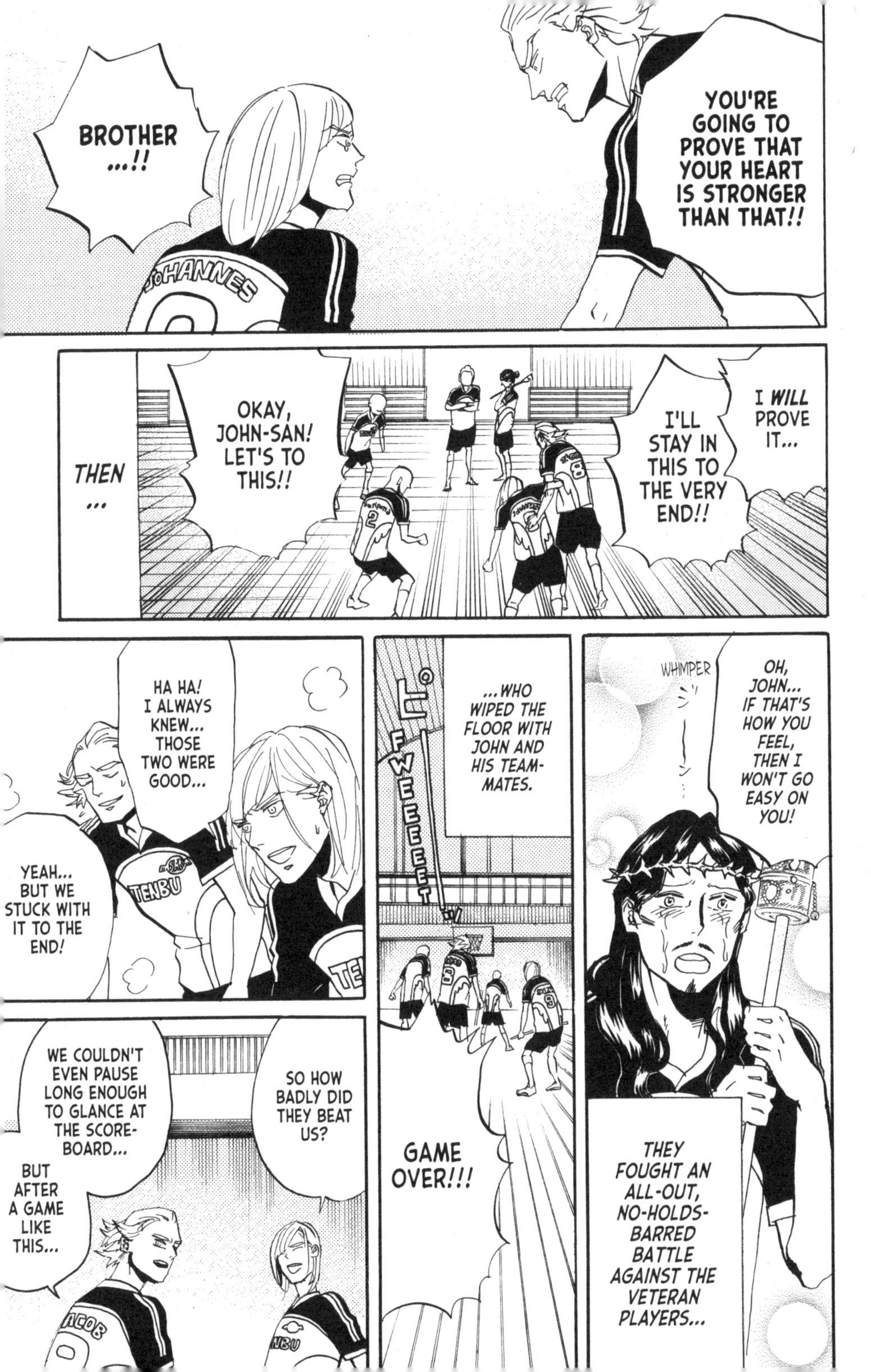
YOU'RE GOING TO PROVE THAT YOUR HEART IS STRONGER THAN THAT!!
BROTHER ...!!
I WILL PROVE IT...
I'LL STAY IN THIS TO THE VERY END!!
OKAY, JOHN-SAN! LET'S TO THIS!!
THEN ...
WHIMPER
OH, JOHN... IF THAT's HOW YOU FEEL, THEN I WON'T GO EASY ON YOU!
THEY FOUGHT AN ALL-OUT, NO-HOLDS-BARRED BATTLE AGAINST THE VETERAN PLAYERS...
...WHO WIPED THE FLOOR WITH JOHN AND HIS TEAM-MATES.
FWEEEEET
GAME OVER!!!
HA HA! I ALWAYS KNEW... THOSE TWO WERE GOOD...
YEAH... BUT WE STUCK WITH IT TO THE END!
SO HOW BADLY DID THEY BEAT US?
WE COULDN'T EVEN PAUSE LONG ENOUGH TO GLANCE AT THE SCORE-BOARD...
BUT AFTER A GAME LIKE THIS...

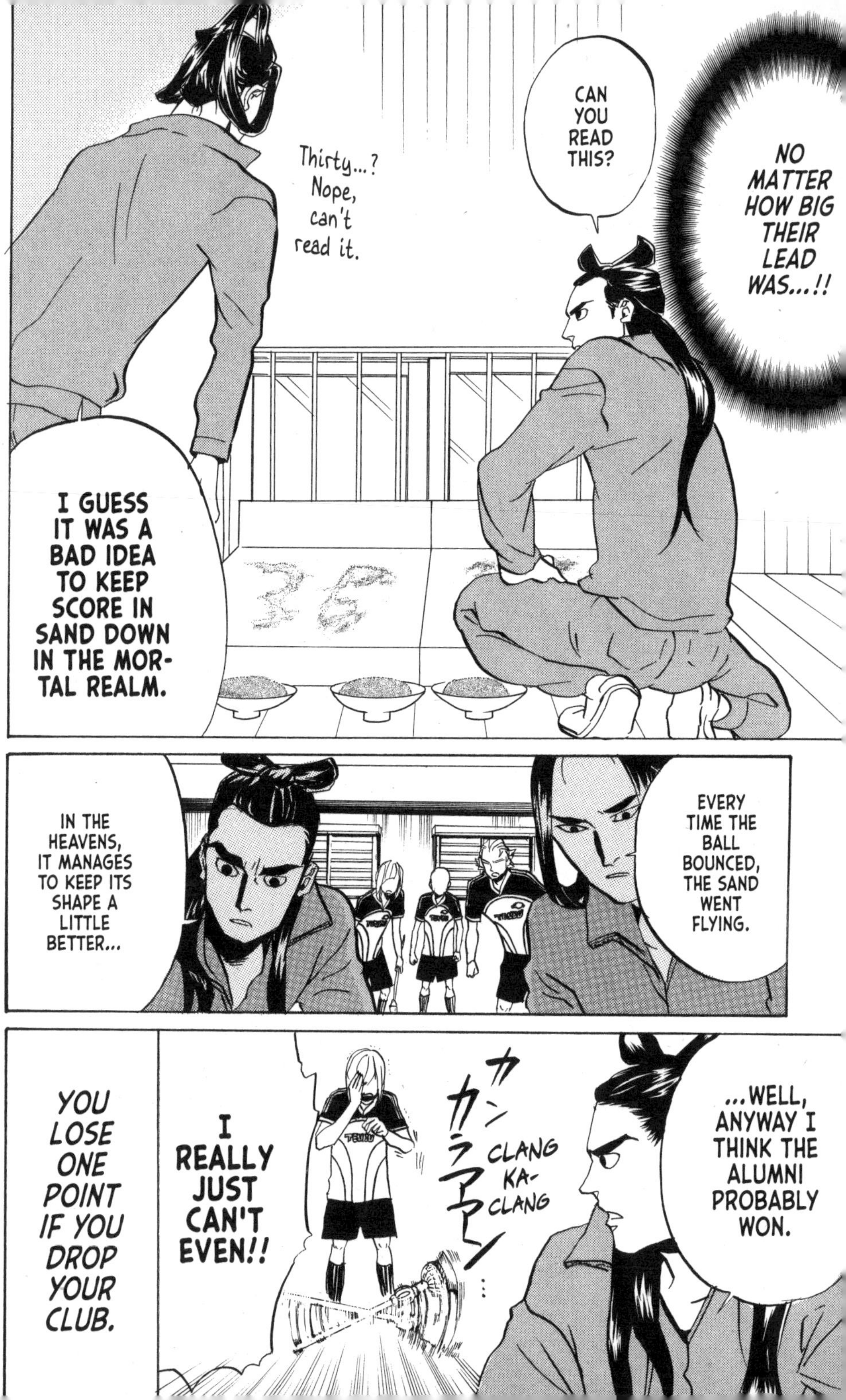
NO MATTER HOW BIG THEIR LEAD WAS...!!
CAN YOU READ THIS?
Thirty...? Nope, can't read it.
I GUESS IT WAS A BAD IDEA TO KEEP SCORE IN SAND DOWN IN THE MOR-TAL REALM.
EVERY TIME THE BALL BOUNCED, THE SAND WENT FLYING.
IN THE HEAVENS, IT MANAGES TO KEEP ITS SHAPE A LITTLE BETTER...
...WELL, ANYWAY I THINK THE ALUMNI PROBABLY WON.
カン
カラァ〜ン…
CLANG KA-CLANG
I REALLY JUST CAN'T EVEN!!
YOU LOSE ONE POINT IF YOU DROP YOUR CLUB.

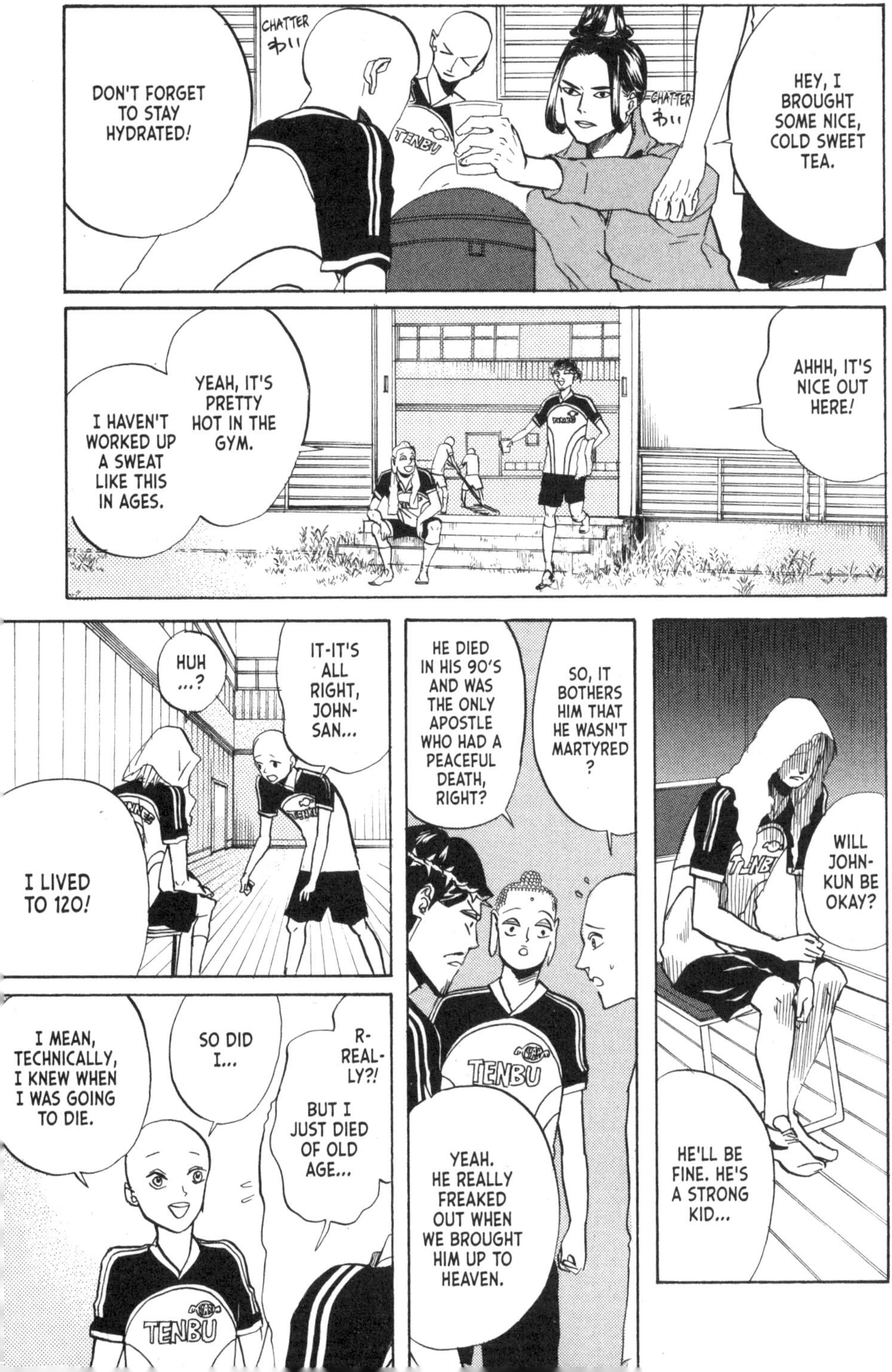
HEY, I BROUGHT SOME NICE, COLD SWEET TEA.
CHATTER わい
CHATTER わい
DON'T FORGET TO STAY HYDRATED!
AHHH, IT'S NICE OUT HERE!
YEAH, IT'S PRETTY HOT IN THE GYM.
I HAVEN'T WORKED UP A SWEAT LIKE THIS IN AGES.
WILL JOHN-KUN BE OKAY?
HE'LL BE FINE. HE'S A STRONG KID...
SO, IT BOTHERS HIM THAT HE WASN'T MARTYRED?
HE DIED IN HIS 90'S AND WAS THE ONLY APOSTLE WHO HAD A PEACEFUL DEATH, RIGHT?
YEAH. HE REALLY FREAKED OUT WHEN WE BROUGHT HIM UP TO HEAVEN.
IT-IT'S ALL RIGHT, JOHN-SAN...
HUH ...?
I LIVED TO 120!
R-REALLY?!
BUT I JUST DIED OF OLD AGE...
SO DID I...
I MEAN, TECHNICALLY, I KNEW WHEN I WAS GOING TO DIE.

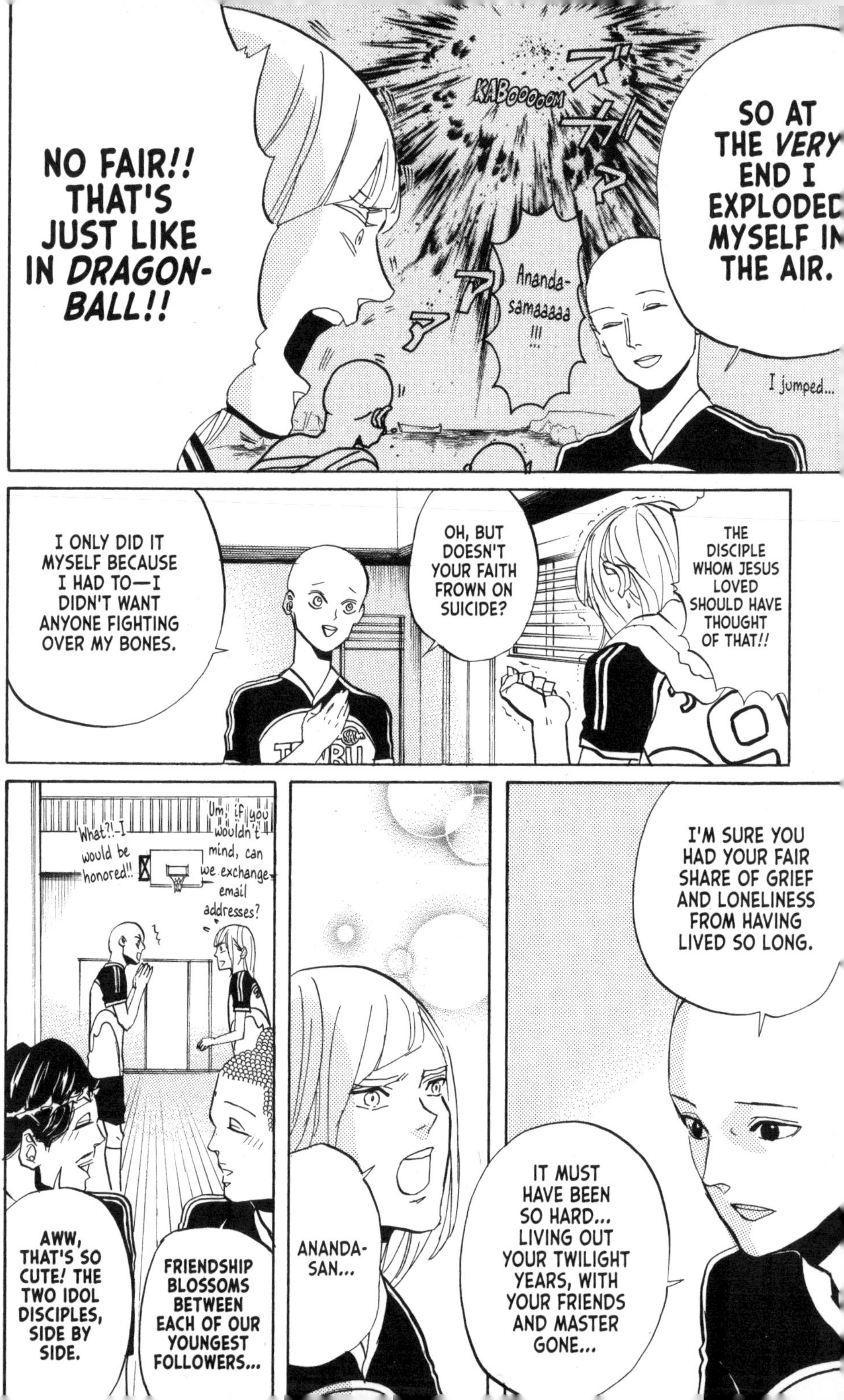
SO AT THE VERY END I EXPLODED MYSELF IN THE AIR.
I jumped...
KABOOOOOM
Ananda-samaaaaa!!!
NO FAIR!! THAT'S JUST LIKE IN DRAGON-BALL!!
THE DISCIPLE WHOM JESUS LOVED SHOULD HAVE THOUGHT OF THAT!!
OH, BUT DOESN'T YOUR FAITH FROWN ON SUICIDE?
I ONLY DID IT MYSELF BECAUSE I HAD TO—I DIDN'T WANT ANYONE FIGHTING OVER MY BONES.
I'M SURE YOU HAD YOUR FAIR SHARE OF GRIEF AND LONELINESS FROM HAVING LIVED SO LONG.
IT MUST HAVE BEEN SO HARD... LIVING OUT YOUR TWILIGHT YEARS, WITH YOUR FRIENDS AND MASTER GONE...
ANANDA-SAN...
Um, if you wouldn't mind, can we exchange email addresses?
What?! I would be honored!!
FRIENDSHIP BLOSSOMS BETWEEN EACH OF OUR YOUNGEST FOLLOWERS...
AWW, THAT'S SO CUTE! THE TWO IDOL DISCIPLES, SIDE BY SIDE.

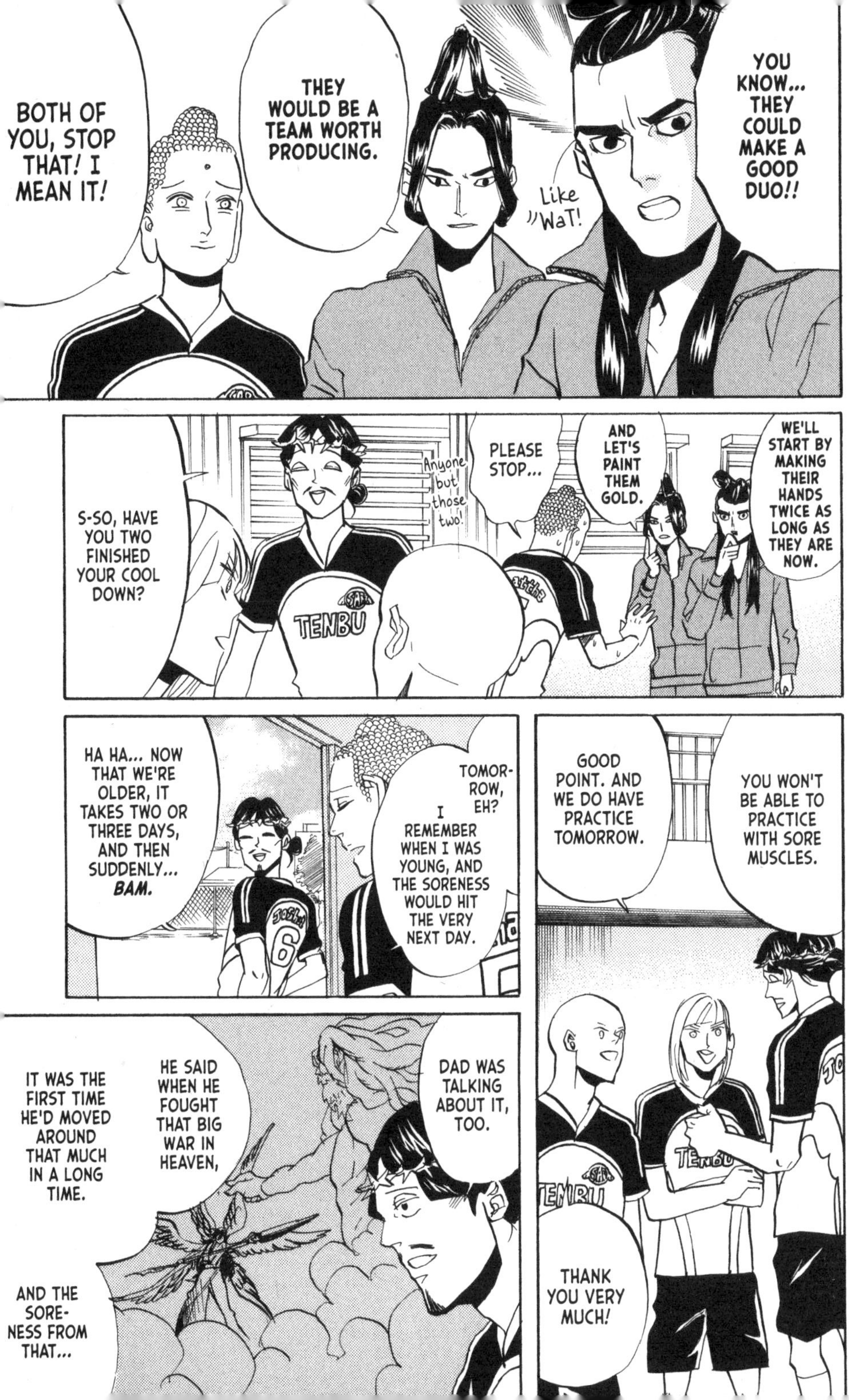
YOU KNOW... THEY COULD MAKE A GOOD DUO!!
Like WaT!
THEY WOULD BE A TEAM WORTH PRODUCING.
BOTH OF YOU, STOP THAT! I MEAN IT!
WE'LL START BY MAKING THEIR HANDS TWICE AS LONG AS THEY ARE NOW.
AND LET'S PAINT THEM GOLD.
PLEASE STOP...
Anyone but those two!
S-SO, HAVE YOU TWO FINISHED YOUR COOL DOWN?
YOU WON'T BE ABLE TO PRACTICE WITH SORE MUSCLES.
GOOD POINT. AND WE DO HAVE PRACTICE TOMORROW.
THANK YOU VERY MUCH!
TOMOR-ROW, EH?
I REMEMBER WHEN I WAS YOUNG, AND THE SORENESS WOULD HIT THE VERY NEXT DAY.
HA HA... NOW THAT WE'RE OLDER, IT TAKES TWO OR THREE DAYS, AND THEN SUDDENLY... BAM.
DAD WAS TALKING ABOUT IT, TOO.
HE SAID WHEN HE FOUGHT THAT BIG WAR IN HEAVEN,
IT WAS THE FIRST TIME HE'D MOVED AROUND THAT MUCH IN A LONG TIME.
AND THE SORE-NESS FROM THAT...

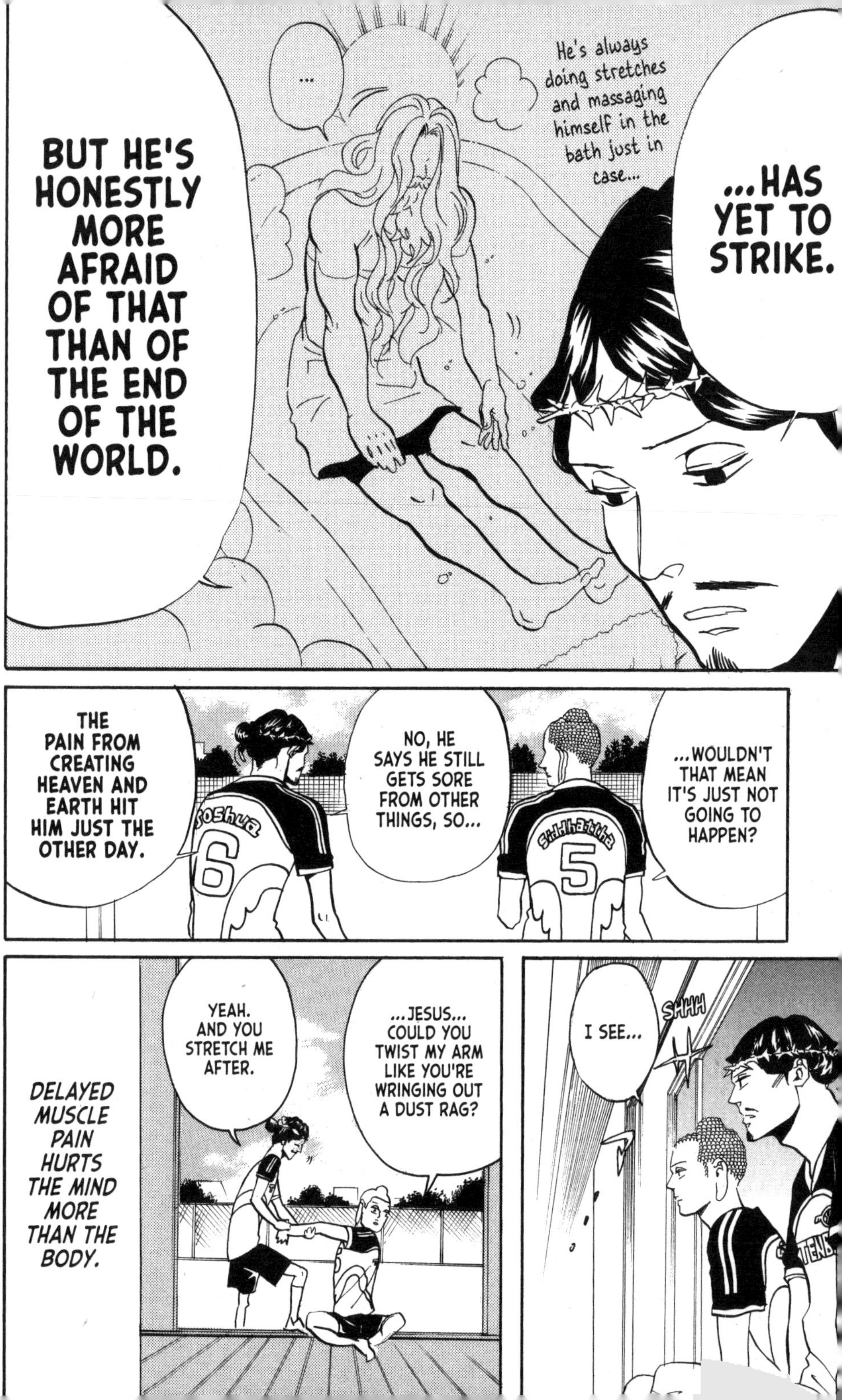
...HAS YET TO STRIKE.
He's always doing stretches and massaging himself in the bath just in case...
...
BUT HE'S HONESTLY MORE AFRAID OF THAT THAN OF THE END OF THE WORLD.
...WOULDN'T THAT MEAN IT'S JUST NOT GOING TO HAPPEN?
NO, HE SAYS HE STILL GETS SORE FROM OTHER THINGS, SO...
THE PAIN FROM CREATING HEAVEN AND EARTH HIT HIM JUST THE OTHER DAY.
SHHH
I SEE...
...JESUS... COULD YOU TWIST MY ARM LIKE YOU'RE WRINGING OUT A DUST RAG?
YEAH. AND YOU STRETCH ME AFTER.
DELAYED MUSCLE PAIN HURTS THE MIND MORE THAN THE BODY.

Heaven Offices Produces: Zennis Duo

"JA!"
Refer to my hairstyle
Nod to their religion
Triple his hotness with triple the faces!
Add two pairs of arms.
Add around 30kg to each of their weights. (Best if it's enough to get wrinkles in their chins!)
Tucked away inside the body
Golden!!

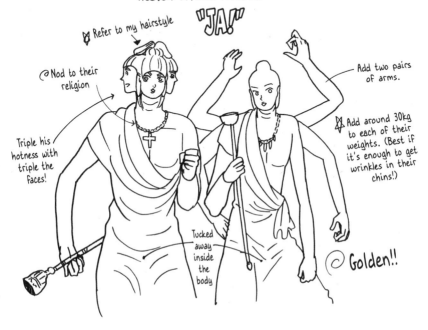

CHAPTER 41 TRANSLATION NOTES

Mandala, page 225
Mandalas are used in various South Asian religions to show sacred geographies or to visually depict the hierarchies among Buddhas, deities or other holy figures. In Japan, mandalas will often depict a kind of heavenly "court" at which presides an specific set of Buddhas or Bodhisattvas to be called in a ritual or other practice, in their order of importance.

Zennis, page 227
The Japanese name of this game is *Shomujo*, short for *shogyō mujō*, which refers to the impermanence of all things.

SAR Tenbu, page 228
SAR stands for *Sōgō Anoyo Rengō*, which is the Japanese name of the United Afterlife Alliance. Tenbu is the Japanese for Heaven Office.

Kūkai, page 228
Kūkai is the Japanese Buddhist monk who founded the Esoteric Shingon ("true word" or "mantra") school of Buddhism. He lived from 774-835.

Sons of Thunder, page 228
When listing the Twelve Apostles, Mark 3:17 says of James and John, "He [Jesus] surnamed them Boanerges, which is, The sons of thunder." This was likely because of their intense personalities.

The legendary Nyorai model, page 229
Buddha's spoon for this game is based on the Buddhist weapon and ritual object, the vajra. A vajra represents the indestructibility of diamond and the irresistible force of the thunderbolt, and the word refers to a weapon of the gods. *Nyorai* is a word that refers to Buddhas, from the Sanskrit *tathagata*, mean "one thus come," meaning one who has passed into the state of enlightenment. The clubs used by the other athletes are based on the bell that is often seen accompanying the vajra. Jesus's club is modeled after a Tibetan prayer wheel.

The disciple whom Jesus loved, page 230
The Gospel of John never names John the Apostle in its narrative, but uses the phrase "the disciple whom Jesus loved" to describe an unnamed disciple, likely an apostle, several times. The end of the book states that it was the testimony of that beloved disciple, thus pointing to John as the disciple in question. Incidentally, the word used for "loved" is a conjugated form of "agape."

James the Greater, page 231
Jesus had two apostles named James, and to differentiate them, they were sometimes called James the Greater and James the Lesser. In this context, "great" means he was older or taller, not that he was more important. It does not necessarily indicate that he was older than John (only that he was older than that other James), however it is assumed that he was John's older brother because he was always mentioned first.

Jacob and Johannes, page 232
The reader may have noticed that the names on the back of James' and John's jerseys don't exactly match the names that have been used in the dialogue. The names used in the Japanese translation of the New Testament are Yakobu and Yohane, which are more closely related to the names Jacob and Johann. Jacob is an old Hebrew name, which changed as it went from Hebrew, to Greek, to Latin, to French, to English into James, the name that has been used in English translations of the New Testament (which was written in Greek) since as early as the 14th century. Other language editions retain the Hebrew name, as does the Old Testament, which was written in Hebrew. Similarly, John is the English version of the Hebrew name Yohanan. The Latin version is Johannes.

The death of John the Apostle, page 237
According to Roman Catholic tradition, John died of old age in Ephesus around AD 100. A church was built on the site believed to be his tomb, but now only ruins of it remain. There are also theories that he did not die, but sleeps underground, making the dust holy with his breath, as well as theories that he was taken up to Heaven without tasting death. He was the only one of the original Twelve Apostles to escape a violent death.

Exploded in midair, page 238
Ananda was traveling at the end of his life, and as his final moments approached, he was met at a river by several different parties who hoped to claim his remains as relics. Realizing that dying on either side of the river would anger the party on the other side, he used his supernatural powers to levitate into the air and cause his body to go up in flames, sending pieces of himself to both sides of the river, thus keeping all parties happy.

WaT, page 239
WaT, short for "Wentz and Teppei," is a Japanese pop duo made up of Eiji Wentz, who is half German-American and half Japanese, and Teppei Koike.

SAINT☆YOUNG MEN

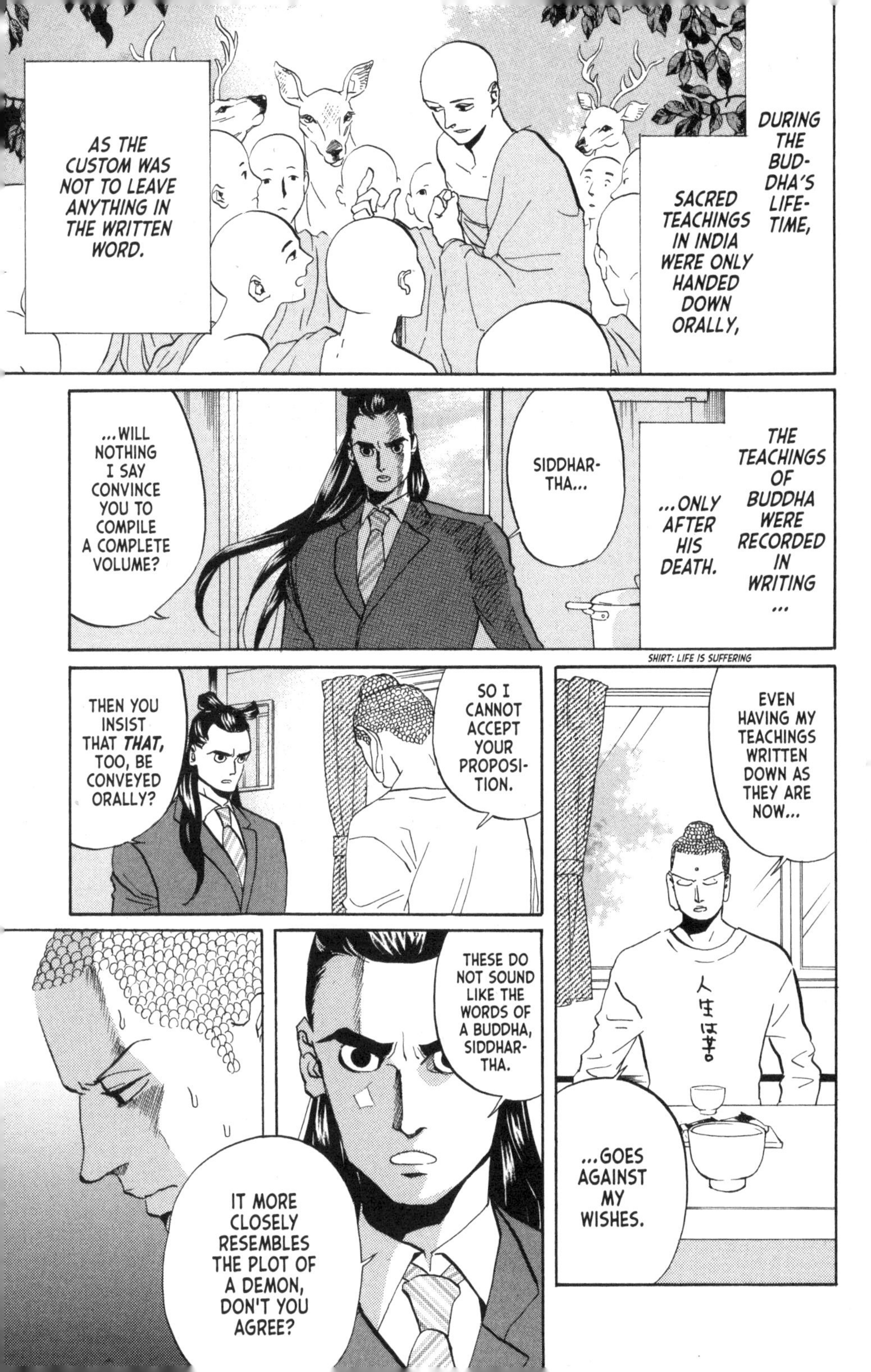
DURING THE BUDDHA'S LIFE-TIME,
SACRED TEACHINGS IN INDIA WERE ONLY HANDED DOWN ORALLY,
AS THE CUSTOM WAS NOT TO LEAVE ANYTHING IN THE WRITTEN WORD.
THE TEACHINGS OF BUDDHA WERE RECORDED IN WRITING ...
...ONLY AFTER HIS DEATH.
SIDDHAR-THA...
...WILL NOTHING I SAY CONVINCE YOU TO COMPILE A COMPLETE VOLUME?
SHIRT: LIFE IS SUFFERING
EVEN HAVING MY TEACHINGS WRITTEN DOWN AS THEY ARE NOW...
人生は苦
...GOES AGAINST MY WISHES.
SO I CANNOT ACCEPT YOUR PROPOSI-TION.
THEN YOU INSIST THAT *THAT*, TOO, BE CONVEYED ORALLY?
THESE DO NOT SOUND LIKE THE WORDS OF A BUDDHA, SIDDHAR-THA.
IT MORE CLOSELY RESEMBLES THE PLOT OF A DEMON, DON'T YOU AGREE?

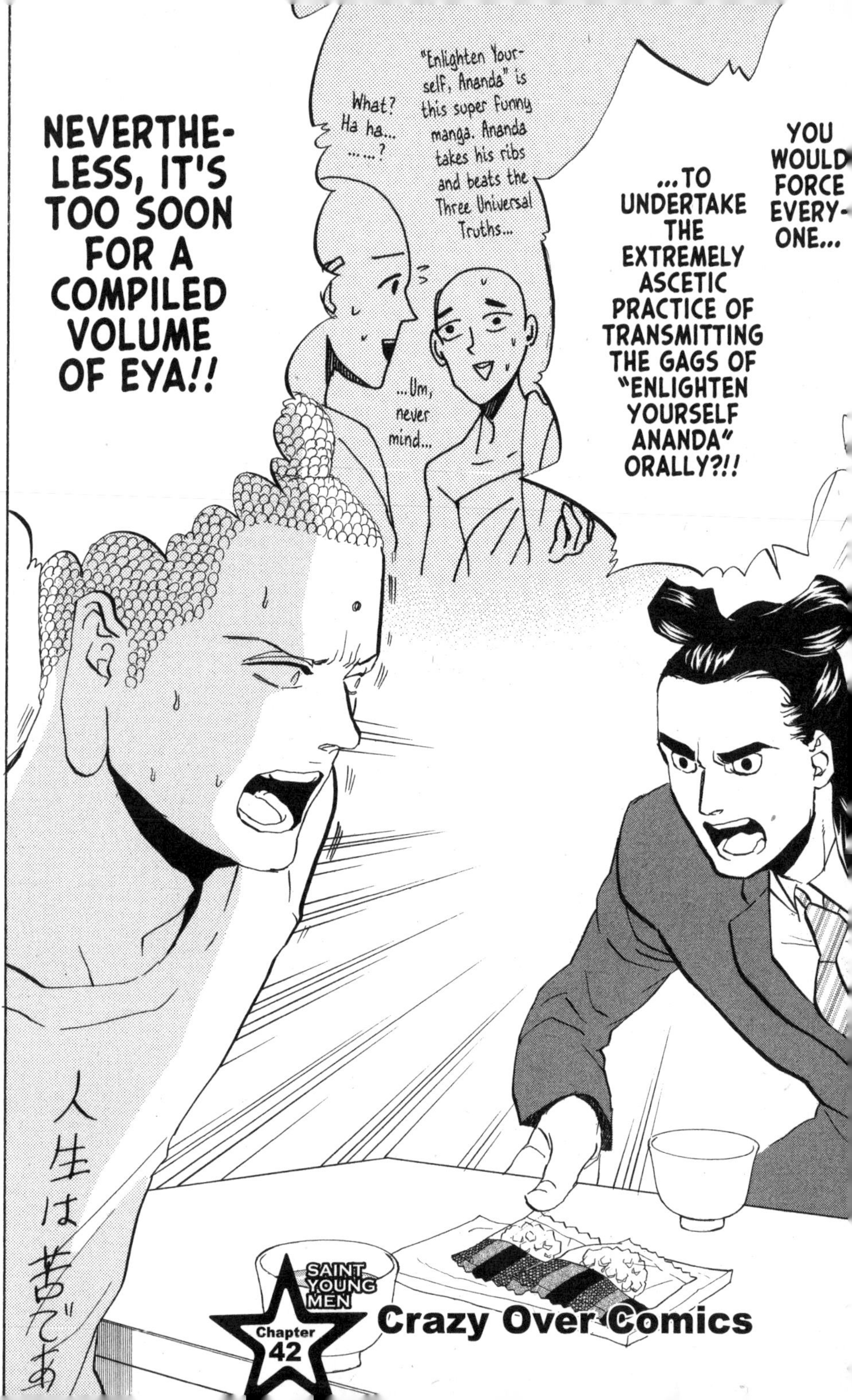
YOU WOULD FORCE EVERY-ONE...
...TO UNDERTAKE THE EXTREMELY ASCETIC PRACTICE OF TRANSMITTING THE GAGS OF "ENLIGHTEN YOURSELF ANANDA" ORALLY?!!
"Enlighten Your-self, Ananda" is this super funny manga. Ananda takes his ribs and beats the Three Universal Truths...
What? Ha ha... ......?
...Um, never mind...
NEVERTHE-LESS, IT'S TOO SOON FOR A COMPILED VOLUME OF EYA!!
人生は苦であ
SAINT YOUNG MEN
Chapter 42
Crazy Over Comics

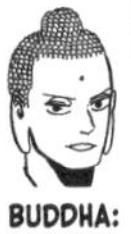

BUDDHA: FAVORITE CHART IS A LINE CHART. IT'S AMAZING TO BE ABLE TO TELL THE CHANGES IN A SITUATION JUST BY LOOKING AT THE RISE AND FALL OF THE LINES.

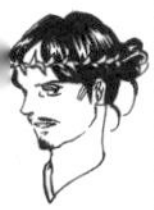

JESUS: FAVORITE CHART IS A PIE CHART. IT'S AMAZING TO BE ABLE TO TELL PERCENTAGES JUST BY LOOKING AT THE SECTIONS OF A CIRCLE.

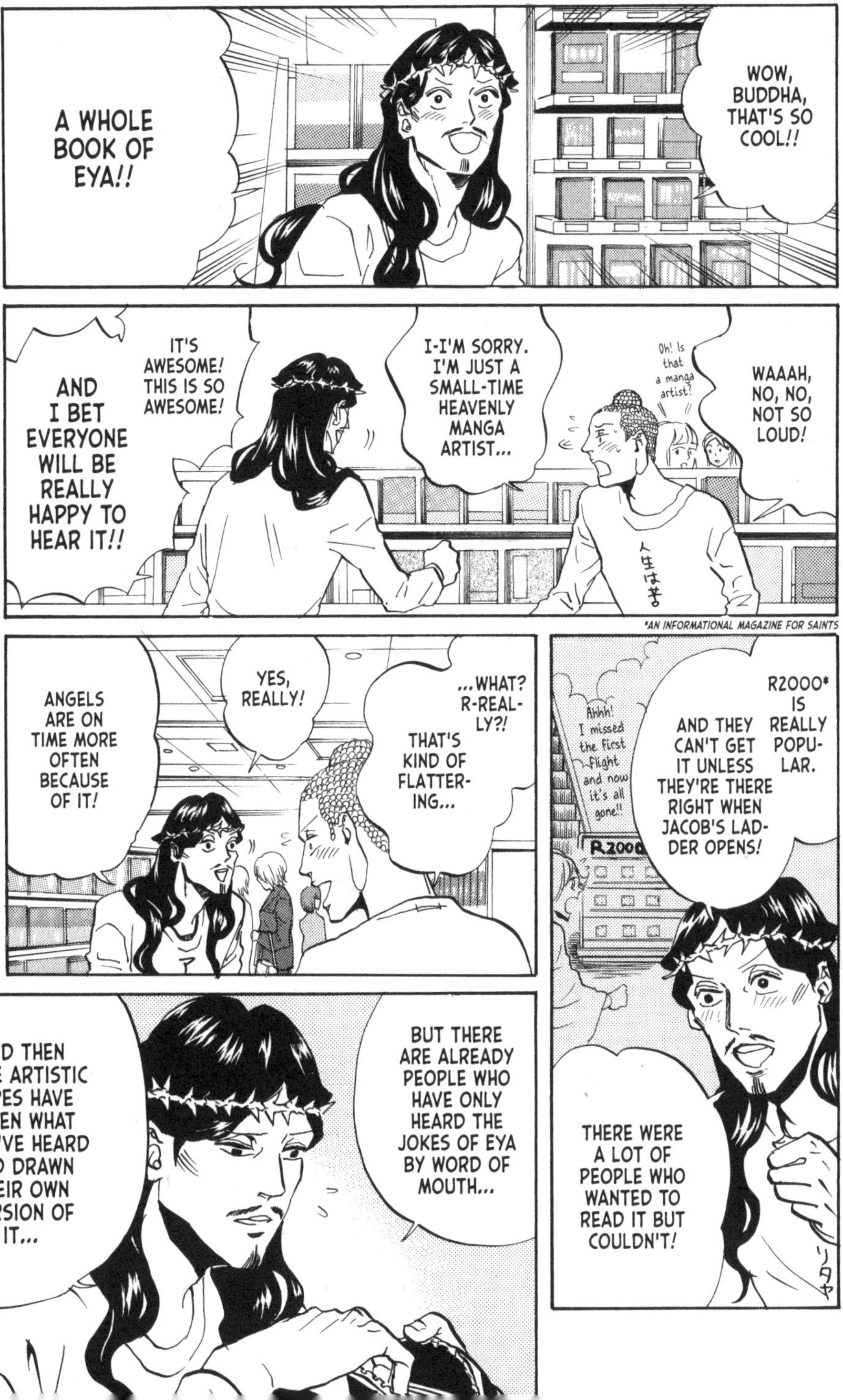
WOW, BUDDHA, THAT'S SO COOL!!
A WHOLE BOOK OF EYA!!
WAAAH, NO, NO, NOT SO LOUD!
Oh! Is that a manga artist?
人生は苦
I-I'M SORRY. I'M JUST A SMALL-TIME HEAVENLY MANGA ARTIST...
IT'S AWESOME! THIS IS SO AWESOME!
AND I BET EVERYONE WILL BE REALLY HAPPY TO HEAR IT!!
*AN INFORMATIONAL MAGAZINE FOR SAINTS
R2000* IS REALLY POPULAR.
AND THEY CAN'T GET IT UNLESS THEY'RE THERE RIGHT WHEN JACOB'S LADDER OPENS!
Ahhh! I missed the first flight and now it's all gone!!
R2000
THERE WERE A LOT OF PEOPLE WHO WANTED TO READ IT BUT COULDN'T!
...WHAT? R-REALLY?!
THAT'S KIND OF FLATTERING...
YES, REALLY!
ANGELS ARE ON TIME MORE OFTEN BECAUSE OF IT!
BUT THERE ARE ALREADY PEOPLE WHO HAVE ONLY HEARD THE JOKES OF EYA BY WORD OF MOUTH...
AND THEN SOME ARTISTIC TYPES HAVE TAKEN WHAT THEY'VE HEARD AND DRAWN THEIR OWN VERSION OF IT...

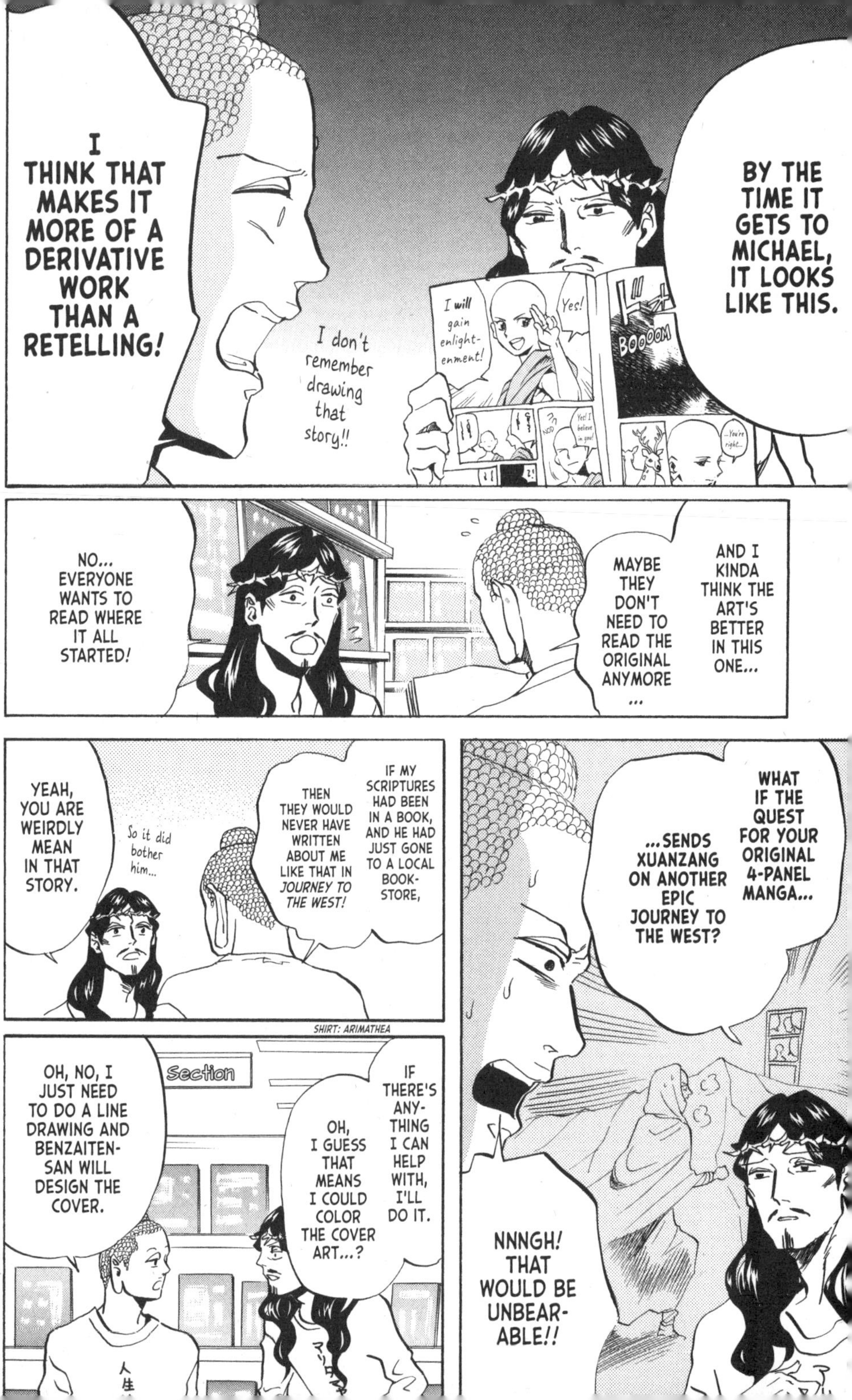
BY THE TIME IT GETS TO MICHAEL, IT LOOKS LIKE THIS.
Yes!
I will gain enlight-enment!
BOOOOM
Yes! I believe in you!
...You're right...
I don't remember drawing that story!!
I THINK THAT MAKES IT MORE OF A DERIVATIVE WORK THAN A RETELLING!
MAYBE THEY DON'T NEED TO READ THE ORIGINAL ANYMORE...
AND I KINDA THINK THE ART'S BETTER IN THIS ONE...
NO... EVERYONE WANTS TO READ WHERE IT ALL STARTED!
WHAT IF THE QUEST FOR YOUR ORIGINAL 4-PANEL MANGA...
...SENDS XUANZANG ON ANOTHER EPIC JOURNEY TO THE WEST?
NNNGH! THAT WOULD BE UNBEARABLE!!
IF MY SCRIPTURES HAD BEEN IN A BOOK, AND HE HAD JUST GONE TO A LOCAL BOOK-STORE,
THEN THEY WOULD NEVER HAVE WRITTEN ABOUT ME LIKE THAT IN *JOURNEY TO THE WEST!*
So it did bother him...
YEAH, YOU ARE WEIRDLY MEAN IN THAT STORY.
SHIRT: ARIMATHEA
Section
IF THERE'S ANY-THING I CAN HELP WITH, I'LL DO IT.
OH, I GUESS THAT MEANS I COULD COLOR THE COVER ART...?
OH, NO, I JUST NEED TO DO A LINE DRAWING AND BENZAITEN-SAN WILL DESIGN THE COVER.

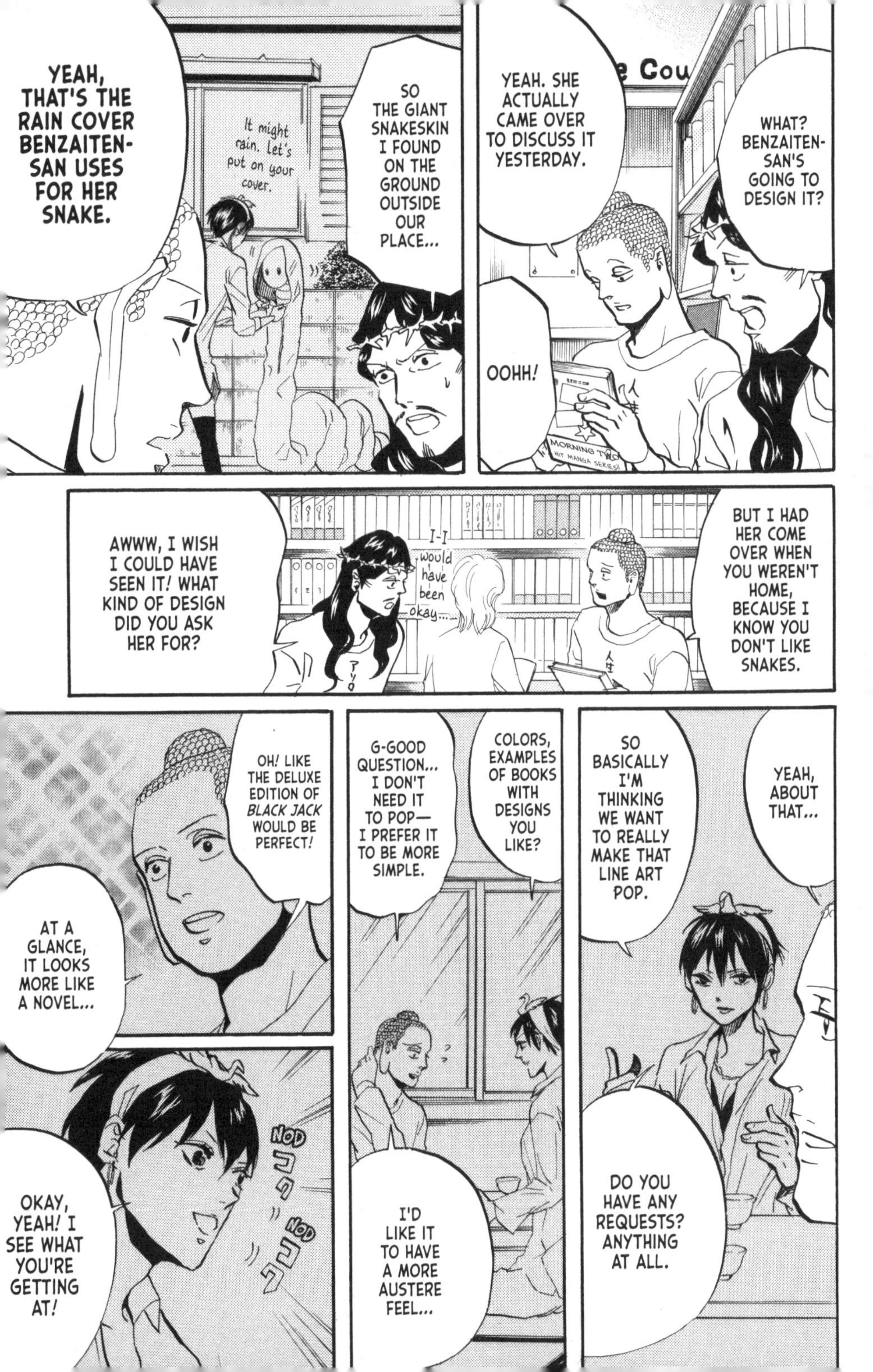

WHAT? BENZAITEN-SAN'S GOING TO DESIGN IT?
YEAH. SHE ACTUALLY CAME OVER TO DISCUSS IT YESTERDAY.
OOHH!
SO THE GIANT SNAKESKIN I FOUND ON THE GROUND OUTSIDE OUR PLACE...
YEAH, THAT'S THE RAIN COVER BENZAITEN-SAN USES FOR HER SNAKE.
It might rain. Let's put on your cover.
BUT I HAD HER COME OVER WHEN YOU WEREN'T HOME, BECAUSE I KNOW YOU DON'T LIKE SNAKES.
I-I would have been okay...
AWWW, I WISH I COULD HAVE SEEN IT! WHAT KIND OF DESIGN DID YOU ASK HER FOR?
YEAH, ABOUT THAT...
SO BASICALLY I'M THINKING WE WANT TO REALLY MAKE THAT LINE ART POP.
DO YOU HAVE ANY REQUESTS? ANYTHING AT ALL.
COLORS, EXAMPLES OF BOOKS WITH DESIGNS YOU LIKE?
G-GOOD QUESTION... I DON'T NEED IT TO POP— I PREFER IT TO BE MORE SIMPLE.
I'D LIKE IT TO HAVE A MORE AUSTERE FEEL...
OH! LIKE THE DELUXE EDITION OF *BLACK JACK* WOULD BE PERFECT!
AT A GLANCE, IT LOOKS MORE LIKE A NOVEL...
NOD
NOD
OKAY, YEAH! I SEE WHAT YOU'RE GETTING AT!

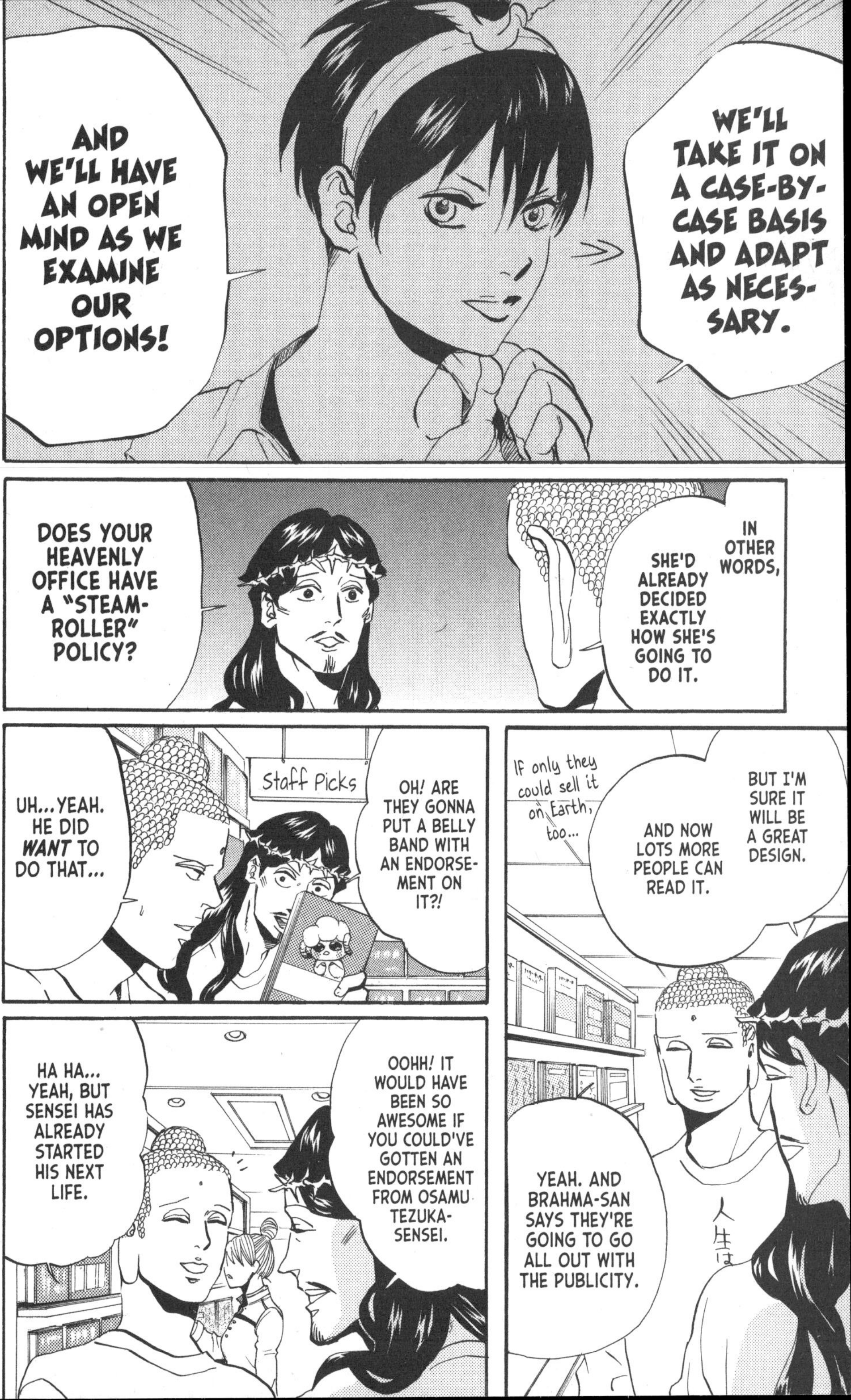
WE'LL TAKE IT ON A CASE-BY-CASE BASIS AND ADAPT AS NECES-SARY.
AND WE'LL HAVE AN OPEN MIND AS WE EXAMINE OUR OPTIONS!
IN OTHER WORDS,
SHE'D ALREADY DECIDED EXACTLY HOW SHE'S GOING TO DO IT.
DOES YOUR HEAVENLY OFFICE HAVE A "STEAM-ROLLER" POLICY?
BUT I'M SURE IT WILL BE A GREAT DESIGN.
AND NOW LOTS MORE PEOPLE CAN READ IT.
If only they could sell it on Earth, too...
YEAH. AND BRAHMA-SAN SAYS THEY'RE GOING TO GO ALL OUT WITH THE PUBLICITY.
人生は
Staff Picks
OH! ARE THEY GONNA PUT A BELLY BAND WITH AN ENDORSE-MENT ON IT?!
UH...YEAH. HE DID *WANT* TO DO THAT...
OOHH! IT WOULD HAVE BEEN SO AWESOME IF YOU COULD'VE GOTTEN AN ENDORSEMENT FROM OSAMU TEZUKA-SENSEI.
HA HA... YEAH, BUT SENSEI HAS ALREADY STARTED HIS NEXT LIFE.

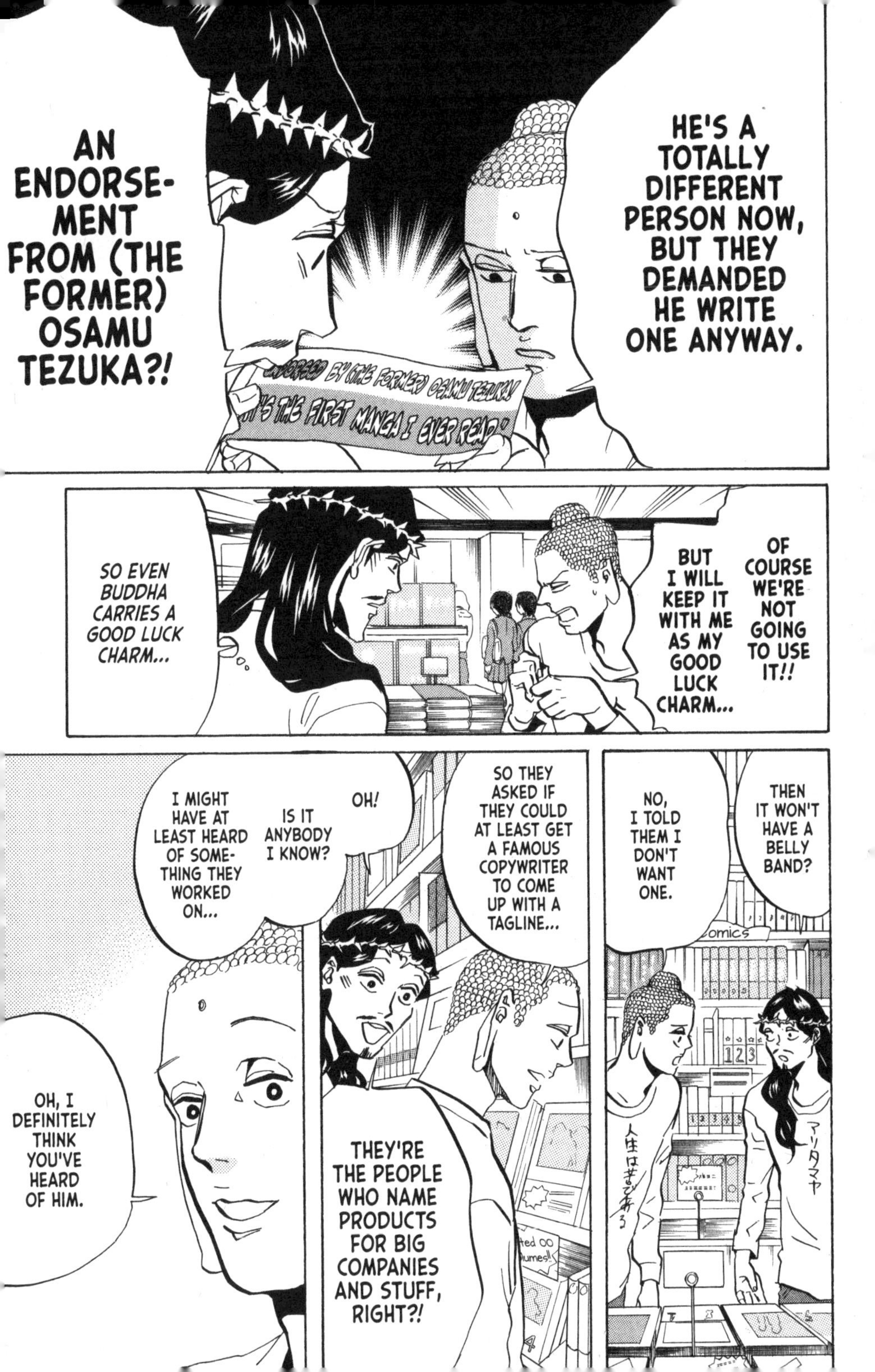
HE'S A TOTALLY DIFFERENT PERSON NOW, BUT THEY DEMANDED HE WRITE ONE ANYWAY.
AN ENDORSE-MENT FROM (THE FORMER) OSAMU TEZUKA?!
BY (THE FORMER) OSAMU TEZUKA!
THE FIRST MANGA I EVER READ
OF COURSE WE'RE NOT GOING TO USE IT!!
BUT I WILL KEEP IT WITH ME AS MY GOOD LUCK CHARM...
SO EVEN BUDDHA CARRIES A GOOD LUCK CHARM...
THEN IT WON'T HAVE A BELLY BAND?
NO, I TOLD THEM I DON'T WANT ONE.
SO THEY ASKED IF THEY COULD AT LEAST GET A FAMOUS COPYWRITER TO COME UP WITH A TAGLINE...
THEY'RE THE PEOPLE WHO NAME PRODUCTS FOR BIG COMPANIES AND STUFF, RIGHT?!
OH!
IS IT ANYBODY I KNOW?
I MIGHT HAVE AT LEAST HEARD OF SOME-THING THEY WORKED ON...
OH, I DEFINITELY THINK YOU'VE HEARD OF HIM.

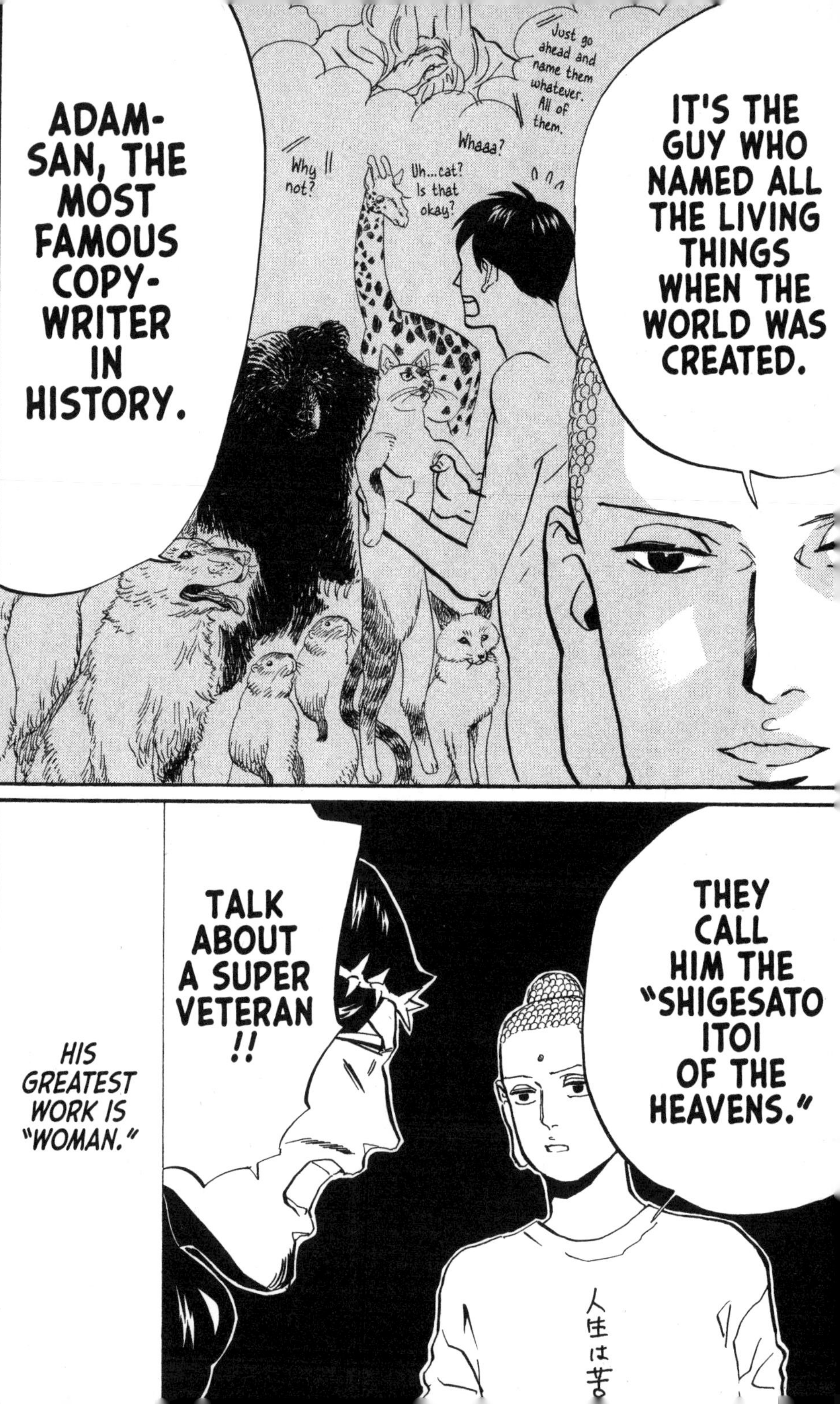
IT'S THE GUY WHO NAMED ALL THE LIVING THINGS WHEN THE WORLD WAS CREATED.
Just go ahead and name them whatever. All of them.
Whaaa?
Uh...cat? Is that okay?
Why not?
ADAM-SAN, THE MOST FAMOUS COPY-WRITER IN HISTORY.
THEY CALL HIM THE "SHIGESATO ITOI OF THE HEAVENS."
TALK ABOUT A SUPER VETERAN!!
HIS GREATEST WORK IS "WOMAN."
人生は苦

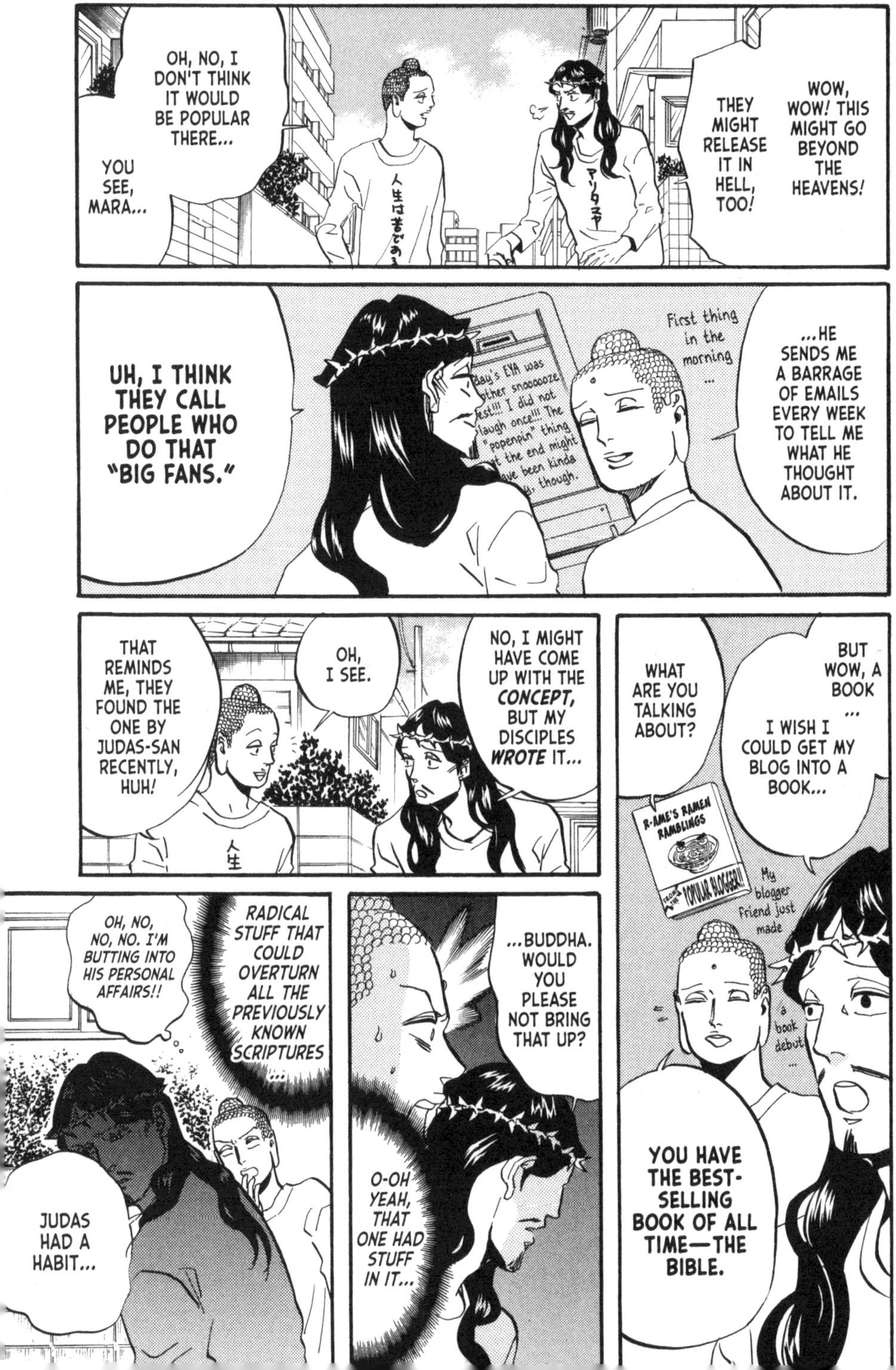
WOW, WOW! THIS MIGHT GO BEYOND THE HEAVENS!
THEY MIGHT RELEASE IT IN HELL, TOO!
OH, NO, I DON'T THINK IT WOULD BE POPULAR THERE...
YOU SEE, MARA...
First thing in the morning...
...HE SENDS ME A BARRAGE OF EMAILS EVERY WEEK TO TELL ME WHAT HE THOUGHT ABOUT IT.
UH, I THINK THEY CALL PEOPLE WHO DO THAT "BIG FANS."
BUT WOW, A BOOK...
I WISH I COULD GET MY BLOG INTO A BOOK...
WHAT ARE YOU TALKING ABOUT?
R-AME'S RAMEN RAMBLINGS
FROM THE POPULAR BLOGGER!!
My blogger friend just made a book debut...
YOU HAVE THE BEST-SELLING BOOK OF ALL TIME—THE BIBLE.
NO, I MIGHT HAVE COME UP WITH THE *CONCEPT*, BUT MY DISCIPLES *WROTE* IT...
OH, I SEE.
THAT REMINDS ME, THEY FOUND THE ONE BY JUDAS-SAN RECENTLY, HUH!
...BUDDHA. WOULD YOU PLEASE NOT BRING THAT UP?
O-OH YEAH, THAT ONE HAD STUFF IN IT...
RADICAL STUFF THAT COULD OVERTURN ALL THE PREVIOUSLY KNOWN SCRIPTURES...
OH, NO, NO, NO. I'M BUTTING INTO HIS PERSONAL AFFAIRS!!
JUDAS HAD A HABIT...

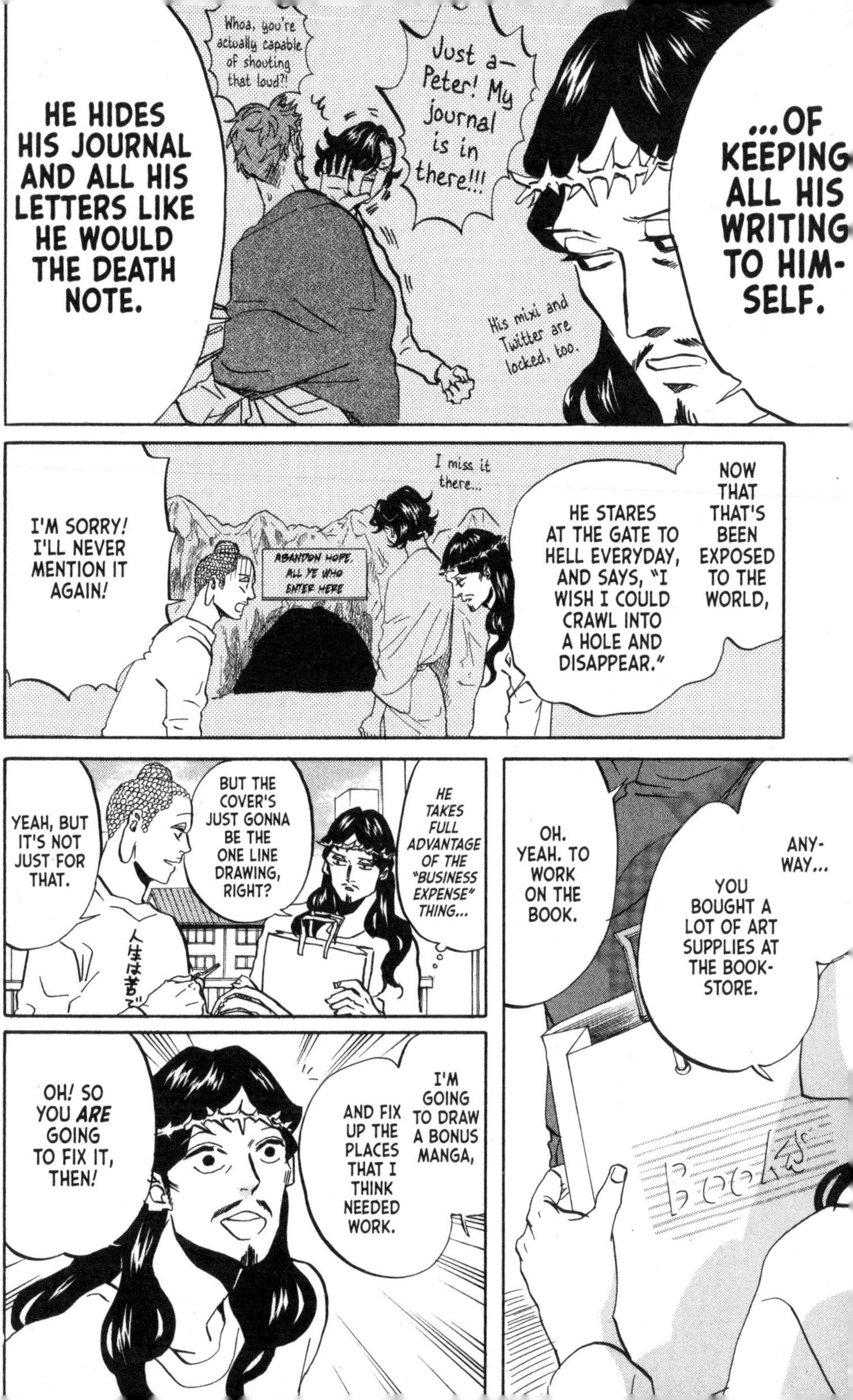

...OF KEEPING ALL HIS WRITING TO HIMSELF.
Just a— Peter! My journal is in there!!!
Whoa, you're actually capable of shouting that loud?!
His mixi and Twitter are locked, too.
HE HIDES HIS JOURNAL AND ALL HIS LETTERS LIKE HE WOULD THE DEATH NOTE.
NOW THAT THAT'S BEEN EXPOSED TO THE WORLD,
HE STARES AT THE GATE TO HELL EVERYDAY, AND SAYS, "I WISH I COULD CRAWL INTO A HOLE AND DISAPPEAR."
I miss it there...
ABANDON HOPE ALL YE WHO ENTER HERE
I'M SORRY! I'LL NEVER MENTION IT AGAIN!
ANY-WAY... YOU BOUGHT A LOT OF ART SUPPLIES AT THE BOOK-STORE.
OH. YEAH. TO WORK ON THE BOOK.
HE TAKES FULL ADVANTAGE OF THE "BUSINESS EXPENSE" THING...
BUT THE COVER'S JUST GONNA BE THE ONE LINE DRAWING, RIGHT?
YEAH, BUT IT'S NOT JUST FOR THAT.
I'M GOING TO DRAW A BONUS MANGA,
AND FIX UP THE PLACES THAT I THINK NEEDED WORK.
OH! SO YOU *ARE* GOING TO FIX IT, THEN!

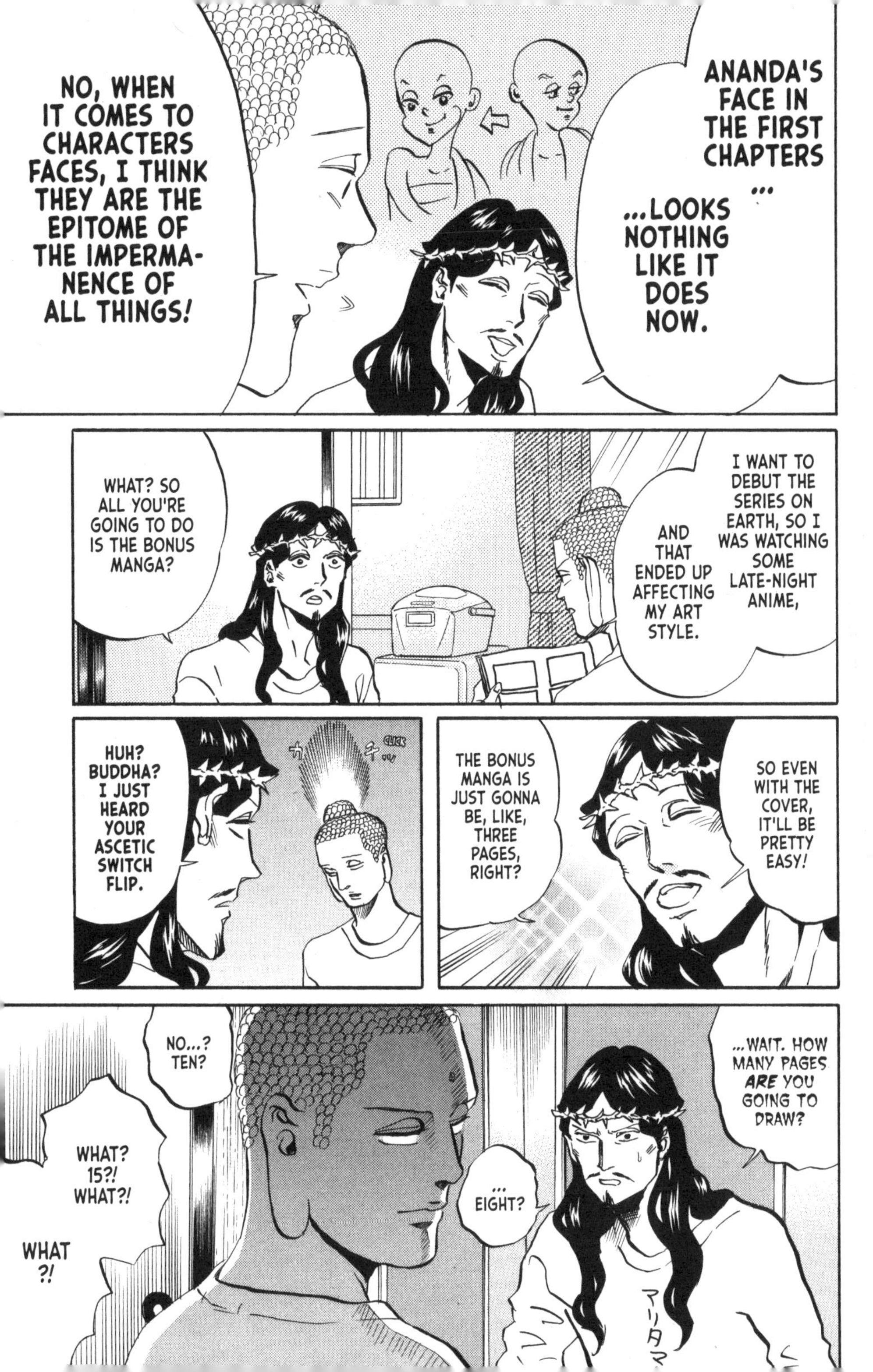
ANANDA'S FACE IN THE FIRST CHAPTERS ...
...LOOKS NOTHING LIKE IT DOES NOW.
NO, WHEN IT COMES TO CHARACTERS FACES, I THINK THEY ARE THE EPITOME OF THE IMPERMANENCE OF ALL THINGS!
I WANT TO DEBUT THE SERIES ON EARTH, SO I WAS WATCHING SOME LATE-NIGHT ANIME,
AND THAT ENDED UP AFFECTING MY ART STYLE.
WHAT? SO ALL YOU'RE GOING TO DO IS THE BONUS MANGA?
SO EVEN WITH THE COVER, IT'LL BE PRETTY EASY!
THE BONUS MANGA IS JUST GONNA BE, LIKE, THREE PAGES, RIGHT?
CLICK
HUH? BUDDHA? I JUST HEARD YOUR ASCETIC SWITCH FLIP.
...WAIT. HOW MANY PAGES ARE YOU GOING TO DRAW?
... EIGHT?
NO...? TEN?
WHAT? 15?! WHAT?!
WHAT ?!

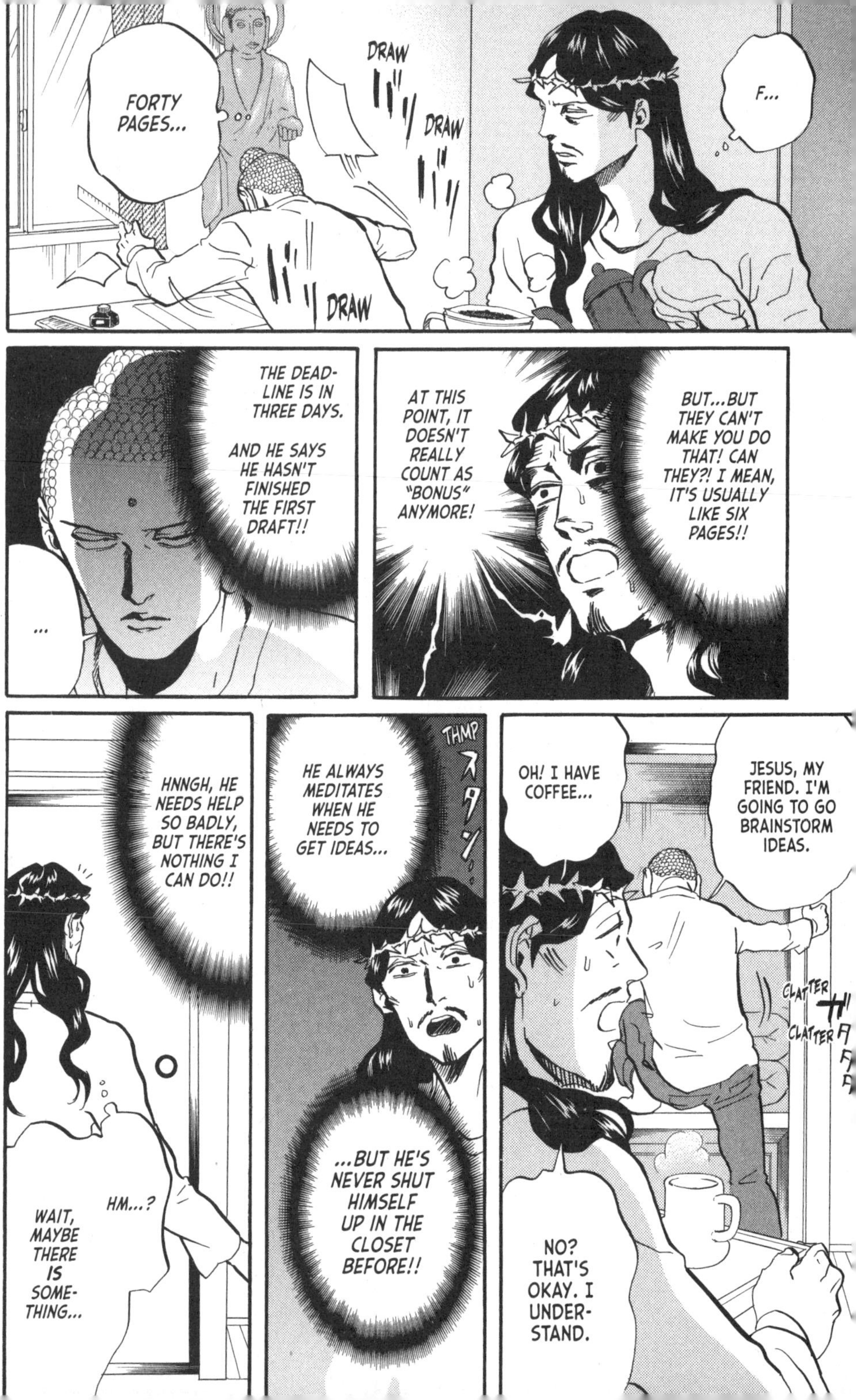
F...
DRAW
DRAW
FORTY PAGES...
DRAW
BUT...BUT THEY CAN'T MAKE YOU DO THAT! CAN THEY?! I MEAN, IT'S USUALLY LIKE SIX PAGES!!
AT THIS POINT, IT DOESN'T REALLY COUNT AS "BONUS" ANYMORE!
THE DEADLINE IS IN THREE DAYS.
AND HE SAYS HE HASN'T FINISHED THE FIRST DRAFT!!
...
JESUS, MY FRIEND. I'M GOING TO GO BRAINSTORM IDEAS.
OH! I HAVE COFFEE...
CLATTER
CLATTER
NO? THAT'S OKAY. I UNDERSTAND.
THMP
HE ALWAYS MEDITATES WHEN HE NEEDS TO GET IDEAS...
...BUT HE'S NEVER SHUT HIMSELF UP IN THE CLOSET BEFORE!!
HNNGH, HE NEEDS HELP SO BADLY, BUT THERE'S NOTHING I CAN DO!!
HM...?
WAIT, MAYBE THERE IS SOMETHING...

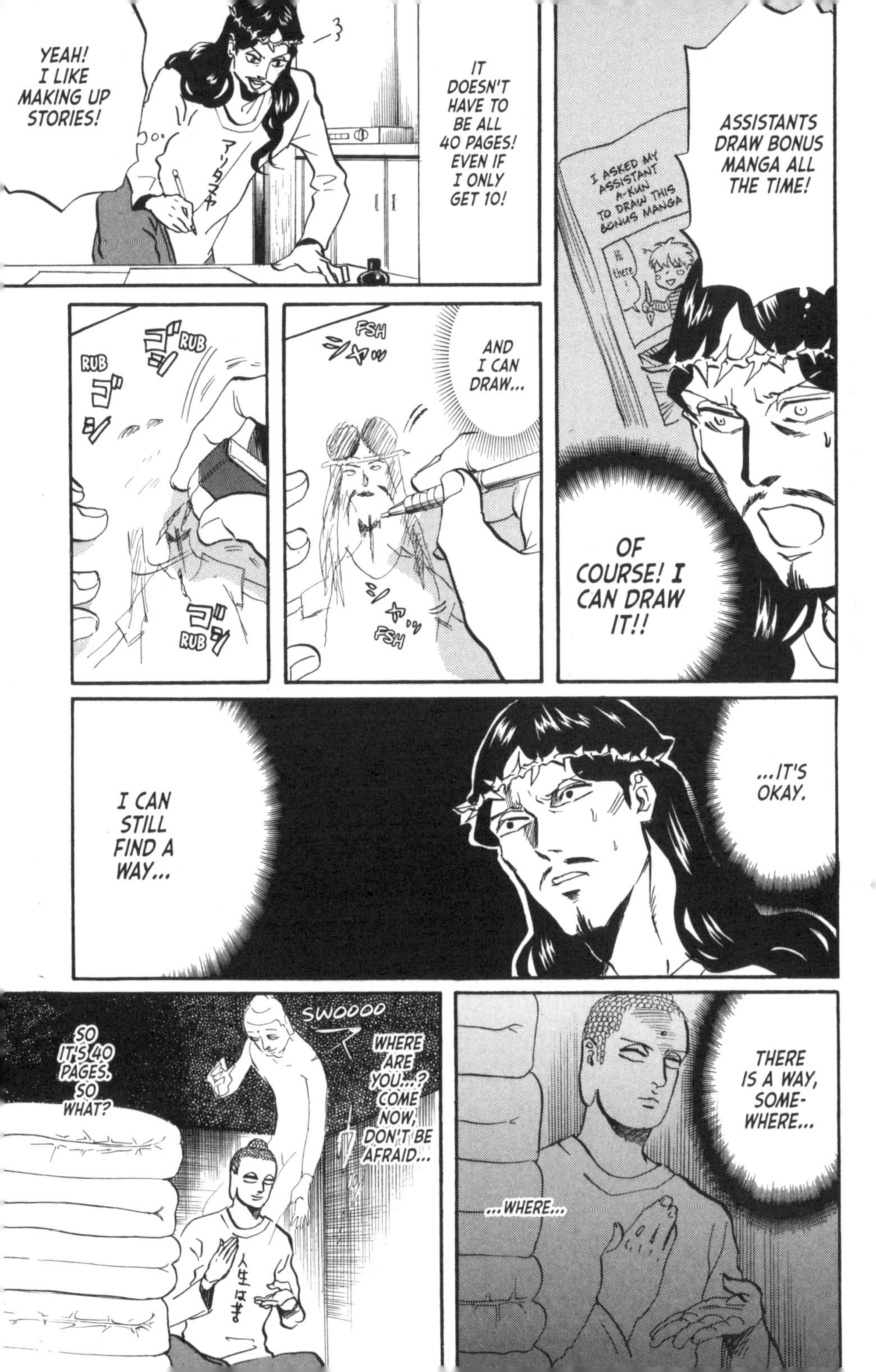
ASSISTANTS DRAW BONUS MANGA ALL THE TIME!
I ASKED MY ASSISTANT A-KUN TO DRAW THIS BONUS MANGA
Hi there!
OF COURSE! I CAN DRAW IT!!
IT DOESN'T HAVE TO BE ALL 40 PAGES! EVEN IF I ONLY GET 10!
YEAH! I LIKE MAKING UP STORIES!
AND I CAN DRAW...
シャッ FSH
シャッ FSH
ゴシ RUB
ゴシ RUB
ゴシ RUB
...IT'S OKAY.
I CAN STILL FIND A WAY...
THERE IS A WAY, SOME-WHERE...
...WHERE...
SWOOOO
WHERE ARE YOU...? COME NOW, DON'T BE AFRAID...
SO IT'S 40 PAGES. SO WHAT?

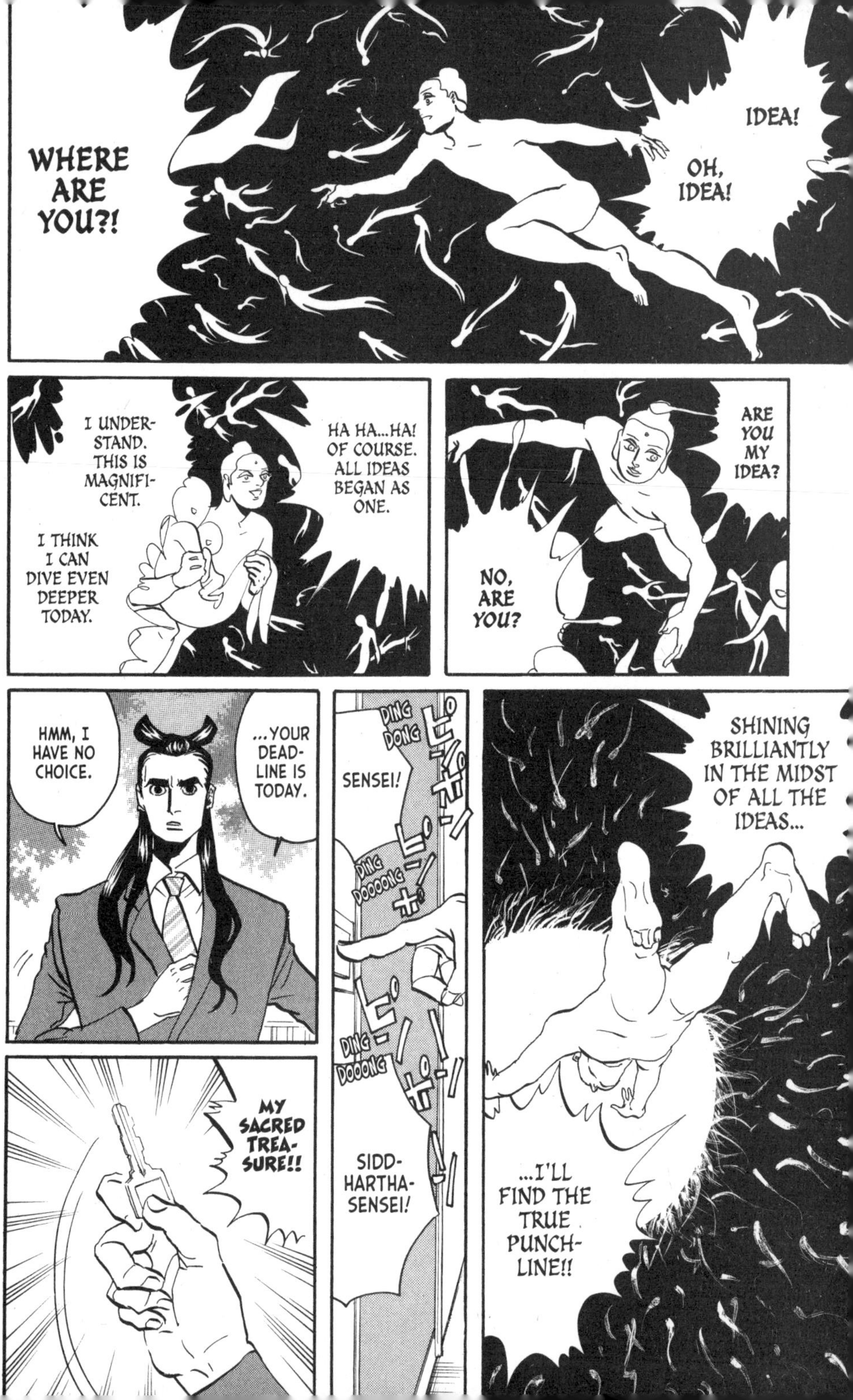
IDEA!
OH, IDEA!
WHERE ARE YOU?!
ARE YOU MY IDEA?
NO, ARE YOU?
HA HA...HA! OF COURSE. ALL IDEAS BEGAN AS ONE.
I UNDER-STAND. THIS IS MAGNIFI-CENT.
I THINK I CAN DIVE EVEN DEEPER TODAY.
SHINING BRILLIANTLY IN THE MIDST OF ALL THE IDEAS...
...I'LL FIND THE TRUE PUNCH-LINE!!
DING DONG
SENSEI!
DING DOOOONG
DING DOOONG
SIDD-HARTHA-SENSEI!
...YOUR DEAD-LINE IS TODAY.
HMM, I HAVE NO CHOICE.
MY SACRED TREA-SURE!!

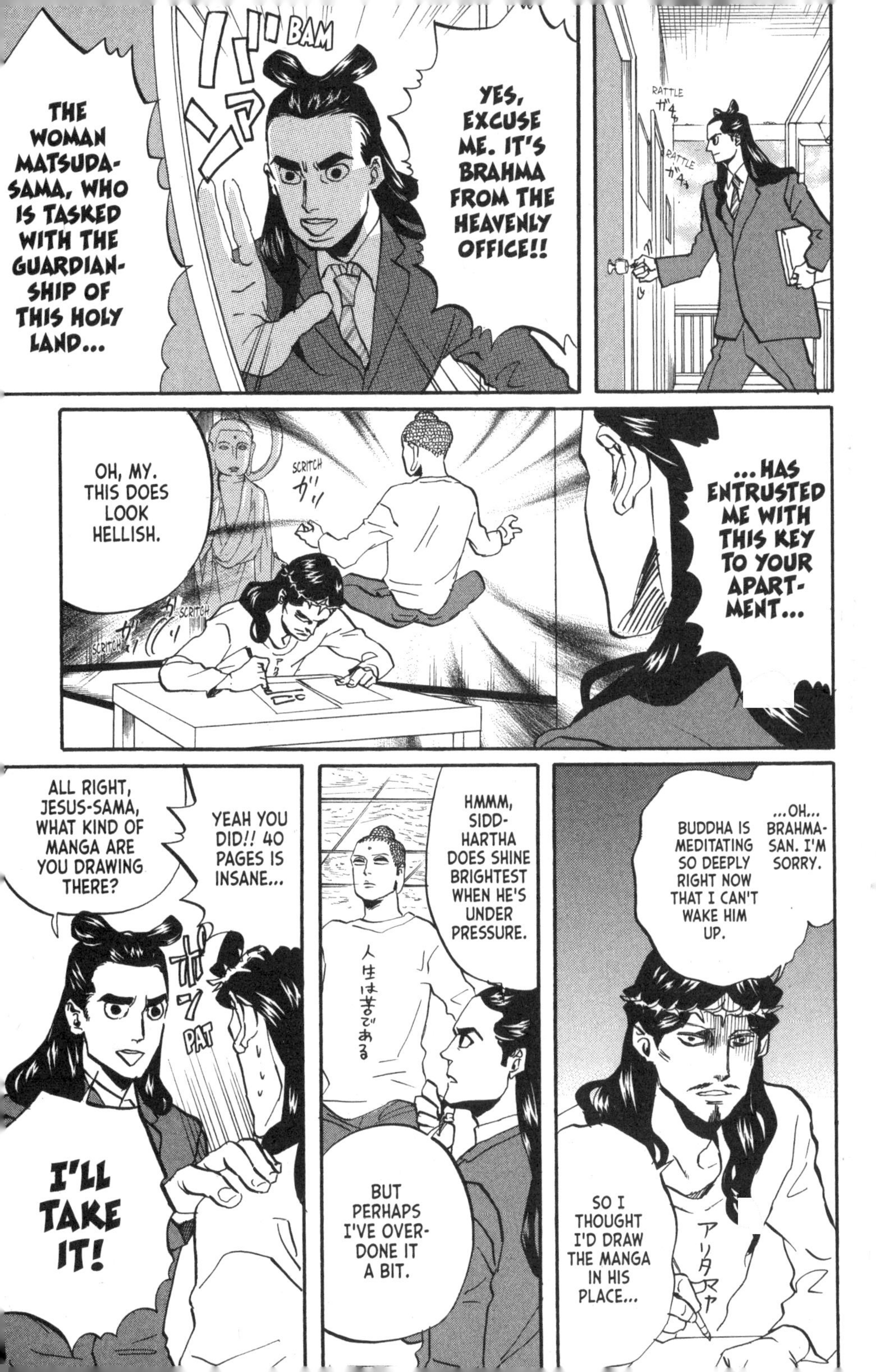
RATTLE
RATTLE
BAM
YES, EXCUSE ME. IT'S BRAHMA FROM THE HEAVENLY OFFICE!!
THE WOMAN MATSUDA-SAMA, WHO IS TASKED WITH THE GUARDIANSHIP OF THIS HOLY LAND...
...HAS ENTRUSTED ME WITH THIS KEY TO YOUR APARTMENT...
SCRITCH
OH, MY. THIS DOES LOOK HELLISH.
SCRITCH
SCRITCH
...OH... BRAHMA-SAN. I'M SORRY.
BUDDHA IS MEDITATING SO DEEPLY RIGHT NOW THAT I CAN'T WAKE HIM UP.
SO I THOUGHT I'D DRAW THE MANGA IN HIS PLACE...
HMMM, SIDDHARTHA DOES SHINE BRIGHTEST WHEN HE'S UNDER PRESSURE.
人生は苦である
BUT PERHAPS I'VE OVERDONE IT A BIT.
YEAH YOU DID!! 40 PAGES IS INSANE...
ALL RIGHT, JESUS-SAMA, WHAT KIND OF MANGA ARE YOU DRAWING THERE?
PAT
I'LL TAKE IT!

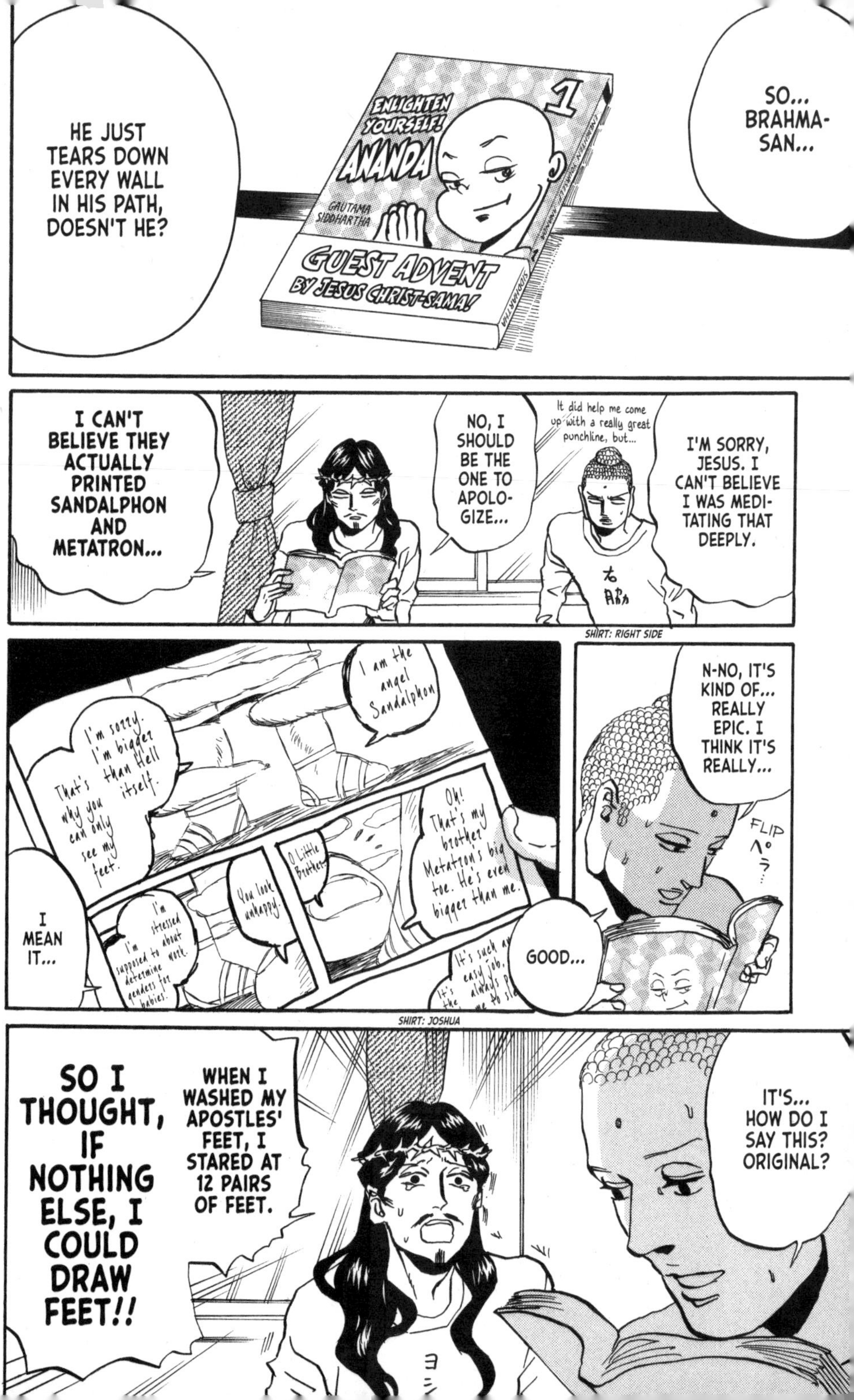
SO... BRAHMA-SAN...
ENLIGHTEN YOURSELF! ANANDA
1
GAUTAMA SIDDHARTHA
GUEST ADVENT BY JESUS CHRIST-SAMA!
SIDDHARTHA
HE JUST TEARS DOWN EVERY WALL IN HIS PATH, DOESN'T HE?
I'M SORRY, JESUS. I CAN'T BELIEVE I WAS MEDITATING THAT DEEPLY.
It did help me come up with a really great punchline, but...
NO, I SHOULD BE THE ONE TO APOLOGIZE...
I CAN'T BELIEVE THEY ACTUALLY PRINTED SANDALPHON AND METATRON...
SHIRT: RIGHT SIDE
N-NO, IT'S KIND OF... REALLY EPIC. I THINK IT'S REALLY...
FLIP
GOOD...
I am the angel Sandalphon
I'm sorry. I'm bigger than Hell itself. That's why you can only see my feet.
Oh! That's my brother Metatron's big toe. He's even bigger than me.
O Little Brother
You look unhappy.
I'm stressed about work. I'm supposed to determine genders for babies.
I MEAN IT...
SHIRT: JOSHUA
IT'S... HOW DO I SAY THIS? ORIGINAL?
WHEN I WASHED MY APOSTLES' FEET, I STARED AT 12 PAIRS OF FEET.
SO I THOUGHT, IF NOTHING ELSE, I COULD DRAW FEET!!

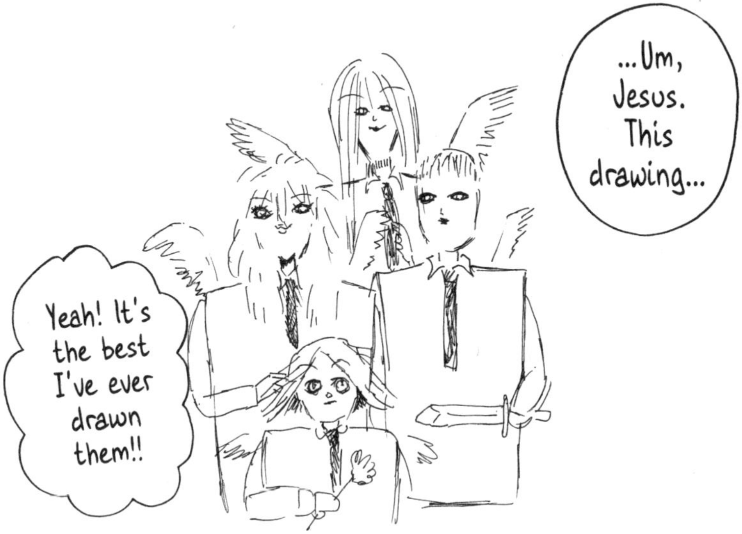
...Um, Jesus. This drawing...
Yeah! It's the best I've ever drawn them!!

CHAPTER 42 TRANSLATION NOTES

Journey to the West, page 248
Journey to the West is a famous novel from the 16th century inspireed by the tale of Xuanzang, a Buddhist priest who travels to the West to obtain sacred Buddhist texts. The story starts by telling about Sun Wukong, the Monkey King, and the mischief that he wrought in the Heavens. Wukong's victims enlist the help of the Buddha in subduing this troublemaker, so Buddha makes a bet with the Monkey, wins the best, and imprisons Sun Wukong in a mountain for centuries.

Arimathea, page 248
Joseph of Arimathea is the man assumed responsibility for the body of Jesus after the crucifixion. He is so named because he came from Arimathea, a city of Judea.

Morning 2, page 249
This is the magazine in Japan where Saint Young Men was originally serialized.

Adam, page 252
This story is told in the Bible as follows: "And out of the ground the Lord God formed every beast of the field, and every fowl of the air; and brought them unto Adam to see what he would call them: and whatsoever Adam called every living creature, that was the name thereof." (Genesis 2:19)

Shigesato Itoi, page 252
Shigesato Itoi is a Japanese copywriter, game designer, and actor, among his many other credits. He has been writing copy since the 1980s, and is known in the US for designing the Super Ninterndo game EarthBound.

The Gospel of Judas, page 253
The Gospel of Judas was translated from a papyrus scroll that was found in Egypt in the 1970s and eventually translated in the early 2000s. The scroll has been carbon-dated to around 280 AD, and is believed to be a Coptic translation of an earlier Greek text which describes Judas as Jesus's favorite disciple, having done what he did in accordance with instructions from Jesus himself.

Sandalphon and Metatron, page 260
Sandalphon is known as the Tall Angel, because he's so tall, it would take 500 years to walk the distance that is the length of his body. His is seen as the protector of unborn children, and the one who assigns gender. His brother Metatron is the greatest of all angels.

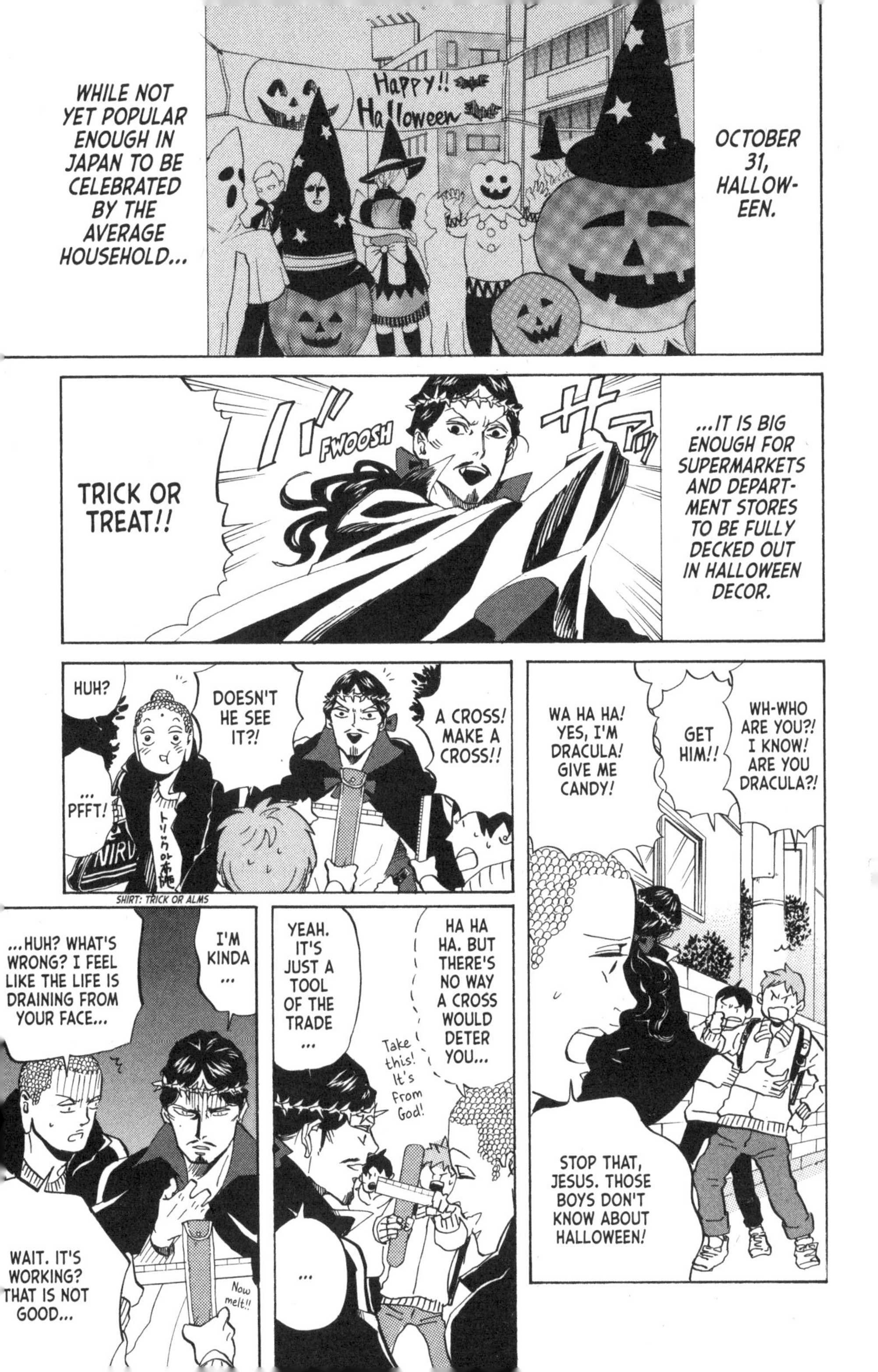
OCTOBER 31, HALLOWEEN.
Happy!! Halloween
WHILE NOT YET POPULAR ENOUGH IN JAPAN TO BE CELEBRATED BY THE AVERAGE HOUSEHOLD...
...IT IS BIG ENOUGH FOR SUPERMARKETS AND DEPARTMENT STORES TO BE FULLY DECKED OUT IN HALLOWEEN DECOR.
FWOOSH
TRICK OR TREAT!!
WH-WHO ARE YOU?! I KNOW! ARE YOU DRACULA?!
GET HIM!!
WA HA HA! YES, I'M DRACULA! GIVE ME CANDY!
STOP THAT, JESUS. THOSE BOYS DON'T KNOW ABOUT HALLOWEEN!
A CROSS! MAKE A CROSS!!
DOESN'T HE SEE IT?!
HUH?
... PFFT!
SHIRT: TRICK OR ALMS
HA HA HA. BUT THERE'S NO WAY A CROSS WOULD DETER YOU...
YEAH. IT'S JUST A TOOL OF THE TRADE...
Take this! It's From God!
...
I'M KINDA...
...HUH? WHAT'S WRONG? I FEEL LIKE THE LIFE IS DRAINING FROM YOUR FACE...
WAIT. IT'S WORKING? THAT IS NOT GOOD...
Now melt!!

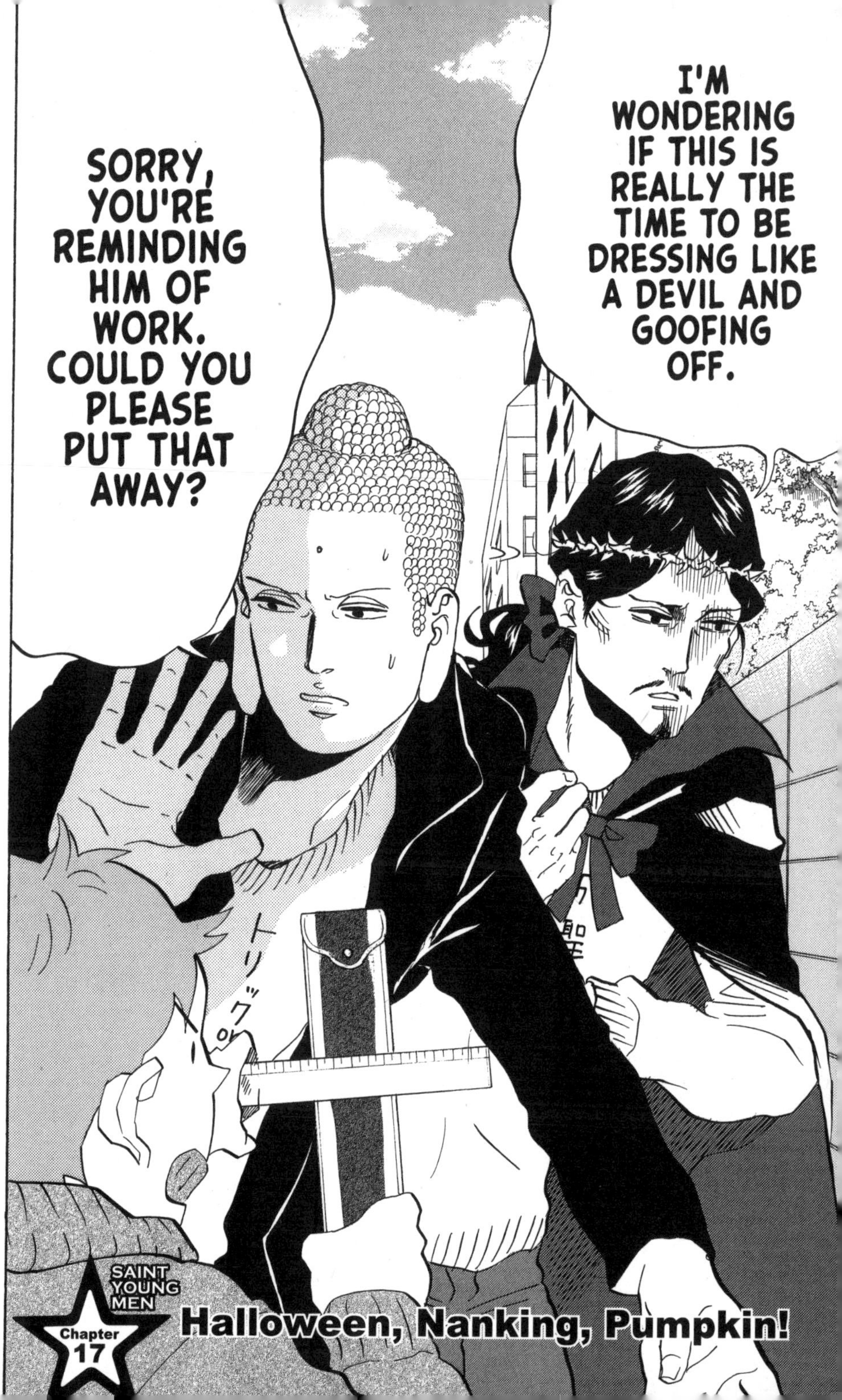
I'M WONDERING IF THIS IS REALLY THE TIME TO BE DRESSING LIKE A DEVIL AND GOOFING OFF.
SORRY, YOU'RE REMINDING HIM OF WORK. COULD YOU PLEASE PUT THAT AWAY?
SAINT YOUNG MEN
Chapter 17
Halloween, Nanking, Pumpkin!

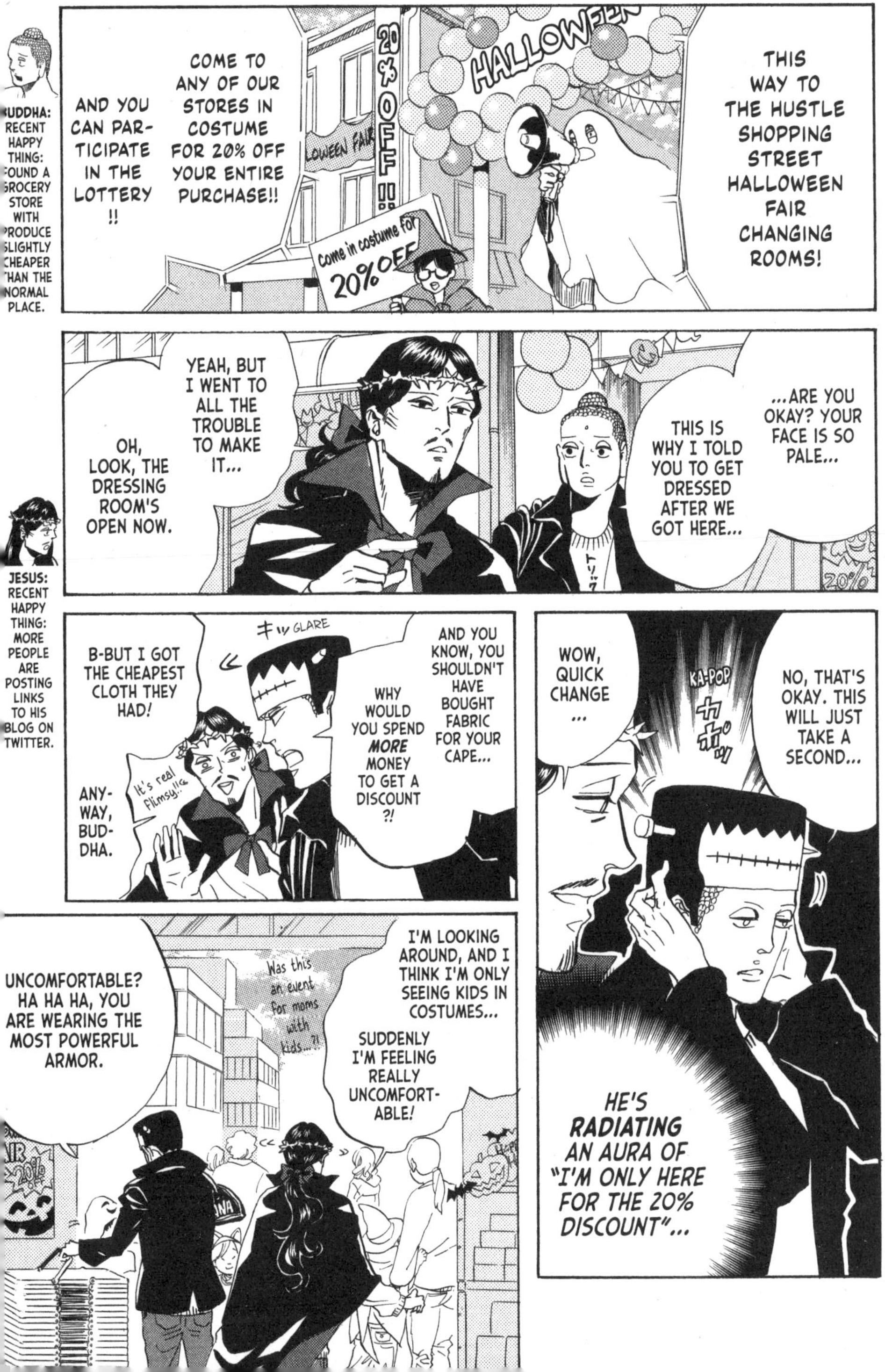
BUDDHA: RECENT HAPPY THING: FOUND A GROCERY STORE WITH PRODUCE SLIGHTLY CHEAPER THAN THE NORMAL PLACE.
JESUS: RECENT HAPPY THING: MORE PEOPLE ARE POSTING LINKS TO HIS BLOG ON TWITTER.
HALLOWEEN
THIS WAY TO THE HUSTLE SHOPPING STREET HALLOWEEN FAIR CHANGING ROOMS!
20% OFF!!
LOWEEN FAIR
COME TO ANY OF OUR STORES IN COSTUME FOR 20% OFF YOUR ENTIRE PURCHASE!!
AND YOU CAN PARTICIPATE IN THE LOTTERY!!
Come in costume for 20% OFF
...ARE YOU OKAY? YOUR FACE IS SO PALE...
THIS IS WHY I TOLD YOU TO GET DRESSED AFTER WE GOT HERE...
YEAH, BUT I WENT TO ALL THE TROUBLE TO MAKE IT...
OH, LOOK, THE DRESSING ROOM'S OPEN NOW.
NO, THAT'S OKAY. THIS WILL JUST TAKE A SECOND...
KA-POP
WOW, QUICK CHANGE...
HE'S RADIATING AN AURA OF "I'M ONLY HERE FOR THE 20% DISCOUNT"...
AND YOU KNOW, YOU SHOULDN'T HAVE BOUGHT FABRIC FOR YOUR CAPE...
WHY WOULD YOU SPEND MORE MONEY TO GET A DISCOUNT?!
GLARE
B-BUT I GOT THE CHEAPEST CLOTH THEY HAD!
It's real flimsy!!
ANYWAY, BUDDHA.
I'M LOOKING AROUND, AND I THINK I'M ONLY SEEING KIDS IN COSTUMES...
SUDDENLY I'M FEELING REALLY UNCOMFORTABLE!
Was this an event for moms with kids...?!
UNCOMFORTABLE? HA HA HA, YOU ARE WEARING THE MOST POWERFUL ARMOR.

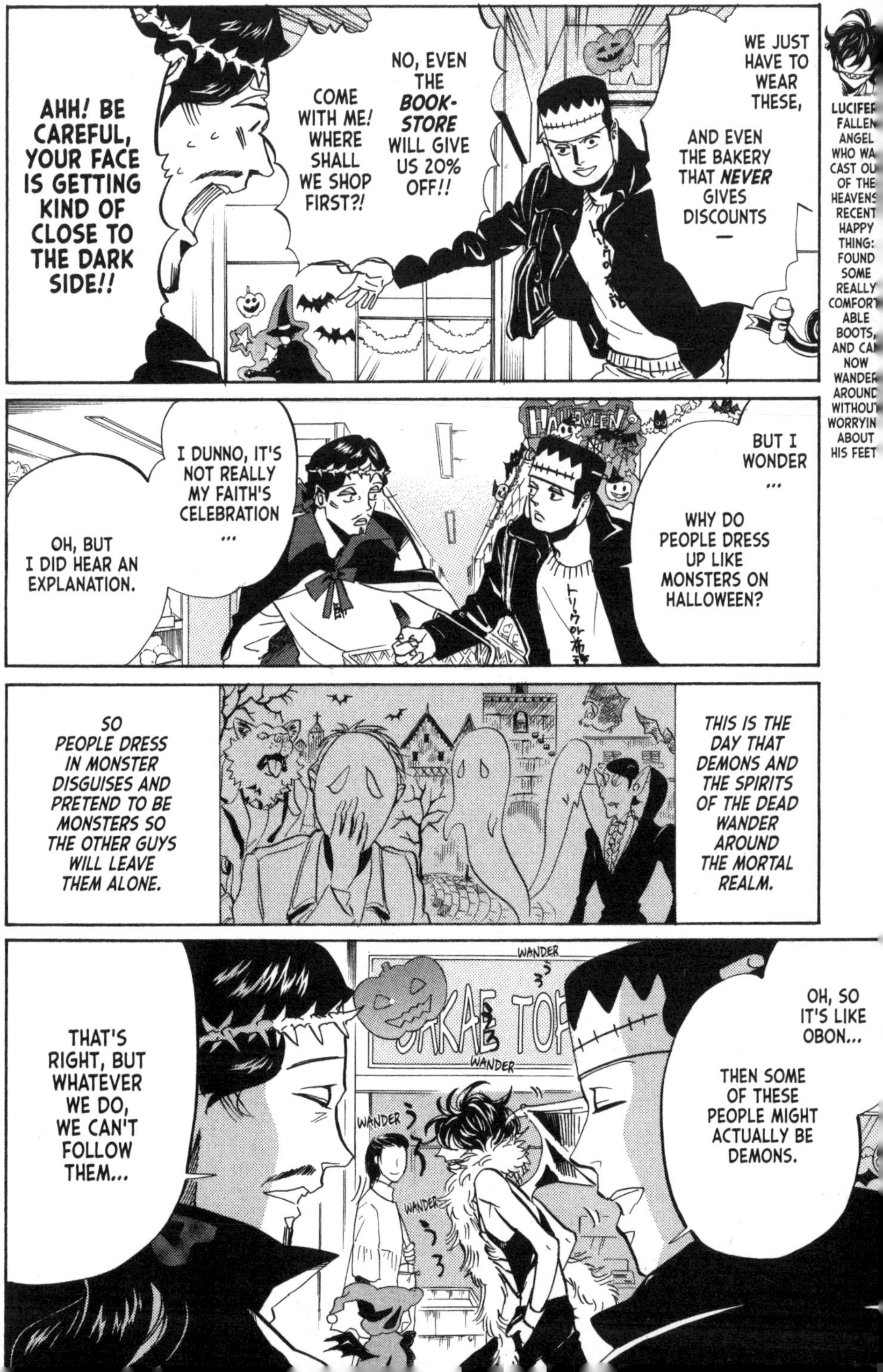
LUCIFER FALLEN ANGEL WHO WA CAST OU OF THE HEAVENS RECENT HAPPY THING: FOUND SOME REALLY COMFORT ABLE BOOTS, AND CA NOW WANDER AROUND WITHOUT WORRYIN ABOUT HIS FEET
WE JUST HAVE TO WEAR THESE,
AND EVEN THE BAKERY THAT NEVER GIVES DISCOUNTS —
NO, EVEN THE BOOKSTORE WILL GIVE US 20% OFF!!
COME WITH ME! WHERE SHALL WE SHOP FIRST?!
AHH! BE CAREFUL, YOUR FACE IS GETTING KIND OF CLOSE TO THE DARK SIDE!!
HALLOWEEN
BUT I WONDER...
WHY DO PEOPLE DRESS UP LIKE MONSTERS ON HALLOWEEN?
I DUNNO, IT'S NOT REALLY MY FAITH'S CELEBRATION...
OH, BUT I DID HEAR AN EXPLANATION.
THIS IS THE DAY THAT DEMONS AND THE SPIRITS OF THE DEAD WANDER AROUND THE MORTAL REALM.
SO PEOPLE DRESS IN MONSTER DISGUISES AND PRETEND TO BE MONSTERS SO THE OTHER GUYS WILL LEAVE THEM ALONE.
OH, SO IT'S LIKE OBON...
THEN SOME OF THESE PEOPLE MIGHT ACTUALLY BE DEMONS.
WANDER
WANDER
WANDER
WANDER
THAT'S RIGHT, BUT WHATEVER WE DO, WE CAN'T FOLLOW THEM...

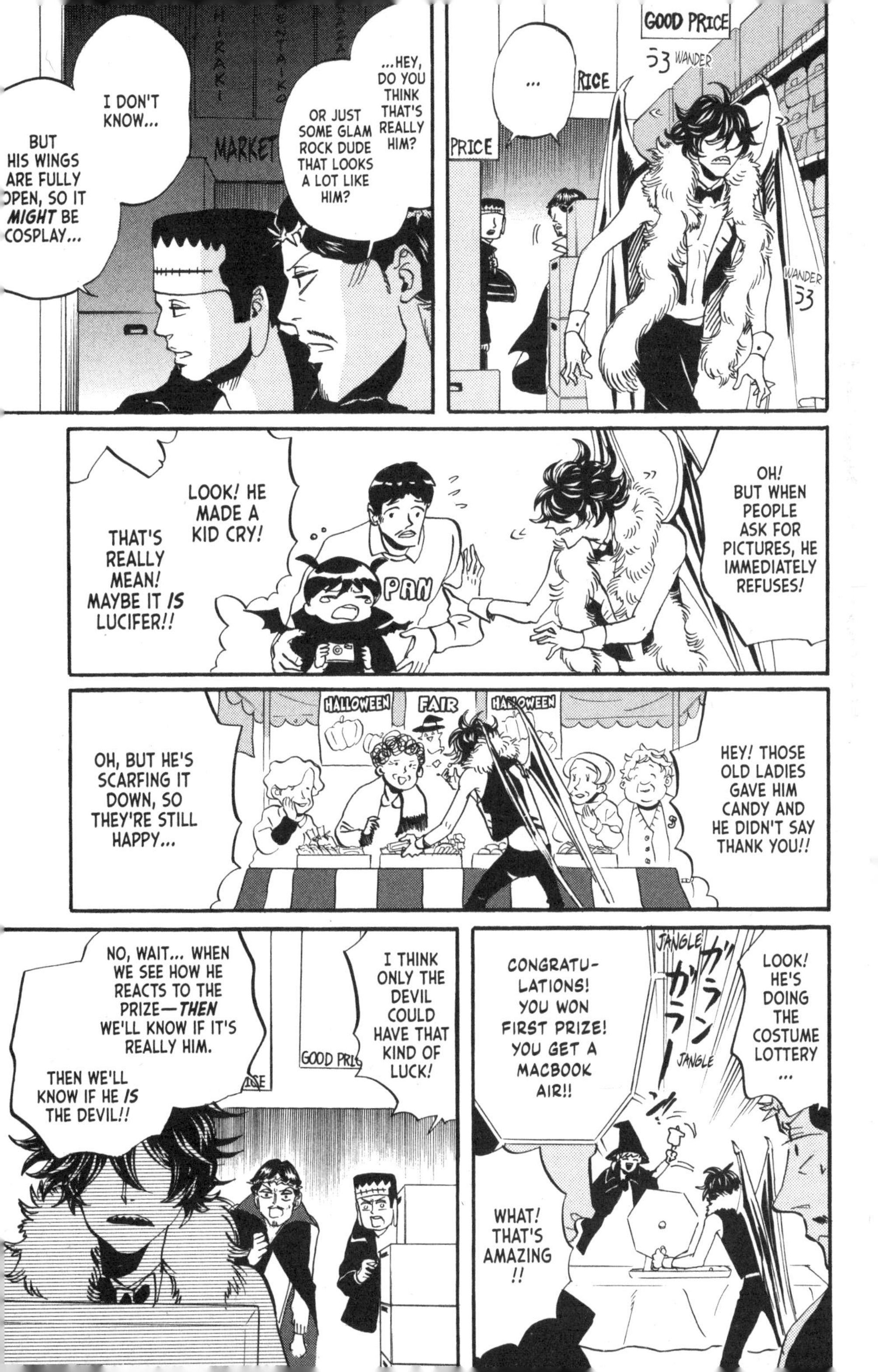
GOOD PRICE
RICE
PRICE
...
うろ WANDER
WANDER うろ
...HEY, DO YOU THINK THAT'S REALLY HIM?
OR JUST SOME GLAM ROCK DUDE THAT LOOKS A LOT LIKE HIM?
MARKET
I DON'T KNOW...
BUT HIS WINGS ARE FULLY OPEN, SO IT *MIGHT* BE COSPLAY...
OH! BUT WHEN PEOPLE ASK FOR PICTURES, HE IMMEDIATELY REFUSES!
LOOK! HE MADE A KID CRY!
PRN
THAT'S REALLY MEAN! MAYBE IT *IS* LUCIFER!!
HALLOWEEN FAIR HALLOWEEN
HEY! THOSE OLD LADIES GAVE HIM CANDY AND HE DIDN'T SAY THANK YOU!!
OH, BUT HE'S SCARFING IT DOWN, SO THEY'RE STILL HAPPY...
LOOK! HE'S DOING THE COSTUME LOTTERY...
JANGLE ガラン
JANGLE ガラー!!
CONGRATU-LATIONS! YOU WON FIRST PRIZE! YOU GET A MACBOOK AIR!!
WHAT! THAT'S AMAZING!!
I THINK ONLY THE DEVIL COULD HAVE THAT KIND OF LUCK!
GOOD PRI
NO, WAIT... WHEN WE SEE HOW HE REACTS TO THE PRIZE—*THEN* WE'LL KNOW IF IT'S REALLY HIM.
THEN WE'LL KNOW IF HE *IS* THE DEVIL!!

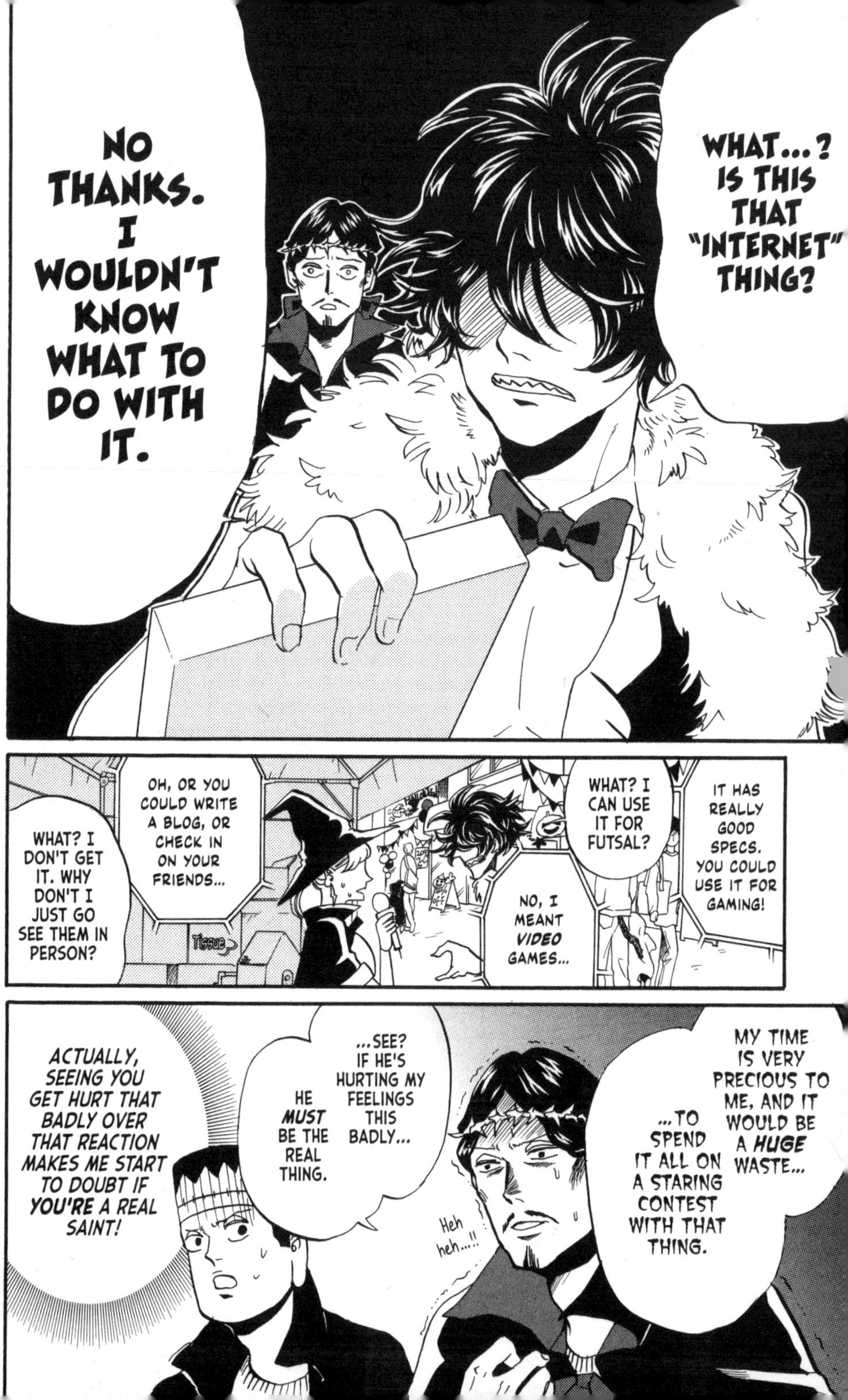
WHAT...? IS THIS THAT "INTERNET" THING?
NO THANKS. I WOULDN'T KNOW WHAT TO DO WITH IT.
IT HAS REALLY GOOD SPECS. YOU COULD USE IT FOR GAMING!
WHAT? I CAN USE IT FOR FUTSAL?
NO, I MEANT *VIDEO* GAMES...
OH, OR YOU COULD WRITE A BLOG, OR CHECK IN ON YOUR FRIENDS...
WHAT? I DON'T GET IT. WHY DON'T I JUST GO SEE THEM IN PERSON?
Tissue
MY TIME IS VERY PRECIOUS TO ME, AND IT WOULD BE A *HUGE* WASTE...
...TO SPEND IT ALL ON A STARING CONTEST WITH THAT THING.
Heh heh...!!
...SEE? IF HE'S HURTING MY FEELINGS THIS BADLY...
HE *MUST* BE THE REAL THING.
*ACTUALLY, SEEING YOU GET HURT THAT BADLY OVER THAT REACTION MAKES ME START TO DOUBT IF **YOU'RE** A REAL SAINT!*

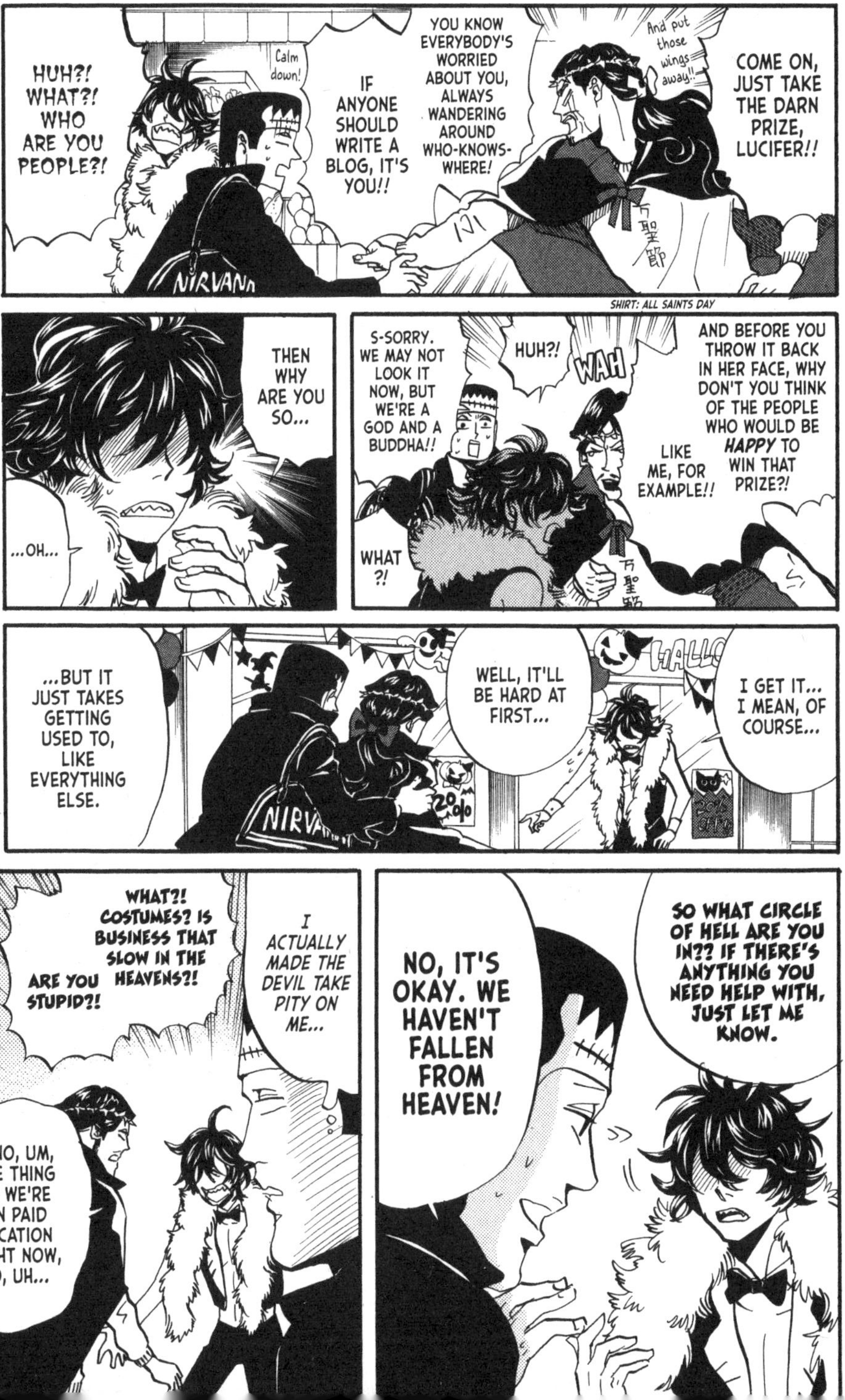
COME ON, JUST TAKE THE DARN PRIZE, LUCIFER!!
And put those wings away!!
YOU KNOW EVERYBODY'S WORRIED ABOUT YOU, ALWAYS WANDERING AROUND WHO-KNOWS-WHERE!
IF ANYONE SHOULD WRITE A BLOG, IT'S YOU!!
Calm down!
HUH?! WHAT?! WHO ARE YOU PEOPLE?!
SHIRT: ALL SAINTS DAY
AND BEFORE YOU THROW IT BACK IN HER FACE, WHY DON'T YOU THINK OF THE PEOPLE WHO WOULD BE *HAPPY* TO WIN THAT PRIZE?!
LIKE ME, FOR EXAMPLE!!
WAH
HUH?!
S-SORRY. WE MAY NOT LOOK IT NOW, BUT WE'RE A GOD AND A BUDDHA!!
WHAT?!
THEN WHY ARE YOU SO...
...OH...
I GET IT... I MEAN, OF COURSE...
WELL, IT'LL BE HARD AT FIRST...
...BUT IT JUST TAKES GETTING USED TO, LIKE EVERYTHING ELSE.
SO WHAT CIRCLE OF HELL ARE YOU IN?? IF THERE'S ANYTHING YOU NEED HELP WITH, JUST LET ME KNOW.
NO, IT'S OKAY. WE HAVEN'T FALLEN FROM HEAVEN!
I ACTUALLY MADE THE DEVIL TAKE PITY ON ME...
WHAT?! COSTUMES? IS BUSINESS THAT SLOW IN THE HEAVENS?!
ARE YOU STUPID?!
N-NO, UM, THE THING IS, WE'RE ON PAID VACATION RIGHT NOW, SO, UH...

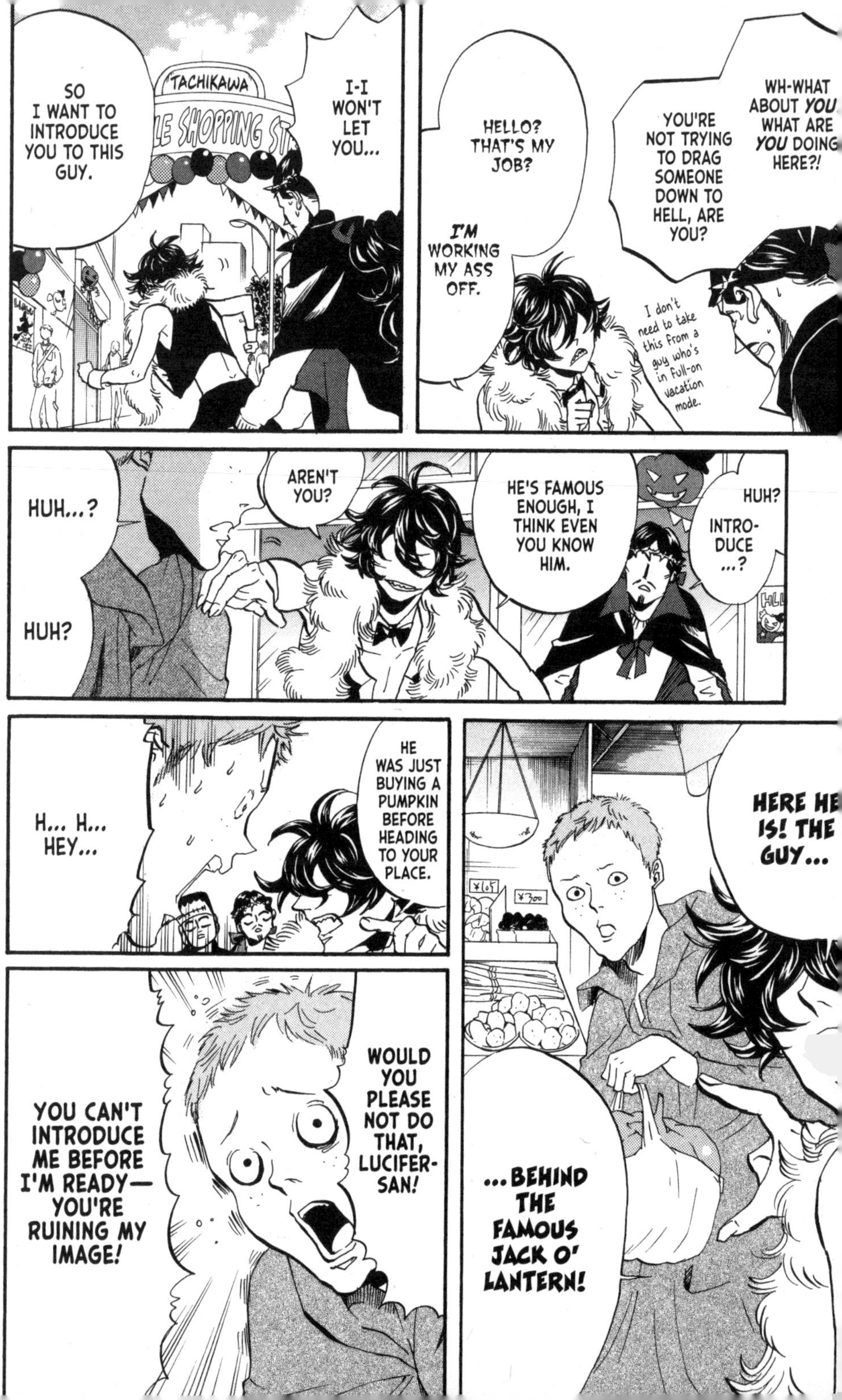
WH-WHAT ABOUT YOU WHAT ARE YOU DOING HERE?!
YOU'RE NOT TRYING TO DRAG SOMEONE DOWN TO HELL, ARE YOU?
HELLO? THAT'S MY JOB?
I'M WORKING MY ASS OFF.
I don't need to take this from a guy who's in full-on vacation mode.
I-I WON'T LET YOU...
TACHIKAWA
SO I WANT TO INTRODUCE YOU TO THIS GUY.
HUH? INTRODUCE...?
HE'S FAMOUS ENOUGH, I THINK EVEN YOU KNOW HIM.
AREN'T YOU?
HUH...?
HUH?
HERE HE IS! THE GUY...
...BEHIND THE FAMOUS JACK O' LANTERN!
HE WAS JUST BUYING A PUMPKIN BEFORE HEADING TO YOUR PLACE.
H... H... HEY...
WOULD YOU PLEASE NOT DO THAT, LUCIFER-SAN!
YOU CAN'T INTRODUCE ME BEFORE I'M READY— YOU'RE RUINING MY IMAGE!

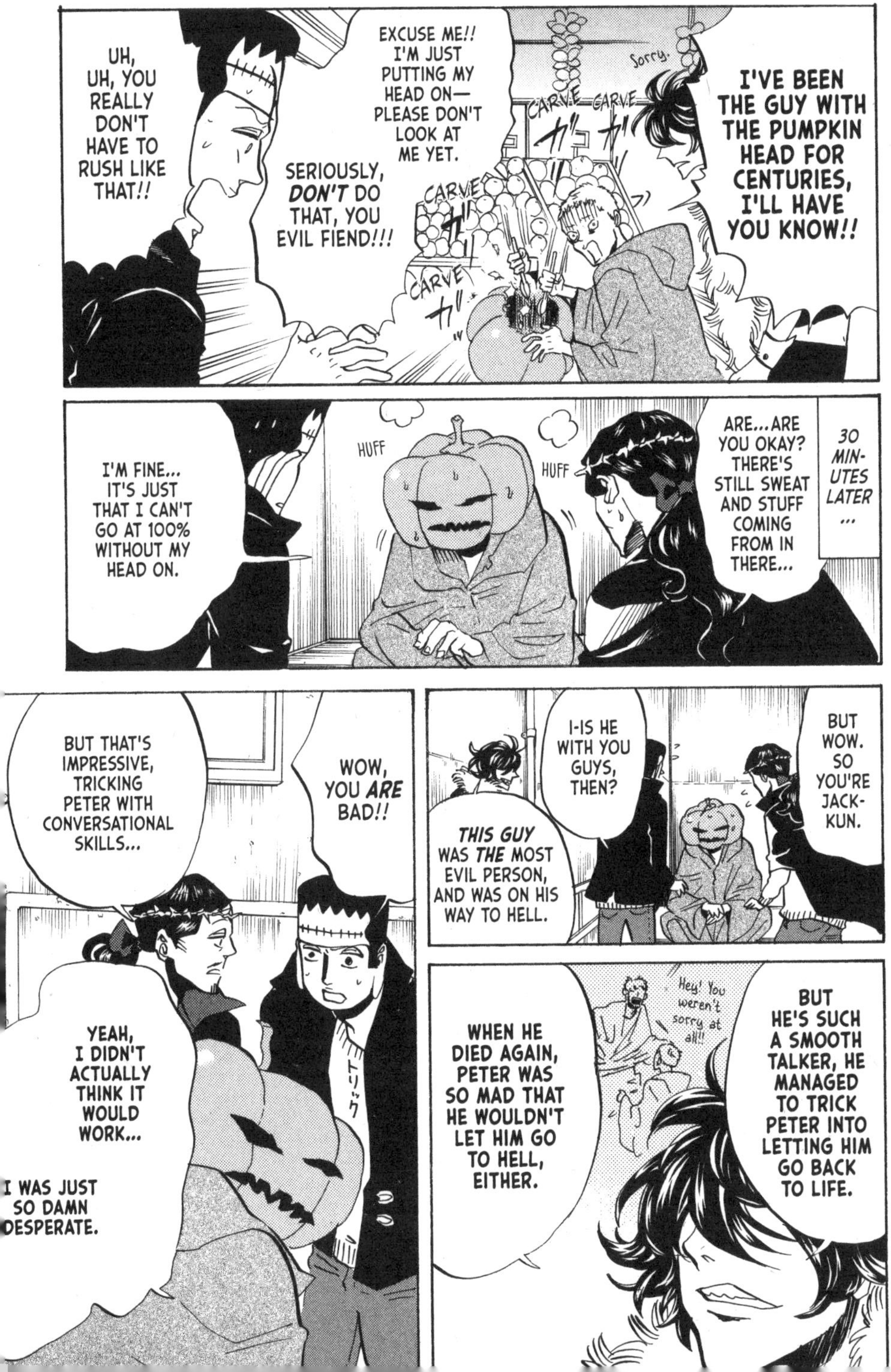
I'VE BEEN THE GUY WITH THE PUMPKIN HEAD FOR CENTURIES, I'LL HAVE YOU KNOW!!
Sorry.
CARVE CARVE
EXCUSE ME!! I'M JUST PUTTING MY HEAD ON— PLEASE DON'T LOOK AT ME YET.
SERIOUSLY, ***DON'T*** DO THAT, YOU EVIL FIEND!!!
CARVE
UH, UH, YOU REALLY DON'T HAVE TO RUSH LIKE THAT!!
CARVE
30 MIN-UTES LATER...
ARE...ARE YOU OKAY? THERE'S STILL SWEAT AND STUFF COMING FROM IN THERE...
HUFF
HUFF
I'M FINE... IT'S JUST THAT I CAN'T GO AT 100% WITHOUT MY HEAD ON.
BUT WOW. SO YOU'RE JACK-KUN.
I-IS HE WITH YOU GUYS, THEN?
THIS GUY WAS ***THE*** MOST EVIL PERSON, AND WAS ON HIS WAY TO HELL.
BUT HE'S SUCH A SMOOTH TALKER, HE MANAGED TO TRICK PETER INTO LETTING HIM GO BACK TO LIFE.
Hey! You weren't sorry at all!!
WHEN HE DIED AGAIN, PETER WAS SO MAD THAT HE WOULDN'T LET HIM GO TO HELL, EITHER.
WOW, YOU ***ARE*** BAD!!
BUT THAT'S IMPRESSIVE, TRICKING PETER WITH CONVERSATIONAL SKILLS...
トリック
YEAH, I DIDN'T ACTUALLY THINK IT WOULD WORK...
I WAS JUST SO DAMN DESPERATE.

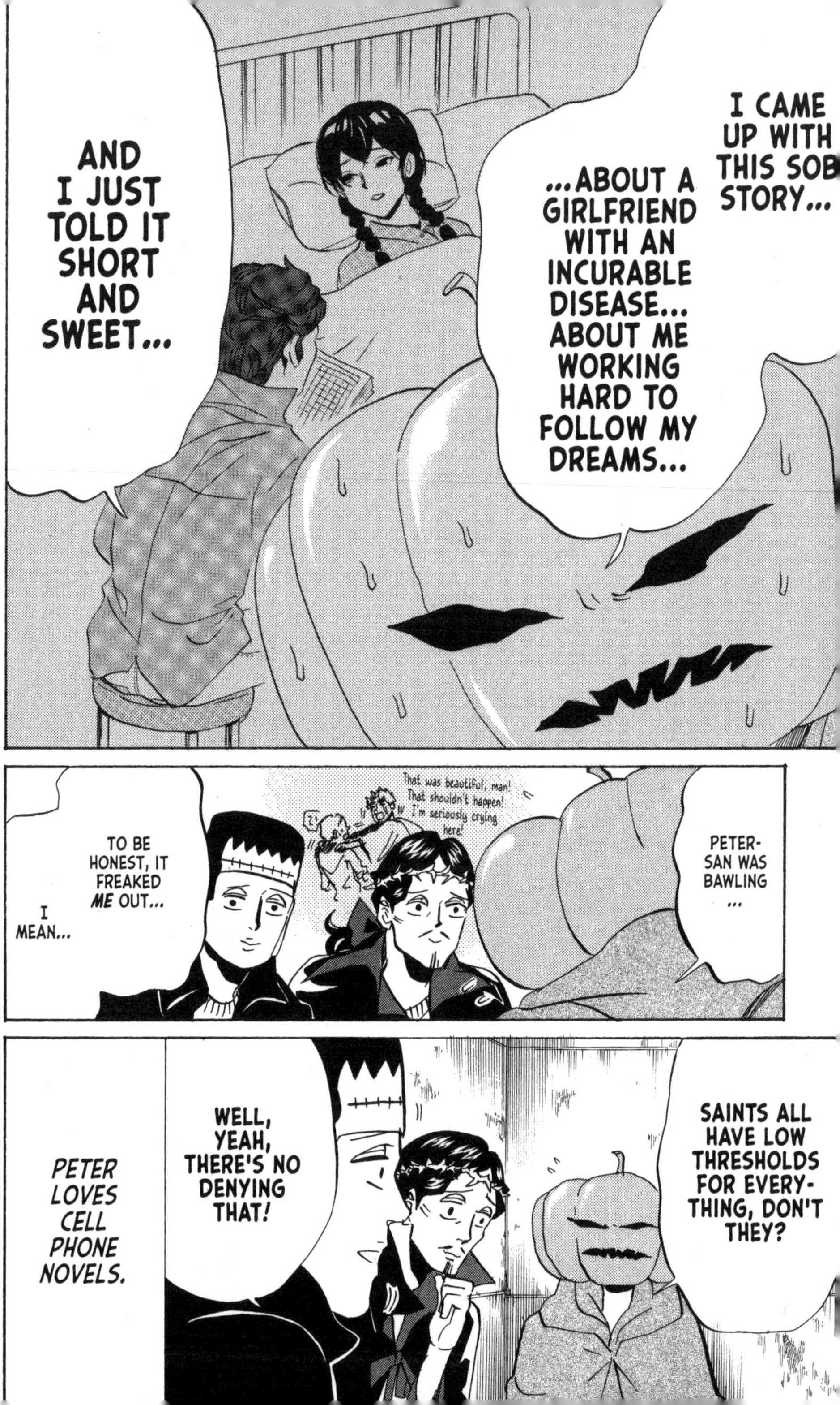
I CAME UP WITH THIS SOB STORY...
...ABOUT A GIRLFRIEND WITH AN INCURABLE DISEASE... ABOUT ME WORKING HARD TO FOLLOW MY DREAMS...
AND I JUST TOLD IT SHORT AND SWEET...
PETER-SAN WAS BAWLING ...
That was beautiful, man! That shouldn't happen! I'm seriously crying here!
TO BE HONEST, IT FREAKED *ME* OUT...
I MEAN...
SAINTS ALL HAVE LOW THRESHOLDS FOR EVERY-THING, DON'T THEY?
WELL, YEAH, THERE'S NO DENYING THAT!
PETER LOVES CELL PHONE NOVELS.

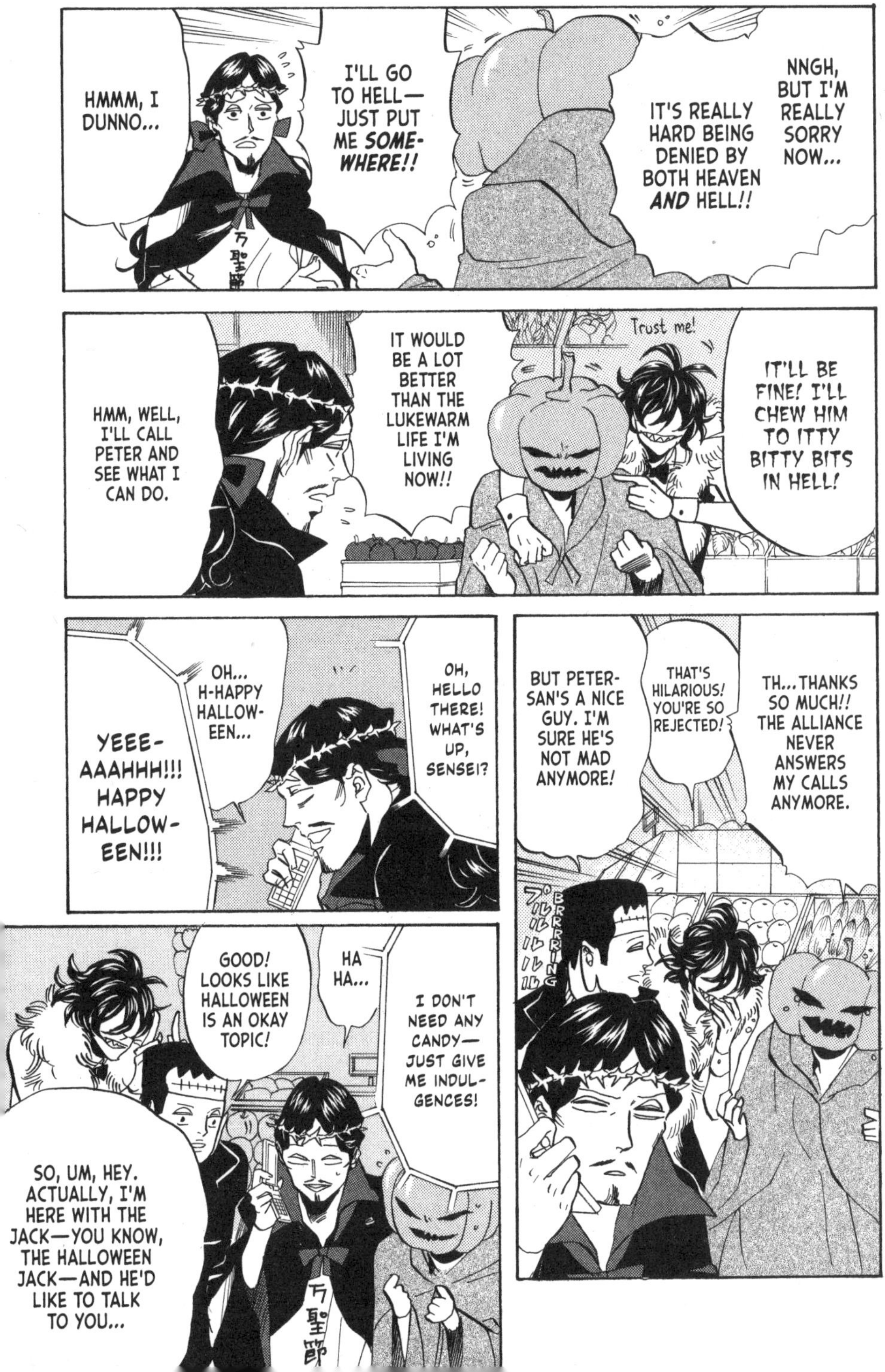
NNGH, BUT I'M REALLY SORRY NOW...
IT'S REALLY HARD BEING DENIED BY BOTH HEAVEN *AND* HELL!!
I'LL GO TO HELL—JUST PUT ME *SOME-WHERE!!*
HMMM, I DUNNO...
Trust me!
IT'LL BE FINE! I'LL CHEW HIM TO ITTY BITTY BITS IN HELL!
IT WOULD BE A LOT BETTER THAN THE LUKEWARM LIFE I'M LIVING NOW!!
HMM, WELL, I'LL CALL PETER AND SEE WHAT I CAN DO.
TH...THANKS SO MUCH!! THE ALLIANCE NEVER ANSWERS MY CALLS ANYMORE.
THAT'S HILARIOUS! YOU'RE SO REJECTED!
BUT PETER-SAN'S A NICE GUY. I'M SURE HE'S NOT MAD ANYMORE!
BRRRING
OH, HELLO THERE! WHAT'S UP, SENSEI?
OH... H-HAPPY HALLOW-EEN...
YEEE-AAAHHH!!! HAPPY HALLOW-EEN!!!
I DON'T NEED ANY CANDY—JUST GIVE ME INDUL-GENCES!
HA HA...
GOOD! LOOKS LIKE HALLOWEEN IS AN OKAY TOPIC!
SO, UM, HEY. ACTUALLY, I'M HERE WITH THE JACK—YOU KNOW, THE HALLOWEEN JACK—AND HE'D LIKE TO TALK TO YOU...

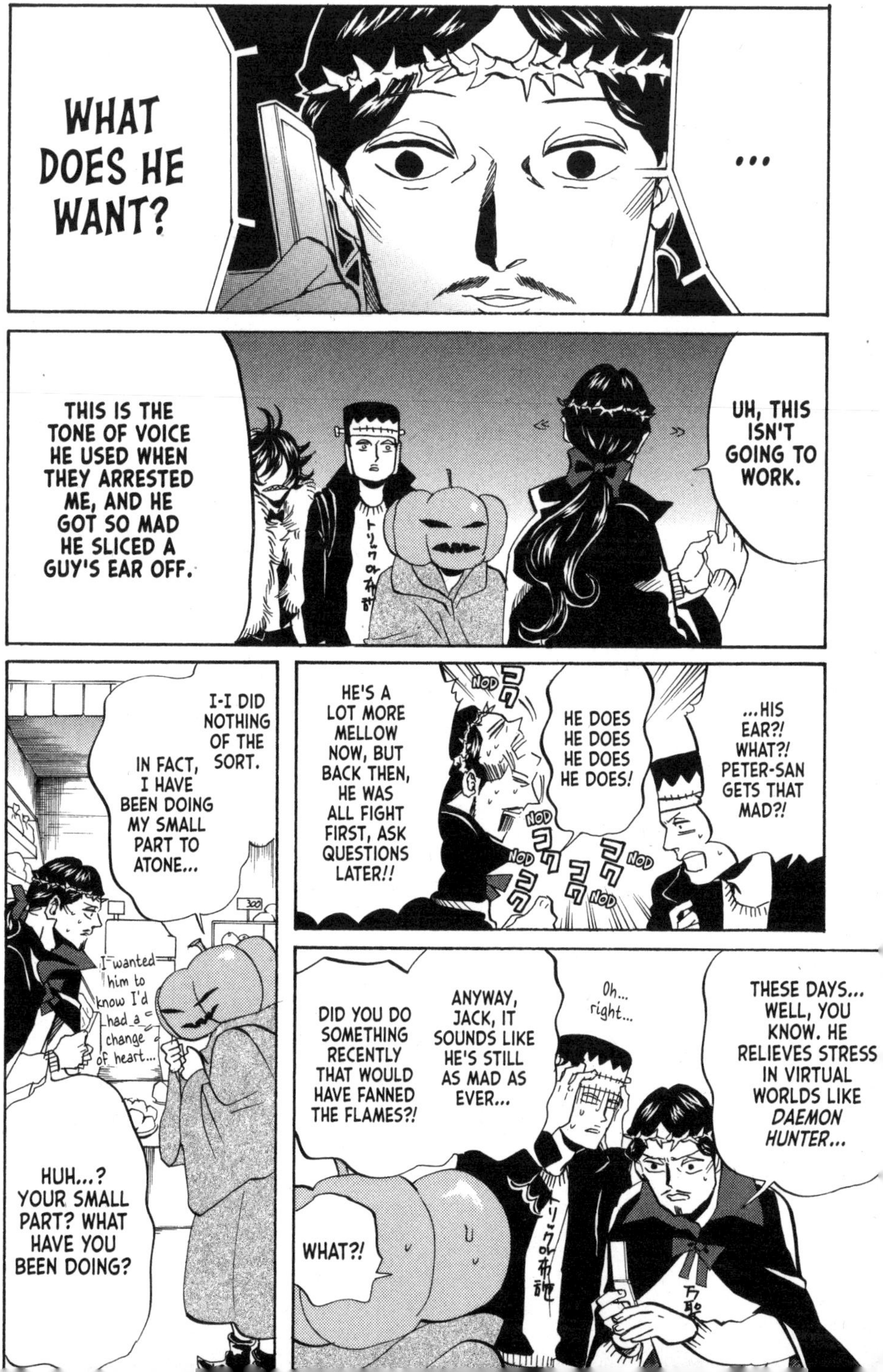
...
WHAT DOES HE WANT?
UH, THIS ISN'T GOING TO WORK.
THIS IS THE TONE OF VOICE HE USED WHEN THEY ARRESTED ME, AND HE GOT SO MAD HE SLICED A GUY'S EAR OFF.
...HIS EAR?! WHAT?! PETER-SAN GETS THAT MAD?!
HE DOES HE DOES HE DOES HE DOES!
NOD コク
NOD コク
NOD コク
NOD コク
NOD コク
HE'S A LOT MORE MELLOW NOW, BUT BACK THEN, HE WAS ALL FIGHT FIRST, ASK QUESTIONS LATER!!
THESE DAYS... WELL, YOU KNOW. HE RELIEVES STRESS IN VIRTUAL WORLDS LIKE *DAEMON HUNTER*...
Oh... right...
ANYWAY, JACK, IT SOUNDS LIKE HE'S STILL AS MAD AS EVER...
DID YOU DO SOMETHING RECENTLY THAT WOULD HAVE FANNED THE FLAMES?!
WHAT?!
I-I DID NOTHING OF THE SORT.
IN FACT, I HAVE BEEN DOING MY SMALL PART TO ATONE...
I wanted him to know I'd had a change of heart...
HUH...? YOUR SMALL PART? WHAT HAVE YOU BEEN DOING?

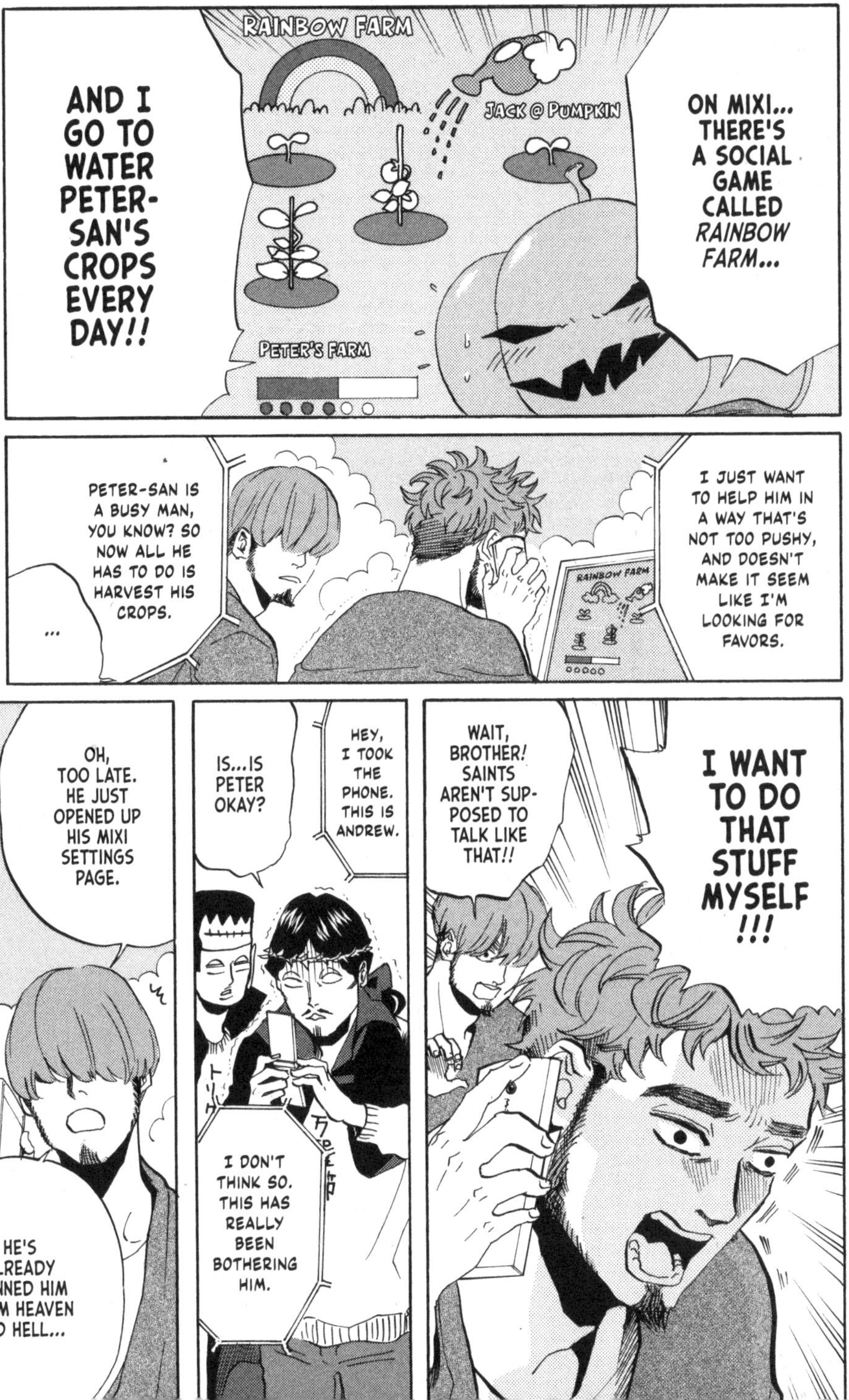
ON MIXI... THERE'S A SOCIAL GAME CALLED *RAINBOW FARM*...
RAINBOW FARM
JACK @ PUMPKIN
PETER'S FARM
AND I GO TO WATER PETER-SAN'S CROPS EVERY DAY!!
I JUST WANT TO HELP HIM IN A WAY THAT'S NOT TOO PUSHY, AND DOESN'T MAKE IT SEEM LIKE I'M LOOKING FOR FAVORS.
RAINBOW FARM
PETER-SAN IS A BUSY MAN, YOU KNOW? SO NOW ALL HE HAS TO DO IS HARVEST HIS CROPS.
...
I WANT TO DO THAT STUFF MYSELF!!!
WAIT, BROTHER! SAINTS AREN'T SUPPOSED TO TALK LIKE THAT!!
HEY, I TOOK THE PHONE. THIS IS ANDREW.
IS...IS PETER OKAY?
I DON'T THINK SO. THIS HAS REALLY BEEN BOTHERING HIM.
OH, TOO LATE. HE JUST OPENED UP HIS MIXI SETTINGS PAGE.
HE'S ALREADY BANNED HIM FROM HEAVEN AND HELL...

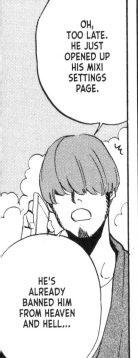

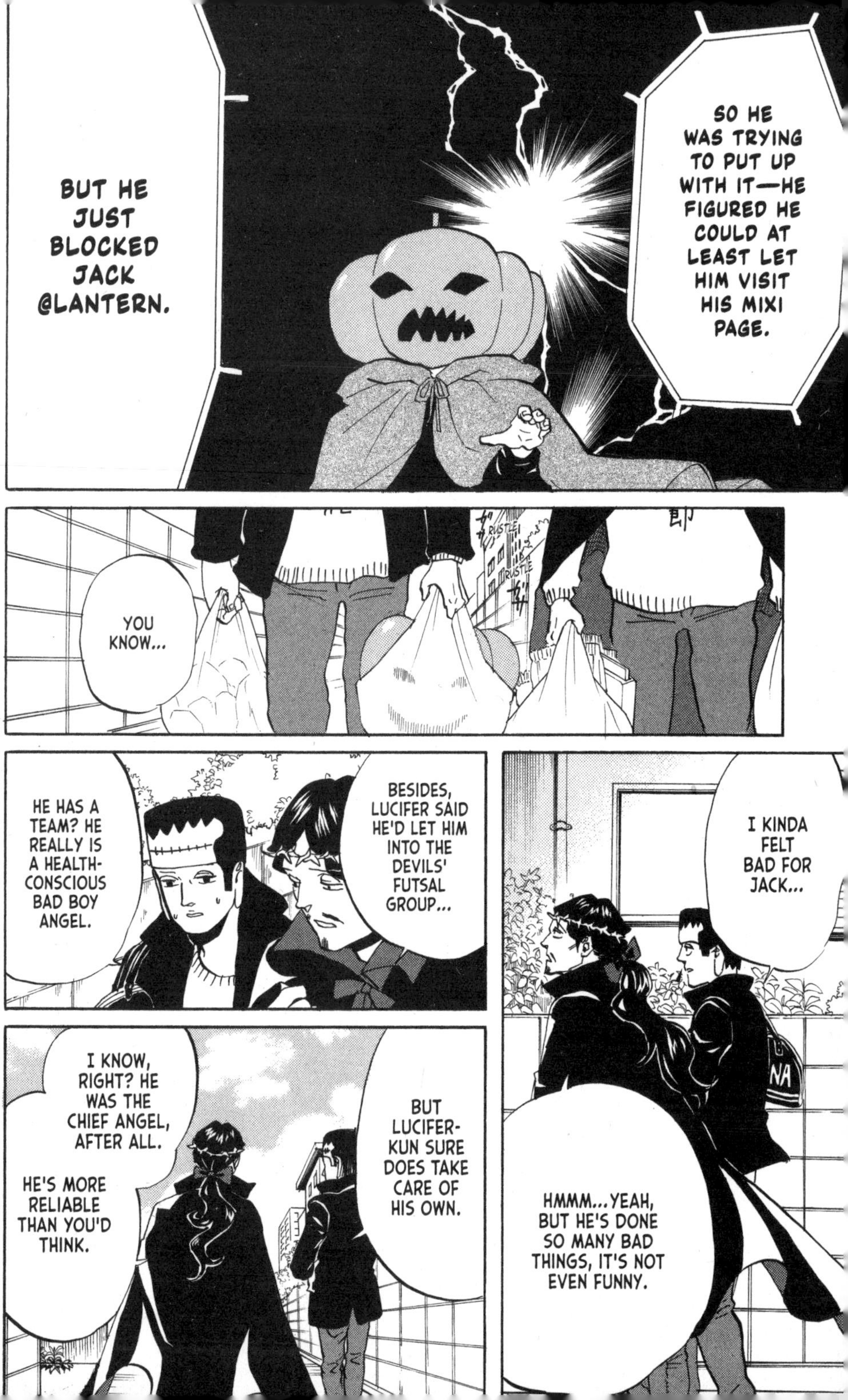
SO HE WAS TRYING TO PUT UP WITH IT—HE FIGURED HE COULD AT LEAST LET HIM VISIT HIS MIXI PAGE.
BUT HE JUST BLOCKED JACK @LANTERN.
RUSTLE
RUSTLE
YOU KNOW...
I KINDA FELT BAD FOR JACK...
HMMM...YEAH, BUT HE'S DONE SO MANY BAD THINGS, IT'S NOT EVEN FUNNY.
BESIDES, LUCIFER SAID HE'D LET HIM INTO THE DEVILS' FUTSAL GROUP...
HE HAS A TEAM? HE REALLY IS A HEALTH-CONSCIOUS BAD BOY ANGEL.
BUT LUCIFER-KUN SURE DOES TAKE CARE OF HIS OWN.
I KNOW, RIGHT? HE WAS THE CHIEF ANGEL, AFTER ALL.
HE'S MORE RELIABLE THAN YOU'D THINK.

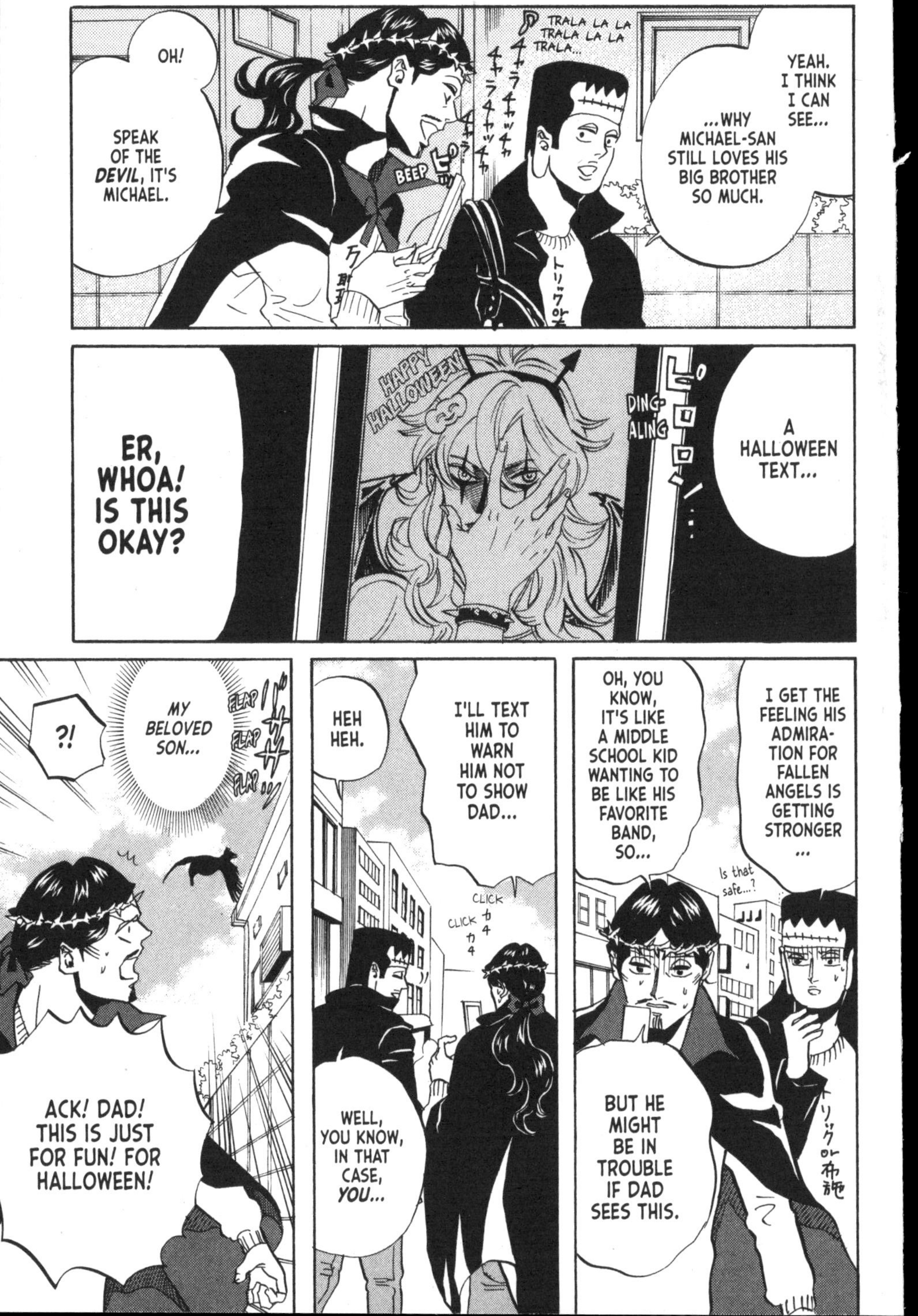
YEAH. I THINK I CAN SEE...
...WHY MICHAEL-SAN STILL LOVES HIS BIG BROTHER SO MUCH.
TRALA LA LA TRALA LA LA TRALA...
BEEP
OH!
SPEAK OF THE *DEVIL*, IT'S MICHAEL.
A HALLOWEEN TEXT...
DING-ALING
HAPPY HALLOWEEN
ER, WHOA! IS THIS OKAY?
I GET THE FEELING HIS ADMIRATION FOR FALLEN ANGELS IS GETTING STRONGER ...
Is that safe...?
OH, YOU KNOW, IT'S LIKE A MIDDLE SCHOOL KID WANTING TO BE LIKE HIS FAVORITE BAND, SO...
BUT HE MIGHT BE IN TROUBLE IF DAD SEES THIS.
I'LL TEXT HIM TO WARN HIM NOT TO SHOW DAD...
HEH HEH.
CLICK
CLICK
WELL, YOU KNOW, IN THAT CASE, *YOU*...
MY BELOVED SON...
FLAP
FLAP
FLAP
?!
ACK! DAD! THIS IS JUST FOR FUN! FOR HALLOWEEN!

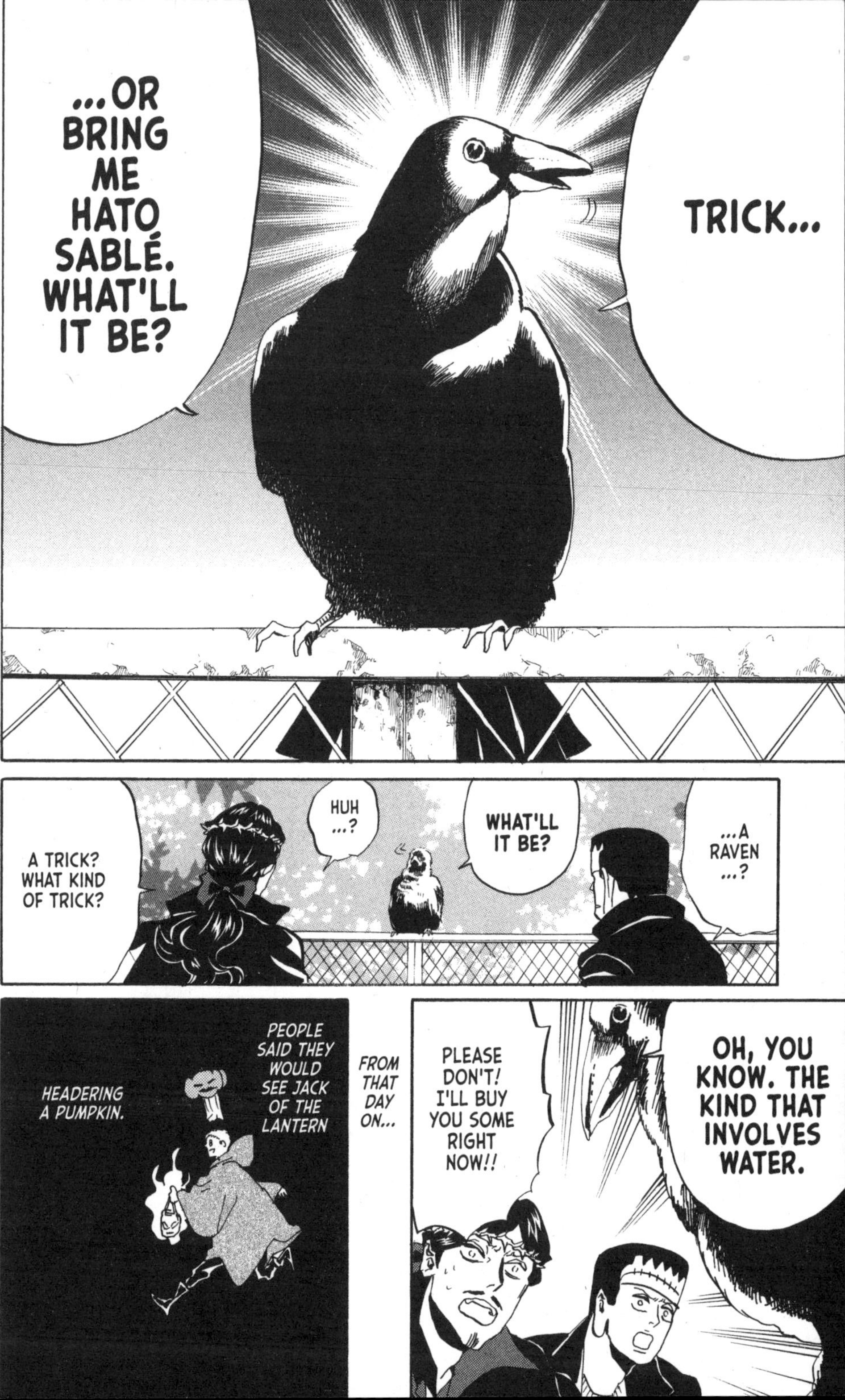
TRICK...
...OR BRING ME HATO SABLÉ. WHAT'LL IT BE?
...A RAVEN ...?
WHAT'LL IT BE?
HUH ...?
A TRICK? WHAT KIND OF TRICK?
OH, YOU KNOW. THE KIND THAT INVOLVES WATER.
PLEASE DON'T! I'LL BUY YOU SOME RIGHT NOW!!
FROM THAT DAY ON...
PEOPLE SAID THEY WOULD SEE JACK OF THE LANTERN
HEADERING A PUMPKIN.

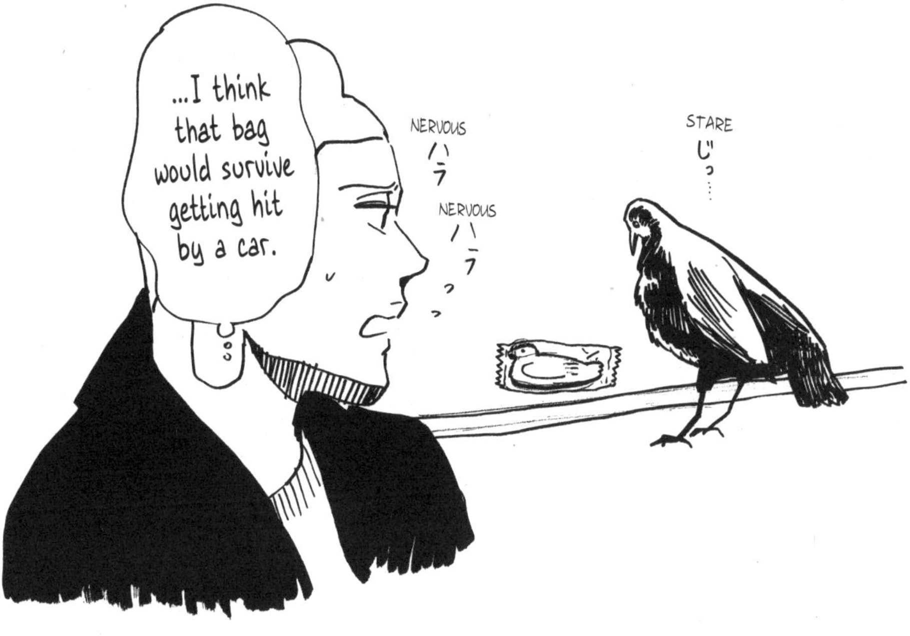
STARE
じっ……
NERVOUS
ハラ
NERVOUS
ハラ
...I think that bag would survive getting hit by a car.

CHAPTER 43 TRANSLATION NOTES

Halloween Fair changing rooms, page 265
It's generally frowned upon in Japan to walk around in costume outside of cosplay/event venues. For this reason, event venues often set aside changing rooms so that attendees can change into costumes after their arrival.

Halloween, page 266
While the name Halloween comes from All Hallows Eve, meaning "the evening before All Saints Day" (a Christian observance), the traditions associated with it come from the Celtic festival Samhain, which was a New Year's festival. On this night, the boundary between the world and the Otherworld—the realm of the supernatural—thinned.

All Saints Day, page 267
All Saints Day is a day dedicated to all saints.

Cell phone novels, page 272
As the name suggests, a cell phone novel is a novel written via cell phone. Because of the way Japanese writing works, it is possible to fit a fair amount of information into a text message even with character limitations. The main genres are fantasy and romance.

Sliced a guy's ear off, page 274
As per John's account of Jesus's arrest: "Then Simon Peter having a sword drew it, and smote the high priest's servant, and cut off his right ear," (John 18:10).

SAINT☆YOUNG MEN

◄ KAMOME ►
SHIRAHAMA

Witch Hat Atelier

A magical manga
adventure for
fans of Disney
and Studio
Ghibli!

Witch Hat Atelier © Kamome Shirahama/Kodansha Ltd.

The magical adventure that took Japan by storm is finally here, from acclaimed DC and Marvel cover artist Kamome Shirahama!

In a world where everyone takes wonders like magic spells and dragons for granted, Coco is a girl with a simple dream: She wants to be a witch. But everybody knows magicians are born, not made, and Coco was not born with a gift for magic. Resigned to her un-magical life, Coco is about to give up on her dream to become a witch...until the day she meets Qifrey, a mysterious, traveling magician. After secretly seeing Qifrey perform magic in a way she's never seen before, Coco soon learns what everybody "knows" might not be the truth, and discovers that her magical dream may not be as far away as it may seem...

KC
KODANSHA
COMICS

A BELOVED CLASSIC MAKES ITS STUNNING RETURN IN THIS GORGEOUS, LIMITED EDITION BOX SET!

This tale of three Tokyo teenagers who cross through a magical portal and become the champions of another world is a modern manga classic. The box set includes three volumes of manga covering the entire first series of *Magic Knight Rayearth*, plus the series's super-rare full-color art book companion, all printed at a larger size than ever before on premium paper, featuring a newly-revised translation and lettering, and exquisite foil-stamped covers.

A strictly limited edition, this will be gone in a flash!

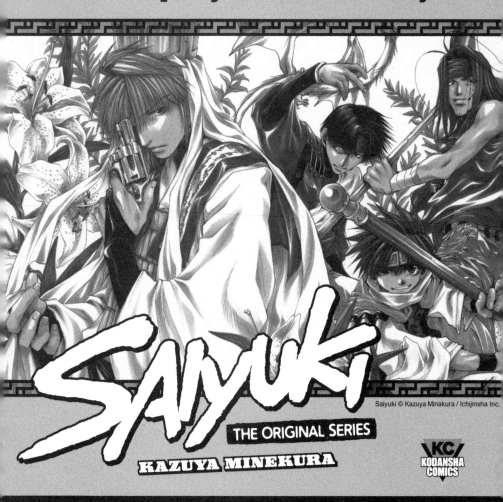

PERFECT WORLD 1

Rie Aruga

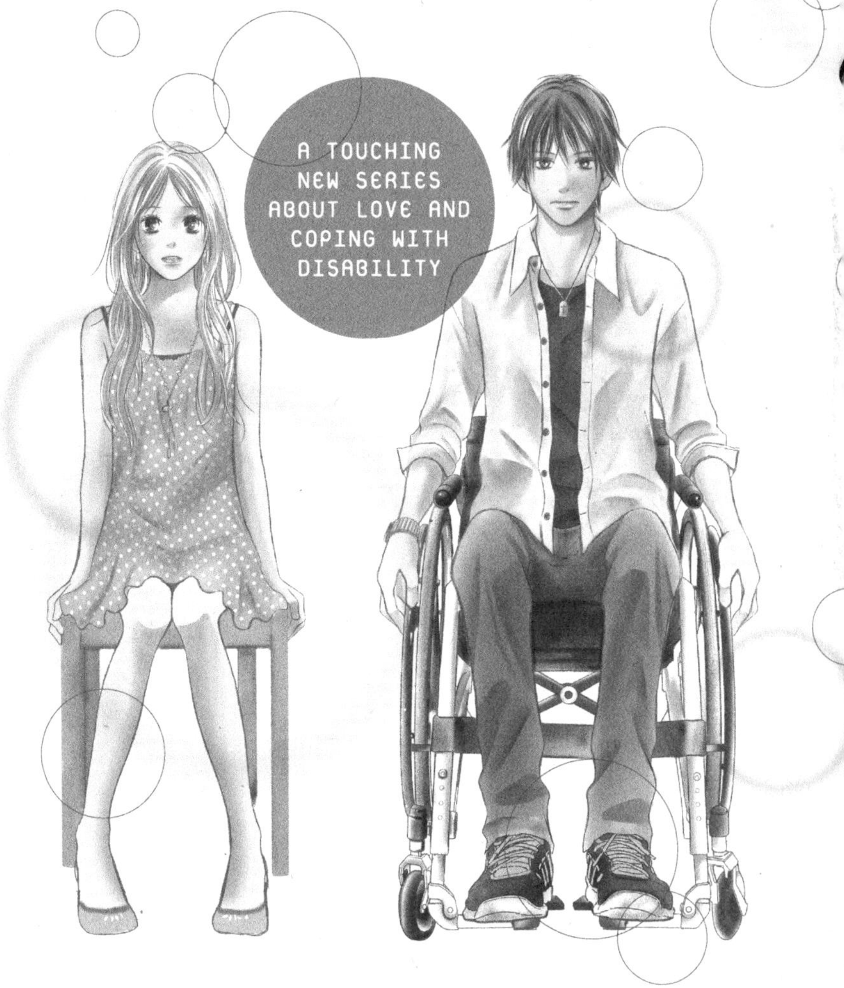
A TOUCHING NEW SERIES ABOUT LOVE AND COPING WITH DISABILITY

An office party reunites Tsugumi with her high school crush Itsuki. He's realized his dream of becoming an architect, but along the way, he experienced a spinal injury that put him in a wheelchair. Now Tsugumi's rekindled feelings will butt up against prejudices she never considered — and Itsuki will have to decide if he's ready to let someone into his heart...

"Depicts with great delicacy and courage the difficulties some with disabilities experience getting involved in romantic relationships... Rie Aruga refuses to romanticize, pushing her heroine to face the reality of disability. She invites her readers to the same tasks of empathy, knowledge and recognition."
—Slate.fr

"An important entry [in manga romance]... The emotional core of both plot and characters indicates thoughtfulness... [Aruga's] research is readily apparent in the text and artwork, making this feel like a real story."
—Anime News Network

KC KODANSHA COMICS

The adorable new odd-couple cat comedy manga from the creator of the beloved *Chi's Sweet Home*, in full color!

Praise for Chi's Sweet Home

"Nearly impossible to turn away... a true all-ages title that anyone, young or old, cat lover or not, will enjoy. The stories will bring a smile to your face and warm your heart."

—School Library Journal

Sue & Tai-chan

Konami Kanata

Sue is an aging housecat who's looking forward to living out her life in peace... but her plans change when the mischievous black tomcat Tai-chan enters the picture! Hey! Sue never signed up to be a catsitter! *Sue & Tai-chan* is the latest from the reigning meow-narch of cute kitty comics, Konami Kanata.

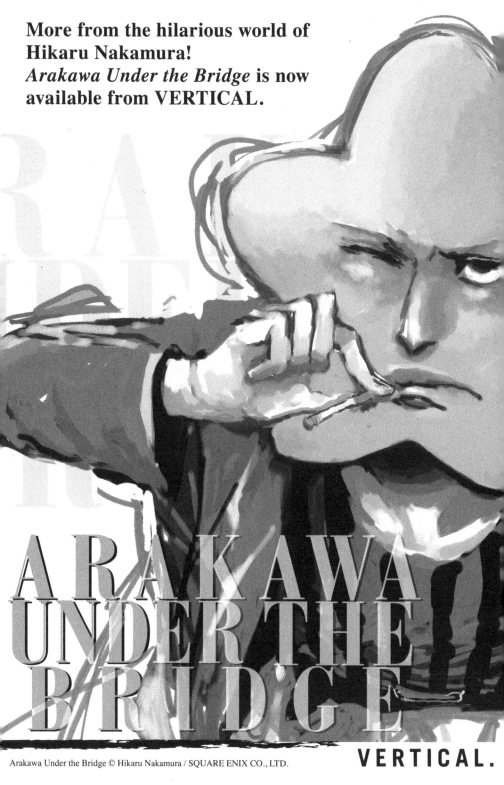

Saint Young Men 3 copyright © 2010 Hikaru Nakamura
English translation copyright © 2020 Hikaru Nakamura

Published in the United States by Kodansha Comics, an imprint of Kodansha USA Publishing, LLC, New York.

Publication rights for this English edition arranged through Kodansha Ltd., Tokyo.

First published in Japan in 2010 by Kodansha Ltd., Tokyo as *Seinto oniisan*, volumes 5 & 6.

ISBN 978-1-63236-976-5

Original cover design by Hiroshi Niigami (NARTI;S)

Printed in the United States of America.

www.kodanshacomics.com

9 8 7 6 5 4 3 2 1
Translation: Alethea Nibley & Athena Nibley
Lettering: Lys Blakeslee
Editing: Nathaniel Gallant
Kodansha Comics edition cover design by Phil Balsman

Publisher: Kiichiro Sugawara
Vice president of marketing & publicity: Naho Yamada

Director of publishing services: Ben Applegate
Associate director of operations: Stephen Pakula
Publishing services managing editor: Noelle Webster
Assistant production manager: Emi Lotto, Angela Zurlo